CW01371157

THE BLACKWELL HISTORY OF
MUSIC IN BRITAIN

General Editor Ian Spink

Volume 6
THE TWENTIETH CENTURY

The Blackwell History of Music in Britain

General Editor IAN SPINK
*Professor of Music, Royal Holloway and Bedford New College,
University of London*

1 The Middle Ages[†]

2 The Sixteenth Century
Editor ROGER BRAY

3 The Seventeenth Century
Editor IAN SPINK

4 The Eighteenth Century
Editors H. DIACK JOHNSTONE
ROGER FISKE

5 The Romantic Age 1800–1914
Editor NICHOLAS TEMPERLEY

6 The Twentieth Century
Editor STEPHEN BANFIELD

[†] Projected
Information on request from the publishers

Music in Britain

THE TWENTIETH CENTURY

edited by
STEPHEN BANFIELD

BLACKWELL
Reference

Copyright © Blackwell Publishers Ltd 1995
Editorial organization © Stephen Banfield 1995

The right of Stephen Banfield to be identified as
editor of this work has been asserted in accordance
with the Copyright, Designs and Patents Act 1988.

First published 1995
First published in USA 1995

Blackwell Publishers Ltd.
108 Cowley Road
Oxford OX4 IJF
UK

Blackwell Publishers Inc.
238 Main Street
Cambridge, Massachusetts 02142
USA

All rights reserved. Except for the quotation of short passages for the purposes of criticism and review, no part of this publication may be reproduced, stored in a retrieval system or transmitted, in any form or by any means, electronic, mechanical, photocopying, recording or otherwise, without the prior permission of the publisher.

Except in the United States of America, this book is sold subject to the condition that it shall not, by way of trade or otherwise, be lent, resold, hired out, or otherwise circulated without the publisher's prior consent in any form of binding or cover other than that in which it is published and without a similar condition including this condition being imposed on the subsequent purchaser.

British Library Cataloguing in Publication Data
A CIP catalogue record for this book is available from the British Library

Library of Congress Cataloging-in-Publication Data
The Twentieth Century
The Blackwell History of Music in Britain; 6
Bibliography
Includes index
1. Music–Great Britain–History and criticism
I Banfield, Stephen. II Series
ML285.B58 1988   780'.941   88-19352
ISBN 0-631-17424-9 (v. 6)

Typeset in 11 on 12 pt Linotype New Baskerville
by Seton Music Graphics Ltd
Printed in Great Britain by
T. J. Press (Padstow) Ltd, Padstow, Cornwall

This book is printed on acid-free paper

CONTENTS

Contributors vii
Acknowledgements ix

Introduction STEPHEN BANFIELD 1

PART I   Music in Context   7

  1 British Music in the Modern World ARNOLD WHITTALL   9
  2 The 'Problem' of Popular Music RICHARD MIDDLETON   27
  3 The Marketplace CYRIL EHRLICH   39

PART II   Popular Music   55

  4 The 'Jazz Age' DEREK SCOTT   57
  5 The Rock Revolution RICHARD MIDDLETON   79
  6 Music for the Stage PATRICK O'CONNOR   107
  7 Film and Television Music DAVID KERSHAW   125
  8 Amateur Musicians and Their Repertoire DAVE RUSSELL   145

PART III   Art Music   177

  9 Instrumental Music I PETER EVANS   179
  10 Instrumental Music II JIM SAMSON   278
  11 Music and Drama MATTHEW RYE   343
  12 Vocal Music STEPHEN BANFIELD   402

PART IV   Music and Scholarship   501

  13 Criticism and Theory CHRISTIAN KENNETT   503
  14 The Revival of Early Music HARRY HASKELL   519

List of Sources   531
Index   555

CONTRIBUTORS

STEPHEN BANFIELD is Elgar Professor of Music at the University of Birmingham and author of *Sensibility and English Song* and *Sondheim's Broadway Musicals*.

CYRIL EHRLICH is Emeritus Professor of Social and Economic History at Queen's University, Belfast. His books include histories of the piano, the music profession and the Royal Philharmonic Society.

PETER EVANS, Professor of Music at Southampton University until his retirement in 1990, has written a major study of Britten's music and contributed to *The New Oxford History of Music*.

HARRY HASKELL, an editor at Yale University Press, is author of *The Early Music Revival* and editor of the forthcoming anthology *The Attentive Listener: Three Centuries of Music Criticism*.

CHRISTIAN KENNETT, currently teaching at Goldsmiths' College and the University of Westminster, studied at Southampton, Sussex and Reading Universities and has recently submitted his PhD on pitch-class set theory.

DAVID KERSHAW, Senior Lecturer in Music at the University of York, is Director of the University's Film Music Resource Centre.

RICHARD MIDDLETON, Staff Tutor and Senior Lecturer in Music at the Open University, is the author of *Studying Popular Music* and co-editor of the journal *Popular Music*.

PATRICK O'CONNOR was a consulting editor to *The New Grove Dictionary of Opera* and is a regular contributor to *Gramophone*.

DAVE RUSSELL is Senior Lecturer in the Department of Historical and Critical Studies at the University of Central Lancashire; he is the author of *Popular Music in England, 1840–1914: a Social History* and a number of articles and essays on cognate topics.

MATTHEW RYE, a former assistant editor of the *Musical Times*, is currently on the editorial staff of *BBC Music Magazine*. He also works as a freelance writer and music critic and is a major contributor to

CONTRIBUTORS

the *Rough Guide to Classical Music on CD* and *Rough Guide to Opera* (forthcoming).

JIM SAMSON is Badock Professor of Music at the University of Bristol. He has published books on Szymanowski, Chopin and early twentieth-century music, together with articles on the analysis and aesthetics of music.

DEREK SCOTT is author of *The Singing Bourgeois,* a study of Victorian song, and various articles on nineteenth- and twentieth-century popular music; he is Director of Music at the University of Salford.

ARNOLD WHITTALL, Professor of Musical Theory and Analysis at King's College London, has written extensively about British music in his books *Music Since the First World War* and *The Music of Britten and Tippett,* as well as publishing major articles on Birtwistle, Dillon, Maw and Maxwell Davies.

ACKNOWLEDGEMENTS

Every effort has been made to trace all the copyright holders, but if any have been inadvertently overlooked, the publishers will be pleased to make the necessary arrangement at the first opportunity.

The publisher is grateful for permission to reproduce the following:

Ex. 4.2   'It's the talk of the town'
Music by Jerry Livingston and words by Marty Symes and Al Neiburg. © 1933, Santly Bros Inc, USA. Reproduced by permission of Keith Prowse Music Pub Co Ltd, London, WC2H 0EA.

Ex. 4.3   Sid Phillips, *Dinner and Dance*
© 1938 by Campbell Connelly & Co Ltd, 8-9 Frith Street, London, W1V 5TZ. Used by permission. All rights reserved.

Ex. 5.1   'Jumpin' Jack Flash'
© 1968 by ABKCO Music In, New York, USA. Exclusive sub-publication rights for the world exc. USA and Canada controlled by Westminster Music Ltd, London, SW10 0SZ. Used by permission. International copyright secured. All rights reserved. This copy authorized for sale outside the USA and Canada only.

Ex. 5.2   'She loves you'
Words and music by John Lennon and Paul McCartney. © Copyright 1963 Northern Songs. Reproduced by permission of Music Sales Ltd. All rights reserved. International copyright secured.

Ex. 5.3   'Strawberry fields forever'
Words and music by John Lennon and Paul McCartney. © Copyright 1967 Northern Songs. Reproduced by permission of Music Sales Ltd. All rights reserved. International copyright secured.

Ex. 5.4   'Anarchy in the UK'
© Warner Chappell Music Ltd., London, W1Y 3FA. Reproduced by permission of International Music Publications Ltd.

Ex. 5.5   'I should be so lucky' by Mike Stock/Matt Aitken/Pete Waterman. © 1987 SAW Songs. All rights for the world administered by BMG Music Publishing Ltd.

Ex. 5.6   'Dub be good to me'
Words and music by James Harris III and Terry Lewis. © 1987, Flyte Tyme Tunes Inc/Avant Garde Music Pub Inc, USA.

ACKNOWLEDGEMENTS

Reproduced by permission of EMI Music Publishing Ltd, London, WC2H 0EA.

Ex. 5.7 'Handsworth Revolution' (Gabbidon/McQueen/Brown/Riley/Nesbitt/Hind/Martin). © 1978 Blue Mountain Music Ltd, 47 British Grove, W4 2NL. International copyright secured. All rights reserved.

Ex. 5.8 'Now be thankful' (David Swarbrick/Richard Thompson). © 1970 Warlock Music Ltd. International copyright secured. All rights reserved.

Ex. 6.2 Novello, 'The wings of sleep'
© Warner Chappell Music Ltd., London, W1Y 3FA. Reproduced by permission of International Music Publishers Ltd.

Ex. 6.3 Coward, 'Poor little rich girl'
© Warner Chappell Music Ltd., London, W1Y 3FA. Reproduced by permission of International Music Publishers Ltd.

Ex. 6.4 Strachey, 'These foolish things'
Reproduced by kind permission of Boosey & Hawkes Publishers Ltd.

Ex. 6.5 Bart, 'Who will buy?'
© 1960 Lakeview Music Publishing Co Ltd., London, SW10 0SZ.

Ex. 6.6 'Memory'
Music by Andrew Lloyd Webber. Text by Trevor Nunn after T. S. Eliot. Music Copyright 1981 by The Really Useful Group Ltd. Text Copyright by Trevor Nunn/Set Copyrights Ltd. Reproduced by permission of Faber Music Ltd, London.

Ex. 7.1b Ketèlbey, 'Amaryllis'
© 1924 Bosworth & Co Ltd, London.

Ex. 7.2 *Warsaw Concerto*
Music by Richard Addinsell. © 1942, Reproduced by permission of Keith Prowse Music Pub Co Ltd, London, WC2H 0EA.

Ex. 7.3. *Carry on Henry*
Music by Eric Rogers from the Peter Rogers Production.

Ex. 7.4 *Diamonds are Forever*
Music by John Barry. © 1971 EMI United Partnership Ltd, London, WC2H 0EA. Reprinted by permission of CPP/Belwin Europe, 5 Bushey Close, Old Barn Lane, Kenley, Surrey, England.

Ex. 7.5 *The Cook, the Thief, His Wife and Her Lover*
Music by Michael Nyman © By permission of Chester Music Ltd.

ACKNOWLEDGEMENTS

Ex. 8.1b	Gregson, *Connotations* Reproduced by kind permission of Boosey & Hawkes Music Publishers Ltd.
Ex. 8.2	Bourgeois, *Blitz* © By permission of Chester Music Ltd on behalf of R. Smith & Co.
Ex. 8.4	Appleford, 'Living Lord' © 1960 Josef Weinberger Ltd. Reproduced by permission of copyright owners.
Ex. 8.5	Bedford, *The Rime of the Ancient Mariner* © 1979 by Universal Edition (London) Ltd.
Ex. 9.1	Vaughan Williams, Symphony no. 4 in F minor © 1935 Oxford University Press. Reproduced by permission.
Ex. 9.2	Vaughan Williams, Symphony no. 6 in E minor © 1948 Oxford University Press. Reproduced by permission.
Ex. 9.5	Ireland, Piano Concerto © By permission of Chester Music Ltd.
Ex. 9.6	Bridge, *Enter Spring* © for USA by Faber Music, London.
Ex. 9.7	Bax, Symphony no. 1 © Warner Chappell Music Ltd., London, W1Y 3FA. Reproduced by permission of International Music Publishers Ltd.
Ex. 9.8	Bax, Symphony no. 5 © Warner Chappell Music Ltd., London, W1Y 3FA. Reproduced by permission of International Music Publishers Ltd.
Ex. 9.9	Brian, Symphony no.2 Reproduced by permission of the Havergal Brian Estate/United Music Publishers Ltd.
Ex. 9.10	Walton, Viola Concerto © 1936 Oxford University Press. Reproduced by permission.
Ex. 9.11	Walton, Symphony no. 1 © 1936 Oxford University Press. Reproduced by permission.
Ex. 9.12	Rawsthorne, Symphonic Studies © 1946 Oxford University Press. Reproduced by permission.
Ex. 9.13	Rawsthorne, Symphony no. 3 © 1965 Oxford University Press. Reproduced by permission.
Ex. 9.14	Tippett, Symphony no. 1 © 1948 by Schott & Co Ltd.

ACKNOWLEDGEMENTS

Ex. 9.15   Tippett, Symphony no. 2
© 1958 by Schott & Co Ltd.

Ex. 9.16   Rubbra, Symphony no. 2, 1st movement
By permission of Chester Music Ltd.

Ex. 9.17   Berkeley, Symphony no. 2,
© by permission of Chester Music Ltd.

Ex. 9.18   Britten, Variations on a Theme of Frank Bridge
Reproduced by kind permission of Boosey & Hawkes Music Publishers Ltd.

Ex. 9.19   Britten, Cello Symphony
Reproduced by kind permission of Boosey & Hawkes Music Publishers Ltd.

Ex. 9.20   Bridge, String Quartet no. 2
© Frank Bridge. Reproduced by permission of Stainer & Bell Ltd, London.

Ex. 9.21   Bridge, Piano Trio no. 2
© Frank Bridge. Reproduced by permission of Stainer & Bell Ltd, London.

Ex. 9.22   Bax, Viola Sonata
© Warner Chappell Music Ltd, London, W1Y 3FA. Reproduced by permission of International Music Publishers Ltd.

Ex. 9.23   Berkeley, Quintet for piano and wind
© By permission of Chester Music Ltd.

Ex. 9.24   Rawsthorne, Violin Sonata
© 1948 Oxford University Press. Reproduced by permission.

Ex. 9.25   Tippett, String Quartet no. 2
© 1944 by Schott & Co Ltd.

Ex. 9.26   Britten, String Quartet no. 2
Reproduced by kind permission of Boosey & Hawkes Music Publishers Ltd.

Ex. 9.27   Ireland, 'Moon-glade' (*Decorations*)
© J. Ireland. Reproduced by permission of Stainer & Bell Ltd, London.

Ex. 9.28   Bridge, Piano Sonata
© Frank Bridge. Reproduced by permission of Stainer & Bell Ltd, London.

ACKNOWLEDGEMENTS

Ex. 9.29   Tippett, Piano Sonata no. 1
© 1954 by Schott & Co. Ltd.

Ex. 10.1   Simpson, Symphony no. 3
Reproduced by kind permission of Complete Music Ltd.

Ex. 10.2   Tippett, Concerto for Orchestra
© 1964 by Schott & Co. Ltd.

Ex. 10.3   Wellesz, Symphony no. 6
© 1966 by Ludwig Doblinger (Bernhard Herzmansky) K. G. Wien, München.

Ex. 10.4   Searle, Symphony no. 2
© B Schott's Söhne.

Ex. 10.5   Wood, Cello Concerto
© By permission of Chester Music Ltd.

Ex. 10.6   Bennett, Oboe Concerto
© 1970 by Universal Edition (London) Ltd.

Ex. 10.7   Lutyens, *Quincunx*
© Hazel Giebel.

Ex. 10.8   Goehr, Violin Concerto
© 1967 by Schott & Co Ltd.

Ex. 10.9   Goehr, *Little Symphony*
© 1964 by Schott & Co Ltd.

Ex. 10.10   Maxwell Davies, Second Taverner Fantasia
Reproduced by kind permission of Boosey & Hawkes Music Publishers Ltd.

Ex. 10.11   Birtwistle, *Tragoedia*
© 1967 by Universal Edition (London) Ltd.

Ex. 10.12   Birtwistle, *Silbury Air*
© 1979 by Universal Edition (London) Ltd.

Ex. 10.13   Ferneyhough, String Quartet no. 2
© 1981 by Hinrichsen Edition, Peters Edition Ltd, London. Reproduced by permission of the publishers.

Ex. 10.14   Holloway, *Seascape and Harvest*
Reproduced by kind permission of Boosey & Hawkes Music Publishers Ltd.

Ex. 10.15   Dillon, *Überschreiten*
© 1986 by Hinrichsen Edition, Peters Edition, Ltd, London. Reproduced by permission of the publishers.

ACKNOWLEDGEMENTS

Ex. 10.16 Finnissy, *Banumbirr*
Reproduced by permission of United Music Publishers Ltd.

Ex. 10.17 MacMillan, *The Confession of Isobel Gowdie*
Reproduced by kind permission of Boosey & Hawkes Music Publishers Ltd.

Ex. 10.18 Martland, *Babi Yar*
© 1989 by Schott & Co. Ltd.

Ex. 11.1 Boughton, *The Immortal Hour*
© Rutland Boughton. Reproduced by permission of Stainer & Bell Ltd, London.

Ex. 11.4 Vaughan Williams, *Sir John in Love*
© 1930 Oxford University Press. Reproduced by permission.

Ex. 11.5 Vaughan Williams, *Riders to the Sea*
© 1936 Oxford University Press. Reproduced by permission.

Ex. 11.6 Britten, *Peter Grimes*
Reproduced by kind permission of Boosey & Hawkes Music Publishers Ltd.

Ex. 11.7 Britten, *Billy Budd*
© Reproduced by kind permission of Boosey & Hawkes Music Publishers Ltd.

Ex. 11.8 Tippett, *New Year*
© 1989 by Schott & Co. Ltd.

Ex. 11.9 Searle, *The Diary of a Madman*
© B. Schotts Söhne.

Ex. 11.10 Casken, *Golem*
© 1991 by Schott & Co. Ltd.

Ex. 12.1 Vaughan Williams, *Dona nobis pacem*
© 1936 Oxford University Press. Reproduced by permission.

Ex. 12.2 Holst, *Hymn of Jesus*. Stainer and Bell.

Ex. 12.3 Dyson, *The Canterbury Pilgrims*
© 1930 Oxford University Press. Reproduced by permission.

Ex. 12.4 Walton, *Belshazzar's Feast*
© 1941 Oxford University Press. Reproduced by permission.

Ex. 12.5 Howells, *Hymnus paradisi*. Novello.

ACKNOWLEDGEMENTS

Ex. 12.6	Britten, *War Requiem* Reproduced by kind permission of Boosey & Hawkes Music Publishers Ltd.
Ex. 12.7	Bax, *This Worldes Joie* © 1927 Murdoch & Murdoch & Co. Chappell Music Ltd, London. Reproduced by kind permission of International Music Publishers Ltd.
Ex. 12.8	Patric Standford, *Stabat Mater*, Novello.
Ex. 12.9(a)	E. J. Moeran, *Songs of Springtime*, 'Love is a sickness'. Novello.
Ex. 12.9(b)	Britten, *Five Flower Songs* Reproduced by kind permission of Boosey & Hawkes Music Publishers Ltd.
Ex. 12.10	Smalley, 'The crystal cabinet'. Novello
Ex. 12.12(a) and (b)	Marsh, 'Not a soul but ourselves . . .'. Novello.
Ex. 12.13	Ireland, 'Greater love hath no man'.
Ex. 12.14	Howells, 'Gloucester', *Nunc dimittis*. Novello.
Ex. 12.15(a)	Britten, *Rejoice in the Lamb* Reproduced by kind permission of Boosey & Hawkes Music Publishers Ltd.
Ex. 12.15(b)	Tippett, *Nunc dimittis* Schott & Co Ltd, London.
Ex. 12.15(c)	Britten, *Missa brevis* Reproduced by kind permission of Boosey & Hawkes Music Publishers Ltd.
Ex. 12.15(d)	Payne, 'A little passiontide cantata'. Novello.
Ex. 12.16(a)	Warlock, 'The lover's maze' Oxford University Press. Reproduced by kind permission.
Ex. 12.16(b)	Quilter, *Four Songs of Sorrow*. 'In spring'.
Ex. 12.18(a)	Finzi, *Before and After Summer* Reproduced by kind permission of Boosey & Hawkes Music Publishers Ltd.
Ex. 12.18(b)	Ireland, 'The trellis'. Stainer and Bell Ltd.

ACKNOWLEDGEMENTS

Ex. 12.19(a), Britten, 'Early one morning'
(b) and (d) Reproduced by kind permission of Boosey & Hawkes Music Publishers Ltd.

Ex. 12.19(c) Grainger, 'Early one morning'
© 1991 Bardic Edition for USA and all countries. All rights reserved.

Ex. 12.20 Tippett, *The Heart's Assurance*
© 1992 Schott and Co Ltd, London.

Ex. 12.21 Berkeley, *Five Housman Songs*
Chester Music Ltd. London.

Ex. 12.22 Hugh Wood, *Robert Graves Songs.*

Ex. 12.23(a) Maxwell Davies, *From Stone to Thorn*
Reproduced by kind permission of Boosey & Hawkes Music Publishers Ltd.

Ex. 12.23(b) Maxwell Davies, *The Medium*
Reproduced by kind permission of Boosey & Hawkes Music Publishers Ltd.

Ex. 12.24 Birtwistle, *Nenia, The Death of Orpheus*
Universal Edition (London) Ltd.

INTRODUCTION

STEPHEN BANFIELD

The twentieth century is nearly over, and there will be many who, like Thomas Hardy in the nineteenth, will look for a new one which 'if not sublime, / Will show, I doubt not, at its prime, / A scope above this blinkered time'. Yet in most respects it has not been a bad time for music in Britain. London has remained one of the concert and opera capitals of the world, perhaps now pre-eminent, home to an unrivalled number of classical and early musicians and their orchestras, ensembles and scholarship. If the cultural nexus of this élite tradition begins to feel like an extension of Heathrow Airport, it also continues to benefit not only from a more or less common musical language that makes such exchange possible but, specific to Britain, a public service broadcasting history that privileges it: the BBC is inescapably one of the half dozen most important phenomena – let us be blunt and call them facts – to bear in mind about music in Britain in the twentieth century. Another is that what made the BBC possible, technology, has caused a tremendous *growth* of music, admittedly not affecting Britain alone but giving it a head start when it was still the senior industrial nation in the early part of the century (for instance, in the production of both classical and popular gramophone recordings). A further fact is the English language, which has operated to enormous national advantage in the vernacular field, shaping the rise of commercial popular music and musical theatre as an Anglo-American phenomenon; nothing in the smaller, economically declining country may have been able to match Hollywood and Tin Pan Alley, but Wembley has competed with Woodstock and the West End with Broadway, and Britain has produced the Beatles to match Elvis Presley, Lloyd Webber to challenge Irving Berlin.

What, then, happened to *Das Land ohne Musik?* On the high ground again, the two world wars were ill winds indeed, but the very fragmentation of national traditions that accompanied them – of Austro-German hegemony with the First World War and, less suddenly because it was more cosmopolitan, of the Franco-Russian cultural alliance as time went on – blew considerable good for many national repertoires. Elgar and Vaughan Williams may not have travelled well, but further into the twentieth century, where the competition is less between countries than between the new and the old, Britten has held the international stage with his operas as well as anyone since Puccini, Janáček and Berg, at least until American minimalism came along. Britten at the moment of *Peter Grimes* is a fourth primary fact in the case, for with him the country could at last not only host a musical league of nations but had won itself a seat on its council.

Against the fragmentations of the twentieth century there is probably more continuity than our litanies of modern life care to acknowledge. Fact five, I would argue, is Tippett, or something that Tippett, who will be celebrating his 90th birthday in the year of publication of this book, triumphantly represents: a memory, an experience and an artistic compass that span the century in all its contradictoriness. A Suffolk childhood with horses and traps and servants none the less echoed to the sounds of 'Alexander's ragtime band'; a craft first learnt from Stanford's composition textbook and much exercised on folksong took on the intellectual demands of Jung and Stravinsky: a contemporary world with which to engage led him from Trotsky to gay liberation via conscientious objection, nuclear protest and flower power. That this has been a constancy of quest rather than a following of fashion is evidenced by the music itself, for it speaks with a voice initially hard won but without radical change over seven decades and somehow equal to them all. It also speaks optimistically – a rare thing in twentieth-century high art – and one is thankful that he has lived long enough to see at least some of the optimism justified on the world stage in the early 1990s (see Tippett 1991: 270–71).

Is this where we look to locate Britishness? Certainly Tippett's musical voice is British, with an accent consciously cultivated and only half rebelling against Vaughan Williams and Holst in the 1930s. But Tippett would be the first to acknowledge the problematics of the question. It is our sixth fact, and the one for which we look with greatest anticipation to the twenty-first century to provide a sequel or a fixed perspective: that the twentieth century has turned everything it touches into some structure of exclusion, some awareness (or unawareness) of an opposing Other, nowhere more so than in Britain.

INTRODUCTION

This, the curse of subjectivity, is of course the root condition of this book, in its attempt to bind both century and nation (how absurd to want to cut off discussion with Tavener's *The Apocalypse*, or to separate British jazz from its American resources); and I not only predict therefore that the reader will remain unsatisfied with the volume but propose that she or he must. If the twentieth century, in a central, pivoting political moment of which Britten was a kind of cultural correlative, has provided the supreme opportunity for national self-definition – that is, the moment when Britain saw that it was standing alone against the world in 1940 – every other moment has persistently posed the question of what 'it' was or is. Music had done its fair share of excluding, and all of the facts itemized above exclude someone or other. This is why there will be no direct discussion of 'Britishness' in music here, for it is virtually impossible to conceive such a quality, let alone locate it, in wholly or strictly inclusive terms. 'Englishness' excludes the Welsh, Scots and Northern Irish. 'Britishness' can easily exclude immigrants, ethnic communities, and cosmopolitan intellectuals and artists who happen to live here; or, if premised upon language, history, climate or geography, it begins to include not just the Irish but half the globe. This is not to say that the elusive quality will not continue to be sought; indeed, it should be, if music wishes to retain its power to forge identities. But if the Britishness of British music is to represent the whole nation and the whole century, think of how much it must encompass: Birtwistle and Delius may not now seem so far apart, but what about Birtwistle and bhangra? When everything has settled down, shall we find anything that has been holding it all together? Hymns and chants in school assemblies or on the football terraces? Television jingles? The quest for this philosopher's stone seems fruitless, yet it persists in the thinking of a composer such as Turnage (notably in *Greek*) and is not dishonourable.

It also persists in the work of scholars. Something that must be acknowledged here is the groundswell of academic studies of Englishness as a twentieth-century cultural formation that has gathered force during the years in which this book was in the making, for this new thinking and writing has found music, so often the poor relation in contextual research, at the centre of things. Elgar, Parry, even Sir Frederick Bridge now appear in senior historians' footnotes, and the reader is referred to Colls and Dodd 1986, Hobsbawm and Ranger 1983, Holt 1989, R. Porter 1992, Samuel 1989 and Williams 1973, as well as the more specifically musical investigations of Harker (1985), Stradling and Hughes (1993) and Boyes (1993).

Most of these books draw on the range of intellectual traditions and developments that constitute current critical theory, and it is not just Marxism that now persistently challenges history. Indeed, we can welcome the fact that, as from 1994, it is no longer just the British who control the historiography of British music, for its first substantial foreign contribution, Meinhard Saremba's *Elgar, Britten & Co: eine Geschichte der britischen Musik in zwölf Portraits*, has just been published.

The struggle for musical hegemony has been going on for most of the century in Britain in terms of a shifting conflict between respectable and unrespectable art, mostly between high and low, often between patronage and commerce and sometimes between amateur and professional. First there was the attempt to define popular music by excluding the music hall, urban folksong and (I would add) musical comedy and by patronizing the idealized rural folk. After the Second World War the wind shifted and the battle was between international and national standards, with serialism and jazz keeping largely out of each other's way at the top but in contradistinction to everything homespun at the bottom. The weathercock veered around again in the 1960s with new blocs built on youth and its racial alliances. Now there is gender. The year 1994 saw, at the Proms, the first professional performance since the 1930s of Ethel Smyth's opera *The Wreckers*, strongly foreshadowing *Peter Grimes* in its dramaturgy and, as Natalie Wheen put it in her radio commentary, raising all sorts of questions about who owns musical history; but the point was not that it might have converted Brittenites but that it brought with it a new audience – women, feminists, lesbians and gays – for whom this was simply not the issue.

Up to a point this may all be a problem only for historiography – do the people in the street really care whether their music is authentic, or whether it is British? Nevertheless, the taxonomy of music has sooner or later always involved money, and it begins to look as though the late twentieth century has also been the period in which the mutual exclusion of patronized and commercial art, as well as, perhaps, professional and amateur – a distinction developed formidably over three-quarters of the century with the rise of Arts Council, BBC and educational funding on the one hand and the music industry on the other – has broken down. The National Theatre now puts on musicals. Classic FM becomes just another genre station.

The late twentieth-century whole world of music thus betokens equality to some, rampant consumerism with its attendant loss of

INTRODUCTION

authority and real values to others. But we need to bear in mind that the very existence of musical genres and constituencies that can be defined (as the record shops do), even if not ranked, excludes those who do not appear to have them. Amateurs may have remained that vast body of 'hidden musicians', as Dave Russell reminds us in Chapter 8, but both amateur and professional music as adjuncts to, say, religion, may hide even more those Asian identities that do not use either. It would be ironic if, by the twenty-first century, it were beginning to look as though, rather than different musics providing representative badges for communities or (though this now sounds Utopian) helping to bridge them, to be thought of as not 'owning' any music at all were the real cultural exclusion. What if absence from studies such as this book were beginning to stigmatize *Gemeinschaften ohne Musik?*

This is a study shaped very much by its own history, which needs explanation. Arnold Whittall originally edited the volume for the Athlone Press in the mid- to late 1970s and with great skill and labour elicited a complete manuscript that had reached the publishers by the end of 1981 but not soon enough for production before Athlone dropped the series, having issued only Volume V. The script languished until Alyn Shipton rescued it for Blackwell, along with Volumes I – IV, in 1987. At this point Arnold, acutely aware of how quickly perspectives on contemporary music shift even during a short delay in publication, had had enough, and I was asked by Ian Spink if I would take the volume over. I agreed. The original script contained seven substantial chapters on art music, and I was very keen to retain the best of these, one of which also happened to be the longest and struck me as an outstanding, pioneer treatment of a central repertoire. But I was also keen to expand the scope of popular music and contextual coverage, the former (hitherto treated by Richard Middleton in one large chapter) not least because Nicholas Temperley had shown the way in his Volume V, the latter by separating off some of the issues dealt with by Arnold Whittall in his own opening chapter, and both of necessity by way of elisions elsewhere. The seven art music chapters were thereby reduced to four, of which Peter Evans's and Jim Samson's are expansions of their original coverage to include instrumental and chamber music as well as orchestral, and Matthew Rye's and my own are completely new. Both Richard Middleton and Arnold Whittall were invited and agreed, with reserves of graciousness, steadfastness and expertise at which I can only marvel, to write replacement chapters covering in greater detail and enhanced perspective some of their previous areas, the remainder of which were entirely reformulated as new, independent contributions from Cyril Ehrlich, Derek Scott, Patrick O'Connor, David Kershaw, Dave Russell, Christian Kennett and Harry Haskell.

At the time I felt rather pleased with this new configuration, and it is only in the short period by the calendar but journey of a lifetime by way of intellectual education that has been mine and, I suspect, the lot of others since 1988 that I have come to ask myself why there are no contributions from women or chapters on them; why the consideration of art music, still separated from popular, still accounts for more than two-thirds of the book and subjects itself by and large to encyclopaedic discourse, technical and critical, rather than contextual meaning; why composers rather than performers or even institutions are the stuff of discussion in some areas, not others; why jazz is partitioned in popular territories; why early twentieth-century composers tend to get lost in the cracks between this and the previous volume; why electro-acoustic music is not separately treated; and why the whole host of conceptual misgivings referred to in this introduction did not occur to me at the outset. I must stress, therefore, that the responsibility for these proportions and perspectives and the limitations, perhaps affronts to some, that inhere within them are wholly mine. My contributors worked within these bounds.

At any rate, a certain portrait of music in Britain in the twentieth century has now been completed, and there may still be much to be proud of in its scope and its details, many of which have been limned for the first time, once the unstable physiognomy of the sitter has been acknowledged.

It remains also to acknowledge the dedication and compliance of all the contributors to this volume, to thank them for responding positively to my requests, criticisms, suggestions and deadlines, to apologize to them for the delays that beset my own work on the volume, and to express my considerable gratitude to Alyn Shipton and his colleagues at Blackwell's for their support, guidance and patience and to Ingrid Grimes for her devoted copy-editing. Finally, I wish to express my debt to Arnold Whittall, who did so much of the work that has made eventual publication possible. I hope he is not too disappointed with what we have done to his original vision.

Stephen Banfield
Birmingham, September 1994

PART I
Music in Context

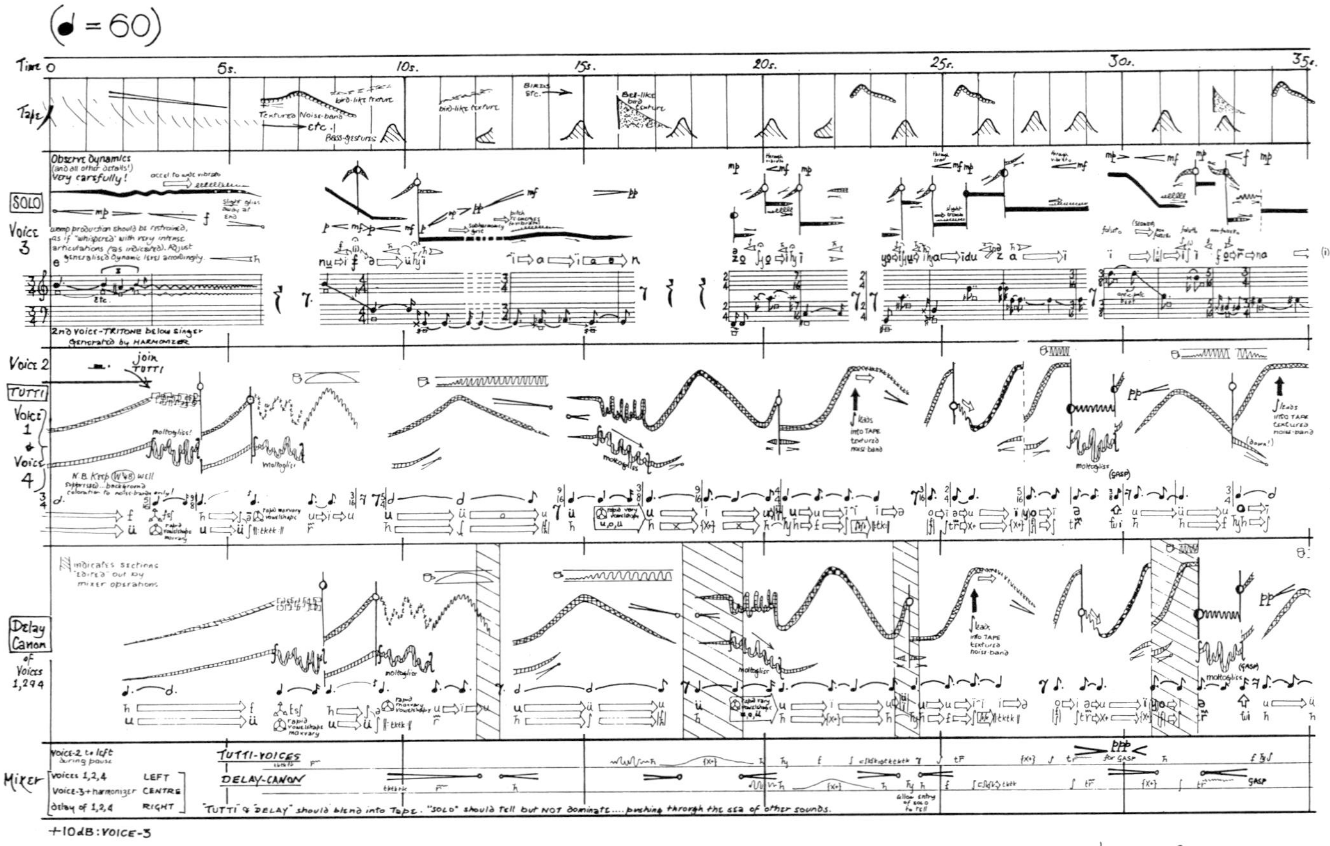

Vox II Trevor Wishart Page 8

Chapter 1

BRITISH MUSIC IN THE MODERN WORLD

ARNOLD WHITTALL

I: Concepts of Modernity

Martin Wiener, the cultural historian, has written that 'for a long time the English have not felt comfortable with "progress"', and that 'the end result of the nineteenth-century transformation of Britain was . . . a peaceful accommodation . . . that entrenched pre-modern elements within the new society and gave legitimacy to anti-modern sentiments' (1981: 5, 7). From this perspective it may be concluded that, for much of the twentieth century, British art at its most characteristic has reflected the essentially passive conservatism of British society. The supreme confidence that went with Britain's imperial expansionism was irrevocably shattered by the cataclysm of the First World War, inducing a deep disillusionment and leading to an interwar period of 'political feebleness and cultural stagnation' (Mellers and Hildyard 1989: 19). Only with the gradual recovery of economic prosperity some 15 years after the end of the Second World War was a cultural climate of greater tolerance and variety created, within which progressiveness – or at any rate permissiveness – could find a place. And even if the 'legitimacy of anti-modern sentiments' can no longer be assumed, there remains, according to the critic Richard Toop, an 'all-purpose anti-intellectualism' that 'is still very much embedded in the collective psyche of the musical establishment' in Britain (1988: 4), and accounts for the tendency to prefer the undemanding to the challenging. Such arguments have received much support, as well as criticism. In my view they are not so much wrong as oversimplified, and this becomes clear if we consider twentieth-century British music more directly in relation to the concept of modernity.

MUSIC IN CONTEXT

We may adopt the conventional use of 'modern' in music history, to refer primarily to the most recent developments, or we may prefer the usage of general historians and social theorists, for whom 'modern' signifies the entire post-renaissance period. In either case, however, the music historian may still find it useful to test the powerful argument of the social theorist Anthony Giddens that 'we have not moved beyond modernity but are living precisely through a phase of its radicalization' (1991: 51). What is involved here is not simply the description of musical style, with the music of certain composers sounding more 'modern' – fragmented, disjointed, dissonant – than that of others, but an explanation of the structures that support style. For it is precisely when particular structural principles and technical procedures can be demonstrated (and perceived) that the true nature of musical modernism may be determined. For Giddens, modernity is not a matter of the absence of evident and pervasive hierarchies and integrating elements, but rather of particular tendencies to fragmentation being 'complemented by countertendencies towards integration and wholeness' (p. 96). Social theorists argue 'that the very dissonances and fragmentations of [modern] society do compose a larger co-ordinating structure and that historical change, in its very rapidity, is strengthening this structure' (Sennett 1991: 6), and cultural historians may also conclude that it is the degree and nature of dissonance and fragmentation in art that make it modern, or modernist, and not the total absence or suppression of any co-ordinating or integrating formal processes. In this sense, it is the speed of change and the absolutely fundamental role of 'dissonances and fragmentations' that are the important constituents of twentieth-century modernity – 'radicalized modernity', in Giddens's terms. Yet these do not exclude every possibility of a 'larger co-ordinating structure', despite the arguments of some theorists committed to the notion of an already evident 'post-modernism'.

A concept of musical modernity as the enhanced – unprecedented – confrontation between unity and diversity, and the consequent intensification of ambiguity, is one of which composers are well aware. To take a relatively recent instance, Jonathan Harvey has discussed his music in a way that presents a dialogue between his concern with eternal spiritual values and the very specific contemporary technical possibilities found in state-of-the-art computing systems at IRCAM (outside the UK). This dialogue reaches inevitably and productively into the composer's aesthetic predilections. On the one hand his desire 'is to integrate ever more and more' (Harvey 1986: 180). On the other hand, in discussing how that desire is best pursued, he shows particular awareness of the inevitable and inherent ambiguities which arise, for the listener, when unities are diversified. Writing of his own recent music, Harvey comments that 'the timbres clarify the structure. In general they draw attention to the fact that a shape is the same as in a neighbouring melody by preserving the timbre invariant, at least at its purest stage.' Nevertheless, 'the sense of ambiguity in timbre is present during the transitions, and it is also present in the composite melodies which are both one thing and two things simultaneously' (pp. 187–8).

We may well be able to find evidence in music of all periods and styles for the interplay of unity and diversity, similarity and difference, ambivalence and explicitness – for the presence of elements 'which are both one thing and two things simultaneously'. Yet twentieth-century modernism, or radicalized modernity, strongly prepared as it was by the increasingly diverse and ambivalent formal designs and harmonic practices of the nineteenth century, offers a distinctive version of an aesthetically recurrent phenomenon – not least in the way that truly 'modern' structures of the kind that concern Harvey coexist with more extreme designs where the 'desire to integrate' is more positively resisted. From this theoretical standpoint, it might seem that British musical life, as well as British musical composition, has been characterized at least as much by a resistance to radicalized modernity as by an embrace of it: in other words, that Wiener and those who think like him are right after all. Yet an important modification of this view becomes possible if we cease to compare Britain with Germany or France, and test the hypothesis that British musical life found an appropriate place for modernism in British compositions at the appropriate time: that is, later rather than sooner. It seems clear that a full assimilation of international twentieth-century modernism – by composers as well as listeners – was not possible before British music had established a strong and independent identity which, to many of those responding to the music when it was new, counted as no less 'modern' in its character and methods than much that was more obviously radical and progressive in the music of other countries.

MUSIC IN CONTEXT
II: Modernism in Early Twentieth-Century British Musical Life

It cannot seriously be argued that British compositional achievement during the nineteenth century matched at every stage the best that Europe had to offer. However, while music on the European mainland during the first decade of the twentieth century seemed in many respects like an overripe, inflated echo of the strengths and glories of the age of romanticism, in some ways decadent, in other ways seeking strenuously to advance and change, music in Britain gave evidence of a new maturity: not without its own adumbrations of decadence (Delius) and innovation (Vaughan Williams), but most essentially, with Elgar, discovering something long sought, rather than seeking to survive and prosper in the shadow of past greatness. As one critic looking back from the immediate post-Second World War period recognized, Elgar's great achievement was to help English music 'gain confidence' (A. E. F. Dickinson 1951: 240), and it is the fact that this long-delayed confidence emerged just as British society in general was losing its imperialist *élan* that encourages assumptions of an association between confidence and conservatism. The confidence Elgar encouraged was the confidence to be independent of well-assimilated German models, and the tendency of critics before 1914 to praise Elgar as a more appealing modernist than either Strauss or Mahler (see Crump 1986: 170) underlines his success at creating a sense of the stylistically new and the vital while avoiding any hint of avant-garde structural experiment. The belief that Elgar had drawn more valid and legitimate conclusions from the masterworks of Wagner and Brahms than any of his German contemporaries remained strong at the time of his death.

For example, the *Musical Times*'s Elgar obituary implied that his greatest achievement – and most legitimately 'modern' trait – was to have ensured that musical romanticism found its fulfilment in Britain, not Germany:

For us . . . he prolonged the standing tradition, maintaining it against the hammerings of Strauss, the insidiousness of Debussy, and the provocations of Stravinsky; and he did so not by an appeal to our conservative instincts but by showing what new adventure and discovery lay in the old ways . . . It cannot be doubted that Elgar's music, by its strength, weight and popularity, acted as a bulwark against the too ready influx of modernism, and that the present British school owes much of its steadiness – as compared with what we see going on elsewhere – to Elgar's example.
(Grace and McNaught 1934: 306–9)

This masterpiece of nationalistic special pleading serves to reinforce the sense of confidence in the rightness of what Elgar had achieved; and it was this emerging confidence, even before 1914, that helped to facilitate a relatively tolerant attitude to those European avant-garde tendencies of which British music itself was in general felt to have no need.

Music historians have rightly emphasized the fact that British – or at least London – musical life in the early twentieth century was not notably more backward-looking or hostile to innovation than that of other centres. Critics were willing to testify that the 'extremes of dissonance' in Strauss's *Elektra* (first performed in England under Beecham in February 1910) 'were justified . . . by dramatic context' (J. Irving 1988: 68–9), and after Henry Wood's celebrated world première of Schoenberg's Five Orchestral Pieces op. 16 in September 1912, Ernest Newman wrote – and probably lived to regret it – that 'the next vital development of music will be along the lines of the best of Schoenberg'. Although the conservative composer Charles Wood was reduced to incomprehending laughter by op. 16, Philip Heseltine found 'a strange fascination', and Percy Grainger wrote of 'the greatest revolution I have witnessed. He opens great and rich freedoms for all of us composers' (quoted in Lambourn 1987: 423–4).

To some, not least the members of the Society of British Composers, the successful performances of recent works by Skryabin, Debussy and Stravinsky, as well as Schoenberg, were damning evidence of an abiding prejudice against the British composer (see Foreman 1987: 2–3). Yet it was precisely in the immediate pre-1914 years that the music of Elgar and Vaughan Williams began to make its mark, whereas, with the exception of Holst, those British composers most directly stimulated by the work of Schoenberg and other progressives – Bernard van Dieren, Percy Grainger, John Foulds and Frank Bridge – were relatively marginal figures. It is tempting to argue that the reason for this failure of a British modernism based on European models to take root was not musical but political: the First World War; but the tendency to shun all things radical, as well as all things German, was already well established before 1914, and on balance it would seem that the war merely reinforced it. And for the best part of 40 years after the war, the fact that much of the most radical and progressive European music could be heard in Britain (principally under the aegis of the BBC) did not mean that such music was assimilated by the major composers in the sense of being crucially influential on their work. One reason for this becomes apparent if we examine how the leading inter-war composer, Ralph Vaughan Williams, viewed the concept of modernity.

III: Vaughan Williams on Nationalism and Modernism

In 'Gustav Holst: an Essay and a Note' (1920), Vaughan Williams's starting-point is the view that 'the modern world needs a modern vocabulary, but the vocabulary will not make the modern mind' (1953: 64). It follows that to describe Richard Strauss as 'a modern of the moderns' is only superficially true, because 'his mind is as early Victorian as that of his father-in-music Liszt'. Similarly, 'Delius, in spite of his bewitching harmonic experiments (or is it because of them?) belongs mentally to the [18]80s'.

Vaughan Williams evidently distinguishes between 'mind' and style: and what makes Holst modern in a sense that applies to neither Strauss nor Delius is 'the simple fact that he is a modern Englishman and that his music is in direct relation with real life' (p. 68). The contrast is between a late romanticism (Strauss, Delius) that lacks such a relation, and an attitude whereby

the interests, responsibilities and realities of life are not a hindrance but a stimulus – they are the very stuff out of which Holst has knit his art, the soil on which it flourishes . . . Life and art are to Holst not enemies but the complements of each other. (p. 69)

Although Vaughan Williams's argument remains vague, he is clearly distinguishing between late romanticism as an escapist, decadent phenomenon and modernity as sane and socially responsible: functional, in essence. Holst is shown to be both pragmatic and uncompromising: whether 'nobly diatonic' or exploiting strong harmonic clashes, he 'does nothing by halves' (p. 74). As Vaughan Williams sees it,

it is of the essence of modern music, as of all modern thought, to drive straight to the root of the matter in hand without artifice or subterfuge; to let the matter rule the form, not the form the matter; to obtain our rules from practice, not our practice from rules. (p. 78)

Vaughan Williams undoubtedly obtained his definition of 'modern' from Holst's practice, not from some broader theoretical position, and he felt justified in doing so, not because Holst was the most radical example he could find, but because he seemed to embody national virtues in their purest form. More than a quarter of a century later ('A Minim's Rest', 1948), Vaughan Williams looked back on the 'great resurgence of music here in England', and ascribed its 'life-giving power' to

> all the composers of this renaissance from Parry to Britten, different and often antagonistic as their aims are, hav[ing] this in common – that they realize that vital art must grow in its own soil and be nurtured by its own rain and sunshine. (R. Vaughan Williams 1963: 168)

It was precisely such sentimental equations of pure nationalism with musical vitality (and progressiveness) that cut deeply, and by no means always negatively, into British musical life between the wars and for some time after 1945. In 1930 William Glock was told by Vaughan Williams and Herbert Howells, who interviewed him when he applied for a bursary to study with Schnabel in Berlin, that 'there was no need to look abroad for a teacher' (Glock 1991: 19). By 1965, a young Turk like Peter Maxwell Davies was reacting to such insularity with vehement protestations to the effect that composers educated exclusively on home ground were, by definition, 'wellnigh uneducated' (1965: 22). It is understandable that in wartime Vaughan Williams should declare that 'all that is of value in our spiritual and cultural life springs from our own soil' (1963: 155); but his argument that British composers 'have been ruined by abdicating their birthright in their most impressionable years' (p. 158) would cut little ice in the internationalist cultural climate after 1945. The signs are that the best composers since that time have not been those who have begun with ideas about personal or national traditions, but those who have responded to the stimulus of great (usually non-British) music, and built a strong personal language on this broad foundation. As Michael Tippett observed in 1967:

> the nationalist impulse was part and parcel of an attempt to come free of teutonic musical and sometimes, also, political domination . . . However, the movements that began as nationalist became by the middle of the century markedly internationalist. (1980: 109)

It was through such internationalism that musical modernism came into its own, supplanting the 'alternative' modernism advocated by Vaughan Williams, whose principles were cultural ('sanity and social responsibility') rather than structural. Even in the case of a composer such as Tippett, who has not been shy to express cultural attitudes and beliefs – the preface to *The Mask of Time* (1983) is a good recent example – the structural consequences of these attitudes and beliefs seem on the face of it more productive of properly modernist characteristics than was the case before 1945.

IV: Between the Wars

The characterization, cited earlier, of the inter-war period as one of 'political feebleness and cultural stagnation' is too sweeping, simply because it fails to acknowledge the contexts within which Vaughan Williams's nationalism was placed, and which challenged as well as confirmed it. That musical life experienced a conservative backlash can be confirmed by remarks of the leading critic and radical sympathizer Edwin Evans (1874–1945), writing in 1926 about the early 1920s:

We were then hearing more modern music than any capital in Europe, and I believe, any city in America . . . Today we hear very little that is new unless we go abroad in search of it; we have lost contact with the current of musical opinion at home and the conservatives hold practically undisputed sway . . . in London, the unprecedented activity of those post-war seasons has left an aftermath of musical indigestion. Perhaps we overdid it.
(Gillies 1989: 37)

Lewis Foreman has also underlined the anti-progressive instincts at work in British music between 1920 and 1940, observing that the BBC was by no means an undimmed beacon of enlightenment, at least as far as British composers were concerned:

There was a tendency for any assessment, once made, to be irreversible . . . Sir Adrian Boult [1889–1983] was a Director of Music at the BBC of remarkably wide sympathies, whose placing of Vaughan Williams on a pedestal confirmed the latter's position in British music for the rest of his life. (1987: 154)

Whether or not Foreman is correct to imply that Vaughan Williams received more than his fair share of promotion and prominence (at the expense, among others, of Havergal Brian), it seems right for promoters of British music during the inter-war period to have focused on its own relatively new world of late romanticism and nationalism, while not positively seeking to suppress the more promising signs of internationalism as they became more insistent during the 1930s. This was a time in which various talents were able to assimilate such powerful influences as Sibelius and Hindemith (Walton), Berg and Bartók (Bridge), and Stravinsky (Britten and Tippett), while Vaughan Williams himself deepened and enriched his own personal brand of nationalist conservatism. From the perspective of progressive modernism, Vaughan Williams's contrasts may be all too obviously and securely integrated, his structures conformist, his ideas limited: yet his voice and his spirit were authentically contemporary. As William McNaught declared, praising the new Fourth Symphony, 'the modernism is never of the darksome, fourth-dimensional, understand-me-if-you-can order. It is daylight modernism, done with a clear brain and a sure hand' (1935: 452). Such comments are nicely representative of the suspicion of the extravagant, the expressionistic, the experimental, that dictated the course of British music's mainstream until the 1960s.

It may well be that the most potent precedent for the creative internationalism that emerged after 1960 is found in such works of Frank Bridge as the String Quartet no. 3 (1926) and *Phantasm* (1931), although the expressionistic associations of Bartók and Berg which they possess were less immediately influential than the continuation of those responses to Stravinskian neoclassicism which can be detected intermittently in the likes of Bliss, Lambert, Britten and Tippett during the inter-war period. The fact that Bridge was still being criticized by the *Musical Times* in 1934 for his use of 'modern tricks' indicates the confidence of the critics that the best British music had survived the onslaught of progressive modernism unscathed. Even those writers who took pride in acting as the goads of the establishment, such as Sorabji and Lambert, were united with that establishment in arguing for the preservation and further development of an essentially romantic kind of music. For these writers, the demon was Stravinsky, the angel Sibelius; and although Lambert took pains not simply to dismiss Schoenberg and Berg out of hand, his conclusions were unambiguous:

Of all contemporary music that of Sibelius seems to point forward most surely to the future. Since the death of Debussy, Sibelius and Schönberg are the most significant figures in European music, and Sibelius is undoubtedly the more complete artist of the two. However much one may admire Schönberg's powerful imagination and unique genius, it is difficult not to feel that the world of sound and thought that he opens up – though apparently iconoclastic – is *au fond* as restricted as the academicism it has supplanted. Sibelius's music suffers from no such restriction. (1934, R/1966: 277)

Lambert was at least half right in this bold prophecy. Sibelius has indeed played a role in British music extending well beyond the obvious connection between his (and Nielsen's) mode of symphonic expression and that of Robert Simpson. At the same time, however, Schoenberg's 'powerful imagination' has had an even more profound impact, and Stravinsky has remained a vital example in the spheres of rhythm and form long after the more obvious stylistic echoes of his neoclassicism have faded away. The result, after 1960, has been a rapprochement with modernism which has allowed a fruitful strain of relatively traditional romanticism to survive and prosper despite being overtaken, in aesthetic and technical terms, by an expressionism and, in some cases, an anti-organicism, all the more vigorous and iconoclastic for having been suppressed for so long.

V: *Permissives and Progressives after 1945*

When William Glock (*b* 1908) wrote, in 1952, that 'we are beginning to see that it is Schoenberg and Stravinsky, above all, who have defined the crisis of contemporary music and of the contemporary spirit without fear or compromise' (1952: 3), his words contained the seeds of a modernist manifesto (already anticipated, for example, in the pages of *Music Survey*) to which established figures like Britten and Tippett could subscribe, as well as the younger radicals then active at various colleges of music and summer schools. And when, seven years later in 1959, Glock became the BBC's Controller of Music, he was in a position to respond to a need of which he was well aware, as much as to create a need, for more and better performances of relatively radical modern music. These performances, especially those under Boulez, made it possible to hear modern classics on a fairly regular basis, and created a context in which new British compositions, often stimulated by those classics, could be tried out. At the same time critics, historians and academics, such as Donald Mitchell, Wilfrid Mellers and Reginald Smith Brindle, who wrote positively about modern developments and provided guidance in contemporary techniques for fledgling composers, contributed to the normalization of once-shunned modernisms.

Even so, the general change in the cultural climate around 1960, from which music benefited, was less one of conscious and widespread enthusiasm for the radical, as of a new spirit of liberalism, or permissiveness – a spirit that could benefit from increasing material prosperity. Roy and Gwen Shaw have proclaimed with confidence that

> ideologically, the permissive society of the sixties stemmed from the coming together of two separate traditions, humanism and . . . a late romantic desire to banish controls, break down barriers and give everyone unfettered freedom to 'do his own thing' and push experience to its limits. (1988: 25)

The concern to underline any kind of continuity between something apparently new and the cultural forces of the past may represent unease with and incomprehension of the new as much as anything else. Yet the Shaws are right to distinguish between the fashions of stylistic innovation (especially evident in the way popular music was transformed between 1950 and 1970 from the relatively genteel to the explosively energetic) and the underlying cultural forces which do indeed embody such persistent artistic aspirations as the desire to further essentially humanistic ideals and 'to banish controls, break down barriers'.

As far as serious music is concerned, it is undeniable that without the post-war pioneering advocacy of advanced music by conductors like Walter Goehr and Adrian Boult, critics like Hans Keller and Donald Mitchell, animateurs like William Glock, and the compositional pioneering of, in particular, Elisabeth Lutyens and Humphrey Searle, the so-called 1960s generation would have found it more difficult to reap the rewards of the new permissiveness and prosperity. (Whether or not such pioneering advocacy, coupled with economic and social changes, made the reaping of rewards *too* easy is an interesting but hypothetical question.) In any case, in serious music the 1960s 'revolution' was more a matter of destabilizing a prevailing conservatism than of sweeping it away in order to welcome the avant garde into its kingdom. These were above all years of expansion and exploration: the attempts to revive interest in neglected composers like Frank Bridge and Havergal Brian, and – on the part of young composers – the search to build anew on the foundations of late romanticism and expressionism as well as on more recent technical advances in serialism or experimentalism. Already, between the death of Schoenberg in 1951 and the death of Vaughan Williams in 1958 (preceded a few months earlier by the death of the long-silent Sibelius), the focus on Stravinsky as Greatest Living Master yielded the disorientating sight of a senior figure fundamentally reassessing his own language in the light of enthusiasm for Webern, and a lively respect for much of what the post-war generation of European composers, led by Boulez and Stockhausen, was achieving after the invigorating if intemperate dismissal of most of what had gone before. Yet even in Continental Europe, as the case of Henze made clear, it was not a simple matter of avant-garde radicalism sweeping all before it. 'The Past' soon began to mount a rearguard action, and in Britain the new creative energy that seemed to surface around 1960 had much to do with a sense that new, fruitful accommodations between past and present could still be achieved.

Vaughan Williams's musical style was always likely to die with him, not least because it was clear by 1958 that the finest phase of his work had closed in 1947 with the Sixth Symphony. But that did not mean that it was no longer possible to write more-or-less tonal symphonic music. Robert Simpson's early symphonies and quartets achieved the remarkable (for sceptics disposed to embrace the progressive creed) feat of seizing the essence of a still vital tonal tradition. In Simpson's eyes Nielsen and Sibelius were not simply latter-day late romantics but the main custodians, for the post-1914 musical world, of the timeless values of tonality and organic symphonic design. And these values, even when shorn of the specific stylistic qualities exploited so resourcefully by Simpson himself over more than 40 years, have proved to be an essential, continuing element in British music throughout the second half of the century, helping to prevent the complete domination of progressive modernism, while contributing to that startling diversity of modes of expression that is itself a characteristic of modern culture in its most radical phase.

At the time of Vaughan Williams's death Benjamin Britten was generally accepted as the leading British composer. Britten can now be seen as exemplary in his internationalism, his adaptability, and in the way in which that adaptability strengthened rather than diluted his personal voice. From the mixture of 12-note and tonal elements to the use of controlled indeterminacy and of chant-derived materials, Britten advanced significantly beyond the particular eclectic stylistic and technical features that had formed his language in the 1930s, yet, as his most passionate and articulate advocates have insisted, this is still a music in which the background of tradition – and traditional tonality – remains decisive. During the 1960s, Britten appeared to many younger composers to be far more cautious and circumspect than that remarkable late developer Michael Tippett, whose modernist willingness to abandon tonality and embrace mosaic rather than organic formal principles seemed comparable to those procedures of Stravinsky, Varèse or Messiaen that the young Birtwistle, in particular, was beginning to build on with such confidence. It would be the mid-1970s before Britten's own style, with its Mahlerian, Bergian and Bartókian features, would prove of equal inspiration, in the context of the broad and deep eclecticism evident in such composers as Robin Holloway, Oliver Knussen and Colin Matthews.

In their very different ways, both Britten and Tippett showed British composers born in or after the 1930s that the 'modern world' was a world at last coming to terms with modernism in its more radical manifestations, and bringing that response in from the fringes to the centre. The composers born in the 1930s have certainly not remained equally committed to the pursuit of modernism – the work of Crosse and Maw is ample proof of that – yet even these composers demonstrated an ability to digest the radicalism of Schoenberg and Webern, and to take note of the efforts of the post-1945 avant garde. The 1930s generation of radicals was notable above all for its instinctive attraction to features of older music and compositional practice that could serve its purposes: not simply Schoenberg's serialism, Messiaen's modality, Stravinsky's rhythmic disjunctions or Varèse's formal discontinuities, but also the patterns of change-ringing, the complex contrapuntal devices of the Ars Nova, the motivic potential of Gregorian Chant. The resulting music was therefore not only internationalist in style but historically heterodox in its sources. Such pluralism was enhanced during the 1960s and after by the persistence of so many diverse features – everything from Cageian surrealism to the new late romanticism. In the modern musical world, synthesis of such divergent tendencies is not in question. But considerable interaction between them has occurred, in the context of remarkable technical and technological advances.

VI: Modernity and Pluralism

British musical life was at its most bracingly pluralist between the mid-1960s and the mid-1970s. Not only was the expressionism of Maxwell Davies and Birtwistle at its most vigorous, but an experimentalism centring on the activities and enterprise of Cornelius

Cardew also flourished, while more traditional modes of expression continued to be memorably explored by relatively senior composers – Tippett, Britten, Simpson. That this was also a time of particular success for British popular music reinforces the sense of a remarkable confidence and creativity, in which modernist ideals were very much to the fore. These were the golden days of progressive permissiveness, so it is tempting to seek parallels between the social and political changes that began to emerge during the mid-1970s and subsequent developments in the arts.

After 1979, with the return of a right-wing Conservative government, British social and political life reflected an increasing unease with the kind of liberalism that had been prevalent since the 1960s. Those seeking neat parallels between Art and Life may find it striking to read the following: 'The tonal backlash is gaining ground. From Robin Holloway to Wolfgang Rihm there's a sentiment abroad that we've had enough of what many see atonal music as: inhuman, indulgent experimentalism.' (Harvey 1980: 699)

Jonathan Harvey was well aware that tonality as such had never been away. Rather, what concerned him was evidence that composers who might hitherto have been regarded as accepting the lasting validity of the atonal revolution were beginning to recant, like so many lower-middle-class voters forsaking socialism for Thatcherism. From that perspective, one of the most disconcerting statements would have been that of Peter Maxwell Davies, writing of his First Symphony (1976) that the first movement had a 'pivotal tonal centre of F, with a "dominant" of D♭', which he hoped would be 'immediately hearable', and acknowledging the significance of Schumann and Sibelius (as well as Boulez) for his own symphonic enterprise (see Griffiths 1982: 159–60). Maxwell Davies's evolution from a style in which the found objects of tonal tradition tended to be parodied and fiercely juxtaposed with the living atonal language of the present into a syntax founded on a concept, however idiosyncratic, of tonality, might indeed have heralded the general collapse of modernism, of pluralism, and even of internationalism. In fact, however, the modernist quality in Maxwell Davies's music was enhanced by this development, and his symphonic works from the later 1970s onwards have retained sufficient contrapuntal complexity and harmonic density for the perception of basic 'tonal' features to be much more problematic than the recognition of more elementary formal and textural contrasts. From this the general point emerges that although the modernist pluralism of the 1990s is different from that of the 1960s, and less boldly defined by its extremes, it undoubtedly exists and, for the moment, continues to prosper.

During the 1980s many informed musicians came to prefer Birtwistle's brand of modernism, with its powerfully sculpted textural juxtapositions and superimpositions, to Maxwell Davies's. Yet Maxwell Davies continued to be admired for his social involvement and commitment. True political radicals shared his ambition to make serious music accessible to children and a wider general public, even while they might deplore the strain of liberal paternalism evident in Davies's ability not to compromise his own 'élitist' stance as a composer while doing so. They themselves, however, disillusioned with what they came to regard as the aesthetic impotence of the post-war avant garde – neatly summarized in Cardew's book title, *Stockhausen Serves Imperialism* (1974) – seemed to run out of creative steam even before events in the wider world in the late 1980s changed the political and ideological climate so decisively. Though the New Simplicity retained its attractiveness for some composers whose prime outlet was the traditional concert hall – Howard Skempton and Steve Martland, for example – the aim to reach as wide an audience as possible was probably best met by Michael Nyman's transference of minimalist techniques into the world of film music, through his association with Peter Greenaway. By comparison, the attempts of Cardew and others to spread radical political ideas by means of a music that had many traditional aspects to it were no more successful than the similar efforts of Alan Bush earlier in the century. Indeed, the intellectual climate of the 1980s, as far as music was concerned, remained more orientated towards art as a psychological or existential entity than either a political or metaphysical one – though in respect of the latter Jonathan Harvey remains a notable exception. Other British composers who share vital elements of Harvey's technical background (in particular the interest in serialism and electronics) are less metaphysically-minded: for example, Nigel Osborne, Brian Ferneyhough, Michael Finnissy and George Benjamin. As with the earlier British modernists – Birtwistle, in particular – any extra-musical subject matter in their compositions is more likely to be broadly humanist in perspective, even when a strong sense of ritual is present, and some sense of the transcendent survives.

One result of the stylistic pluralism evident in recent British music has been a revived polemics. In particular, Richard Toop has sought to distinguish between a group of composers he regards as the 'logical inheritors' of the organicist principles of the Western classical tradition and so tending to be without honour in their own country, and others – 'neo-romantics', 'ritualists', and 'subminimalists' – who, from Toop's position as the advocate of the 'New Complexity', are betrayers rather than inheritors, and suffer from the endemic British disease of complacently giving audiences what they want. The argument is that an 'establishment' – the BBC and Arts Council-supported commissioning and performing bodies whose normal sphere of operations is the London South Bank – prefers to promote the music of Robin Holloway, Oliver Knussen, Colin Matthews, Robert Saxton and Judith Weir rather than that of Michael Finnissy, Chris Dench, Richard Barrett, James Dillon, and their principal mentor-in-exile, Brian Ferneyhough. The point is not that these composers are wholly neglected, but that their support lacks the enthusiasm, the sense of rightness, that goes with the promotion of the other 'team'.

Toop succeeds admirably in demonstrating that his chosen composers do not only think about music, but also actually compose it, in ways that justify his claims about their (modernist) continuity with the past. At the same time, however, a comparable legitimacy (in the sense of building on, not rejecting, tradition) can be granted to the composers in the opposite camp, as well as to those – Harvey, John Casken – who occupy the middle ground in the sense of being neither so unremittingly 'complex' nor so explicitly 'romantic' ('neo' or otherwise) in orientation. Such extreme contrasts in style between composers of comparable aesthetic legitimacy is precisely what is needed for British music to remain properly 'modern' in the final years of the twentieth century. Such contrasts are seen in terms of conflict by some, of coexistence by others, especially if they believe that neither ideology has a monopoly of good or bad.

One particularly impassioned definition of modernism declares it to be

the one art that responds to the scenario of our chaos. It is the art consequent on Heisenberg's 'Uncertainty principle', [the art] of the destruction of civilization and reason in the First World War, of the world changed and reinterpreted by Marx, Freud and Darwin, of capitalism and constant industrial acceleration, of existential exposure to meaninglessness or absurdity. (BRADBURY and MCFARLANE 1976: 27)

Such a definition will appeal to those who seek a clear and all-embracing link between Art and Life, and to those who see the twentieth century as uniquely tension-ridden and unstable. The danger is that such a definition sees art as at best neutral, a mirror held up to the horrors of the modern world, whereas what admirers of modernism in music find most exciting and convincing is the way in which factors making for tension and confrontation are turned to positive artistic account, producing at times a precarious sense of balance, at times a new coherence, if still some way short of the hierarchic integrations of the classical, tonal past. Richard Toop writes of Brian Ferneyhough that

> much of the forcefulness and richness of the *Carceri* pieces arises both from the conceptual obstacle courses that the composer sets himself in the realization of individual layers, and from the violent collisions between these layers. (1987: 626)

The point is precisely that this music is not simply built from layers of textures in violent collision, but that the structure creates a 'forcefulness and richness' that are positively and powerfully expressive. The layers do not (as they might) generate a chaotic absurdity. Even when Ferneyhough himself speaks of the desire to give 'a certain plausibility to the concept of coherence which will later be destroyed' (Toop 1990: 59), he is far from offering an abject admission that his music is merely the helpless embodiment of 'the scenario of our chaos': he is describing a structural principle whose dramatic effect creates a memorable artistic experience.

It is possible to feel that, whereas Ferneyhough's ultra-complex compositions challenge coherence all too successfully, the explicit integrations of, for example, a Robert Saxton are achieved at the expense of vital expressionistic forcefulness. Birtwistle, Casken and Harvey seem at the time of writing the most satisfying and the most impressive British exponents of a modern – atonal – equilibrium between tendencies to ambiguous atonality and the kind of integrative coherence that is most explicit in varieties of minimalism (John Tavener, Graham Fitkin). Harvey's 1980 article, quoted above, continues with the affirmation that

> in my view the [tonal] backlash will be shortlived, because the deeper human meanings of atonality have hardly begun to be understood, although they are of the utmost importance for our growth as a civilization. Once understanding grows, there will be no stopping it. (p. 699)

Harvey's prophecy relates to his belief that 'in a musical language which is highly ordered, and yet which floats above the seething world of tonal becoming, we have a representation of this spirit world' – first outlined in the music of Webern – 'potentially more direct and precise than was possible in the tonal era' (p. 699). Yet it is an essential aspect of music in the modern world that 'tonal becoming' retains its power, its ability to stimulate the musical imagination, no less strongly than atonality, if only a living style can be devised. A highly personal yet undeniably tonal work as ambitious, vital and memorable as Nicholas Maw's *Odyssey* (1973–87) cannot simply be dismissed as anachronistic or irrelevant. In its richness and diversity, twentieth-century British music expresses a healthy scepticism about whether the future will bring to birth the new order imagined by Harvey, or a continuation of that pluralism which the twentieth century itself has evolved and explored. The 'modern world' of the twenty-first century will provide the answer.

Chapter 2

THE 'PROBLEM' OF POPULAR MUSIC

RICHARD MIDDLETON

'All the mass-based entertainment in the world cannot add up to a half-pennyworth of great art.'

(Michael Tippett)

I: Categories of Music

Most societies, certainly all class societies, recognize different categories of music, some 'higher', some 'lower'. Usually, however, distinctions are related to differences of social function or social group, and are not regarded as problematic; only in the twentieth century has popular music, in its modern guise – what Tippett calls 'mass-based entertainment' – become a 'problem'. It is precisely the historical developments characteristic of this period, notably the mass democratization of society and the commodification of culture, that explain why this is so; and any effort to understand it must be historically specific.

Defining popular music is notoriously difficult (see Middleton 1990: 3ff). The proliferation of crossovers today – Brian Eno, Steve Martland, Mike Westbrook, Michael Nyman and many others – makes this especially clear.

But this is a phenomenon that can be traced back, through Richard Rodney Bennett, Carl Davis, Malcolm Arnold, John Dankworth, to the beginnings of our period (Eric Coates, Cyril Scott, Billy Mayerl . . .), and to Elgar and before. Locating 'light music' and theatre music often creates confusions (what is Richard Addinsell's *Warsaw Concerto* or Andrew Lloyd Webber's *Phantom of the Opera?*), as does the substantial, if ever mutating, 'national residual' category: music that everybody knows, from 'Land of hope and glory' to 'We shall overcome', from 'You'll never walk alone' to the '*William Tell* theme'.

Commercialism cannot be the crucial factor. Again this is crystal-clear today, as mass marketing of 'classical' music explodes. Commercial sponsorship is widely accepted; the Arts Council (1985) speaks the language of 'investment' and 'productivity'; Nigel Kennedy and others are sold with production and image-making techniques derived from the pop industry; opera draws rock-stadium audiences. But again there is a history: for example, the marketing of David Munrow or, earlier, of Britten', 'promoted ... as single-mindedly as Unilever would promote a new washing powder' (Cole 1978: 56).

'Nymphs and shepherds', Ernest Lough's 'Hear my prayer', Caruso and Fritz Kreisler were huge sellers in the early years of the record industry, and from the beginning of the century, 'art' musicians had no hesitation in accepting subsidy from the more profitable 'popular' side of the business (Peacock and Weir 1975: 43). In truth, from well before this date, the whole musical field existed within the principles of the market – even if some sectors were unhappy, even rebellious, about this.

If we try different distinctions, we find they are no less elusive. The 'incompetence' attributed to some popular musicians, fuelled by a venerable tradition of artists who cannot play or sing, who fake performances, whose harmonies, orchestrations or records are really created by anonymous professionals, is a product of a lack of understanding of changes wrought by new technologies and production methods; how the music comes into existence is actually of no significance. Besides, in many cases – singers as varied as Annie Lennox, Van Morrison, Cleo Laine and Anne Briggs, for example – consummate artistry is readily apparent if only appropriate criteria are applied. Turning, then, to value distinctions, we find that these are seldom rigorously argued (is all 'art' music automatically good?). Even style differences are less conclusive than might be supposed, and often work as codes for cruder explanatory grids, discredited by ethnomusicologists, which operate with distinctions between simple and complex, banal and original, or primitive and civilized (see Blacking 1976, 1987).

In fact, the musical categories are *discursively* constructed, products of *ideology*. The seemingly opposed concepts of art-music canon on the one hand, commercialized, corrupted popular music on the other, developed symbiotically, but slowly, during the nineteenth

THE 'PROBLEM' OF POPULAR MUSIC

century, as responses to industrialization. Macdonnell (1860) still had to explain to an educated readership how 'classical' music differed from opera and ballads (it was intellectually more demanding). Concert programmes continued mixed right up to the end of the century. The social accommodation between the aristocracy and new bourgeoisie, coupled with the prevailing idea of music as a social grace, tended to drain all categories of the bite of difference (Banfield 1981a: 14–18). Even 'vulgar' genres, it was often thought, had their appropriate social place, and in any case the hierarchy was readily traversed through the ladder of 'self-improvement'. Only tremendous turn-of-the-century changes in political, social and economic life turned Matthew Arnold's earlier warnings into common currency. The beginnings of mass democracy, socialism, the modern leisure apparatus, the mass media: all signalled that the age of the common man had arrived. Against an intellectual context of Nietzschian anxiety about the threat of the totalitarian crowd, 'mass culture' and, in élitist self-defence, 'art for art's sake' emerged together, bred by 'competitive commerce' from the 'fatal division of men into the cultivated and degraded classes' (W. Morris 1962: 139). 'Highbrow' and 'lowbrow' were born, and by the 1920s the new structure mapped by these new terms was firmly in place.

The role of the mass media was crucial. All types of music were dragged from previously separate locations and assembled in the same social space, where they both defined and were forced to respond to each other. The BBC, for example, 'undertook the standardization, classification and placing in rank order of the *whole field of music*' (Scannell 1981: 259). While Constant Lambert regretted that 'classical music is vulgarized and diffused through every highway and byway, and both highbrow and lowbrow are the losers' (1934: 235), the greater hardships were suffered by the popular side. The debate between high and low 'was in truth a disguised dialogue on the state of society' (Bigsby 1975: 20), arising out of the threat of general access to leisured culture. 'Discourses of art . . . depend on the "commercialization" of "mass" culture to set up, by contrast, their own superiority. If "mass" culture did not exist, high culture would have invented it (arguably it *has* invented it)' (Sinfield 1989: 176). The category of popular music, then, is the scapegoat required by the attempt to defend an élite tradition of artistic integrity against the pressures of modern society.

MUSIC IN CONTEXT
II: Attacking Popular Music

General attacks, drawing usually on a confused compendium of ideas about cultural provenance, moral effect and aesthetic value, have been common. The 'cesspool of popular music' (Rosselson 1979: 42), this 'disease' with its 'unworthy rubbish' and 'disgusting sounds' (Dwyer 1967: 115), 'primitive and uncouth' (Tippett 1974: 154), is aimed at listeners of 'bottomless vacuity', their 'open, sagging mouths and glazed eyes, [their] . . . hands mindlessly drumming in time to the music' revealing a 'generation enslaved by a commercial machine' (P. Johnson 1964: 17). Earlier (in 1942) Bliss wanted the BBC to segregate these 'Calibans' on a 'dirt tract', a 'continual stream of noise and nonsense put on by untouchables' (Scannell 1981: 258). By comparison, Macpherson's language in 1910 ('shallow', 'ephemeral', 'obvious') was restrained (1940: 11–12), linking him to late Victorian critiques (see Middleton 1981: 63).

Most commonly, however, condemnation has been directed against specific styles. Between the wars the 'barbaric rhythms' and 'foul noises' of jazz, as Sir Hugh Allen called them (quoted in 'Feste' 1921: 98), were a constant subject of critical discourse. Jazz was 'noisy and incredibly stupid' (Sir Hamilton Harty, in LeMahieu 1988: 116), 'propaganda for vulgarity' and 'deliberately evil' (J. W. N. Sullivan, quoted in 'Feste' 1932: 410). 'A subject for the pathologist', jazz put itself 'outside the pale of music' (Sir Arthur Bliss, W. H. Hadow, in Cole 1978: 146), especially when indulging the 'whinings and sobbings of the so-called "crooners"' ('Feste' 1932: 410). In the fifties, rock 'n' roll received similar treatment. Wain described fans 'screaming aimlessly, like animals' at 'this big phony slob . . . gyrating up and down' (Sinfield 1989: 168). Elsewhere we learn that 'our teddy-boys and girls are essentially primitives, untouched by the Western European culture of which they ought to be the heirs instead of merely the waste by-products', and rock 'n' roll is compared to 'certain forms of music [which] induce mass-hysteria in certain primitive peoples' (anon 1956: 203). As this suggests, racism is rarely far away from this discourse – though its language has seldom been so blatant in recent decades as it was in the 1920s, when African-American musicians were routinely described as 'savages' and 'Sambos' (see, for example, 'Feste' 1924: 797), their music as having a 'debasing effect' on 'the prestige of the white races' (Henry Coward, quoted in anon 1926: 78). For Clive Bell, 'niggers' could be 'admired artists without any gift more singular than high spirits'; 'so why drag in the intellect?' he asked (LeMahieu 1988: 116–17).

It is characteristic that new styles have been attacked because they seem to threaten an established style – and the structure of the musical field associated with this – even if, at a previous stage, this too had been subject to quite similar attack. Steve Race found 'rock-and-roll technique . . . the antithesis of all that jazz has been striving for over the years – . . . good taste and musical integrity' (1956a). Between the wars, when jazz was the enemy, it was often compared adversely to music hall, which had by then come to be seen as possessing 'honest sentiment' and 'sound tunes'; it was indigenous and traditional, coming from the grass roots, unlike imported dance music (Scholes 1938: 601; see also Bonavia 1928). But earlier, for Parry and Sharp, it was music hall that was the enemy, and its prey was folksong, while for Robert Blatchford, in 1894, the 'real music' against which music-hall 'howling' was counterposed lay even further back, in a culture when glee and madrigal singing was commonplace (see Frith 1983: 40). At each stage, a seemingly settled musical field, having assimilated a previous incursion and put it – socially and culturally – in its place, is threatened by further upheaval, forcing historical relocation of the mythical Golden Age (whose ideological potency, however, remains undiminished). But in this historical schema jazz and rock are special, and hence attract special vehemence. Unlike music hall, the 'well-made' inter-war popular song and the mainstream post-war ballad, they have threatened not only the stability of the existing relationships between musical categories but also the very definition of what music, in the European tradition, is and how it is made.

III: A Changing Culture

In the aftermath of the First World War, antipathy to popular music was grounded in fears about materialism, egalitarianism, social and cultural homogeneity and Americanization – all of which seemed aspects of each other.

Elitists such as T. S. Eliot and F. R. Leavis, whatever their differences of motive and policy, were agreed that culture should be a hierarchy and that high culture must be reserved for a minority, who understood its carefully cultivated standards. The rest, 'docile, smiling and obedient . . . [were] capable only of mass indignation, herd pleasures and community singing' (Lambert 1934: 181); their lot was the 'uninterrupted bawling' of the loudspeaker (Leavis and Thompson 1937: 108). The great spectre was 'levelling down': 'in our headlong rush to educate everybody, we are lowering our standards' (Eliot 1962: 108). Even on the left many agreed, pitching an idealized vision of working-class life against the threat of the passive consumerism of Americanized mass culture (Waters 1989–90).

Such a response to the crisis could lead to missionary work among the lower orders, as with the attempt, drawing on the considerable influence of Cecil Sharp, to propagate 'traditional' music and dance in schools and elsewhere (see Harker 1985). Similarly, for the paternalistic BBC of John Reith's dreams, 'few [listeners] knew what they wanted, fewer what they needed' and radio's job was 'giving people what one believes they should like and will come to like . . . the supply of good things will create the demand for more . . . the amenities of culture are available without discrimination' (quoted in Minihan 1977: 207; LeMahieu 1988: 146–7). Reith despised entertainment, including popular music, and the BBC treated it critically (cleaning it up, trying to suit it to the respectable middle-class hearth) and, at the same time, as the first rung on a ladder of cultural improvement.

As a BBC official put it, 'Every man wants in his heart to be a highbrow' (LeMahieu 1988: 147). This belief controlled the programming and presentation policies for 'classical' music, with their educational aims, and led to the highly popular 'music appreciation' talks broadcast by Percy Scholes and Walford Davies.

The BBC's 'democratization of music' strategy was part of a broader project, its ideological roots traceable to Victorian ideas of 'improvement'. The wider 'music appreciation' movement; the development of Associated Board exams, rural music schools, new school music teaching methods, childrens' concerts; the competitive festival movement; the importance of concert programme notes, such as those of Tovey; the educational programmes run by the big record companies: together these can be seen as a general attempt, at this time, to broaden the social base for 'good' music while counteracting the attractions of 'cheap' entertainment. At the BBC this led to continual conflict between programme planners and the Music Department, which was increasingly concerned to improve performance standards and widen the repertoire, in short, to appeal to connoisseurs, rather than educate Bliss's 'Calibans'. By the late 1930s, the cutting edge of their campaign was provided, firstly, by chamber music and, secondly, by unfamiliar modern works – for their derision was directed at the hackneyed orchestral repertoire with popular (*sic*) appeal as much as light and dance music.

What the Music Department was fighting, we can now see, was the outline of a new common culture, a 'middlebrow' culture, part of which was an 'attempt of the BBC to make classical music popular (and popular music classical by vetoing the more dubious material)' (Pearsall 1976: 14). The *Radio Times* wanted listeners who 'were not only tolerant but eclectic in their taste . . . who can . . . enjoy either Bach or Henry Hall' (quoted in Scannell and Cardiff 1991: 206), an attitude embodied in the first disc jockey, Christopher Stone, whose anti-élitist catholicity of taste was designed not to provoke; it was 'the equivalent of a bath and a change for the tired man's and the tired woman's mind' (Stone 1933: 88). The BBC's 'idealized version of a fragile, never fully realized, middle-class cultural tradition which it then proclaimed to be the natural and authentic culture of the nation' (LeMahieu 1988: 182) lay close to J. B. Priestley's 'broadbrow' strategy, rooted as that was in a rosy Edwardian Golden Age. And, in a wider perspective (the taming and 'civilizing' of jazz; the formalizing and domesticating of the new 'barbaric' dances of the 1920s; the blurring of the light/classical boundary), it can be seen as part of an attempt to 'settle' the new, disruptive popular musics within a re-mapped hierarchy, drawing the crude high/popular bifurcation into a more subtle, manageable field structured by older ideas of cultural unity and value. The watershed was probably the late 1920s, when enthusiasm for 'symphonic jazz', cultivation of 'syncopation' by Lambert and others, and the serious jazz criticism of Spike Hughes seem to be symptoms of a historical node, whose crossovers (as we would now call them) then quickly lost any radical potential and slid into comfortable consensus. By the mid-1930s, the BBC was codifying 'popular music' itself, distinguishing between 'music for connoisseurs' (jazz, swing), 'music for entertainment' and 'music for dancing' (Scannell and Cardiff 1991: 191–3).

This settlement was transitional and could not survive the upsurge of populism released by the war (and prefigured in changes to the BBC's programming policy in the late 1930s), the renewed pressures of 'Americanization' that followed, and the growing importance of working-class people in the cultural market. Resistance took on extra vehemence as the cultural economy's adjustment of social focus made it clear that mass culture would increasingly be organized around the 'lowest' values. Waugh's novels document the new terrain, 'flat as a map' (quoted in Hebdige 1981: 41), and the laments ring out: 'we shall have to . . . live a Woolworth life hereafter' (Harold Nicolson, quoted in Sinfield 1989: 45). 'It was the simultaneous articulation of *accessibility* and *reproducibility* (a million streamlined Chevrolets, a million streamlined radios) which finally proved disturbing to so many cultural critics' (Hebdige 1981: 54), for it led to 'barbarism with electric light . . . a cockney tellytopia, a low-grade nirvana' (C. Curran, quoted in Chambers 1985: 4). The influence of Leavisism expanded (see D. Thompson 1964, R/1973), its posing of 'critical discrimination' against the 'false needs' aroused by advertising and the 'standardized pulp' sold to satisfy them becoming something of a middle-class orthodoxy. On the left, Orwell saw the 'comeliness' of traditional working-class life threatened by the 'cheap palliatives' of Americanized mass culture (Orwell 1937, R/1962), while Hoggart, similarly, contrasted the 'shiny barbarism', 'candyfloss world' and 'spiritual dry-rot' of rock 'n' roll and the 'juke-box boys' with the 'warm and shared humanity', the folk-like 'archetypal quality', of the 'big-dipper' vocal style found in the working men's clubs of his youth (Hoggart 1957).

Such poorly focused anxiety and nostalgia offered little more than a variant on what was now a fully fledged analytic paradigm, developed from romantic–modernist ideology: on the one hand, intransigent, 'authentic' art; on the other, everything else. (Such a position was never as rigorously argued in Britain as it was, elsewhere, by T. W. Adorno, but its assumptions permeated the culture of the 1940s and 1950s: see, for instance, Tippett 1974.) William Glock's single-minded campaign at the BBC to make Radio 3 the voice of the modernist élite built on the logic of the three-channel hierarchy established in 1946 (and no doubt the tiny audience – less than 1 per cent – confirmed the implied social analysis). Assaults on this system often served, ironically, to shore it up – at least at first. For a long time, folk music had been presented as an 'authentic' alternative to the commercial song system, and hence could serve as a 'popular art'. In the 1930s, a minority adopted jazz – 'real' jazz, black American jazz, as distinct from what seemed to them the vapid imitations peddled by British dance bands – as an alternative art, at once uncommercial and expressively honest, and culturally rebellious. This enthusiasm was associated particularly with a new intelligentsia, grammar-school educated, lower middle class, excluded by or uninterested in traditional high culture. Philip Larkin was one of them. 'This was something we had found for ourselves, that wasn't taught at school . . . and having found it, we made it bear all the enthusiasm usually directed at more established arts' (Larkin 1970: 3). By the 1950s, jazz – thoroughly mixed up with the Art Schools, Beat poetry and leftist politics – was the basic sound of middle-class bohemia (as in *Look Back in Anger*). Rock music, born partly in the same ambience, took from the examples of folk and jazz the ideas of authenticity and of bohemia. Its artists claimed the legacy of romantic critique. Amid the social upheavals and 'cultural revolution' (Marwick 1991) of the 1960s, its legitimation proceeded fast. By 1963, William Mann was reviewing the Beatles in *The Times* (27 December), and Richard Buckle in *The Sunday Times* (29 December) proclaimed them 'the greatest composers since Beethoven'. The BBC, after earlier reluctance, capitulated. Serious critical writing became common. Academic studies, journals and societies followed, and some university departments introduced popular music as well as jazz to their syllabuses. The Beatles' *Sgt. Pepper* album (1967) was widely admired and the jazz-rock band Soft Machine appeared at the 1970 Promenade Concerts. But this time the question whether upheaval would settle back into renewed consensual hierarchy was to be much less easily decided.

Could the conceptual distinction between 'high' and 'low' survive such constant revisions of boundaries? For a 1964 Government White Paper it was 'a question of bridging the gap between what have come to be called the "higher" forms of entertainment and the . . . brass band . . . the music hall and pop group – and to challenge the fact that a gap exists'. But Raymond Williams still insisted that, while 'jazz is a real musical form . . . the latest Tin-Pan drool . . . [is] not exactly in the same world' (Williams 1965: 364); and Donald Hughes (1964, R/1973: 153) went back to re-drawing hierarchies, distinguishing between 'folk' ('genuine, spontaneous'), 'Radio One pop' ('stereotyped . . . assembly-line product') and 'progressive pop' ('pop as a culture, in which a developing growth may take place'). At the same time, the possibility that both the laws of commodity production and of the romantic ideology of self-expression were now universalized throughout the musical culture might suggest that 'the interplay of artifice and authenticity is central to everyone's lives . . . In looking at the shifting ways in which the love–hate relationship of the artist and society has been worked out in pop, we simply find the dialectic in graphic outline' (Frith and Horne 1987: 180).

MUSIC IN CONTEXT
IV: After Hierarchy?

In a sense, the Cold War struggle – the need to validate 'democracy' – meant that cultural equality *had* to be conceded. And if the choice was between 'Bolshevism' and 'Americanization', it was obvious which direction British society would follow. Cultural libertarianism and economic affluence were two sides of this coin. According to pop art theorist Lawrence Alloway, in 1959, 'the aesthetics of plenty oppose a very strong tradition which dramatizes the arts as the possession of an élite' and propose instead a 'long front of culture', 'the exercise of multiple choices across a wide spectrum' (quoted in Hewison 1986: 46). It became difficult to maintain grounds for value distinctions.

Under what some call a postmodern system, authority has collapsed no less in culture than in society and politics. Universal access to the ceaseless flow of images and reproductions destroys uniqueness and even the sense that a given piece of music (say) has any connection with 'reality'. The triumph of commodity form means that all sense of aesthetic difference is mocked by the homogenizing effects of exchange values. The growing visibility of Asian and African-Caribbean musics, added to the existing proliferation of available styles, historical and subcultural, increases the sense of an unavoidable relativism. The triumphs of 'sociologism' and 'ideological critique' (see, for instance, Shepherd et al. 1977), and the influence of ethnomusicology, in higher education and to some extent on school teachers, provide intellectual underpinnings for this perspective. Protests became plaintive rather than self-confident, Lord Goodman in 1966 lamenting that 'the pop groups are winning the battle' against 'the worthwhile things in life' (quoted in Sinfield 1989: 283) and his successor as Arts Council Chairman, Roy Shaw, attacking the idea that 'anything goes' as a threat to 'all objective standards of taste' (Shaw 1978: 6); or else they turned eccentric (R. C. Taylor (1978) regrets the acceptance of jazz because this removes its capacity to mock the pretensions of high art).

Nowhere is the trend clearer than in schools. Attempts to introduce popular music to CSE syllabuses, followed by the introduction of the GCSE, which made stylistic and cultural pluralism one of its fundamental principles (see Green 1988), led to the 1991 proposals for National Curriculum music, based, with impressive impartiality, on 'a wide variety of past and present musical cultures, styles, idioms and traditions' (anon 1991a: 10). These proposals, together with the controversy they aroused, reveal much about both underlying tendencies and resistance to them. The Minister's request that more attention should be paid to the 'repertoire, history and traditions of music' was a thinly veiled demand for more 'great art'; in the *Guardian* musicologist Geoffrey Chew attacked the elevation of Chuck Berry at the expense of Beethoven (5 March 1991), and critic Michael Kennedy pilloried the capitulation to the 'commercial pop industry' and to 'free-for-all mediocrity' (*Daily Telegraph*, 14 February 1991); while right-wing philosophers Roger Scruton and Anthony O'Hear formed a Music Curriculum Association to demand courses 'concentrating on our [sic] proper musical heritage from Palestrina onwards' (*The Times Educational Supplement*, 22 February 1991). Many 'classical' composers and performers – including Tippett, Boulez and Birtwistle, Simon Rattle, Charles Groves and Colin Davis – were supportive, however, and 83 per cent of public responses to the proposals were too. Nevertheless, the government's National Curriculum Council watered them down and insisted on a predominant profile for the 'Western heritage'. The Minister's final proposals represented something of a compromise – though he did not bow on the principle that 'the dominant examples for study . . . [should come from our] own cultural tradition'.

The theoretical tools to explain such developments are to hand – though they have not been applied rigorously and in detail to music. Ever since Benjamin's pioneering analysis (1970), it has been clear that mass reproduction and dissemination of art-objects destroys their 'aura' of uniqueness and autonomy, locating them instead in mundane everyday life alongside other kinds of commodity, and replacing aesthetic hierarchies with quasi-political struggle. 'We moderns have no safe principle of selection, so we collect . . . The cathedral of culture . . . [is] now a supermarket' (Eisenberg 1987, 18, 24). As Mannheim (1956) explains, this development is part of a more extensive destruction of 'distance' resulting from the comprehensive democratization of experience and social relationships; mystery is unmasked, and everybody and everything are, in principle, subjected to an egalitarian coexistence. At the same time, social power continues to be unequally held, and possession of the bourgeois 'aesthetic disposition', reproduced and transmitted through class-privileged modes of socialization and education, continues in its role of building 'cultural capital', marking social distinction and excluding those with unapproved tastes (Bourdieu 1980). As the collapse of cultural divisions accelerates, therefore, legitimation procedures become ever more frantic, the 'most arbitrary distinctions . . . [being] drawn up into fiercely patrolled aesthetic boundaries' (Chambers 1985: 21).

A hesitant mix of old and new criteria abounds. Probably few 'serious' musicians are now antagonistic to popular music as such; but many perhaps share Robert Saxton's insistence, while rejecting 'hairshirt' modernism, that 'artistic integrity' demands the rejection of 'light listening': to give people 'only what they want', to 'go along at one . . . level', leads to 'a pretty awful cul-de-sac' (Saxton 1991). Responses to Pavarotti's giant Hyde Park concert in July 1991 revealed that many critics, unable either to escape or to cope with the implications of a culture marked by radical democratization of styles and at the same time by continuing disparities of status, fell back on old dogmas, mouthed mechanically, no longer linked to the social realities which gave them birth, but hurled desperately into the aesthetic void. Reactions varied from snook-cocking populism ('He delighted us with a rousing rendition of O Sole Mio, which even I had heard of because it was made famous by the Cornetto advert on TV', *Sun*), to élitist sneer ('With the popular songs, the banal is close at hand – in Mama he is almost the ice-cream tenor', *Financial Times*), to petit-bourgeois self-congratulation ('Mick Jagger's appeal is limited to the basics because he is a slob. Pavarotti, if at all, is a slob only in girth. Hyde Park 1991 is youth's revenge on Woodstock 1969', *Daily Telegraph*; all 1 August 1991).

Given this level of confusion, prognosis and prescription are equally difficult. Pluralism, however desirable, leaves a strange feeling of emptiness. '"No more walls" is a fine slogan, but not if you want to build a home' (Eisenberg 1987: 87). If comparative evaluation is to be rehabilitated, on new grounds, it may be necessary to find ways of reclaiming those parts of the modernist project that are still of use – notably a belief in the capacity of the human species for self-directed progress – while accepting the postmodern insight that culture is a game everyone is entitled to play.

Chapter 3

THE MARKETPLACE

CYRIL EHRLICH

I: A Revolution

The twentieth century has absorbed a revolution in the economics of music. Fundamental patterns of consumption, manufacture and distribution have been realigned, sustaining an enormous growth in the *use* of music. Mechanized sound has replaced live performance as the normal experience, and there has been a precipitous decline in any desire for self-improvement by cultivation of 'good taste'. In 1914 most people acknowledged an ascending order of popular, 'middlebrow' and 'highbrow' music, without question. Repertoire and 'canon' (the exemplary works) were small and therefore easily assimilated. A measure of Elgar's achievement was simply that he was the first Englishman to enter those restricted lists. It was common to pay at least lip-service to the necessity of improving taste: as intrinsically worthwhile, and as a necessary part of that social conditioning, or 'civilizing' process which had begun in Victorian times (see Jevons 1883). Even music-hall entrepreneurs, operating in what was then the largest sector of show business, took pride in occasionally raising the tone with 'good' music. Advocates of 'musical appreciation' sought actively to hasten progress.

Such attitudes and aspirations survived until the late 1960s, and for a brief period seemed capable of fulfilment, with leadership from the BBC (see Glock 1991: 200–13). They were then undermined and eventually swept away by powerful market forces and a new discourse which blended cultural relativism, populist rhetoric and hype. Easily capturing the young, it brainwashed opinion-makers and teachers who rapidly came to dread an image of 'élitism'. In this manner immemorial habits of assessing, defending, and influencing hierarchies of taste were reversed. Mechanization was not the primary cause of this cultural revolution, which began with the economic, social and political upheavals of the 1920s, but it stimulated an insatiable demand for sounds, and transformed the essential product.

In 1914 the music business centred upon dots on pages: written, published, sold, and performed throughout the land (see Roth 1969). The organ loft presided over this keyboard and sheet-music culture, in a still powerful church and handful of universities, while brass bands and choirs exulted in the musicality of 'somewhere further north'. But it was the piano that exercised widest domain. A common article of furniture and 'great respectablizing instrument', it was central to all domestic and most public music; its ownership more widespread than in any other European country (see Ehrlich 1976, R/1990: 88–107). Sheet music was widely marketed, with shops in the smallest towns. Then as mechanization took command, pianos and pages disappeared from homes and places of entertainment. The ability to read dots ceased to be a common accomplishment, or even obligatory among professional musicians. Eventually tape replaced paper, and music publishers became primarily concerned with the negotiation of property rights. Technology usually takes time to assimilate and British institutions always die hard, so the pace of change was initially slow. It came first through gramophone, silent cinema, and radio, arousing some apprehension but offering no substantial challenge to the old system. To appreciate the subsequent chronology of resistance and submission we must scrutinize that system at its height, when structure and *Weltanschauung* (appropriate terms for British institutions in a Teutonic intellectual climate) were intact and seemingly impregnable.

II: The Old Profusion

The Edwardian infrastructure of music consisted of buildings, institutions and processes through which musicians, as producers, and the public, as consumers, came to the marketplace. Despite conventional squeamishness (wages and fees, like sex, were clothed in euphemism and never openly discussed), music-making was already thoroughly commercialized in England, as foreign visitors often remarked; and lines of 'professional' demarcation were jealously guarded. It was a necessary obsession, for music, unique among occupations, attracted amateurs disdaining payment and professionals trying to earn a living. This infrastructure, bequeathed by Victorian commercial vigour, an indifferent government, cultural poverty and cheap labour, was before all else profuse. As an investment for the future it was a strange portfolio, some elements destined soon to perish, others to continue yielding benefits or troubles into the 1990s.

Unequivocally useful were the buildings that later generations would cherish, mourn, and revive. The Albert Hall (1871) was too large, unremunerative (many seats were privately owned) and acoustically bizarre to win much favour from musicians and audiences until late twentieth-century London grew to respect this quintessentially Victorian place, its sound improved, as an indispensable venue for large events. More immediately popular were the Bechstein (later Wigmore) Hall (1901) and Queen's Hall (1893). The latter was ideal for symphony concerts, replacing inadequate venues and remaining central to musical life until bombed in 1941. It was never properly replaced in London, though a worthy successor was created in Birmingham half a century later. The Wigmore Hall had a more chequered history, surviving as the capital's most civilized and cherished auditorium for recitals and chamber music. In contrast to these artefacts of high culture, but no less precious a legacy, were the theatres built as music halls by Frank Matcham all over the country (see Ehrlich and Walker 1980: 21–35). Several would be lovingly restored as opera houses during the extraordinary late twentieth-century boom in that art, including Belfast (1895), Buxton (1903), and the London Coliseum (1904).

Satisfactory buildings were the product of competent architects and cheap labour, both scarce in later years. Cheap labour also featured throughout a sprawling system which was generally undiscriminating and exploitative. A pervasive glut – an excess of supply over any conceivable level of demand – was the prevailing condition of musical life. The vicious circle of profusion and mediocrity began with a surfeit of facilities for instruction and examination. Conservatoires, some loosely described as 'national', and private teachers prepared students for a preposterous list of degrees and diplomas. Little of this instruction was linked to active musical life; or well enough funded to recruit adequate staff and students. There was everywhere a surfeit of instrumentalists, most of whom had to supplement income by taking pupils, who would in turn seek cash from playing and more pupils.

London enjoyed a surfeit of concerts and a very short season of opera. The latter was sometimes of high quality, but socially exclusive, through dress and ticket prices. Slightly more democratic were the symphony concerts whose promoters were beginning to compete for a wider audience, only to find it limited in extent; perhaps diminishing as a result of transport improvement and suburbanization. Instrumentalists were recruited to man (there were hardly any women) an array of impressively named orchestras: Philharmonic Society, Queen's Hall, London Symphony, New Symphony, and the like. Seemingly permanent, but insufficiently funded to provide regular employment for the required complement of 100 or more players, these bodies were inherently unstable, their personnel shifting and often interchangeable. A demoralizing 'deputy' system was ubiquitous, reflecting a constant search for more remunerative work. London players therefore learned to make a virtue of necessity by regular displays of accomplished sight-reading. Conductors, representing a new international breed of virtuoso interpreter, were most successful if they became similarly adept at improvisation. Henry Wood (1869–1944) was the workhorse of England's stable, Thomas Beecham (1879–1961) the thoroughbred who brought genius and funds, in equal richness, to the most brilliant of all twentieth-century performing careers. These distinctive traits of ill-disciplined profusion in London orchestral life were to persist, when all else changed, to the end of the century, requiring a Beecham to impose coherence, brilliance, even style upon loose assemblies. Outside London, oratorio was still the main event and concert life was exiguous. Orchestras offered short seasons in seaside resorts, and in a handful of provincial cities, notably Manchester where the Hallé was Britain's closest approximation to a stable orchestra with regular employment, playing to a loyal audience. Large numbers of players were in Midland and northern towns – the Musicians' Union began there – where life was generally harder than in London, with fewer opportunities and lower remuneration.

Malthusian excesses were the natural condition of an open market. The musician's traditional protection, by means of restrictions upon apprenticeship and limited access to instruments and instruction, had long disappeared. In their absence, entry to the most open of crafts was constrained solely by inclination and talent, the latter not much of a limitation since the expectations of consumers were low, though they were beginning to rise. Considerations of youth, nationality and gender, which limit entry to every other occupation, were either irrelevant or in fast retreat. Child players were common, sometimes prodigious, and often acclaimed; foreigners had long been welcome, indeed preferred; and women were allowed through a few doors: as teachers and singers, of course, but also increasingly as pianists and solo violinists. An overabundance of labour led inevitably to its exploitation. Wages, working hours and environment were often comparable to those suffered in such 'sweated industries' as clothing, which so exercised Edwardian reformers. Orchestra pits in music halls throughout the land were rarely better than sweatshops and, despite the proximity of audiences, equally immune from scrutiny. Such conditions had recently been made notorious, a necessary preliminary to reform, by Joseph Williams's brilliant muckraking during the highly public music-hall strike of 1907, with picket lines manned by famous 'stars'. This was a leap towards the creation of an effective union, and its subsequent arbitration offered some prospects of improvement for the lower orders (see Ehrlich 1985: 164–81).

Similarly placed, though they would have rejected so demeaning a comparison, were the teachers, the largest group of 'professional musicians'. Morbidly preoccupied with status, the music teachers had been conditioned to cherish a paraphernalia of qualification: from external university doctorates based entirely upon 'paperwork', to licentiateships and associateships of diverse academies. Few such 'letters' had much bearing on the ability to command fees by attracting a paying audience, and none protected the owners' employment. Represented with pomp but no muscle by a 'professional' association which had long sought equivalence to doctors and lawyers, the great majority of these vulnerable people were perforce an embodiment of the shabby genteel (see Ehrlich 1985: 121–41, Carr-Saunders and Wilson 1933). The testing and certification of external students through local examination centres was a massive and uniquely British undertaking, with outposts throughout the Empire. It was the most representative, ridiculed and obsolescent feature of the old system. If many of its candidates never contemplated employment as musicians, seeking only an accoutrement, predominantly female, of *petit bourgeois* culture, there were still thousands who endured its drills in the hope of qualifying for gainful employment.

Leading 'professors', including several august names of the 'English musical renaissance', were not immune from the system's destructive powers. Accustomed to mind-numbing routines of teaching and examining, some held multiple appointments in order to supplement modest stipends. A few established a niche in fashionable society by marrying well, attracting a manageable list of prosperous lady pupils, and penning a marketable oeuvre of ballads, 'tutors' and salon pieces. (Berger 1913 is an unintentionally revealing

MUSIC IN CONTEXT

guide to this world.) For the majority, without such resources, ceaseless teaching was the common lot, at home and in institutions which attached images of excellence to mediocre realities. Conservatoire rituals were conducted mostly at elementary levels with pupils who needed to be able to pay fees and assume a modicum of gentility, for it was essential to steer clear of the lower orders. Government financial support was negligible, scholarships rare, and there could be no serious attempt, even at the 'national' academies, to trawl for gifted children without consideration of cash and class, and teach them to be musicians. In 1901 a reporter predicted that few of the 4000 or so students at 'the three colleges' (the Royal College, the Royal Academy and Trinity) would ever 'become anything better than drudging governesses' and described 'the great blot upon musical London' as 'the overtraining of the unfit, the exploitation of the unworthy' (G. Burgess 1901: i, 60). A decade later little was changed. No successful soloist had yet emerged from the national conservatoires but, like the socially inferior and vocationally superior army school at Kneller Hall, they were beginning to train competent wind players and rank and file violinists. Despite the presence of gifted teachers, like Tobias Matthay (1858–1945), and some patronage for exceptional children (Mathilde Verne's pupil Solomon (1902–88) is the outstanding example), the cultural environment of London did not nurture musicianship. Those who were sufficiently endowed with talent, aspiration, or at least funds, sought it abroad. A few, such as the fine Scottish pianist Frederick Lamond (1868–1948), and the violinist Marie Hall (1884–1956), established careers, though never with the drawing and earning power of the leading foreign virtuosi. The outstanding English violinist, Albert Sammons (1886–1957), received no formal training.

For composers the environment was singularly inhospitable. Like other musicians they were forced to piece a living together from diverse employments, sapping energies away from creative work. A few could meet their publishers by crossing firm 'bridges built between business and friendship' (J. N. Moore 1987 i: vii). But when something less than genius or high earning potential was at stake, the structure tended to be rickety, and the going hard; it was best to have a private income (see Banfield 1981a: 28). British composers had no performing right society like SACEM, whose London representative collected fees when French works were played. A few British publishers exercised the right; but anyone wishing to do so was required to announce it on the front page of each piece. Most

THE MARKETPLACE

publishers of popular music stated, in contrast, 'This song may be sung in public *without fee or licence.*' Royalties were typically sold outright to small family businesses whose pinchpenny attitudes towards intellectual property and contractual obligations were bound by few legal constraints. A notorious case was Coleridge-Taylor's sale to Novello of the hugely popular *Hiawatha*, which choral societies ranked next only to *Messiah* and *Elijah*. A subsquent appeal on behalf of his widow and children led to a long newspaper correspondence which let chinks of light into a secretive and unregulated commerce (see *The Times*, 22 November – 15 December 1912; *The Musical News*, May 1913; *The Author*, June 1913).

Music publishers had to allow for high risks, but these could be offset by easy gains from oratorio, musical comedy, music-hall and parlour songs, and simple piano and 'educational' music (see Roth 1969, Boosey 1931). There were about 40,000 new titles a year, each printed in runs of at least 200. Popular hits often sold 200,000 copies. An indication of the market's size and profitability was the extent of piracy and the violence with which it was fought. Approximately one million copies of pirated music were seized on the streets in the early 1900s, often after pitched battles between vendors and publishers (see Ehrlich 1989: 8–12, Coover 1985). If commercially successful composers such as Stephen Adams (Michael Maybrick) and Leslie Stuart occasionally suffered from the law's inadequacies, the less fortunate or astute were forced into a market similar to Gissing's Grub Street. Note-spinners, many of them women, provided unlimited supplies of cheap domestic labour without any protection from unions or the law (see D. Scott 1989: 60–80). In 1906 piracy was restrained by an interim Musical Copyright Act, sufficient to appease the publishers; but copyright law needed thorough reform if Britain was to meet new international obligations. The Berne Convention had been revised, extending protection to 50 years after the composer's death – a fact of enormous significance to the economics of twentieth-century music – and the need to announce claims on performing right was also modified. The government consulted publishers and found them divided about reform; this reflected both limited perceptions of new opportunities and rational differences of self-interest. A few, such as Novello, were still primarily selling and hiring large numbers of parts to choral societies. Some firms, far from demanding cash for performance, actually paid popular entertainers to sing their songs, and then advertised 'as sung by . . .' on the front cover. Although William

Boosey later claimed to have foreseen that eventually 'a composer's performing rights might be even more valuable than his publishing rights' (1931: 175), this was not commonly perceived. Nor did British publishers take much interest in another sign of changing times: evidence about trade in pianolas, cylinders and discs submitted to the Committee whose report preceded a new Copyright Act in 1911 (anon 1909). They were also blind to accounts of SACEM's 'dazzling' success in Paris with the proceeds from music at 'picture shows' (Ehrlich 1989: 15).

For some musicians the environment was therefore beginning to improve by 1914. Union activity and industrial arbitration had started to civilize the climate of industrial relations for orchestral instrumentalists. Parliamentary reform had tidied up an antiquated, confusing and arbitrary set of laws, establishing clearer ground rules and facilitating the collection of new sources of income: not ensuring them, for that would take considerable organization. But the great mass of musicians were unaffected by such initiatives and reforms. For them nothing seemed capable of correcting the fundamental cause of their impoverishment: a chronic excess of supply.

III: Adjustments

After 1914 the market's imbalance was adjusted, even corrected for a time, by spectacular events. The war removed 'enemy aliens', including many of the better-paid musicians, with obvious benefits to native practitioners. There were new opportunities for women: not only as solo pianists and violinists, a long-established niche, but as rank and file players who needed only practical experience to demonstrate equal ability with men. One lady was even allowed to lead a major orchestra. Such experiments were short-lived; ancient prejudices regained their hold with the peace. More significant for the changing balance of supply and demand was a new form of entertainment which offered employment throughout the industry. The silent cinema functioned as if it had been designed for musicians. Far from being silent, it required a ceaseless flow of music which could not yet be produced mechanically. In all other respects cinemas exploited every advantage of mass production for a world market. So long as no soundtrack was available musicians were indispensable, their services required simultaneously everywhere, for most of the year, in contrast to the traditional short seasons and tours. At every level of competence and ensemble, from 'fleapit' pianists or trios with drums, to *quasi* symphony orchestras in the principal city theatres, instrumentalists found jobs throughout the country. And there were corresponding opportunities for composers and publishers, as sheet music had to be bought, or hired, in huge quantities.

The Performing Right Society, established in 1914, provided a new source of income. More than 2500 cinemas were licensed by the mid-1920s, when music-hall licences fell to 30 (Ehrlich 1989: 36). An entirely fresh form of entertainment thus had the paradoxical effect of reinforcing the old infrastructure of music while providing a base for the new. It absorbed surpluses of labour and paper and, since demand was centred upon existing skills and repertoire, gave both financial and cultural underpinning. The diet was mainly light and 'light classical', with a few exotic 'novelties'. The most successful composer was Albert Ketèlbey, whose *In a Persian Market*, also familiar in music hall and tea shop, probably received more performances than any other work in the history of English music, with the possible exception of the national anthem. By 1928 Edwin Evans could reasonably describe the cinema as 'the most important musical institution in the country' (E. Evans 1929: 65). It gave most of the public their main listening experience, employed some 80 per cent of instrumentalists, and dominated publishers' catalogues (Ehrlich 1985: 194–200, 1989: 35–8).

Then talkies arrived and the market collapsed practically overnight; players were dismissed and sheet music destroyed by the tonne. Within a few years some 15,000 players had lost their jobs. Victims of technological, not cyclical unemployment, they could expect no reinstatement when the country recovered from depression. Accustomed to old-fashioned and anonymous routines, few could grasp new opportunities in radio and recording studios, dance and 'showbands'. There was particular distress in northern industrial districts, where a majority was trapped and the slump was most serious and persistent. Only young, skilled and enterprising musicians could escape to London, which was becoming the undisputed centre of a new entertainment industry. Music flourished through the 1930s but it was rejecting many elements of the old system; including the teachers, most of whom experienced not dole queues but genteel underemployment. Generally unremarked by inter-war chroniclers of despair, their plight was caused by factors more complex and profound than the immediate impact of a new technology, but similarly irreversible. New patterns of consumption, leisure and social emulation were destroying the roots of their livelihood. Music lessons declined in the same way as they had risen, along with piano ownership (see Ehrlich 1990: 184–92). Learning an instrument became an expression of musical, rather than social, aspiration.

Harsh times enforced higher standards at a time when public expectations were being raised by an unprecedented flow of good performances on radio and gramophone records. The BBC's influence was paramount. It saved the Proms in 1927, provided modest subsidies for opera and, in 1930, created the nation's first permanent symphony orchestra, initiating full-time contracts, adequate rehearsals, and an enlightened approach to repertoire (see Kenyon 1981 *passim*). It also attempted to mould tastes, a policy that divides historians. Eschewing the vulgar and meretricious, opposing an Americanization of popular culture, it offered, in Reith's essential phrase, 'what people will like tomorrow'. 'No one', said Arthur Bliss in 1932, 'can fairly ask for anything better, and no one in any other broadcasting centre of the world can hope to get as much' (Roscow 1991: 63). Alternatively the BBC's music policy can be viewed with scepticism. It reflected 'a preferred image of its own cultural identity' and reached only a tiny minority. (The quotation is from the invaluable LeMahieu 1988: 186; see also Scannell 1981.) Beyond dispute is the fact that, with rising income from licences and immunity from commercial competition, the BBC provided unprecedented quantities of music, and was uniquely free from market constraints: an immunity that outraged pillars of the musical establishment (see Kenyon 1981: 46–8). But even they agreed about the objectives of improvement in an age of 'musical appreciation', its representative book, perhaps, Scholes's *Oxford Companion to Music* – concise and breezily confident about what constituted 'good' music; unscholarly and eager to communicate with everyman.

The old infrastructure had been jolted but its associated hierarchy of taste was still firmly in place. Indeed it derived fresh sustenance from the cultural euphoria of the Second World War and seemed poised to underpin a new era in the arts. Whereas inter-war governments had imposed further burdens upon music with an entertainment tax, now all would be sweetness and light, under the guidance ('pump-priming' was the fashionable Keynesian term) of an Arts Council. Covent Garden was reinstated; the Festival of Britain introduced the South Bank as a new venue; music would become a generously endowed handmaiden to the welfare state.

THE MARKETPLACE
IV: Subsidies and the New Profusion

Technology developed rapidly after the war, each innovation presenting opportunities to musicians, not simply destroying jobs. It provided wide-ranging employment for studio musicians, including some of the best instrumentalists: sight-reading skills were again at a premium. It created a great orchestra (Walter Legge's Philharmonia), financed a huge extension of repertoire, and helped raise concert standards by funding rehearsals. London's studios, which had led the world in the first decade of electrical recording, continued to do so with each phase of development: long-playing records, reeled tape, television, stereo, FM radio, cassette, video, compact disc. Small innovatory 'hi-fi' manufacturers flourished, despite the collapse of the conservative wireless industry which had been established between the wars. Along with ceaseless technological innovation came an enormous increase in music's earning power. Modern levels of productivity (output per unit of input) and therefore of income at last came within the musician's grasp (see Baumol and Bowen 1966, particularly Chapter 7). A few became 'seriously' rich, for the first time in British history. Many – not only the denizens of pop – earned high incomes: an equally significant, but less noticed break with the past. A large proportion of these funds came from performing right. If it had ever been true to say that 'control over performance' was 'more expensive than it is worth' (Krummel 1981: 52), that time had long past.

By 1990 the PRS had some 24,000 members and its net distributable income exceeded £106 million (anon 1990; for earlier years and analysis see Ehrlich 1989 and Peacock and Weir 1975). Although a separate organization (the Mechanical Copyright Protection Society) was responsible for additional 'mechanical' royalties, the PRS derived the great bulk of its funds from performances associated with technology: television, radio, discos, and so forth. In a 'soundbite' culture it was also inevitable that substantial income, even for serious music, would flow from peripheral use. It accompanied advertisements on the new commercial radio and television. It became obligatory for background sound throughout broadcasting and films; the latter, of course, dating back to the 1930s. Often such usage was unintended by the composer, bringing adventitious income: excerpts from Holst's *The Planets* were ubiquitously attached to space adventures (see Ehrlich 1989: 164). Backed by international co-operation between collecting societies, and further legislative reforms in 1957 and 1988, such developments brought immense benefits to composers and publishers.

Less attention has been devoted to these arcane but crucial aspects of music's recent economic history than to the more diverting activities of the Arts Council. From modest beginnings with a tiny staff dispensing a few thousand pounds it became a considerable patron, developing a solid bureaucracy and an image of high purpose. At first confidence in high culture provided it with a skeleton of rational purpose, clothed in rhetoric and abundant statistics. As the skeleton shattered, under pressure from cultural relativism and bickering between the regions and the metropolis, the clothing gave scant protection. Policies became arbitrary and subject to frequent reversals and ceaseless controversy. Enthusiasts debated the level and distribution of funds, brandishing figures that cannot be fairly summarized; they agreed only that grants were insufficient, comparing poorly with such munificent governments as those of Sweden, France and Austria. Detached observers were hard put to discern consistent patterns of dispensation, except for a pronounced bias towards London, particularly in the most expensive field of opera, where comparative costs and artistic standards in the various companies increasingly bore little relation to the size of grants. If the politics of music subsidies were transparent, their economics defied coherence; for how could the market's logic of choice be replaced, or even supplemented, by an alternative logic in a diffuse, anarchic culture? By the 1990s a beleaguered Arts Council had, perhaps surprisingly, survived the Thatcher years and still functioned as a source of cash, of periodic inquests by journalists and politicians, and, not least, of employment for administrators, including some music graduates. (On the birth of the Arts Council, see Leventhal 1990; on the economics, King and Blaug 1976; on politics, a debate between Lord Gowrie and Sir Denis Forman in *The Listener*, 28 March, 4 April, 2 May 1985; on political and cultural inadequacies, Hutchison 1982; and various writings by J. Pick, particularly Pick 1981 and 1991. In defence of the Arts Council, see a veritable library of its own publications, including anon 1984.)

More remarkable than new incomes and subsidies, though linked to them, was an efflorescence of British performance, and a reversal of the international trade balance. Its most familiar manifestation was the rock explosion of the 1960s, when America ceased to dominate popular music. Yet the simultaneous emergence of serious musicians was no less astonishing. For centuries, with few exceptions, the country had imported its favourites and exported little, except for the occasional singer who acquired a foreign technique and name. Between the wars a handful of British instrumentalists and conductors had begun to attract foreign audiences; but the country was still starved of opera, with worthy, slight and incongruous exceptions at Sadler's Wells, Glyndebourne, and the tattered British National Opera Company. There were still few star instrumentalists and not a single first-class string quartet. A generation later British conductors, soloists, orchestras and ensembles of every size and style, including the newly fashionable 'authentic', were acclaimed throughout the world. Opera companies, power houses of musical culture, were busy throughout the country.

There is no convincing explanation for this extraordinary reversal of every previous trend. Was it a transmogrification of national temperament, a break in that carapace of phlegm and reticence which had served Blitz survivors and guardians of Empire, but stifled eloquence in the performing arts? Was it, more simply, the natural result of doing justice, at last, to latent talents, providing more cash and better training, with less regard for parental resources and background? Facilities had certainly improved beyond recognition in extent, and largely in quality. Some of the old institutions for formal training in music could now afford better staff and students, and were more open to foreign influence, London was beginning to rival Manchester. There were a few great teachers and charismatic role models: Max Rostal, William Pleeth, David Munrow, above all Jacqueline du Pré (1945–87). There were new specialist places for young talent, like the Menuhin and Chetham schools. Opportunities in higher education were transformed, essentially as a by-product of the expansion of universities and polytechnic colleges, most of which had music departments, where the paradigm of study shifted from counterpoint to analysis. More informally and at least as fruitfully there was new access to skilled coaching: the National Youth Orchestra, a showcase and breeding ground for exceptional talent; summer schools like Dartington; master classes and more generous opportunities for study abroad. Even the schools began to connect with music, employing competent peripatetic teachers, linking to the youth orchestra movement, and abandoning inter-war practices which had been quite unrelated 'to the living world of music outside school' (percussion bands, bamboo pipes and cheap recorders). Then they were overwhelmed by pop. (The quotation is from Fletcher 1987: 29 – an indispensable source.).

Despite later retrenchment, these decades were, by any previous standard, a period of largesse and achievement. They also brought a new profusion and imbalance. More accomplished than the old system, but equally plagued by inflexibility and glut, the new system similarly failed to make equable adjustments of supply to demand. Certification was no longer a primary purpose, but students seeking a degree or diploma were faced with upwards of 70 alternative institutions. The number of orchestras, instrumental groups and soloists grew to exceed any possibility of sufficient gainful and rewarding employment: how, for example, could a young string quartet's rehearsals be financed? Not from the fees afforded by provincial music societies; briefly, perhaps, by a university 'residence'. New surfeits came from a proliferation of competitions, attracting patronage and temporary excitement, without building permanent audiences; assisting a few careers but giving false promise to many: pianists the cruellest case.

There were attempts to chart realities. Two Gulbenkian Reports proposed a rationalization of training institutions, and were promptly shelved (anon 1965 and 1978). Periodic talk about reducing duplication by creating 'centres of excellence' merely excited ancient rivalries (see *The Times*, 6 March, 22 March and, appropriately, 1 April 1986). The Peacock Report's careful analysis of orchestral funding was similarly dissipated (1970). As with other Arts Council deliberations there were too many vested interests at stake for voluntary resolution. Choice could be imposed only by markets and government. The former could impose solutions by force, and explore new fashions of selling. 'Image' and 'demographics' became primary concerns. Could 'nostalgia' and 'heritage' be sold to an ageing population? Could serious music be packaged with a pop-like gloss; a few stars targeted for short bursts of earning power? None of this was likely to do much to correct fundamental imbalances in the system.

Baumol's law dictated that music outside the canning factories could no longer survive except by subsidies. They came from the BBC, the government, and business sponsorship, in that rapidly descending order of importance. All were under threat. The latter had so far proved of dubious benefit. Much less generous than in the USA, it was volatile, customarily wedded to those activities least in need of support, and sometimes damaging to artistic integrity and public utility: notably at Covent Garden. The BBC's future as a patron of music was in greater jeopardy than at any time in its history, with existing commitments under fire; so a return to Reithian policies was inconceivable. The creation of demand by musical appreciation was no longer on the agenda, even among musical publicists. In contrast to a previous generation's Scholes, *The New Grove*, a superb achievement in its own right, was representative of *fin de siècle* preoccupations: 20 volumes of exhaustive, remote scholarship. Serious music was peripheral to the proposed National Curriculum for schools and, of course, outdistanced by pop among university and polytechnic students. It would fall to the government, and possibly the industry itself (as in France and Germany) to provide generous funding. But that would require not so much a great sacrifice by the taxpayers (perhaps a lottery), as a style of commitment wholly at variance with the prevailing culture. The time was ripe for 'Britain's first national arts strategy' (*The Independent*, 6 September 1991).

PART II
Popular Music

Chapter 4

THE 'JAZZ AGE'

DEREK SCOTT

I: The 'Jazz Age' Begins

The word 'jazz' became current in the USA in 1917 (Schuller 1968: 63), and in Britain in 1919 the *Daily Mail* spoke of 'this jazz age', describing people 'dancing as they have never danced before, in a happy rebound from the austerities of war' (quoted in Graves and Hodge 1940, R/1985: 38). Jazz was the term increasingly used to refer to syncopated dance music, the ragtime idiom which met with moral outrage from 'respectable' society when it invaded Britain in 1912. The sensational success of the American Ragtime Octette that year rested on ground prepared by blackface minstrels, who had used syncopation sparsely for years. Ragtime itself had been in existence in the USA since the 1890s, but neither then nor in 1904–7, called by Schuller 'the golden age of ragtime' (1968: 282), did it sustain an impact in Britain. Its success in 1912 was consolidated by the revue *Hullo, Ragtime*, and by Irving Berlin's highly acclaimed visit in 1913.

British bands formed in response: previously, dance music was the province of the German bands established in Britain since the nineteenth century. The first to lead a British modern dance band was Archibald Joyce, who recorded for HMV in 1912. The new bands were little affected by the visit of the self-consciously anarchic Original Dixieland Jazz Band in April 1919, despite its 15-month stay and Columbia recordings. It was different, however, when Paul Whiteman and His Orchestra appeared in the revue *Brighter London* at the London Hippodrome in 1923, and concern about Americanization of taste in popular music increased rapidly. As the demand for dancing grew, particularly while dining out, those experienced in the style of American bands were sought after: Bert Ambrose (1897–1971) returned from New York to lead the band at London's Embassy Club in 1920, and Bert Ralton followed suit in 1921 to form the Savoy Havana Band (for further details of musicians, bands and venues, see Colin 1977; Godbolt 1984; McCarthy 1971; Rust 1972). The Savoy added a second band, the Savoy Orpheans (led by Debroy Somers), in 1923, which, together with that of Jack Hylton (1892–1965), imitated Whiteman's 'symphonic syncopation'.

A typical 1920s dance band was ten strong: two trumpets, trombone, three reeds (clarinets and/or saxophones), piano, banjo, tuba, and drums. Some, like the Savoy Orpheans, were bigger than this from the beginning; others, like Hylton's band, expanded (to 21 players, including a harpist, by 1933) or, like the BBC Dance Orchestra, shrank – from 16 under Jack Payne (1899–1969) to 13 under Henry Hall (1898–1989). White performers dominated. The black Versatile Four (two banjos, piano and drums) had performed in clubs from 1913 and recorded, but no great attention was given to the visit of the black Southern Syncopators in 1919 (though the young Sidney Bechet was among them), and while small black bands were not uncommon in London clubs by 1920 (including Africans and West Indians as well as African-Americans), the legacy of blackface minstrelsy weighed heavily upon them. That black dance bands were still judged by minstrel standards in 1915 is evident from the following contemporary review: 'Jordan's Syncopated Orchestra at Newcastle's Empire Theatre are unquestionably one of the smartest combinations since minstrelsy was in its prime' (quoted in Rye 1990: 47). An early jazz musician like Louis Armstrong, performing to a white audience, could not disentangle himself from minstrel 'business'. How else, he must have considered, do Blacks perform to Whites? Only when a paradigmatic shift in aesthetics allowed a perception of black music as something opposed to a shallow, white 'commercial' music, would a white audience be ready for the very different stage presence of Miles Davis.

The music of dance bands spread to a wider audience via songsheets, radio and records. If the category 'Variety and Concert Party' (the latter referring to troupes familiar from seaside shows) came top in a *Daily Mail* popularity ballot in 1927 while dance bands came fourth (Hustwitt 1983: 20), dance bands were none the less big business: the Café de Paris reaped a profit of £27,485 from supper dances in 1927 (Clegg 1986), and that year Ambrose was reputedly offered £10,000 per annum to move to the Mayfair Hotel with his band (Miller and Boar 1982: 139). Dance bands were also responsible for the boom in the record industry in 1928, whose duration may be disputed (for contradictory figures concerning 1929, see

THE 'JAZZ AGE'

Hustwitt 1983: 22–3, and Gronow 1983: 62–3) but whose outcome was clear when subsequent bankruptcies and mergers left the future to two big firms, EMI and Decca. Moreover, dance-band music, unlike music hall, won over a large fraction of the middle and upper classes, and this happened, perhaps, because a new generation, young enough to have avoided decimation in the First World War, was ready to identify with a new music from the New World. It is scarcely surprising that they favoured songs with romantic, escapist, or even frivolous lyrics in contrast to drawing-room ballads whose high moral tone would be associated with the patriotism and duty for which so many had recently sacrificed their lives.

Leisure provision regarding two major new forms of recreation, dancing and film-going, became increasingly centralized between the world wars: Associated Dance Halls built 'Locarnos' throughout Britain, and British Gaumont or Rank owned most of the cinemas. In the 1930s, dance halls, named Palais, Winter Gardens, Locarno, or Astoria, were everywhere (Billy Cotton (1899–1969), Joe Loss (1909–90), and Oscar Rabin (1899–1958) led the foremost Palais bands). It was through dance that much of the commercial popular music of this period was consumed and gained meaning. Even the Original Dixieland Jazz Band first performed in Britain with a male and female dancer.

The most popular dances immediately after the First World War were the foxtrot, one-step, shimmy (*ca* 1922), blues (1923), and Charleston (1925). The tango and Boston were pre-war, but the former remained popular. The visit of the Argentinian Filipotto and Ariotto Tango Band is commemorated in Lawrence Wright's publication *The Savoy Tango Album* of 1926. Gerald Bright (1904–74) adopted the pseudonym 'Geraldo' to front his Gaucho Tango Orchestra at the Savoy in 1930. There were two kinds of tango, the Spanish habanera variety with the rhythm heard in Primo Scala's recording of 'Serenade in the night' (Jimmy Kennedy, 1937) (Ex. 4.1a), and the Argentinian variety with the rhythm heard in Henry Hall's recording of 'Play to me, gypsy' (music Karel Vacek, English words Kennedy, 1934) (Ex. 4.1b). An unusual feature of the performance of tangos was the convention of ending with a loud dominant seventh.

Jack Payne's 1931 recording of Moises Simon's 'The peanut vendor' was one of the first to introduce Cuban rhythms to British dancers; it was a *son*, but danced as a rumba. The rumba proper was present by 1932, the date of Ambrose's recording of 'When Yuba plays the rumba on his tuba' (Herman Hupfeld). A favourite rumba

POPULAR MUSIC

Ex. 4.1   Dance Rhythms

(a) tango

(b) tango

(c) rumba

was 'Sidewalks of Cuba' (Ben Oakland, Mitchell Parish and Irving Mills), and on Lew Stone's recording the characteristic clave rhythm (Ex. 4.1c) can be heard. It is a two-bar rhythm, an additive rhythm in the first bar (of a kind already familiar from the Charleston) followed by a divisive rhythm in the second. There was a tendency for some composers to write rumbas consisting of an almost incessant 3 + 3 + 2. The rumba version of Frank Magine's 'Balloons' by the 'novelty' composer and pianist Billy Mayerl is a case in point; and even when he incorporates divisive rhythms he opts for the reverse clave pattern of 2 + 2 + 4 followed by 3 + 3 + 2. Other Latin rhythms arrived when Edmundo Ros formed his Rumba Band in 1940; he later added calypsos. Then came the mambo, a speciality of the Kirchen Band.

This does not exhaust the variety of popular dances during the period under discussion. The band most concerned to keep abreast of dancers' needs was that of Victor Sylvester (1901–78) who, as a dancer himself, had won the World Ballroom Dance Championship in 1922; he was also the author of *Modern Ballroom Dancing* (1928). His records were prized by dancers for their 'strict tempo', a term Sylvester made his own. He moved with the times, catering for jive in 1944 with recordings made by his Jive Band, an outfit featuring trumpeter Tommy McQuater (*b* 1914) and trombonist George Chisholm (*b* 1915). Sales of his records are eloquent testimony to the popularity of dancing: they exceeded those of every other band by 1955, having reached 27 million (Colin 1977: 75).

THE 'JAZZ AGE'
II: The Growth and Diffusion of Jazz

Attempts to frame empirical definitions of jazz have proved unfruitful (see Gridley et al. 1989). Such definitions are often formed to weed out false from true, fake from real. Decisions about what is *not* jazz are therefore crucial to an understanding of what *is* jazz. Consequently, jazz exists in a dialectical relationship with other musical activities, and changes in the latter affect the meaning of the former.

In the late 1920s a cultural formation emerged determined to define jazz in a particular way. Indeed, but for the fact that 'jazz' had stuck as a label for syncopated music, a more dignified term, such as 'rhythm style', would have been preferred for the music that members of this formation wished to privilege. Its key figures were Edgar Jackson, editor of the then monthly *Melody Maker*, and bandleaders Bert Firman and Fred Elizalde. Jackson attempted to distinguish as true jazz, music innovative in style, containing improvised solos. As committed to the idea of progress as any modernist of the concert hall, he heard evidence of it in the records of white rather than black musicians, interpreting performances by the former as innovative and polished, and by the latter as retrogressive and crude. In his review of Duke Ellington's *Black and Tan Fantasy* in *Melody Maker*, March 1928 (quoted in Godbolt 1984: 42), he stated that he had considered previous records by Ellington's band to be 'highly crude'. It is ironic that the tune he now found 'far above the average in melody' was Bubber Miley's minor version of the refrain of Stephen Adams's drawing-room ballad 'The Holy City' (1892).

The influence of white American bands like Red Nichols and His Five Pennies suffuses the early Zonophone recordings Bert Firman (*b* 1906) made with his Dance Orchestra and, especially, with the Rhythmic Eight (not always eight in number). These 1926 recordings, with their improvised solos, lay claim to be the first British examples of jazz complying with Jackson's redefinition of that term. They include his best-known recording, of DeSylva, Brown and Henderson's 'Black bottom (of the Swanee River)', with its telling, though brief, bass saxophone solo from Adrian Rollini. Firman was first influenced by the two-beat ragtime style, but moved to a four-beat style before the decade ended: compare, for example, 'Mississippi mud' (Harry Barris) of 1928 with 'Painting the clouds with sunshine' (music by Joe Burke) of 1929. The four-beat bar allows greater variety of syncopation and a more interesting bass part. The first chorus of 'Painting the clouds with sunshine' sounds like classic

New Orleans three-part polyphony, except that the clarinet and trumpet are joined by a tenor saxophone instead of trombone (for details of personnel on these and other recordings, see Rust 1969, and Rust and Forbes 1987, R/1989).

Fred Elizalde (1907–79) started a jazz group with his brother as a student at Cambridge in 1927, then led a band at the Savoy that included ex-members of the California Ramblers. A 'progressive' feature of some of Elizalde's recordings is their move away from 'paraphrase improvisation' – a term coined by Hodeir (1956: 144) to describe improvisation based on the original melody – towards improvisation around chord changes. The technique can be heard in 'Misery Farm' (C. Jay Wallis) of 1928 (with the singer Al Bowlly (1899–1941), whose first engagement in Britain was with this band). Elizalde was voted number one in a *Melody Maker* poll in November 1928, indicating that the paper had become a focal point for jazz enthusiasts. Opinions elsewhere differed: the BBC stopped broadcasting his band in spring 1929, and the Savoy management terminated his contract in the summer (Colin 1977: 45). His music was not at home in the cultural environment of the upper-class hotel, and was obviously regarded as morally suspect by the BBC; yet Elizalde's aspirations for jazz extended to his writing concert suites.

Other important figures in British jazz at this time were Philip Lewis, who recorded for Decca in 1929 with the Rhythm Maniacs, and Patrick 'Spike' Hughes (1908–87), who recorded for Decca in the early 1930s with his Dance Orchestra (at first called the Decca-Dents, a name pointing to the disapproval some felt for the music). Both of these bands included Americans. Hughes's records met all the criteria of the latest 'real' jazz: 'It's unanimous now' (Sam Stept and John Green), for example, is four-beat, full of improvisation around chords, and contains jazz devices like the two-bar chase (one solo succeeding another at two-bar intervals). The double bass (played by Hughes, hence his nickname) propels the music in a way impossible for brass bass. The newness of the sound of the double bass in jazz, and the jazz style of playing it, is the subject of 'Pick and slap' (1930). He plays a tin bass, not quite believing recording technology had advanced sufficiently to pick up the conventional bass. Hughes encouraged improvisation around chords by sometimes giving soloists chord symbols only (L. Thompson 1986). His imaginative arranging is revealed in his attention to detail, noticeable in the poetic touches so often added to endings. His compositions show the same distinctive mind: note, for example, the dorian inflexions to *A Harlem Symphony* (1931). Hughes was enthusiastic about black jazz musicians, a symptom of a changing mood and future challenge to Jackson's theoretical paradigm. Many of Hughes's compositions were recorded by a band organized by Benny Carter in the USA in 1933. Shortly after, he turned to jazz journalism, then to writing on classical music (Elizalde, too, turned to a classical career and, for a while, so did Firman).

Hughes's jazz stood as far outside the dominant musical aesthetics of the time as did Elizalde's. An event in 1932, however, showed evidence of the growing oppositional cultural formation given identity by *Melody Maker*. On 18 July, Louis Armstrong began his British visit by performing at the London Palladium. He came without a band of his own and was part of a variety bill. The reception ranged from surprised bewilderment to the ecstasy of *Melody Maker* readers whose excitement had been stirred up beforehand. Yet *Melody Maker* did not superficially glamorize jazz stars; Armstrong was harshly criticized on his next visit (1933) when he was considered to be sacrificing his art to showmanship. Indeed, when Ellington visited with his band in 1933, *Melody Maker* arranged a special concert for jazz *cognoscenti* at the Trocadero Cinema, Elephant and Castle. Ellington wrote of that occasion, in his book *Music Is My Mistress*, as follows:

We were to avoid 'commercial' numbers and apparently on this occasion we lived up to expectations because Spike Hughes, the foremost critic at that time, didn't criticize us at all. Instead, he criticized the audience for applauding at the end of solos and in the middle of numbers! That's how serious it was. (quoted in Godbolt 1984: 111)

Ellington had begun his visit as Turn Number 13, last on the bill, at the Palladium: something he took easily in his stride. His puzzlement at the Trocadero concert is another matter. As late as 1939 he was proclaiming 'Sure I'm commercial' (*Melody Maker*, 13 May: 9). He seems to have remained unaware that being 'uncommercial' was crucial to the arguments of Jackson and Hughes (the latter writing under the pseudonym 'Mike' in *Melody Maker*), who were struggling to achieve recognition for jazz as a form of 'art' music. This also explains Hughes's dislike of applause during jazz performances: it constituted irreverent behaviour not tolerated in the concert hall. Ironically, the person responsible for bringing Ellington to Britain was Jack Hylton who, by so doing, indicated that he did not think Ellington embraced an aesthetic opposed to his own; later that year, in fact, they shared a bill in Paris.

POPULAR MUSIC

Fans of 'real' jazz were not well served by the radio: the BBC broadcast a mere twenty minutes of Armstrong's performance at the Palladium on the London Regional Programme (28 July 1932). Ellington, too, was confined to a single broadcast on the Regional Programme during his first visit. Fortunately, records were available: Columbia started a Hot Jazz Records series in 1927, Parlophone following suit with a Rhythm Style series in 1928. The specialist record shop Levy's in Whitechapel started releasing records on their own independent label in 1927. As part of the broadening interest in jazz in the 1930s, a network of Rhythm Clubs spread throughout Britain (Rhythm Club No. 1 was founded in London in 1933). The Radio Rhythm Club of 1940, which became the BBC Jazz Club, was the first serious acknowledgement of a jazz audience by the BBC. Harry Parry (clarinet) formed the first Radio Rhythm Club Sextet, which included George Shearing (*b* 1919) who, however, did not fully develop his renowned 'locked-hands' technique (right-hand melody doubled in left hand with a chord sandwiched between) until 1949 (Feather 1988: 195). Buddy Featherstonhaugh (tenor saxophone) took over with a new Radio Rhythm Club Sextet in 1943.

Melody Maker, founded in 1926, and *Rhythm*, which began as a drummer's paper in 1927, were the most popular papers with jazz enthusiasts. They both included musical quotations, suggesting that musical literacy was expected of their readership. *Melody Maker* became more concerned with jazz when it changed owners from dance-music publisher Lawrence Wright to the Oldham Press, who also took over *Rhythm* (which ceased publication in 1939). The *Gramophone*, launched in 1923, offered Jackson space for jazz record reviews. Two specialist monthlies, *Swing Music* and *Hot News*, both launched in 1935, were short-lived: the former survived fitfully till autumn 1936. Sales were never high, and to defray costs by advertising 'commercial' music went against the grain.

Until the mid-1930s, a steady stream of American jazz musicians visited Britain: Cab Calloway, Coleman Hawkins and Joe Venuti were among those arriving in 1934. The next year, however, the Ministry of Labour, under pressure from the Musicians' Union, banned visits by American bands. The only way round the ban was for jazz musicians to pretend to be variety performers. This subterfuge was easiest for pianists and accounts for Fats Waller's appearance at the Palladium in 1938. The ban was ineffective against American servicemen playing jazz off-duty while stationed in Britain during the Second World War. Yet it lasted until 1954, and before it ceased

THE 'JAZZ AGE'

there was a notorious court case concerning illegal performances by Bechet and Hawkins.

In the early 1930s, despite efforts by Jackson, Hughes, and others, jazz was still being defined by reference to dance music: 'I have played dance music with genuine sincerity of purpose,' claimed Hylton, 'for I believe that in many ways clever and melodious "jazz music" portrays the spirit of this age' (1934: ii). This is not to say jazz was being used as an undiscriminating term. The criteria underlying the aesthetic values of Stanley Nelson's *All About Jazz* (1934), for example, may seem very different from Jackson's, but are alike in that each writer sees jazz evolving along approved lines. Nelson makes the revealing comment, 'from the jungle to the ballroom is a long step and jazz has undergone a refinement in keeping with such a transition' (quoted in Godbolt 1984: 150). Jackson's own notions of progress and refinement marginalized the efforts of many black musicians whom he considered had not progressed sufficiently 'from the jungle'. Constant Lambert, in 1934, argued against jungle metaphors by stressing the substantial contribution made to jazz by Jewish musicians (the extent to which Jews were drawn to jazz as an 'outsider's music' is certainly of sociological significance). However, Lambert's aesthetics being those of the dominant culture, he not surprisingly states, 'the next move in the development will come, almost inevitably, from the sophisticated or highbrow composers', because they alone can rid jazz of its 'nightclub element' the way Haydn rid the minuet of its 'ballroom element' (1934: 227). It is difficult to understand how this would work with Ellington's *Hot and Bothered*, which Lambert so admired. He was merely replacing one disparaging label (jungle music) with another (nightclub music). Elizalde, in contrast, pleaded for jazz to be thought of as 'an art apart, and not in any way comparable to the classics' (1929: 393).

Dance bands of the 1930s did produce some records to delight 'real' jazz enthusiasts. ''Leven thirty Saturday night' (Earl Burnett, Bill Grantham and Jess Kirkpatrick), arranged for Ambrose's band in 1930 by Lew Stone (1898–1969), provided for lots of jazzy violin and dazzling playing from American clarinettist Danny Polo. The usual dance-band output, however, was rarely as hot. Singers, especially crooners exploiting an amplified intimacy made possible by the microphone, were becoming more important; anonymous vocal refrains were simultaneously disappearing. Al Bowlly built his reputation with the New Mayfair Dance Orchestra (the HMV studio band), led by Ray Noble (1903–78), singing romantic Noble compositions like 'Love is the sweetest thing' (1932) and 'The very thought of you' (1934). Some singers were beginning to improvise: on Hylton's recording in 1933 of 'It's the talk of the town' (music Jerry Livingston, words Marty Symes and Al Neiburg) Eve Becke improvises when repeating the final eight bars (see Ex. 4.2, which gives the last 16 bars).

Ex. 4.2 'It's the talk of the town'
(Livingston/Symes/Neiburg), as performed by Eve Becke

British dance bands did not simply imitate American models, especially if they had a skilful arranger like Lew Stone. Comparing his arrangement of *Solitude* (1934) with Ellington's only slightly earlier New York and Chicago recordings reveals significant differences. He adopts a faster tempo, which means the piece will be too short if its 32-bar *AABA* structure is played just twice as in the Ellington performances. Stone opts for a repeated *AABA*, then a two-bar guitar break followed by *BAA*. This allows more solo improvisation, but it is not handled haphazardly: Nat Gonella's muted trumpet *obbligato* (improvised countermelody) during the varied ensemble restatement of *AABA* develops into a trumpet solo in the *B* section. In complementary fashion, Albert Harris's guitar break is followed by *BA* with guitar *obbligato*. Then the final ensemble performance of *A* echoes the opening texture and timbre, unifying the piece. Stone's adroit use of *obbligato* owes much to his experience of its effectiveness in vocal refrains; he employed it frequently in recordings made with Bowlly two years earlier.

THE 'JAZZ AGE'

The extent to which improvisations are pre-planned in danceband performances of the 1930s varies. Improvisations on different takes of a recording can show marked similarities, as with Lew Stone's band on takes E 1004-B and E 1004-C of 'By the fireside' (Ray Noble, James Campbell and Reginald Connelly). Elsewhere they show considerable variety, as happens with the same band on 'My sweet Virginia' (music Vincent Rose, words Ray Klages and Jack Meskill), comparing takes E 1024-B and E 1024-C. For jazz enthusiasts a spontaneous-sounding improvisation, such as Gonella's *obbligato* to Dorothy Carless's singing on Ray Noble's 1934 recording of 'Oh, you nasty man' (Ray Henderson, Jack Yellen and Irving Caesar), was what made a dance band worth listening to. Otherwise the familiar 32-bar *AABA* form and the style of arranging, especially the thickening of a melody with parallel harmony, could become too formulaic.

In the 1930s black musicians became more visible. Cotton employed trombonist Ellis Jackson, who had been in Britain since 1907, and Garland Wilson played the piano with Payne's band. As for black singers, Paul Robeson was living in London, Leslie Hutchinson ('Hutch') sang to his own piano accompaniment in variety, and Alberta Hunter joined Jack Jackson's band at the Dorchester Hotel in 1934. Hunter had worked with many top Chicago and New York jazz musicians, but Adelaide Hall moved to London with even more impressive jazz credentials in 1938. Benny Carter was employed as an arranger for Henry Hall in 1936–7, thanks to efforts by Leonard Feather and Spike Hughes. Coleman Hawkins was active in Europe and often in Britain (like Ellington, he was invited first by Hylton). The Harlem Knights, led by Guyanan clarinettist Rudolph Dunbar, was one of the first black dance bands to be broadcast in Britain (from the Cossack Club).

Reginald Foresythe (1907–58), a black British composer of African and German descent, led a white band at the 400 Club, London, in 1933. His compositions attempted to fuse jazz and classical techniques; an example is *Swing for Roundabout* (1936). Stone made an impressive arrangement of Foresythe's *Garden of Weed*, with its 'advanced' harmonies, for his own band in 1934. Ken 'Snakehips' Johnson, a Guyanan dancer, formed his Emperors of Swing in 1936 with Jamaican trumpeter Leslie Thompson. Johnson was killed when the Café de Paris was bombed in 1941, but West Indian clarinet virtuoso Carl Barriteau, who had performed with Johnson, formed his own band. Cyril Blake and His Jig's Club Band also recorded in the early 1940s.

Blake had come to Britain with Will Marion Cook's Southern Syncopated Orchestra in 1919 and stayed.

Other well-known black musicians of the 1940s were West Indian drummer Ray Ellington (1915–85), who played with Harry Roy (1900–71) before forming his famous quartet; drummer Edmundo Ros from Trinidad, whose first residency was at the Cosmo Club; and singer Archie Lewis from Jamaica, who met Geraldo while working for ENSA and recorded many romantic numbers with him. The number of West Indian musicians in Britain increased when mass migration from the Caribbean commenced in 1948. The first distinctly Caribbean event was the performance by a steel band, the Trinidad All Steel Percussion Orchestra, at the Festival of Britain in 1951 (for information on West Indian musicians in Britain, 1900–1960, see J. Cowley 1990).

Women, black or white, are noticeably absent as instrumentalists or composers in the history of British dance bands. There are striking exceptions: Kathy Stobart (*b* 1925) played various members of the saxophone family, notably with Vic Lewis's Kenton-style big band in 1948–9 and 1951–2; and Ivy Benson (1913–93) had several hit records in the 1940s with her All Girls Band (which included trumpeter Gracie Cole). An entirely female band, however, was a novelty and circumscribed women instrumentalists. Female vocalists were a different matter. Some of them – for example, Elsie Carlisle, Vera Lynn and Anne Shelton – became international stars performing with Ambrose.

III: Alternatives to the Dance Band

What was once called 'light music' is now labelled 'easy listening'. Besides suggesting dance-band music (for which it was the preferred term of the dominant cultural institutions), light music often implied an easily assimilated classical rather than jazz idiom (also termed 'light classical'). Albert Ketèlbey (1875–1959) was a pioneer: his 'characteristic intermezzo' *In a Monastery Garden* (1915) was one of the earliest of his short descriptive works to become categorized as 'light music'. His pieces generally evoke either exotic locales or religious melancholy, *In the Mystic Land of Egypt* (1931) exemplifying the one and *Sanctuary of the Heart* (1924) the other. In many ways his music is deliberately incidental to the narrative.

THE 'JAZZ AGE'

Ketèlbey was not alone in composing short pieces with generic descriptions such as 'narrative poem', 'descriptive intermezzo' and 'characteristic melody'; others were Leo Torrance, Mary Nightingale, Ernest Austin, Evan Marsden, and Ambroise Farman. Some, such as Kenneth Alford, composed topical pieces, like *The Vanished Army* (1919).

A major influence on Ketèlbey's style was the drawing-room ballad, so it is understandable that he converted compositions such as *In a Monastery Garden* and *The Sacred Hour* (1929) into sacred ballads by inventing lyrics. The ballad was still thriving in the First World War decade, well-known examples being 'Shipmates o' mine' (music Wilfrid Sanderson, words Edward Teschemacher) of 1913, 'Roses of Picardy' (music Haydn Wood, words Fred Weatherly) of 1916, and 'The bells of St Mary's' (music A. Emmett Adams, words Douglas Furber) of 1917. In 1926, however, Herbert Greenhalgh, discussing the effects of wireless, asserted, 'amateurs no longer flock to buy ballads and pianoforte pieces with which to impress their friends . . . It is dance music that is in demand today' (1926: 128). But dance rhythms were inappropriate for sacred texts, which probably accounts for the fact that sacred ballads possessed the greater staying power.

The ballad declined but did not become extinct, and British women composers continued to be more involved with this genre than with dance music: Betsy O'Hogan, for example, had a notable success with 'Old Father Thames' in 1933. In *Ceol Mara (Songs of the Isle of Lewis)* of 1935, Duncan Morison continued the practice of turning Hebridean songs into drawing-room ballads that had occupied Marjorie Kennedy Fraser (1857–1930) for the first three decades of the century. 'Pseudo-Celtic' would seem a fair description of the results, since the originals are often radically transformed. In particular, the rhythmic character of waulking songs, originally emphasized by the regular beating of the damp cloth, is lost in Fraser's versions: 'The seagull of the Land-under-Waves', for example, becomes an impressionistic 'Celtic twilight' piece.

William Boosey found his Ballad Concerts less well attended during the 1930s, and some singers of this material were taking to the 'halls', as did Peter Dawson (1882–1961). This style of music, however, continued to resonate in operetta, especially in the songs of Ivor Novello. It can also be heard in the compositions of Eric Coates (1886–1957). Although best known today for his march *The Dam Busters* (1954), Coates had been composing 'light orchestral suites' since before the First World War. He composed ballads, too, a favourite being 'The green hills o' Somerset' (1916), with words by veteran lyricist Frederick Weatherly. Coates's music was heard frequently on the radio: the marches 'Knightsbridge', from his suite *London* (1933), and *Calling All Workers* (1940) became the most familiar of radio signature tunes. Indeed, however difficult it may be to place him and Ketèlbey within the development of 'aligned' popular taste, it must be recognized that statistically, in terms of their earnings, they have been among the most popular composers of all (see Ehrlich 1989: 37–8, 106, 164).

One of the best-known light orchestras was that of Annunzio Mantovani (1905–80), a classical violinist of considerable technique. He came to attention broadcasting with his Tipica Orchestra in the 1930s, and began recording for Decca in the 1940s (playing regularly at Butlin's holiday camps in the summer). His New Orchestra of 1951 was a sensation. He and Ronald Binge (1910–79) used their imaginative arranging skills to create a luxurious texture from 40 players, employing devices such as the celebrated 'cascading strings'. The pioneer of the sentimental massed-string sound was George Melachrino, but Mantovani was first to exploit recording-studio effects. Other leaders of light orchestras were Jack Byfield and Dorothy Summers. During the Second World War Geraldo, too, started a light orchestra (the Geraldo Concert Orchestra). Apart from playing their own repertoire, these orchestras accompanied singers of ballads and light opera, as on the records of the husband and wife duettists Anne Ziegler and Webster Booth.

Dance bands recognized no clear-cut division between the repertoire of light orchestras and their own: Hylton's band had Coates's *The Selfish Giant* and *The Three Bears* in its repertoire (Rust 1972: 61) and Payne had Pierné's *Entrance of the Little Fauns*. *The Teddy Bears' Picnic* was a purely instrumental intermezzo (composed by an American, J. W. Bratton) until Jimmy Kennedy added words to provide Henry Hall with a novelty record for Christmas 1932. The song 'Moonlight and roses' was adapted from Edwin H. Lemare's Andantino in D♭ by Ben Black and Neil Moret (*ca* 1925). Some performers felt equally happy in a dance-band or light orchestral context: one such was Gracie Fields, who ran the gamut from music-hall comedy to light classical. Her recording of the Bach–Gounod 'Ave Maria' in 1934 was a best seller.

The accordion band was a novelty form of dance band. The instrument was popularized by the Macari Brothers, an Italian variety act, one of whom formed an accordion band, Macari's Dutch Serenaders (Whitcomb 1986: 175–6). Harry Bidgood formed Don

Porto and His Novelty Accordions in 1932 and his most famous band, Primo Scala and His Accordion Band, two years later. He was also leader of Rossini's Accordions (formed 1935), with whom the young Vera Lynn (*b* 1917) sang. The point of all these aliases was to enable him to record for several labels simultaneously, keeping the secret from the public by using different arrangers for each band. Accordion bands did not consist solely of accordions; there was a rhythm section (for example, piano, bass and drums), and often a xylophone, which sounded effective in its brittle tone against sustained accordion chords. The same held true of mandolin bands and banjo bands, though a bass banjo might feature in the rhythm section of the latter. Tangos were the predictable favourites of accordion bands, as blackface minstrel songs were the obvious choice for banjo bands.

In the 1930s the accordion ousted the ukulele as the most popular amateur instrument. Not that the ukulele disappeared; in the hands of virtuoso Max Nesbit it astonished audiences in variety theatres, and in its banjolele form it became the well-known instrument of George Formby (1904–61). The accordion's popularity was boosted by Arthur Tracy, the 'Street Singer', an American who came to Britain in 1935 and stayed four years, appearing in films and making records.

Two instruments related to the accordion deserve brief mention. The concertina had a champion in Percy Honri, one of the leaders of the music-hall strike of 1907; he was still touring variety theatres in the 1930s with his wife, who accompanied on accordion and sang. The melodeon became popular in the Western Isles of Scotland; its rudimentary harmonic capability (the same as a mouth organ) was turned to advantage in performances of melodically and rhythmically conceived Gaelic dance tunes.

IV: *Swing, Revivalism and Bebop*

Two ensembles formed in 1935 are praised by Brian Rust for keeping alive the spirit of improvisation and small-band jazz (1972: 96): Nat Gonella and His Georgians, and Joe Daniels and His Hot Shots. Daniels (*b* 1908) was formerly Harry Roy's drummer. He and his Hot Shots continued to record fitfully throughout the war, their records selling as successfully in the USA as in Britain. Gonella's Georgians were formed originally from colleagues in Stone's band. Gonella (*b* 1908) had fallen under the spell of Armstrong in 1930, as a member of Cotton's band. He imitated Armstrong's melodic and rhythmic mannerisms, his tone and vibrato effects, as well as his vocal techniques of growling and 'scatting' (a quasi-instrumental vocalise), but he added an effervescent quality very much his own.

While jazz fans were keen on the 'hot', there were many who preferred 'sweet' music. The hot versus sweet opposition surfaced in the mid-1930s. In 1934 Maurice Winnick began to imitate the gentle, sweet style of Guy Lombardo and His Royal Canadians (who, apart from Guy and his brothers, were American). This smooth, sophisticated music was soon favoured in plush hotels. Winnick's band replaced Roy's at the Mayfair in 1936, then moved to the Dorchester in 1939. What upmarket hotels and clubs did not like was the new swing music. The Heralds of Swing relived Elizalde's Savoy experience when their jazz proved unacceptable to the clientele of the Paradise nightclub in Regent Street in 1939. This ten-piece band, which included McQuater and Chisholm, was intended to be Britain's first regularly organized jazz ensemble. Despite high expectations, it lasted but a few months.

The beginning of the swing era is usually dated from the immense success of Benny Goodman's version of Jelly Roll Morton's *King Porter Stomp* in 1935, an arrangement that concluded with an exciting call-and-response riff chorus (an antiphonal passage based on a short melodic–rhythmic idea). British swing came a few years later: Sid Phillips (1902–73) can be heard responding to the new style in his composition *Dinner and Dance* (1938) for Lew Stone's band. After a 4-bar introduction, it consists of three 32-bar choruses (the second containing a spectacular clarinet solo by Joe Crossman) separated by interludes and followed by a final chorus which begins as an exciting tutti with trombone countermelody but, after a dramatic rising scale on clarinet, is interrupted by an 8-bar coda featuring a *diminuendo* and *crescendo* (a typical Glen Miller device). The piece is based on a riff tune, that is, one built from a constantly repeated motif, usually two bars long and tenacious concerning pitch (Ex. 4.3). Examples of riff-like repetition exist in dance music of the 1920s, but what was rare became the norm in swing.

According to Schuller, the formula 'worked to death' by American swing bands consisted of a relentless four-to-the-beat bar, riffs constructed to fit any of the primary triads, and the fade-out ending (1968: 276–7): Glen Miller made a career out of it. The Skyrockets' recording of *Saturday Night Jump* (1943) by British composer Gordon Rees is indebted to the Miller model and comprises a riff tune, riff-

Ex. 4.3   Sid Phillips: *Dinner and Dance*

style accompaniments to solos, riffs thickened by parallel movement, and prominent 'pushed notes' (accented notes played just before the beat). It lacks other Miller hallmarks, like call and response, but most of all it lacks his energetic drive. The following were known for playing swing in the early 1940s: Oscar Rabin, Joe Loss, Harry Roy, Harry Leader, Nat Gonella and his New Georgians, the Squadronaires, the Skyrockets, and (occasionally) Geraldo. In the mid-1940s big band boogie woogie was popularized by Harry James in the USA, and was soon added to the repertoire of those above. Two outstanding small swing bands, Danny Polo and his Swing Stars and George Chisholm and his Jive Five, were formed in the late 1930s but did not survive the outbreak of war. Ken Johnson's Emperors of Swing lasted, as previously noted, until Johnson's death in 1941. A final mention should go to Leonard Feather's bizarre Ye Olde English Swynge Band, which gave the swing treatment to traditional airs.

War was declared as swing was making inroads in Britain. Some performers responded quickly to swing, like Stone; others called it a day: Roy Fox (1901–82) left for Australia in 1938, and Hylton disbanded in 1940, after unsuccessfully trying out the new style with Coleman Hawkins (with whom he recorded two sides in 1939). Dance bands lost members in the call-up. Ambrose's entire brass section virtually disappeared, re-emerging later in the RAF Dance Orchestra, the Squadronaires. Led by Jimmy Miller, this was a greatly admired swing band. Chisholm and McQuater were star attractions; the former also created imaginative arrangements for them. The Skyrockets (the No. 1 Balloon Centre Dance Orchestra) was another dynamic RAF band, led by trombonist Paul Fenhoulet. There were also services' bands in the army and navy.

When the Forces' Programme started in 1940, it included far more dance music than the BBC had offered before. Not that this proved expensive, since the BBC paid dance-band musicians at the Musicians' Union minimum rate of £12 per week (Mairants 1980: 55), less than many conscripts were earning. Geraldo's band and the voice of Dorothy Carless became familiar from wartime radio; the former had been appointed Supervisor of the ENSA Dance Band Division.

It was, however, Ambrose's ex-singer, the more innocent-sounding Vera Lynn, who was promoted as the 'Forces' Sweetheart'. During the war, Miller was an ever-increasing influence, especially when stationed in Britain with his massive Army Air Force Band in 1944.

After the war, the theoretical paradigm based on progress and refinement was shifting to another based on notions of authen- ticity, causing black jazz to be accorded priority over white. John Hammond's reports from America (published in *Melody Maker*) were influential, as was the interest in early jazz awakened by reissues of old records and compilations of discographies. Evidence of this shift is seen in the enormous impact of George Webb's Dixielanders, an amateur band that performed regularly at a pub in Barnehurst, Kent. Harking back to King Oliver, they played in collective improvisatory style, but had an outstanding clarinettist in Wally Fawkes. They became a centre of attention for those seeking an authentic working-class culture, and were considered the guardians of oral rather than literate music-making. Their anthem, 'When the saints go marching in', was taken up by the many revivalist bands appearing in the later 1940s, for example, the Yorkshire Jazz Band (Leeds), Sandy Brown's band (Edinburgh), and the Crane River Jazz Band (Twickenham). These bands stressed their allegiance to early black New Orleans jazz, rejecting 'progress' on the one hand and 'Archer Street jazz' on the other. (Archer Street in London was a kind of open-air labour exchange for musicians, patrolled by agents at lunchtime, and 'Archer Street jazz' suggested jazz played for commercial gain rather than from conviction.) Professionals playing in Dixieland style, like Harry Gold, were spurned by the diehards for what they saw as an attempt to profit from 'real' jazz. Lewis and Parnell's Jazzmen, formed in 1944, also played Dixieland, but their association with 'Archer Street jazz' meant that their technical superiority to Webb's band was condemned as 'slick professionalism'. The Young Communists 'adopted' Webb's Dixielanders as the standard-bearers of proletarian culture (member-ship of the Communist Party of Great Britain reached its peak at 56,000 during 1945–8, and three Communist MPs sat in the Commons). However, when Graeme Bell and His Australian Jazz Band visited in 1948 and introduced the novelty of dancing to revivalist jazz, the enthusiastic reception was a sign that the intellectual left was losing its hegemony over the music. Furthermore, revivalism had to face the challenge of bebop.

The stirrings of a new kind of jazz were evident when Vocalion (part of Decca) began a jazz-orientated 'S' series in 1936. In April

THE 'JAZZ AGE'

1937 they released 'Lady be good' (Gershwin) by a small ensemble which included Count Basie and Lester Young. The latter's tenor saxophone solo, an original and irregularly phrased improvisation departing entirely from Gershwin's melody, heralded a new direction in jazz, leading to bebop. In December 1939, while experimenting with the higher intervals of the chords to Ray Noble's 'Cherokee' (1938), Charlie Parker moved further in creating the new style, and an improvisation on this tune won him an ovation on New York's 52nd Street in 1942 (Shapiro and Hentoff 1966: 354–60). Bebop was an attempt to create a black 'art' music, a project building upon the artistic successes of the Harlem Renaissance. Jazz was to become an alternative modern 'art' music by being true to its own values rather than those of the European classical tradition. Esquire released records of Parker in Britain, and some of Dizzy Gillespie's modernist experiments appeared in Parlophone's Rhythm Style series in 1947. The Club Eleven, Carnaby Street, was founded in 1948 to cater for the new interest. Key figures were Ronnie Scott (tenor saxophone), Hank Shaw and Leon Calvert (trumpets), Tony Crombie (drums), and Denis Rose (piano, trumpet, and bebop analyst).

Many young boppers joined 'Geraldo's Navy' – a reference to the bands he organized for P & O liners – for the purpose of visiting 52nd Street. Steve Race was an early champion of bebop, and so was Edgar Jackson (presumably because it represented 'progress'). Another enthusiast was Leonard Feather (1914–94); but, all said, more critics favoured revivalism. Nevertheless, clubs began to appear for bop fans, who sported an image of fashionable youth in contrast to the corduroys and woolly jumpers of 'trad' fans. Soon the diluted bop of Tito Burns and others appeared alongside that of the uncompromising Ronnie Scott and John Dankworth.

Ralph Sharon's *Boptical Illusion* (1950) for piano, tenor saxophone, guitar, bass and drums demonstrates the 'advanced' harmonies, sinuous melodic lines and abrupt rhythmic interjections that characterize bebop. His improvised piano solo is given in Ex.4.4. The progression Fm^7–E^7–$E\flat$ in bars 8–9 of this solo is a typical example of tritone substitution in bebop, whereby a chord that forms part of a conventional cycle-of-5ths progression ($B\flat$ here) is replaced by one a tritone away (E^7). Tritone substitution may have been discovered through bebop's espousal of the 7th chord with flattened 5th ($G^{7(-5)}$, for instance, contains the same notes as $D\flat^{7(-5)}$), though what was new was its frequency of use rather than the device itself.

Ex. 4.4   Ralph Sharon: *Boptical Illusion*

V: *Conflict, Commercialism and Continuity*

The term 'mouldy fig' was used by jazz modernists to describe Dixielanders. According to Feather (1988: 88), it was not he who coined the term (as often reported) but an *Esquire* correspondent in June 1945. The prime venue in London for traditionalists was 100 Oxford Street. Ironically, the commercial success they despised proved more wounding than the gibes of modernists. The 'trad' boom was regarded as a sell-out by revivalists; admirers of Ken Colyer, for example, felt distaste at the commercial success of Chris Barber, since they considered the music a challenge to the establishment: 'Ken had equated traditional jazz with left-wing protest and it

THE 'JAZZ AGE'

was to the sound of a New Orleans marching band that the Ban-the-Bomb columns kept their spirits up on the road from Aldermaston' (Melly 1989: 60). Barber's ideas were different, and he had no qualms about being booked to play for a Tory fund-raising event. This should be no surprise since, as Simon Frith has commented, 'Even before jazz became the sound of 1950s bohemia, it was clear that its British class-base was not the proletariat' (1988a: 59). It is significant that two of the major figures in early British jazz, Elizalde and Hughes, were both Cambridge graduates. And it was Eton-educated Humphrey Lyttelton (*b* 1921) who took over Webb's band.

Nevertheless, the concept of selling out remains an important yardstick in the aesthetics of jazz. Traditional versus 'traddy-pop' became a new opposition designed to distinguish good from bad, real from fake. Despite the fact that almost all recorded jazz can in some sense be called commercial, since a disc is undeniably a commodity, the non-commercial is always the authentic, always the most elevated. Schuller, for example, speaks of 'real jazz and commercial derivatives of jazz' (1968: 54), Rust remarks that 'the average dance band on either side of the Atlantic was not a jazz band and had no pretensions in that direction' (1972: 7), and Godbolt mentions 'the wide difference between ordinary dance music and the vitally alive and creative music called jazz' (1984: 150). This elevated quality is not simply a matter of technical skill, otherwise many revivalist bands would have fallen short of it. Rather, the argument is indebted to the nineteenth-century concept of 'art for art's sake'; indeed, Schuller calls Armstrong's *West End Blues* (1928) 'music for music's sake' (1968: 89).

The music discussed in this chapter did not suddenly cease in 1955 because of a 'rock revolution'. Ted Heath (1900–69) was featured with his band in the first British rock 'n' roll film, *It's a Wonderful World* (1956). The Squadronaires did not disband till 1964. Joe Loss, who started as a bandleader in 1930, was still fronting a band in the 1980s. Jazz traditionalists Kenny Ball (*b* 1930), Chris Barber (*b* 1930) and Acker Bilk (*b* 1929) had many successes in the earlier 1960s and still remain active. John Dankworth, like other modernists, was only just building a reputation in 1955, and the Ronnie Scott Club (Frith Street) is now world-famous and has opened a second venue in Birmingham. Even the maligned drawing-room ballad topped the charts in 1969 when Rolf Harris sang 'Two little boys' (music Theodore Morse, words Edward Madden, 1903). A recording of a piece of different style but similar vintage, George Botsford's

Black and White Rag (1908), launched an international career in 1952, that of Winifred Atwell (1914–83), a child prodigy from Trinidad who turned to playing boogie after encountering difficulties beginning a concert career; and another pianist, Russ Conway (*b* 1927), very much in the light music tradition, achieved his first hit even later, in 1957 (*Side Saddle* followed in 1959).

Nor were the Beatles the first artists from the UK to achieve major chart success in the USA: in 1952 Vera Lynn's 'Auf Wiederseh'n sweetheart' (music Eberhard Storch, words John Sexton and John Turner) was the first disc to be a no. 1 hit in both countries (starting a fresh Vera Lynn craze); and in 1954 David Whitfield (1925–80) became the first male vocalist to sell a million discs in the USA with 'Cara mia' (Tulio Tranpani and Lee Lange).

The dance music of the 1920s was kept alive in the 'swinging sixties' by groups like the Temperance Seven. George Martin no doubt allowed his experience as their arranger to influence the Beatles when he arranged for them in turn: 'When I'm sixty-four' (1967) shows how a 1920s flavour can be assimilated into the rock idiom. Today, the original dance music of the 1920s and 1930s is performed by bands such as the Pasadena Roof Top Orchestra and the Piccadilly Dance Orchestra.

Chapter 5

THE ROCK REVOLUTION

RICHARD MIDDLETON

I: A Revolution?

The dominant popular music style since 1955 has been rock (defining this rather broadly). This dominance can be measured in commercial success, influence on other styles, media visibility and cultural weight. The most disparate contexts – from 'society' gossip column or charity fund-raising event to school concert and military band programme – reveal its impact, while television theme tune and commercial, film soundtrack, supermarket Muzak and pub jukebox confirm its normative status no less than the ubiquitous chart-based flow of pop radio. If this period has a musical *lingua franca*, it is rock. Commonly, rock's relative effacement of previous styles is represented as a revolution, a major shift in musical norms, cultural focus and aesthetic values. Nik Cohn catches some of this in the moment of its first impact: 'Rock 'n' roll was very simple music. All that mattered was the noise it made, its drive, its aggression, its newness . . . This wasn't just stupidity . . . It was a kind of teen code . . . that would make rock entirely incomprehensible to adults' (Cohn 1969: 30). While a lot of later rock became more complex, a strong tendency remained, in the rock culture itself, to root the music in exclusivity, a kind of 'righteous difference'; as Pete Townshend of the Who put it, 'What we are trying to do in our music [is] protest against "show biz" stuff, clear the hit parade of stodge' (N. Jones 1965: 11). Outraged critics such as Steve Race were no less convinced of the gravity of the challenge:

> . . . for sheer repulsiveness coupled with the monotony of incoherence, [Elvis Presley's] 'Hound Dog' hit a new low in my experience . . . There must be some criteria left, even in popular music . . . How much further can the public be encouraged to stray from the artistry of an Ella Fitzgerald, or the smooth swinging musicianship of a Frank Sinatra?
>
> (Race 1956b: 5)

But the tide could not be held back. Most subsequent observers have agreed that 'the radical differences between rock and the popular music that preceded it produced radical changes in the structure of the whole musical field' (Laing 1969: 64).

However, whether these changes constituted a *revolution*, and if so of what kind, is a complex issue. It has been plausibly suggested (van der Merwe 1989) that virtually all the essential features of rock music were present, if only embryonically, in Anglo-American popular music even before the twentieth century. Conversely, some Tin Pan Alley style features, such as the sentimental ballad genre and the *AABA* form, survive in rock, together with periodic structures and harmonic patterns derived from even older, more widespread practices (see A. Moore 1993, Chapter 2). Many rock musicians, from Tommy Steele to Status Quo, have absorbed elements of older show-business practices into their music, their image, their stagecraft. Other performers, more traditional in type – Tom Jones, Shirley Bassey, Petula Clark, Peter Skellern – have not found it difficult to take just enough from rock (often merely the rock beat; sometimes elements of vocal timbre and phrasing) to assimilate themselves to 'modern' norms. Chart-orientated pop often betrays the influence of pre-rock models of assembly-line composition and novelty or sing-along genres; it would be hard to describe Paul McCartney's 'We all stand together' (with the Frog Chorus: 1984), Slade's 'Merry Xmas everybody' (1973) or even the Beatles' 'Yellow submarine' (1966) as 'revolutionary' in musical style. Rock rebellion has been blurred by social acceptance (epitomized by the 1987 Conservative Party general election rally singing John Lennon's utopian *cri de coeur* 'Imagine') and by commercialization; aggression finds it hard to survive the embrace of corporate capital, and subversion loses its force when classic anthems of rock integrity such as Cream's 'I feel free' (1966) and Eric Clapton's 'Layla' (1972) are used on television commercials to help sell motor cars. (The rock theory term for this is *co-option*, and the antinomy of 'rock' and 'pop', widely used since the mid-1960s though seldom precisely defined, attempts to capture the conflict between 'rebellion' and 'authenticity' on the one hand, 'sell-out' and 'commercial bubblegum' on the other.) Besides, the subversive stance itself – the insistence on expressive and moral freedom typical of the rock ideology – can easily be connected with well-established aesthetic paradigms in the lineages of romanticism.

In point of fact, the debate over the 'rock revolution' is a live one at the time of writing, and is tangled up with a parallel argument over the so-called 'death of rock' (see Frith 1988a, 1990; Goodwin 1990; Grossberg 1990; Laing 1991; Bradby 1993; Fornäs 1995). One of the tasks of this chapter is to place rock in popular music history and in the context of general musical life since 1955.

No one recording could adequately exemplify the stylistic variety within the rock/pop spectrum (for more comprehensive analysis see Middleton 1972; Durant 1984: 167–233; Hatch and Millward 1987; Wicke 1990; A. Moore 1993). But the Rolling Stones' 'Jumpin' Jack Flash' (1968) displays most of the essential features (see Ex. 5.1). The verse–refrain form is introduced by an instrumental I–IV-based motif and this recurs to break the structure between verses 2 and 3. The break could well have been the occasion for a guitar solo; in fact, the record ends with prolonged improvised guitar duetting over the I–IV pattern, which fades out (a typical technique). The basic textural framework is organized around characteristic drum patterns, themselves focused on a prominent accented offbeat ('backbeat'); driving rhythm guitar chords; and an electric bass part switching between a mainly rhythmic function in the verses and typical 'walking' shapes in the refrains, which fill in the rhythmic and harmonic gaps. Above this, the verses are tied together by a continuous lead guitar riff, while in the refrains lead guitar 'fills' answer the singer, creating a typical antiphonal ('call-and-response') relationship; both techniques derive from blues. Mick Jagger sings with 'natural' voice, 'dirty' tone, irregular rhythmic nuancing and plentiful pitch inflexion, all features originating, again, in African-American music. Vocal harmonies – widely used in rock – appear in the refrain. The tonality is major/modal. Harmonically both the drone chord of the verse and modal progression of the refrain exemplify common practices (others are 12-bar blues and derivatives, and cycle-of-5ths sequences). The pitch contours of both riff and vocal are equally characteristic, with their focus on flat 7th and 'blue' 3rd, and their pentatonic 'ladder-of-3rds' shapes (see van der Merwe 1989: 120–25, 177–83). Again, the main source for all these techniques is African-American rhythm 'n' blues. As far as overall sound is concerned, electric amplification is a defining condition, just as multi-track recording, which gives us both the enveloping total mix and the clear audibility of individual voices, plays an important role.

Even a cursory comparison of this piece with typical inter-war popular songs, or even more with nineteenth-century types (see Temperley 1981: 63–134), reveals the scale of the change in musical language. At the same time, as mentioned earlier, the main melodic, harmonic and rhythmic features can be found in embryo in corners of the pre-rock repertoire. What is important here is the extent to which they permeate the music and the explicitness of the way they are used; they are now dominant, linking the 'folk' traditions of black Americans in a relatively direct and remarkable way to urban, consumer-capitalist society in which traditions of that sort had

Ex. 5.1 The Rolling Stones: 'Jumpin' Jack Flash'
selective transcription of opening verse and refrain

THE ROCK REVOLUTION

seemingly been destroyed. Important too is the context, for this defined the specific shape that the musical characteristics took. The development of rock is inseparable from technological, economic and social changes. Amplified instruments (especially the electric guitar); magnetic tape (which turns 'composition' into the infinitely flexible editing of sounds and recording 'takes'); electronically manipulated and synthesized sound (eventually on synthesizers but even before that through a variety of processes and accessories): these are intrinsic to rock's sound and production methods. 'Jumpin' Jack Flash' was 'written' by group members Mick Jagger and Keith Richards not on paper but orally; the music was created in (studio) performance, the performance fixed on tape. Specialist songwriters decline in importance, collective production methods involving musicians, producers and engineers become central. Form of dissemination is also important. While sheet music retained some economic significance up to the mid-1950s (see Henson and Morgan 1989), it was already being superseded by the seven-inch single and LP album (and later the cassette and CD). Music publishers moved from selling scores to negotiating and protecting rights (and in any case often came to be owned by record companies) (see Frith 1988b). Rock was the first music to be conceived with dissemination on record in mind; the nuances of performance, and of particular performers, assumed a new prominence, along with the 'non-notatable parameters' of musical syntax (key features of the African-American source-styles). The spread of radio, especially the ubiquitous transistor, helped universalize distribution and create new listening contexts, especially after the BBC reorganization of 1967 which, in the wake of government legislation banning the innovative pirate radio stations flourishing in the preceding years, created Radios 1 and 2. And since 'airplay' is vital to chart success, the universality of radio also conditioned musical production in various ways. Not the least important factor here is the way that records must be fitted into the policies and programme styles associated with particular disc jockeys; DJ styles have varied – from the middle-of-the-road chumminess of Jimmy Young on Radio 2, through the Radio 1 populism of Tony Blackburn, to the countercultural iconoclasm of John Peel – but their importance as mediators is unquestionable. (On radio, see Hind and Mosco 1985; Barnard 1989; *Popular Music* 1990.)

The enormous impact of the mass media meant that by the 1970s rock was inescapable. The record industry was already sizeable in the early 1950s but enjoyed an extraordinary boom in the 1960s and early 1970s. Between 1955 and 1977 annual sales of singles grew from 50 million to 83 million, sales of LPs from 9 million to 122 million; by 1975, 3000 different singles were issued every year, and 3000 pop albums – and pop accounted for some 90 per cent of record sales; while a typical early 1950s hit sold only 30,000, 'Rock around the clock' (1955) was the first single to sell a million and Paul McCartney's 'Mull of Kintyre' (1977) exceeded 2 million (Frith 1978: 11,12; Harker 1980: 68, 69, 226). Despite periodic recession in the 1980s and 1990s, the general scale of activity is not radically altered today – though there have been changes in the structure of the market and in products (away from singles towards cassettes, albums, CDs and videos); pop/rock is very big business and it is in its esssence a mass musical form (see Scaping 1991; Negus 1993).

Through the period as a whole, its audience has overwhelmingly been youth. In 1978, Frith reported (1978: 12) that over 80 per cent of record buyers were under thirty and more than 75 per cent of pop sales were to 12– to 20-year-olds. While a middle-aged market has increased in importance since then, images of 'youth' still dominate pop styles and sales strategies. Of course, earlier in the century young people had often seemed to be disproportionately involved in music-related activity (especially dancing), but rock was the first music to be aimed specifically at them and associated with them. Rock 'n' roll was, clearly, teenage music; the symbiotic bond between 'pop' and 'youth' has not been broken since. It is widely agreed that some kind of 'cultural revolution' took place in Britain in the late 1950s and the 1960s; and that youth culture was one of its cutting edges (see Nuttall 1968; Melly 1970; B. Martin 1981; Marwick 1990: 110–81). Despite later vicissitudes associated with economic difficulties and ideological reaction, its main features remain in place. Grounded in a 'platform of security' produced by increased affluence and the Butskellite welfarist consensus; in a widening of opportunities and ambitions derived from the effects of the 1944 Education Act and from the influence of a media 'window on the world' (especially on North America); and in a strategic shift towards an economy driven by consumerism, cultural production grew in quantity and variety, broadened in social appeal and accessibility, and relaxed its structure of moral and aesthetic values to the point of fragmentation. Late capitalism's thrust towards total commodification of cultural processes and a contemporaneous democratization of both production and consumption possibilities seem to be interlinked sides of this major realignment, with youth and its music at the forefront.

THE ROCK REVOLUTION
II: From Rock 'n' Roll to Progressive Rock

The pop story has been well told elsewhere (see Cohn 1969; Gillett 1970, R/1983; Chambers 1985) and only a brief sketch is possible here.

Fed by the presence of American troops (and their radio), by imported American records and films, and, negatively, by economic austerity, the appeal of American popular culture in the post-war period was immense, particularly to the working-class young. Energies previously suppressed by a rigid class structure did not bear their full fruit, in music at least, until the appearance of the Beatles in the early 1960s; before then, American models remained predominant.

Rock 'n' roll was basically the African-American rhythm 'n' blues and 'jump' dance-music styles of the 1940s, somewhat simplified, their lyric subject matter re-orientated, for a white adolescent audience. Congruent types of white country music – honkytonk and rockabilly – were also influential. The blues-shaped vocals, simple, non-developmental harmonics, repetitive structures and hypnotic rhythm became the primary source of all rock styles. Some US stars toured Britain – Bill Haley in 1957, Jerry Lee Lewis in 1958, for instance – and notorious (and much exaggerated) 'riots' accompanied screenings of Haley's films, *Blackboard Jungle* (1955) and *Rock Around the Clock* (1956). But the BBC stayed aloof, and the major source for the music was records: Haley's 'Rock around the clock' was a hit in 1955, and Elvis Presley, whose records were first heard in Britain in 1956, created the rock singer archetype – most British rock 'n' roll performers modelled themselves on him.

Blues singers also visited, responding to an enthusiasm that had grown out of skiffle's interest in folk-blues (see Chapter 8). (Though skiffle was largely amateur, it enjoyed brief commercial success in 1956–8, notably through the hits of Lonnie Donegan.) Muddy Waters, Sonny Boy Williamson and John Lee Hooker all came in the late 1950s and early 1960s. Rhythm 'n' blues clubs appeared, and by 1963 groups performing the harsh, aggressive, 'down-home' blues of Chicago were emerging on to the rock scene, the most celebrated being the Rolling Stones. After this, successive contemporary African-American styles, from soul through funk and disco to house and rap, were quickly absorbed here, and copied (see Marks 1990); they formed the central youth dance music of the period, the staple of the discotheque, from the mod 'noonday underground' (Hebdige 1979: 53) of the mid-1960s south-east through the 'secret subculture' (p. 25) of the 'northern soul' clubs of northern England to the 'acid house' parties of the late 1980s. From the 1960s on, white American rock music also had considerable influence and popularity in Britain. But by this time the traffic was two-way; British performers and songs were achieving startling success in the USA, often with original developments of the source-styles, and the ground for subsequent Anglo-American world popular music hegemony was laid.

Studies of rock 'n' roll reception (e.g. Bradley 1992) confirm that the music represented some kind of revolt – in cultural and moral values: freer, more erotic use of the body, as well as of the voice, was central. This impression is amplified by the music's association with those apostles of working-class street 'flash', the teds. But while the British record industry quickly accustomed itself to the new trend, for the most part their singers – Tommy Steele, Terry Dene, Marty Wilde, Billy Fury, Cliff Richard – were mediocre, imitative, lacking charisma and unrelaxed in the idiom. Often their bands were made up of session musicians. Several – Steele (b 1936), for example – ended up as variety entertainers, and Richard (b 1940), following his model, Elvis Presley, turned into a middle-of-the-road performer of pop ballads.

Not until the generation of the early 1960s, led by the Beatles, was there a substantive British response to rock 'n' roll. These groups, many hundreds of them, centred on Merseyside and other provincial cities, had learned by playing skiffle, copying American rock 'n' roll records and imitating the Shadows, the first electric guitar band (see Leigh 1984). The Beatles were special not so much because of any superior ability as performers but because of their manner – cool, self-mocking, witty – because they wrote most of their own songs (or at least leading group members John Lennon (1940–80) and Paul McCartney (b 1942) did), and because they added new musical qualities to rock 'n' roll: tunefulness, harmonic sophistication, a native 'folkiness'. Their immense success from 1963 onwards opened the way for many others, and the resulting assault on the professional music industry establishment had lasting effects. They proved that young, self-taught provincials, even if working-class, could make music – often accomplished music – and could seize the moment, to initiate new cultural style; 'merseybeat' was the most significant sign so far (following skiffle) of a profound democratization of musical activity. Gerry and the Pacemakers, Freddy and the Dreamers, the Hollies, the Swinging Blue Jeans, the Dave Clark Five, Herman's Hermits and many others followed the Beatles to commercial success, in America as well as Britain.

THE ROCK REVOLUTION

Early Lennon–McCartney compositions (see Mellers 1973; O'Grady 1983; Riley 1988) create a new kind of adolescent love song, drawing on American sources – rock 'n' rollers like Little Richard, Chuck Berry and Buddy Holly, the black vocal groups of New York and Detroit, the vocal harmonies of the Everley Brothers country duo, rockabilly singer Carl Perkins – but fusing them with the simple diatonic tunes and modal tendencies of Anglo-Irish Merseyside traditions, and with the more complex harmonic language and sectional forms of older types of commercial popular song. In performance the Beatles could be wild and raw, but their records as a rule have a sweeter, more lyrical feel; anguished blues pitch inflexion is complemented, and often replaced, by modal purity and an innocent enjoyment of sensuous tonal harmony. In 'She loves you' (1963) the simple, diatonic first phrase of the verse (Ex. 5.2a), with typical, mostly parallel vocal harmony, is repeated, then followed by a third phrase with modal implications (Ex. 5.2b). After a fourth phrase containing a chromatic inflexion (IVm^6), the refrain's tune is solidly modal and repetitious, like a folk-chant, forcing modal harmony; and in the introduction and coda this results in a 'bitonal' relationship in which an added-6th chord reconciles the modal E and the tonal G major (Ex. 5.2c).

Ex. 5.2   The Beatles: 'She loves you'

Where the Beatles synthesized, the early rhythm 'n' blues groups – the Rolling Stones, the Yardbirds, the Animals, followed soon after by the Spencer Davis Group, Them, the Move, the Who, the Kinks – seemed uncompromising. Learning, in many cases, by playing with pioneers of the British blues movement – Alexis Korner, Cyril Davies, John Mayall, Graham Bond – they transferred the aggressive anguish and macho sexuality of Chicago blues to themes of adolescent alienation and desire (quintessentially in the Stones' 'Satisfaction' of 1965). The Stones' image was to remain defiantly iconoclastic – with Mick Jagger (*b* 1943) the first British singer to match Elvis Presley as a symbol of eroticism and revolt – but their songs developed an individual style; similarly, the Kinks absorbed elements of music hall, and the Who, leading mod band, evolved a theatrically violent manner epitomized by the classic 'My generation' (1965). Cream, including ex-Yardbird guitarist Eric Clapton (*b* 1945), played highly influential, virtuoso blues-based rock including lengthy improvisation, Clapton going on to become the most celebrated rock guitarist, extending the instrument's potential for fast runs, expressive bending of pitch and 'vocalized' effects. Jimi Hendrix (1942–70), equally influential, developed a startling, electronically mediated blues guitar through novel and expert use of wah-wah pedal, tremolo arm and feedback (see Murray 1989).

By the late 1960s, this blues-based lineage had the elements in place to fashion a separate, identifiable genre, 'heavy rock', and this in turn fed into the 'heavy metal' styles of the 1970s, 1980s and 1990s (see Walser 1993). Heavy metal bands – Black Sabbath, Thin Lizzy, Iron Maiden, Judas Priest, Motorhead and many more – see themselves as guardians of the heroic core of rock; their music is loud, aggressive, built on thundering bass riffs and simple harmonies (often drones or two-chord alternations), and featuring melodramatic vocals and exhibitionistic guitar solos. The style can be found at its formative stage (*ca* 1970) in the heavy rock of such groups as Deep Purple and Led Zeppelin. Here too are the roots of typical heavy metal themes: male chauvinist sexuality, sado-masochism, pagan myth, satanism; though by the 1980s these were more often portrayed with a knowing theatricality, the concerts having more to do with cathartic camaraderie than serious moral subversion.

In 1965–6, many rock groups, swept along by the media image of 'swinging London', by the boom in music-industry activity and by the lure of new technological possibilities, began to break the bounds of the existing rock language. The Beatles' development at this time was both symptomatic and an inspiration. On the *Rubber Soul* (1965) and *Revolver* (1966) albums, new influences appear (Indian music, folk music, classical music); there are new sorts of instrumentation (strings, brass, keyboards); many songs have an added harmonic and structural complexity; and studio techniques (electronic treatment of sound, overdubbing and collage) are important. (The Beatles did not perform live after 1966.) These trends climax in *Sgt. Pepper's Lonely Hearts Club Band* (1967), where they are carefully mixed to produce a degree of coherence over the whole album. *Sgt. Pepper* set off a rash of concept and narrative LPs (such as the Who's 'rock opera' *Tommy* (1969)); in the longer term it had the effect of forcing listeners to question their preconceptions about the differences between popular and art music, and also encouraged fragmentation of the rock/pop language and audience.

The double-single 'Penny Lane'/'Strawberry fields forever' (1967) is also in the *Pepper* mode. In 'Strawberry fields' the unconventional harmonic progressions, phrasing and rhythmic patterns (see Ex. 5.3) are only the starting-point for a compelling evocation of a sound-world as mysterious as the subject matter is opaque.

Ex. 5.3 The Beatles: 'Strawberry fields forever'
opening verse

The setting draws not only on guitars and drums but also cellos, trumpets, piano, mellotron, table harp and assorted percussion. Many of the sounds have been altered electronically, and they are mixed together through a complex multi-tracking process to produce a texture sometimes impenetrably dark, other times open and fragmentary, with individual sounds (cello glissandi, for instance) and motifs suddenly appearing out of the mists. The effect is by turns frightening and ethereal, and the mystery is deepened by the coda, an effective collage of vocal, instrumental and electronically processed sounds in different keys and tempi. This is clearly a scored piece, even though the scoring has taken place largely in the recording studio.

As 'Strawberry fields' suggests, there were intimate if complex links between 'progressive rock', as it was soon called, and the 'counterculture' of the time (see Willis 1978: 83–169, Whiteley 1992). The influence of American hippies, of West Coast 'acid rock' and Bob Dylan's folk-rock, of drug culture and pseudo-oriental mysticism, was widespread. Some groups, such as Pink Floyd, were as much part of a wider London avant-garde 'underground', centred on clubs like the UFO, as of pop music. Pink Floyd's music fused rhythm 'n' blues with electronic sounds, often using tape effects to construct large-scale collages on grandiose themes. The concept album *The Dark Side of the Moon* (1973) successfully explores one of their favourite subjects – 'space' – while later *The Wall* (1979) tackles another: the alienation and lack of communication in modern society. In a good deal of progressive rock, the influence of classical music – on textures, extended sectional forms, thematic integration and development, and in some cases on actual idioms – became common, appearing in many recordings by the Nice, the Electric Light Orchestra, Genesis, Yes, Emerson Lake and Palmer, and Procul Harum. Extreme instrumental virtuosity was cultivated by some bands – Ten Years After, Family, King Crimson, for example, not to mention Jimi Hendrix's 'psychedelic blues-rock' – while others (Donovan, Jethro Tull) were influenced by 'contemporary folk'; jazz-rock fusions, coupling rock rhythms and electric instruments with jazz improvisation techniques, were also important (Soft Machine, Colosseum, John McLaughlin).

As the counterculture disintegrated, in the early 1970s, progressive or 'art rock' lost much of its broad appeal – though a substantial audience remained. Much the same was true of heavy rock. In both cases, records tended to become ever more expensive and complex, performances to demand increasingly elaborate stage, light and sound effects. Eventually a distinct genre of often overblown 'stadium rock' can be distinguished (Queen, Ultravox). Both progressive and heavy rock are serious; their ideologies are organized around concepts of 'self-expression', 'honesty' and 'originality'. This was hardly what the new generations of youngsters – christened 'teenyboppers' – wanted, and in the early 1970s a simpler pop music was aimed at this market. Derived from early 1960s pop, with an admixture of visual and performance 'glitter', the records of Slade, the Sweet, T. Rex and the Bay City Rollers made clear that the pop/rock dichotomy was now firmly in place – though Elton John (*b* 1947) and Rod Stewart (*b* 1945), the most commercially successful singers of the 1970s, demonstrated that pop accessibility could be combined with older traditions of songwriting craftsmanship in the one case, the gritty, passionate vocal techniques of soul singing in the second (for example, in the classic 1975 'rock ballad' 'Sailing').

III: From Disco to Rap

The turn from progressive rock's stress on listening to a renewed emphasis on the dance function was confirmed in the second half of the decade by the rise of disco, the popularity of American records complemented by the success of British groups like the Bee Gees (for instance, in the film *Saturday Night Fever* (1977)). Disco, a slimmed-down electric-soul focusing on fragmentary, rhythmically orientated textures over an endless, mechanically precise beat, re-asserted the importance of pop music's African-American roots. The influential David Bowie (*b* 1947) drew on disco and soul after 1975; earlier, though, a simple rock 'n' roll musical style had been used to support an intriguingly constructed visual and performance persona whose ambiguities and irony aimed to query the cultural and gender stereotypes of rock stardom. Particularly in *The Rise and Fall of Ziggy Stardust and the Spiders from Mars* (1972), Bowie presented himself in quotation marks. Rock's sense of authenticity was seriously undermined. Far from protesting against show-biz, to recall Pete Townshend's words, Bowie made it clear that rock was show-biz.

Punk rock (1976–7) pursued this point (see Vermorel and Vermorel 1978; Coon 1982; Laing 1985; Marcus 1993). Influenced by the situationism of impresario Malcolm McClaren, with its roots in dada (see Marcus 1989), the Sex Pistols, the Clash, the Damned, the Stranglers and many more deliberately insulted audiences and media; their antisocial antics, bizarre appearance and provocative subject matter, their short, high-speed, ultra-loud songs with shrieked vocals, feedback-loaded 'buzzsaw' guitar tone, painfully thumped drums, almost monosyllabic bass lines and calculated crassness of syntax, were all meant to outrage not only mainstream social and aesthetic values but also rock's pretensions. A carefully constructed incompetence, together with a rejection of all studio trickery, reclaimed pop music for the do-it-yourself amateur. The formation of many new, small record companies, asserting their independence from the music industry moguls, had long-term effects, for, even after many had re-embraced the industry through takeover and distribution deals, they dramatized the point that modern technology makes it possible for virtually anyone to make a record. But the energy of punk itself quickly dissipated as its two rather different wings – quasi-proletarian street protest and bohemian, neo-formalist experiment – split apart. The high-volume banalities, the furious, sneering vocal and nihilistic message of the Sex Pistols' 1976 record 'Anarchy in the UK' (Ex. 5.4) epitomize so-called 'dole-queue rock'; but its aesthetic shock tactics (distortion, noise, painfully unrelenting eight-to-the-bar thrash) probably had longer-lasting influence on the many radical post-punk bands of the 1980s.

Ex. 5.4 The Sex Pistols: 'Anarchy in the UK' opening verse

Based on a network of independent record companies evolving from punk's restructuring of the industry, these bands – Joy Division, New Order, Simple Minds, the Fall, the Cure, the Smiths and many less well known – came to be associated with a distinct category, 'indie' music, despite a wide variety of styles.

In a broader context, punk marked the transition from economic boom to a more fractious, unsettled period. In the Thatcherite 1980s, 'commitment', stylistic or expressive, was suspect (though the

THE ROCK REVOLUTION

rise of 'charity rock', epitomized by Band Aid's 'Do they know it's Christmas' (1984), suggests that its appeal survived). From the 'new pop' early in the decade (Culture Club, Duran Duran, Wham, Spandau Ballet, ABC) through the 'electro-pop' synthesizer groups (Depeche Mode, Human League) and the disco-based sensuality of Frankie Goes to Hollywood and the Pet Shop Boys to the late 1980s assembly-line dance-songs of production team Stock, Aitken and Waterman, the varied styles of the pop mainstream unite around a hedonistic though often ironic consumption of the aural surface, grounded on a knowing use of the assembled repertoires of pop history (see Rimmer 1985, Reynolds 1990).

Closely involved in this project was the 'promo' video, its beginnings usually dated to Queen's 'Bohemian rhapsody' (1975), and by the early 1980s regarded as virtually essential to chart success (see Hustwitt 1985; Frith 1988a: 205–25; Straw 1988; Goodwin 1992; Frith et al. 1993). While the origins of music video can be traced to earlier forms of film and television music, its specific techniques and functions reflect the fact that the large record companies were by now parts of multi-media leisure-industry corporations looking to make cable and satellite television an integral component of home entertainment set-ups (the success of MTV, the US 'music television' channel, led to the establishment of European imitators from 1982 onwards). For all its wide variety of visual techniques and forms, the pop video's relationship to advertising is usually obvious, and at its heart is a sort of 'portraiture', the musicians almost always being presented for consumption visually as well as aurally, the focus of a rejuvenated 'pin-up culture' (Straw 1988: 252).

At the same time, such groups as the Pretenders, Madness, Eurythmics, with the charismatic singer Annie Lennox (b 1954), and the Communards, with the equally startling falsetto technique of Jimmy Somerville (b 1961), demonstrated that it was possible to combine chart success with passion and older virtues of rock performance. Even so, it is worth considering the possible merits of seemingly banal hit songs. Stock, Aitken and Waterman's 'I should be so lucky', a 1988 hit for television soap opera star Kylie Minogue, has no pretensions to be more than a functional dance-song and uses a bagful of clichés (see Ex. 5.5).

Over a heavy, purely supportive bass line and drum-machine rhythm, electronically precise and virtually syncopation-free, the verse is built on a repeating, commonplace modal progression, while the refrain lays a pentatonic vocal over an equally commonplace

POPULAR MUSIC

Ex. 5.5　　　　　　　Kylie Minogue: 'I should be so lucky'
　　　　　　　　　　　opening verse and refrain

cycle-of-5ths sequence. The singing is anonymous. But the 'hook' ('I should be so lucky') works effectively as a 'gesture', its intonational shape matching the shape of the verbal cliché but at the same time lifting it from the merely everyday into musical memorability. The circling patterns of both harmonic sequences, together with the tonal switches – the unprepared jump from A to B major, the sequentially descending transition from B to C, the jump from C back to A when the refrain gives way to the next verse – create the sense of a constantly shifting harmonic perspective, an unending journey; together with the skilfully filled out, swirling texture (keyboards;

backing vocals) and hypnotic beat, this insistent continuity, typical of disco-styled pieces, threatens to sweep even the most reluctant listener, let alone the enthusiastic dancer, away.

The refocusing of popular music on dance, indicated by the success of disco and of 1980s pop, is confirmed by the emergence in the second half of the decade of a so-called 'dance music' style-category (see Langlois 1992; Bradby 1993). Growing from the consistent popularity of black American dance records in British clubs, and absorbing the impact of further American imports (rap – spoken lyrics over a rhythm backing – from New York; house – a more electronically manipulated derivative of disco – from Chicago), this style is premised on the important role of the club DJ and the record producer (the two functions increasingly blurring into each other), and on an acceptance of the fact that, given modern technology, sounds from whatever source can be legitimate raw materials for a confessedly 'artificial' production process. 'Scratching' (sounds and rhythms created through manipulating record turntables), 're-mixes' (often drastic), 'sampling' (re-use, often in radically altered forms, of fragments from existing recordings) and computer-programmed rhythms and 'loops' are symptoms of the new aesthetic. Melody and harmony are downplayed, rhythm, sound and texture foregrounded. The work of M/A/R/R/S ('Pump up the volume', 1987), Soul II Soul ('Back to life', 1989), KLF (Kopyright Liberation Front), Pop Will Eat Itself and Bomb the Bass is representative of the new techno-dance, while Derek B and the Wee Papa Girl Rappers were among the best British rap performers.

Many of the key features are pulled together in Beats International's haunting 1990 hit, 'Dub be good to me' (see Ex. 5.6). A 'rapped' introduction (imitating a radio DJ: 'you're listening to the boy from the big bad city, this is jam hot', and ending with a sequenced fade) recurs midway through the song and at the end, breaking the otherwise seamless flow of rhythm and quasi-improvised melody.

The conventional verse–refrain form actually runs continuously since both sections are built over the same bass riff and I–IV chord sequence, which are virtually unceasing. However, so far back are the keyboards mixed that the harmonies are all but implicit, allowing the bass, the quite intricately polyrhythmic drum patterns and the modal vocal to dominate, and resulting in a clearly articulated web of rhythms and fragmentary melodic phrases. After the rap break, backing vocal (mostly echoing the hook, 'just be good to me'), bluesy harmonica and trombone solo all twine round

POPULAR MUSIC

Ex. 5.6   Beats International: 'Dub be good to me'

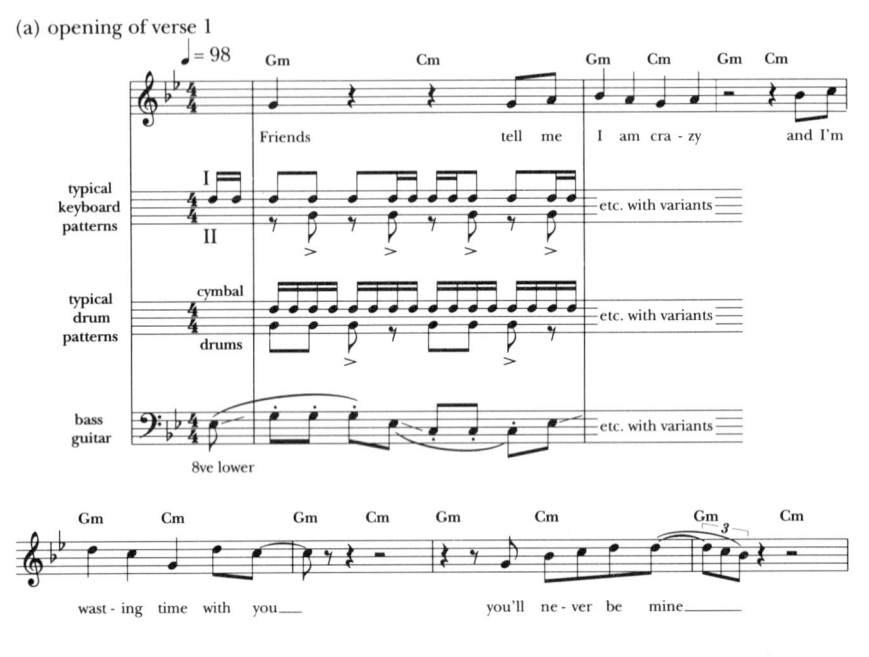

(a) opening of verse 1

[musical score: vocal line with lyrics "Friends tell me I am cra-zy and I'm wast-ing time with you you'll ne-ver be mine", typical keyboard patterns I and II, typical drum patterns (cymbal and drums), bass guitar 8ve lower, chord symbols Gm Cm alternating, ♩ = 98]

(b) hook

[musical score with lyrics "Just be good to me", chords Cm Gm]

the lead vocal. Throughout, spots of radio 'static' are overdubbed, as if we are hearing the music as part of the city 'soundscape' – indicating the deliberately 'constructed' nature of the piece.

This record is a drastic re-composition of a 1984 American song – just as 'I should be so lucky', while a British recording in all important respects, is sung by an Australian; in the last years of the century, British pop works unavoidably within a multi-national Anglophone context. There is another connection, the emphasis on dance rhythm relating both records back across the years of rock history to the simplicities of early rock 'n' roll. At the same time, the differences between them mark out some of the style variance within present pop. The harmonic patterns, sequential structures and lush sound of 'I should be so lucky' reach back in some ways to pre-rock, Tin Pan Alley conventions, while the relative withdrawal from harmony and the spare texture of 'Dub be good to me', with its foregrounding of rhythm and timbre, reveal the more radical potentials inherent in rock 'n' roll.

IV: In the Margins

Pop/rock dominates but it does not monopolize. Relatively hidden but intensely active, and at times influential on the more commercial mainstream, three spheres in particular demand note: black music, jazz and folk music.

The continuous popularity and influence of black American music has already been mentioned. A British blues scene survived the decline of the 1960s blues boom (see Brunning 1986), throwing up impressive singers like Jo Ann Kelly. Soul, funk, disco and hip-hop have not only dominated the dance floors; they have profoundly affected instrumental idioms, textures and production values in pop and rock, not to mention many singers, from Joe Cocker to Paul Young, Steve Winwood to George Michael and Billy Ocean. American gospel music is a strong influence on the British gospel now thriving in the black community (see Broughton 1985).

At the same time, British black people have developed a lively music culture of their own (see P. Oliver 1990a). With the large-scale African-Caribbean immigration of the fifties, West Indian clubs with a programme of jazz, rhythm 'n' blues and calypso were soon established. Recording of calypso mostly pre-dates 1955 but continued until 1960 (J. Cowley 1990). In the 1960s, new hybrid styles, particularly from Jamaica, arrived on imported records. With them came the 'sound system' (large mobile discotheques for dances and parties) and later 'toasting' (the Jamaican equivalent of rap) and 'dub' (complex re-mixes – often instrumental so that spontaneous toasting could be added). Ska was a fusion of indigenous Jamaican mento and American rhythm 'n' blues; as it gave way to rock-steady, then reggae, the tempo slowed, the rhythms became more complex, the mood more intense (see S. Clarke 1980; Johnson and Pines 1982; Hebdige 1987; S. Jones 1988). Rastafarian themes were common in the 1970s, for example in the work of the highly influential Bob Marley (1945–81), but later in the decade a 'softer' style, 'lovers' rock', in which women singers were prominent, split away from 'roots' reggae. Recording of ska and reggae in Britain, for the home market and for export to the West Indies, dates from the early

1960s, and before long British groups emerged, notably Aswad, Misty, Steel Pulse and Matumbi. By the eighties, a specifically British reggae style could be discerned, in the work of these bands and of 'dub poets' Smiley Culture and Linton Kwesi Johnson.

The main features of 'roots' reggae can be heard in Steel Pulse's 1978 recording, 'Handsworth Revolution' (see Ex. 5.7).

The bass is prominent, both melodically and in dynamic level, and its riff is typical in its rhythmic irregularity and its 'gappiness'. The guitars ('dry', scratchy, trebly) and keyboards, as well as the

Ex. 5.7   Steel Pulse: 'Handsworth Revolution'
opening of verse 1

percussion (the basic cymbal framework embroidered with quaver/semiquaver drum patterns, not shown in the transcription), have parts that are primarily of rhythmic interest, and there is a strong emphasis on weaker beats (three; four) and on the offbeat quaver. The moderate-tempo, eight-to-the-bar chug, with offbeat accents and a tendency to staccato playing, gives the characteristic reggae 'groove'. Over this intricate, precise, dense but holey texture, the vocal has a notable and contrasting rhythmic fluidity. This is serious, emotionally intense music, its apparent repetitiveness – much criticized by detractors – acting as a gateway to the unique sound-world and mastery of improvised nuance that lie within, and pulling the listener away from the harmonic and melodic fringes, deep into the centre of the texture.

By and large, reggae has remained a music apart, rooted in the values and lifestyle of black culture. But the influence of its rhythms and textures on pop and rock musicians increased from the 1970s on, and there have been moments of greater visibility, notably the mid- and late 1960s when ska was popular with mods and skinheads, the late 1970s when reggae's popularity with punks coincided with Bob Marley's peak of fame, and the early 1980s when the multi-racial Two Tone bands of the Midlands – the Specials, the Beat, UB40 – took their own adaptations of ska and reggae to a mass audience. Whether the same pattern will be followed by the analogous hybrid styles developed in the British Asian community – indipop and bhangra – remains to be seen (see Banerji and Baumann 1990).

British jazz achieved its most notable moment of commercial visibility around 1960, when, in the hands of Acker Bilk and Kenny Ball, 'trad jazz', a novelty version of the revivalist style, became fashionable and a mass record seller. After 1963, traditional jazz returned to the status of an amateur and semi-professional pub music, though several players schooled in the revivalist movement – Humphrey Lyttelton, Alex Welsh (1929–82), Sandy Brown (1929–75), Bruce Turner (b 1922), Tony Coe (b 1934) – broadened their approach and repertoire, and led successful careers playing 'mainstream' jazz. At about the same time, the first fully fledged 'modernists' were emerging from the early 1950s experiments, notably reed-players Ronnie Scott (b 1927), Tubby Hayes (1935–73), Joe Harriott (1928–72), Don Rendell (b 1926) and John Dankworth (b 1927) – who also became a well-known arranger and composer – and drummer Phil Seamen (1926–72). (Involved too was singer Cleo Laine (b 1928), but her remarkable vocal range and breadth of interests and techniques took her subsequently – like Dankworth – into a wider spread of musical enterprises.) These players laid the ground for the explosion of activity that occurred in the sixties. It is impossible to mention all the important figures in what became a broad stylistic spectrum (see Carr 1973; Cotterell 1976; Godbolt 1989; entries in Carr et al. 1988). This stretches from masterly improvisers like saxophonists John Surman (*b* 1944) and Alan Skidmore (*b* 1942), trumpeter Kenny Wheeler (*b* 1930) and pianist Keith Tippett (*b* 1947) to composers as varied in style as Mike Gibbs (*b* 1937), Graham Collier (*b* 1937) and Mike Westbrook (*b* 1936); from musicians with links to the classical avant garde – pianist Howard Riley (*b* 1943), bassist Barry Guy (*b* 1947) – to pioneers of 'free jazz', influenced by the open structures, spontaneous, post-tonal improvising and extended instrumental techniques of Ornette Coleman, Cecil Taylor and Archie Shepp, such as guitarist Derek Bailey (*b* 1932), percussionist John Stevens (*b* 1940) and saxophonist Evan Parker (*b* 1944). Outstanding bandleaders were Stan Tracey (*b* 1927), a sometimes violent, sometimes sensuous 'Jackson Pollock of the piano' (Carr 1973: 2) and composer of the classic suite *Under Milk Wood* (1965), and Westbrook, who, in a series of large-scale works, expanded the boundaries of his music, drawing on rock, classical and theatre music as well as a variety of jazz styles.

After a period of relative decline, a revival of jazz activity and popularity began in the mid-1980s. The demise of progressive rock left a gap for a 'thoughtful' music; at the same time, the success of African-American styles on the dance floor led many in the direction of jazz. As in the USA at this time, the chief concern of many young players was with learning techniques and repertoire rather than blazing original trails; the most favoured focus for this rather backward-looking, classicizing spirit was the modal jazz of John Coltrane and the hard bop of Art Blakey and Sonny Rollins – saxophonists Andy Sheppard (*b* 1957), Courtney Pine (*b* 1965) and Steve Williamson (*b* 1965) are examples here – while pianists Django Bates (*b* 1960) and Jason Rebello (*b* 1969) displayed a more eclectic range of influences. Similarly freewheeling were the impressive big bands Loose Tubes and the Jazz Warriors. Saxophonist Tommy Smith (*b* 1967) looked to Europeans like Jan Garbarek as well as to American traditions. But if the main achievements of these musicians so far are technical mastery and stylistic agility, there is enormous promise for the future. At the same time, some recent groups – Pinski Zoo, Roadside Picnic, the John Rae Collective – are drawing on rock, funk and even folk as well as jazz traditions, suggesting the possibility of new musical blends.

The British folk revival (see Laing et al. 1975; Boyes 1993; Munro 1984; also Chapter 8), from its beginnings in the 1950s, developed, and for the most part kept to, its own infrastructure of amateur-run clubs, but it also threw up several notable professional reinterpreters of the 'traditional' repertoire: Jean Redpath, Martin Carthy, Anne Briggs, Shirley Collins, and, among *a cappella* groups, building on the example of the Copper family of Sussex, the Young Tradition and the Watersons. Owing partly to the simultaneous influence in the clubs of blues, white American folk styles, American folk-rock and 'contemporary folk', some musicians acquired a more eclectic repertoire, a more 'popular' approach; Pentangle and the Incredible String Band are examples. At the same time, this upsurge of activity and new influences resulted in the beginnings of a continuing line of singer–songwriters, performing self-composed songs on contemporary themes to, usually, acoustic guitar accompaniment; the line runs from Ewan MacColl (1915–90) and Ralph McTell (*b* 1944) through Richard Thompson(*b* 1949) to Billy Bragg (*b* 1957). With the Liverpool group the Spinners and, in Scotland, the Corries (who created the country's unofficial national anthem, 'Flower of Scotland'), popularization took a more frankly commercial turn.

British folk-rock had little direct connection with its American namesake; rather, it grew out of indigenous attempts to perform 'traditional' and traditional-styled songs with electric instruments, rock rhythms and textures, and pop excitement. Fairport Convention led the way, in the late 1960s, followed by Steeleye Span; both groups contained notable musicians – singers Maddy Prior and Sandy Denny, instrumentalists Dave Swarbrick and Ashley Hutchings, as well as Carthy and Thompson – many of whom went on to join a variety of subsequent bands. Their music had significant influence on progressive rock; and indeed, in a way, it makes explicit an underlying stylistic congruence. For instance, in Fairport Convention's 1970 single 'Now be thankful' (see Ex. 5.8), composed by Thompson and Swarbrick, the tune's modal tendencies, irregular metre and phrase-lengths, and parallel chord movements (all derived from 'traditional' song but common too in rock) fit easily with rock drumming and electric guitar fills; the vocal harmonies in the refrain point equally to folk and rock practice, and the singing style – with rock-influenced syncopations and pitch inflexions – does not seem incongruous. More recently, Run Rig proved the same point with Scottish Gaelic material.

POPULAR MUSIC

Ex. 5.8 Fairport Convention: 'Now be thankful'
verse 1 and refrain

[Musical notation with lyrics:]

When the stone is grown too cold to kneel, in crys-tal wa-ters I'll be bound, cold as stone, wear-y to the sounds u-pon the wheel. Now be thank-ful for good things be-low. Now be thank-ful to your ma-ker for the rose, the red rose blooms for all to know

This period has also seen a flowering of neo-traditional instrumental music. Of course, Scottish instrumental music was in any case still very much alive; but alongside run-of-the-mill functional dance playing (epitomized by Jimmy Shand), and significantly influenced by Irish groups like the Chieftains, an older repertoire has been revived; and the Scots-Irish Boys of the Lough (with the remarkable fiddler Aly Bain), the McPeake family of Belfast, and others have carried the music to new levels of virtuosity, textural complexity and delicacy of ensemble. In England too, a seemingly declining tradition has been resurrected, with such groups as the Albion Band, the Oyster Band and Blowzabella playing polkas, waltzes, jigs and step dances, adding electric instruments and, in some cases, influences from blues, rock and even further afield. In the north, piper Katherine Tickell and concertina player Alastair Anderson have taken Northumbrian instrumental music to new audiences (and produced new material).

THE ROCK REVOLUTION
V: Context and Conclusions

By the 1980s, the fragmentation and fluidity of the pop audience were its clearest characteristics. Virtually all the styles of the music's 30-year history mingled pluralistically together, each one a badge of identity as well as a marketing label. Revivals were as common as nostalgic 'oldies' radio programmes; many musicians drew on past styles – often ironically, self-consciously – for raw material and historical associations; among critics the discourse of postmodernism was mobilized to cover the situation (see Redhead 1990). In the wider popular music field, black music, jazz and folk were not the only important 'marginal' styles. 'World music' neatly categorized the growing interest in popular musics from Third World countries. Country music maintained a large audience and an active (though relatively 'secret') performing scene – especially in rural areas, in Scotland and Ireland (where similarities to native traditions stimulated enthusiasm), and in some large cities (Liverpool, Glasgow, London). While the British repertoire was centred on American material, some musicians produced their own songs too. Adult Oriented Rock (AOR), through such performers as Phil Collins (*b* 1951), Fleetwood Mac and Dire Straits, catered for middle-ageing rock fans with a taste for a more 'mature', 'thoughtful' species of rock than that provided for younger listeners, while a variety of Middle-of-the-Road (MOR), Easy Listening and Old Time styles flourished, as demonstrated by the popularity of variety, 'palm court' and pre-rock-style dance bands, such as those of Billy Cotton, Joe Loss, Mantovani and Max Jaffa, and of the BBC's Radio 2 channel with its programmes of 'evergreens', ballad singers, swing bands and cinema organs.

At the same time, crossovers proliferated. Progressive rock star Peter Gabriel (*b* 1950) was influenced by 'world music', abrasive post-punk songwriter Elvis Costello (*b* 1954) by country music; the Pogues and the Mekons crossed folk with punk, while Sky, including concert guitarist John Williams, played soft-rock versions of classical pieces; Courtney Pine mixed modern jazz and reggae, and Working Week fused it with 1980s dance-floor rhythms. 'New Age' music (see Schaefer 1990) – 'spiritual' mood music built on repetitive structures and soothing instrumental textures – has an ancestor in the large-scale studio compositions of Mike Oldfield (*b* 1953), such as *Tubular Bells* (1973), but also draws on the work of American minimalists like Philip Glass – for instance in the 'ambient music' of

Brian Eno (b 1948) (see Tamm 1989). In the case of classical avant-garde composers such as Steve Martland, Trevor Wishart and Graham Fitkin, influence has moved in the opposite direction across the popular/serious divide. Altogether there is the feeling – usually picked out as a defining feature of postmodernism – that any limits to eclecticism have vanished.

Popular music history is now not only linear (in the sense that, say, heavy metal could not have preceded rock 'n' roll) but also cumulative. The immense mass of music produced and consumed is made up of an enormous variety of types, and, ironically, the tendency in the commercial sector towards total commodification of musical activity, with a strategy of narrowing choice, goes along with a decided democratization of access and opportunities, for both music-making (see Finnegan 1989, Cohen 1991) and listening. Admittedly, this democratization is heavily gender-conditioned. In practice and in ideology, rock/pop culture, like the music industry itself, is overwhelmingly male-dominated. In the 1960s, notable performers like Dusty Springfield could never free themselves from the stereotyped positions and subjects to which women have been largely confined. Punk's challenge to gender stereotypes, especially through such female performers and bands as Poly Styrene, Siouxsee and the Banshees, and the Slits, freed things up somewhat and made possible (for example) the success of the enigmatic, theatrical style of singer-songwriter Kate Bush (b 1958). But change has been slow (see Steward and Garratt 1984, Bradby 1993). The sociology of consumption is complex. Despite the partial success of subcultural theorists in linking particular musics to particular social groups (see Hall and Jefferson 1976; Willis 1978; Hebdige 1979), it is clear that styles often cross class (and gender and age) boundaries – though gender may be the least permeable, with boys and girls in the pop audience apparently often responding to different genres, performers and aesthetics (see Frith and McRobbie 1978). A dominant feature, for both listener appeal and the trajectory of musicians, is the alliance, or dialectic, between models of working-class 'street' romanticism on the one hand, *petit bourgeois* bohemianism on the other; often the latter is mediated by the art schools, which have been of great importance in pop (see Frith and Horne 1987). It is this confluence, and its relationship with the commercial marketplace, that distinguishes the social geography of popular music in this period from that of classical music, set in its context of traditionally more privileged, institutionalized middle-class intellectualism: though the latter sphere has fed popular music to some extent, particularly the 'serious' areas of jazz and folk.

The sociological complexities arise in part because of mass media effects. At the same time as electric technologies encourage neo-oral musical processes, prompting comparisons between modern popular and 'traditional' folk musics (see Laing et al. 1975: 83–136, Cutler 1985), they also democratize and universalize access to repertoires and techniques, threatening any notions of connection between specific styles and specific communities, and rendering social 'ownership' of music difficult to protect. Already in 1970, the history of pop was described as 'revolt' turning into 'style' (Melly 1970); in truth, the very conditions of the cultural economy were bringing into question any sense of that 'authenticity' on which all musical revolution is based – even though many musicians and fans, especially in rock, folk and world music, still cling to a belief in the concept (see Redhead and Street 1989). Given that any music can now be readily 'stolen' from those who consider it embodies *their* feelings and identity, a better model for popular music consumption today is probably that of 'appropriation' (see Middleton 1990: 139–40).

A good deal of listening is probably not 'committed' in any sense but rather takes place 'in distraction', to use a phrase of Walter Benjamin (1970: 242); musical experience is focused not on the individual entity but on the 'field', made up of a fluid mix of sounds, tunes, rhythms, compositions, which ultimately merges into the general soundscape. The traditional aesthetics of the finite artistic object may not furnish the most appropriate criteria. Parallel to this development runs the increasingly 'constructed' quality of popular records themselves. The important role of the producer is already clear in the 1960s, George Martin, producer of the Beatles, being the obvious example (see G. Martin 1979). In a way, the history of popular music since 1955 could be written through an account of the contributions of producers – Joe Meek, Mickie Most, Trevor Horn; Chris Blackwell and Dennis Bovell in reggae, Joe Boyd in folk-rock, for instance; and by the late 1980s, the masters of sampling, computerized mixing and other studio techniques – such as Paul Oakenfold – stand right at the centre of some genres, at the same time as consummating the shift of popular music out of designated moments of aesthetically validated coherence into the fluid soundtrack of everyday life. In the realm of musical technology at least, then, recent developments substantiate and build on the revolution set in motion by rock 'n' roll (see Durant 1992, Beadle 1993).

Ideologically, though, these very developments raise questions over established rock myths. As youngsters abandon records in favour of marathon 'raves' (if not computer games), swapping vocal charisma and guitar heroes for the ecstatic soundscapes of anonymous producers, aesthetic rebellion for endless rhythm loops, there is a sense in which the 'death of rock' might arguably seem close. On this level, the postmodern refusal of significance typical of much current pop practice can appear more revolutionary than rock itself.

Assessing the longterm impact of rock on musical history is thus quite difficult. However, despite recent shifts in style and practice, despite (elsewhere in the popular musical field) the continued recuperation of pre-rock elements, there seems little doubt that fundamental rock/pop 'gestures' arising from conjunctions of phrase-types, rhythms, harmonic patterns, textures and vocal intonations have come to constitute a stylistic baseline, against which alternative conventions are heard. In a longer time-span, this hegemony appears as a further stage in a progressive African-American takeover of British popular music starting around 1840 with minstrelsy, and related historically to a growing crisis in European bourgeois culture, ideologically to complex strategies evolving in that culture for dealing with its usually repressed, Dionysian 'other' (see Middleton 1972; Frith 1988a: 45–63; Pickering 1986).

It is less fruitful, however, to see this as some kind of capitulation to 'Americanization', or still less as a symptom of the 'decline of the West', than as a distinct stage in the evolution of a long-lived plebeian stratum in the musical geology of Western culture itself, formed not only through interactions with contemporary cultivated musics but also through a complex network of cross-influences linking Europe, North America and Africa, beginning at least as early as the seventeenth century (see van der Merwe 1989; Middleton 1990: 117–22). Within British society, the rock stage of the process has operated through a sometimes fractious *modus vivendi* worked out between the forces of late-capitalist consumerism and the 'long revolution' (Raymond Williams) of cultural democratization. In a wider context, the enormous world influence of British popular music since the 1960s, emanating from a country which, though politically enfeebled and socially unsettled, retains neo-imperialistic habits in the economic and cultural spheres, takes its place as a contribution to the establishment of a global mainstream musical language, with which, for better or worse, all music cultures now have to come to terms.

Chapter 6

MUSIC FOR THE STAGE

PATRICK O'CONNOR

I: *The American Influence*

In 1914 the future of the British musical comedy, and to a lesser extent the form of the popular song in its music-hall context, appears to have been threefold: there was music obviously based on the American example, music that still took its form from the European operettas, all of which were in turn parodies of 'grand' opera, and music that clung to the rigid formula of the verse-and-chorus style typical of the music-hall song. In time this three-way trend was blurred by the dominance of the international music publishing business, so that songs that might seem to the public to belong to their homegrown musical culture were in reality cleverly adapted versions of foreign titles.

The American influence had leapt ahead on 16 May 1903, when an 'All-Negro musical comedy', *In Dahomey* by Jesse A. Shipp, opened at the Shaftesbury Theatre, London, produced by its stars, Bert Williams and George Walker, with music by Will Marion Cook, composer of 'I'm comin', Virginia' and other famous songs. It was by no means the first time that Londoners had heard African-American performers, nor was it the very beginning of the craze for American popular song based on black music: ten years earlier, all London had been taken by the song 'Ta-ra-ra-boom-de-ay', which came from a black American source (see Collins 1932: 15, Macqueen-Pope 1949: 300–302). However, the success of *In Dahomey*, with its songs such as 'Swing along', 'Brown skin baby mine' and 'Emancipation Day' and its cakewalk finale, was the first signal that a new, all-American type of musical play might be in the offing. In particular, the success in London and Paris of Walker's wife Aida Overton anticipated the later triumphs of such black stars as Florence Mills and Josephine Baker by a quarter of a century.

POPULAR MUSIC

The popularity and exclusively homegrown nature of the British musical comedy were at their peak in 1903. The newly reopened Gaiety Theatre in the Aldwych and Daly's in Leicester Square were the showcases for the musicals of Lionel Monckton, Paul Rubens, Leslie Stuart and many others, whose mixture of ballads, comic patter songs, kissing duets and rollicking marches made palatable for a more polite, middle-class audience the same sort of material that for the working class, bohemians, or more raffish aristocracy was to be found in the music hall.

The more obviously theatrical and rigid form of the musical comedy was to an extent replaced during the years immediately preceding the First World War by the revue. Although this genre had been attempted several years earlier (notably in London by Seymour Hicks with *Under the Clock* (1893) and most successfully in Berlin at theatres such as the Metropol, and of course in Paris at the Folies Bergère and Moulin Rouge), the freer format, in which songs by diverse hands and sketches, ballets, sometimes even a mini-operetta might be strung together with little or no obvious connection, held obvious attractions for performers and impresarios. Particularly during wartime, when members of the public might be too distracted to sit through an entire musical play, it preserved the spirit of the music hall with its rotating acts while overlaying it with the design and ensemble elements of the musical. In London the revue was especially wedded to the success of ragtime in such shows as *Hullo, Ragtime!* and *Hullo, Tango!* and *The Passing Show of 1912*, all of which featured, albeit not exclusively, the music of American composers, namely Berlin, Kern and Shelton Brooks.

The ragtime craze was at its height from 1912 (see Chapter 4), but songs by or in imitation of American rag composers were being introduced to British audiences for several years beforehand by music-hall performers such as Victoria Monks ('John Bull's girl'), whose recordings demonstrate an accurate knowledge of the style adopted by female African-American performers. Another British star, Ida Barr (1882–1967), who had appeared for two seasons in New York, was often credited with introducing 'true' ragtime songs to England, including Berlin's 'Everybody's doing it!' By 1912, Marie Lloyd (1870–1922) satirized the fashion in her song (by George Arthurs and Worton David) 'The Piccadilly trot' with its references to a new dance that 'doesn't come from Yankee land'.

One of the forces that changed the format of variety and music-hall entertainment was the erosion of the idea of exclusive material.

MUSIC FOR THE STAGE

Stars like Marie Lloyd always purchased their songs outright from the composers, and thereafter no professional performance could be undertaken without their permission. By 1912 it was more likely that an artist like Ida Barr would buy only two years' rights on a number, such as on her greatest hit, Nat D. Ayer's 'Oh! you beautiful doll'. Although Ayer was American, his impact on the London musical stage during the First World War was immense, with his songs for the *Bing Boys* revues, including 'If you were the only girl in the world' and 'Let the great big world keep turning'. These and many First World War songs, such as Rubens's 'Something in the atmosphere' (from *Tina*, 1915), Monckton's 'Neville was a devil' (*Bric-à-brac*, 1915) and Ayer's 'Widows are wonderful' (from his 1917 show *Yes! Uncle*), some with syncopated, ragtime-influenced accompaniments, are part of the gradual Americanization of the British popular song. It must be noted, however, that they were sung at the time, even by American performers such as Shirley Kellogg and Elsie Janis, very much in the operetta/musical comedy tradition. By 1916 the gradual Americanization of British musical theatre was so great that even in Charles Collins's and Fred W. Leigh's 'Don't dilly dally on the way' (a song often wrongly attributed to the Edwardian

Ex. 6.1   'Don't dilly dally on the way' (Collins/Leigh)

music hall but in fact belonging to the First World War) features specific to an imitation rag can be heard, perhaps not so much in the widely used duple-rhythm accompaniment as in the syncopation and secondary dominant at *x* in Ex. 6.1.

II: Between the Wars: Novello and Coward

During the First World War several composers emerged who were to be the dominant forces in the inter-war musical theatre in Britain. Foremost among them was Ivor Novello (1893–1951). Coming from a musical, slightly churchy background, he had already published 20 songs when at the outbreak of war he was encouraged to try a patriotic number. 'Till the boys come home' ('Keep the home fires burning') was an immediate success and led to his engagement to provide music for *Theodore and Co.*, produced at the Gaiety in 1916. Customarily for the period, the numbers were by several composers, but Novello contributed 13. Among the others were songs by Melville Gideon, who with Novello, and later Noël Coward and Vivian Ellis, was the most durably successful composer of theatre music in London in the immediate aftermath of the war.

Novello's songs were for the most part either romantic slow waltzes, rather in the manner of Rubens, or satiric, deceptively simple 'point' numbers. 'It's just a memory' from *Arlette* (1917) and 'I said goodbye' from *Tabs* (1918), sung by Beatrice Lillie, are examples of the former; of the latter, 'And her mother came too' from *A–Z* (1921) and 'There's an angel watching over me' from *Who's Hooper?* (1919) demonstrate the ease with which he could set becoming melodies to lyrics designed to be timed by comic singers who, while they had adequate singing voices, were more concerned with verbal enunciation than vocal line.

In several of these early revues and plays Novello chose to satirize the fashion for ragtime and 'jazz' (for example, 'The wedding jazz' in *Who's Hooper?*, 'Raggedy doll' in *Puppets* (1924) and 'Baby blues' in *Charlot's 1925 Revue*). But his greatest and most enduring successes in the musical theatre were in the 1930s and 1940s when, going completely against the trend of Americanization, he reacted with a series of operettas harking back to the pre-1914 Viennese tradition: *Glamorous Night* (1935), *Careless Rapture* (1936), *Crest of the Wave* (1937) and above all *The Dancing Years* (1939) and *Perchance to Dream* (1945). These were melodramatic, spectacular shows which drew upon popular ideas of news events and illustrated them with high-flown operatic duets and with ballads obviously designed for a life outside the theatre as popular songs. *Glamorous Night* mixes the story of the invention of television with a revolution in a central European kingdom resembling Romania; *The Dancing Years* is about the rise of fascism and anti-Semitism. Of the duets, 'Fold your wings' from *Glamorous Night* and 'The wings of sleep' from *The Dancing Years* are representative; of the ballads, 'We'll gather lilacs' from *Perchance to Dream*, originally a duet for two female voices, became the most popular. Novello tapped a hitherto ignored seam of reactionary, sentimental yearning on the part of his audiences to escape from the current trend towards swing (just as Lloyd Webber in our own time frequently bypasses rock) and return to what seemed like 'The land of Might Have Been', in the words of the song he contributed to *Our Nell* (1924), one of the later musical plays by Harold Fraser-Simson (1873–1944). Just as Fraser-Simson's music for *The Maid of the Mountains* (1917), *A Southern Maid* (1920) and *The Street Singer* (1924) was largely influenced by that of Lehár (and in the case of the song 'Love will find a way' from *The Maid of the Mountains* was a direct parody of the *Merry Widow* waltz), so Novello's romantic operettas recalled Puccini.

If this element of commercial pastiche suggests that British light theatre music at this time was cynical and depressing, it is because the separation of the musically inquisitive public from the theatre-going one was sufficiently rigid to prevent such an innovative musician as Billy Mayerl (1902–59) from achieving a success in the theatre comparable with that of his solo piano music. Nevertheless his stage works, including *Nippy* (1930) and *Over She Goes* (1936), were well received and provided material for his solo piano repertoire as well as his dance band.

The virtual closure of Covent Garden as a venue for opera for long periods during the 1920s and 1930s (the theatre was given over to film, pantomime, revue and other entertainments) perhaps encouraged a notable rise in the number of comic operas written then, though not one of them has achieved a lasting place in the repertoire. Most significant in the 1920s was the famous revival of John Gay's *The Beggar's Opera* at the Lyric, Hammersmith, in Frederic Austin's arrangement in 1920. Also worthy of mention are *Young England* by Hubert Bath (1883–1945), in which the Victorian favourite Hayden Coffin made a late appearance in 1915, *Jolly Roger* by Walter Leigh, with George Robey as Bold Ben Blister, which ran for six months at the Savoy in 1933, and *The Blue Peter* by Cecil Armstrong Gibbs (1889–1960). This last had a libretto by A. P. Herbert, who was later to prove a great asset in musicals and who also wrote the libretto for *Tantivy Towers* by Thomas Dunhill (1877–1946), given at the Lyric, Hammersmith, in 1931 with Maggie Teyte. Teyte played in a number of light operas, among them Kennedy Russell's *By Appointment* (New Theatre, 1934), in which she was Mrs Fitzherbert to the Beau Brummell of Gavin Gordon. Roger Quilter (1877–1953) was another distinguished composer who worked in light opera; his *Julia* was given at Covent Garden in 1936, and his music for the children's play *Where the Rainbow Ends* (Savoy, 1921) was, with the play itself, for many years a Christmas favourite.

By the 1930s the success or failure of a musical play was largely dependent on the acceptance of its numbers by the dance orchestras and recording companies. While there was nothing new about this, it inevitably prevented Novello from developing more interesting and interwoven musical scenes (assuming that he might have done so – *Arc de Triomphe* (1943) does contain a mini-opera on Joan of Arc). But another factor is important: since Novello himself usually played the leading man's part in his own shows, and he was not a singer, he did not on the whole provide large concerted finales (in which he would have been unable to partake); and they would have shown up the inadequacy of the singing actors' techniques compared with those of his favourite prima donnas, Mary Ellis and Olive Gilbert, for whom he wrote his most ambitious songs (see Ex. 6.2 from 'The wings of sleep' (*The Dancing Years*)).

Novello's career paralleled that of Noël Coward (1899–1973) in many ways; but musically they might have been chosen to represent two of the three major trends during this period. While Novello was the logical inheritor of the romantic operetta and musical comedy traditions, growing out of Offenbach, Strauss and their British equivalent, Sullivan, Coward, for all his apparent sophistication and worldwide popularity (something that eluded Novello), was a Londoner, and his songs, though he too attempted the romantic vein, are at their very best when in direct line from the music hall. Though he originated the speaking voice which has become such an often parodied style, his quick-fire delivery and tongue-twisting rhymes might have been penned by the same lyricists who had once produced numbers for Harry Champion or Wilkie Bard, cockney character comedians with the timing and musical skill that suggested not rehearsal but improvisation and are part of Coward's heritage.

MUSIC FOR THE STAGE

Ex. 6.2   Novello: 'The wings of sleep' (*The Dancing Years*)

[musical score: Tempo di Berceuse; MARIA CÄCILIE KURT sings "Soon as the shades are fall-ing gent-ly, call-ing you to rest;"]

Like Novello, Coward began by writing songs for revues ('The story of Peter Pan' in *Tails Up!*, 1918) but to begin with he contributed only the lyrics. Unlike Novello, Coward had no formal musical training and relied upon transcribers and arrangers. His prodigious early success as a playwright, lyricist, composer and actor dates from the seasons 1923–5 when in quick succession he wrote and starred in *London Calling!* (1923, which contained 'Parisian Pierrot'), *The Vortex* (1924), *Hay Fever* (1924, in which Coward did not appear) and *On With the Dance* (1925). This last, as well as containing the song 'Poor little rich girl', also had a ballet, 'Crescendo', danced and choreographed by Massine. Coward's career switched back and forth between melodrama, comedy, revue and eventually operetta. His works proved to be stageworthy in other countries and his songs have entered the international folklore of popular song. Like Cole Porter's, Coward's songs are variable in their melodic attraction and a promising lyric does not always produce the equal musical response. His most successful early songs, as well as the two already mentioned (to which one should add 'Dance, little lady', 'World weary' and 'A room with a view' from *This Year of Grace* of 1928), all drew upon the rhythms of the dance crazes of the time, foxtrot and black bottom (see Ex. 6.3, from 'Poor little rich girl'). *This Year of Grace* also included a song, performed by Jessie Matthews, 'Teach me to dance like Grandma'. This theme pointed the way towards Coward's first and most successful attempt at a romantic operetta, *Bitter Sweet* (1929). The device of the story, a tale told in flashback by its main character, sung in London by Peggy Wood and on Broadway by Evelyn Laye, also allowed for the juxtaposition of contemporary dance tunes with the waltzes which are the main musical topic and also play their part in the story. Musically, the most inventive passage

Ex. 6.3   Coward: 'Poor little rich girl' (*On with the Dance*)

[Steady rhythm]

Cock-tails and laugh-ter   But what comes aft-er?   No-bod-y knows.

You're weav-ing love in-to a mad jazz pat-tern, Ruled by pan-ta-loon.

is in the opening scene when the chorus of young people sing stanzas of a Charleston, intertwined with the aged heroine's first aria, 'The call of life'. 'I'll see you again' from *Bitter Sweet*, 'Someday I'll find you', introduced into the action of *Private Lives*, 'I'll follow my secret heart' from *Conversation Piece* and 'Where are the songs we sung?' from *Operette* were Coward's favourites among his own tunes. As slow waltzes they all have enough melody and charm to have ensured them a life outside the shows for which they were created, but they lack the rhythmic pulse that distinguished Coward's finest comedy numbers, and as each one is in its way a pastiche to furnish a plot device they cannot compete with the best of Lehár, Kern or even Oscar Straus, all of whom were composing at exactly the same time. It is impossible to believe that Coward, in his construction of *Bitter Sweet*, was not influenced by Kern's *Show Boat*, which had been given in London the year before, just as *Conversation Piece* was conceived as a vehicle for the French singing actress Yvonne Printemps and indeed contains a direct quote from Hahn's *Mozart*, her most famous role in French *opérette*.

Coward's musicals written after the Second World War had decreasing success, although each one contains at least one memorable song; it is significant, however, that the best of these are not the pseudo-romantic love songs and waltzes but numbers that hark back to the music hall and revues of Coward's youth. 'Chase me, Charlie!' in *Ace of Clubs*, 'Poor Uncle Harry' in *Pacific 1860* and the sequence of London songs written for Tessie O'Shea in Coward's final musical, *The Girl Who Came to Supper*, created on Broadway in 1963 but never produced in London, showed Coward's strength as a composer–lyricist in the tradition not of the central European operetta but of the London variety stage. 'The star of the evening was Tessie O'Shea,' wrote Coward in his diary on 11 December; 'I have never heard such cheering. It was truly thrilling to see that rumbustious, bouncing old-timer, after some years of limbo, come back and tear the place up' (quoted in Payne and Morley 1982: 552). Much earlier Coward had written a one-act play, *Red Peppers*, for himself and Gertrude Lawrence to perform as part of the sequence *Tonight at 8.30*. Their performances as a pair of ageing song-and-dance comics playing in seaside music halls had an edge and an affection missing from Coward's more obviously sophisticated work.

III: Ellis, Gay and Others

Vivian Ellis (*b* 1903) had a more conventional musical background and schooling than either Novello or Coward, yet his progression from writing songs for revues to writing musical comedies and then operettas was similar. He allowed the popular American style to influence his work more subtly and in his first major success, *Mr Cinders* (1929), he composed the song with which his name has continued to be associated and which has been revived by numerous singers since Binnie Hale first performed it, 'Spread a little happiness'. This show translated successfully into German as *Jim und Jill* and was produced in Berlin and Vienna. Ellis's clearer understanding of the possibilities of jazz and modern dance music was further advanced by *Follow a Star*, written as a vehicle for 'the last of the red-hot mommas', Sophie Tucker; it included 'If your kisses can't hold the man you love', in which Tucker mixed her customary blues-influenced singing with the *Sprechgesang* essential to her storytelling method.

Ellis's later pre-war shows, *Jill Darling* (1933), with its famous duet 'I'm on a see-saw', *Streamline* (1934) and *Under Your Hat* (1938), all developed his sure musical instincts without creating a new or innovatory genre. This is perhaps the main reason why, despite the occasional revival, not one of the musicals by Novello, Coward or Ellis has secured a place in the permanent repertoire or been performed with more than short-term success in other countries.

After the Second World War, Ellis found the ideal librettist in A. P. Herbert, who had written the lyrics for *Streamline* (including the risqué 'Other people's babies'). Together they came up with *Big Ben* (1946), *Bless the Bride* (1947), *Tough at the Top* (1949), and *The Water Gipsies* (1955). *Bless the Bride* came nearest among these to establishing a new post-war British operetta tradition, all the more remarkable in the face of the new wave of competition that had arrived from America with the first London staging of Rodgers and Hammerstein's *Oklahoma!* in 1947. The brash dancing and singing style of this, and its energetic reshaping of what a musical might achieve, effectively put paid to the pre-war operetta and musical comedy style. Although most of the seasoned practitioners continued to produce work (more or less in line with their existing style), the overwhelming impact of the Rodgers and Hammerstein shows and the first London productions of Gershwin's *Porgy and Bess* (1952) and Loesser's *Guys and Dolls* (1953) seemed to sound the death-knell for a homegrown musical theatre.

This was no surprise, for the music hall and variety stage had already been first usurped by the cinema and then weakened by the popularity of American-style dance bands and vocalists. The two most innovative and enduring of the later music-hall stars, Gracie Fields (1898–1979) and Max Miller (1894–1963), both emerged during the 1920s. Fields always retained the music-hall style with the comedy and pathos numbers for which she is remembered, such as 'I took my harp to a party' by Noel Gay (1898–1954), composer of the musical *Me and My Girl* – the only British show to have had a modern long-run revival. She secured her own longevity with a mixture of standards from overseas, even including an English-language version of the Edith Piaf/Marguerite Monnot 'La vie en rose'. Miller's songs, on the other hand, were rooted in the pre-war music-hall tradition, the most famous, 'Mary from the dairy', being a collaboration between Miller and the composer–lyricist Jimmie Walsh, best remembered for 'Don't have any more, Mrs. Moore' (written with Harry Castling).

The erosion of this folkloric music-hall style, and its eventual demise along with the last of the London halls, Collins on Islington Green and the Metropolitan in the Edgware Road (both of which survived until the late 1950s), paralleled the disappearance of the seaside Pierrot and concert-party shows which were also an essential part of the popular musical theatre of the late Victorian and Edwardian eras. Coward, in a scene from *Cavalcade*, suggests the atmosphere at one of these entertainments, whose format was also used by more sophisticated urban groups such as Pellissier's Follies and later The Co-optimists founded in 1921 by Davy Burnaby. Although the dominant musical force in this 'Pierrotic entertainment' was the American composer Melville Gideon, for the entire decade of the 1920s The Co-optimists – which at different times included Stanley Holloway, Gilbert Childs, Laddie Cliff, Phyllis Monkman and Betty Chester – provided a unique alternative entertainment, with a witty, almost cabaret-like style.

Of other composers, most of whose work is now totally forgotten and unperformed, it is worth mentioning Philip Braham (1882–1934), whose 'Limehouse blues' was first sung by Teddie Gerard and later by Gertrude Lawrence and Jessie Matthews; Martin Broones (1892–1971), who wrote three of the final shows produced at the Gaiety: *Gay Deceivers* (1935), *Seeing Stars* (1935) and *Swing Along* (1936); and Jack Strachey (1894–1972), perhaps the British composer whose songs for the theatre are most worthy of reappraisal. In *Lady Luck* (1927) Strachey wrote 'Blue pipes of Pan', the most elegiac commentary upon the confrontation between 'rag' and 'classic' music, and for the revue *Spread It Abroad* (1936), to the lyrics of Eric Maschwitz, he composed 'These foolish things', first sung by Dorothy Dickson and destined to become a worldwide standard, interpreted by singers as diverse as Billie Holiday, Jean Sablon and Bryan Ferry (see Ex. 6.4).

Ex. 6.4   Jack Strachey: 'These foolish things' (*Spread It Abroad*)

[Slowly]

A tink-ling pi-a-no in the next a-part-ment,— Those stumb-ling words that told you what my heart meant,— A fair-ground's paint-ed swings.— These fool-ish things Re-mind me of you.

IV: From the Second World War to Lloyd Webber

The Second World War only increased American domination of the musical and dance-band repertoire, though one contribution to London musical comedy came from Richard Tauber, who composed *Old Chelsea* (1943), 'a musical romance', adding his name to the distinguished group of foreign composers who wrote shows specially for London, of which one might also mention Cole Porter's *Nymph Errant* (1933), Kurt Weill's *A Kingdom for a Cow* (1935) and André Messager's *Monsieur Beaucaire* (1918). The influence of *Oklahoma!*, with its shift away from the more relaxed pre-war musical comedy manner towards a through-composed, larger-scale type of production, was a step in the direction of the biggest change that overtook music for the stage. It is generally held that the first Broadway musical to use amplification was *West Side Story* (New York 1957, London 1958). What this did was to alter completely the requirements for voice and indeed for vocal training necessary for the singing actor. (In 1964, with the London pop revolution in full swing, the veteran Ida Barr returned to the West End for a few weeks in a 'public house entertainment', *Nights at the Comedy*. She sang Irving Berlin's 'Everybody's doing it', as she had in 1910. When she made her entrance, gestured towards the standard microphone and announced 'Take that *thing* away', she brought the house down.) In the interim period, between the end of hostilities in 1945 and the sudden upturn in British popular music during the 1960s, the most successful composers for the theatre all evoked some nostalgic past, either by the settings for their plays, the format or the reactionary idiom chosen. Coward's logical successors were the comic duo Michael Flanders (1922–75) and Donald Swann (1923–94). Like Coward's, their songs depended upon a peculiarly English method of delivery, and while nothing in their output has the brilliance of Coward's best melodies, songs like 'The gnu' and 'The gasman cometh' belong firmly to the tradition of the Victorian song-and-supper, passed down through music hall, via Coward's West End successes and back to the concert platform at the New Lindsey Theatre Club in Notting Hill Gate where in 1956 the pair started.

It was at another theatre club, the Players', that Sandy Wilson (*b* 1924) first had his 1920s pastiche musical *The Boy Friend* (1953) produced. This enjoyed a lasting success on both sides of the Atlantic and has been revived many times. While the songs are unashamed evocations of specific numbers from the 1920s – for instance, 'A room in Bloomsbury' is a modern echo of 'A tiny flat in Soho Square' from *Lido Lady* and 'Poor little Pierrette' recalls Coward's 'Parisian Pierrot' – the show had a freshness and originality that singled it out. Wilson's *Valmouth*, based on the novel by Ronald Firbank, has never enjoyed the same popularity, although it is a more personal and sophisticated adaptation of decadent literature. Almost at the same time as *The Boy Friend*, *Salad Days* by Julian Slade (*b* 1930) carved out another niche for sentimental English whimsy. The composer who most adeptly mixed the new, amplified American style with the established English music-hall and bar-room tradition was Lionel Bart (*b* 1930). *Fings Ain't Wot They Used T' Be*, *Blitz*, *Maggie May* and above all *Oliver!* proved to be a renaissance for the London musical, although music critics found much to doubt in Bart's work, Arthur Jacobs, reviewing *Blitz*, writing that 'the musical bridge-passages and backgrounds, especially, are of a barely imaginable crudity' (1962: 496). Be that as it may, Bart's masterpiece, *Oliver!*, is impressive both for the way in which he condenses the story within the constraints imposed by the musical format and for its ambitious mixture of voices – unlike Novello and Coward, Bart seems at his best in ensemble passages (see Ex. 6.5, from 'Who will buy?' with its crossover echoes of Vaughan Williams and modal freedom). In 1991 *Oliver!* was recorded with an operatic cast; though the work has yet to enter the repertoire of an opera company, it is a tribute to its enduring strength that this seems a likely proposition.

While Bart's theatricality sometimes seemed over-commercial, the short-lived successes of other musical theatre works of the late 1950s and early 1960s, such as Anthony Newley's *Stop the World – I Want to Get Off*, David Heneker's *Half a Sixpence* and Ron Grainer's *Robert and Elizabeth* were all, like the pieces tailor-made for the stars of the 1900s, so dependent on their leading players' personalities that their chances of survival seem slim. Just as the combined threat of the cinema, radio and gramophone had eroded the popularity of the music hall, depriving it of the younger musicians and performers for whom in the past it had been the most natural and lucrative outlet, so the rise of the international pop industry, and in particular its domination of the music to be seen and heard on television, seemed for a while to herald the demise of the musical theatre.

It was surely the lack of apparent enthusiasm from a large or youthful audience that discouraged, for instance, Paul McCartney and John Lennon, or most of the successful popular British songwriters of the time, from bothering with musicals. Composers from an academic background were more attracted by the less obviously theatrical formats now on offer (*Tommy* (1969), the Who's rock opera, and the eventually cult-status *Rocky Horror Show* by Richard O'Brien (*b* 1942) belong to this era); however, it was a composer from such a school, Andrew Lloyd Webber (*b* 1948), who changed the whole face of musical theatre. Starting with his school play *Joseph and the*

Ex. 6.5   Bart: 'Who will buy?' (*Oliver!*)

Amazing Technicolor Dreamcoat, first given by the pupils of Colet Court in 1968, the subsequent commercial, worldwide successes of his other collaborations with Tim Rice, *Jesus Christ Superstar* (1971), *Evita* (1978) and *Cats* (1981), showed him overtaking the example of Novello in creating a genre that transcended the formally approved theatre of its day and made a hybrid form of popular song, drawing on elements from popular classics, opera (the original classification of *Evita* and *Jesus Christ Superstar*), rock and musical comedy. Reviewing the first performance of *Jesus Christ Superstar*, Ned Rorem wrote:

POPULAR MUSIC

Webber's score derives totally from the music of others, but eclecticism is no sin and greater than he have fed off what's around . . . Much of the recipe is accented with jagged 5/4 and 7/8 meters favored by America in the 1940s . . . His originality, like anyone's, lies in the ability to take a chance and win. His color is the color of speed . . . If one can assert that the most touching portion from the great classical cantatas are slow and introspective, then *Superstar*'s grandeur owes nothing to the past . . . Where the text would indicate to anyone but Webber a reflective pause, a hush, he goes hog-wild. His color then is the maintenance of fever pulse, a *trouvaille* utterly appropriate to the story's tension, and reminiscent only of itself. (1974: 84–5)

Lloyd Webber's most reflective, most memorable later songs were, conversely, slow ballads: 'Don't cry for me, Argentina' in *Evita*, 'Memory' in *Cats* (Ex. 6.6), 'Love changes everything' in *Aspects of Love* and 'With one look' from *Sunset Boulevard*. The challenge such songs present to the classically trained, non-amplified singer, as Gwyneth Jones's recording of 'Memory' demonstrates, balances Lloyd Webber's music as delicately between operetta and musical theatre as the serious works of Coward and Novello. The many aspirants who have succeeded him, notably Howard Goodall (*b* 1960) with *The Hired Man*, have only made his achievements both as impresario and composer more impressive.

Lloyd Webber's successes were paralleled by those of several musicals by non-British composers working in London, especially Claude-Michel Schönberg's *Les misérables*. First given in Paris in 1980, the original production had little of the impact that it made in its English version first at the Barbican and then at the Palace Theatre. The impresario Cameron Mackintosh, who produced Schönberg's subsequent *Miss Saigon*, written for London, also persuaded Stephen Sondheim to revise his 1971 *Follies* for a London production (1987). The influence of Sondheim, as composer and even more as lyricist, on a new generation of writers and performers – for instance the group Fascinating Aida and the duo Kit and the Widow – pointed a way towards a textually intricate songwriting style in contrast to the almost universally bland lyrics fashionable in rock and pop. A new and ferociously political musical drawing on this and the more traditional ballad forms was Paddy Cunneen's *Lady Betty*, to a libretto by Declan Donnellan, presented by Cheek-By-Jowl at the Almeida in 1989.

As the century draws to a close, the theatrical milieu open to aspiring composers and performers is so transformed from that

MUSIC FOR THE STAGE

Ex. 6.6 Lloyd Webber: 'Memory' (*Cats*)

available in 1914 that comparisons simply between musical styles seem irrelevant. A musical may now reach the stage only either through the medium of recordings (several of Lloyd Webber's pieces were recorded before they were staged), the guarantee of huge audiences, or the co-operation of international production companies. Nevertheless, the musical styles that were once peculiar to each country or region, together with the cross-fertilization provided by the advent of recording and broadcasting, have renewed the vitality of the stage musical. The same composers and players who might once have provided incidental music for stage plays at a time when most large theatres employed musicians regardless of whether or not the play called for music, may now find their employment in television. Whereas songwriters for the music hall might once have sold the copyright of their work for a few pounds to a singer or theatre manager, now the chances of success with a recording involve them in elaborate contracts with agents and producers. Singers trained at a conservatoire may find that their talents are needed in musicals, advertising or backing for a pop record, and singing actors with no formal musical training may be placed side by side with established opera stars.

Meeting the record producer Peter Wadland for the first time in London in the late 1960s, Noël Coward introduced himself with the words, 'I wrote *Bitter Sweet.*' That he should have chosen this example of his work, talking to someone who was born nearly 20 years after its première, confirms that it was in the musical theatre that he held the highest esteem for his own creations. 'There had been little or no sentiment on the London musical stage for a long while,' Coward wrote in 1937. 'It seemed high time for a little romantic renaissance' (1937: 335). Experimentation with the possibilities afforded by modern amplification and electronic music has, it would seem, hardly yet begun in the field of music for the stage, but despite such overwhelming influences from outside, the chances that in future the traditions of sentimental operetta on the one hand and satiric verbal dexterity on the other will continue to be the dominant forces in Britain seems likely.

Chapter 7

FILM AND TELEVISION MUSIC

DAVID KERSHAW

I: *Music to the Silent Film*

Here's a chord you can't do without, he said, if you're a picture palace pianoplayer. You use it for fights, burst dams, thunderstorms, the voice of the Lord God, a wife telling her old man to bugger off out of the house and not come back never no more. And he showed me. C E flat G flat A. Or F G sharp B D. Or E G B flat C sharp. Always the same like dangerous sound, he said, as if something terrible's going to happen or is happening (soft for going to happen, loud for happening) . . . and you can arpeggio them to make them like very mysterious. (A. BURGESS 1986: 28)

At the turn of the century, before the age of complete film shows, films were shown in the context of a varied programme of other musical and dramatic entertainments, and live music was provided by small 'orchestras' often numbering only two or three players. There is no evidence of films having been publicly screened without the support of such accompaniment, which served not only to mask the sounds of the projector, the street and the customers, but also to anaesthetize the audience to both the deficiencies and the disturbing novelty of the medium. Within two months of the first public film screening in Great Britain, the Empire and Alhambra Music Halls were in April 1896 showing films accompanied by their orchestras (Manvell and Huntley 1975: 265). On 23 November 1897 a Royal Command Film Performance was given at Windsor Castle by Prof. Jolly's Cinematographe and the Empire Theatre Orchestra.

Pit musicians accustomed to 'following' and offering musical support to, and comment upon, the action of a drama or speciality turn would have had no difficulty in catching both mood and individual gesture when similar variety acts were presented on film; hence from the beginning it was customary for an accompaniment sympathetic to the film's subject matter to be found from within the large repertoire of incidental music available to theatre music directors. 'In the old days of the theatre the incidental music in a melodrama was very prominent and, up to a point, important; one of its principal intentions was that of the fat boy "to make yer flesh creep" . . . Music was unblushingly used to brighten up an entrance, strengthen an exit, emphasize the action and wheedle a salt tear in the pathetic scenes' (E. Irving 1959: 147).

The use of 'special effects' was also customary at this time, well before the introduction of theatre organs a decade later. The minimum 'orchestra' would comprise pianist and percussionist–either two players, or the one player doubling on a 'trap drum combination' consisting of gong, drum, cymbals, pedal triangle and beater. A large range of realistic imitation effects was commonly available, including anvil, lion roar, dog bark, horse hoofs and tearing cloth, and would have been used to enhance the immediacy of all film presentations.

Not until the First World War did music-hall promoters fully exploit the commercial potential of cinema or invest in purpose-built 'electric palaces' or 'bioscope theatres'. As film technology developed and film makers were emboldened to attempt longer films, so the need became apparent for a dedicated musical repertoire.

It became increasingly difficult for the music director (or 'fitter') to meet the demand for suitable continuous music, with the result that in the smaller establishments the same tired numbers were heard with monotonous regularity. Film distributors answered a need by circulating with their films 'cue sheets' which recommended a suitable selection of music. Timings would be given for each item. The music director would then either purchase the specified numbers (see Ex. 7.1), or would find similar music from within his library. The first such 'Suggestions for music' had been issued with Edison films in 1909.

During the following 20 years many publishing houses exploited the market by offering 'cinema music' listed according to mood and situation. All was grist to the mill. Beethoven's *Coriolanus*, for example, was recommended as 'suitable for tree-felling or lumber-rolling' (E. Irving 1943: 225). Two much-used catalogues of 'mood-music' were those published by Giuseppe Becce (1919) and Erno Rapée (1924). While the standard of performance and the commitment of the musicians in the smaller 'flea-pits' was often low, in the plusher cinemas large professional orchestras were retained or hired. During the 1920s, by which time the industry was well established, and with music's important contribution to the success

FILM AND TELEVISION MUSIC

Ex. 7.1 (a) 'for Pathetic and Sad Scenes' A. Czibulka: 'Hearts and flowers'

(b) 'for Light, Pretty Scenes'
Ketèlbey: 'Amaryllis' (Graceful Dance)
(Bosworth's Loose Leaf Film-Play Music Series, Book 1)

of a film fully recognized, major films were supplied with specially tailored compilation scores for orchestra. Eugene Goossens relates how he conducted 65 members of the LSO engaged at the Royal Opera House to accompany the silent film *The Three Musketeers* (1921). He plundered the music library of Goodwin and Tabb for lesser-known symphonic repertoire, discovering August Enna whose unidentifiable music 'fitted anything, and also conveyed a spurious impression of great emotional depth, making it very suitable for my purpose' (1951: 183–5). Most accompaniments drew largely upon standard nineteenth-century classics and light classics; as a result, many people were first introduced to this repertoire in the cinema. It was also common for orchestras to perform music before the screening and during the intermission.

By the end of the 1920s it was generally recognized that film had achieved the status of an art form, one that – unlike theatre – was potentially international, given the absence of spoken dialogue. In Europe, the USA and Russia, major feature-length films had become the norm. For a small minority of these – notably *Birth of a Nation* (Breil/Griffith), *Napoleon* (Honegger), *Battleship Potemkin* and *October* (Meisel), *The Big Parade* and *Ben Hur* (Axt), and *New Babylon* (Shostakovich) – scores had been specially compiled or composed, clearly in the expectation that the financial outlay would be recouped by the anticipated international distribution.

Had silent film endured a few years longer, it is likely that, as had already occurred abroad, major British composers would have written special scores for feature films, much as those of an earlier generation (Stanford, Elgar, and Delius) had written incidental music for the theatre. Indeed, 'serious' composers, accustomed to the luxury of writing music unconstrained by the exact timings and integration with effects and dialogue required in sound film, would have found composing for silent film less of a block to their natural creative flow.

But as it is, there are no extant British silent-film scores of significance. All that remain are publishers' cue sheets and numerous 'mood-music' selections. Authentic reconstruction of silent-film performance must have recourse to these printed materials. It is worth remarking that, with few exceptions, scores of any kind are unavailable to students of sound films, for, having no commercial value once their music had been committed to film, they were consigned to oblivion by production company and composer alike unless, as occasionally happened, a concert suite could be devised from a reworking of cues.

FILM AND TELEVISION MUSIC
II: Transition to Sound Film

Since 1900 and the promotion of vaudeville stars in the Phono-Bio-Tableau Films, attempts had been made to synchronize music with film. Between 1906 and 1910 a large number of films with synchronized sound on record immortalized variety performers such as Vesta Tilley and Harry Lauder. But the deficiencies of pre-electric amplification saw a lull in such promotions until sound-on-film won the day on 27 September 1928, when Warner's *The Jazz Singer*, featuring Al Jolson, became the first 'talkie' screened publicly in London. (Although only in part a talking film – it still used intertitles – there were several songs and snatches of conversation.) It met with a mixed reception, being dismissed by one critic as 'merely a temporary craze, like broadcasting and greyhound racing' (Adams 1929). First in America, then internationally, a standard for sound-film projection was agreed, and a new era began as cinemas were 'wired for sound'. The demise of silent film and its accompaniment took place virtually overnight, resulting in unemployment for thousands of musicians.

In the opinion of film theorists of the time such as Arnheim, Spottiswoode, Eisenstein and Pudovkin, aesthetic losses were not offset by commensurate gains. The first sound films were, in comparison with the better silent-film productions, unimaginative in their editing, with the slower pacing of the action conditioned by the dictates of recording technology. The fascination for the general public of seeing and hearing already popular stars – actors, singers and comedians – on film was such that commentators feared for the survival of film as an art form. Musically, little changed immediately. Transitional films such as Alfred Hitchcock's *Blackmail* (1929) were released in both sound and silent versions. And although the days of the live cinema orchestra were gone (replaced, if at all, by the lone organist arising from the pit at the console of a 'mighty Wurlitzer'), those few players remaining to record for film were directed by the same men – Hubert Bath, Louis Levy and Ernest Irving – for whom they had earlier performed live. Levy, for example, moved from the Shepherd's Bush Pavilion Theatre to become music director for Gaumont–British Studios, also at Shepherd's Bush.

In all essentials, the function of film music did not change, its primary purpose still being at once to define and universalize the film's mood by providing a sympathetic musical ambience; secondarily it gave a feeling of continuity which the filmed image-succession itself lacked; and in conjunction with sound effects it created a sense of 'presence' which simulated the reality of a live performance. Over succeeding decades musical styles did of course change radically; but while the sound of film music has always been individual to its era, its gestural language has remained consistent, and not distant from the language used for similar situations in other musico-dramatic forms such as theatre and ballet.

It is regrettable that few scores have been critically esteemed for their contribution within a film. When composers have reworked their film music into concert suites (one of the earliest being Bliss's *Things to Come* of 1935), it is these that have been evaluated as autonomous music. The functioning of music within the complex of film action, difficult as it is to describe without recourse to screening the film itself, has rarely been attempted, a notable exception being the several citations of Walton's music to *Henry V* (see Manvell and Huntley 1975: 92–107, Palmer 1972: 250).

The film scores of British composers have received scant attention, the major reference works rarely caring even to list the films on which a composer has worked. This is partly due to a British snobbery about the perceived lowly status of film composition, an attitude unfortunately shared by some composers, who regarded such work as a well-paid chore necessary to buy time for 'serious' music. To an extent this attitude is justified: since composers are customarily not introduced to the film-in-progress until it has been finally edited, it cannot be expected that they will necessarily sympathize with the film's narrative style and ideology; they may well need to suspend disbelief when putting 'suitable' music to picture. This music may therefore be inimical to their own individual style; their skill is usually that of the accomplished pasticheur, one who can adapt the phraseology of familiar musical genres to the peculiar constraints of film. 'A little honest plagiarism is often an advantage' (E. Irving 1943: 230).

Theorists were rightly insistent on the integration of music with effects and dialogue, and they recognized a role for silence, something that the silent film itself could not allow. While music was often overused in early sound films, certain irksome restraints were at this stage imposed upon composers. Until the technology had developed to a point where conventional orchestrations could be satisfactorily recorded, it is hardly surprising that concert-hall composers were not attracted to the medium. 'To write specially with a view to the deficiencies of recording technique is to upset the natural order of things . . . It is not for the composer to play handmaiden to the engineer' (Lambert 1934: 257–8).

FILM AND TELEVISION MUSIC

From the mid-1930s film-recording techniques achieved a quality of orchestral sound not inferior to that of 78 rpm discs, the immediate comparator. By this time, several significant British composers of concert music were becoming attracted to the medium, notably Arthur Bliss with *Things to Come*, mentioned earlier, and William Walton with *Escape Me Never* (1935). Others who began writing for film in the 1930s, and whose careers also continued into the next decade, included Arthur Benjamin (*The Man Who Knew Too Much*, 1934), William Alwyn (*The Future's in the Air*, 1936), John Greenwood (1889–1975) (*Elephant Boy*, 1937), and Richard Addinsell (1904–77) (*Goodbye Mr Chips*, 1938). Many composers were intrigued by the new medium, and initially worked more for the experience than for significant financial reward. Those whose careers were spent largely in film music remained the less well known but are ultimately the more significant in that their understanding of the craft was extensive. Key figures in British film music were Muir Mathieson (1911–75), a conductor and music director of over 600 films, Louis Levy (1893–1957) and Ernest Irving (1878–1953), both composers and music directors. All three exerted a profound influence in encouraging composers to work in the medium, and in advising and assisting them at all stages. They raised both the quality of film music and its critical estimation. Mathieson attributed this recognition to Bliss's entry (at H. G. Wells's invitation) into film music composition. 'We never looked back after that' (Mathieson and Mitchell 1947: 60).

In this decade the documentary film movement, led by John Grierson at the GPO Film Unit, was important to novice film composers. Grierson (1898–1972), strongly influenced by Russian theorizing on the creative use of sound in films, was open-minded about the contribution of music, and encouraged its imaginative integration with dialogue and effects. Remarkable for such experimental intermeshing are *Song of Ceylon* (1934), which was actually edited to a 'sound-score' composed by Walter Leigh, and *Coal Face* (1935) and *Night Mail* (1936), both with poetry by W. H. Auden and music by Benjamin Britten. In *Coal Face* Britten employed an unusually large battery of percussion, including 'the reversed sound-track of a cymbal struck with a hard beater to achieve the "whoosh" effect of a train' (J. Evans et al. 1987: 132). This compositional incorporation of noise shows Leigh's and Britten's awareness of earlier 'noise music', ranging from the Futurists to Satie's *Parade* (1917), Arthur Honegger's *Pacific 231* (1924), Alexander Mossolov's *Music of the Machines* (1927) and Walther Ruttmann's film *La mélodie du monde* (1929).

As in the silent era, British feature films continued to compete with Hollywood productions, the battleground now being a new genre, the musical, whose escapism proved welcome both in the Depression and during the war. Although technically inferior, British musicals were assured box office success by featuring major dance bands such as those of Ambrose (*Soft Lights and Sweet Music*, 1937), Henry Hall (*Music Hath Charms*, 1936), Jack Hylton (*She Shall Have Music*, 1935, and *Band Wagon*, 1940) and Harry Roy (*Everything Is Rhythm*, 1936), and stage comedians and music-hall and radio stars, including Jack Buchanan, Gracie Fields, George Formby, Jack Hulbert, Jessie Matthews and Max Miller. Thanks to its convincing period atmosphere (of the music halls of the 1860s) and a suitably effervescent score assembled by Ernest Irving, Lord Berners, Billy Mayerl and others, Ealing Studios' musical *Champagne Charlie* (1944) achieved a refreshing individuality.

III: The War Years

The talent already shown by British directors in documentary film production was exploited at the beginning of the war by the Ministry of Information, which commissioned the production of films which

were shown compulsorily in every cinema in the country. This gave an unparalleled opportunity to up and coming composers who were invited to write suitable music. Every week in every cinema from those early days, there has been at least one score by a first rate British composer to which, willingly or unwillingly, consciously or unconsciously, the film audiences have listened. Whatever their tastes, music has been played to them which otherwise they might never have heard . . . Today you can fill any hall with Beethoven and Tchaikovski largely, I think, because their musical imagination has been stimulated by hearing first rate music in the cinema. (Mathieson and Mitchell 1947: 56)

Richard Addinsell's *Warsaw Concerto* (from the film *Dangerous Moonlight*, 1941) was instanced by Mathieson as a fine example of such film music (see Ex. 7.2). Kaikhosru Sorabji, however, berated such spoonfeeding:

When is a Concerto not a Concerto?

The answer is: When a film forms all over it, and when it gets struck by the very dangerous Moonshine of Hollywood, and when the great, tripe-

Ex. 7.2 Richard Addinsell: Theme from the *Warsaw Concerto*

hearted democracy thinks it is going all classical and highbrow as it sits and listens, in the Palmers Green or Peckham Rye Pallas-Athenaeum, to the multitudinous masterpieces of Mr Richard Addinsell, having had, naturally enough till then, not the slightest idea how nice and easy 'nice' music was to listen to. (SORABJI 1947: 17)

At the age of 69 Vaughan Williams was prevailed upon by Mathieson to write for the semi-documentary *49th Parallel* (1941). This was followed by *Coastal Command* (1942), and in 1948 by *Scott of the Antarctic*, the music for which was later to be reworked into his *Sinfonia antartica*. Vaughan Williams found music a 'Cinderella of the film arts . . . too apt to become just an afterthought', and looked forward to a time when the composer would 'take his place with the author, the photographer, and the designer from the inception of the idea' (Vaughan Williams, quoted in Cameron 1947: viii). He urged 'real' composers to enter the new collaborative medium and wrest it from mere hacks. However, he never really came to terms with the restrictive disciplines of composing for film. Indeed, he had written the music for *Scott of the Antarctic* even before receiving timings from Irving, who had subsequently to 'move it about inside the film, applying some of it to incidents for which it was not designed' (E. Irving 1959: 176).

Walton's busy career as a film composer (he wrote altogether 14 film scores and was thus no dabbler) achieved an early high point in 1945 with *Henry V*, followed in 1948 by his second collaboration with Laurence Olivier, *Hamlet*. More than Vaughan Williams, Bax and Bliss, Walton recognized (if he did not relish) the specialized skills of film composition. Mathieson paid tribute to Walton's 'extraordinary ingenuity' in *Hamlet* in effecting transitions from 'source' music (a lightly scored sarabande) to 'background' music (for full symphony orchestra) in the players' scene, and back again (Mathieson, 1948: 63).

From among a large number of significant feature film scores written in this decade a representative selection of their composers includes: Alwyn (*Desert Victory*, 1943); Bath (*Love Story*, 1944); Clifton Parker (1905–89) (*Western Approaches*, 1944); Richard Addinsell (*A Diary for Timothy*, 1945); Rawsthorne (*The Captive Heart*, 1946); Ireland (*The Overlanders*, 1946); Bliss (*Men of Two Worlds*, 1946); Walter Goehr (*Great Expectations*, 1946); Berners (*Nicholas Nickleby*, 1947); Lambert (*Anna Karenina*, 1947); Bax (*Oliver Twist*, 1948); and Brian Easdale (*b* 1909) (*The Red Shoes*, 1948, an Oscar-winning score famous for its extended ballet sequence).

It was Irving who persuaded a wary John Ireland to write his only film score, *The Overlanders* (Irving also orchestrated it), and Mathieson who, on behalf of the Ministry of Information, approached the recently appointed Master of the King's Musick, Arnold Bax, first to write for *Malta GC* (1942) and then for *Oliver Twist*. Bax, however, remained unhappy that his music was subordinated to narration in *Malta GC*, and was consequently reluctant to accept the later commission.

IV: Post-War Years

The middle 1950s saw the gradual emergence of television as a competitor to the cinema, although for many years it offered no serious alternative to composers as a regular source of income. Throughout this decade the feature film scores of established composers continued to be heard, alongside the work of newcomers such as Francis Chagrin (1905–72) (*The Colditz Story*, 1954), Tristram

Cary (*b* 1925) (*The Ladykillers*, 1955), John Addison (*b* 1920) (*Reach for the Sky*, 1956), Malcolm Arnold (*The Bridge on the River Kwai*, 1957), and James Bernard (*b* 1925) – who composed the music to *The Quatermass Experiment* (1955), and *The Curse of Frankenstein* (1957), the film with which Hammer Studios began its profitable series of horror films.

Bernard's full-blooded gothic–romantic scores, built on pervasive leitmotifs and generously laced with tritonal dissonance, like those of other composers for the genre – Christopher Gunning, Don Banks, Harry Robertson and David Whitaker – endowed Hammer productions with a flamboyant splendour which their production values did not otherwise attain. Benjamin Frankel, a composer whose prolific film career began in 1934 and included Ealing Studios' satirical comedy *The Man in the White Suit* (1951) and *Mine Own Executioner* (1947), provided a score for *Curse of the Werewolf* (1961) which incorporated traditional tonal and melodic gestures within a compositional method deriving from serial procedures. Elisabeth Lutyens similarly contributed serial-inflected scores to *Paranoiac* (1963), *The Skull* and *Dr Terror's House of Horrors* (both 1965). An equally popular contemporary genre, one rooted in the music-hall tradition, arrived in 1958 with the first of the numerous *Carry On* films where sexual innuendo and high jinks were naughtily underscored by Bruce Montgomery (1921–78) and Eric Rogers (1921–81). Rogers's Merrie England music for *Carry On Henry* (1971) achieved in its way as deft an integration of pseudo-old and new as did Walton's celebrated score for *Henry V*. The main-title music (what else but variations on 'Greensleeves'?) is a *tour de force* in mood setting, interlocking up-tempo sections for jazz orchestra with metric and harmonic devices from the sixteenth century. Musical as well as verbal one-liners are the stuff of this genre, fusing in the cartoon-derived technique of 'Mickey-Mousing' – as when Barbara Windsor (Bettina, a buxom 'knowing' wench) and Sid James (the lecherous King) get to grappling:

> '[My mother] says I must save myself until I have a husband.'
> 'Well, that's alright. I'm a husband.'
> [Pause for thought]
> 'That's right! You are, aren't you?'
> 'Yes!'
> [Music enters as they laugh. Bettina throws herself on the King who falls back. His leg rises and trembles in passion; his garter bursts; Bettina releases him; he gradually sits up . . .]
> 'Cor!'

Ex. 7.3 Eric Rogers: *Carry On Henry* (aural transcription)

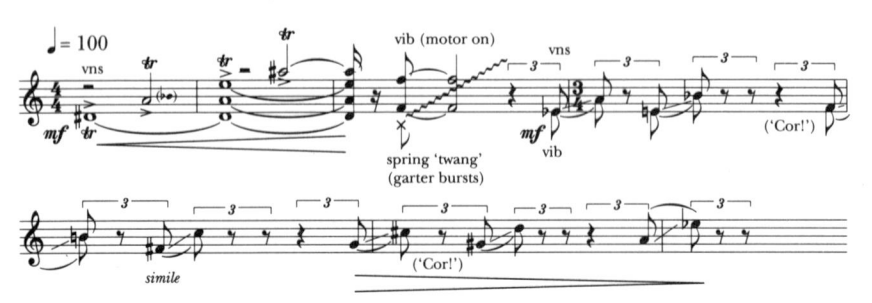

The phenomenal success with American teenagers in 1955 of the rock music of Bill Haley and the Comets, first in *The Blackboard Jungle* and then the following year in *Rock Around the Clock*, alerted producers to the existence of a new, relatively affluent market. Rock gave release to the pent-up frustrations of British adolescents schooled in the immediate post-war years of austerity. In cinemas in the States rebellious patrons 'danced in the aisles, they tore up seats during screenings, and scores of police were usually on hand for the sell-out performances. Efforts were made to ban [*Rock Around the Clock*] in this country and the fact that rock's instant notoriety was branded by religious and media buffoons as decadent and carnal only enhanced its appeal' (Dellar 1981: 10). *The Tommy Steele Story*, subtitled *Rock Around the World*, which appeared in 1957, told how Britain's first rock star rose to show-biz fame. Its score and songs were 'pieced together in just one week' (Dellar 1981: 165). A similar vehicle was given to Cliff Richard in *Expresso Bongo* (1959), *The Young Ones* (1961) and *Summer Holiday* (1963). There followed numerous pop musicals featuring, among others, Billy Fury, Helen Shapiro, Craig Douglas, Joe Brown, and Mark Wynter. Shortly after directing Shapiro and Douglas in *It's Trad, Dad!* (*Ring a Ding Rhythm*) (1962) Richard Lester achieved major successes with *A Hard Day's Night* (1964) and *Help!* (1965) featuring the Beatles. In the spirit of *A Hard Day's Night* was *Catch Us If You Can* (1965) with the Dave Clark Five.

V: Diversification

The 1960s was the decade of the Beatles, culminating in film with a feature-length animation *Yellow Submarine* (1968) inspired by the songs of Lennon and McCartney. It was also the decade of the James

Bond movies, beginning with *Dr No* (1962) and continuing over a 20-year period. After *Dr No* the name of John Barry (*b* 1933) was associated with most of the Bond films. In the pre-title montage sequence with which *Diamonds Are Forever* (1971) begins, Barry succeeds in defining mood (the bass guitar's dour rhythmic ostinato signalling both Bond's relentless sexual predation and his licence to kill) and location (Japan and Cairo), and in 'stinging' and Mickey-Mousing action. Ex. 7.4 demonstrates how close and complex is the integration of all montage elements – screen action, effects, dialogue and music – in this sequence, and that the intrinsic/extrinsic distinction (otherwise frequently termed diegetic/non-diegetic, featured/incidental, or source/background) is often fruitfully blurred. Barry won Oscars for his scores to *Born Free* (1965), *The Lion in Winter* (1968) and *Out of Africa* (1985) and has become one of the most sought-after and prolific British film composers. Richard Rodney Bennett's film scores – *Billy Liar* (1963), *Billion Dollar Brain* (1967), *Far from the Madding Crowd* (1967), and *Secret Ceremony* (1968) – also began to achieve international recognition. John Dankworth contributed jazz-inspired scores to *Saturday Night and Sunday Morning* (1960), *The Servant* (1963), *Darling* (1965), *Morgan: a Suitable Case for Treatment* (1966), and *Accident* (1967). John Addison scored for *Tom Jones* (1963), Ron Goodwin (*b* 1925) for *Those Magnificent Men in Their Flying Machines* (1965). Goodwin was also brought in to compose a new score for *Battle of Britain* (1969) following the rejection of all Walton's music save a four-minute sequence, 'Battle in the air'.

Ken Russell's biopics, both those for the television programme *Monitor* on Delius and Elgar and those for the cinema such as *The Music Lovers* (1970), on Tchaikovsky, and *Mahler* (1974), later included the fictional *Tommy* (1975) with a score by Pete Townshend and the Who. The Who also contributed to the soundtrack of the musical *Quadrophenia* (1979). Peter Maxwell Davies wrote for two films in 1971, *The Devils* and *The Boy Friend*, both directed by Ken Russell. Richard Rodney Bennett scored for *Nicholas and Alexandra* (1971), *Lady Caroline Lamb* (1972), *Murder on the Orient Express* (1974), and *Yanks* (1979).

The American composer Carl Davis, resident in England, designed pastiche scores to many major silent features of the 1920s, including D. W. Griffith's *Broken Blossoms* (1919), Erich von Stroheim's *Greed* (1923), Fred Niblo's *Ben Hur* (1925) and Abel Gance's *Napoleon* (1927). More remarkably, these films were screened not only on television but to capacity audiences in London. Similar scores have been written or reconstructed by Ben Mason, Paul Robinson and Alan Fearon.

Ex. 7.4 John Barry: *Diamonds Are Forever* (aural transcription)

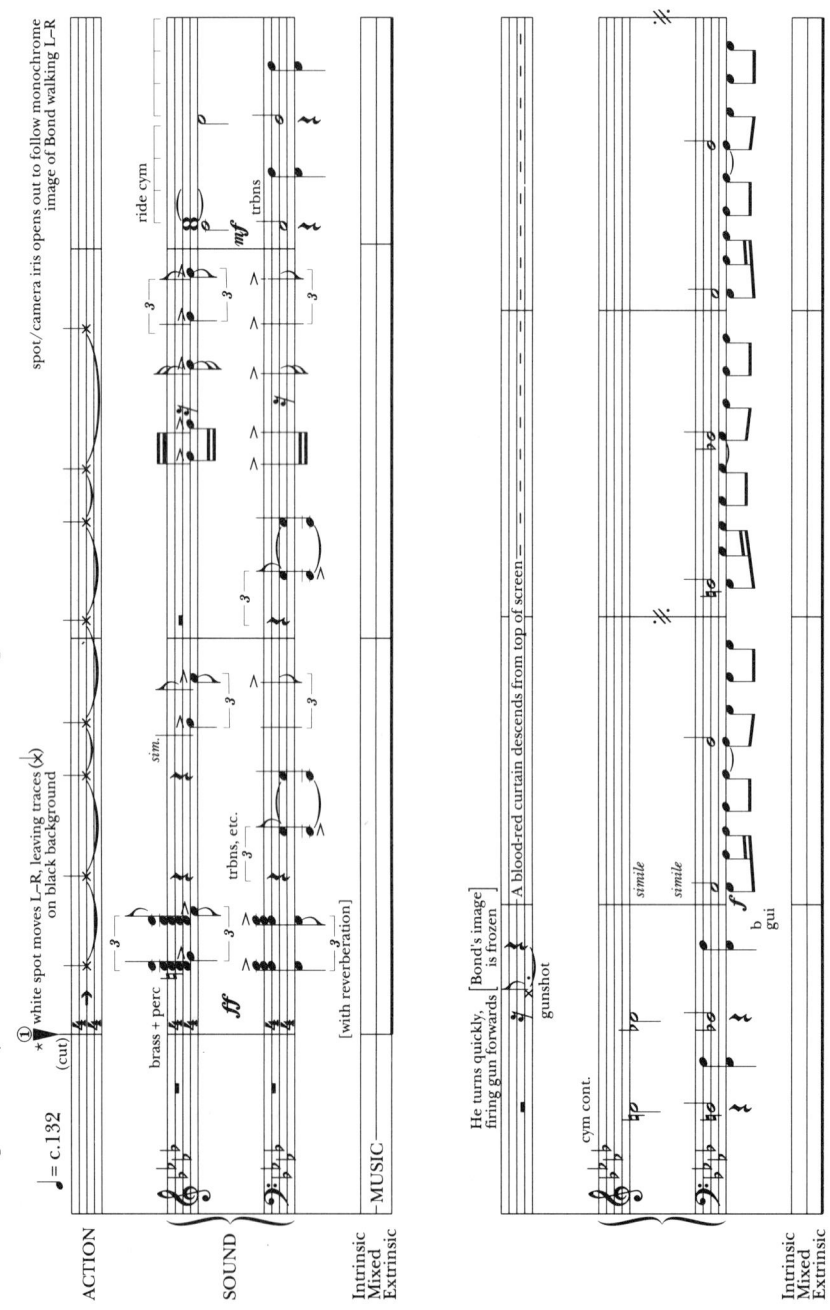

* * this figure anticipates the main title music sung by Shirley Bassey.

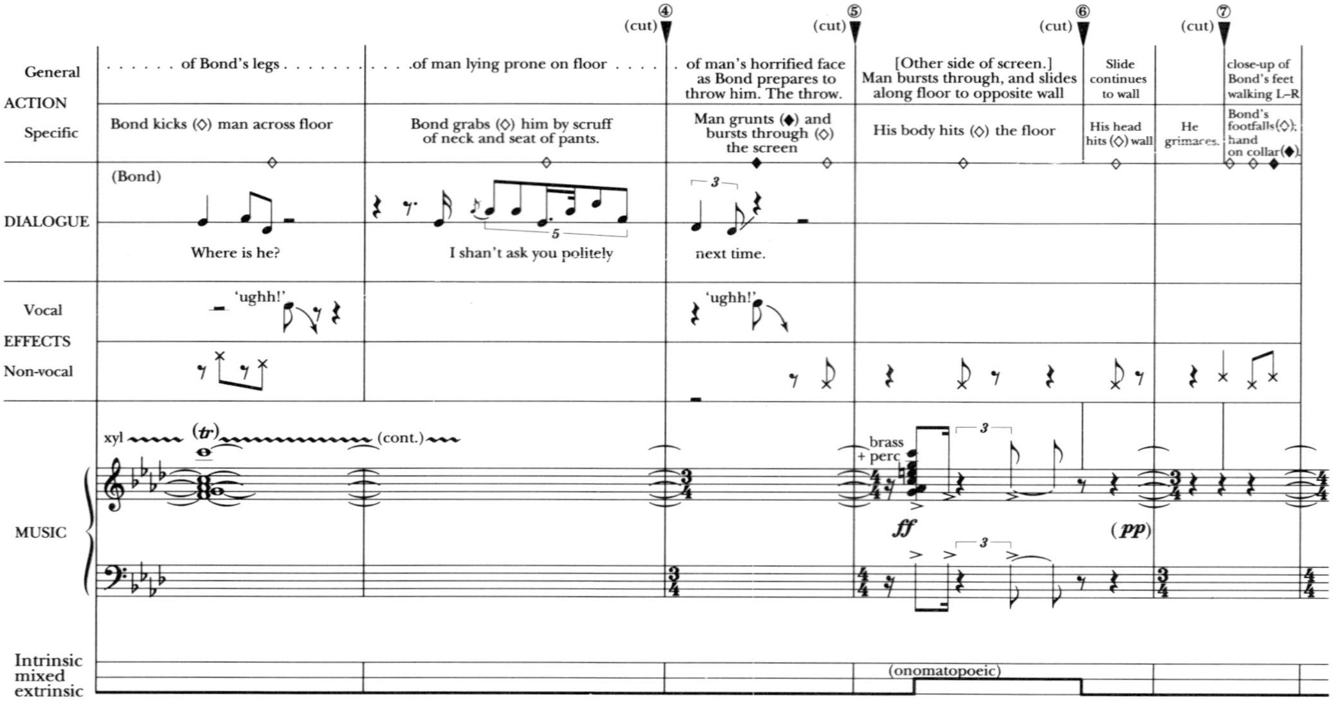

(cut) ④
(cut) ⑤
(cut) ⑥
(cut) ⑦
General
ACTION
Specific
DIALOGUE
Vocal
EFFECTS
Non-vocal
MUSIC
Intrinsic
mixed
extrinsic
. . . . . . of Bond's legs . . . .
Bond kicks (◇) man across floor
(Bond)
Where is he?
'ughh!'
xyl
(tr)
(cont.)
. . . .of man lying prone on floor . . . .
Bond grabs (◇) him by scruff of neck and seat of pants.
I shan't ask you politely
5
. of man's horrified face as Bond prepares to throw him. The throw.
Man grunts (◆) and bursts through (◇) the screen
3
next time.
'ughh!'
[Other side of screen.] Man bursts through, and slides along floor to opposite wall
His body hits (◇) the floor
brass + perc
3
ff
(onomatopoeic)
Slide continues to wall
His head hits (◇) wall
(pp)
He grimaces.
close-up of Bond's feet walking L–R
Bond's footfalls(◇); hand on collar(◆)

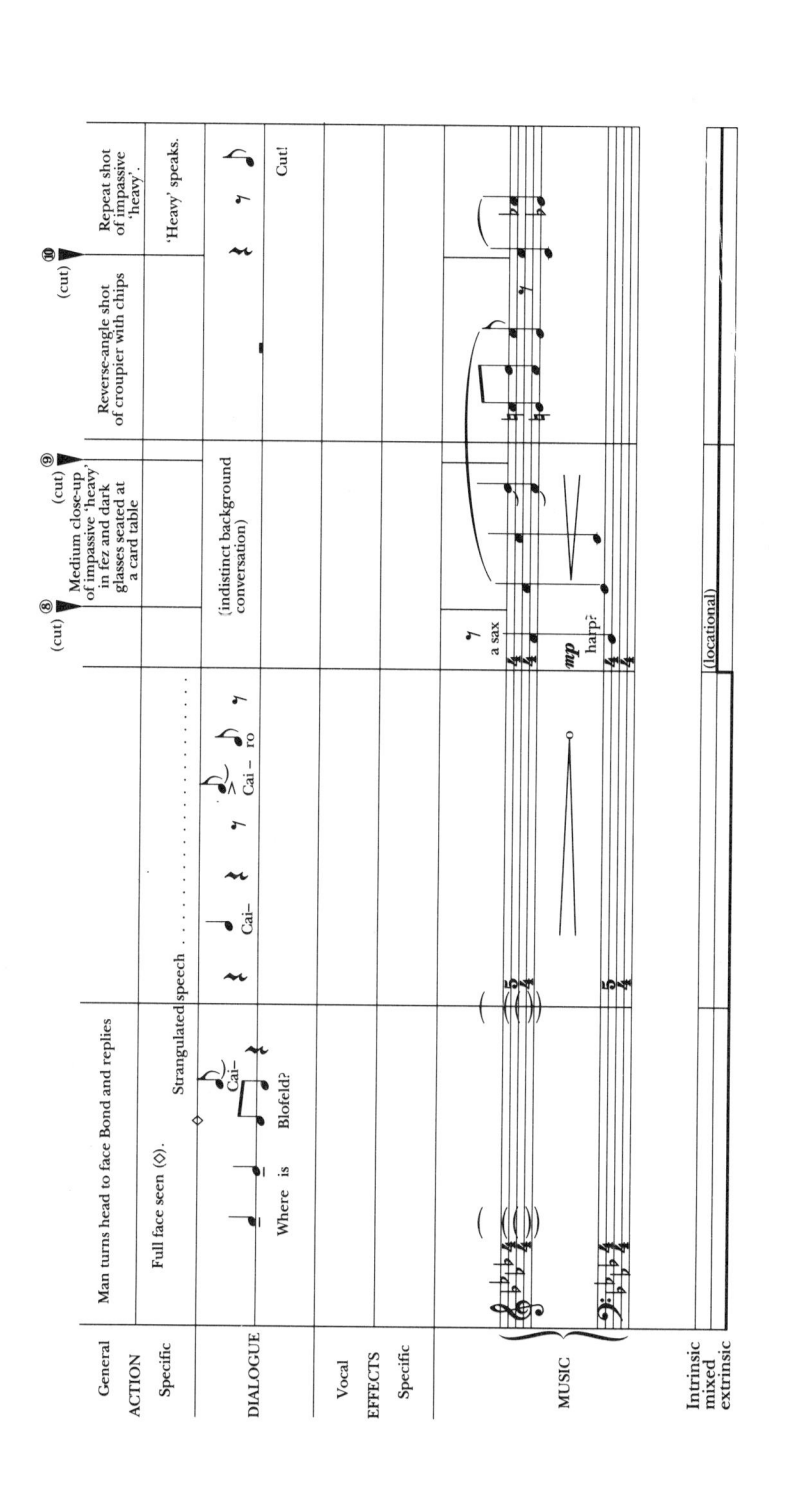

		▶ ⑧ (cut)	▶ ⑨ (cut)		▶ ⑩ (cut)
ACTION General	Man turns head to face Bond and replies		Medium close-up of impassive 'heavy' in fez and dark glasses seated at a card table	Reverse-angle shot of croupier with chips	Repeat shot of impassive 'heavy'.
Specific	Full face seen (◊).	Strangulated speech...........			'Heavy' speaks.
DIALOGUE	Where is Blofeld?	Cai- Cai- ro	(indistinct background conversation)		Cut!
Vocal					
EFFECTS Specific					
MUSIC			a sax mp harp?		
Intrinsic mixed extrinsic			(locational)		

POPULAR MUSIC

In the 1980s Stanley Myers (1930–93) became known as composer to such films as *Moonlighting* (1982), *The Honorary Consul* (1983) and *Prick Up Your Ears* (1987), but the British film industry was by then in continuing decline, despite major successes such as *Chariots of Fire* (1984), *Gandhi* (1982), *A Passage to India* (1984) and *The Killing Fields* (1984), this last with music by Mike Oldfield. The promotion of British Film Year in 1985 did much to raise the profile of present and past achievements but did not secure the essential finance to allow significant production. The later 1960s and early 1970s had seen the rise of an independent avant-garde cinema, centred in Britain on the London Filmmakers' Cooperative. Their films rejected the conventional narrative framework and representation of the dominant ideology in favour of a concentration on the filmic material and upon its shaping of time, often in broad analogy to musical structuring. The work of Malcolm Le Grice (*b* 1940) exemplifies such concerns (see Le Grice 1977). Such experimentation was later assimilated by mainstream cinema (particularly in commercials and music videos). Michael Nyman worked extensively with the avant-garde director Peter Greenaway in *The Draughtsman's Contract* (1982), *Drowning By Numbers* (1988), *The Cook, the Thief, His Wife and Her Lover* (1989), and *Prospero's Books* (1991). The predominantly self-subsistent, anempathetic music to the revenge tragedy *The Cook, the Thief, His Wife and Her Lover* is characteristic of Nyman's ritualistic, repetitive scores. Ex. 7.5, already frequently heard with slight variation, occurs at the end of the film, beginning with the intertitle 'Friday'. The thief's wife has arranged a special meal for her boorish husband, namely the body of her bibliophile lover, murdered by the thief and served up by the cook. The music impassively underscores the thief's bluster: 'What's going on in here? Why do I suddenly have to come into my own restaurant like a stranger? Special invitations! Ha, ha, ha!' Its climactic recurrence (heightened by an icily dispassionate trumpet solo) is particularly impressive, when for the only time in the film its pace coincides with screen action: the funereal tread of the processing guests.

Increasingly, British composers looked abroad for work in film, at home turning their attention to music for television. In addition to commissioned scores, there remained a steady demand for 'library music'. This is no other than the present-day equivalent to the vast catalogues of 'mood-music' available to music directors during the silent film period. An example of such off-the-shelf library music was Johnny Pearson's score used for the long-running Yorkshire vet series *All Creatures Great and Small*.

FILM AND TELEVISION MUSIC

Ex. 7.5   Nyman: *The Cook, the Thief, His Wife and Her Lover*
                          (aural transcription)

Television music (featured or background) is commissioned not only for programmes, films and series, but also for signature tunes, station identification signals, interval music, station opening and closing music, music used in test transmissions, and commercials. The composition of music ('jingles') for signature tunes and for commercials demands versatility and a special 'nose' for the identity of the product, it being essential not only to establish a memorable motif within a second or so, but one that can withstand repeated hearings. Johnny Johnston's music for the 'Mild green Fairy Liquid' commercial (1958) was still to be heard in the mid-1980s. Christopher Gunning's 'Martini' theme (1971; subsequently rescored in numerous guises) has enjoyed similar longevity, at one time entering the Top Ten charts. Tony Hatch's signature tune to the Australian soap opera *Neighbours* and Johnny Pearson's *News at Ten* 'ident' also achieve this essential memorability.

By the mid-1980s reputations were increasingly made on the basis of television credits: George Fenton was known not only for his Oscar-nominated scores to *Gandhi* (1982) and *Cry Freedom* (1987) but also for his music to television productions as various as *Jewel in the Crown*, *Bergerac*, and *The Trials of Life* (a fully synthesized score). Other composers noted for their television credits include Geoffrey Burgon, Robert Farnon, Patrick Gowers, Ron Grainer, Ronnie Hazlehurst, Nigel Hess, Wilfred Josephs, Stephen Oliver, Elizabeth Parker (BBC Radiophonic Workshop), Jim Parker, Rachel Portman, and Tim Souster. In an intensely competitive profession, film and television composers are becoming increasingly responsive to the rapidly developing music technology, which has now made it possible for them to notate and record a synchronous film score on their own digital equipment, either for use as a producer's 'demo' guide before recording with live musicians or indeed as an electronically synthesized final product. Their control of the medium has never been greater.

Chapter 8

AMATEUR MUSICIANS AND THEIR REPERTOIRE

DAVE RUSSELL

I: The Field

Early twentieth-century Britain inherited rich traditions of amateur music-making. They divided broadly into six albeit often overlapping areas. Best known to later generations, perhaps, are the formal bodies: choral societies, wind bands and the like. A second sector comprised the far less well documented instrumental groups, untrammelled by formal constitutions and rules and serving mainly as dance bands in a variety of settings. Music-making in church and chapel both by choir and congregation formed another crucial component, as did domestic music-making, informal activity such as singing in pubs, the street and at sporting events and, finally, music in schools. This chapter, using 'amateur' simply as a convenient shorthand denoting those for whom music was essentially a spare-time activity, not a career, examines the development of these strands in the light of the radically altering social and economic conditions within which they have operated. (On 'amateur', see Finnegan 1989: 12–18, Hutchison and Feist 1991: 6–16.)

II: Victorian Musical Societies in Decline

By 1900 the vigorous network of amateur musical societies in Britain embraced such diverse elements as choral and operatic societies, orchestras, brass, military and pipe bands, bugle and drum and fife bands attached to uniformed youth movements, concertina bands and handbell teams. A dearth of statistical evidence hampers detailed measurement of this configuration over the course of the twentieth century, but overall, steady decline appears to have been the norm for most types of organization.

Best guesses indicate falling numbers of brass bands from perhaps 6000–8000 in 1914 to 4000–5000 in 1939 and 2000 in 1990 (D. Russell 1991: 58–60). Even hazy estimation of the national scope of other types of organization is impossible, but local figures are suggestive. Huddersfield and its immediate environs, for example, supported approximately 40 choral societies and six or seven amateur (adult) orchestras at any one time between 1900 and 1914. By the 1980s the figures had fallen to 15–20 and two to three respectively. At the same time, amateur musicians have generally lost their once central place in local musical life and much of the community respect and status that accompanied it; they have become 'hidden musicians' (Finnegan 1989). In the 1920s, leading brass bands could attract several thousand people to open-air concerts. By the 1960s attendances were so reduced that top bands abandoned these engagements. At least until the 1930s, and later in some areas, success in musical competitions was capable of generating levels of celebration now more normally associated with returning professional sports teams, but such demonstrations have become very rare. Media coverage has also diminished, particularly since the 1950s.

Concern for the amateur musical society's health and status was first voiced from about 1906, but it was between the wars, particularly from the mid-1920s, that patterns of decline were firmly established (D. Russell 1987: 242–8). Some of the more marginal institutions virtually died out, few concertina bands, for example, surviving beyond 1939. Of the more established forms, the amateur orchestra and the larger, mixed-voice choral societies were the first to experience difficulty, the musical press expressing increasing concern about recruitment and, more crucially, loss of audiences, from about 1925. By 1938 even as renowned a choir as Henry Coward's Sheffield Musical Union had been forced to amalgamate with another society (Mackerness 1974: 141–8). The brass band movement entered its crisis phase almost a decade later than these other groups, initially protected by deep-rooted patterns of family-based recruitment and lesser dependency on audience revenue. By 1938, however, the *British Bandsman* was recording dissolutions on a hitherto unknown scale, claiming the loss of over 50 bands in Lancashire alone during the year (D. Russell 1991: 59).

The extent of all these problems is further indicated by the establishment of numerous bodies dedicated to the protection of amateur musical life. These included the University Council of Music in Wales (1919), vital in assisting unemployed amateurs in the 1930s,

AMATEUR MUSICIANS AND THEIR REPERTOIRE

the Rural Music Schools movement (now the Benslow Trust) begun by Mary Ibberson in Hertfordshire in 1929, and the National Federation of Music Societies, launched by the Incorporated Society of Musicians with Carnegie Trust backing in 1935 in order to protect those ISM members training and conducting choirs and orchestras from loss of income (anon 1949: 126–33, 198; anon 1951: 8, 30–1).

The Second World War caused so much disruption that clear patterns are not discernible in its immediate aftermath. However, in the mid-1950s the pace of decline visibly accelerated. Even organizations of national repute were not immune, as the Huddersfield Choral Society's experience illustrates (Table 8.1).

Table 8.1

Membership of the Huddersfield Choral Society 1950–1990

Year	Members
1950	326
1955	312
1960	280
1965	238
1970	239
1975	212
1980	218
1985	224
1990	218

Source: Huddersfield Choral Society Annual Reports, Kirklees Central Library

The loss of members in the early 1960s is especially striking. Analysis of other choirs and orchestras, admittedly in the same region, shows broadly similar trends. The Huddersfield statistics suggest at least a stabilization since the mid-1970s and a national survey in 1991 showed affiliation to various umbrella groups for amateur musicians rising in the 1980s (Hutchison and Feist 1991: 20–21). However, if editorials in the specialist press are any indication, informed insiders seem pessimistic about the long-term recovery of either numbers or status.

Numerous factors have contributed to this process of decline. The malign influence of inter-war economic dislocation upon amateur music has been exaggerated by commentators and, in fact, the almost continuous rise in the living standards of the majority of the population from 1920 and particularly from the 1950s, with resultant enhanced consumer choice, has proved a more significant economic challenge (D. Russell 1991: 77–80). The process of secularization has been a further factor, one of specific importance to choral societies. In a society placing ever less emphasis on highly visible, public displays of personal religiosity, the larger choirs with their essentially sacred repertoires rapidly lost their once central entertainment function. This process had begun before 1914, but when combined with the emergence of the other economic and social factors it made the choral societies particularly vulnerable to the loss of audience. At the same time, the shrinking church population has reduced the pool of trained singers, exemplified by the fact that the percentage of singers over 60 in Welsh male voice choirs doubled to 32 per cent during the course of the 1980s, with the number under 30 falling to only 6 per cent (Hutchison and Feist 1991: 29).

The most potent force for change, however, has been the massive increase in the technological media from the 1920s. At one level the sheer weight of alternative forms of musical reproduction must have proved something of a disincentive to music-making of all types, and not simply among potential bandsmen and choristers. In 1990 the 'average Briton' watched 23.51 hours of television per week, and even allowing for the generality of such figures and for the fact that some of this time may simply have replaced that previously absorbed by other 'passive' activity or filled leisure hours that earlier generations did not have, it is surely likely that some of it would have been used for music in earlier periods (*Social Trends* xxii (1992): 177). Above all, new technologies have played a major role in the dissemination of the American-influenced styles of popular music dominant since the second decade of the twentieth century. In essence, many of the older forms of voluntary society were simply marginalized by powerfully promulgated rival forms, by a massive change in taste. The problems faced by brass bands in the late 1930s were a specific manifestation of this: they were attempting to recruit from the first generation of young males fully exposed to the gramophone, radio and 'talkies', with many young musicians and audience members far more attracted by the dance band as a form of musical expression. Television, transistor radios and portable record players had a similar impact in the crucial decade after 1955.

The social structure of amateur societies has, like their social position, changed considerably. Those drawing most heavily on the working-class community in the early twentieth century now exhibit far broader membership profiles, a tendency most marked in brass bands since the 1950s and 1960s and also evident in some orchestras and male voice choirs. This mainly reflects complex changes in class structure wrought by educational and technical processes, whereby individuals and families previously defined in occupational terms as 'working-class' have attained higher social status via promotion, change in job specification and enhanced educational opportunity, rather than any substantial recruitment from the established middle classes.

Shifts in gender balance have also been highly significant. In 1900, although mixed voice choirs were fairly equally balanced, women's choirs were not common and women comprised only a tiny proportion of most amateur orchestras. The brass band and most other instrumental groups were decidedly male republics. Since the 1920s, women have predominated in mixed choirs, comprising from then on about 60 per cent of the choral population. By 1990 they had attained a similar share in the amateur orchestral population (Hutchison and Feist 1991: 26). 'Ladies" choirs, often stimulated by the initiatives of the National Federation of Women's Institutes (1915) and the National Union of Townswomen's Guilds (1929), have increased in number, representing one of the few substantial growth areas of British choral culture this century. Women or, more accurately in the initial stages, girls first appeared in brass bands in the very late 1930s, eventually representing a substantial minority within the movement by the 1990s. Women have also become increasingly active in Scottish pipe bands and in the revival of handbell ringing.

However, although all this represents considerably expanded leisure opportunity for women, it does not necessarily herald any fundamental shift in women's social place. Often, increased access has arisen only owing to the declining number of male recruits, women thereby forming a reserve army of labour in the sphere of leisure as well as employment. At the same time, in high-status groups with plentiful male recruits, such as championship section brass bands, women began to be accepted only in the 1980s, and indeed still encounter hostility in some quarters.

The amateur operatic society was the one Victorian musical institution to avoid most of the problems troubling other groups from the 1920s onwards. Although escalating costs and competition from television caused concern from 1945, this form of musical theatre has remained remarkably virile. An estimated 1,970 companies attracted 4.7 million people to 18,500 United Kingdom performances in 1989–90 (Hutchison and Feist 1991: 37). In the inter-war period their essentially light-hearted repertoire and use of costume and make-up were well suited to a society seeking still respectable yet less overtly 'improving' forms of entertainment. At the same time operatic groups have maintained favour by providing music initially popularized by professionals but rarely available in live professional performance thereafter, thus meeting a market need more centrally than many other organizations.

New forms of voluntary musical society have, of course, emerged during the period since 1914. Kazoo bands, usually known as 'jazz' or 'comic' bands, outlandishly named (for example, the Treorchy Zulus) and even more outlandishly dressed, were in vogue between the early 1920s and late 1930s, especially in areas of high unemployment (Bird 1976; Wharton and Clarke 1979). A variant has emerged since the 1960s in the juvenile marching band, although this is perhaps more akin to an organized youth movement than a musical society, given its intention of providing a 'safe' leisure outlet for the adolescent girls who constitute the largest membership (Grieves 1989: 3).

Another recent addition, with more serious musical intent, is the steel band. Ironically for an institution initially acting as a focus for rival gangs of poor black youths in Port of Spain, steel or 'pan' playing was adopted from the 1950s by schools in areas with a sizeable African-Caribbean population as a strategy for enhancing both multi-racial and musical education. Exposure to steel bands at school has greatly extended the steel band's constituency beyond the Caribbean community. 'No other non-native instrumental ensemble has flourished so strongly in these islands', it has been argued, and indeed, by the late 1980s, some believed that white musicians had probably attained numerical ascendancy in the British steel band movement (Chatburn 1990: 118, 133). Further important growth points from the 1970s include male and female barbershop singing, and the symphonic wind band, with at least 12,500 players in 420 bands in 1990, testimony to the growth of wind tuition in schools (Hutchison and Feist 1991: 43). Overall, however, although these various developments have expanded the range of amateur music, they have not compensated for the decline in either the number or status of the older forms.

III: Choral and Band Repertoire

While many of the older voluntary bodies have experienced difficulty in the changing social climate, their musical horizons and technical capacity have for the most part been substantially broadened and raised. The focus here will be on specialist repertoires not dealt with elsewhere in this volume.

The brass band's musical activity demonstrates both considerable change and continuity. The instrumentation has remained remarkably and, for some, infuriatingly static, the only changes to the typical 24-piece nineteenth-century contesting band being the addition of an extra B♭ solo cornet in the 1950s and the increased use of percussion in contests since 1973 (A. Myers 1991: 169–95). Much nineteenth- and early twentieth-century repertoire has maintained its place, especially certain marches. Key figures here include brass band specialists such as James Ord Hume (1864–1932) and William Rimmer (1862–1936) and composers from the military world, particularly Kenneth Alford (1881–1945), immortalized by 'Colonel Bogey' (1914). Nevertheless, a central feature of the period from around 1910 has been the creation of a distinct repertoire of custom-composed band music with obvious artistic intent. Initially, this involved the commissioning of test-pieces from contemporary composers by contest organizers and band music publishers seeking a beneficial alliance with the musical establishment, and resulted in National Championship test-pieces from Holst (*Moorside Suite*), Elgar (*Severn Suite*), Ireland (*A Downland Suite* and *A Comedy Overture*), Bliss (*Kenilworth*) and Howells (*Pageantry*) between 1928 and 1937. In the 1960s a second spate of commissions, many from arts organizations and individual bands, often county youth bands, began to generate works by Musgrave, Simpson, McCabe, Horovitz, Bourgeois and Birtwistle among others.

In general, however, collaboration between individual 'serious' composers and the brass band has been limited, often largely confined to the production of a single work, although in the 1920s and 1930s Thomas Keighley (1869–?) and Cyril Jenkins (1889–1978), and more recently Derek Bourgeois (*b* 1941), have been exceptions (Howarth and Howarth 1988: 125–47). A combination of the medium's perceived low social and artistic status and adherence to a specific instrumentation that not all find appealing have been mainly responsible for this. A more sustained contribution has come from the following quarters: writers normally bracketed in the field of light music such as Percy Fletcher (1879–1932) and Gilbert Vinter (1909–69); a small but influential group of academically trained composer-practitioners such as Elgar Howarth (*b* 1935) and Edward Gregson (*b* 1945); and composers who have emerged from within the movement itself or from associated fields such as the Salvation Army. The

POPULAR MUSIC

most striking example of the last is Eric Ball (1903–89), whose works, notably *Resurgam* (1950), have proved immensely popular.

These new compositions, whatever their source, have greatly extended the technical ability of bandsmen, testing the whole band rather than allowing soloists to shoulder the burden as they had done before 1900. Ex. 8.1a and b, extracts from test-pieces of 1900 and 1981 respectively, illustrate this well.

Ex. 8.1a 'Gems from Sullivan's Operas', arr. J. Ord Hume (1900)

Ex. 8.1b Edward Gregson: *Connotations* for brass band

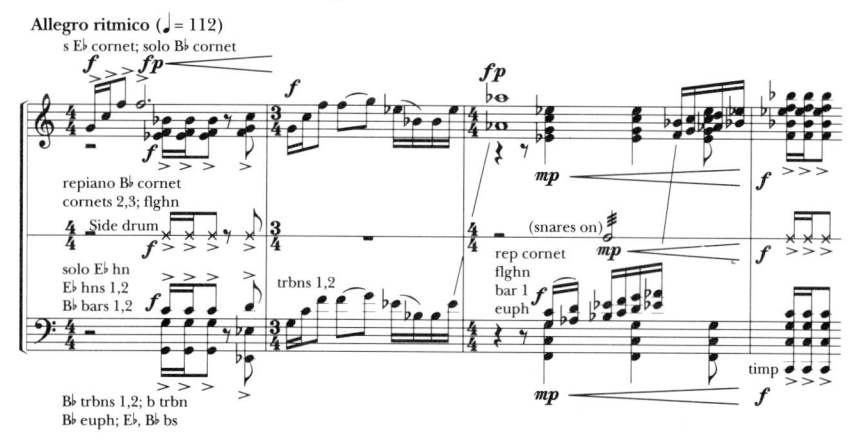

Similarly, from the early 1960s sustained attempts have been made to familiarize players and audiences with some modern currents, composers like Vinter, Howarth, Bourgeois and Gregson working within fairly conservative bounds while giving in Gregson's words 'a flavour of the contemporary idiom' (Brand 1979: 141). The opening chords of Bourgeois's *Blitz*, for example, fit this prescription (Ex. 8.2). A few have gone further, notably Birtwistle in the bleak, dissonant and controversial *Grimethorpe Aria* (1973), Paul Patterson in *Cataclysm* (1973), with its aleatoric passages, and Robert Lennon, whose *Songs of the Aristos* marries band and electroacoustic music (Brand 1979: 139–51; Howarth and Howarth 1988: 148–62).

It is extremely doubtful, however, whether much of this recently composed music has made a deep impression on either performers or audience. Many players still see themselves as defenders of a specific musical tradition with an instrumentation and language rooted in the nineteenth and early twentieth centuries, and one of the most progressive bands of recent decades surprised a new conductor by wanting to play 'much more conventional material, traditional material – a march, an overture, an old-fashioned cornet solo, ending up with the "1812"' (A. Taylor 1983: 203). Similarly, although works like Gregson's *Connotations* (1977 – see Ex. 8.1b) have passed into the mainstream repertoire, most others have not, an amalgam of the older band repertoire, of Broadway musicals, contemporary ballads and the 'light music' compositions and arrangements of national and folk-songs by composers such as Gordon Langford (*b* 1930) being more to the taste of most audiences (Gammond and Horricks 1980: 80–81).

POPULAR MUSIC

Ex. 8.2   Derek Bourgeois: *Blitz*, op. 65

The choral repertoire has perhaps been more marked by regional and local variation and more prone to the tastes of individual conductors than the brass band movement, which has always been driven more directly from the centre. The emphasis placed on arrangements of Scottish folksongs by the Glasgow Orpheus Choir under Hugh Roberton (1878–1952) is a case in point. Interestingly, the male voice choir has, like the brass band, had only a relatively limited relationship with mainstream art composers, although Granville Bantock and, once again, Cyril Jenkins have been exceptions. As with bands, it is tempting to argue that at least part of the cause stems from the *social* distance between choir and composer.

Most of the small and medium-sized mixed and male voice choirs have embraced a far broader range of music than had been the case before the First World War. Increased levels of concert work and, as with brass bands, the rise since the 1970s of entertainment contests demanding multiple test-pieces in 'contrasting styles' have been important here. Among the most notable additions have been spirituals, common from the 1920s, settings of folksongs (although this had begun before 1914), arrangements of nursery rhymes and children's songs, especially the settings by Michael Diack much used by 'Ladies" choirs and, in recent decades, songs from musicals and popular standards by Lennon and McCartney, Bacharach, Paul Simon and others. Many of Elgar's mixed-voice partsongs, often rearranged for other voice settings, have retained popularity.

Savoy opera lies at the core of the amateur operatic tradition, the two indeed virtually synonymous at least until the 1930s. Many societies performed Gilbert and Sullivan almost exclusively in the first two or three decades of the century, save only for the odd piece by a local composer or 'starter' works like *Rajah of Rajpore*. Baily's comment that amateur performance of Gilbert and Sullivan 'has done a great deal to strengthen the hold of these operas on the British public' is an understatement (L. Baily 1973: 59). In the early 1990s, after the Savoy operas, which still comprise about 15–20 per cent of all performances, the Broadway musicals of the 1940s and 1950s, especially *South Pacific*, *Carousel* and *Oklahoma!*, are the most frequently performed works, although shows from earlier periods, notably *The Merry Widow*, have a strong place and new pieces are continually being absorbed.

A significant minority of companies have also performed grand opera, a few exclusively so. In the inter-war period the Falmouth Opera Singers and the Glasgow Grand Opera Society gained national reputations for their performance of previously neglected or unperformed works. Falmouth's record included Purcell's *King Arthur* (1924) and Gluck's *Orfeo ed Euridice* (1925), and the Glasgow Society under Scottish composer Erik Chisholm gave the British première of Berlioz's *The Trojans* in 1934 (Roscow 1991: 144–5, 137–9). This pioneering amateur tradition took on a new guise in the 1980s as amateur groups paralleled professional attempts to make opera accessible to wider audiences. The Yorkshire-based Airedale Opera, for example, took *The Barber of Seville* to four small Yorkshire and Lancashire towns in 1990–91 (Mentor 1991: 9).

The repertoire of the larger oratorio choirs contains some clear continuities from the Victorian and Edwardian periods. *Messiah*, an indispensable part of Britain's musical Christmas and essential to the balance sheets of numerous societies, has remained by a great distance the most performed and best-known oratorio, *The Dream of Gerontius* probably its closest rival. Many Victorian favourites, however, had ceased being performed by the 1920s, including *Samson, St Paul, The Seasons, The Last Judgment* and Rossini's *Stabat mater*. To an extent these lost ground to new compositions, but the declining status of oratorio at the expense of orchestral and instrumental music over the course of the century has meant primarily that expansion of the repertoire for oratorio choirs, especially from the 1970s, has been based on exploration of the pre-1900 canon. Once again, an important sector of the British musical community has not engaged with the musical languages of the later twentieth century. The Brahms and Fauré Requiems are among the more frequently performed outcomes of the search, and it is interesting that an overtly secular society has shown such interest in this music in recent decades. Many commentators have noted that declining religious attendance has not been accompanied by a general diminution in basic religious beliefs; perhaps one of the choral societies' unintended functions, and indeed that of a number of other bodies that engage with sacred music, has been to play a small part in maintaining people's broad sense of religion.

IV: Small Groups: Dance Bands, Pop Groups and the Folk Revival

Possibly the most dynamic growth in the field of amateur music since 1920 has emanated from the world of small, informally constituted bands, often dedicated to the performance of American or American-influenced popular music. Small groups separate from the formal societies had existed in profusion in the nineteenth century. Most were essentially dance bands led by fiddle, melodeon or concertina and, particularly away from major urban centres, often performing traditional tunes. Many carried on into the 1930s and later, especially in some English rural areas, among the Irish and Jewish communities in mainland Britain and in many parts of Scotland and Northern Ireland, where they happily coexisted with the new American-style bands, indeed sometimes borrowing their repertoire. There was certainly sufficient demand for Scottish dance music in the 1930s to allow Fife miner and button-accordionist Jimmy Shand to turn professional (O'Connor 1991: 150–51; Emmerson 1971: 112–14).

AMATEUR MUSICIANS AND THEIR REPERTOIRE

What distinguished the new arrivals from the 1920s, however, was their general reliance on new American-style repertoires and instrumentation, trumpet and saxophone emerging as the favoured lead instruments. The first such bands were established by the early 1920s, quickly growing in number to meet the expanding social dance market. By the 1930s there were thousands, ranging from scratch groups to semi-professional bands with dance hall and hotel residencies and appearances in the *Melody Maker* dance-band competitions (Hustwitt 1983; Pritchard 1988; R. Thomson 1989). Along with jazz bands, they held sway until the mid-1950s, when a range of alternative forms emerged, notably skiffle – rarely taken seriously by commentators but briefly a genuine mass amateur movement providing an entry point into music for many young men – followed from the late 1950s by the multifarious and mainly guitar-led pop, rock, folk and country groups. Largely male-dominated, dance and jazz bands and pop and rock groups have mostly comprised 18- to 30-year-olds, with this age group especially important at seminal moments when new forms of popular music have emerged. Most dance bands of the 1920s, revivalist jazz bands of the 1940s and pop groups of the 1950s and early 1960s were composed of teenagers and those in their early twenties, although once established, most genres have retained some practitioners as they grow older.

Much of the small-group repertoire has essentially followed that offered by the professional role models discussed elsewhere in this volume. This is not to deny the potential for proselytization, innovation and creativity among amateur popular musicians. The first revivalist jazz bands such as George Webb's Dixielanders were essentially amateur (Godbolt 1984: 200–207; see also Chapter 4). Some of the most striking examples of creativity at amateur level stem from ethnic minority musics, where exposure to Western styles has led to the forging of new genres. In the 1970s, for example, the Derby-based Ukrainian folk band Odessa adopted electric instruments and percussion to accompany Ukrainian folksongs, resulting in a possibly unique folk-rock style (Khan 1977: 48–9). A more wide-ranging example is afforded by the development of bhangra since the early 1980s. Although professional record producers have exerted important influence, in its modern guise as an amalgam of Punjabi folk music and Western disco it owes much to amateur and semi-professional players. Unlike most successful pop bands, leading bhangra groups such as Alaap and Heera have maintained an effectively amateur status, influenced by a combination of economic constraints and a sense of community service (Banerji and Baumann 1990: 150–52).

Although, as these examples illustrate, 'folk music' has interrelated with African–American music in profitable ways, folk musics do represent a separate current in the popular repertoire, and one in which the contribution of non-professionals has been central. (On the vital issue of defining 'folk', see Pickering 1990.) Most minority ethnic groups in Britain have made vigorous attempts to maintain folk-music cultures, often organizing classes for children such as those sponsored by the Irish traditional music association, Comhaltas Ceoltoírí Eireann, since 1945. Eastern European communities, sometimes driven by concern over the obliteration of folk cultures by state intervention in their homelands, have been notably active in this area (Khan 1977: 41–52).

The period from the mid-1950s witnessed a surge of interest in British 'folk' or 'vernacular' music (Boyes 1993; MacKinnon 1993). In Scotland and Ireland, especially in rural areas, this took the form of an intensification of interest in a strong living culture but in England and Wales it was a revival of a highly marginalized one. A Sussex singer recalled that by the 1930s, among young people, 'far from being appreciated[, traditional] songs even met with a good deal of antipathy' (Copper 1971: 184–5; Woods 1979). In many regions of Scotland and Ireland, however, folk music and dance had remained central, nowhere more so than in the Shetland Islands, where a distinctive and popular form of fiddle playing heavily influenced by Norwegian music had maintained deep roots. Leading exponent Tom Anderson (1910–91) was training 170 Shetland school children in folk fiddle by the 1970s, worrying some who felt that the healthy state of Shetland fiddling 'was detrimental to the study of the violin in its classical context' (Popplewell 1984: 251; C. MacDonald 1991: 8).

In England and urban Britain limited lines of communication between folk and the wider musical culture were kept open in the 1940s and early 1950s by the BBC and the English Folk Dance and Song Society (1932), but the key point in the revival came around 1956–7 when sections of the skiffle movement seeking an expanded repertoire encountered evangelizing revivalists, most notably Bert Lloyd (1908–82) and Ewan MacColl. Skifflers brought with them guitars, establishing the instrument as central to a tradition within which it had little previous standing.

The emphasis placed by MacColl, Lloyd and others on the value of traditional British music stemmed at least in part from their

AMATEUR MUSICIANS AND THEIR REPERTOIRE

Communist allegiances: along with many others on the left, they saw the music as a counterweight to the supposedly de-politicizing products of the American entertainment industry (Harker 1985: 250). Whether they shared that political perspective or not, many people turned enthusiastically to folk music. MacColl's Ballads and Blues Club in High Holborn which opened in 1953/4 (accounts vary) was probably the first 'folk club', and a national network of several hundred clubs was in existence by the mid-1960s. While never a mass movement, the revival initially attracted a working-class following, MacColl claiming that a survey of his club in 1967 revealed 67 per cent of members as manual workers under 24. By the 1980s, however, Finnegan could say of Milton Keynes's folk community: 'If any of the local musical worlds could be regarded as "middle class" it was that of folk music' (MacColl 1990: 293; Finnegan 1989: 68).

Although riven by arguments over authenticity and the supposed superiority of one type of music over another, folk clubs often operated a very liberal musical policy, embracing by the late 1960s 'contemporary folk', acoustic blues and ragtime alongside traditional music. Their encouragement of 'floorsingers', members of the audience singing two or three pieces, made them an important training ground for public performance. Somewhat depressed by the late 1970s, folk music, especially traditional music, enjoyed a revival in the 1980s as part of the wider 'roots' or 'world music' movement, although the number of clubs may have fallen during this decade. The 1970s and 1980s also witnessed a growing interest in ritual dance and its music (*English Folk Dance and Song Society Directory*, 1981, 1985, 1991).

One of the most striking features of all small-group amateur music has been its preference for a whole gamut of informal self- and group teaching methods rather than the more formal teacher-controlled music lessons associated with the art music traditon. Many popular musicians have received formal teaching, but many more have learnt by playing along to records or tapes, by watching fellow musicians and by self-study of instructional tutors and, more recently, videos. Much of this takes place without recourse to traditional notation, musicians playing by ear or using alternatives such as guitar tablature, where notes are represented as fret numbers on the relevant string (see Ex. 8.3). Providing study aids for this market, particularly for guitarists, has become an important specialist element of the music publishing business. Bert Weedon's *Play in a*

Day, its sales of over 2 million copies since its publication in 1957 an indication of the size of the guitar-playing population, is surely one of the key music educational texts of the century (Weedon 1991).

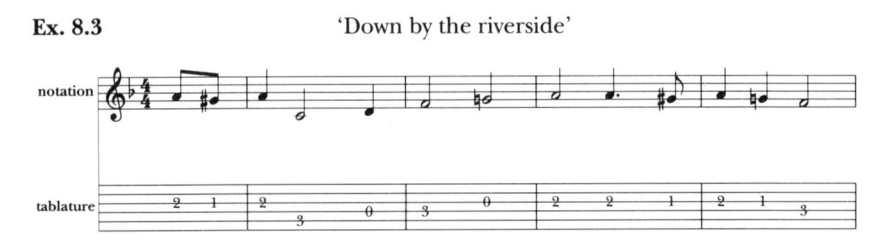

Ex. 8.3   'Down by the riverside'

V: Domestic and Informal Community Music

Both individual and group domestic music-making were major features of social life at almost all levels of Victorian and Edwardian society, and here lies another area of amateur musical heritage radically altered from the 1920s. An informed student of the period has talked of 'the collapse' of domestic music-making by the early 1930s (Ehrlich 1985: 209). This comment clearly refers to the piano-based, parlour-centred tradition, and in that context the argument is incontrovertible. Musical instrument manufacture and retail statistics, a valuable guide to the health of such domestic activity, reveal that annual British consumer expenditure on instruments and sheet music fell from an estimated £9 million in 1924 to £6 million in 1930 and £5 million in 1935, while, significantly, expenditure on radios and gramophones rose in the same 11-year period from £7 million to £27 million (Ehrlich 1976: 188–90). Taken alongside the panicky utterances of underemployed private music teachers, these figures lend weight to the idea of the inter-war period as one of profound change for amateur musicians.

It should of course be remembered that the 'parlour' tradition was only one type, albeit the most common, of domestic music-making, and among certain groups such as travellers, and in rural areas, especially in Scotland and Northern Ireland, other traditions continued unabated into the 1920s and beyond. Much domestic music-making had, though, fallen victim to changed circumstance. As the above figures show, competition from the new technological media was once again a major factor, although the situation was exacerbated by the piano's loss of social cachet in the face of new status symbols, the motor car in particular (Ehrlich 1976: 184–5). Local statistics, Huddersfield again serving as a case study, show how deep-seated these changes in musical habit were. In 1937 the number of local musical instrument dealers, tuners and repairers, tradesmen largely dependent on the domestic market, stood at 19; by 1954 the figure had fallen to seven. Only in the 1980s did the trend reverse, the 11 entries in a 1987 directory perhaps offering another hint that the late twentieth century has witnessed a slight revival in levels of music-making.

The 'home' obviously continues to play a role as a centre for musical education, practice and performance. Some sections of the community admittedly have little share in all this for economic and/or cultural reasons. As in the nineteenth century, the very poorest have largely found any sustained involvement in what is often an expensive hobby difficult, while many of Britain's Muslims, especially those from strongly orthodox rural communities, have traditionally shown little interest in domestic music-making with its 'worldly' overtones (Khan 1977: 85; J. Baily 1990: 157–8). For the majority, however, there are many options. New instruments, especially the guitar and electronic organs and keyboards, some of the latter equipped with earphones to allow performance with minimal household disruption, have emerged since the 1950s, filling the gap left by the piano, in itself still a far from uncommon feature of British houses. The organ-with-headphone suggests a change in the nature of domestic music-making, the rise of solo playing at the expense of the communal element. Obviously, ensemble singing and playing still take place; the home is an important focus for amateur chamber groups and for the performance of Indian classical musics, to give just two examples, but solo modes seem to predominate. It is also likely, partly as a corollary of this, that the home has become more of a site for the practice of music eventually to be performed elsewhere than a locale for the performance of a finished product.

'Informal community music', an ungainly term, is used here as a convenient umbrella under which to group the inchoate collection of practices embracing music made in pubs, at social clubs, in the street and at public gatherings. Performers in these locales have been termed with good cause the 'real "hidden" music-makers', bequeathing very little written evidence and attracting precious little scholarly attention (I. Russell 1990: 90). The most common mode of such music-making is singing. The public house has long been a major location (and also for instrumental performance), its activity sometimes focused on solo performance, sometimes on spontaneous group sing-songs. Not dissimilar patterns can be discerned in various working men's clubs, social clubs, pensioners' groups and so forth. The pub and club repertoire has always been dependent to a degree on geographical and social location, a study of Suffolk pub singing in the 1930s demonstrating differences even within one building, farm labourers singing mainly country songs in the taproom, farmers and tradesmen parlour ballads in the best room (Dunn 1980: 47–8). The street, another Victorian musical arena, remained a centre for performance well into the century, Ewan MacColl recalling that light operatic arias were included in the repertoire of the 'back entry singers' of Salford (MacColl 1990: 68). Public gatherings afforded further opportunity, Arthur Bliss noting the quality of pre-match singing, probably of hymns and contemporary popular songs, among rugby crowds in Wales and Cornwall in the 1930s (Roscow 1991: 143).

Bliss seems to have been describing spontaneous singing, but public gatherings were also the occasion for formally organized large group singing. The Victorians had long favoured mass hymn-singing, often to raise money for charities, particularly hospitals, but during the First World War such activity was armed with a more secular repertoire and dignified by the new North American label of 'community singing'. The *Daily Express* became heavily associated with this phenomenon via a much publicized series of gatherings at the Albert Hall in 1926 and sponsorship of the singing at Wembley FA Cup finals. It was at the 1927 final that song-leader T. R. Farrell closed the singing with 'Abide with me', thus establishing one of Britain's most commented-on, if little investigated, socio-musical rituals (Scholes 1938: 211–12; Garland 1957: 125–9).

Despite vigorous exceptions such as the South Yorkshire pub carolling tradition, most of these types of music-making have probably been in overall decline since the 1950s (I. Russell 1970, 1973). The opportunity for pub performance, for example, has no doubt diminished since the 1960s. New marketing styles have resulted in the introduction of jukeboxes and architectural devices, especially the amalgamation of rooms into single bars, which make the organization of singing harder, particularly as singing outside of a specially designated room is now often deemed rowdy (the popularity of Japanese karaoke sessions from the late 1980s runs counter to this trend but hardly amounts to a reversal). Increased access to mechanical means of musical reproduction, improvements in home comfort and changing concepts of appropriate public behaviour have largely ended street singing. Some sports crowds still sing but in soccer at least this aspect of spectating has largely been hi-jacked by the 'ends', the younger fans congregated behind the goals. This was demonstrated in the 1970s when the organized pre-cup final sing-song was gradually abandoned because younger fans consistently chose to sing (very loudly) their own songs rather than those on the *Daily Express* songsheet, an effective comment on attitudes to formal community singing.

VI: Church and Chapel

Church and chapel were at the heart of much nineteenth-century popular musical life, as training grounds for secular musical societies and providing an important element in many people's musical experience through both congregational singing and the sacred choral concerts which punctuated the religious calendar. Clearly this stemmed from the centrality of organized religion in contemporary society. However, from the late nineteenth century and more particularly over the course of the twentieth, Britain has evolved into what is frequently termed a post-Christian society, the proportion of the British population attending church falling from some 40–50 per cent in 1851 to only 11 per cent in 1980 (Brown 1989: 213). While allowing for considerable regional and denominational variation, since about 1965 all indices of formal religious activity have 'presented a picture of massive crisis' (Gilbert 1980: 77).

These fundamental changes could hardly have failed to exert profound influence upon patterns of church music-making. Most obviously, churches have often experienced difficulty in recruiting musicians. Young male choristers have proved notably difficult to recruit, especially since 1950, women thereby making up a far higher proportion of choir membership than in 1900 (Long 1972: 338–90; Temperley 1979: 337–8; Finnegan 1989: 212). A more recent problem has been the shortage of organists, which gave rise to the National Learn-the-Organ Year campaign of 1990. This was successful at least in the short term, encouraging some 1700 people to take up the instrument and overseeing the publication of a new tutor (Barrett 1989; Hale 1991). Partly because of recruitment difficulties, the number of church and chapel choirs has fallen in the last 25 years, a fact that also reflects the increasing tendency for congregations to combine with others in order to make services viable, and the demolition and deconsecration of churches stranded by population shifts and changing sensibilities. Between 1970 and 1987 the number of British congregations fell from some 53,500 to 49,500 (Brierley 1988: 154). Certain aspects of the churches' function as entertainment centres have also diminished. At least until 1939, the sacred concert, with *Olivet to Calvary* and *Crucifixion* the Easter favourites, *Messiah* almost obligatory at Christmas, seems to have held its own. From that point it has become increasingly rare. In 1952, for example, eight Bradford churches and chapels gave Christmas performances of *Messiah*. By 1965 the number had fallen to four, by 1975 to one. In 1985 the local press had no record of church or chapel performance of the work.

There have been countervailing tendencies at work. Many of Britain's non-Christian faiths make extensive use of music, while certain Christian sects such as the so-called 'Black Churches' which have grown considerably also place a strong emphasis on it; the consequent expansion of British gospel music has been an important growth point within amateur music in the 1970s and 1980s (Broughton 1985). Many churches encourage small instrumental ensembles, such as recorder groups, which help compensate for the lack of a choir or supplement its work. It is also of considerable importance that the twentieth century has witnessed increased congregational involvement in church singing where this had not previously been the dominant practice or had passed out of fashion; it has been one of the most striking developments in Anglican church music (Routley 1964: 99–100). This trend, established before 1914, was accelerated by the First World War, army chaplains appreciating the congregational need for maximum involvement. By 1922, the Archbishops' committee report *Music in Worship* could claim that 'the ideal in all parish churches is congregational singing', an ideal arguably the norm by 1950 (Temperley 1979: 327).

The best generalization in regard to formal worship music might therefore be that fewer specialist musicians 'perform' to considerably diminished congregations which, however, are more musically active than at the beginning of the century. At the same time, the decline of sacred and other church concerts amounts to a substantially reduced role for the church as a centre of musical production. Overall, the sense of declining numbers and influence is predominant.

The churches' constant need to attract followers has resulted in a number of liturgical changes which have influenced the nature of church music. Most striking has been the elevation of parish communion within the established church to a position of pre-eminence, a process largely carried out between 1939 and 1965 (Temperley 1979: 332–3). Many choirs have thus become less well versed in the musical liturgy associated with morning and evening services. Increased congregational singing has also led to some important changes in the nature of performance. More sensitive supporters of congregational singing such as Vaughan Williams and Percy Dearmer appreciated that choirs and organists might be angered by an apparent diminution of their roles, and were careful to allow for certain verses to be sung by choir alone, sometimes in full harmony. Another fruitful compromise has been the provision of descants (Temperley 1979: 324–5).

As with most other areas of voluntary musical culture, the twentieth century has witnessed a substantial broadening of repertoire among almost all denominations. Increased public access to the media has once again played an important role, programmes such as BBC Radio's *Sunday Half Hour* (1941) and BBC Television's *Songs of Praise* allowing for the rapid dissemination of new hymn tunes. Certain developments in repertoire, particularly the engagement with pop music, can be located in the churches' concern over their position in society. A key pioneer here was Rev Geoffrey Beaumont (1905–71), whose *Anglican Folk Mass* (1956), a setting of the liturgy of the Eucharist, caused heated debate following its televising in 1957. A group of like-minded Anglican clergymen and composers founded the Twentieth Century Church Light Music Group to sponsor works which would have a direct appeal to those, especially the young, who, it was believed, found the church too formal and traditional (Routley 1964: 163–4).

Many of the pieces, mainly hymns, that resulted were written by amateur enthusiasts, although some serious composers also contributed, notably Malcolm Williamson with *Adoremus, Procession of Palms* and his collection *Hymn Tunes* (1962). Much of this music might be better termed 'light' than 'pop', if the latter word is used co-terminously with the idioms of the charts favoured by the youth market, Routley noting the similarity between the Sanctus from Beaumont's Mass and Coates's *Dam Busters* march (p. 166), Long that the Mass 'breathes, perhaps somewhat feebly, the spirit of Fred Astaire and Ginger Rogers' (1972: 434). The musical language of much of this music is well captured by the 'Broadway' feel of the tune 'Living Lord' by Patrick Appleford (*b* 1924) (Ex. 8.4); its popularity illustrates that the type has gained a constituency of sorts, though it failed to penetrate as extensively as had been hoped. In some denominations, use of contemporary idioms caused serious tensions. The Joystrings, a Salvation Army female guitar and vocal group that enjoyed two top 40 records in 1964, so upset one minister that he had his church re-dedicated after they had performed in it (Boon 1978: 159–64). Pop and light music have found their greatest devotees among the most evangelical congregations and the independent or 'house' churches featuring in the religious landscape from the 1980s. One modern work deserving special mention is Sydney Carter's 'Lord of the dance', contemporary religious poetry set to a Shaker hymn tune, whose widespread use by most denominations (and schools) has made it a late twentieth-century standard.

Substantial gains have stemmed from the interchange between mainstream composers and the churches. The work of writers such as Britten and Howells is discussed elsewhere in this volume (see Chapter 12), but what might be termed functional, quotidian church music has benefited too. Perhaps the most lasting contributions stem from the first folksong and early music revivals of the late

Ex. 8.4   Patrick Appleford: 'Living Lord'

nineteenth and early twentieth centuries. *The English Hymnal* of 1906, edited by the Anglo-Catholic Percy Dearmer (1867–1936) with Vaughan Williams as music editor, was important in extending the musical vocabulary of the Anglican church and, indeed, some nonconformist churches as the book gained purchase among them from the 1920s. Its stock of tunes included Genevan psalms, English folksongs and their derivatives, and pieces by Tallis, Gibbons and Lawes. The interdenominational *Songs of Praise* (1925), edited by the same team with the addition of Martin Shaw (1875–1958), continued this process as well as adding many new hymns using diatonic and modal devices in strong reaction against the classic Victorian tunes (Long 1972: 424). Nonconformist church music has benefited from the input of the largely self-taught Eric Thiman (1900–75), a Congregationalist and an enormously popular composer of hymns, simple anthems and extended choral works who sought to raise the standard of church (and other amateur) musicians while working within a comfortable harmonic and melodic language.

In the final analysis, however, it is continuity rather than change that marks church repertoire. While much of the new music, whether it be the new hymns in *Songs of Praise* or the light music of the 1960s, has not gained widespread popularity, almost 30 per cent of the tunes in the 1950 version of *Hymns Ancient and Modern* were composed between 1850 and 1880. Temperley has commented that Cyril Taylor's tune 'Abbot's Leigh' from the 1951 *BBC Hymn Book*, one of the most popular new tunes of the century, contains little in musical language that would have 'surprised or dismayed the Victorians' (1979: 340, 343). The increasingly influential evangelical musical agenda – *Mission Praise* (1985) and *Junior Praise* (1986) were the most commonly used hymnbooks in the Anglican church by 1990, according to one major survey – while changing emphasis and broadening repertoire, will ultimately reinforce the musical status quo (anon 1992: 275). Church music perhaps more than any other type is laden with a heavy burden of associated meaning which has imposed firm limits to change.

VII: Music in Schools

Twentieth-century (state) school music has largely been organized around three sometimes conflicting, sometimes complementary paradigms: it has been a vehicle for transmitting certain musical traditions and social values, for stimulating individual creativity, and for making schooling 'relevant' to the wider society (Carlton 1987; Swanwick 1988: 10–17; Rainbow 1989). For much of the period to the 1950s, and indeed beyond for many teachers and certainly many politicians, the former idea predominated; enthusiasts for areas as apparently diverse as folksong and dance and western art music encouraged them as, among other things, a necessary defence against the supposedly detrimental influences of a burgeoning mass culture. Cecil Sharp added a substantial patriotic gloss to his defence of folksong in school, arguing that we could not produce 'citizens distinctly national in type . . . if we bring up our children on German kindergarten games, Swedish dances and foreign music' (C. Sharp 1912: 13).

An ever-broadening repertoire of teaching techniques was deployed to disseminate musical and cultural heritage. Perhaps the major development was music appreciation, 'music' clearly defined here as Western art music. Although of pre-war origin, it came of age when the Gramophone Company (later HMV) published Percy Scholes's *Learning to Listen* in 1921. Although it was viewed with hostility by devotees of class singing, the dominant form of classroom music before 1914, many teachers greeted it enthusiastically, especially the army of non-specialists for whom the weekly singing lesson was a worrying enterprise. Another set of initiatives focused on instrumental activity. Margaret James's bamboo pipe movement, featuring Mediterranean shepherd-style bamboo pipes made by the pupils, gained some popularity from the mid-1920s, only to submit to interest in the recorder and the unavailability of imported bamboo in the late 1930s. The percussion band also gained the approbation of inspectors and policy-makers, and from 1930 came the earliest sustained attempts to start school brass and wind bands (Rainbow 1980; Paynter 1982: 8–12; D. Russell 1991: 63). These new approaches obviously undermined the dominance of singing and, as early as 1927, the Board of Education encouraged use of the timetable appellation 'music' in preference to the then current 'teaching of singing' (Fletcher 1987: 30).

In an important sense these developments in instrumental teaching, with their rather more generous view of children's needs and potential, helped prepare the way for increased emphasis on the second of the contending paradigms as, from the 1950s and 1960s, the so-called 'creative' music movement gained ground. Influenced by music educators such as Carl Orff but also reflecting wider educational currents which emphasized child-centredness and a less restrictive curriculum, teachers encouraged composition via a process of refined improvisation. Many teachers received further stimulation in this respect from the contemporary avant garde (Paynter 1982, Appendix 1). By the end of the 1960s teachers were being asked to consider yet another perspective, as exponents of 'pop music in school', led by Keith Swanwick's *Popular Music and the Teacher* (1968) and Graham Vulliamy and Ed Lee's *Pop Music in School* (1976), focused on the need to relate class music to children's wider musical experience. The mortal enemy that the music teacher had battled against since 1870 was to be embraced.

By the 1980s the great expansion of both range and approach led to a diversity of classroom practice and to what one leading theorist termed a 'pick and mix' curriculum (Swanwick 1988: 17). The problems and possibilities stemming from such a plethora of teacher choice greatly exercised GCSE curriculum designers who, from the inception of the exam in 1986, attempted to give due attention to many facets of music. They have encouraged consideration of pop music, previously often viewed as suitable only for supposedly 'less able' CSE pupils, and allowed improvisation as an alternative to sight-reading, to give but two examples. Debates about the desirability of such a catholic approach have been at the heart of much of the controversy surrounding the National Curriculum, a controversy often rooted in an overtly political agenda (anon 1991b).

The above relates specifically to classroom teaching, but other important dimensions of school music have emerged. A key feature since 1945 has been the extensive provision of instrumental tuition funded by the local authority, often reinforced (and sometimes underpinned) by recourse to private tuition. This has divided educational theorists, some regarding it as the 'most significant musical advance in post-war education', others appreciating its importance but worried that it has detracted from the needs of the majority. Similar disputes have arisen over extra-curricular activity (Fletcher 1987: 33; Paynter 1982: 8; Green 1988: 79). Whatever the merits, the scale of both elements is undeniable. Mainly as a result of school tuition, entries for the examinations of the Associated Board – itself a peculiarly British institution whose pervasiveness deserves the historian's investigation – doubled in the decade to 1976 to reach 244,000 and stood at 345,000 in 1989 (Swanwick 1988: 11; Hutchison and Feist 1991: 44). Finnegan's survey of about half the schools in Milton Keynes estimated that perhaps 10–15 per cent of local children were involved in extra-curricular music in the early 1980s (Finnegan 1989: 198–200).

Inequalities of experience are, of course, apparent. At least until the 1960s and sometimes beyond, these developments bypassed many children. A chronic shortage of trained music teachers in the period to 1945, a problem that has recurred at intervals ever since, limited the extent of change. Moreover, much initial experimentation took place only in the primary sector, the 1963 Newsom Report recording classroom provision of music in only about one half of the secondary schools it surveyed (Paynter 1982: 12–13). Similarly, provision has always tended to be lowest in boys' schools. It was not until the 1940s that music gained any real foothold in the curriculum of boys' secondary schools and boys' opportunities to follow it as an examination subject at 16+ have often been severely restricted, at least outside the mixed comprehensive (anon 1973: 11, 13, 29). Girls also tend to predominate in school choirs and bands, especially among younger age groups.

Evidence concerning the social class base of school music is less obvious. Finnegan's local study suggests that a supportive family background and the enthusiasm of individual music teachers, not class, have been the key determinants of a child's musicality. However, it is difficult to believe that many children from the poorest homes have enjoyed access to the full range of school music given the deterrent costs often involved (Finnegan 1989: 202–3). Crucially, at many times but particularly from the 1980s, teachers have claimed that limited resources have hindered both delivery of new teaching strategies and maintenance of existing provision. The problems of local authority peripatetic instrumental teaching services in the 1980s were a well-publicized example. A 1991 survey suggested that, depending on which set of statistical criteria was used, the level of provision between 1980 and 1990 showed at worst a constant level of provision, at best 'a trend that has shown a general improvement'. However, it also pointed up considerable degrees of local variation and showed the vulnerability of services in moments of political retrenchment (Stimpson 1991). The 6–7 per cent of children in private education have generally experienced far better provision than their state school counterparts. In 1980, for example, while the 800-pupil Marlborough School employed six full-time and 21 peripatetic music staff, the equivalent figures in the 1300-pupil neighbouring comprehensive school were 2 and 1 respectively (Griggs 1985: 68–9).

Repertoire can be dealt with only in general terms here. Until about 1950, most children's experience of making music in school was still devoted to singing, and largely rooted in Western art music from about 1600 to 1900 and British folksong and national song. Some collections of the latter had remarkably long lives, a third edition of Stanford's *The New National Songbook* (1905) appearing as late as 1958, the selection of songs unaltered, only the piano accompaniments changed. Since then opportunities for instrumental performance have increased and the variety of music on offer has widened enormously. A further striking feature of the period has been the amount of music written for children, often aimed initially at specific schools, by composers of stature. Particularly in the last two decades, such writers have shown increasing sensitivity to the needs of non-specialists. The work of David Bedford, a composer with extensive secondary schoolteaching experience, has been important here. His one-act opera for children, *The Rime of the Ancient Mariner*, features kazoos, wine glasses, bottles, bird-warblers, a sound effects choir and a variety of non-standard notations (see Ex. 8.5).

For all the new developments, however, a survey of music in the first three years of operation of some 60 comprehensive schools undertaken in the early 1980s showed that many teachers still privileged a narrow band of art music in their teaching (Green 1988: 56–80). Similarly, although the Associated Board's syllabuses do insist on at least some engagement with twentieth-century currents as well as including a small amount of light and popular music in the lower grade examinations and even at intermediate and higher levels for instruments such as the saxophone, in general choices are weighted towards art music from Purcell to the early twentieth century.

What is unclear is the extent to which musical skills developed in school have been carried through into adult amateur musical activity. The recruitment problems faced by church choirs, choral societies and many orchestras are suggestive. It would be particularly interesting to see which musical pathways have been taken by children learning popular school instruments such as the recorder which have a limited constituency outside schools. These are complex and ill-understood issues, but it is possible that school music is, for many, exactly that, something separate from music 'out there', a kind of rite of passage, and an unpopular one at that according to some surveys, to be abandoned in favour of other leisure activities on leaving school (Swanwick 1988: 141).

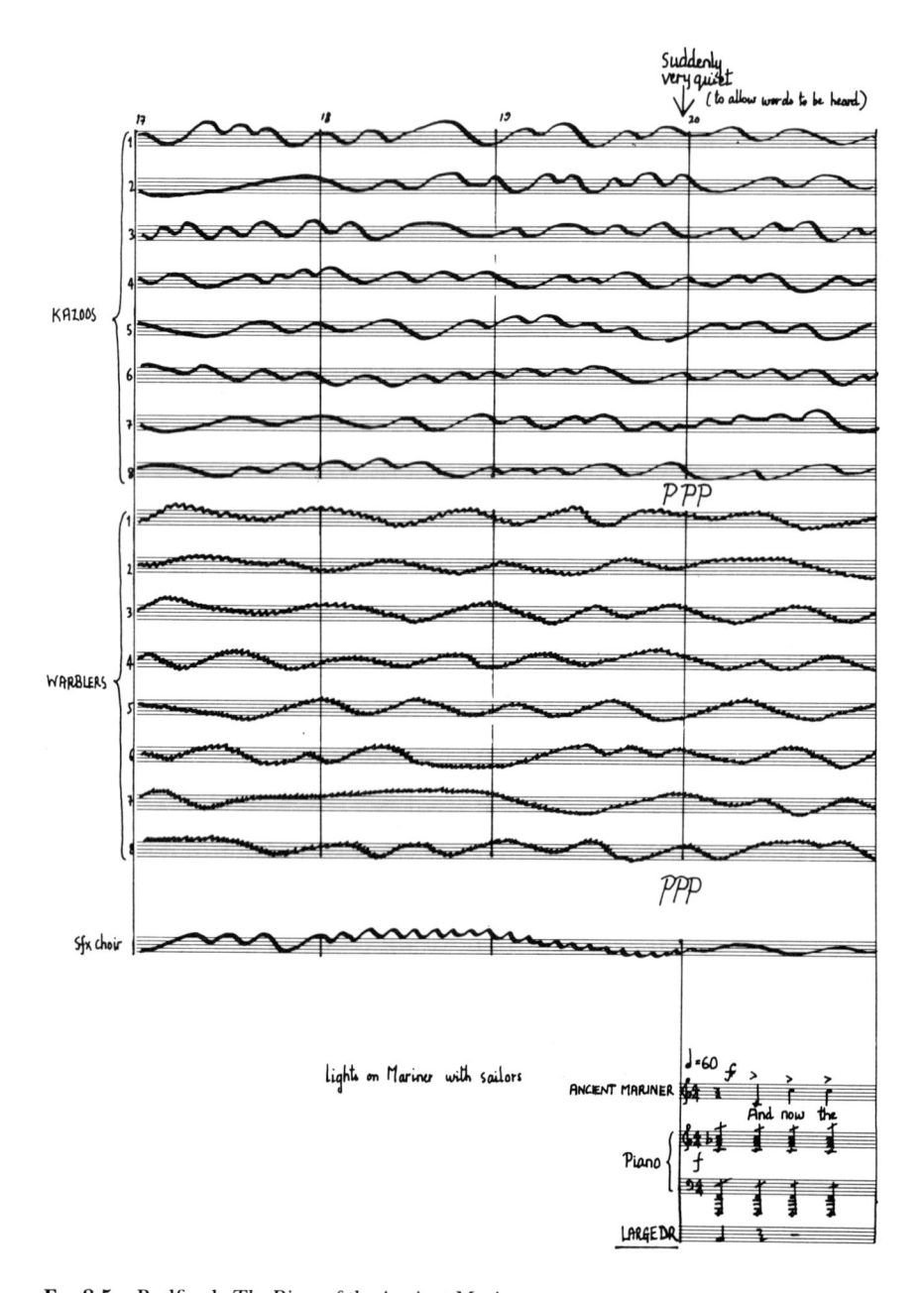

Ex. 8.5 Bedford: *The Rime of the Ancient Mariner*

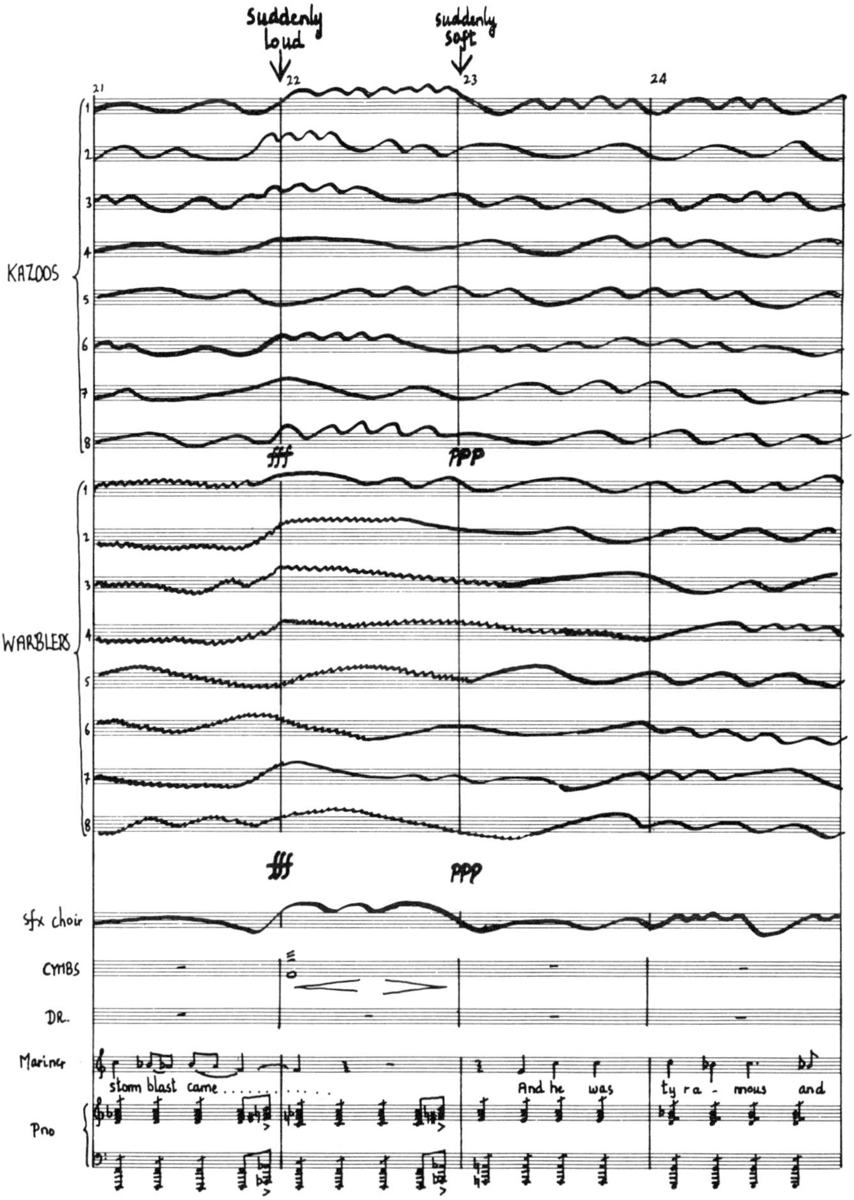

suddenly loud
suddenly soft
21
22
23
24
KAZOOS
WARBLERS
fff
ppp
fff
ppp
Sfx choir
CYMBS
DR.
Mariner
storm blast came . . . . And he was ty ra - mous and
Pno

POPULAR MUSIC

VIII: Overview

Amateur music-making in late twentieth-century Britain is far healthier than pessimistic delineators of mass culture have assumed. Finnegan speculated that 5–6 per cent of Milton Keynes's population was musically active in the 1980s; a 1991 survey suggested a combined membership of 300,000 for 17 national umbrella organizations concerned with formally organized musical performance (Finnegan 1989: 298; Hutchison and Feist 1991: 20–21). This positive picture, however, requires setting in historical context. The issue is complex, but it is likely that the decline within the older voluntary organizations and many areas of church, domestic and informal music-making has not been compensated for by the rise of new forms of amateur performance.

Individuals from a wide social spectrum have followed musical pursuits, probably only the poorest finding access limited; consequently, some commentators have played down issues of class when analysing twentieth-century, especially late twentieth-century, amateur music. Significantly, however, participation rates in formal amateur music-making have clearly been highest among the most affluent groups in recent decades, and while Finnegan argues that most musical worlds are not class-specific, her evidence suggests that some of them actually are (anon 1990: 153; Finnegan 1989: 45, 68, 99, 312, 314). Class can also cut across the musical taste of minority ethnic groups, one writer recalling being 'stoned' by a Southall audience expecting folk dance but receiving classical, which carries strong élitist connotations for many South Asians (Khan 1977: 81). While obsessive focus on class is to be avoided, future research must still pay heed to it.

Divisions along gender lines are striking. Women appear to have been most welcome in and/or most attracted to areas of music-making forced to absorb them in order to survive (some brass bands, church choirs) or bestowed with an aura of respectability and suitability by long accretion of social custom (choral societies, school music groups). They have been most unwelcome and/or most unattracted to those bodies with connotations of masculine gaiety (brass bands not run on the 'family' model) or rebellion and immorality (rock bands). Music throughout the twentieth century has thus both reflected and reinforced patriarchal social relationships, if at the same time, especially since the 1980s, forming the site of some challenges to them.

AMATEUR MUSICIANS AND THEIR REPERTOIRE

A marked pluralism typifies the late twentieth-century repertoire, the broad nineteenth-century base further widened most notably by popular musics drawing on the aesthetics of jazz and rock. Almost all areas of amateur musical life have embraced this music to some degree, albeit sometimes only in search of 'relevance'. However, the availability of so many different types of music, coupled with the ease of access to means of mechanical reproduction, has tended to fracture taste along lines of personal and generational preference. Sacred music and art music probably have a less secure place in the popular repertoire than was the case in 1914 and indeed until as late as the 1950s, although art music still has great kudos for those seeking musical respectability and status. Most art music produced after about 1920 has had only minimal impact on popular tastes.

The period has seen a major shift in styles of musical education, away from formal teacher-centred lessons based on traditional notation, towards greater group and self-tuition utilizing informal learning techniques. Levels of musical literacy as defined and measured from the late nineteenth century may therefore have fallen, even tonic sol-fa, that important Victorian amateur aid, declining in use, probably by 1939 and certainly from the 1950s; but other strategies have developed. Contrary to some opinion, a concern with raising standards has remained. In those areas of amateur music-making characterized by a sense of belonging to a movement, the great stress on making 'better' music has often involved the adoption of correspondence courses and exam systems, the trappings of professional bodies such as colleges. A similar concern for standards can be found in the informal sectors, most guitarists, for example, moving a long way from the simple chord-strumming that often sufficed in the mid-1950s. The musical competition, from the network of eisteddfods and competitive festivals to dance band contests, has been vital in raising standards and broadening horizons across the whole arena of amateur music and has also helped hold and revive interest in certain types of performance, such as Welsh *penillion* singing, and instruments, including the Northumbrian small pipes and the Gaelic small harp or *clarsach*.

One point is undeniable. Amateur musicians have been crucial figures in twentieth-century musical life, stimulating the musical service industries, forming the seedbed for future generations of professionals, and, above all, serving as an important artistic force in their own right. Whole traditions, especially what might be termed 'folk' traditions, often owe their lifeblood to amateurs. Brass bands and choirs have stimulated composition which otherwise would not have existed. Important areas of music, such as revivalist jazz and Savoy opera, have maintained or regained currency largely through amateurs. This record is worthy of respect.

PART III
Art Music

Chapter 9

INSTRUMENTAL MUSIC I

PETER EVANS

Orchestral Music

I: Vaughan Williams and Holst

Turning his attention to British music at the end of a European survey, Cecil Gray asked with heavy irony, 'Why, indeed, should we go abroad for things which we can turn out just as well at home?' He went on, 'In the same way that Stanford and Parry provided us with second-hand Brahms, Cyril Scott provides us with imitation Debussy; Holbrooke and Bantock have followed Strauss, and in the music of Goossens, Bliss and Berners we find our English Ravel, Stravinsky and Satie' (1924: 251). Gray's resounding verdict, that 'the outcome of their combined efforts . . . is precisely nil', seems to be endorsed by the neglect these British composers share today. Excluded from his pairing exercise were Holst and Vaughan Williams, the one because of his compendious and 'mediocre' pastiche, the other because an apparent 'almost sublime incompetence' masked a personality 'wholly and without admixture English' (p. 252).

The view that music was a declining art, prevalent in Europe before the old century had closed, gained currency in Britain rather later, most notably through Gray's writings and those of Constant Lambert between the wars (Lambert 1934). They were not embittered conservatives, but men unusually familiar with the music of the Continental pioneers, and the short shrift allowed their own countrymen makes clear how little they shared that vision of an English 'renaissance' which sustained composers and critics of more parochial sympathies. Yet their pungent discontent may even have helped to confirm in their prejudices musicians already reluctant to plunge too far into the troubled waters of European styles.

An interesting sidelight on some of these styles is afforded by George Dyson's study (1924). The comment made by this traditionally based composer on excerpts from his Continental contemporaries' work is intelligent and often shrewd, but he treats them as curios, without much regard for the wider contexts in which the techniques operate. In the work of many British composers the same impression persists – that radical developments are being observed from without, but that here and there useful pickings may be made in order circumspectly to 'modernize' their own styles. The short focus favoured by Dyson tended to distort theoretical studies in Britain, perhaps because they were usually conducted by men whose day-to-day musical thinking was on the scale of the hymn and the chant. Their view of 'harmonization' as the central compositional process created the ogre of 'modern harmony', reviled by the conservative and wooed by the daring, sometimes with little regard for a comprehensive harmonic logic. The topical question whether folksong could be a fructifying element in a composer's style was a particular aspect of a general problem: harmonic resources ranging from the ascetically modal to the luxuriantly chromatic, so long as they were merely *applied*, could not readily be embodied in that hierarchical system which, from Bach to Wagner, related the chord to the work.

Delius already departed significantly from Wagnerian harmonic principle in that his chords are essentially local phenomena, sensitively coloured and spaced but accountable for their nature only in terms of immediate chromatic adjacencies: in effect, he was a melodist with a gift for harmonic beautification, as were also, for example, Grieg and the folk-like Bartók. But if harmonic ingenuity was to underpin long-term structure, piquant chords were less crucial than ramified harmonic principles. This is not the place to outline the case for regarding Debussy, Stravinsky and Schoenberg as pioneers, but Dyson's arguments suggest that even those British composers who looked to such European models might find answers to the wrong questions.

Placed at opposite ends of Gray's spectrum of ridicule, Holst and Vaughan Williams have more commonly been bracketed together, and have enjoyed more sustained public interest than the rest of that generation which had arrived at artistic maturity by the outbreak of the First World War. A further paradox is that Vaughan Williams's openness to – and ability to pay for – Continental guidance (from Bruch and Ravel) should have developed that 'wholly English' character which Gray did not find in the parochially trained Holst. By now we can see in the styles of both composers complex personal amalgams, the melodic contours of English folksong playing a more sustained formative role in that of Vaughan Williams.

INSTRUMENTAL MUSIC I

Both were pupils of Stanford, but Ralph Vaughan Williams (1872–1958) considered himself a disciple of Parry. The point is not trivial, for while Holst and Vaughan Williams both acquired the professional competence that Stanford's 'constructive intolerance' (Vaughan Williams and Holst 1959: 100) could wring from the hardy, Vaughan Williams, however he might explore developments abroad, would guard himself against Stanford's stylistic opportunism with Parry's moral injunction to 'write . . . as befits an Englishman and a democrat' (p. 96). As a musical prescription the words have no obvious meaning, but Parry's own example suggests that they imply an obligation to address primarily one's own countrymen, in elevating tones, while taking care not to alienate them by surrendering too abjectly to the ecstasy of the creative process. Self-denial is called for, typically in renouncing the hedonism of hyper-chromaticism and glittering orchestration. Gestures are valued for what they withhold – hence the oblique openings, the modest perorations, the rarity of importunately anguished dominants. The 'clean' diatonic discord, often in an appoggiatura context, becomes the stoical token of yearning: in later Parry it may be associated with a modality that owes nothing to folksong.

In his *Sea Symphony* (1909) Vaughan Williams testified eloquently to his belief that Parry's *Blest Pair of Sirens* was the 'finest work' in all British music (p. 97), but other influences are at work. Elgar's can be definitively isolated chiefly in orchestral finesse, since much we regard as quintessentially Elgarian can be found in Parry too. The symphony's juxtaposition of distant triads foreshadows a method, at variance with the reliance on Wagnerian fluidity in transitional contexts. Incongruous though such chromatic means may be, their end, a state of dissolution, was worth striving for by a potential symphonist. (Holst, in contrast, treated the arts of transition as superfluous contrivance, and the later Vaughan Williams was sometimes too ready to follow his example.)

Before embarking on the true symphony, Vaughan Williams tested the orchestral potentialities of two formative influences – folksong and Tudor music. Of the three *Norfolk Rhapsodies* of 1905–7, only one was spared, in an abbreviated form; the Fantasia on a Theme by Thomas Tallis (1910) was similarly pruned, though it can still seem to tread the same ground once too often. The elaborate string textures are impressive and Tallis's tune offers flexibility of metre and Phrygian modality; in extrapolating from it Vaughan Williams essays neither the fertile cross-rhythms nor the impelling dissonances of Tudor polyphony. His archaisms are more extreme yet more approximate – a burgeoning *rubato* solo line, stemming ultimately from plainsong, and shifting triads as uniform colouring of melody; organum is less relevant than Debussy's example.

Restore to the Fantasia's technical repertoire the aspiring appoggiatura dissonances of Parry and Elgar and we have the varied resources of the slow movement in *A London Symphony* (1914; revised 1920 and 1935); despite a wayward tonal scheme, the work feels symphonic rather than rhapsodic. But the very success of the outer-frame device (prologue–epilogue) confirms the rather unfocused impression made by the finale proper. Just before the Epilogue it effectively recalls the first movement's crucial tonal stress (G major on an E♭ bass), and within the first movement that theme has powerfully articulated the main stages of a sonata plan; the Fourth and Sixth Symphonies were to re-create this frenzied opening gesture. However, it is the prologue's impassive pair of 4ths (D–G; A–D) which influences the copious subsidiary material, some of it claiming by its popular tone too independent a place in our experience.

Programmatic requirements, while not tiresomely specific, no doubt account for this tone. By the same token, we might take the *Pastoral Symphony* (1922) to distil the folk influence, though the rhapsody for violin and orchestra, *The Lark Ascending* (1914), more simply invites such a claim. The symphony's originality is less in doubt than its success: Vaughan Williams's preference for unassertive opening and *niente* close is here extended to three out of four movements, all predominantly quiet, leisurely and thick of texture. Even the scherzo is not fleet until its coda, but its firm thematic contours provide a definition blurred elsewhere. Pentatonicism, with its ambiguity of final, rhythmic groups that freely mix triplets and duplets and suppress strong downbeats, harmony that parallels melody or juxtaposes triads for colour rather than tonal strategy: all these discourage the listener from bringing to the play of events the mental agility demanded by traditional sonata dialectic. Yet at a subdued level the structures sound traditional, even to the recapitulation's correction of the exposition's tonal displacement. Refuting facile arguments about folk derivation, the expansive central paragraphs retain more traditional notions of 'development' than Debussy favoured – though a Debussian self-renewing organic process might have been more appropriate. But, eleven years after Elgar's ardently valedictory Second Symphony, the *Pastoral Symphony* demonstrated that British composers might still cultivate the symphonic ideal without invoking a jaded rhetoric.

Vaughan Williams dedicated his Fourth Symphony (1935) to Arnold Bax, the composer who had taken up this challenge in the intervening decade. Yet Bax's symphonies control a rhapsodic flow quite differently from the *Pastoral Symphony*: if in the latter we must penetrate beyond a surface monotony, in Bax we may be disconcerted by the rich profligacy of colouring. Vaughan Williams's Fourth Symphony appears to banish rhapsodizing, yet in the arbitrary assembly of some of its textures old attitudes persist. The urgent new tone comes from exploring new materials, in particular from trying to harness the energy latent within the semitone (see Ex. 9.1a). Several consequences of this – the prevalence of major-plus-minor triads, the synthetic mode containing both 3rds (a gapped scale with clear folk links) and the tendency for two tonal planes to coexist (see Ex. 9.1d) – invite comparison with Bartók, if not with his schematic unification of such elements. How empirically Vaughan Williams arrived at them may be seen in his ballet score, *Job* (1930), where angular chromatic features represent Satan (compare Parry's 'harsh din'), and the composer sought now to subjugate symphonically such recalcitrant musical forces. Obsessive though the symphony is in its materials, it is notably orthodox (classicistic even to several acknowledgements of Beethoven's Fifth as a model) in its structural shapes. Tonal relations are typically kept within the circle of minor 3rds (see the Scherzo's circuit, D minor–B major/B minor–F minor/A♭ minor–A♭ major [trio]), allowing more pliable horizontal and vertical tonal juxtapositions (see Exx. 9.1e and f) than would a sustained exploration of the semitonal antithesis of Ex.9.1b. That example shows the 'tonic' position asserted at the first-movement reprise, but the outcome of the movement is escapist, its cadence theme savouring the Ex. 9.1d scale and attendant false relations in a withdrawn D♭. So extreme a tension is not shrugged off: its return in the symphony's closing bars answers an expectation, even if the final gesture (recalling the close of Holst's 'Mars') dismisses rather than resolves.

The pervading sense of frustrated energy derives less from harmonic semitonal conflict than from the horizontalized motif, Ex. 9.1c. This constricted, non-achieving shape is countered by one that almost recklessly invades musical space, only to arrive again at the harmonic *cul de sac* (see Ex. 9.1g). Though there is much material more generally related to the modal/tonal ideas outlined above, some of

ART MUSIC

Ex. 9.1 Vaughan Williams: Symphony no. 4 in F minor

(g) [musical notation: ff, +8va]

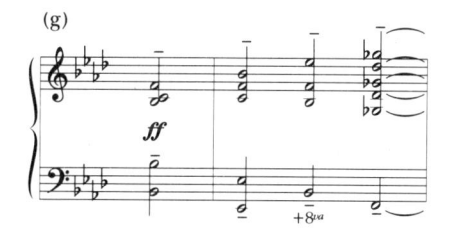

it even folk-like in melodic repertoire (see Ex. 9.1f), in every movement these two motifs play a decisive role. Perhaps the composer's finest symphonic achievement is the intricate argument, thematic and tonal, that links the scherzo and finale; the obvious debt to Beethoven is creatively repaid. The 'Epilogo Fugato' is provoked by the magnificently timely *deus ex machina* of Ex. 9.1c, after the finale's main theme, Ex.9.1e, in its attempts to perorate, has arrived at frenzied stalemate. The devouring of each finale theme by this motif – fertile at last in encounters with itself – is graphic, and its anarchic counterpoint thrusts powerfully towards the cataclysmic resurgence of the opening proposition.

Reacting against such vehemence, in his Fifth Symphony (1943) Vaughan Williams banished the goad of chromatic tension, exalted the ideal of long and sinuous pentatonic line and readmitted the 'forthright' diatonic harmony familiar in his choral style. The effect is much more plastic than in the *Pastoral Symphony*: fluent polyphony is no longer restricted to developmental sections, yet the material has more memorable contour. The first movement retains faint 'sonata' links, though a simple ternary impression is stronger, and the beautifully elusive modality of the opening, in remaining finally undetermined, endorses the composer's label, 'Preludio'. Compensating for its very flat reading of a putative D, the middle movements are centred on A; less demonstrative ideas than in the previous symphony are worked into some of the composer's best-realized designs. The closing passacaglia, new in shape rather than moods, gives D a primacy that unforcedly calls for a clarification of first-movement material in this transfigured atmosphere.

A quickened interest in the symphony produced four further essays during the remaining 15 years of Vaughan Williams's life. General opinion brackets Symphony no. 6 (1948) with its two predecessors, at the peak of his achievement. If the raw ideas are as provocative as those of the Fourth Symphony, their working out is rougher. The will to create panic tensions by protracted adherence to a single *Affekt*, as in the tortuous chromatic line straining against a brutally rhythmicized pedal in the slow movement, or the wraith-like string writing of the Epilogue, is weakened by routine formal patterns, their subsidiary ideas often being pallid formulas of shifting triads. The most irregular design is the first movement: of a typical three-stage exposition all the second group is dropped from the restatement, which follows without development. As the reprise is inconspicuous, a dramatic point is made when the movement's initial F minor/E minor conflict erupts at the peak of the third subject's plump assertion of a mixed-mode E. That initial semitonal friction has consequences in the rest of the symphony too. The tonal scheme of the exposition has been heavily weighted to the flat side (see Ex. 9.2a; every change is effected without modulatory graces) and the F minor/E minor issue is recalled in the slow movement (in relation to a tonic B♭ minor) and at the transition from scherzo to finale. The Epilogue's weaving string lines generate tonal ambivalence from one basic mode (see Ex. 9.2b and compare Ex. 9.1d above); at the Holstian ending the semitonal oscillation, depressed to the E♭ major/E minor level, creates an emotional vacuum. The tritonal shift for both inner movements functions melodically in another wide-ranging scherzo theme, but the splenetic fugal artifice seems arbitrary, the juxtapositions of tritonal tetrachords (i.e. of E and B♭ – compare Holst's 'Mercury') remain inert, and blank 5ths are the stock harmonic filling. A merely improvisatory treatment of local detail, remorseless over-scoring and excessive length mar the impact of this symphony: impossible to forget, it juxtaposes uncertainly the composer's most urgent expression and a disdain for technical finesse approaching irresponsibility.

Ex. 9.2   Vaughan Williams: Symphony no. 6 in E minor

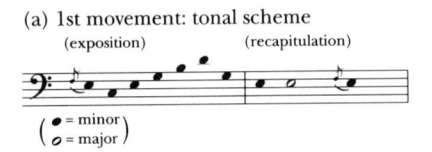

(a) 1st movement: tonal scheme
     (exposition)   (recapitulation)

(● = minor)
(o = major)

(b) 4th movement

The *Sinfonia antartica* (1952) is more comfortably eloquent and its uninhibited use of pitched percussion and women's voices provides an attractive variety of timbre. The five movements have titles and quotations to channel our response to a cycle less concerned with inter-thematic issues than its predecessors. Exotic sonorities recur in the percussion writing of the Eighth Symphony (1956) but its other resources are standard, whereas the Ninth (1958) requires triple woodwind, three saxophones and a solo flugelhorn. The cued alternatives allowed are no longer of that extraordinarily wholesale kind ('the bass clarinet and double bassoon can be omitted' – *London Symphony*) which Vaughan Williams and even Holst felt morally obliged to offer in early scores. The modest orchestra of the Eighth Symphony is treated selectively in its Scherzo, for wind, and its Cavatina, for strings. As in the *Antartica*, the sonata idea is rejected, but the opening variation set (on two melodic principles rather than a theme) has strong arched correspondences; only the wide range of moods creates a tempo of experience unexpected at this stage in a symphony. The following movements retard this dramatically by their uniformity of *Affekt* as well as of orchestral colour. So the final Toccata, in which all the extra percussion engage, appears gratingly high-spirited; that sensitive balance in the cycle of moods which distinguishes Symphonies 3 to 6 has been lost.

The Ninth Symphony confirms this impression that the habits of composition have outlasted the impulse. The alternative degrees of its scalic material are more various than in the Sixth Symphony, but semitonally related centres are less dramatically explored; again E minor/F minor (or F major) is the opening proposition, and a strong element of E♭ compounds the final antithesis. Neither materials nor structures are as memorably shaped, though the first movement's coda imaginatively reinstates the initial pedal to support a synthesis of themes. The finale's shape is unique, three distinct thematic stages being heard twice before they prove preludial to a theme less tersely treated; as this moves to climax, the opening profile of the symphony becomes an ever clearer counterpoint, and it dominates a broad epilogue. There may be too many ideas in this movement, but it is in their rather bald juxtaposition that the *gaucherie* lies, and the problem is recurrent in Vaughan Williams's symphonic output. Thematic material often seems to have been conceived in a series of unrelated creative spurts; so subsidiary ideas prove redundant (Symphony no. 6, first movement) or contextually incongruous (no. 2, first movement, or no. 4, finale), and many passages simply offer a general class of theme that could with neither more nor less cogency be slotted into another context. The composer's programme notes suggest he held a constricted view of the classical sonata principle, though the formulas he thought it to imply sometimes serve him well. Of classical long-term tonal design he makes little sustained use, but in the creation of tonal ambiguity and tension by synthetic modes his achievement is individual and consistent.

Gustav Holst's last completed orchestral movement was a Scherzo, intended for a symphony that would have been contemporary with Vaughan Williams's Fourth, had Holst (1874–1934) lived to complete it. The two men's scherzos reveal many likenesses – the rotations of a tight little chromatic cell (persisting as an ostinato much longer in Holst), fluctuating readings of the 6/8 metre, similar tutti orchestration of essentially two-part writing, and some debt to Holst's 'Mercury'. Vaughan Williams's trio, a *fugato* on a very Holstian version of his 4ths theme, can interrupt the rhythmic surge of a scherzo big enough to include subsidiary ideas that intensify the momentum. Holst's modest proportions exclude a true trio, and his lyrical interlude is melodically contrived, but even episodes that maintain the scherzo pulse dissipate its driving force. By 1933 Holst's health was undermined; *Hammersmith*, a scherzo written three years earlier, had been more strongly characterized. Even so, the Vaughan Williams shows the symphonist's control in the slow unfolding of rapid music, while one cannot easily imagine a symphonic context for Holst's scherzo.

Indeed, Holst had avoided the purely orchestral symphony since his early *Cotswolds Symphony* of 1900. The overture and the two concertos of the 1920s stress their rejection of classical example, and the suite is the commonest type among his mature scores. Its juxtaposition of 'characteristic' musics was practised by Holst within, not just between, movements. As many moments in *The Planets* confirm, he had little enthusiasm for the arts of transition, yet his favourite devices – the ostinato melodies, harmonic circuits and rhythms, the pedals, the persistent five- and seven-beat metres – draw embarrassing attention to the moment at which they stop. Reiteration is certainly more appropriate to such finite material than organic development, but Holst, despite learning from Stravinsky in other areas, never elevated into a structural method the brusqueness of his juxtapositions. Like Vaughan Williams's failure to learn the wider lessons Debussy could have taught him, this recalls that short focus typified by Dyson's analyses.

In his single reference to the composer, Lambert notes a 'complete absence of anything approaching Dykes-like harmonies in Holst's music' (1934: 283), and the slick but miniature chordal engineering of the hymnbook may well have influenced Holst's mistrust of smooth progressive mechanisms. But his early attempts to exorcize Wagnerian influences from his music suggest that, like some other English musicians, he may have been too sensitive to the local effect of chromatic progression to observe the higher organizing levels on which Wagner's harmony operates. Consequently, ingenuity in devising contexts for unusual chords may not extend to making their relationships fundamental. Indeed, piquant foreground harmonies often have to be supported on a framework (revealed by the bass) of entirely conventional 5ths-movement if any sense of progress is to be achieved.

Holst's stylistic amalgam remains idiosyncratic even though its sources are diverse. After a folksong pot-pourri, the *Somerset Rhapsody* (1907), oriental enthusiasms dominated for some years, notably in the *Hymns from the Rig Veda* and *Sāvitri*. They have no orchestral equivalent, the Algerian suite, *Beni Mora* (1910), and the *Japanese Suite* (1915) being concerned with exoticisms of colour rather than of thought. But these required the invention of appropriate musical imagery, and in *The Planets* (1914–16) he was able to draw on an established repertoire. No less resourceful was the deployment of a vaster orchestra than Elgar, then the unchallenged British orchestral virtuoso, ever used. Though Holst claimed that Berlioz's treatise laid the foundations of his skill, his years as a trombonist (like Bridge's as a violist) developed an acute ear for sonority. His scores impress by this precision rather than by originality of disposition: tuttis rarely radiate the affirmative glow of Elgar's, and never the sensual sheen of Strauss's, while even his most mysterious quiet textures rely on flatter colours than Debussy's, or Schoenberg's in the Five Pieces. His unconventional instruments earn their favoured moments by lending routine support elsewhere, and the treatment of the others is orthodox: there are two natural and no artificial string harmonics in the whole of *The Planets* and not a single wind pitch as daringly exposed as Stravinsky's celebrated opening bassoon C.

Holst's conversion of essentially static materials to dynamic purposes is often drastically simple; in 'Mars' it is the more potent for that. In the sonata-like scheme shown in Figure 9.1, pitch references are to the long pedals which underpin the movement (see Ex. 9.3a),

ART MUSIC

and semitonal or tritonal frictions between these and the sliding triadic movement above inevitably give to each a 'dominant' quality. Thus a restatement in which all three themes appear above a G pedal does not signify tonal reconciliation, for some 50 literal reiterations of the one bludgeoning rhythmic figure, already perverse in its regular irregularity, induce an explosive tension. Disappointingly, this vast potential is finally defused in a progression which, whatever its superficial tonal stresses, is explained by the bass in decorously orthodox terms (see Ex. 9.3b).

Fig.9.1 Holst: 'Mars' (*The Planets*), formal and tonal scheme

A	B	C	B devel.	A; C/B	Coda
on G	on C	fluid	on G♯; on B	on G	on G >(in?)C
39	18+8	30	8 6	50+8	19

Ex. 9.3 Holst: 'Mars' (*The Planets*)

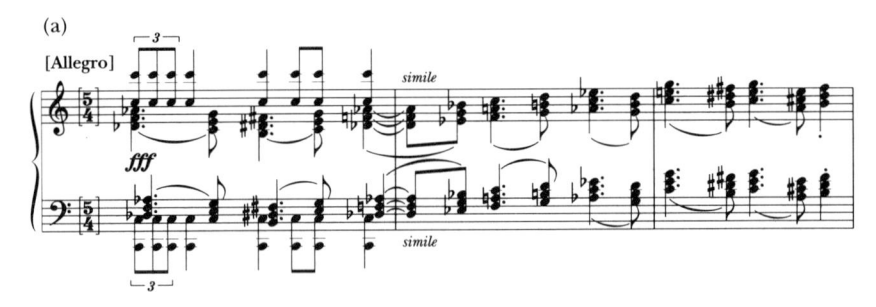

Though its shape is still simpler (*AB*; abbreviated *AB*; coda on *A*), 'Venus' is more subtle in twice preparing by the bass descents of the *A* section a tonic achieved only in the long pedal of the coda; the cycle of 5ths, too, is more imaginatively used in the dominant 9ths above this pedal. But it is with this piece that discrepancies of style obtrude: when the narcotic undulations give way to the solo violin theme, the change in harmonic method bumps us back to Earth. The syncopated accompaniment evades fully committed chromatic progression, but the minor 9th plus minor 13th of its climax is importunate, while the oboe phrase takes us still nearer the expressive conventions of the ballad. The juxtaposition of triads, or of scalic tetrachords, of B♭ and E in 'Mercury' suggests a parallel with Bartók and a precedent for Britten, but true motion has to be generated by subsidiary material; the *Petrushka*-like central idea draws on Russian 'changing backgrounds'. 'Jupiter' is pointedly sectional despite its near-sonata design (the big tune dominating middle section and coda); its syncopated white-note contexts neatly bridge the gap between Stanford and *Portsmouth Point.*

The opening of 'Saturn' sensitively matches properties of chord and timbre, and finely controlled timing prepares the final superimposition of ostinatos. Contrasted use of a whole-tone segment is made in the four-note motto which dramatically punctuates 'Uranus', a piece to which Vaughan Williams's galumphing contexts owe much. Of Holst's own debts, that to Debussy's *Nocturnes* is declared with the wordless female chorus of 'Neptune', yet this movement is the most consistently original: even the clarinet's folk-like melody creates no incongruity in this essentially athematic piece, the emergence of the voices having beautifully covered the moment at which the basic harmonic tension (of superimposed minor triads a major 3rd apart) has been relaxed. 'Neptune' represents an emphatic break with conventional correspondences in favour of a single span, subtly nuanced rather than articulated by successive events.

The Planets seems to prepare for developments that never took place in Holst's orchestral writing. The Fugal Overture (1922) and Fugal Concerto (1923) carry Holstian fingerprints in detail and broader conception, yet the effect of both works is qualified by a neo-baroque reference in fugal texture and figurative patterns that seems defensive rather than, as with the contemporary Stravinsky, wittily opportunist. Their best features, the crossing of asymmetric rhythmic groups and some adroit tonal ambiguities, register more acutely than similar procedures in *The Planets* because of the new wiry textures.

Egdon Heath (1927) is no less sparse, but jettisons the spurious optimism of the fugal pieces. From their busy chatter Holst retreats to a quietism unrelieved by the quasi-mystical sonorities of the slow music in *The Planets*. He presents and varies a little, but scarcely develops, a chain of ideas, making no attempt to conceal brusque joins. Of the two climaxes the second is markedly less affirmative, and summary restatement follows after the incursion of a folky contour; in that its rhythm is folky too, the effect is stranger than the comparable moment in 'Neptune'. This hint of a warmer tone is potent yet equivocal in its bitonal obliquity to the structural dominant pedal. The whole work shows Holst expressively in command of tonal ambivalence, rather than merely fascinated by its mechanisms. The opening synthetic mode presents a frozen tonal situation typical of almost all that follows: it contains pitches proper to each of three modes – G phrygian, B♭ dorian and D♭ lydian (see Ex. 9.4). The tritone G–D♭, often underpinned in the shape of two 4ths (D–G; A♭–D♭) is the most pervasive pitch reference, but without obtruding schematicism; similarly, the ostinatos and scalic basses never congeal into cliché. In remaining creatively vigilant throughout its brief span, and in rejecting conventional views of balance (in dynamics as well as momentum), Holst in *Egdon Heath* fuses in a true amalgam elements that elsewhere declare too readily their heterogeneous origins.

Ex. 9.4   Holst: *Egdon Heath*

II: Ireland, Bridge and Bantock

To Stanford's conservative eclecticism both Vaughan Williams's dogged insularity and Holst's experimentalism must have appeared an affront. More directly inspired by Stanford's teaching are the music of John Ireland (1879–1962) and the earlier work of Frank Bridge (1879–1941), for they are founded in entirely orthodox progressive harmony, embellished with higher-diatonic or chromatic dissonance, yet cautiously admit echoes of the great Continental pioneers. Ireland ranges from side-slipping Debussian sonority to brittle Stravinskian figuration, but shows no increasing commitment to such stimuli: on the contrary, in the final scores his truest sympathies seem to be embodied in the sighing appoggiatura usages of Parry and Elgar. As with other composers of his generation, an innate preference for rhapsodic spans may at times be suppressed in favour of classicizing forms, but tonal moves tend still to be governed by immediacy of effect rather than by a balance of tensions.

INSTRUMENTAL MUSIC I

In the prelude *The Forgotten Rite* (1913), a simple arch is braced by the conversion of a pentatonic horn call into a unifying motif. The symphonic rhapsody *Mai-Dun* (1921), another evocation of a prehistoric world, is more ambitious in structure and emotional scope, and Ireland also cast his *Legend* for piano and orchestra (1933) as a single quasi-programmatic cycle. These Lisztian sympathies reappear in the rhetorical dialogue between soloist and orchestra that opens the more orthodox Piano Concerto (1930) and in the recitative-like prefigurings of the main theme in the *Concertino pastorale* for strings (1939); though these portents are curiously denied by the genial movements that follow, the Concerto gives them some credibility later when first-movement material and key disturb the song of the second movement. And in turn the song and its key are recovered as last episode in a finale that rounds off a discursive but ultimately convincing tonal cycle. A quotation from the orchestra's second subject in the first movement will exemplify some features of Ireland's style – the decorated repetition (rather than immediate sequential extension) of a short phrase, creating a harmonic stasis eventually relieved by cycle-of-5ths movement, the association of a jauntily mechanized pattern with chromaticized accompaniment detail (appoggiaturas that create false relations being particularly common) and the metrical freedom within uniform barring (see Ex. 9.5).

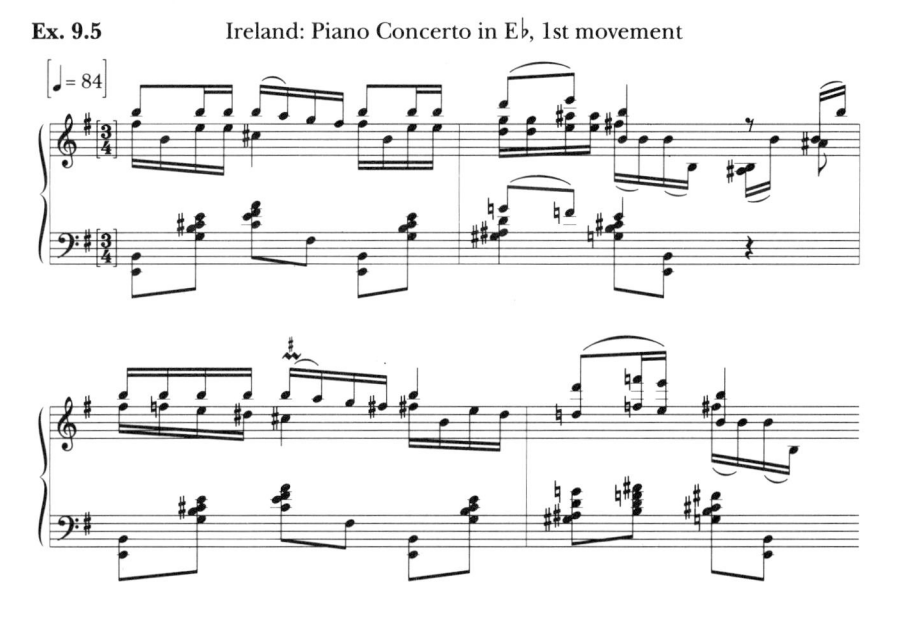

Ex. 9.5 Ireland: Piano Concerto in E♭, 1st movement

ART MUSIC

Divorced from the stimulus of the piano, Ireland rarely attempted such figurative detail in his orchestral works: the two comedy overtures, A *London Overture* (1936) and *Satyricon* (1946), assert high spirits chiefly through rhythmically buoyant treatment of simple diatonic ideas. Similar formulas, with a clear debt to Walton in the preparation of explosive dominants, are used in the final Toccata of the *Concertino pastorale*, Ireland's most successful motoric piece. Invention runs strongest in the almost bitonal tensions of the opening Eclogue, while the Threnody reveals the individuality of tone Ireland could retain within well-worn English expressive conventions.

The reputation of Frank Bridge was kept alive for decades after his death by a handful of piano pieces and songs, though Ireland was at his most imaginative more consistently in those media than Bridge; in chamber and orchestral music the reverse is true. Yet when Ireland's *London Overture* and Piano Concerto were still performed occasionally, Bridge's major orchestral scores were overlooked: five years after Bridge's death, in a warmly appreciative notice, Westrup seems to have known neither *Enter Spring* nor the cello concerto, *Oration* (1946a: 75). Between the Suite of 1908 and the unfinished Symphony of 1940–41, both for string orchestra, Bridge wrote no orchestral works with such bald, unevocative titles. He also produced no true symphonic poem after *Isabella* (1907), but his continuing acknowledgement of programmatic stimulus, albeit shadowy, may have disadvantaged his music in the 1930s, when the symphony gained prestige from a fashionable anti-romanticism – however dependent on a romantic sequence of moods the music stuffed into the form. Bax, for example, is in his symphonies less subject to a classically disciplined view of thematicism and structural balance than is Bridge in nominally 'rhapsodic' works.

This is not to say that Bridge's structural predilections are classicistic. As we shall see in his chamber music, the Lisztian composite movement, favoured by W. W. Cobbett in his quixotic attempt to found a second great literature of English fantasias, still attracted Bridge even after he had distinctively adapted the traditional cycle in his quartets; but he never employs the single-movement plan to evade developmental responsibilities. The price he pays for a fastidious use of unifying cells is that long lines, impulsive in intent, may lack the 'spontaneity' we attribute to what proves to be memorable. Bridge can set against this a more refined control of harmonic unity than other English eclectics (Holst or Bax) demonstrate, and a richer harmonic range than the drastically unified resources of Vaughan Williams.

INSTRUMENTAL MUSIC I

His use of the romantic orchestra reflects the inside experience of conductor as well as player: even at high dynamic levels Bridge's scores sound lithe, avoiding excessively doubled harmonic padding. The scoring of the symphonic suite *The Sea* (1910–11) is more sensitive than that of any British contemporary, Holst included. The quality of the invention is more variable. Expressive added notes in 'Seascape' sound through more transparent contexts than Delius's, but a reversion to conventional progression is disturbing both here and in the scherzo. Fauré's influence in the flute melody of 'Moonlight' gives way to Debussy's, and Sibelius is glimpsed in the string textures of the final 'Storm', a piece that melodramatically juxtaposes rather inert material.

Enter Spring (1927), described as a 'rhapsody', satisfies programmatic expectations in details like the birdsong which precedes the central expansive song, and in the splendour of sound when that melody returns as coda. A subtler symbol of burgeoning growth is heard in the innumerable offshoots of a few melodic and rhythmic cells which in the two main spans replace the broad melodic paragraphs of earlier works. Techniques of derivation are elastic, but used so unremittingly they forge palpable connections between quite remotely related figures. Ex. 9.6a shows a typical texture from early in the Allegro and Ex. 9.6b–d some of the shapes that have preceded it. This is chromatic music, but almost entirely without that fatalistic drift of semitonally falling bass which, characterizing Delius, served other English lyricists to similar nostalgic ends (see, for example, the Bax quoted at Ex. 9.7b below). And there are fewer heightened dominants (chords 2 and 4) than whole-tone collections, pure (7, 9) or with one foreign pitch (3, 8, 10). These create a feeling of disengagement so that tonal objectives appear neither sought nor agonizingly postponed, but rather incidental. Unfortunately, the motivic interconnections and the persistent compound metre combine with this tonal neutrality in too undifferentiated a flow of event. On the other hand, as chords 1 and 6 confirm, purely diatonic collections (often with a core of perfect 4ths) are not incongruous within this scheme; indeed, the opening of the Andante melody, Ex. 9.6e, is pronouncedly English in tone because of its loving protraction of an oblique diatonic situation.

Oration (1930) is more diverse in melody and tempo and sharper in harmonic profile. Now the augmented triad is built upon to produce bitonal (even bi-triadic) as well as whole-tone chords; the major triad with flattened 6th added below, which colours the

ART MUSIC

Ex. 9.6 Bridge: *Enter Spring*

(d)

(e)

elegiac march on a ground, verticalizes the major/minor 3rd cell that is even more fundamental to the melodic constructions than in *Enter Spring*. This march is the inner frame of a large, essentially symmetrical composite movement; tonal stresses remain expressive rather than structural, much of the expository Allegro returning at the same pitch level. The centre of the arch refers to the main subject within a macabre *scherzando* tonally tangential to the timpani's pedal G. There are pointers towards Britten in this work – in details (compare the distorted military music with that of Britten's Violin Concerto; also the cadenzas of both concertos), in the quasi-programmatic cycle (see Britten's op. 2 Phantasy) and in the fusion of memorial and protest for the victims of war. Bridge finally rejects a perfect arch, adding an Epilogue in which the opening bars' wandering triads find a serene monotonal outcome in the D that has been no more than presumptively central. This 'elegiac concerto' represents a powerful argument in the revivalists' case for Bridge. Its grave eloquence controlled by motivic economy is almost unparalleled within the 'phantasy' tradition; nor could Bridge himself regain this imaginative level in the *Phantasm* for piano and orchestra of the following year.

Despite a generous breadth of stylistic reference, the composers who studied at the Royal College of Music never lost a certain emotional decorum that owes something to Parry's moral precepts as well as Stanford's technical example. The products of the only alternative teaching available in England, that of Frederick Corder at the Royal Academy of Music, show less reserve, but rather an anxiety to catch up with the grandest romanticism of the (no longer very) New German School. Corder's pupils acquired a harmonic palette rich if not revolutionary, an exuberant orchestral technique and a liberal view of structural obligations. Corder and his wife had made singing translations of Wagner, and his operatic enthusiasms fired several of his pupils. Granville Bantock (1868–1946) launched his career with an opera to a text by Corder, but most of his large output was in media that were more practicable in Britain. His orchestral writing takes its departure from the Liszt symphonic poem, even those works labelled as symphonies (*Hebridean*, 1915; *Pagan*, 1928; *Celtic*, 1940) reflecting his reliance on exotic programmatic stimulus. Extremely professional workmanship too often highlights reach-me-down invention. *Dante and Beatrice* (1910), for example, shows skilful combination of themes, long harmonic paragraphs and Lisztian *fugato*, but an unbalanced tonal structure; loose rhapsody (harp arpeggios, solo violin cadenzas, and so on) assists the crucial tonal shift from C minor to D♭, a key which then remains in force. The 'orchestral drama' *Fifine at the Fair* (1911) is less attitudinizing, though its scoring is more self-consciously virtuoso than Elgar's; the much divided string section and its *tremolandi* are Sibelian, while the scherzo writing is almost as deft as Berlioz's. But where Tchaikovsky or Elgar would have slimmed the sound to capture a whimsical note, Bantock over-scores, and grandiose cadenza interludes again weaken the structure. His later comedy-overtures after Aristophanes, *The Frogs* (1935) and *The Birds* (1946), are still heard occasionally.

III: Two Symphonists: Bax and Brian

Bantock and other Corder pupils of great, if eclectic, facility, Joseph Holbrooke (1878–1958) and Benjamin Dale (1885–1943), were contemporaries of Vaughan Williams, yet by the time he had reached the height of his powers, during the 1940s, their music was almost forgotten. Of the RAM composers, only Arnold Bax (1883–1953) still attracted audiences, above all for his large body of orchestral music. Like Bantock, he cultivated both symphonic poem and symphony, but his avoidance of titles for the latter recognizes a more pronounced distinction between the genres. Before Vaughan Williams's (not to mention Brian's) remarkable concentration upon symphony in his last years, Bax's seven symphonies constituted the most sustained attempt to add to the opulent romantic symphony a recognizably English sub-species. Bax might have contested this description since, although of pure English stock, he drew much of his inspiration from Celtic sources and wrote verse under an Irish pseudonym. While a folk influence is evident in many of his second-group melodic lines, it rarely has a formative effect on the luxuriant harmony. Although in some respects (orchestration being the most obvious) Bax's music displays a professional fluency denied, or rejected by, the wilfully clumsy Vaughan Williams, it betrays less concern for consistency of language. Whether using folky idioms or more angular lines, his melody rarely has an inescapable harmonic corollary. Bax is a redoutable harmonist, but the price paid for his sleight-of-hand is that little sounds utterly inevitable: to reharmonize Debussy is to destroy delicate inner relationships; even with Delius a certain logic restricts the possible fillings between top line and semitonally descending bass; but in many Bax contexts, while the chords are splendidly rich, others would be no less plausibly so. The point seems ludicrously censorious since Bax's Central European contemporaries were evolving harmonic languages far more tenuously related to tradition. But just because his chords, unlike theirs, are finally referable to orthodox functions and tonal environments, their exuberance can cloy.

In the symphonic poems the problem is less acute, since harmonic colours are often protracted by lavish undulating decoration. An occasional debt to Debussy never persists into tutti scorings, and with harmony moving by chromatically eased progression, the rhetoric remains traditional. Structure may rely upon a programmatic sequence, yet remain comprehensible in terms of Lisztian composite forms. Thus *The Garden of Fand* (1916) contains within its framing seascape an allegro punctuated by, and later perorating in, broad folky melody. In the same year as *Tintagel* and *November Woods* (1917), Bax produced his Symphonic Variations for piano and orchestra. They bear titles, yet the balancing of a wide range of moods in a large-scale cycle with no controlling programme justifies the description 'symphonic' and forms a bridge to the composer's central achievement.

His First Symphony appeared in 1922, the year of Vaughan Williams's *Pastoral*; the contrast between the two men's orchestral ideals has been noted. Bax establishes a three-movement layout, omitting the scherzo – a type Vaughan Williams continued to cultivate with increasing resource. Contrary to facile assumptions, Vaughan Williams's block movements of simple triads may inhibit rapid motion less than the more 'connected' chords of Bax, since these, being acoustically more complex, need time to develop their individual colouring. In the bitonal aggregate that opens his First Symphony, Bax may seem to be on common ground with Vaughan Williams (first movements of Symphonies 2, 4, 6 and 9), but only in the coda are the bitonal implications given much force. It is the rhythmic cast of this *feroce* opening gesture that dominates later events, together with the general melodic contour (not necessarily retaining its 3 4 0 intervallic constitution) and that of the next two-bar motif (see Ex. 9.7a). A restless energy sustains their varied presentation in and around E♭ minor before a patent transition (Bax's often are) prepares for a second group in E; its opening strain is shown at Ex. 9.7b. Melodically this begins as though pentatonic, adds a lydian 4th, and then winds through the pure major collection, but harmonically these nuances are uniformly disregarded in a welter of chromatic sub-progressions. Even so, the impression of an orthodox antecedent (I–V) is stabilizing, yet the following phrases, incorporating a homophonic subsidiary idea (another common move), dissipate that effect in a wayward stream of beautiful incident: the opening strain returns only as codetta. Development is clearer in its sources than in its overall expressive meaning, but the route to restatement is a forcefully orthodox II–V–I. The abbreviated recapitulation assimilates the second group to E♭, and its shadowy references to the main motif are suddenly clarified by the coda. The finale picks up first-movement threads again, its *marcia trionfale* diatonicizing the main motif, but with much new material too, the total impression is diffuse. This is less true of the Second Symphony (1926), not because its thematicism is less prodigal, but because four contrasted shapes presented in the portentous introduction maintain a crucial relevance throughout the work, whether intruding upon movements nominally shaped by quite other themes (first-movement Allegro and slow movement) or transforming character to serve as primary material (finale). The feeling that the most important events are linked across the whole cycle in this way draws attention away from Bax's practice of representing in only an attenuated form the later stages of structures still recognizably traditional in outline. The tonal progress of the cycle is less clear-cut than the title-page suggests ('in E minor and C') but it effectively supports the thematic argument in spurning symmetrical correspondences.

Though tonally conflicting harmonic aggregates are still the recurrent token of emotional stress, the Second Symphony is less given to vehement protestation than the First, while in the Third (1928–9) Bax makes much greater use of diatonic harmony, including

Ex. 9.7   Bax: Symphony no. 1, 1st movement

(a) Allegro moderato e feroce

(b) *Cantabile*
Moderato espressivo

block triadic movement. The sound remains typically more complex than that of Vaughan Williams, yet his influence is suggested also by the slow movement's modal horn tune (though not its later, sensuously beautiful treatment) and by the stylized country-dance tune in the finale. Again many ideas from the opening Lento remain active in the Allegro, and almost 300 bars pass before the song-like paragraph with chromatic accompaniment which usually signals Bax's second group. This too is spaciously expounded, so a melodramatic intrusion of the opening motto is all that postpones a recapitulation moving again from Lento to Allegro. The B♭ close clarifies earlier obliquities; these and the exposition's voluminous thematic exploration seem necessary consequences of a form from which 'development' as a substantial central stage has been eliminated. The initial tense homophony of the finale is less memorable than its eventual transformation as chordal background of a protracted (and finely orchestrated) epilogue, in which the symphony's first, and most momentous, theme gives a focus to the nostalgia.

The Fourth Symphony (1930–31) is founded with a new directness in E♭, with slow movement in E. The abrupt thematic address is also new, but the use of an elaborately mixed major mode staves off platitude; even so, another *marcia trionfale* peroration stresses how tawdry Bax's most affirmative moods can prove. The Fifth Symphony (1931–2) reinforces its dedication to Sibelius by the rhythmic cast of the first movement's Lento frame. Later tributes concern orchestral texture rather than structural method, for Bax's view of expansive form is altogether more open-handed, not to say prodigal, in its thematic events. But tonal argument is unusually consistent, the relationship of the Lento's E minor to the main Allegro's C♯ minor providing the model for an axis system (turning about the minor-3rd keys) that regulates the chief tonal buttresses. The Allegro's head-motif is yet again (compare Symphonies 1 and 3) a minor 3rd within a major (see Ex. 9.8). This cell and an associated semitonal key conflict have proved central to some of this century's tautest musical argument, yet Bax's recognition of their unifying powers is desultory: when quite other ideas flow to mind, he sees no reason to stem them. Even the hymnic epilogue can only with sophistry be traced back further than the finale's introduction. The tendency of these slow epilogues to impair the formal balance may account for a new finale design in the Sixth Symphony (1934) – slow introduction, scherzo-and-trio, slow epilogue. It is best overcome in Bax's last symphony (no. 7; 1938–9), where epilogue closes variations and developmental interludes on a coolly diatonic theme. The first movement still presents a plethora of first-group ideas, but the tonic pedal over which some of them appear creates a strong frame when it returns as a coda. The mixed-mode descent of one theme, stressing $^\sharp\hat{4}$, $^\natural\hat{3}$ and $^\flat\hat{3}$, brings to mind Vaughan Williams's Fourth Symphony finale. To juxtapose the two works is again to observe Bax's greater fluidity of gesture and colour, Vaughan Williams's more obstinate concentration on points at issue.

One composer of the same generation remains to be considered, who, being self-taught, owed allegiance to neither Stanford's nor Corder's ideals. This lack of institutional training may help to explain why the music of Havergal Brian (1876–1972) remained in such

Ex. 9.8   Bax: Symphony no. 5, 1st movement

obscurity; Elgar's belated triumph against similar odds is one measure of a technical scope and an imaginative power unmatched in the next generation. For whatever reason, whereas the music of, say, Bantock enjoyed success before the First World War, even if it fell a victim to changing tastes thereafter, Brian's never gained a firm hold at all. Since he cultivated into extreme old age a stoical indifference to the neglect of his works, their development related little to the mainstreams of either British or Continental musical thought. Brian's astonishing fertility as a symphonist after the age of 80 required critics to assess as new music the work of a composer whose true contemporaries were beginning to qualify for centennial reassessment. The claim for Brian as 'the most prolific writer of symphonies since Haydn' (M. MacDonald 1974: 7) may be irrefutable, but the problems of evaluating his 32 essays in the form have been intensified by the sparsity of performances and the limited availability of scores.

ART MUSIC

His earlier symphonies reflect the post-Wagnerian association of profundity with size. In the *Gothic Symphony* (1919–27) three orchestral movements are followed by a gigantic setting of the *Te Deum*, for soloists, choruses, orchestra and brass bands. To feel that so lofty an undertaking should have yielded a masterpiece does not quell doubts prompted by the music itself. That many of its ideas lack memorability might even be a virtue if their function was to generate a process of organic development as spacious as the work's scale promises. Yet Brian's preferred method is to juxtapose rather than to develop, blurring a mental image of the immediate in relation to the whole. His orchestral imagination, while it rarely makes the vast resources appear fundamentally necessary, is often most effectively deployed in the creation of bold sonorous contrast. His tonal shifts too may be impressively unexpected, but an interest focused so much on the means of articulation can wither in the course of unremarkable ideas.

The Second Symphony (1930–31) is purely instrumental, though its demands remain grandiose. Its opening Adagio establishes a type of cryptic or menacing gesture to which later Brian continues to have recourse, and the eruption of the Allegro is forcefully tangential in tonality. The second group, however, fully defines by the major mode the E adumbrated by the introduction's mysterious drone. Collapse into the obvious is reinforced by the theme itself: rhythmically monotonous, melodically fettered to the basic triad except for one swing to the flat submediant, and articulated by a chromatic cliché beloved of ballad composers, it is orchestrated with a forest of accompanimental details that tend to cancel out (see Ex. 9.9). The grand expressive intentions of the scherzo and funeral-march finale are confounded less by banal invention than by a disparity between the size of the movements and that of the constituent melodic/harmonic units.

In the next few years Brian's symphonic output included two more works setting texts – the Fourth with chorus, the Fifth with solo baritone. From the *Sinfonia tragica* of 1948 dates the remarkable acceleration of his late years. This transfer of his habitual prodigality from individually massive projects to a long series of much slighter designs (notably the single-movement symphonies) may stem not so much from considerations of practicality – when the series began, his work seems to have had no prospects of performance – as from a recognition that he was writing simply for his own satisfaction. What this old man's music lacks, if we compare it with Verdi's or Haydn's, is the impression of a ruthless self-criticism won from the experience

Ex. 9.9   Brian: Symphony no. 2 in E minor, 1st movement

of countless performances. The brevity of the Eighth Symphony (1949), for example, does not represent a distillation: on the contrary, paragraphs that appear to demand spacious treatment are constantly abandoned in favour of contrasted ideas. Apt epithets for each section are easier to find than an interpretation that embraces so many kinds of music. This is not to deny common thematic shapes or the ultimate centrality of the B♭ defined by the opening drone (compare Symphony no. 2), though the immediacy of tonal juxtaposition still counts for more than long-term tensions. Even before he had outlived his contemporaries, Brian was an elusive creative figure. A response of indifference to activity on so heroic a scale seems less generous than one of antipathy, yet a cross-section of his works prompts no expectation of richly individual music awaiting discovery.

ART MUSIC

IV: The Generation of Walton, Bliss and Lambert

Of the same generation as the composers discussed so far, Lord Berners (1883–1950) invites classification rather with the Walton of the 1920s, and with Constant Lambert. Like Lambert he was most at ease in ballet scores, and in some songs his determined satire finds its mark. But in neither of his major orchestral works, the *Fantaisie espagnole* (1919) and the Fugue in C minor (1934), do stolidly competent orchestration and essentially conventional harmony (chromatically sliding dominant 7ths are taken to be self-evidently mordant) permit the lean ironies of *Façade*, let alone the elegant wit of Stravinsky's distortions.

It was with Satie that Cecil Gray paired Berners (1924: 251). No less inept by now appears the matching he found for Stravinsky – with Bliss. One of the few composers to have served in, and survived, the First World War, Arthur Bliss (1891–1975) was thus left almost without contemporaries, and he is difficult to place stylistically. Such composition teaching as he received was RCM-orientated, yet hankerings after an Elgarian bravura are clear in the orchestral work that made his name, the *Colour Symphony* (1922, revised 1932); an attempt to balance moods classically is compromised by their explicitly symbolic functions, reminiscent of *The Planets*. His is a less adventurous mind than Holst's, harmonic movement being essentially orthodox and melodic rhythmic invention too contrived (see, for example, the two fugue subjects in 'Green'). Gestures are uncomfortably big for the short spans, and the restless orchestral disposition errs towards the overblown. But in 'Blue' are acknowledged the sympathies of an English pastoralist, however veneered by Ravelian smartness and some metrical quirks.

And these sympathies give a persuasive ardour to the Music for Strings (1935) without stifling textural invention of an incisive kind; here the moods and the scale match very successfully. The Piano Concerto (1939) represents the opposite extreme. Too much depends on flatulent reiteration of the main theme's mannered head-motif, while the second subject's E, following B$\flat$, fails to generate fruitful tonal argument, since this wilting lyrical idea has to be revived by decorative modulation. Lyrical and dramatic qualities are better played off, with some debt to the scheme of Walton's concertos, in the Violin Concerto (1956), though melodic platitude sometimes threatens. In the short and emotionally uniform movements of his ballet scores, Bliss's technical skills are applied to unaffectedly simple ideas. His strongest concert work, *Meditations on a Theme by John Blow* (1955), organizes eight variations on the programmatic thread of Psalm 23; an ambitious scale does not demand ambitious structures, and the orchestration is more selectively colourful than in the symphony.

There is a significant dearth of British composers born in the 1880s and 1890s but an efflorescence in the first decade of the new century. Most of this generation, too young to be sacrificed in the First World War, lived through the Second. Their Continental contemporaries, composers such as Fortner, Hartmann and Petrassi, adopted a policy of retrenchment and synthesis after major upheavals in Western musical thought and practice; even Dallapiccola's rich achievement was founded more on assimilation than on experiment, and only Messiaen's idiosyncratic progress gave much hint of still further territories to be cultivated. In Britain, insulation from the European radicals, the celebrated 'time lag', allowed the 1900s generation some sense of creative adventure, but in essence they were as cautious as their colleagues abroad; there was no explorer among them to match Holst, and until Tippett's full maturity no visionary prepared, like Vaughan Williams, to risk charges of monumental bungling rather than lower his aim. A respectable level of technical skill was common, though its sources might be diverse; the standard orchestra served their needs well, symphony and concerto being preferred to the freer, programmatic forms. It was left to a younger generation, emerging after the Second World War, to attempt synthesis based on intimate knowledge of the European models. Yet if their elders shunned revolt, several of them showed a capacity for self-renewal which prevented their merely pandering to the expectations of the growing, but endemically wary, audience for orchestral concerts in Britain.

William Walton (1902–83) never lost the place he won with that audience before the war, though in the common critical view his later scores, no less elegantly finished, too complacently reproduced features he had made highly personal. *Portsmouth Point*, an overture written in 1925 and played at the Zurich ISCM Festival in the following year, helped to consolidate in Britain the reputation Walton had gained with *Façade* for irreverent wit and modish technical equipment. As so often in this country, 'modish' meant other, smarter, people's fashions. The orchestral textures favoured by English composers in the early 1920s were turgid, the characteristic gait slow and reflective; Vaughan Williams's *Pastoral Symphony* and Bax's first

ART MUSIC

two symphonies had graduated more certainly beyond the scale than the moods of rhapsody, and even Bliss's vehemence was ponderous. So the varied metres, noisily reiterated figurations and incisively scored textures of Walton's overture inevitably suggested that Stravinsky (*Les noces* had been performed two years earlier) and Hindemith (see the *Kammermusik Nr 1* of 1922) were to prompt him on the stage of European music. Wise so long after the event, one observes that the breezily nautical C major pentatonics do not so much parody as indulge a simple strain of diatonic melodic invention, and that the explosive opening chords form an added-note progression rather than a Stravinskian petrifaction of contradictory functions.

Cosmopolitan pretensions were already renounced in the conversion of a projected ballet score for Diaghilev into the *Sinfonia concertante* of 1927. In so short a work weighty introduction and epilogue disturb the balance, giving a sectional feeling that cannot be attributed to clumsy transition. Indeed, the structural rhetoric is often more impressive than the thematic invention, though in the slow movement the typical short, twisting phrases are fused into a warmly lyrical polyphony; the climactic appoggiaturas intensify a debt to Elgar already plain in the introduction. The finale adumbrates the motoric figuration and the 4th-aggregates of the Viola Concerto's scherzo. But in the Concerto (1929) this is placed centrally, and the new-found lyricism saturates the opening slow movement (a sonata with abridged restatement) and the finale. As even the latter is leisurely, the work might succumb to a nostalgic lassitude but for an upheaval late in the movement that creates a unique and powerfully tragic form. Above a subdominant pedal an orchestral *fugato* on the refrain expands into an epic polyphonic development of all the finale material; its climax subsides to a dominant pedal on which the refrain as bass ostinato attends the soloist's recall of first-movement themes, and a tonic pedal brings a distillation of the whole work's thematic and tonal character. This is not only Walton's finest close (in what many regard as his finest work) but the most convincing of all those 'epilogues' in which British composers have sought to impose unity on their works by an ultimate reversion to first ideas. The device is so satisfying here because the unity is inherent, not a sentimental contrivance. The soloist's first theme sets up not only a general type of curve, countering steps by large, gesturing intervals, but various cells which remain active in the other movements; Ex. 9.10 shows some derivatives. The initial but, as Tovey pointed out (1936: 222), entirely logical collision of sharp and

INSTRUMENTAL MUSIC I

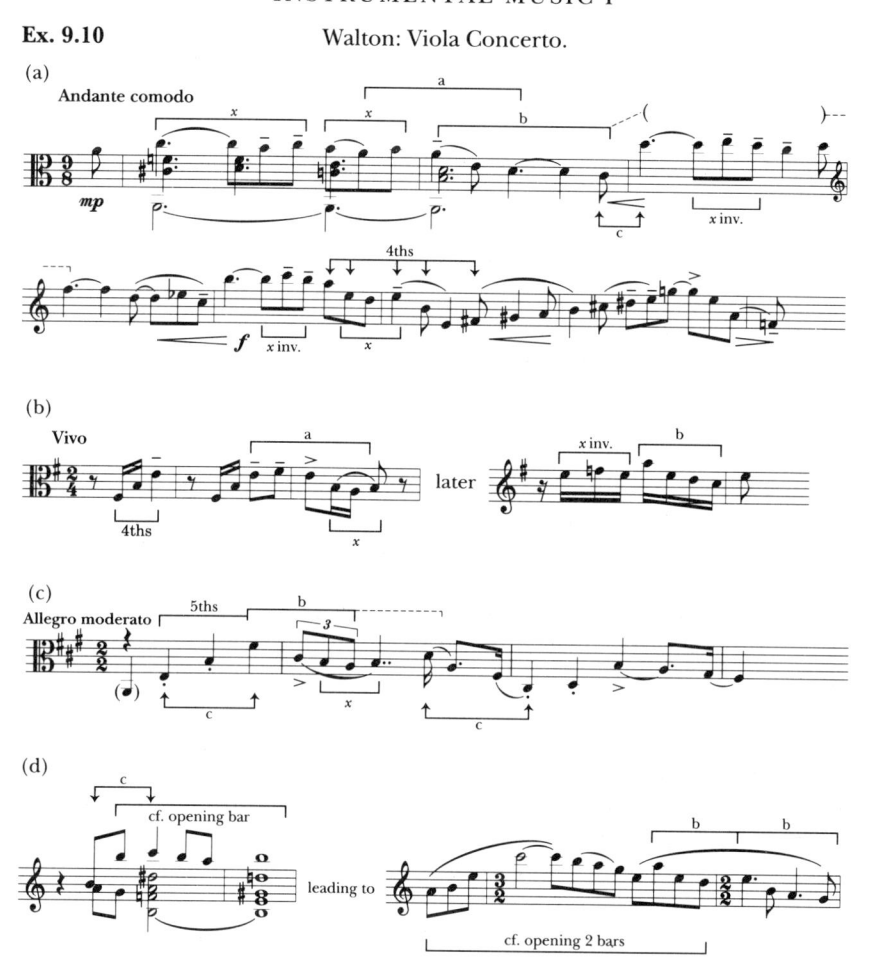

Ex. 9.10   Walton: Viola Concerto.

natural degrees is elevated into an opposition of mode, colouring many contexts and symbolizing at the close the major/minor relationship of the outer movements; and even the epilogue's pedals simply telescope a process by which much of the concerto has been articulated. The sombre tone, perfectly adapted to the viola's strengths and weaknesses, is reinforced by the scoring, rich in sinuous counterpoints of lower woodwind and horn; the modified score of 1961 clarifies some detail, but its lightening of the atmosphere typifies the composer's later withdrawal from the impassioned melancholy of the Viola Concerto. To proceed beyond its tonal groundplan, A minor–E minor–A major, one would have to chart

ART MUSIC

many temporary poles. These balance to confirm the fundamental centre, but the lack of any sustained antithesis gives a nervous quality to the music. Rejecting the elaborate chromatic circumnavigation of a key, Walton stabilizes an area by a diatonic cycle of 5ths or by a pedal. Typically, however, he uses pedals more dramatically to *postpone* tonal commitment, even apparent dominants often proving piquantly deceptive. Such methods were to be more severely tested when Walton essayed a symphony, on the grandest scale.

While Walton was engaged on this First Symphony, his friend, Constant Lambert, published *Music Ho!* (1934), its disillusioned reading of modern music brightened only by a closing testimony to the beneficial role Sibelius's influence might play in future developments. Dedications by Bax and Vaughan Williams imply some indebtedness to Sibelius. Walton's most glaring debts – themes turning about long-held notes but preceded or followed by rapid slides, obsessive accompaniment patterns, plangent woodwind 3rds, dense lower-string textures – are less significant than his first movement's Sibelian conflation of material expounded in spaciously defined stages into a single recapitulatory span. But the originality of this movement consists in the deployment of pedals on a scale not remotely approached in Sibelius. Though one pedal may bear a succession of tonal meanings, a remarkably clear account of the tonal structure is provided by charting pedal points (see Ex. 9.11a.).

This proves to be classically based not only in the literal monotonality of that summary restatement (the penultimate deflections in Ex. 9.11a represent the coda) but even to the structural colon on the V of V before the exposition's second group. In fact, much of that group's material is presented tangentially (note the E pedal, for example), yet such delay before the unequivocally rooted dominant-

Ex. 9.11 Walton: Symphony no. 1, 1st movement.

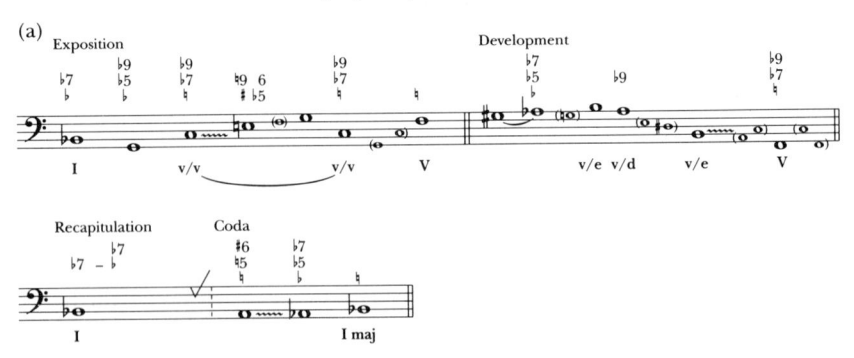

as-tonic can be paralleled in Brahms. The diagram omits various scalic connections in the bass, but it also oversimplifies the movement's crisis: after the development's last pedal in its sharp-side explorations, a frenzied search for the home dominant cuts loose from such moorings to telling effect. At Ex. 9.11b is shown the structural V–I which follows, the V being typically overlaid with ♭9 reiterations of the principal melodic shape and the I stressing its characteristic ♭7, but with the minor 3rd held back for the unwinding of the restatement's magisterial line. Many elements, melodic and rhythmic, are variously counterpointed in both subject groups, but subtle interrelationships prevent diffuseness. The vast energy of this movement (in which gestures as big as those of Ex. 9.11b appear self-evidently proportionate) is initially accumulated with the help of a driving accompaniment rhythm, but that surface momentum is unnecessary after our inner rhythm has adjusted to the projecting force of the pedals; it returns only to celebrate the final major chord. Though this feels unexpectedly affirmative, in fact dissonance levels have been neither high nor perplexing: harmonies set askew to the pedal and containing their own appoggiatura clashes (often 'falsely related') represent Walton's extreme. It is the magnificent sense of scale that gives this movement so dominating a place in English symphonic writing.

A long scherzo is similarly founded on a framework of pedals (the penultimate dominant lasts a hundred bars), and the fragmentary thematic ideas are so furiously recharged with energy by displacements in foreground and background metre and twisted harmonic relationships that no 'trio' relaxation is offered, and very little literal restatement. The slow movement achieves pathos, after Sibelian climactic sonorities, with the modal ambiguity of the closing recall of the flute's opening lament: is the C♯ which broods over this movement (in the symphony's plan B♭ minor–E minor–C♯ minor–B♭ major) really a tonic or a dominant? But at this tempo some of the pedals hang fire, and the rhetoric is over-insistent. The finale introduction reinstates this inflated note in oddly dissociated gestures, while later attempts to propel fast music without pedal tensions relapse into episodic small-talk; genially academic fugue generates more vital rhythmic propulsion but the lofty coda appears inadequately motivated.

The year's delay between the performance of the first three movements in 1934 and the completion of the symphony reflects some crisis of the creative will. During the following years Walton began to draw the confidence and incentive to compose chiefly from his existing works. Such self-scrutiny carried the risk of converting manner into mannerism, though it facilitated a polish none of his contemporaries could rival. The Violin Concerto (1939) adopts the movement plan of the Viola Concerto, making great play with the preparation in the finale of a context that prompts the return of the first movement's main theme. Since this theme again epitomizes the work's tone, the later concerto is much blander. There are now three gesturing 7ths, the single peak comes pat in the third of four square phrases, and the close on the dominant (contrast the Viola Concerto's subdominant) compliantly invites repetition rather than extension; the use of both a countermelody (source of subsidiary theme here and main theme in the finale) and a lilting rhythmic figure (diluting that in the symphony) ensures easier propulsion than in the earlier concerto, as do appoggiatura dissonances that are titillating rather than acute. To extend comparisons into the passage work (see, for example, figs. 5 to 9 in the Viola Concerto and 10 to 13 in the Violin Concerto) yields similar results. But the luminosity of scoring marks a new level of Walton's orchestral skill.

After the symphony's monolithic scherzo, the brilliant one here seems overloaded with subsidiary ideas, seductive though their 'popular' vein may be. The dry opening of the finale confirms an affinity with Prokofiev (compare his Third Piano Concerto) which Lambert had identified earlier in Walton's career (1934: 151), while the closing stages are reminiscent, not just in the accompanied cadenza, of Elgar's Violin Concerto. But the narcissistic treatment of the first-movement theme circumvents the problem of the finale as an autonomous structure; and nostalgia so practised can cloy. When Walton uses the 'epilogue' device for a third time in his Cello Concerto (1956), the recall of first-movement themes more intricately structured places far greater expressive weight on the bitonal chordal motto which coloured the accompaniment. Yet the finale's cogent variations on a monumental theme could have been rounded off convincingly in their own terms.

This theme reflects a concept of melody building strongly indebted to Hindemith in rhythm, phrase development and tonal fluidity. Seven years later Walton's Variations on a Theme by Hindemith adopt that composer's view of variations as contrasted characters imposed on essentially unchanged linear successions (see *The Four Temperaments*, 1940). Meanwhile Walton had in 1960 written a second symphony, in a Bax-like pattern of sonata allegro, slow movement and final passacaglia. A colourful accompaniment formula, modelled on that of the Cello Concerto, contains in its pitches (D, C♯, B♭, A) the intervallic nucleus from which most of the first movement's thematic material is fashioned: the economy is palpable, but the derivatives, whether swooning *cantabile* gestures or twitching rhythmic figures, rarely build paragraphs proportionate to the length of the whole. The simple identity between verticals and horizontals suggests a cautious interest in Schoenbergian principle, acknowledged in the passacaglia's 12-note theme. But its opening six pitches endorse the first movement's G minor and the final A♭ inflects back to it, and in ten variations the ground is never transposed, though it appears in retrograde inversion; despite some harmonic conflations, the attendant detail has no concern for serial propriety. Only in the coda, following a *fugato*, does the ground explore new tonal levels, and characteristically these are underpinned by a home-dominant pedal, initiating a slow cadential progression below the ebullient surface. A new kind of thread has not transformed Walton's old kind of fabric.

However perverse the judgements may now appear with which Constant Lambert (1905–51) so exuberantly sprinkled the pages of *Music Ho!*, his acquaintance with a remarkably catholic range of contemporary music remains impressive. Yet close scrutiny of compositional processes was not to his taste, and when we turn to his own music it becomes clear that cultivated intuitions have not been supplemented by decisive pre-compositional strategies. Music for Orchestra (1927) pays tribute to its dedicatee, Lord Berners, in a C minor *fugato* that opens the main movement. A few jazzy syncopations notwithstanding, this is disappointingly conventional even by comparison with *Portsmouth Point*, to which its laboured brio is indebted. The Concerto for piano and nine players (1931) straddles the boundary between chamber and orchestral style: most of the instruments share duets with the piano, yet a rich tutti sonority is also available, based on the homogeneous sound of three clarinets. Varieties of colour sustain the jazz-derived manner better than in Lambert's Piano Sonata, and, though formal schemes are improvisatory (in the classical rather than the jazz sense), the invention is always engaging – witty in the crisp irregular metres and affecting in the blues-tinged melody. Inscribed to Vaughan Williams, the *Aubade héroïque* (1942) pays tribute in the opening rhapsodizing for unaccompanied cor anglais; alternations of 'nature' and distant 'warlike' symbols have a touching appeal, yet seem oddly simplistic after we have read Lambert the critic.

It may be that in a short life, much of it devoted to ballet composition and conducting, Lambert never found time to test the compositional consequences of his propaganda for Sibelius;

certainly he never approached the scale of musical thinking at which the budding symphonist's model became relevant. But E. J. Moeran (1894–1950) was probably directly inspired by Lambert's homilies to the composition of his most ambitious work, the Symphony in G minor of 1937. Until then, Moeran had betrayed no influences from beyond the English scene other than an enthusiasm for Irish melody and poetry. Like Bax, he was born in England, but his descent gave him stronger claims on Irish sources; yet it was the experience of collecting Norfolk folksongs that left the strongest mark on his melodic invention. His first orchestral score, *In the Mountain Country* (1921), was written during studies with John Ireland. It avoids the inertia of much rhapsody, the central pentatonic melismata creating slow-moving harmonic successions below the scherzo-like momentum. Two pieces for small orchestra, *Lonely Waters* and *Whythorne's Shadow* (1931), show Moeran's ability to add imaginative trimmings to a tune: whether he affected the bluff root triads of Vaughan Williams or the chromatic basses and empirical harmonic superstructure of Delius (or disconcertingly interleaved one with the other), an initially melodic invention could direct the piece.

So a symphony of some 45 minutes' duration suggests an astonishing confidence in Lambert's panacea. Debts to Sibelius stand out even more conspicuously than did Walton's – the wandering woodwind 3rds, the rhythmic cast and portentous falling 5ths of the slow-movement theme, the *tremolando* string textures of the finale and almost every detail of the scherzo, which Westrup accurately related to Lambert's preferred model, Sibelius's Fourth (1946: 182). The first movement seems less derivative, yet here the composer endorses Sibelius's view of symphony as progressively concentrated, 'free from the tautological emotional repetitions of romantic music cast in the classic mould' (Lambert 1934: 318). Restatement is shadowy, drastically abbreviated and tonally oblique, but the delayed return of the tonic area is then celebrated in a vast coda, virtually a pedal; and now the crucial material is discovered to be neither the elegant fusion of folky contour and neoclassical accompaniment that opened the work nor the ardently harmonized song of the second group, but a pentatonic cell (typically G–F–D(–C)) which, inconspicuously present in both, and more openly heard in subsidiary themes, finally predominates. It shapes the finale's main theme, later giving point to the inevitable epilogue – a wistful recall of first-movement material. But more powerful still is its appearance at the climax of the slow movement, for it reasserts pentatonic

G minor against a C♯ pedal that prepares the return of the movement's own E minor. In these two movements, proportions are sometimes inflated by elaborating static harmonic situations, but Moeran shows an unexpectedly assured control of the big span.

He never exercised it again so ambitiously. The Rhapsody for piano and orchestra (1943) reverts to earlier structural methods though the piano denies his characteristic lyricism the determining role it assumes in the string concertos (for violin, 1942; for cello, 1945), with an attractively Irish melodic tinge in both. The Sinfonietta (1944), for orchestra of classical proportions, revives the Sibelian echoes, fusing them with neoclassical patterning in an interesting first-movement design. By comparison the Serenade (1948) is glib and a little tired in its folky melody and archaizing dance metres.

Another Ireland pupil, Alan Bush (*b* 1900), pointedly dissociated himself from the decorous rhapsodizing with which Moeran became known. The capacity for taut argument shown in his *Dialectic* for string quartet (see below, p. 258) was still rare among British composers, and his work tended to be written off as unacceptably dry. Only with the belated awakening after the Second World War to the rigour of much European music were audiences here encouraged to listen as closely as such music demands – and by then Bush's own development, prompted by the social commitment of a left-wing idealist, had brought a pronounced simplification of language. Yet his view of the popular remains more elevated than the people have ever seemed to find congenial; perhaps the polemical intentions of a 'Leningrad' symphony are more readily accepted, if only at an exotic level, than those of a 'Nottingham' Symphony, Bush's second symphonic essay (1948). Its predecessor, the Symphony in C (1939–40), reviews a troubled political era in a brooding Prologue and three movements of vehement debate. Yet even the cataclysmic end of the slow movement is constructed solely from the initial three pitches of that 12-note row which gives this movement a pioneer place in British ventures into dodecaphony. Though all four forms of the complete row appear, Bush's practice is not serial, different row segments being used in turn to secure a highly concentrated motivic discourse. Textures are contrapuntal without surrendering to fortuitous intervallic relations, and a remarkable dynamism of rhythm sustains the tension. Equally neglected is Bush's Piano Concerto (1938), possibly because of the modification of the genre by the introduction of a chorus for the finale. But the Violin Concerto (1947), drawing on Bush's lyrical generosity without abandoning his care for finely related detail, might have been expected to remain before the public, had not the fortunes of his music tended to turn more on political sympathies than on artistic judgments.

V: Rawsthorne and Tippett

Though less committed to the symphony than Arnold Bax, Alan Rawsthorne (1905–71) is known, like him, almost entirely for his instrumental music. Like his contemporary, Rubbra, he handles orchestral forces with great assurance yet the invention does not owe much to the suggestibility of timbre. Already in his first ambitious score, the Symphonic Studies (1939), Rawsthorne's personal tone can be recognized. Despite inflexions of opposite tendencies, towards a more diatonic, even English pastoral, lyricism (Second Symphony), or towards 12-note usages (Third Symphony and the late chamber music), that tone was to be little modified throughout his career.

First impressions of a wiry polyphony need to be qualified: strong though the treble/bass polarity is, and etched in detail the intermediate strand(s), the music is typically controlled by an elaborately fashioned top voice which juxtaposes diatonic segments in a rapid quasi-chromatic flux. Hindemith inevitably comes to mind, the more so since both composers favour neo-baroque rhythms and sequential patterning. But Rawsthorne relies less on successive 4ths to keep tonal allegiance fluid, and in the vertical dimension neither Hindemith's quartal harmonies nor their mediating role in a hierarchical system are reproduced. Rawsthorne's harmonic system recognizes greater and lesser densities, but there is otherwise curiously little variation in the nature of his chord building. This stems, like the dominating lines themselves, from a constant process of association and dispersal between tonally conflicting triads, represented in full or part. The augmented triad is often central to the process, its inherent ambiguity being given sharper profile when its various major 3rds stake firm tonal claims by adding pitches to themselves – inevitably setting up false relations and other semitonal discrepancies in the aggregate (see Ex. 9.12). These shifting ambiguities make for a mobility rare in British music of Rawsthorne's generation, but blur distinctions of expressive intention: too often this music satisfies by its easy textural flow but remains enigmatic, even apparently uncommitted, at any deeper level. However, by

Ex. 9.12   Rawsthorne: Symphonic Studies

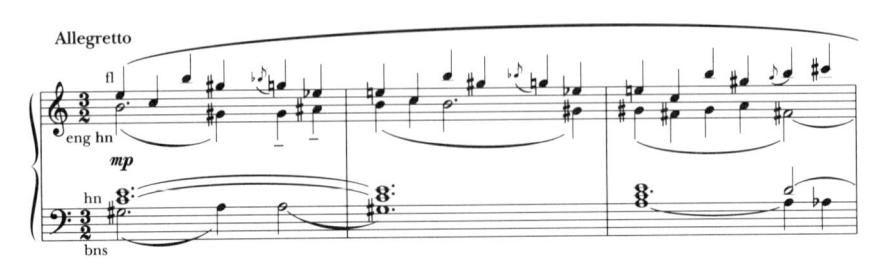

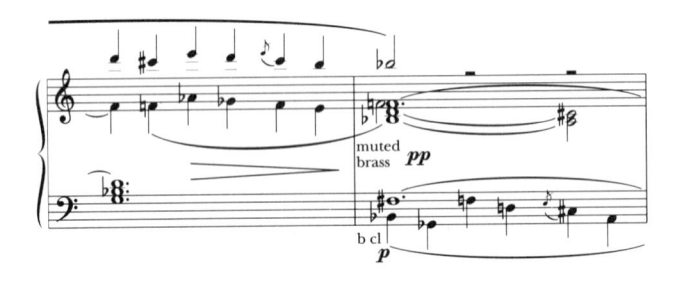

giving structural prominence to a single tonal area he can achieve affirmative statements; by relating the fluctuating tonal implications to two opposed centres he can maintain powerful tensions. But the kind of tension dependent on a basic contrast in the nature and tonal orientation of *successive* but logically continuous events – in short, the sonata dialectic – is less well adapted to this language. His early work shows a preference for variation types and for composite movements, defining absolute, even inert, contrast between blocks of material.

As the Symphonic Studies make clear, this implies no aversion to development. Each of the five sections, arranged in *ABABA* correspondences, engages one or more figures from the opening complex in an expansive orchestral dialogue. This complex is summarized in its initial pitches, B–E–C♯–A–F, but the derived figures all acquire independent life, now preserving intervallic identities, now modifying intervals within recognizable contours. The most unifying harmonic colour is the augmented triad plus minor 3rd of pitches 2–5, yet the centricity of B is never in doubt, nor the logic of the only pure major triads of B, at the end of the third and fifth sections. The orchestral sound is never voluptuous: climaxes are hard-edged, and the expert wind scoring is most original in the rather wintry ostinato textures of the second section (Ex. 9.12).

Chromatic alteration creates here an introverted, almost desolate mood which becomes characteristic; the languorous dance in the Oboe Concerto (1947) is marked *con morbidezza*. But in Rawsthorne's first popular success, the First Piano Concerto (with strings and percussion, 1939; with full orchestra, 1942) the flow of mechanized figurations in Capriccio and Tarantella makes pert rather than wry the endless tonal cross-cutting. The variations of the central Chaconne form a continuous expressive arch, based on ascending repetitions of the descending ground. The piano concerto's brittle manner was relaxed in the First Violin Concerto (1948) in favour of lyrical and *scherzando* idioms recalling those of its dedicatee, Walton. However, such apparent plagiarisms as the soloist's falsely related 6ths are in fact an almost inevitable product of the harmonic methods outlined above. Two large movements both juxtapose material at different tempi, emphasizing the rhetorical, rather than the developmental, possibilities of their basic intervallic shapes.

More successful in making a slow motto decisively active in the following fast movement is the Concerto for String Orchestra (1949), texturally one of the composer's most immaculate works; its neo-baroque device is drily pointed rather than (as too often in Hindemith) earnestly agile. Clearly Rawsthorne's restrained expressivity is nearer *Affekt* than unbridled subjective imagery; his titled pieces are neither rhapsodies nor tone poems but overtures, of which even the most extended, *Cortèges* (1955), makes no call on programmatic minutiae. The Second Piano Concerto (1951), texturally more enterprising than the first, harnesses the bravura clatter to suave *cantabile* lines. Its Intermezzo announces that warmer, more wayward tone which colours Rawsthorne's music of the 1950s, and the finale offers unapologetically diatonic tune and catchily varied metre. No British piano concerto has ever won the popular enthusiasm reserved for a handful of works; this concerto seems better fitted than those of Ireland and Bliss to compete for it.

Between the Symphonic Studies and the Third Symphony (1964), Rawsthorne's strongest music was a response to the innate contrasts of the concerto genre. As the First Symphony (1950) shows, he recognized a special challenge in the symphony without always finding the means to rise to it. The opening *tempestuoso* surge quickly fades into figurative small-talk, and, deprived of a soloist, the *cantabile* can lack fervour; here it is almost eliminated in the abridged reprise. The Lento relies entirely on a semitonal undermining of triads and furtively altered melodic degrees to create the most persuasive music in the symphony. The Second Symphony (1959), later entitled 'Pastoral', is less aspiring but more assured. Its opening motto, superimposing an A♭ triad on an E minor triad, is germinal in first and last movements; melodically too the finale, a setting for soprano and orchestra of a sixteenth-century sonnet, draws on the first movement, transforming patterned instrumental lines into vocal declamation. The extreme simplicity of this setting and the wistful radiance of its diatonic 7ths and 9ths approach the mainstream of English lyricism; in the Country Dance shifting drone 5ths even recall Vaughan Williams's bucolic manner. But the slow movement's *affrettando* gestures suggest a fundamental expressive limitation: too often a conception potentially tragic is realized as merely morose.

Most of the orchestral works of Rawsthorne's last period avoid this failing in their restriction to divertimento-like tone and proportions; those written for youth orchestras make a special bid for approachability. But in adding two concertos and a final symphony to his output, he tested the relevance to his own idiom of some 12-note practices. Those of the two-piano Concerto (1968) seem a substitute for a strong creative impulse, but the Cello Concerto (1965) recaptures the rich lyricism of the violin concertos. The Third Symphony (1964) is his largest and most tightly unified, not so much by the *attacca* links between its four movements as by the vigorous defence of the initial E asserted by the timpani. A substantial first movement deploys a 12-note row (Ex. 9.13a, *x*) without schematicism; despite restated contours (see Ex. 9.13b), the effect is often almost athematic, but of an unbroken evolution. In the 'Alla Sarabanda', E is consistently opposed by its semitonal neighbours, and Rawsthorne's longest scherzo follows, admirably transparent in sound. A quasi-serial width of interval in the finale jostles with figurative work nearer neoclassical ideals; grandiose peroration on E typically fades to a more equivocal close, in which semitonal frictions are eased but not dispelled.

The composer now seen to be the most adventurous musical thinker of this British generation, Michael Tippett (*b* 1905), matured stylistically still later than Rawsthorne. Almost all his early music, including a symphony contemporary with Walton's first, had been suppressed; only with the Concerto for Double String Orchestra (1939) did he retain an entire piece as fully representative of his musical thought. Its present secure place in a line of popular English string works emphasizes the folky qualities of the slow movement and of the Concerto's apotheosis, where broad major-mode harmonies

Ex. 9.13 Rawsthorne: Symphony no. 3, 1st movement

and song-with-dance invite an uncomplicated response. But pentatonic contours and traditional harmony (very English in its ardent appoggiaturas – see the finale's second subject) are a foil to a more original feature – variable metres. Since Walton's early ebullience had waned, even a uniform irregularity of metre had been little cultivated, but Tippett's counterpointing of irregular stresses discovers an entirely original buoyancy, a sensation that many bars pass in which one's feet do not touch the ground. The two orchestras offer endless varieties of antiphony, but intense linearity ensures that textures never congeal. Forms are essentially orthodox, exemplifying Tippett's tendency to shape the second half of a piece by juxtaposing literal or transposed paragraphs from the first. When statements are so often expansive rather than definitive, this can reduce the sense of adventure. And the chosen transpositions may lack logical force when the switches turn so automatically, as in the finale (see Figure 9.2).

Fig.9.2 Tippett: Concerto for Double String Orchestra,
3rd movement, formal and tonal scheme

Exposition					Development	
A_1 A_2	Transition	B	A_1 A_2		using C (= B/A synthesis)	
a G	→	A♭	b A		A/a then via d f b♭ g♯ b a c♯	

Recapitulation				Coda	
A_1 A_2	Transition	B	A_1	new expansion	on D (apotheosis)
g♯ F♯	→	B♭	c♯	C	C

A comparable process in the opening Allegro of the First Symphony (1945) ensures that there is neither a single crucial tonal caesura nor a 'second subject' otherness within the nervously tense succession of ideas spun from the opening 14 bars; string homophony finally stems this flow into cadential channels, later enlarged in a warm coda prophetic of Tippett's first opera. On the other hand, development as a mid-point activity is recognizable in unusually extensive spans of event and frequent interpolation of the opening 4ths in pointedly flat areas. Whatever his spiritual debt to Beethoven, Tippett accepts that his proliferating textures are incompatible with classical periodicity, yet the baroque device he borrows in the slow movement is the highly periodic passacaglia. Like baroque composers who controlled as a ground, or in fugue, their most poignant resource, the chromatic segment of the minor scale, Tippett tests and restrains his chromaticism (see the fugues in the String Concerto and the Second Quartet). His ground multiplies the traditional chromaticized tetrachord, producing a tritonal key-circuit, and this is subjected to comparable operations at the higher level of the successive variations (see Ex. 9.14). The florid superimpositions are too diffuse and rhythmically quirky quite to match this strength of design. But the scherzo, contrasting a mosaic of simple, cleanly coloured blocks with a trio of burgeoning string polyphony, vindicates Tippett's mechanistic view of structure. The finale is far from mechanistic in its eventual yoking of the opening darting semiquavers and the later slow, ruminative curve; both are introduced in fugal terms and incorporate the 4ths aggregates that integrate the symphony. The magical sonorities of the close (in fact left open – on V) offer most to those who know what they foreshadow – the worlds of Tippett's first two operas.

The 'Ritual Dances' from *The Midsummer Marriage* realize that promise in abundance. Invention scarcely less generous has been

Ex. 9.14   Tippett: Symphony no. 1, 2nd movement

lavished on the torrential arabesques of the Fantasia Concertante on a Theme of Corelli (1953), though the juxtaposition of baroque and Baroque detail is not always comfortable. To set its string textures beside those of the String Concerto is to observe a radical stylistic shift in which the opera has been decisive. Two major orchestral scores refine the new character and point towards the further modification achieved with *King Priam*. Arthur Bliss's impression of Tippett's Piano Concerto (1955) as of 'spring meadows and orchards in blossom in some Blake-like world' (1965: 34) would seem apt even if we had never experienced the piercing visions of *The Midsummer Marriage*; these are surely Tippett's most unremittingly beautiful sonorities. But the dream induces a narcotic response: after we have bathed for two movements in these lapping 4ths, endlessly postponing the disenchantment of tonal banks still reassuringly within reach, the energy and soloistic swagger of the finale, normally *de rigueur* in a piano concerto, appear factitious. The outer movements apply Tippett's block transfer methods to classical prototypes but each has memorable felicities. In the first movement the magic sonority of horn and celesta effects the reprise, and the finale announces its central episode with a great dominant pedal, aerating the structure as do Beethoven's in his Fourth Concerto, the impetus towards Tippett's own. More puzzling in shape is the slow movement, a prodigiously long, slow canon between wind instruments, with a metrically conflicting undertow in bass strings and cascading piano figurations. The antithetical A and E♭ areas at the dénouement anticipate an important relationship in *King Priam*, though no programmatic clues elucidate this impassioned context. They play equal and opposite roles in relation to the vast C which spans the work.

A still vaster C booms through opening and close of the Second Symphony (1957). Pulsating rhythms distil the experience of a Vivaldi concerto overheard – which has also suggested, with no trace of pastiche, the driving string semiquavers; and C's centrality is reinforced by the phalanx of dominants and subdominants surrounding it in the brass. Tonal and textural contrast identifies the luminous second theme, but its flat bias (A♭; D♭ on restatement; E♭ transformation in coda) is balanced by a sharpened recurrence of the main theme (E; A on restatement) before a third, monolithic idea, more arresting than the token development around it; this returns in the coda, followed with superb finality by what is evidently more a ritornello than a first subject. Of the slow movement's four ideas, the first two are associated by their surrounding harp and piano arabesques, the second two by a cross-cutting technique; the pairs are varied facets of one contrast – between coldly bright trumpet solo and warmly dark string *cantabile*. The whole strophe is reworked in the other half of the movement, at first simply transposed and with reversed orchestral colourings (trombone/violins replace trumpet/cellos), but more momentously with the second pair: the dramatic intrusion of the nervous repeated notes from the very opening reduces the exchanges to fragments, exposing an element already hinted at – quiet horn harmony. This mediation between sonorous extremes also resolves tonal tensions, to end in A♭ (V on I); the closing stage of the process is shown at Ex. 9.15. The scherzo, in D, surpasses earlier feats of variable metre, preserving clarity even when the diverse ideas are synthesized; after a tense climax, *da capo* literalism is vestigial. The finale is still more a straight-line structure, almost a collage of figures and textures. Though supporting evidence implies C as the destination of the opening bass Es, only after a richly lyrical episode has abandoned the bass area entirely is a way found down to that pitch. Inevitably the coda revives memories of the symphony's opening, but not as a nostalgic epilogue. Both Tippett's later symphonies have more embracing aspirations, yet the Second may be thought his best realized orchestral design.

Ex. 9.15 Tippett: Symphony no. 2, 2nd movement

VI: *Rubbra, Finzi and Berkeley*

While Tippett returned to symphony at well-spaced intervals, to test the 'absolute' validity of stylistic territory won in verbal–dramatic contexts, the career of Edmund Rubbra (1901–86) is principally charted by symphonies. A common debt to R. O. Morris's contrapuntal discipline and the revitalizing rhythms of Tudor polyphony might suggest similar objectives, yet even at its most polymetric Rubbra's texture could never be mistaken for Tippett's. Nor could his harmonic/tonal processes: that Stravinskian element in Tippett which makes each span of activity, frenzied or rapt, appear to circle about stasis, is replaced in Rubbra by patient yet relentless motion, not always with a clear destination in view. Tippett's superimposed dominants and subdominants in equipoise may simply abandon a flat area for a sharp one (or vice versa) from time to time; Rubbra's franker key-assertions are constantly undermined by deft modulation. The scherzo of his Fifth Symphony (1948) reiterates a genial eight-bar dance tune of undisturbed major modality, interest being sustained by some 30 clear-cut modulations that occur between the initial and the final D major.

Such fluidity of essentially orthodox modulatory technique inevitably limits the role of fundamental tonal shifts or oppositions in building dramatic tensions. But it is clear from the nature of their material that Rubbra's structures, while often respecting sonata symmetries, place little reliance on a dichotomy of thematic types and associated tonal areas. Even when a pointed contrast is set up, the new idea tends to be assimilated into the onward flow of the old: see the wind homophony in B♭ minor that follows the E major polyphony of the Third Symphony (1939). As Rubbra's early apologists stressed, his textural ideals owe more to the renaissance motet or the viol fantasy than to the disjunct propositions and vertical bias of the classical style. Yet symphony became his preferred medium, and polyphonic forms are not unduly prominent. Even in the first two symphonies the texture rarely exceeds three 'real parts', and thereafter Rubbra quite rarely writes orchestral polyphony in any strict sense. His characteristic layout is hierarchical, compounded of an expansive top line, a secondary middle strand related to this or developing a subsidiary figure, and a bass moving restlessly by step – whether in wide-ranging scales or oscillations between two pitches. A sense of constant organic growth is vital to the success of the method, and such textures invite an orchestral treatment nearer 'registration' than either repartee or impressionistically blurred sonority.

Yet the later symphonies, less uniform in texture and orchestral treatment, remind us that Rubbra can score colourfully, despite his place in that line of English composers who give that skill a low priority. But in every work there are passages in which conspicuous activity seems to carry a quite blank expressive intention. A similar sense of desertion may sometimes be felt in Shostakovich, a composer who in his contrapuntal vein often approaches common ground with Rubbra; in Shostakovich, however, the range of mood within a symphony is more extreme, so that determinedly faceless music draws its point from searing irony or desperate high spirits surrounding it. Rubbra is a composer without irony, as is confirmed by his total avoidance of archaizing pastiche, whether nostalgically precise or wilfully distorted, in what is in one sense very old-fashioned music. His harmonic vocabulary is small and climaxes are more likely to be glowingly consonant than destructively dissonant. They are achieved by traditional means – the proliferation of rhythmic activity, the expansion or severe contraction of the textural width, the timing of modulations, the developing friction between a fixed element and a free, and so on. Of course, as Wilfrid Mellers showed by examining Rubbra's fluid dominant-7th usage, a small vocabulary need not prevent originality of syntax (1948). Few British composers at work after the Second World War remained as faithful to traditional diatonic collections; of those who did, none matched his fluidity and unpredictability – which is not the same as neoclassical sidestepping of the obvious.

When we have learned the patience called for by Rubbra's long unwinding paragraphs, we may still be uneasily aware that he has chosen to assemble them within a form commonly dependent on a very different conception of the musical 'event'. Ex. 9.16, from the Second Symphony (1937), makes a point in shifting the tonal perspective, but seems resolved, in its stubbornly conjunct motion, not to ingratiate the listener. The Third Symphony's first movement rejects his typical structural flow in favour of a more sectional form – hence its rather self-conscious sonata observances (we have noted its unusually differentiated 'second subject') and its middle section, enclosing development within statements of a new theme. The finale's ending, of variation theme climactically augmented against fugue subject, is one of Rubbra's most effective, and tonally it completes a purposeful scheme across the cycle (E major; A♭ major;

Ex. 9.16   Rubbra: Symphony no. 2, 1st movement

B minor–D major; C♯ minor). In the Fourth Symphony (1941), Rubbra solves the problem of a monolithic form; 'monothematic' would be an inaccurate description of this first movement, but its initial three-note motif remains active in all that follows, and each shape is generated out of its predecessor; not until a brief reprise (in feeling a coda) does the steadily rising intensity flag. There being no slow movement, the finale has an impressively weighty introduction and central interlude, but the allegro section is driven too automatically by those scalic marching basses which remind us that Rubbra was a Holst pupil. Motivic derivations from a three-note cell are again pervasive in the opening movement of the Fifth Symphony (1948) and re-emerge in an epilogue. If Sibelius's Fifth influenced the shape of this composite first movement, Rubbra has weakened the impression of inexorable growth by excessive fluctuations of speed and metre. His slow movement, on the other hand, in its intense span of slowing tempo and proliferating detail, makes notably original use of musical time.

In his concertos (for viola, 1953; and piano, 1956) Rubbra finds solo string lines more compatible with his usual orchestral methods, though their melodic eloquence is restrained. The 'Collana musicale' finale rationalizes his preference for a steadily changing state in tempo and thematicism; the viola's closing industry, where panache might have been expected, typifies Rubbra's sober response to the concerto challenge. In the Piano Concerto this is still more limiting, for he lacks the kind of melodic flair to make a catchy, knockabout affair of the 'Danza alla rondo'; nor can his piano textures rival the seductive quality of Tippett's concerto.

As well as brighter scoring, the Sixth Symphony (1954) admits more overt expressive impulses than hitherto, notably in the slow Canto on lines from Leopardi. This urge towards 'romantic' states of feeling (which we have seen in Rawsthorne too) throws greater weight on harmonic textures, and the normally inhibited melodic spans achieve some relaxation. A four-pitch motto begets another chain-like finale, while in the Seventh Symphony (1957) passacaglia and fugue make for a still tauter succession. Rubbra's anxiety to escape the sheer fluency of his normal practice is evident in the scherzo's metrical asymmetries and blocks of material, and a decision to reassess may be reflected in his withdrawal from symphonic composition for eleven years after this work. By this time, general interest in his work had waned, and his symphonies are now in limbo, unappealing to the revivalists who set most store by opulent orchestral sound, and unadventurous to the radicals. The indisputable originality of his methods may never overcome the sobriety of his materials.

Gerald Finzi (1901–56) was of the same conservative bent as Rubbra. His melody is less cautious, achieving at its best a soaring lyricism that triumphs over a severely restricted harmonic syntax: his gesturing 7ths and higher-diatonic dissonances retain precisely the expressive connotations they had for Parry, while the simultaneous false relation is the peak of his chromatic repertoire. He shares Rubbra's gift for stealthy modulation, but harnesses it less certainly to structural effect: the first movement of the Clarinet Concerto (1949) demonstrates this, together with a disproportion between momentarily aggressive tuttis and the imperturbable lyrical flow of the solo writing. Finzi ventured diffidently outside the field of vocal music in which most of his best work was done, but towards the end of his life his grasp of absolute designs became surer; his Cello Concerto (1955) promises a development that was cut short. Its opening movement essays epic gestures and proportions, and an enhanced harmonic range at first supports the new breadth. But the momentum flags, and the lyrical stream of second-group events seems merely to displace rather than to challenge the first group's assertiveness; only after the cadenza is the initial potential realized in the spacious cadential moves. The slow movement's major-mode diatonicism could be dated half a century too early, yet it rings true. The flat bias is so strong that recapitulation in E♭ regains the original D only at the closing tonic pedal; placed between the A minor and A major of the outer movements, this tritonal stress helps to weld a strong tonal arch. The attempt in the Rondo to adapt his diatonicism to more exuberant ends dims Finzi's characteristic radiance.

The few British composers born in the century's first decade who studied abroad include no Schoenberg pupil; only two minor figures, Walter Leigh (1905–42) and Arnold Cooke (*b* 1906), studied with Hindemith, and Lennox Berkeley (1903–89) was the only Boulanger pupil of note. Though Britten, with whom Berkeley collaborated on a set of orchestral dances, *Mont Juic* (1937), might affect a comparable insouciance, it was never more than one weapon in a varied armoury, whereas Berkeley remained faithful throughout much of his career to the contained ideals instilled by Nadia Boulanger's teaching. Fastidiously clean textures prevail, often setting elegant melody faintly awry to classicistic repeated-chord accompaniments. Nothing persists to the point of importunity: without the arrogance of Stravinsky's juxtapositions of material, Berkeley's are often scarcely less offhand. The effect of inconsequence is stronger, indeed, when there is neither the logic of Stravinsky's cross-cutting method nor so consistent a tension within the harmonies. It might seem that Berkeley was destined to be *par excellence* a composer of instrumental diversions, yet as early as 1940 he produced a symphony and had already written ambitiously for chorus and orchestra. His expressive range widened at the suggestibility of texts, and the dramatic contingencies of opera (*Nelson*, 1953) encouraged a new breadth of statement.

The Serenade for Strings (1939) is deftly pointed in its quick music, while its two slow movements, invoking respectively Poulenc and Fauré, twist tonality to touching effect. Their ultimate melodic derivation is from a French tradition of popular (rather than folk) song, and despite faint 'epilogue' memories of the opening theme, the Serenade disowns the aspiration and heavy nostalgia of so much British music of its time. Turning to symphony, Berkeley moved no nearer Vaughan Williams or Walton; but Stravinsky's own Symphony in C was just being written, and the neoclassicism of Berkeley's First Symphony is more reminiscent of the drily invigorating Roussel. The first movement presents a confusing sequence of subsidiary ideas, accompaniment patterns and tonal implications, but much stems from the 4 3 0 cell of the opening unison statement, and fresh developments continue busily after its recapitulation. The aseptic chromaticism of the slow movement is oddly affecting, and the divertimento-like movements around it find a congenial place for frank accompaniment patterns and block formal assembly. Not surprisingly, the Divertimento in B♭ (1943) and the Sinfonietta (1950), with their token initial sonatas and their slow movements that exploit tonal ambivalence for piquancy rather than anguish, are better balanced pieces.

Between these works the Piano Concerto appeared in 1947. Its busy flow of figurations fills out the form without too many subsidiary ideas, and major/minor inflexions or superimpositions have 'blue' connotations to match jazz-derived syncopations. A self-conscious common touch is evident in the slow-movement refrain, of piano-octave melody and mildly dissonant string harmonies, but the finale's relaxed note, more crudely struck, is not improved upon by contrapuntal working-out. The Flute Concerto (1952) seems better suited to Berkeley's textural and structural predilections.

Berkeley's Second Symphony (1958) has a more satisfying breadth of phrase, a less overtly entertaining manner, than its predecessor. Its first Allegro gains weight, not prolixity, from the Lento frame, and a spaciously proportioned scherzo follows. But it is the unfussy textures of the slow movement which best show the composer's new command of symphonic continuity; by its close the initial tonal ambiguity has been enriched to an unforced ambivalence of 3rd-related keys (see Ex. 9.17). The Third Symphony (1969), in one movement, is short because of a reluctance to cover old ground again: thus the final Allegro adapts material from the first section to quite new purpose, the intervening Lento scarcely exceeds 30 bars. The harmonic resources gain strength and consistency in the superimposition of conflicting triadic units, and such tensions brace far broader spans in the Fourth Symphony (1977). Its opening Allegro quarries much material from the slow introductory shape, and its central slow movement flows purposefully across the constituent variations. The finale opens with a great wedge that wrenches away from E major. It is exceptional in Berkeley for the amount of literal recapitulation, yet the stamp of a large-scale work, not an inflated one, is unmistakable, and the coda's hammering home of the wedge so as now to secure the E it originally unsettled makes for his most convincing symphonic climax.

Ex. 9.17 Berkeley: Symphony no. 2, 3rd movement

VII: Britten and Others

Of the composers who had earned a serious claim on the interest of conductors and audiences by the outbreak of the 1939–45 war, Benjamin Britten (1913–76) was notably the youngest. At just that time he had moved to North America, where several of his major orchestral scores were written. Whatever personal and political motivations were involved, a contributory factor was the suspicion fostered by critics of the day (and prevalent among British musicians much later) that the remarkable technical fluency of this young composer must inhibit qualities they found more lovable. His lineage was acceptable enough, back to Stanford through both Ireland at the RCM and Frank Bridge, but the difficulty of categorizing his work was as unsettling as the evidently justified self-confidence it displayed. A natural musicality superior to that of any British composer of modern times had been nurtured by Bridge against the background of his own widened stylistic horizons. At this stage, therefore, Britten preferred to accept the lot of a tradition-less composer rather than embrace local traditions that might be stifling.

His Sinfonietta (1932) is more appropriately discussed with his chamber works. Ideals of full orchestral sound ranging from Stravinsky to Berg were tested in the song cycle *Our Hunting Fathers* (1936) but Britten's opportunity to address an international audience in an orchestral work came with a string score, the Variations on a Theme of Frank Bridge (Salzburg Festival, 1937). Ignoring the British exemplars of Elgar, Vaughan Williams and Bliss, he aimed at a cosmopolitan virtuosity, to which his gift for witty pastiche gave him a stronger claim than any British composer had yet advanced. Inevitably, this cultivation of a range of genre musics relegated to a secondary role both the motivic skills and the structural subtlety of his earlier chamber music. Behind the astonishing variety of highly polished string scorings, however, these still exercise a strengthening influence, and in the coda, his most personal tribute to his teacher (see Hindmarsh 1983: 44–5), Britten deploys a wholly creative tonal irony rather than modish satire (see Ex. 9.18). But a marked distinction was to persist between music in which he could develop a brilliant aptitude, and music whose character depended upon its inner evolution. So we may consider separately Britten's variation and sonata types – even though they are often cross-fertilized. The line established by the *Bridge Variations* continues with the *Diversions* for piano (left hand) and orchestra of 1940. Here the challenge lies in circumventing the limitations of one-handed pianism in as many ways as possible. The idea varied is half the cycle of 5ths, ascending C to F♯, and its reversal – continuing to ascend in 4ths. This formula covers a wide range of the keyboard, while its traditional function, to cover a

Ex. 9.18   Britten: Variations on a Theme of Frank Bridge

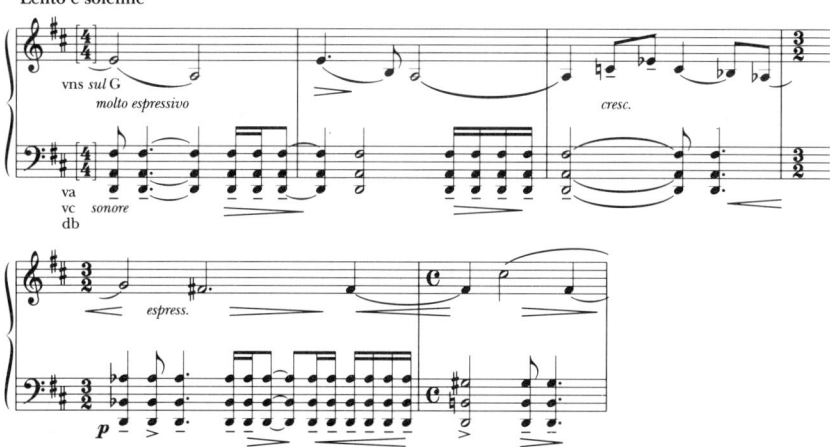

wide range of keys, is used to promote tonal designs more sophisticated than those of the Bridge set. The humour has taken on a drier tone, and in his last American score it seems a little acid: the *Scottish Ballad* for two pianos and orchestra (1942) is a dramatic juxtaposition, sometimes superimposition, of Scottish psalm-tune, lament, march and reel, undermining the general pentatonicism with merciless bitonality. Best known of all Britten's orchestral genre pieces are the variations on a Purcell theme, *The Young Person's Guide to the Orchestra* (1946). Written after his return to England, when the success of *Peter Grimes* had encouraged him and his audience to their warmest relationship, it satisfies customary expectations of each instrument's qualities and resources in turn. How unwise it is to generalize about Britten's response to technical challenge may be seen by comparing the concluding fugue of this work with two others: here the brilliance lies in the irrepressible profusion of entries flung into the texture, in the *Bridge Variations* fugue the wit is in the entries' failure to accumulate polyphony (instead a rhythmic heterophony is produced), while the fugue, with prelude and postlude, for 18-part strings (1943) remains primarily a testimony to ingenuity.

Britten is conspicuous among British composers of his own and the next generations in showing so little interest in the orchestral symphony. (Neither of his teachers had cultivated the type, nor had the mature Holst, but with Walton's generation the urge for composers to test themselves against this hurdle became more compelling.) Not only the Sinfonietta but the quartets and the Cello Symphony demonstrate that Britten developed a consistent train of thought within the sonata concept, and that this need not rely on the quasi-dramatic promptings of the concerto's opposition of forces or of programmatic titles. As the biggest early scores do so rely, a view gained currency, of the dramatist in search of his *métier*, that overlooked their refinement of argument. If some of the irony of the variations persists, it is a defence to be observed in all the music in which Britten is discovering his own character.

Titled movements in the Piano Concerto (1938) seem to disown classical reference. But the opening Toccata, despite the piano's clanging figurations, is an elaborate sonata with a dichotomy of theme and key (D–E) and a control of long spans by pedals (worth comparing with Walton's). Restatement of both subjects in conflation has less point than in the Sinfonietta, since the second is given an orthodox return too. In the Waltz, the satirical mask is more evident, but the tonal architecture more subtle, turning on an ambivalence that was to be refined in the *Sinfonia da Requiem*. With the Violin Concerto (1939) Britten achieves forms in which the tonal scheme is expressively crucial. Here D (on balance, major) is the goal of both movements but the starting-point of neither. Indeed, the soloist's rather withdrawn lyrical opening establishes F, so that his later, more ardent preference for D (and its ancillary A in a 'second subject' fanfare) runs against the course pursued in the orchestra; militant accompaniment rhythms intensify the friction. 'Development' is not a separate stage in this process, and 'restatement', while palpably the movement's goal, is not restatement; for at this point, after sublimating its baser material into a compelling lyricism, the soloist wins from the orchestra its own expansive version of the original theme in a luminous D major and the more contentious ideas are not recalled. This unique expressive form owes much to 'sonata thinking' – but not its shape. In the finale, Britten forges a passacaglia chain so that a tonally nebulous scalic formula finally achieves the highly personal assertions of D major at the peak and its poignantly inflected form at the close.

After this mobility, the retention in all three movements of the thunderous initial D of the *Sinfonia da Requiem* (1941) appears heavily symbolic. The relentless undertow of 'Lacrymosa' extends the imagery on to the structural plane, yet this is no inert form. Though in one sense a straight-line piece, directed towards crisis, it is powerfully articulated by a sonata-like distinction in thematic roles and tonal stresses. And in the 'Dies irae' scherzo, semitonal tensions vehemently seek to dislodge D minor. It is difficult to think of any British orchestral writing so shocking in its impact: if we compare Vaughan Williams's Fourth Symphony, we see that Britten's juxtapositions are brusquer, the eventual splitting apart of texture more savage, and yet the momentum is greater because of subterranean scalic connections. The emergence of the serenely hymnic 'Requiem aeternam' from this abyss is not programmatically contrived but magnificently logical: its revolving bass audibly pieces together the ruins of the scherzo, now recognizing in them two tonal constituents, B♭ and the D in which the flutes' refrain is cast. This theme, heard before in frenzied exchanges with the saxophone's 'Lacrymosa' distortion in the trio, inevitably prompts the return of 'Lacrymosa' as an exalted central panel in this deeply 'major' close to the cycle.

The urge to write opera and the responsibility of providing pieces for distinguished colleagues to play at the Aldeburgh Festival deflected Britten's interest from large-scale orchestral composition.

ART MUSIC

It is symptomatic that the Sonata for orchestra he interrupted to concentrate on *Peter Grimes* was eventually abandoned (Mitchell and Reed 1991: 1042). But one of his tributes to Rostropovich was conceived on the grand scale, and its title, 'Symphony for Cello and Orchestra' (1963), declares Britten's intention to engage the performers in an equal dialogue comparable to the duo-sonata, rather than to set a grandiose frame around soloistic virtuosity. The first movement, his biggest sonata scheme, strikes an unusual balance between impassioned rhetoric and intense economy of material. Thus the falling semitone of the soloist's opening phrases is retained in transition and sighing second subject, while the orchestral scales that punctuate the first subject persist in octave-transposed form as the pizzicato irritant in the second. The irritant is also tonal, for F major is implied by the pizzicato figures no less than A major by the cello's *tranquillo* melody and its accompaniment; thus two stock secondary keys simultaneously counter the symphony's tonic, D minor. On restatement the leading themes pass to the orchestra, and the tonal circuit is from F minor to D major opposed by B♭. In the coda D remains equivocal only in mode, and in another conflation the soloist projects the first subject against the wind's transition theme. The scherzo is spectral, deriving scurrying lines and articulating chords from one cell of tone-plus-semitone (see Ex. 9.19). On its own the ternary Adagio might seem not quite

Ex. 9.19   Britten: Cello Symphony, 2nd movement

to fulfil the promise of its solemn cello theme, but after a cadenza the secondary theme returns as trumpet tune of the final passacaglia. By its close the aspiring mood of the Adagio has been recaptured and brought to apotheosis. Britten's title is accurate, but it is not always proof against expectations of all-consuming brilliance as the goal of a work that employs the forces of a concerto.

After the Second World War, most of the new composers, such as Fricker and Hamilton, found their point of departure in a stylistic synthesis indebted to the Continental pioneers; their work is discussed in the next chapter. But that of Malcolm Arnold (*b* 1921) pointedly shrugs off any burden of responsibility to the European models it fitfully suggests. An aptitude for popularist, often unwaveringly diatonic invention has served him well in light music, and the calculated flippancy with which he has approached that sacred cow, the English symphony, can be entertaining. But it does not easily survive either developmental processes or the juxtaposition of more aspiring moods, so that an embarrassing incongruity can disturb Arnold's most ambitious structures. In the first movement of the Second Symphony (1953), two tunes are indulged by repetitions in varied surroundings; the key scheme E♭–A–C–E♭ is neatly used so as to give a sonata-ish nuance to rondo-ish events. The scherzo derives melodic and harmonic material quasi-serially from an eight-note idea; as in the first movement, much confidence is placed in superimposed strands of 3rds (here often coalescing into dense 3rd-aggregates) and in juxtaposition of segments. Yet the music moves convincingly, as does the genial finale, albeit by crude means in the contrapuntal encounters of its second theme, a relation of the slow movement's *idée fixe*. It is this Lento in which we notice that, expressive though the theme seeks to be, its reiteration against a series of thinly imagined accompaniments makes the dramatic interludes appear factitious. And neither this earnestness nor the finale's ingratiating jollity prepares for the symphony's pompous coda; the First Symphony (1949) had set the pattern for such uneasy alliance of moods, and it remains typical. But many of Arnold's concertos and dance suites are effective at an undemanding level, while a few works, such as the Seventh Symphony (1973), reflect a heightened intensity of motivation in exploring sombre material.

Another composer just as expert as Arnold in the composition of film scores turned to symphony at the same time, though he was of the Walton–Tippett generation and had written a Piano Concerto as early as 1930. The First Symphony (1949) by William Alwyn (1905–85) typifies the form as cultivated by those composers and promoting institutions that felt no obligation to measure themselves against the wider European scene. It is melodically less racy than Arnold, harmonically more conservative than Fricker, texturally more virtuoso than Rubbra. Perhaps such well-wrought but circumspect music allowed responsibilities towards a nominally new music to be painlessly discharged; even the lack of memorability accorded with policies in which the first performance was all-important. But Alwyn did not merely repeat these recipes. His Second Symphony (1953) abandons standard types for two composite movements; its gestures are less histrionic and the use of tight intervallic cells consolidates relationships and gives a more individual sound. In the Third Symphony (1955) certain intervallic repertoires constitute the total pitch resources of complete movements: the lengthy opening Allegro never admits the four pitches D, E, F and A♭, but fashions from the other eight a network of tangible but unconstrained relations, making use of the ability of this synthetic mode to operate tonally around various pitches (most prominently C, B, E♭ and F♯). Alwyn's imagination seems revitalized by these rich potentialities, and contrives even to overcome the daunting restrictions of the complementary sections in which the remaining four pitches have to generate all events.

B: Chamber and Keyboard Music

VIII: The Cobbett Legacy: Bridge and Ireland

Geoffrey Bush's account of British chamber music in the early years of this century ended with a tribute to W. W. Cobbett, a patron and amateur performer so energetic in his enthusiasms as to have left two substantial memorials – the large body of native chamber music composed to his commission or for his competitions and the *Cyclopedic Survey of Chamber Music* (1929–30) which he edited (Bush 1981: 399). As well as contemporary assessments of the composers Cobbett supported, the encyclopaedia gives some account of the performing conditions for which they wrote (Cobbett 1929–30, i: 203). The professional ensemble of constant membership, solely devoted to the chamber repertoire, was not yet familiar (it became so in Britain only with the success of the Griller Quartet in the 1930s), and the picture is typically of players active in several groups as well as in orchestral playing and teaching. Even so, a list of more than 70 ensembles suggests that professionally performed chamber music was far more widespread than professional orchestral performance. The more gifted amateurs, such as Cobbett himself, might on occasion share the platform with professionals, and many of his editorial footnotes on recent music offer encouragement or warning to that body of fellow practitioners for whom his survey seems primarily intended. But the ways were parting, and he regretfully concludes that such works as the late Bridge quartets must be left to the professionals. Their supremacy was reinforced by broadcasting, for which the small ensembles were considered particularly suitable in the early days, when neither transmission nor reception was equal to the amplest orchestral sonorities; and a quarter of the chamber music broadcast was by native composers (Cobbett 1929–30, i: 212). The decline of the highly cultivated domestic ensemble-playing Cobbett championed became most marked after the Second World War, when it lost ground in the affection of young players to the cult of the youth orchestra. Meanwhile the immeasurable improvement in radio and gramophone reproduction gave the pure listener an unrestricted choice of medium, and here too the headier delights of orchestral music secured for it the dominating place it still enjoys in general musical experience.

So the first four decades of this century represent a heyday for British chamber music. Yet not all the composers whose orchestral music has been discussed were at ease in the more intimate media. Among the Stanford pupils it was not Vaughan Williams and Holst but Bridge and Ireland who rose to the challenges of an idiomatic chamber style. Ireland's mature chamber music is restricted to duo-sonatas and piano trios, in which the piano's harmonic masses carry the burden of the compositional argument. Frank Bridge, a violist with a profound knowledge of the classical repertoire, is subtler in textural balance, while his more sinewy lines can engage in string quartet textures that owe nothing to keyboard thinking. Among the composers who profited from Cobbett's patronage, Bridge was to become stylistically the most adventurous. Even while his idiom remained fundamentally traditional, an exploratory mind can be seen at work. Thus, Bridge not only struck a fresh balance in each example of the 'phantasy' forms but significantly modified his treatment of standard types when he again used self-contained movements. Both the Phantasie for piano trio (1907) and the Phantasy for piano quartet (1910) are mirrored structures, but the

ART MUSIC

quartet is terser and much better integrated: it excludes 'second subject' elements from the framing material, so that the scherzo-ish sequel provides the generating contrast. Development of the main material passes into restatement in mid-theme, giving point to a climactic return of the full theme before the coda synthesizes elements from both sources. The harmonic language is still rooted in traditional chromaticism, sometimes elided, and phrase-lengths rarely confound expectations, but there is a neat wit and complete freedom from that adiposity which piano with strings can induce. In the Piano Quintet, as revised two years later, an independent central movement frames scherzo with Adagios, and the first movement's main shape is finally brought back against a modified version of the finale's first subject; thus an embracing arch is again delineated.

Appearing in the same year, his String Sextet applied these structural traits to pure string textures. Their idiomatic flair had been cultivated in quartet contexts such as the *Noveletten* (1904) and *Three Idylls* (1906), admirably precise in their characterizing sonorities. But the G minor Quartet (no. 2, 1915) marks a new level of technical accomplishment in British quartet writing, not to be surpassed (whatever the more memorable beauties of Elgar's 1918 quartet) till Bridge returned to the medium 11 years later. The centrepiece is now scherzo–andante–scherzo, and the sharing of thematic shapes between the outer movements is more pervasive yet less ostentatious. The chromatic intensity of Bridge's language may create an almost expressionistic surface of rapidly shifting tonal implications or be retarded to an impressionistic languor (see Ex. 9.20). In either case the background is strongly and spaciously planned within a tonal design spanning the whole work: 3rd-relationships are typical, while dominants, notably in the finale development, are so rarely, or so belatedly, fulfilled as to create fine tensions. The immediate sonorous appeal of this quartet (especially its intermezzo) ensured the success of its first performance, but its motivic concentration and harmonic depth of field already invite that more searching response which Bridge's final chamber works were to demand.

Bridge's Second Quartet was dedicated to Cobbett, his next to Elizabeth Sprague Coolidge. It was the generosity of this other influential patron of chamber music that enabled Bridge in the later part of his career to withdraw from professional performance and to compose without too constricting a deference to the taste of British audiences. The Third Quartet (1926) was first performed by the Kolisch Quartet, when those pioneer interpreters of the Second

INSTRUMENTAL MUSIC I

Ex. 9.20 Bridge: String Quartet no. 2 in G minor, 1st movement

Viennese School also introduced Schoenberg's Third Quartet. Bridge can have known neither that nor Berg's *Lyric Suite* while at work on his quartet, though Berg's op. 3 and Bartók's Second Quartet may have influenced its more rigorous thematic and harmonic organization and more tangential tonal reference. Triadic components are still audible, but their centripetal powers are disowned by conflicting implications, not merely concealed by a network of appoggiaturas. Many chords appear cogent for their interval content, whether based upon whole-tone collections or perfect- and augmented-4th superimpositions; echoes of Skryabin in such formations are belied in the wider context by far greater mobility in implied root progression and in directed bass. A concern for consistent intervallic profile is still more evident in the motivic economy which unifies the outer movements. Yet at the Viennese première it was the wistful central movement that was most admired, and the best-realized moods of the work appear the most English, recalling at times the poignant lassitude of Warlock's *The Curlew*, written four years earlier. This is not to question the driving force of Bridge's fast music, but to observe that it is sometimes over-reliant on reiteration, as with the cardinal motif, C–E♭–G–F♯, aptly though this epitomizes a tritonal convergence on F♯ that is fundamental.

Bridge's handling of reversed restatement was further refined in this quartet, but a renewed interest in the symmetries of a large composite movement, soon to shape *Oration*, was exercised first in a trio for two violins and viola, subtitled Rhapsody (1928). Transition between quick and slow sections is subtler than in the early phantasies, and the primarily linear chromatic language is coloured by ubiquitous 0 3 4 cells. The textural possibilities discovered in a problematic medium command the admiration, though the sound is drier than Bridge's habitual sonority; its elusive emotional temper and exacting technical demands have denied this excellently wrought piece many hearings. The Piano Trio of 1929 appears more orthodox in instrumentation and four-movement plan. For once, scherzo and slow movement are independent, though the latter reworks the first movement's head-motif and functions as weighty upbeat to the finale. So there is a palpable logic in Bridge's typical interpolation of first-movement material during the finale's development and in the coda, where it reduces the finale theme to a shadow cast over the C♯ tonic pedal. Pedals support the first movement too, their harmonic superstructure unfolded rather too monotonously in piano arpeggiations. But the fundamental bass references, C♯–E♭–C♯,

INSTRUMENTAL MUSIC I

effectively transfer to the structural level the major 2nd C♯–D♯ that was the crucial dyad in the strings' opening motivic nucleus; as in the Rhapsody Trio, the linear relationships are of minor 3rd within major. How intensively Bridge works these resources in the scherzo can be seen in Ex. 9.21. This movement, in which G asserts priority over C♯ despite endless whole-tone ambiguities, deploys an ingenuity rare in British music of the 1920s with great delicacy and wit.

The Violin Sonata (1932), Bridge's last big 'phantasy' design, is his most elaborate, for the 'sonata' material includes two contrasted introductory elements as well as a three-stage exposition. After the central sequence of slow movement, rhapsodic interlude and scherzo, the recapitulatory process is reordered in terser thematic succession and tonal direction. Westrup wrote that 'the players [of this sonata] must win their delight through hard labour' (1946a: 78), yet the listener is conscious more of its extending expressive horizons than of the controls which prevent its sprawling. The Fourth

Ex. 9.21   Bridge: Piano Trio no. 2, 2nd movement

Quartet (1937) is texturally sparer than the Third, partly because of more frequent parallel movement, and its structural outlines have an almost neoclassical clarity. 'A further and more decisive step along the road to atonality' (p. 77) may be suggested by the harmonic obliquity or ambivalence of opening propositions, but second subjects sharpen the tonal focus. The eventual arrival at a glowingly affirmative D major with added 2nd (adumbrated at the close of the first movement) is entirely convincing, and the whole finale, though rondo-like in the use of its main idea, is among Bridge's tautest designs. His only subsequent chamber work, *Divertimenti* for woodwind quartet (1938), is a set of character pieces, structurally unadventurous and nonchalantly bitonal in their counterpoint.

Though two early string quartets and a sextet have been published posthumously, Ireland's representative chamber output is contained in four sonatas with piano and three piano trios. The first two trios use the conflated form to which the Cobbett competitions gave currency, and indeed the A minor Phantasie won second prize in 1908. Its easy flow is propelled chiefly by piano figurations, and if the thematicism has little pronounced individuality, the structural balance of slow section interpolated into sonata development and animated coda is assured. The First Violin Sonata (1909) is cautiously innovative: orthodox chromatic progression can give way to side-slipping dominant 7ths, and an orthodox sonata allegro is enriched by unusual events – from a D minor tonic, the exposition swerves to B♭ minor, the recapitulation begins in E minor. This sonata won a Cobbett Prize, but not the remarkable *éclat* which greeted its successor, the A minor Sonata, following its 1917 première. Edwin Evans wrote that 'it was as if the music had struck some latent sentiment that had been waiting for the sympathetic voice to make it articulate', and he added that 'its appearance had . . . a stimulating effect upon the whole prospects of British chamber music' (Cobbett 1929–30, i: 21). The interpretation he offered of the sonata's moods tells us more about the aspirations of First World War audiences ('rugged vigour', 'sane idealism', 'humour . . . like that of soldiers') than of what fulfilled them so notably. The first movement's rhythmic head-motif integrates later, more lyrical contexts, and the modest development spins a long line over its series of pedals. After a chromatically tense preamble, the slow movement's restrained diatonic theme emphasizes Ireland's place within a peculiarly English tradition. E♭ is his favoured key for this vein, but here its tritonal opposition to the work's basic tonality is recognized in the passionate A major climax of the middle section. The same relationship in reverse is the controlling tension of the finale's tonal argument, and provokes a more ambitious piece than its chirpy refrain would imply.

In the Cello Sonata (1923) a richly chromatic piano texture threatens the balance at culminating moments, but the cello, particularly suited to Ireland's vein of impassioned lyricism, usually sings eloquently through. Perhaps the impassioned approaches the importunate when the finale draws so constantly upon shapes already worked hard in the first movement, though – as so often in Ireland – given no tonic restatement there. He wrote no more chamber music for 15 years, and the Third Piano Trio (1938) is based on much earlier material. The simplified harmonic language need not be attributed to this, for it reflects a general tendency in the composer's later work. Simplicity does not exclude subtlety, as may be heard in the tonally elusive second subject of the first movement and the unexpectedly ample slow movement. But without the need for such protraction, the Fantasy-Sonata for clarinet and piano (1943) draws more richly on Ireland's imaginative powers; it is perhaps the last direct tribute to Cobbett's ideals, and a worthy one.

IX: A Miscellany

In 1921 Vaughan Williams revised two chamber works conceived before the war. The G minor String Quartet dates back to 1909, when its archaizing modal melody must have been experimental. A sonata plan can be read into the first movement, but the progress is desultory and quartet dialogue minimal; the surprisingly *grazioso* minuet and the jiggish rondo-finale are more successful. Still more like a suite is the Phantasy Quintet of 1914. Its *attacca* links and a token return of Prelude material in the Burlesca finale appear sops to Cobbett (the dedicatee) when set beside Bridge's enlargement of sonata logic to embrace a continuous cycle. Only in 1947 did Vaughan Williams write a second quartet, in A minor; reflecting its dedication to the violist, Jean Stewart, all four movements are led off by solo viola. Their textures lack air – even the Scherzo is only fitfully buoyant – but progression in both modality and tonality gives point to another suite-like succession: the Prelude's tangential A minor is coloured by a 'dominant' hovering around the composer's favoured E minor/F minor juxtaposition, the Romance is in aeolian G minor, the Scherzo eventually settles on F minor and the hymnic Epilogue moves from F to an unblemished D major. The late Violin

Sonata (1954), marred by wooden piano writing, is redeemed by violin passage-work more idiomatic, if unresponsive to colour. The opening Fantasia is in fact a sonata movement, propelled by those minor-3rd shifts prominent in the Fourth Symphony, and truncated reprise of the first subject justifies its return in synthesis with the last of the finale's variations. A less inhibited harmonic palette, scrawny counterpoint, irregular accentuation and cross-rhythm give to the central scherzo an edgy impetus.

Holst's mature chamber output is slighter still. His chief published work, the Terzetto for flute, oboe and viola (1925), is renowned as an essay in polytonality but earns performance as an unassuming divertimento for an unusual ensemble: key signatures differentiate three tonal planes, but their coincident harmony achieves no greater piquancy than does much 1920s music written without prescription.

Herbert Howells (1892–1983), remembered for church and choral music, came to early notice for some chamber works. While their expressive means show Vaughan Williams's influence, their refinement is Howells's own. In the Piano Quartet (1916) textures redolent of Fauré support folk-inspired lines, and shapes are transferred between movements without blurring individuality. The successful Cobbett submission of the following year, a Fantasy for string quartet, seems in its contemplative opening so predestined to serene cadence as to make factitious the energetic music which intervenes before a beautiful coda. One-movement design is more inventively handled in the *Rhapsodic Quintet* for clarinet and strings (1919). The opening gesture, oblique in its modal harmony, is very English, but the mood is complicated by the clarinet's later introduction of an *inquieto* chromatically twisting shape (indebted to Debussy's quartet scherzo), a strategy that gives strength to the ultimate serenity; progressive modification of tempo and contour unifies a single argument. Only in its piquant scherzo does the four-movement quartet, 'In Gloucestershire' (1923), approach such terseness. Elsewhere its dependence on freely expanding melody is too uniformly leisurely, and the most idiomatic quartet dialogue is rare; indeed, some of the most memorable ideas are quasi-orchestral in conception. Though his sonatas with piano (three for violin, one each for oboe and clarinet) lack the pianistic flair of Ireland or Bax, their melodic eloquence is persuasive.

Howells did not qualify for mention in Cecil Gray's diatribe on English music; Eugene Goossens (1893–1962) was satirically dubbed our Ravel. A contrast between the two is already indicated in the circumstance that Goossens, the younger man, finished his apprenticeship with Stanford as Howells began. Precocious technical competence characterized Goossens's early career, and a prodigality curbed only by his success as a conductor. His sympathies were cosmopolitan, but of Ravel's neurotic care for the precise quality of every note his music shows little trace. A workmanlike effectiveness is assured, with whatever harmonic tools come to hand – commonly chromatic, yet fluctuating between impressionistic colouring and a functionalism without long-term objectives. The Phantasy Sextet written for Mrs Coolidge in 1923 ingeniously manipulates a few shapes across a three-in-one framework. Seventeen years later, for the same dedicatee, his Second Quartet is in four movements, limiting cross-reference to the retrospection of an epilogue; the harmonic eclecticism is especially clear in the slow fantasy on the folk tune, 'Searching for lambs'. In both works literal restatement of material disappoints expectations, and *fugato* seems a glib token of intensity. The horizons of Howells are more parochial, but the expressive intentions are more clearly defined and realized.

Still the least known of Stanford's gifted pupils, Rebecca Clarke (1886–1979) was, like Bridge, a professional violist. She shared his player's understanding of chamber dispositions and his fondness for elaborating quasi-dominant harmonies to the point where conflicting tonal fields seem to be implied. But whereas Bridge in a long series of works progressively refined this language, Clarke gave up large-scale composition before perfecting the stylistic synthesis undertaken in the three works on which her claim to rediscovery chiefly rests. The Viola Sonata (1919) is one of the strongest pieces in that British repertoire for the instrument initiated by Benjamin Dale's Suite (1913). A rhapsodizing dorian theme introduces and punctuates a sonata scheme otherwise chromatically fluid. It reappears within the final Allegro, though a long prelude has been founded on an aeolian melody that also functions in the main design. Such fluctuation between textures comparable (to oversimplify) now with Vaughan Williams's, now with Bridge's, produces transitions that too ostentatiously dissolve or too brusquely juxtapose material. The scherzo, texturally sparer and rhythmically fleet, is oblique in scale pattern and harmony; tritone relations in its lyrical episode point towards the 1921 Piano Trio. This work is far from arbitrary in the means by which its outer movements converge on E♭ and its slow movement on G, but these tonal assertions achieve clarified form only after tritonal or semitonal pressures have qualified almost every stage of the argument; the eventual subjugation of the quasi-dorian A of the finale refrain by the E♭ major triad underlying it is particularly felicitous. The Rhapsody for cello and piano (1923) is a composite structure, generous in scale and expressive substance, that carries no hint of the composer's impending withdrawal.

Though the Cobbett competitions were not restricted to RCM composers, they tended to dominate the field. Arnold Bax seems neither to have been associated with Cobbett nor to have found attractive the most typical 'phantasy' formula. His own Fantasy-Sonata for harp and viola (1927), for example, is in four successive movements, rhapsodically linked. Themes are transformed across the cycle and ideas merge into each other, giving an impression of reminiscence rather than earnest development that seems apt in so fancifully coloured a medium. In contrast, his Quartet in One Movement for strings and piano (1922) is quite literally a single sonata structure, in which Bax's predilection for prolific exposition is given its head, before an equally spacious development and a typically abridged restatement; as in some other Bax, it is the first subject that has to await this final stage to gain tonic stability. A suppressed programme rather than a modification of sonata principle may explain the idiosyncratic balance struck in the Nonet (1930) between different kinds of motion in the two movements. Formal correspondences are discernible, but never feel recapitulatory, and the atmospheric textures Bax devises for this large ensemble (string quintet, trio of upper woodwind and harp), notably in the nostalgic conclusion, heighten the impression of a tone poem for chamber orchestra.

But the greater part of his large body of chamber music conforms at least nominally to traditional movement orderings. The first of the four violin sonatas, after successive revisions (1910–45), remains leisurely in its unfolding, its E major radiance intensified by thematic transfer from first movement to last. Inspired by Lionel Tertis's playing, the Viola Sonata (1921) responds with unusual intensity to the instrument's range of timbre. Its opening sonority of low viola melody strangely remote from the piano's floating harmonies (see Ex. 9.22) defines the prevailing character and its return to close the sonata seems predestined. Invention stays strong through an orthodox sonata scheme in which, partly by a pervasive use of ostinato, pentatonics and chromaticisms achieve a compatibility that sometimes eluded Bax. In the central sonata-rondo, hard-driven *scherzando* rhythms and popularist themes stave off banality chiefly because,

Ex. 9.22   Bax: Viola Sonata, 1st movement

although a tonal centre seems always accessible, the harmony is so often set askew to it; the resulting sardonic flavour is to be heard in many of Bax's fast movements. The viola's powerful declamatory statement in the slow finale returns with the rediscovery of the sonata's tonic, and an unforced dissolution into the work's opening theme completes an emotional curve that places the Viola Sonata among Bax's finest achievements.

Bax's four string quartets contain many beautiful moments, but fail as entities to sustain the kind of close reasoning that distinguishes the central tradition in this monochrome medium. 'That organic quality, the intellectual grasp and balance of the whole, which nearly all his contemporaries lack' was what Cecil Gray (1924: 238) found in the work of Bernard van Dieren (1887–1936), a composer who wrote six quartets. Since his creative career postdated his settling in England, van Dieren belongs to the history of British music. The quartets have shared with the rest of his output a neglect unrelieved by the revivalist campaigns accorded to some less interesting figures, an influential factor being the extreme difficulty they present to interpreters. The layout of individual string parts is skilled, but a composite lucidity is unlikely when, as in the first movement of the Second Quartet (1917), each instrument pursues an entirely independent rhythmic and thematic course. Yet textures closer to traditional polyphony, as in the finale, are stolid in their complementary rhythms. The most successful movement is the scherzo, where the violins trace a subdued *moto perpetuo* arch above the expansive duet of viola and cello. The inverse relationship of figurative detail and tempo is made a principle in the improbably titled 'Tempo di minuetto' of the Third Quartet (1918), producing a shape more attractive than the finale's hard-driven but clotted fugue. The Fourth and Fifth Quartets (1923 and 1927), both including double bass (in no. 4 it displaces the cello), continue a process of simplification which leads in the Sixth Quartet (1928) to clarified thematicism and tonal relations; eruptions of complex detail are now restricted to the 'Furioso' finale.

Arthur Bliss's early chamber works were withdrawn; the quartet that appeared in 1941 as his first was in fact his third. Immediately after the First World War some impatience with tradition was declared by such pieces as *Rout*, in which a soprano adds nonsense syllables to a ten-instrument ensemble, and *Conversations* for five instruments. But the iconoclasm is jocular rather than ruthless, and before the end of the 1920s Bliss had turned to more traditional media and rhetoric. Gestures and climactic textures seem too inflated for a quintet (1927) where the oboe provides the solo colour, but structural invention is nimble, as in the finale's accommodation of an Irish jig without solecism, by tonal cross-cuttings and duality of metre. The restoration of key signatures in the Clarinet Quintet (1931) signifies the reimposition of a control much loosened in the Oboe Quintet, and Bliss's expansive neo-romanticism of line is well adapted to the clarinet's character; indeed, the slowish ternary movements (1 and 3) are more rewarding than the fast sonata movements (2 and 4). *Cantabile* eloquence predominates also in the first two movements of the Viola Sonata (1933), reserving virtuosity for the final Furiant. The work's summarizing Coda is a little naive in its reminiscence of earlier events, but the return of the sonata's opening over a dominant pedal and an ostinato based on the finale refrain is convincing; its blatant debt to Walton's Viola Concerto confirms echoes already stirred by the first movement's impassioned false relations. In chamber media, Bliss never surpassed these generous pieces, for the string quartets only sporadically achieve that interplay or that inwardness which are, texturally and spiritually, the highest ideals of the medium. The Second Quartet (1950) is ambitious in scale and address, with forms inventively balanced in thematic and tonal relations, but awkward layout and harmonic stresses artificially imposed on conventional language create a strain irrelevant to the expressive scheme.

Walton's Piano Quartet (1918–19) predates Vaughan Williams's use of 'My bonny boy' in the *English Folksong Suite* by four years, but that melody seems to haunt his opening, and persistently influential, theme. Such reliance on folk-derived material, and on models found in Herbert Howells's Piano Quartet, stamp as immature the tone of this work. Neither the harmonic fluctuations, between modal parallelism and dominants embellished to the point of false relation, nor an over-confidence in the relevance of *fugato* lessen that impression, though both carry prophetic overtones, as does the rhythmic sophistication of the finale. But before the stylistic amalgam to which we relate such features was perfectly fused in the Viola Concerto, Walton's exposure to contemporary European music had a convulsive effect on his own work; if the String Quartet given at the 1923 inauguration of the ISCM represented a battle for modernity, its subsequent withdrawal suggested a truce. Its three linked movements develop totally chromatic material in intensely motivic counterpoint, but the arbitrary harmonic consequences are emphasized by the preference shown at the rare homophonic moments for mild 7th chords. The huge central scherzo hints at the energy later Walton could sustain through reiterated gesture, while the final fugue contrasts a subject disposing eleven pitch classes in conventional contour with one self-consciously bizarre in rhythmic and registral diversity.

Not until 1947 did Walton return to chamber music, with a String Quartet determinedly 'in A minor'. The vehemence of some of its gestures was to prompt a transcription for string orchestra, yet the original never strains the medium, and Walton's lyricism loses its urbanity in the brooding sonorities of the slow movement. Forms are classicistic but not mechanistic, and wiry contrapuntal textures give a tensile strength that Walton's ampler scores no longer consistently achieved. The piano's chordal resources tilt back the balance in the Violin Sonata (1950) towards the cloying elegance of the later concertos. The large scale of its two movements is determined by a long chain of lyrical ideas in the sonata allegro and by an extensive theme in the variation set. Though the first makes effective play with its opening B♭/G minor ambivalence, its tonal profile is lightly drawn, whereas the variations cover, by successive semitonal rises, the ground between their opening E♭ minor and the final recovery of B♭. The process is refined in its detail, and much assisted by the theme's tailpiece, a 13-note phrase (all 12 pitches, plus a repeat of the first) which serves as dominant preparation for each new variation.

E. J. Moeran wrote no chamber work remotely on the scale of his Symphony, working comfortably in the smaller media without over-inflating their content. All three movements of the A minor Quartet (1921) use folk-influenced material, respecting local modalities in its harmonization and rarely venturing to those extremes, of Vaughan Williams's stolid parallelism and Delius's chromatic decline, that defy reconciliation in some of his music. Accompanying textures are prone to formula but counterpoint is virile (with some adroit thematic superimpositions) and metrical ambivalence well sustained in the finale. Ten years later, the String Trio shows still greater assurance: a three-part norm is ill-adapted to lush harmonic embellishment and Moeran writes one of his airiest scores. Perhaps the oboe's pastoral associations prove too beguiling in the Fantasy Quartet (1946): despite its elaborate cycle of tempi and textures, it lacks decisive melodic contrast, and the recurrent folky tags become overworked.

One of the most accomplished craftsmen of the Walton–Tippett generation, Howard Ferguson (*b* 1908) seems to have lacked the assertive creativity his gifts would have justified. Much of his earlier career was devoted to performance (typically the two-piano duo was his preferred context), and he later gave up composition to edit a wide range of keyboard music. All his activities reflect an impeccable musicality which makes his compositions satisfying to the players. The First Violin Sonata (1931) admits English pastoralism without relaxing a fastidious textural disposition referable to Brahms. A delicate astringency of harmonic relations is handled with greater consistency than in its probable model, Walton, approaching a tonal ambivalence that was to become Rawsthorne's favoured territory. Brahmsian echoes are still stronger in the slow movement of the Octet (1933), for Schubert's instrumentation. Its opening sonata design is finely wrought, and the slow movement's gentle expressivity can become incandescent. The scherzo nicely balances agile and reflective elements, but the finale's tarantella rhythms too readily succumb, or become automatic background, to yet more *espressivo*. Tension is maintained by a protracted classical dominant pedal, leading more forcefully than in the violin sonata to recall of the first-movement themes.

At times Ferguson's music can seem handicapped by his detailed knowledge of the great classical exemplars, yet the technical control it brought becomes conspicuous if we compare his work with the slight chamber music output of his friend, Gerald Finzi. The Interlude for oboe quartet (1936) and the Prelude and Fugue for string trio (1938) have very personal touches of harmonic poignancy and a fine linear flow, but their structural ambitions are modest. Finzi's most performed instrumental score is the genial but undemanding suite of *Five Bagatelles* for clarinet and piano.

X: Berkeley, Rubbra and Rawsthorne

Lennox Berkeley's preference for lean textures, with patterned accompaniments in which each harmonic displacement is sensitively judged, attracted him repeatedly to chamber scorings. His success seems most obvious when the associations are with divertimento rather than the more intense processes of the classical quartet. Yet while rigorous development is not impressed upon the listener, nor are those complacently literal reiterations that have satisfied some neoclassicists: Berkeley remains as creatively active in the later as in the expository sections of his movements. His distaste for the superfluous and the bombastic often restricts him to slender proportions, which may correspond to the nature of the material, as in the little String Trio of 1943, or can inhibit potentially more ambitious structures, as in the Second Quartet of the previous year. In these works initial tonal obliquity is progressively elucidated, but the entirely unambiguous point of departure in such pieces as the Violin Sonatina (1942), the Viola Sonata (1945) and the Horn Trio (1954) reassures, without patronizing, a relatively unsophisticated audience; the variation finales in the first and last of these are equally direct in their appeal.

The opening horn 4ths of the Horn Trio prompt comparisons with Schoenberg's op. 9; its derived quartal harmony occasionally suggests Hindemith. But schematicism was always alien to Berkeley's working methods, and this remained so when in the following decades his music drew more on the whole 12-note repertoire. The Oboe Quartet (1967) is markedly free in the range of pitches in circulation, and oscillating 3rds create many ambivalences. The F that supplants the oblique A of the first movement intrudes upon

ART MUSIC

both the D of the fast middle movement and the A of the gentle finale; the final dissolution is equivocal yet satisfying in its reinterpretation of the opening oscillations. In much of the Quintet for piano and wind (1976) Berkeley has moved still further from the disarming tunes and gracefully twisted tonal relationships of his early music. Now the centrality of A has to be inferred in the first movement, despite a rapid flux of implications thrown up in exploring intervallic shapes from the slow introduction; yet cycle-of-5ths progressions still have a role. The scherzo can be assigned to F, its trio to E, but its themes – familiar enough in cast – may use some 11 different successive pitches (see Ex. 9.23). Such sinuosity makes the finale's 16-bar theme, in clarified tonality and routine scoring, seem a throwback. More imaginative roles for piano and wind differentiate the variations, and throughout the quintet the writing is admirably spare. Like the Horn Trio, this piece can modestly, but without embarrassment, keep company with its illustrious predecessors.

If the criticism sometimes made of Edmund Rubbra's earlier symphonies – that their seamless polyphony is too dour a response to modern orchestral potentialities – were just, then we might expect to find such texture better adapted to the monochrome string quartet. In fact, the imperturbable flow of Rubbra's partwriting is typically articulated by a swerve in the harmonic direction, illuminated by a change of timbre; the substitute favoured in his

Ex. 9.23   Berkeley: Quintet for piano and wind, 2nd movement

quartets, of a *subito pianissimo*, can more quickly pall. Earlier pieces like the Second Violin Sonata (1931) show a preference for harmonically orientated textures, with a debt to French as well as English models. Despite professional activity as a chamber-music pianist, Rubbra discovers in his mature works surprisingly few roles for the piano between the extremes of weighty homophony and spindly two-part counterpoint. Such wide-spaced counterpoint can simply ramble, but in the Cello Sonata (1946), one of his most ardent pieces, it propels a buoyant scherzo, an apt foil to the unusually burnished eloquence of the first movement. If the final variation theme appears simplistic, the growth it engenders is strong, and the culminating fugue (on a subject that only out of context suggests pastiche) summarizes emotionally the whole work. Written in the same year, the First Piano Trio compresses a complex cycle of events into one span, whose many sections unfold organically with no debt to the typical 'Cobbett' methods of synthesis. But in many of his chamber works he seems content with *Gebrauchsmusik* ideals and, as in the Oboe Sonata (1959), with conjunct pattern-making that dulls the expressive impact. The string quartets are the product of more sustained reflection, in the case of the First extending over many years. In its revised form (1946), the first movement strikes a fine balance between polyphonically developing and rhythmically gesturing ideas, but the Second Quartet (1952) is more typical in the evolutionary process which renders sonata correspondences incidental within progressive textural change. The ingenuity of its 'Scherzo polymetrico' is somewhat concealed by the common pulse of the stratified metres, but the constrained key scheme (four movements: E♭ major–D major– E minor–E♭ minor/major) is telling. In three movements with no break, the Third Quartet (1964) further enlarges textural resource and has a new tonal mobility and a subtle interplay of tempi.

Alan Rawsthorne's earliest scores were of chamber music and in his last decade these again outnumbered orchestral works. This may reflect the commissions available rather than any pronounced shift of interest from the orchestral composition that had made his reputation. His range of ensembles is wide; most are standard groupings but only the string quartet is repeatedly explored. Works such as the Suite for flute, viola and harp (1968) and the Concerto for ten instruments (1961) pay greater heed to the suggestibility of sonority, without modifying the fundamentals of his language.

Their initial debt to Hindemith was discussed in considering the Symphonic Studies, and the finale of the Viola Sonata (1935) shows the influence less digested. As the composer allowed this movement to stand in 1953, the revision he undertook was presumably not drastic, and the other movements probably represent the early achievement of more personal traits. In playing off slow and fast sections the first movement disowns 'sonata' pretensions: a potential second subject is simply eliminated. The harmonic contradictions that amplify the simultaneous false relation are too constant, as is the lithe figuration on the octatonic scale; indeed, the rarity of two adjacent major 2nds robs this music of traditionally affirmative major-mode implications. The first mature chamber work was probably the lost string quartet of 1939, from which the composer was able to reconstruct only the variations, cleanly finished textural studies that categorize his affective range. After the war, Rawsthorne returned to the small ensemble with a Clarinet Quartet (1948). It lasts less than 20 minutes and all but one (the wind and piano Quintet) of his subsequent chamber works were to be still shorter. An aversion to the garrulous was deeply rooted in the composer's character, yet, however much may be epitomized in initial aphorism, the melodic phraseology is often romantically cumulative, and the lean proportions are achieved by abbreviation, especially of restated material. Thus in the Second Quartet (1954) the first movement's second subject is virtually excised at the recapitulation, the scherzo's *da capo* is no more than a coda. The final variations are progressively shortened, but they form a single rise to climax before a brief ebb to a coda recalls the movement's opening, then its progenitor, the quartet's initial gesture. Rawsthorne's Violin Sonata (1958) is still more tangibly an outgrowth from the Adagio that frames the first movement, since this sets up the friction between chords in tonal fields of D and E♭ that will predominate throughout the sonata (see Ex. 9.24). More veiled in the second movement's elusive dance, it surfaces in episode and coda of the strident Toccata that follows – a sonata with reversed restatement. Finally the Epilogue unfolds a rhapsodic violin line against a background that juxtaposes D minor and E♭ major, and culminates in the rediscovery of the opening Adagio. By the clock a slight work, this is among the most satisfying of British violin sonatas.

The Quintet for piano and wind (1963) shows how small a shift of stylistic balance was needed for Rawsthorne to make unforced use of some aspects of 12-note serial technique. His interest in the potentialities of a single generating shape had been constant, while his tendency to treat harmonic phenomena as meeting-points between

Ex. 9.24   Rawsthorne: Violin Sonata, 1st movement

tonal fields had often rapidly exhausted the 12 pitch classes. To fuse these two preoccupations was to find in Schoenberg a relevant parallel but not a prescriptive model. In the Quintet's first movement the basic shape has 9 pitches; that of the third movement uses all 12, but with recourse to figurations not at all serial. After a 12-note introduction, the finale reverts to the variable scales of earlier Rawsthorne, and it is this primacy still accorded stepwise melody that, as with Bartók, finally alienates him from Schoenberg. Yet the scalic, the bitonal and a quasi-serial distribution of pitches across a contrapuntal web can coexist, as may be seen in the opening of the Third Quartet (1964). Its 'Alla ciacona' brings to an old formula a new richness of harmony, expanding the 'false relation' schematically (for example, by aggregates of minor 6ths: E C / C♯A / B♭F♯ / G E♭). The Quintet for piano and strings (1968) uses another composite structure, while the Oboe Quartet (1970) unifies three movements with a single set. As ever, Rawsthorne fashions tautly argued, texturally immaculate music; whether its emotional reserve will ever be attractive to a general audience seems doubtful but regrettable.

XI: Mostly Quartets: Bush, Tippett and Maconchy

While the string quartet retains its traditional pride of place in the chamber music discussed so far, even Bridge's quartets depend for their immediate impression more on sonorous invention than on rigorous procedure. These priorities are reversed in *Dialectic* (1929), a single-movement quartet by Alan Bush. The judges who selected Bush's A minor Quartet (1924) for a Carnegie Award had commented on its terse style, 'without a superfluous bar or phrase' (Cobbett 1929–30, i: 218), though today one notes rather how smoothly Bush can pass in treating folk-influenced themes from modal to sophisticated modulatory textures. A vestigial modality can be heard in *Dialectic*, but folk melody and contemplative rhapsody have no place in this high-minded argument from thematic first principles. Given the big reservoir of shapes in the long opening unison statement, it is not too remarkable that the five later themes and all subsidiary material can be claimed as derivatives. Such endless regeneration produces congruity, but not parsimony: indeed, neither 'development' as traditionally understood nor the tonal flux stresses the expanded-sonata groundplan behind the foreground prodigality of events. *Dialectic* remains an impressive phenomenon in British music of the period: its panthematicism invites comparison with Schoenberg's developments in the same decade, even though its very English vocabulary is so remote from chromatic saturation. Among Bush's later chamber music, the Three Concert Studies for piano trio (1947), by setting up distinct technical and interpretative objectives for each piece, achieve a colourful sequence. Tonality is now more oblique and the textural possibilities of a medium that had lost status are revitalized by the break with the traditional movement cycle.

Six years after *Dialectic*, Bush's friend Michael Tippett wrote the first quartet that (with a new movement replacing the opening pair in 1943) he thought worthy of publication. Its fugal finale suggests a comparable view of the quartet as the ideal vehicle for concentrating on points at issue rather than colouristic effect. Fugue has always been, since Haydn's op. 20, a special solution of the quartet's textural problem, and it can be a mechanistic one. Tippett's technical skill rises effortlessly to quadruple counterpoint, but instead of limply rotating its permutations, he makes it one extreme in a constantly fluctuating complexity within an often uniform density of activity. Ian Kemp's analysis shows how much

Tippett's unique propulsion owes to the subject's rhythmic structure (1984: 98). The slow movement is more metrically constrained. If its flat-key colour and its unventilated harmony seem a bid for the spirituality of late Beethoven, the shafts of light admitted by abrupt modulations are too frequent to achieve transfiguring power. Nor are key-relationships of clinching force in the 1943 first movement: explosive *fortissimo* lines and contained *piano* lyricism establish an unambiguous sonata duality, yet the tonic A is defined more clearly by the second of these, and its recapitulation at the subdominant has no counterweight. Even before revising this score, Tippett had completed in his Second Quartet (1942) the most limpid of all his works. A classicistic orthodoxy in the disposition of its four movements is not altogether belied by the bland harmonic resources and a tonal scheme that is never obscure, however flexible the modality. Every movement sets up a different norm of rhythmic/metric behaviour, the scherzo's often uniform irregularity of stress patterns being served best by variable bar-lengths, the first movement's independent rhythmic constructions being accommodated for convenience within regular barring. This restless inner life of the contradictory rhythmic groupings brings such levitating joy to a movement restrained in dynamics and genial in its themes that the evident shape of a sonata (with reversed recapitulation) scarcely matches our experience. It is the finale that is braced by pointed dissimilarity of subject matter, though the first subject's sprung rhythm is very pervasive, leaving the opening of the second group to distil, in its tonal remoteness and the rapt harmonies unfolded by its falling 9ths, an otherness that gives this movement deep resonances and justifies its protracted dying fall (see Ex. 9.25). The slow fugue shows Tippett, with the moving vignettes of *A Child of Our Time* just accomplished, able to work out an introvertedly chromatic subject without sentimentality, investing a familiar chordal vocabulary with a new syntax (see Puffett 1986). In the third movement, a single strophe, juxtaposing scherzo and trio elements, appears three times at rising pitch levels: the inner key-relationships change, most actively in the central strophe, but the sense is less of an arch than of a projectile, its target the downbeat affirmation of the finale opening.

The odd-numbered movements of the five in Tippett's Third Quartet (1946) are fugal Allegros; the even-numbered are slow. This symmetry is qualified by a slow introduction to the first fugue and by shadings within the basic contrast of tempo. As in Berg's *Lyric Suite*, the crisis comes when slowest follows fastest, but with none of Berg's

Ex. 9.25 Tippett: String Quartet no. 2, 4th movement

irresolvable drama, for there remains a finale, the most relaxed and airy of the fugues and the work's summarizing affirmation. The first fugue, on a subject of extraordinary length, is necessarily the most spacious, its three stages forming, tonally at least, a ternary shape, much inflected by introduction material. The central fugue, like the first, has four complementary strands, two linked as double subject; lighter textures in the episodic material maintain the *scherzando* character. The second movement is a huge span of melody, intricately articulated by a variety of attendant elements and with no kind of precedent in the quartet literature; Kemp sees here the full flowering of the 'visionary artist' (1984: 194). At an extreme from this serene order is the fourth movement, which in three strophes repeats the journey from crystalline sonority to *appassionato* gestures, and finally explodes in Tippett's most frenzied arabesques. The prodigal detail of this work does not easily lodge in the memory, but the strength of its unique cycle (quite unlike, for example, Bartók's five-movement arches) is unforgettable.

Elizabeth Maconchy (1907–94), a pupil of Vaughan Williams, worked in orchestral and choral media, but is best known for her sustained interest in the string quartet as a vehicle for unremitting argument, based on spare, chromatically introverted motifs. Craftsmanship is assured in her 13 quartets, but they can appear uniform to the point of obsession in their moods; her great seriousness of purpose can stifle qualities of wit and warmth, which are also part of the medium's heritage. When the emotional stimulus is intense, as in the impassioned lament at the heart of the Ninth Quartet (written during the occupation of Prague, where Maconchy had studied), she can transmute it into powerful expression. The scale of her quartets is typically quite small, but she is concerned, not with filling predetermined lengths by predetermined articulation (for example, that of the sonata), but with exploring the possibilities of a small germinal idea. The distinctive shapes of successive movements derive from this, so that the vigilant ear will detect the logic in the final return of opening propositions. Thus, in the Eighth Quartet (1966), the conflation of perfect 5ths on G and C♯ frames a cycle of four short movements, but to account for their strong impression of congruity one must trace the shapes, some tightly knotted, others splintered apart by octave transposition, woven around this nucleus. The identical nucleus opens *Reflections* (1960) for oboe, clarinet, viola and harp, but now the mirror of the tritone produces genially bitonal images. Maconchy could write such luminous entertainment music effectively, but she rarely admitted it to her quartets.

XII: Britten

Britten studied with Bridge during the years of his teacher's most exploratory chamber works – the Third Quartet, the Rhapsody and the Second Piano Trio. Of the chamber scores Britten completed before his op. 1 Sinfonietta two reflect typical aspects of Bridge's practice. The Quartettino (1930) is experimental in its high norm of dissonance and its fitful pitch centricity, but it lacks Bridge's consistency of harmonic character; it is Britten's determined motivic economy that reveals the marvellously observant pupil. The Phantasy Quintet (1932), which won a Cobbett Prize, more circumspectly admits echoes of the pastoral modality which was an RCM orthodoxy, yet still finds subtle means of fusing semitonally distinct strata. The 'phantasy' principle was to be refined later in the same year with the op. 2 Oboe Quartet, but before then Britten used linked movements in the Sinfonietta, completing the first movement's argument at the end of the finale. The composer preferred this work played with single strings, and its modal linearity, often neutralized harmonically by an embracing major 7th or minor 9th, produces a dry sonority that owes nothing to English predilections and little to the strained opulence of Schoenberg's op. 9. But it is in motif development more concentrated than Bridge's, affecting subsidiary strands and transforming nominally recapitulatory areas, that we observe Schoenberg's importance in forming Britten's thought. The oboe Phantasy's unbroken span suggests an undeclared programmatic sequence; its recurrent cryptic march may stem from Bridge's *Oration*, but the tonal stresses have a sharper edge that is already personal. English pastoral decorum in the slow section is tightened as the oboe's rhapsodizing becomes urgent comment on the returning Allegro.

Other early chamber works, the String Quartet in D (1931) and the posthumously published relics of *Alla Quartetto Serioso* (1933), show how Britten's interests could veer between close thematic integration and a graphic 'genre' style. That these need not be mutually exclusive is seen in the Suite for violin and piano (1935) and the *Temporal Variations* for oboe and piano (1936). The Suite is faithful only to the contour of its four-pitch motto, but the variations, intricately organized in thematic cells and tonal cycle, give a richer foretaste of Britten's authentic sound-world.

Five years later, in the official String Quartet no. 1, this sonorous stamp is fundamental. The opening high clusters of lydian D have a tense sweetness that does not feel merely introductory, and the cello's countering low C♮ has far-reaching implications. Successively in D, F and restored to D, these Andantes are the buttresses of the first movement, and it is their contrast with, rather than the interior articulation of, the exposition and development-cum-restatement of the intervening Allegros that provides the structural dichotomy. The middle movements are in F and B♭, a bizarre scherzo and a slow movement that unobtrusively reinterprets sounds and shapes from the first movement. As in many classical finales, great technical refinement is wittily applied to slender epigrams, and the tonal propensities of the whole quartet are reviewed. Britten's impatience with the premature lowering of temperature that a tonicized second group can bring had, since the Sinfonietta, led him to favour the recapitulation of first and second subjects in superimposition: the *ne plus ultra* of this device is found in the Second Quartet (1945).

Three spans of melody, with a common head-motif but each a 5th higher than its predecessor, follow in broken succession before the tonic C is reaffirmed and the spans are more spaciously expounded as first, second and closing subjects. 'Development' has already been intense, but more fragmented derivations are explored before the three subjects rediscover their common origin in simultaneous restatement. Cello arpeggios celebrate a tonic mislaid rather than banished during the middle section (see Ex. 9.26). So drastically conflated a recapitulation of so lengthy an exposition invites us to experience the movement on terms no more than coloured by the sonata thesis. A final 'Chacony' (in tribute to Purcell) provides the counterweight. By grouping the variations in three blocks (harmonic; rhythmic; new melodic counterpoint), separated by solo cadenzas, Britten imposes an embracing principle on an additive form; but so endlessly resourceful are the tonal encounters to which he subjects his untransposed ground that a final block of variations is needed to restore resounding stability to C major.

The three decades between the Second and Third Quartets were those during which Britten built upon the success of *Peter Grimes* with a series of operas that culminated in *Death in Venice*. Most of his other works were no less a response to the suggestibility of texts, their choice prompted by the occasion to be marked or the artistic personality of the performer he saluted. But even without the intermediary of words, this last stimulus could be compelling, and the programming needs of the Aldeburgh Festival encouraged him to write pieces for instrumentalists he wished to invite there. The *Metamorphoses* for solo oboe (1951) find prompts in Ovid for a feat of monodic characterization, and *Lachrymae* for viola and piano (1950) makes an inspired association between the 'semper dolens' nature of the viola's tone and material taken from John Dowland. The process by which pure Dowland is revealed only after a series of variations on the source theme is still more poetically employed in the *Nocturnal* for solo guitar (1963): 'Come, heavy sleep' in literal statement achieves repose after each of the preceding restless fantasies has broken off in mid-strain.

The imaginative powers Britten brings to so unified a concept are more fitfully displayed in the three suites for solo cello (1964, 1967 and 1971) and the Harp Suite (1969), but the same ingenuity in devising new instrumental idioms is at work. Britten's tendency to read his own kind of challenge into fugue (see above, p. 234) results in four contrasted examples, that in the Second Cello Suite

ART MUSIC

Ex. 9.26 Britten: String Quartet no. 2 in C major, 1st movement

especially artful in its dovetailing of polyphonic strata into a monophonic plane. But the simpler *cantando* pieces are just as striking, those in the Third Cello Suite – based on Russian themes – being notably rich. Russian echoes of another kind (Prokofiev and Shostakovich) point the ironies of the 'Marcia' in the Cello Sonata of 1961. The shadowy pizzicato contrapuntal mechanisms and the scalic symmetries of the scherzo are Britten's closest approach to Bartók. These suite-like pieces separate three movements that more certainly provide the specific gravity of a sonata. The opening 'Dialogo' floats gently free of tonal absolutes (its C/E tonal fusions typify one aspect of the lyrical Britten), and the 'Moto perpetuo' finale pursues the tone–semitone alternations that colour much of the sonata so far as to make the emergence in C appear providential. The centrepiece, 'Elegia', uses the same octatonic scale harmonically, to powerfully simple effect.

In some sense all Britten's mature music makes this bid for the simplest presentation consistent with his expressive intentions; even the elaborate Second Quartet carries no trace of the obscurity that pseudo-profundity or imperfect technical control can bring. Even so, to compare it with its successor is to recognize that in his last period (the church parables provide the decisive marker), the delights of complex craftsmanship played a reduced role in his conceptions. Britten's Third Quartet was written in 1975, and the relationship of this last chamber work to his last opera becomes explicit when quotations from *Death in Venice* (1973), as instrumental recitative preceding the closing Passacaglia, make of the finale a commentary on Aschenbach's fate. The ground is Britten's most elemental, its hesitant upward steps inverting back to the flat 7th, while the line spun above amplifies the curve and defines more fully the E major that irradiates this moving swansong. Less overtly, the same curve characterizes the opening 'Duets', in barcarolle rhythms propelled by Britten's beloved 2nds, and shadowy references to the opera intensify recapitulation following a squally outburst. Contrasted scherzos form the inner correspondence in a five-movement arch: 'Ostinato' converts scalic steps into erratically striding 7ths, 'Burlesque' subjects scalic commonplace to a nightmarish development that is far from Britten's habitually cool irony. At the centre, 'Solo' projects a long violin line against major triads impassively arpeggiated by the other instruments in turn; as in much late Britten, what looks alarmingly slender in the score proves memorably expressive. Indeed, the whole quartet yields an experience greater than the sum of its parts. The composer heard it only in rehearsal, and its initial wide circulation may stem from autobiographical implications unique in his instrumental music (culminating in a dying fall that also aspires), but its dominating place in British chamber music seems assured.

XIII: The Piano

By 1914 France could boast a distinguished literature for the piano by composers still active. If the following generation did not equal the achievements of Fauré, Debussy and Ravel, they belonged to a tradition broad enough to nurture piano styles as unlike as Poulenc's and Messiaen's. Britain was denied such models, for the pioneers had a limited sensitivity to the piano's range of colour and texture; too often their writing sounds like a reduction from an ampler medium. And the prevailing character was Germanic: even Stanford's continuo realizations of Purcell sound Brahmsian, and Elgar, so idiosyncratic in orchestral sonority, could appear a Brahms imitator when he wrote for the piano (see his Quintet). Younger British composers, especially if they were skilled pianists, sought to reclaim the instrument's vast range of sonorous character by adopting fresh models, the French being joined by Skryabin as the most influential. The colourful, titled piece, structurally unambitious but alive to the precise quality of sound, was preferred to abstract developmental forms; Ireland and Bridge turned to sonata only when they had outgrown the danger of producing dilute Brahms, while Bax reintroduced Lisztian flamboyance and waywardness to the sonata concept. Apart from Bax, few composers explored repeatedly the sonata's potentialities. Cyril Scott's three sonatas seem rather a confirmation of an endemic prodigality that produced, *The New Grove* tells us, some 160 piano pieces, and not until Tippett do we find a major composer fascinated by the piano's ability to sustain through a single player an elaborate structural argument. The distinctive tendencies noted in surveying the symphonic and chamber works of our period have enough consistency to represent central British traditions; in that sense British piano music seems to lack one.

More than one generation of piano students found in John Ireland's pieces a reassuring introduction to the music of their century. But these modest character pieces are less readily accommodated in today's patterns of recital programming, and only a handful of Ireland's enjoy much currency. Some of the earliest are among these, such as 'The island spell' (1912), a flat-key study in aqueous arpeggiation that derives from Liszt, with Ravel's mediation evident in its pentatonic embellishment of essentially orthodox harmonic functions. 'Moon-glade' (1913), from the same set, *Decorations*, has a more elusive overlay, and the paralleling of minor $^6_3$ arpeggios

Ex. 9.27   Ireland: 'Moon-glade' (*Decorations*)

at the major 6th spins a web of false relations, which never lost their fascination for Ireland (see Ex. 9.27). But, unlike Bridge, he chose not to pursue harmonic ambiguity until it defied aural reference to traditional progression, and at any stage of his work delicately oblique reference may be juxtaposed with the disconcertingly immediate. Indeed, there is a strain of ruminative homophony (to which E♭ contexts seem prone – see 'For remembrance' (Two Pieces, 1921), Prelude (1924), 'In a May morning' (*Sarnia*, 1940–41)) which may remind us uncomfortably how many hours of his professional life Ireland must have devoted to organ extemporization. His racier, popular tone, as in 'Ragamuffin' (*London Pieces*, 1917–20), makes harmonic cliché a matter for some wit, though ironic distortion is foreign to Ireland's earnest temperament. Patterned textures grateful to the player typify his lyric pieces, whether or not their melodic cast is compelling, but a tendency to inflated climax is also recurrent; see, for example, 'Amberley Wild Brooks' (Two Pieces). Only in a few works does Ireland unfold an expansive structure rather than assemble deftly characterized sections. Even the Rhapsody of 1915, in filling out a large sonata scheme, has more room for spacious episode than for development.

But in the Sonata (1918–20), Ireland derives from his first subject a stream of developmental variants that flows on unchecked by a moment of reprise inconspicuous in the absence of any tonic return; the D minor here in an E minor movement reverses the procedure of the First Violin Sonata (see above). Only with the second group is E major firmly asserted, countering its B♭ in the exposition, a tritonal relation magnified in the sonata's movement plan. Both ideas in the slow movement are expanded developmentally at their presentation, yet they lack the memorability of some slender lyric sketches in which he has worked far less upon his material. The finale has the most elaborate design, deploying three subjects in a sonata-rondo plan that allows Ireland to eliminate intensive working-out and to apply to the refrain his nimble technique of character variation. The suite *Sarnia*, subtitled 'An island sequence', is the composer's most sustained response to the beauty and mystery of the Channel Islands. Almost 30 years after 'The island spell', he is satisfied with more conventionally disposed textures and harmonic embellishment, though the ideas are characteristic to the point of self-quotation. The unusually large scale of the three pieces is bolstered by much internal repetition, but the contrasted middle-section material is always strong, and evolutionary enough to avoid

ART MUSIC

that glib ternary symmetry which can make wearisome a succession of lyric pieces.

For decades even more popular than any of Ireland's miniatures, Frank Bridge's 'Rosemary' (from *Three Sketches*, 1906) consigned to relative obscurity the composer's sizeable output of piano pieces just as felicitous in their melodic shape and their elegantly textured use of the full range of decorative chromaticism. Earlier in 1906 he had written a *Dramatic Fantasia*, his first essay in the composite structure recurrent in his chamber music; despite some stiffness in the structural joints, it has panache within well-worn conventions of pianism. But it was not published, and 'characteristic pieces', some more ambitiously conceived, like *A Fairy Tale Suite* of 1917, dominated his piano writing. Admirably crafted though they all are, there is little in them that foreshadows the masterly pacing of the Piano Sonata (1921–4), a work to be explained only in relation to his progress in chamber music. The Sonata was a memorial tribute to a fellow student under Stanford, Ernest Farrar, killed in the First World War. The elegiac tone is most intense in the slow preludial music that twice returns, with increasing anguish. In its apotheosis at the end of the work, the original bell-like G♯s, struck against a progression of minor first inversions, have become major triads on roots consistently a tone above those of the minor chords (see Ex. 9.28a), a relationship made memorable early in the opening movement. More often the parallelism is of complex quasi-dominants (as in the prelude's sighing subsidiary idea, Ex. 9.28b), and in such a context the folk-like strains of the third theme and the perfect 5ths supporting its harmony can appear disingenuous. Development unusually extended for Bridge is also unusually clamorous, and after a reversed recapitulation (admitting a return of the tolling prelude) the passionate first subject becomes an explosive tailpiece. For once a Bridge slow movement is so disconsolate as to offer no *scherzando* relief. The transitional basis of its harmonic language can be heard in the approaches to a clear tonic D by essentially traditional 5ths-moves in the bass, after a tangential opening subject; as the second idea is more directly referable to this tonic, it is the first that must accommodate itself tonally in the (again reversed) restatement. The opening material of the finale depends harmonically on the first-movement prelude and first subject, and the sighing shape is prominent, but monotony is avoided, partly by extensive working-out of the independent second subject. Indeed, this is protracted to do duty for its own recapitulation, allowing the first subject to be

INSTRUMENTAL MUSIC I

Ex. 9.28 Bridge: Piano Sonata, 1st movement

directed towards the close by progressively exposing its origins in, and finally yielding to, the Sonata's initial ideas. Ireland's influence can be felt at times in piano layout and even thematic cast (as in the repetition with grace note of Ex. 9.28b), but in the sombre energy with which it sustains original designs the Bridge Sonata is a towering achievement in the British piano literature. Thereafter he returned to small-scale piano works, some almost as mellifluous as in his early period, though sparer and less prone to touches of conventional brilliance. The whimsical scherzo, *Gargoyle*, is less radical in its fluctuating bitonal formations than the Rhapsody Trio, also of 1928, and the piano encourages figurations more automatic than Bridge's chamber style admits.

Vaughan Williams wrote no solo piano music of substance, but in 1946 he completed an Introduction and Fugue for two pianos. This is almost too literally of substance, for the introduction material, returning to articulate a series of fugal textures, is overloaded with dense triadic parallelism on both keyboards. Some of the fugal writing is delicate, though its parade of devices is relentless, and modulatory switches on the minor-3rd circuit from the basic G minor are too regular. Only fitfully has the medium sparked the composer's imaginative response.

Arnold Bax was scarcely less prolific in the field of pictorial piano writing than Ireland or Bridge, but he never scored the kind of success that linked their names indissolubly to minor pieces. After about 1920 he abandoned this field; just as the symphony came to predominate in his orchestral work, so the sonata became his chief interest in writing for the piano and for his most committed interpreter, Harriet Cohen. His four piano sonatas can be viewed as a schematic progress from a single expanded sonata form, through a Lisztian composite span, then a three-movement sequence still tempestuously romantic, to a final modification of the same plan to match an almost neoclassical sobriety of language. In the resourceful variants that follow each statement and in the amplitude of its development and celebratory coda, the First Sonata (1910; revised 1917–21) shows how Bax's early exuberance of invention could fill out this large scale without help from the fateful intrusion of symbolic themes. Such quasi-programmatic device dominates the Second Sonata (1919), where the most arresting shape of the long, ominous prelude articulates (as in Liszt's Sonata) many of the later juxtapositions in a form that places slow-movement and scherzo elements within a sonata framework. Tension of key in the 'sonata' is slight (second group in the relative minor), so that it is the tonal obliquity of the prelude and the protracted flat submediant of the slow/scherzo sequence that demand tonal reconciliation; similarly, development concerns the prelude and scherzo ideas, culminating in their superimposition. The proportions and the moods of this complex design are convincing, whereas the casual sonata observances in the first movement of the Third Sonata (1926) appear self-indulgent: the initial subdominant bias (copied from the previous sonata) is corrected at the first subject's reprise, but the interior key contrast is provided by two slower lyrical ideas whose total failure to return creates a sectional ternary impression. In the finale, the momentum of a strongly characterized expository dichotomy is dissipated in a slower interlude on a lyrical derivative of the first subject. Such divergences argue a continuing interest in, if uneven control of, unorthodox structural balance, but the Fourth Sonata (1932) suggests a failure of Bax's customary creative ebullience both in its much closer adherence to textbook formal and harmonic precepts and in its trim divertimento textures. But characteristic episodes outshine development in the outer movements, in the first by relegating the first subject to ostinato duties and in the finale by introducing a third subject as centrepiece in a sonata-rondo. The square-phrased middle movement finds an unpretentious charm in the protraction for over half its length of the opening mediant pedal.

Arthur Bliss's Piano Sonata of 1952 is isolated from his early piano sets by 25 years and from his late pieces by another 17. Clearly, the solo piano was not an important medium in the shaping of his musical personality, and his essays are confidently crafted but rather stolid in their timbral qualities. Of the four *Masks* (1924), all but the first use some form of ostinato in building up textural layers. The last piece, by setting its ostinato of parallel 4ths askew to the main harmony, elevates into a consistent feature the clash of triads that is the common limit of Bliss's harmonic exploration; by setting chords into relentless contrary motion he ventures further in the unbarred middle section of the 'Elegy' in the Suite (1925). Such methods are applied in the Sonata to material better adapted to expansive processes. The tonal planning, denying closure to the basic A minor until the finale, is cogent, while the rhetorical balance is more striking than the ideas themselves. More challenging demands might have commended this neglected sonata to virtuoso pianists, though it finally lacks the impassioned individuality that would place it in the rather thin front rank of British piano sonatas.

Apart from his *Duets for Children* (1940), Walton wrote nothing for the piano's monochrome resources. Even his early jazz interests were never realized in keyboard terms, and it was left to Constant

ART MUSIC

Lambert to find common ground between jazz idioms and the classical piano traditions. His Sonata (1929) is a big work, more by quick-witted juxtaposition of short ideas than by structural planning on the grand scale. Its engaging jazz rhythms discourage extended rhythmic development, and the harmonic means are varied with the dexterity of a brilliant improviser. Such nonchalance of procedure confuses the intentions when devices from other traditions obtrude – *fugato*, Lisztian bravura and stentorian apotheosis. The less aspiring central Nocturne, elegantly poised between pathos and irony, is a review of contemporary dance types. Twenty years later, in *Trois pièces nègres pour les touches blanches* (1949; for piano duet), the popular sources of Lambert's inspiration have not changed, even if the white-note prescription keeps his harmony rather tepid; the rhythmic invention achieves great zest within the bounds of amateur skills. Lambert's title recalls the habit of his friend, Lord Berners, whose piano pieces affect French titles. The *Trois petites marches funèbres* (1920), with their insistent ostinatos and arbitrary harmonic surface, probably seemed mordant in the 1920s; by now their orthodox background sounds through.

Presumably the French titles gave Berners some tenuous claim on Gray's label, 'our English Satie'. The composer of French training and truer Gallic sympathies, Lennox Berkeley, dispensed with titles, even of the kind by which previous British piano composers had sought to befriend the domestic pianist; but he continued to make the short character piece, or set of pieces, the basis of his piano output. Not all are domestic in their demands, for the civilized reserve associated with Berkeley's music did not prevent his writing boldly for the virtuoso, in the Piano Concerto but also in Concert Studies for piano (1940 and 1955). His simpler collections, such as Five Short Pieces (1936) and Six Preludes (1945), are as smartly finished as Poulenc's; stylistically they are less wayward, and perhaps less memorable in consequence, but their unobtrusive redirection of the harmonic or the metrical flow belies bland first appearances. The Piano Sonata (1945) enlarges the scale on which ideas are presented, without recourse to the grandiose. Its opening epigrams lose their Stravinskian resonances as they engage in an expansive process so prolonged that the emergence of a clear-cut lyrical foil is surprising. Development-cum-episode is also long, but recapitulation is laconic and so much reworked as to maintain tension until the coda reinterprets the opening epigram. After the middle movements' engaging genre styles, the portentous tone of the harmonically tense introduction that prefigures the finale theme and returns in the coda seems misplaced.

Howard Ferguson's Piano Sonata was finished in 1940, almost a decade after the Violin Sonata discussed on p. 252, yet the lyricism of its central Adagio (overtly Elgarian by the coda) draws on still more restrained harmonic sources, except for brief climactic stresses. These reinstate the semitonal opposition that so persistently distinguishes the two outer movements, investing with a compelling logic the final return of the introduction's majestic gloom. Ultimately the superimpositions of semitonally discrepant triads prove to be less the head-on collisions of Vaughan Williams's Fourth Symphony (compare Ex. 9.1b above) than a vast amplification of a chromatic appoggiatura such as closes Schubert's String Quintet or Brahms's Piano Quintet scherzo. Ferguson's ability to harness its energy to drive urgent paragraphs is impressive. In a much slighter work, the *Five Bagatelles* (1944), he works on aphoristic pitch nuclei, defining contrasted characters in idiomatic but undemanding piano style.

Rawsthorne's nearest approach to a popular tone was in his piano concertos. Deprived of the stimulus of its dialogue with the orchestra, he found less in the piano to stimulate his finest invention. The two best-known sets, *Bagatelles* (1938) and *Four Romantic Pieces* (1953), are representative in their faintly tart harmonic flavour, their balanced melodic shapes and their modest technical level. Even more domestic is the delightful set of piano-duet miniatures, *The Creel* (1940), in which Izaak Walton prompts Rawsthorne's rarely exercised graphic powers. At an extreme both from these sketches and from the trimly pruned neoclassical piano Sonatina (1949) is the Ballade of 1967. This essay in the broad canvas of the single composite movement is characteristically built from alternations of two kinds of material, contrasted in tempo and mood but fairly consistent in their internal tonal tensions; the impassioned rhetoric of its climaxes salutes the style of its dedicatee, John Ogdon.

Writing a birthday tribute to Michael Tippett, Britten added a postscript: 'I wish your piano parts weren't so difficult' (Kemp 1965: 30). Certainly *The Heart's Assurance* cycle demands more of the pianist than anything in the songs of the superbly skilled accompanist, Britten. The further paradox – that it was Tippett, never professionally a performer, who revitalized the piano sonata, while Britten neglected the solo piano almost totally – may suggest that Britten, with the more formulated view of the instrument's potentialities, continued to find them interesting only as they facilitated his imaginative response to texts, whereas Tippett, with far fewer tactile associations, found a challenge in realizing his idiosyncratic invention in terms of a recalcitrant medium. Ian Kemp's claim of Tippett's First Sonata (1938), that 'the keyboard layout of every bar is derived from a particular style or composer' (1984: 137), becomes particularly convincing if we set this work beside its three successors (discussed by Jim Samson in Chapter 10); even so, the musical language, though clamorously diatonic, is already distinctive. The formal sequence progresses curiously, from a set of variations, through a slow movement in which two ideas alternate, and a scherzo with a full sonata range of material and procedure, to a finale still more articulated, as a sonata-rondo. Given the adventurous range of textures by which Tippett imposes definitive character on each variation, some kind of balance is struck between the first movement's unity and the last movement's diversity. Their contrasted methods of enriching the tonic G, by temporary excursions and by embracing tonal circuit, reflect the intervening experience of the slow movement (in A minor), with its rather stiff tonal switches, and the scherzo (in B minor), in which the continuous momentum rushes us exhilaratingly over the points (see Ex. 9.29). Echoes of folk melody and of jazz can be isolated, but in performance they contribute congruously to an affirmative quality that, while jettisoning the nineteenth-century legacy most earlier British piano sonatas still acknowledged, owes little to neoclassical small-talk.

Britten shows a greater debt in 'Funfair', the third piece in his *Holiday Diary* of 1934, where the refrain's high spirits depend on Stravinskian figuration. But the gently tilted major-mode relationships between melody and accompaniment formula in 'Sailing' pre-echo many quintessential Britten contexts, and in 'Night', however reminiscent of Bartók the enclosing mirrored harmonies may be, the fade-out into dreamless sleep of melodic snatches recalled from the earlier pieces provides the first example of a recurrent Britten image. His only other solo piano work, the *Night-Piece* written for the 1963 Leeds Piano Competition, treats it more spaciously. Here Bartók has influenced both the oscillating sextuplet from which the climactic middle section grows and the interludes of fantasy that punctuate the theme's return, but the piece's wider oscillations, between B♭ and B, belong to Britten's own nocturnal poetry. In America he wrote two pieces for the two-piano team of Ethel Bartlett and Rae Robertson. The Introduction and Rondo Burlesca (1940) has arresting sonorities, though its irony is not Britten's most

Ex. 9.29 Tippett: Piano Sonata no. 1, 3rd movement

pointed. Subtler moods are distilled in the *Mazurka elegiaca* (1941), a memorial to Paderewski, by wistfully oblique memories of Chopin.

XIV: The Organ

The difficulties we experience in trying to identify a distinctively British piano style are far less acute when we turn to the organ. Not only the nature of the typical British instrument but the context for which they were written give to many organ pieces from the first half of the century common features that differentiate them from the contemporary organ literature in the rest of Europe. Even the range of mood is circumscribed by the assumption that they will be played before or after an Anglican service, while that tradition of expressively responsive dynamic and timbral shading developed in the accompaniment of psalm-chant and hymn presupposes a taste for harmonically solid textures and a quasi-orchestral succession of sonorities. With the greater availability, if only through radio and gramophone, of true orchestral music, the once popular substitute of the town-hall organ recital lost its appeal, and with it such secular types as Hollins's 'concert overtures'; by the end of the Second World War, an organ recital was likely to appear a church-related activity rather than another kind of professional performance for a general public.

The organ built for the Royal Festival Hall in 1954 stimulated a change of attitude, which a subsequent widespread move towards more wholeheartedly 'reformed' principles of organ mechanism and tonal design confirmed, so that a new generation of performers, answerable to the same professional criteria as all other aspirants to the concert platform, could present reasonably faithful accounts of the great historical organ repertoires. In such a demanding context, much of the music our own traditions could offer proved inadequate to the change of function and inappropriate to the change in tonal ideals, though a welcome consequence was that more composers without ecclesiastical affiliations began to find in the organ a more rewarding challenge.

Before then, the vast majority of organ works were written by musicians who played the instrument in the service of the church, and who were often ill at ease in other media. Only in Herbert Howells do we find a composer of notable achievement across a range of instrumental and vocal types who produced some of his best work for the organ; for other Stanford pupils, such as Ireland and Bridge, the instrument prompted little of their most characteristic invention, and they soon neglected it. Vaughan Williams produced music of stronger profile in his Three Preludes (founded on Welsh hymn tunes) of 1920, though the suggestions he admitted from both the fugal and the chorale-embellishing aspects of Lutheran tradition point up a lack of textural finesse. Howells, more indebted to idioms that stem from cathedral improvisation, is also more fastidious in instrumental dispositions. His earliest works include an Organ Sonata (1911), but it is with the first set of Three Psalm-Preludes (1915–16) that he defines a personal tone. A modality recalling Vaughan Williams is directed harmonically towards higher-diatonic peaks with strong appoggiatura elements that still derive from Parry, while the sense of steady growth through long paragraphs stems from the patient registral unfolding of conjunct lines; the articulation is commonly by bold modulatory swings. Chromatic tensions reserved here for climactic moments become more pervasive in his later work, and the intensification of falsely related chords, together with insistent Lombard rhythms, become rather mannered. Comparison of the third prelude from Set 1 (on 'the valley of the shadow') and the first from Set 2 (on 'De profundis'; 1938) clarifies his stylistic progress. Between these sets, Howells wrote three Rhapsodies (1915–18) and a Second Sonata (1933), his most ambitious organ score. Its big scale is sustained with remarkable panache, though the alternations between dense added-note diatonicism and tight chromaticism can seem arbitrary, and pedal-points too often elaborate stasis rather than generate structural tension. The Six Pieces of 1940 are more variable in quality, recalling in 'Master Tallis's testament' the whimsical archaizing Howells exploited in his two sets of pieces for the clavichord, *Lambert's Clavichord* and *Howells' Clavichord.*

The organist–composers are legion, and much of their work retains its purpose in an environment where a steady supply of unexceptionable music is required. Of those who ventured beyond this scale of activity, two may be cited: Edward Bairstow (1874–1946) and Percy Whitlock (1903–46) each wrote an organ sonata, and Whitlock, though best known for sets of deft but unassuming miniatures, produced a Symphony for organ and orchestra; both sonata and symphony show an unexpected assurance in pacing big forms. Conversely, the major composers without practical involvement tended to write modestly for the instrument; neither Britten in his Prelude and Fugue on a Theme of Vittoria (1946) nor Tippett in his *Preludio* (1946) seems to have envisaged a piece that would significantly outlast the occasion for which it was written.

Chapter 10

INSTRUMENTAL MUSIC II[1]

JIM SAMSON

I: *Prelude*

With the death of Vaughan Williams in 1958, British music lost its leading senior composer. The dual succession was not in doubt. Tippett and Britten were sharply contrasted figures even at that time – contrasted as much in the range and nature of their dramatic and literary inspiration as in musical style. Yet they also had much in common, sharing a belief in the ethical value of music and in the consequent social responsibility of the composer, and turning alike to the idioms of early British music (rather than to more recent national traditions) as a major source of creative inspiration. There was a further parallel, more germane to my concerns in this chapter. Despite the very different nature of their stylistic developments, both composers reached significant turning-points at around the same time – the end of the 1950s. (For a sustained discussion of the music of both composers, including the changes in the music of their later years, see Whittall 1982.)

I will consider those turning-points briefly. Britten's was the less conspicuous, as befits a composer who preferred constant refinement to radical change. His commitment to lyric melody and tonally regulated harmony remained intact in the 1960s, but increasingly it was accommodated to a new-found preoccupation with the unification of melody and harmony, extending at times to a creative interest in

---

[1] It is a pleasure to acknowledge the assistance of Trevor Bray and Philip Grange, both of whom generously shared their expertise on British music. Dr Bray allowed me to see his unpublished manuscript on twentieth-century British chamber music, and several of his observations have found their way into my text. Dr Grange read the manuscript and made numerous helpful suggestions. I am also grateful to Lionel Pike for his helpful advice on the music of Simpson, and for showing me unpublished material.

INSTRUMENTAL MUSIC II

12-note concepts. Following the Cello Symphony of 1963, motivic and intervallic integration came to the fore in Britten's music, in the measure that conventional tonal argument receded. This change of direction was one artist's response to internal creative imperatives. Yet it was also part of a much more general reappraisal of style and technique in the 1960s by British composers of broadly traditional orientation. And on this larger canvas the technical concerns were very much the same – a renovation of tonal harmony allied to a growing interest in 12-note concepts.

The change of direction in Tippett's development following 1958 was characteristically more abrupt and of a different order stylistically. From *King Priam* onwards his music was marked by a rejection of tonally based evolutionary procedures in favour of a juxtaposition and superimposition of sharply differentiated and strongly characterized materials, rather in the manner of cinematic intercutting techniques. There is an ancestry in baroque formal procedures, but a more immediate and relevant background in the music of Stravinsky. Tippett's new formal methods represented a more radical departure from earlier traditions than Britten's, and predictably they found an echo in composers of more progressive bent, notably of the younger generation.

It would not be helpful or realistic to explain these new directions in the music of Britten and Tippett solely in contextual terms. Nevertheless they speak eloquently of a much wider change – even a caesura – in British music in the late 1950s. Vaughan Williams's death marked the symbolic end of a nationalist tradition which was already in terminal decline. The 'pastoral modality' associated above all with his music lingered for a time in the work of several older composers, but its rejection by a younger generation was decisive. In his later years Vaughan Williams had become the bastion of a conservative musical establishment (including the main teaching institutions) which seemed bent on condemning to obscurity and neglect the more experimental figures in British music, and in particular those who took the serial path. Budding composers in post-war Britain were hardly less isolated from progressive Continental trends – though for very different reasons – than their East European contemporaries. And intriguingly the 'cultural thaw' occurred at more or less the same time.

From the late 1950s onwards even the more traditional styles in Britain were increasingly fertilized by 'advanced' techniques emanating from post-war Europe. Serialism in particular began to make belated headway, and in the 1960s the interpenetration of serialism and tonality became a central theme of British music. By then the more progressive trends in Europe (epitomized by the Darmstadt seminar) were centred less on serialism than on the concept of controlled chance in music, and this too had an impact on British composers. The more radical manifestations of *alea*, together with related concerns such as improvised music theatre and possible rapprochements with popular styles, were examined at Darmstadt in the early 1960s and they were embraced by a small but vociferous group of composers in Britain too.

Other themes will emerge from this survey, less directly dependent on either indigenous or European sources – the formal mosaics of late Tippett and Gerhard, the 'dramatic abstracts' of Musgrave and Bennett, the parodistic techniques of Maxwell Davies and the new tonalities of a postmodern age. Ultimately, however, rigid categorization of the achievements of British composers during this period is unhelpful. The best of them pursued an individual path, taking what they needed from a variety of sources and often mediating between contrasted styles and attitudes in the spirit of compromise and synthesis which has been the hallmark of British cultural achievement in the past.

II: The Symphonic Tradition

Style and medium are inextricably linked. The nineteenth-century orchestra took its familiar shape in response to the demands of tonal harmony and tonal melody, and it is hardly surprising that many younger composers – in Britain as elsewhere – considered it an inappropriate vehicle for contemporary idioms. There were also more practical disincentives to the composition of orchestral works, above all the inadequate rehearsal time given by established orchestras to new music. Younger composers often preferred then to write for *ad hoc* forces, better suited to their compositional needs. Hence the appearance of groups that approached the condition of chamber music while still employing a conductor – the Fires of London, the Nash Ensemble and the London Sinfonietta. There was a similar transformation – even a redefinition – of chamber music itself. Here the movement was towards larger groups of non-standard instrumentation, but usually playing without a conductor. The Melos Ensemble and the Music Group of London have been typical, their services to British chamber music ably promoted by societies such as the Park Lane Group and the Redcliffe Concerts for British Music.

Yet for all this reshaping of instrumental forces the symphony orchestra and the string quartet held their ground, and not just as guardians of a classical heritage. Commissioning policies have ensured that even among younger progressive composers the old media will die hard. It seems too that – expediency apart – they still retain their traditional allure as the principal vehicles for epic statements in instrumental music. Unsurprisingly it is among the older generation that the orchestra and string quartet have been employed with greatest respect for historical archetypes. Yet within this general commitment to traditional genres the range of styles may be enormously wide. We need only consider the distance between the frankly romantic, Elgar-inspired symphonies of George Lloyd (b 1913) and the tough-grained, Beethovenian quartets of Robert Simpson (b 1921). (There is no general account of Lloyd's music in books or music journals, though there have been several newspaper profiles.)

In a style-conscious age it is perhaps too easy to condemn those composers whose innate conservatism has been repelled by contemporary idioms; we may in short confuse originality with innovation. The traditional gestures that characterize Rubbra's music, for example, discreetly veil harmonic processes of considerable subtlety and originality (see Ottaway 1971). Equally the ponderous, almost Brucknerian romanticism of Daniel Jones (b 1912) is given a contemporary 'edge' through his exploration of organized rhythmic asymmetries, not unlike the variable metres developed by Boris Blacher (see Wilcox 1984). Havergal Brian, too, in the 20 symphonies that postdate 1958, developed a uniquely personal idiom (characterized by massive tonal conflicts and craggy contrapuntal textures), which none the less retains clear links with classical formal archetypes and conventional tonal expectations (see M. MacDonald 1974–83).

The decade following Vaughan Williams's death was indeed a seminal period in the development of the British symphony, marked above all by a sustained renovation of its traditional tonal resources. Technically two features emerge, linking composers whose music is very different in other respects. In the first place composers often tended to replace a precisely focused tonal argument with a more generalized dialectic of sharp and flat tonal regions, a procedure that had already informed the structure of Tippett's Second Symphony of 1956–7. And secondly there was an obvious concern on the part of many composers of tonal music to come to terms with the possibilities of total chromaticism, as liberated by serialism. Here Walton's Second Symphony (1960) was an eloquent example, its final movement based on a 12-note passacaglia theme which in no way undermines the strong tonal foundation of the music.

These topics were rehearsed in a number of British symphonies composed in the immediate aftermath of 1958. In Alwyn's Fourth Symphony (1959), the two basic modes outline flat and sharp areas which together exhaust the total chromatic (see Hold 1972). They are presented simultaneously at the outset and their later confrontation and attempted synthesis determine the overall tonal argument of the work. There are similar devices in Rawsthorne's Third Symphony, which has already been discussed in Chapter 9.

The Third Symphony of Robert Simpson, dating from 1962, epitomizes the renovative approach to tonal argument found in such works. Although tonality is established through pedal points and long-range linear progressions (see the bass progressions at Figs 76–9 and 83–5 of the second movement), as much as through triadic clarifications, the 5th relationship remains crucial in Simpson's symphony. Indeed the overall conflict between C and B♭ is resolved by the final bars in such a way that derivations from a cycle of 5ths become clear. At the same time an essential feature of the work is the distortion of this 5th relationship into a tritone by means of the semitonal interferences that recur throughout. The bass progression at Figs 80–82 of the second movement is perhaps the clearest expression of this tendency, but a harmonic summary of the opening of the work (Ex. 10.1) illustrates that from the start it is a tritonal bass progression that deflects the music from the initial centre of C to one of B♭. It also demonstrates the alternation of materials built on sharp and flat modes, an alternation that culminates in the second movement's triadic affirmations of B major as an alternative to the principal centres.

Ex. 10.1 Simpson: Symphony no. 3, 1st movement (summary of bars 1–18)

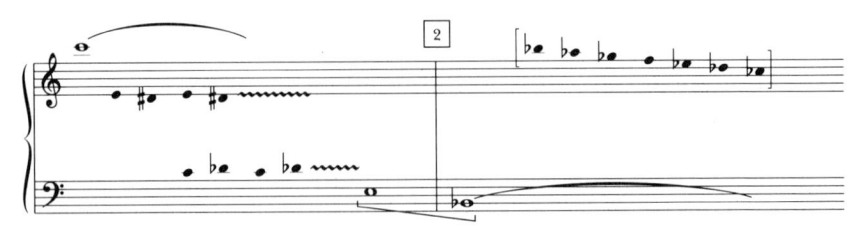

INSTRUMENTAL MUSIC II

Of the older generation of British composers it is perhaps Simpson who has most convincingly made the case for the continuing vitality of the symphonic tradition in a post-tonal world. His Third Symphony perfectly illustrates his control of extended structures, above all his ability to pace an argument, and where necessary to 'mark time' musically. The second (and final) movement forms a single *crescendo* and a barely perceptible *accelerando*, the latter achieved through subtleties of rhythm and metre which have remained a constant feature of Simpson's music. Yet there have been subtle changes in other aspects of his music since the Third Symphony. From the Fifth Symphony onwards, Simpson has followed his mentor Nielsen in an increasing preoccupation with intervallic rather than tonal–triadic structural tensions. As a result he has arrived at a somewhat novel view of tonality. The tonalities of neither the Fifth nor the Seventh Symphonies, for example, are definable in any 'normal' terms, but in each case the ending produces a stability that is in a sense tonal in that there is a real feeling of inevitability about the final A♭ of no. 5 and the C♯ of no. 7.

Most of Simpson's output is instrumental and its backbone is to be found in the symphonies (11 to date) and quartets (15 to date). In both genres he has pursued the same kind of muscular energy and cumulative growth processes that he identifies in the music of Beethoven, Nielsen and Sibelius. As a corpus, the series of quartets is indeed among the most remarkable achievements of post-war music, not least for the variety – both of form and of character – that Simpson manages to achieve within a single medium. They range from the single-movement Seventh Quartet (1977), whose central scherzo defies the modest dimensions of the work to build an astonishingly powerful climax, to the hour-long Ninth Quartet, whose musical argument (a set of 32 variations and fugue on a theme of Haydn) unfolds from first to last over a single unchanging pulse. (For further analyses of Simpson's music see *Tonic*, the journal of the Robert Simpson Society, and E. Johnson 1971.)

Simpson's position is unusual in British music, not so much because he has cultivated the symphony and quartet to such impressive effect, but because in doing so he has re-created for our times something of Beethoven's lofty tone of moral idealism and humanism. For many senior British composers this tone has seemed inappropriate – even unavailable – in a post-Mahler age. And it is striking that in technical terms such composers often seemed to rehearse again in the 1960s some of the basic musical processes that accompanied the massive upheavals of early modernism in European music. To generalize, we find Bartók, Stravinsky and Schoenberg replacing Sibelius and Hindemith as mentors to an older generation of British composers in the post-1958 era.

The later string quartets of Maconchy, for instance, are clearly indebted to Bartók. This influence extends beyond formal design to embrace texture and motivic working, where small germinal motifs generate larger paragraphs in a gradual cumulative fashion often unplanned in advance. Priaulx Rainier (1903–86) proceeded in a similar manner in her later chamber works, though the building blocks here are often characterized in other-than motivic terms. In *Quanta* (1962) for oboe quartet, for example, the musical argument develops from an initial textural and rhythmic shape which is in due course developed into a large mosaic of clearly defined cells, with each lull in the music followed by a new impulse of energy. There are intriguing parallels with the Polish composer Andrzej Panufnik (1914–91), resident in Britain from 1954. Panufnik's early music (from the 1940s and early 1950s) was also much influenced by Bartók, though there were of course specific political reasons for its folkloric basis. Following his arrival in Britain, he gradually refined this idiom in the direction of ever greater abstraction. Works such as the *Sinfonia sacra* (1963) and *Sinfonia votiva* (1981) still have a cellular basis, but the cells are elaborated into 'geometric' configurations of considerable sophistication, with symbolic – even mystical – connotations. (The most detailed study of Panufnik's music is Stasiak 1991; see also Walsh 1974b and Osborne 1984.)

Peter Racine Fricker (1920–90) also changed direction – albeit discreetly – in the late 1950s, having already composed an impressive series of instrumental works characterized by a closely argued motivic working allied to a rigorous, even intellectual, investigation of novel formal possibilities (see the material on Fricker in Hines 1970, and Hoddinott 1970). The String Quartet no. 1 (1949) has a four-in-one movement structure, for instance, while the Violin Sonata (1950) assigns a slower tempo to each successive movement and the Second Symphony (1951) is constructed as a series of 'expanding rondos'. In all these works the interpenetration of melodic and harmonic material was achieved by methods closer to Bartók than to Schoenberg. But from the late 1950s onwards, Fricker showed a creative interest in serialism, allowing fairly rudimentary serial devices (usually employed in rigorously contrapuntal contexts) to enrich rather than radically to modify existing features of his musical thought. After moving to the

INSTRUMENTAL MUSIC II

University of California in 1964, his music, including the Fourth and Fifth Symphonies (1966 and 1976 respectively), if anything acquired a leaner, sparser texture, designed to sharpen the contrapuntal working at the heart of his musical language.

If a single generalization emerges from the work of these older composers of a broadly traditional orientation, it is that a crossroads was reached in the development of conventional instrumental genres in Britain – especially the symphony and string quartet – in the late 1950s. There was a widely held view that these genres could no longer retain their vitality without a thorough-going infusion of new technical developments emanating from Europe, even if in some cases this meant the Europe of half a century earlier. Even the most established styles were shaken by new influences in the late 1950s. For some composers, as for Britten (whose instrumental music is discussed in Chapter 9), this amounted to an enrichment and refinement of procedures that were already well established. For others, as for Tippett, it resulted in a major change of stylistic direction. (The authoritative study of Tippett's music is Kemp 1984; see also D. Clarke 1990.)

Tippett's early music took its stylistic origins in a 'rediscovery' of Tudor music, allied to a lively interest in Beethoven and Stravinsky. From the Concerto for Double String Orchestra (1939) onwards, he cultivated a polyphonic and rhythmic technique that owed much to the madrigalists, together with a modally inflected pitch structure indebted both to Tudor music and to more recent British traditions. This idiom was at its most persuasive in the Second and Third String Quartets (1942 and 1946), which typify respectively his leanings towards a disciplined, 'classical' art on the one hand and a more exploratory, visionary aesthetic on the other. This represents a duality at the heart of Tippett's music, from whatever period, and the tension it engenders is usually, though by no means always, a source of strength. The early tonal phase of his creative development culminated in the Stravinsky-inspired Second Symphony of 1957, but already in that work there were signs of major new directions, and these were consolidated in the subsequent opera *King Priam*. It was above all the particular musico-dramatic problems encountered in that opera that prompted Tippett to depart radically from a tonally based idiom, both in *King Priam* itself, and in the related Second Piano Sonata and Concerto for Orchestra.

The tonal organization of these works is similar in some respects to that of the Second Symphony. The first three sections of the concerto, for instance, alternate flat and sharp sides of the tonal spectrum, each built around groups of perfect 5ths. But although invariance is an important factor in the work's opening movement, the effect is quite different from the generative processes of traditional tonality, which would direct the course of the music in a dynamic way. The collision of invariant pitch areas is rather one aspect of a more fundamental rethinking of formal process, radically different from the developmental forms of the Austro-German tradition. In his single-movement Second Piano Sonata (1962), for example, Tippett allows eight contrasted blocks of material (ranging from massive chords and repeated-note patterns to lyrical arabesques) to alternate – mosaic-like – in a kaleidoscope of multiple combinations. There is no development in any conventional sense of the term.

The Concerto for Orchestra extends this approach to include a superimposition (as well as juxtaposition) of materials, creating multi-layered textures comparable to those found in Stravinsky – the Symphonies of Wind Instruments, for example. The slow movement of the work is more orthodox, but the outer movements, and especially the first, are almost in the nature of experiments in these new formal methods. Nine separate materials are presented in the first movement, each with a specific instrumentation. The 'exposition' of these materials can be presented most clearly in tabular form (Table 10.1), while 'development' consists of alternative juxtapositions and superimpositions of the nine characters. The dangers of fragmentation are considerable, but Tippett minimizes them by preserving some semblance of tonal continuity, by invoking conventional formal archetypes (sonata form in the tripartite scheme, and rondo in the recurrence of the 1a material (Ex. 10.2)), and by establishing close correspondences between separate characters.

Table 10.1   Tippett: Concerto for Orchestra, 1st movement (exposition material)

1st group				2nd group				3rd group			
1a	1b	1c	1a	2a	2b	2c	2a	3a	3b	3c	3a
			1b				2b				3b
			1c				2c				3c
2 fls	tb	3 hns		pf	ob	2 tbns		pf	cl	2 tpts	
hp	pf			timp	e.h.	perc		xyl	bcl	perc	
					bn				pf		
					dbn						

Ex. 10.2

These intercutting and characterization techniques have become a basic feature of Tippett's later music, and they are all the more effective in that they now form part of a much larger synthesis of elements from his earlier style. The opening of the Third Symphony (1972) intercuts between materials marked 'arrest' and 'movement' (see Eliot's *Burnt Norton*: '. . . at the still point, there the dance is, / But neither arrest nor movement'). The opening of Part Two of the work presents five 'characters', clearly differentiated by instrumentation, which remain essentially unchanged in themselves, though they are combined and juxtaposed in a variety of ways. By superimposing them in such a way that each preserves an independent harmonic and contrapuntal life, Tippett suggests technical parallels with Charles Ives as well as Stravinsky. Ives's music has interested him greatly from the later 1960s and the stylistic counterpoint which is essential to the American's work appears in his opera *The Knot Garden* and subsequent works, including the Third Symphony. In addition to the re-creation of blues style in the symphony's second part, Tippett here makes use of a quotation from the finale of Beethoven's Ninth Symphony, a potent pairing of an idiom that for Tippett symbolizes modern man's suffering with the optimism of an earlier age in a searching examination of the possibility of affirmative gestures such as Beethoven's in today's world.

The extra-musical references of the Third Symphony are less obvious in Tippett's later instrumental works, including the Third and Fourth Piano Sonatas, the Fourth Symphony, the Fourth String Quartet and the Triple Concerto. The Fourth Symphony, completed in 1977, is in a single movement, clearly divided into seven sections, and it intercuts between three basic tempi, each with an associated group of 'characters'. Sections 3–5 explore the full potential of the materials of each tempo separately, while the outer four sections intercut more rapidly between the different tempi. Again there are underlying archetypal patterns – rondo and, more strongly, four-in-one sonata form, where section 3 is a slow movement, section 5 a scherzo and section 7 a reprise. Within its compact half-hour span the symphony achieves a powerful synthesis of earlier styles and gestures, from the Tudor-inspired polyphony of the Concerto for Double String Orchestra to the powerful brass writing of the Third Symphony.

The dramatic and lyrical qualities of the Fourth Symphony are emphasized respectively in the Fourth String Quartet and Triple Concerto. The inspiration for the quartet (1978) arose when Tippett heard a passage from one of the late Beethoven quartets used as background music for a television programme. The influence works on several levels, from the foreground level of a recurrent dotted-rhythm pattern reminiscent of the *Grosse Fuge*, to the background level of a general dramatic or psychological 'plot'. This latter is described by Tippett as 'a general progression (repeated) . . . from a web of sound into linear clarity, and from intense stillness breaking out through unwinding into vigour', and it operates both within sections and from section to section. The Triple Concerto (1979) is more obviously nostalgic in tone, looking back at different periods in the composer's creative life. Familiar stabbing brass chords and florid woodwind configurations intercut in its outer movements, while the slow movement, the longest of the three and the heart of the work, recalls the Double Concerto and even more *The Midsummer Marriage*. Yet Tippett's nostalgia is anything but self-indulgent. There are new ingredients in the mix, notably an exotic coloration (prominent in the 'interludes') which was apparently inspired by Balinese music.

Tippett has searched constantly for new ways to realize, extend and renew his inner vision, while at the same time maintaining a lively creative interest in, and dependence upon, the enduring masterpieces of the past. His music, like that of the other senior composers discussed here, demonstrates well that the terms 'traditionalist' and 'progressive' need not be incompatible. Among a middle generation of British 'traditionalists' (those born in the late 1920s and 1930s), the problem of style appears to have been more acute, perhaps because they had wider access to new techniques at an earlier stage of their development. Generalizations are difficult, but it does seem that those composers who remained committed to conservative styles produced few works with the weight of a Simpson, a Rawsthorne or a Tippett. Conversely, an involvement with modern techniques by such composers all too often seems forced and gratuitous, a flirtation with the new rather than the necessary response to a deepening creativity.

We may consider briefly a group of middle-generation composers of traditional leanings. The first symphonies of Kenneth Leighton (1929–88) and John McCabe (*b* 1939), both composed in 1963, form a useful starting-point. They are closely unified and skilfully crafted on all levels. Yet the impression left is hardly a strong one. For all its fluency, Leighton's counterpoint (Hindemithian in origin) lacks the strength and exuberance of Tippett's Second Symphony, while the ostinato accompaniment patterns designed to propel the allegro sections in the first and second movements are a poor substitute for the driving rhythmic energy of Rawsthorne's Third. McCabe's symphony is similarly problematic, despite an effective central movement, 'Dance', in 5/4. The vertical density of the outer movements seems curiously unmotivated and the cyclic devices lack the sense of inevitability that attends similar procedures in Alwyn's Fourth.

It is intriguing to compare the later developments of Leighton and McCabe (see Truscott 1975). Leighton clearly perceived no difficulty with an essentially traditional idiom, and his musical style remained largely unchanged in later years. It is at its best in works such as the piano piece *Conflicts* (1967), whose two themes generate complex webs of counterpoint in a cumulative process of growth and variation. Hindemith still stands behind much of the music, but the influence has been skilfully absorbed, as it has been too in later works such as the Concerto for organ, timpani and strings and the Second Symphony. In contrast, McCabe clearly felt a need to respond to the challenge of more progressive techniques. His music became more adventurous following the First Piano Concerto of 1966, a work marred by the undigested influence of Bartók. Yet despite their more complex rhythms and harmonies and their occasional use of aleatory procedure, the structural basis of works such as the Second Symphony (1971), *The Castle of Arianrhod* for horn and piano (1973) and the orchestral *The Chagall Windows* (1974) remains traditional, extending the thematic methods of earlier works and preserving the outlines of an underlying tonal scheme.

A similar allegiance to traditional structural methods has been a feature of the music of the Welsh composers William Mathias (1934–92) and Alun Hoddinott (*b* 1929) (see Michael Oliver in Foreman 1975: 86–96 for a discussion of both composers). Much of their output is instrumental, often written in response to commissions. The latter point is important, for it underlines an attitude to the business of composing shared with Leighton and McCabe and indeed also with composers such as Malcolm Williamson (*b* 1931) and Wilfred Josephs (*b* 1927). Mathias saw his job, and Hoddinott sees his, as somewhat akin to the earlier Kapellmeister, and their ability and readiness to produce music to order (often at great speed) have commanded admiration while at the same time arousing suspicion. Such facility carries its own penalties and both composers on occasion show themselves much too ready to fall back on easy orchestral pickings and well-tried formal devices.

Of the two, Mathias was perhaps the closer to Leighton in his untroubled acceptance of a relatively conservative musical language.

INSTRUMENTAL MUSIC II

He cultivated a melodious, often dance-based, idiom, whose accessibility reflects his commitment to reaching the widest possible audience. From the Second Piano Concerto (1961) onwards, his highly personal style embraced just about every conventional genre in an extensive catalogue of works, most of them fairly lightweight in character, but some (such as the String Quartet of 1968) revealing a capacity for a more introverted and intense musical discourse. There is little sense of a developing musical language here, and it is perhaps a comment on our age that this has been regarded in many quarters as just cause for criticism. Once established, Mathias's style took occasional new turnings and explored some unexpected byways, but in essence it remained unchanged.

Hoddinott, on the other hand, is closer to McCabe in his apparent need to respond to surrounding modernisms. Yet, on a deeper level, his music too has circled around a number of fairly restricted gestures and techniques, not least the formal palindrome which has reappeared in many different guises (often fused with other formal types) since the Harp Concerto of 1958. The spiky, Hindemithian rhythms and angular melodic outlines of his early Clarinet Concerto (1954) form a recurring characteristic of his music, one that is given its most appropriate expression in lightweight divertimentos but that is present, thinly disguised, in symphonic essays too. A comparison of the finale of the Second Piano Concerto and the opening of the second movement of the Third Symphony (1960 and 1968 respectively) demonstrates how in the later work this kind of movement has been given a face-lift.

Hoddinott's instrumental music has continued to develop stylistically in the 1970s and 1980s. His orchestral palette has been enriched by a growing fascination with the percussion section and, more crucially, he has felt less need to hold in check his dissonant harmonies by means of a strong tonal foundation, often preferring to order them by means of simple serial devices. These changes were already apparent in the Fourth Symphony of 1969, but they are most marked in a group of shorter pieces, including *The Sun, the Great Luminary of the Universe* (1970), the aggressively dissonant, linearly conceived Sixth Piano Sonata (1972) and the orchestral *Passaggio* of 1977. Yet there is little evidence that the new techniques penetrate through to deep levels of creativity in Hoddinott's music. On the contrary they seem at times to be little more than a spicy dressing on basically conservative fare – an engagement with 'modernity' on one level perhaps.

It will be worth contrasting the attitudes and achievements of these four composers with those of another 'traditionalist' of the middle generation. Nicholas Maw (*b* 1935) is a composer whose natural affinity with aspects of romantic traditions has never once been expressed through the second-hand, the conventional, gesture. Yet the difficulties involved in preserving his independence of the traditional concepts on which he must at the same time lean heavily have been formidable, and Maw's small output contrasts strikingly with the ease and fluency of a Hoddinott or a McCabe. Constant revisions and great difficulty in completing works are a measure of the hazards of his particular path, but they also proclaim his integrity. Maw's stylistic maturity has been hard-won. His music has looked in many directions, from the post-Webern avant garde to Britten and Tippett, from pre-serial Schoenberg to neoclassical Stravinsky. Yet this eclecticism has in no sense signified easy flirtations, rather a penetrating investigation into the meaning of twentieth-century stylistic pluralism and a creative search for the context to which his own sympathies as a composer might best relate. (See Whittall 1975 for a good general account of Maw's development.)

The frank romanticism of *Nocturne* and *Scenes and Arias* is less in evidence in Maw's purely instrumental music, but the 'slow movement' embedded in his String Quartet (1965) and the central Threnody from his Sinfonia (1966) present openly the kind of intensely expressive quality that underlies all his music. For all that, Maw himself described the Sinfonia as his 'most neoclassical work', and the work does undoubtedly present a close dialogue with traditional formal types. Its substantial first movement fuses sonata form with a scherzo which appears after the development section, while the finale is a set of nine variations which had originally been intended as part of the Threnody. Even in an avowedly neoclassical work, however, the fertility of Maw's imagination generates its own counterpoint to the expectations set up by such formal types. The scherzo material virtually takes over the recapitulation of the first movement, while the variations of the finale stray from the theme to an extent that calls the term 'variations' into question.

In Maw's Sonata for two horns and strings (1967) the dialogue with a background of tonal forms and procedures ranges even more widely than in the Sinfonia, but the background remains perceptible none the less. Later works, on the other hand, moved in the direction of ever greater and ever more confident independence from such a background. *Life Studies* for 15 solo strings (1973–6) proposes a formal organization that betrays not a trace of sonata thinking. Even more crucial than the element of 'mobility' introduced in the overall distribution of the work's several sections is the reliance in individual movements on an intuitive sense of musical flow that is no longer closely allied to traditional forms. The freely evolving thematicism of these pieces suggests that of all his earlier models it is perhaps the pre-serial music of Schoenberg that has come to have greatest relevance to Maw. At the same time it should be stressed that, as with the Sinfonia, the detailed working of *Life Studies* – its melodic phraseology and its suggestions of structural (albeit not traditional) harmony – sets up associations with tonal literature which Maw obviously values and which are unlikely to disappear entirely from his music.

Maw spent much of the 1970s and 1980s working on his gigantic orchestral work *Odyssey*, given an incomplete performance in 1987 and its first complete hearing two years later. Other works appeared during these years of course, among them the strikingly individual *Personae* for piano, whose masterly six pieces explore a remarkably wide range of expression, from the violent explosions of no. 3 to the placid 'lyrical continuum' of no. 6. But *Odyssey* remains Maw's seminal work to date, and it must stand as one of the most remarkable instrumental compositions ever to appear in Britain. By what can only be described as an immense effort of will, not to say a highly developed intuitive sense of formal balance, Maw has somehow imposed a coherence on this massive structure. Thematic cross-references (grouped around an *Ur*-melody) help us find our bearings. So, too, do the clear formal outlines – a five-movement symphony with an introduction, 'first movement', intermezzo, slow movement (lasting some thirty minutes) and finale. But in the end *Odyssey* remains in the memory as a continuous outpouring of ideas, now sensuous, even voluptuous, in tone, now delicate and restrained, now aggressive and violent, and finally cataclysmic.

III: Serialism and Beyond

The musical language of Nicholas Maw's maturity owed a great deal to the 12-note technique which he abandoned, at any rate in strict form, after his *Six Chinese Lyrics* of 1959. His interest in serialism, shared by many composers whose student years fell in the late 1950s, would have been given little opportunity to develop a decade earlier. The eventual acceptance of the method in Britain owed much to the presence of three major immigrant composers of the older generation, all of them influential not just as composers but as teachers. Of these composers two will be considered briefly at this stage – the Hungarian-born Mátyás Seiber (1905–60) and the Austrian-born Egon Wellesz (1885–1974). The third, Spanish-born Roberto Gerhard (1896–1970), will be discussed later.

Seiber's later music draws together 'Hungarian' elements (owing more to his teacher Kodály than to Bartók) and a highly personal – but strict – application of 12-note technique. Yet for all the command of *métier* revealed by works such as the *Quartetto lirico* (1952), the Elegy for viola and small orchestra (1954) and the Violin Sonata (1960), Seiber's music has somehow failed to achieve the kind of unmistakable profile that would guarantee its survival on our concert platforms. Nor has Wellesz fared much better, though there is a more distinctive voice in his music, and one that might yet emerge if and when the critical climate becomes more receptive.

Like Schoenberg's, Wellesz's serial technique was always concerned exclusively with pitch relationships, and even then primarily of a linear, thematic character. By placing the method at the service of a symphonic idiom derived from Mahler, he gave a lead to several British symphonists who felt the need to come to terms with serialism. The nine symphonies all date from the post-war years, during the period of Wellesz's residence in England, when he felt able to adopt a very flexible attitude to serial procedures. Indeed in the first four symphonies these are totally subordinated to tonal relationships, and only from the Fifth (1955–6) onwards are they explored with reasonable consistency. The feature that is common to all nine symphonies is a technique of extended tonal paraphrase, whereby all or most of the tonal potentialities of a work are indicated at the beginning and later projected to the larger structure of the symphony (Symons 1980).

The opening of the finale of his Sixth Symphony (1965) (Ex. 10.3) demonstrates an attitude towards serialism whose flexibility is characteristic not only of Wellesz's music in general but of a whole range of British music. The violin melody has an obvious kinship with the widely spanning, emotion-laden lines of late Mahler, while the underlying harmonies are reminiscent of Schoenbergian chord-types. Serially the working is carefully designed to create strong links with traditional tonal procedures. The tritonal span ensures invariant terminal points for both prime and inverted forms

Ex. 10.3   Wellesz: Symphony no. 6, 3rd movement

(compare Schoenberg's op. 25 and op. 31), while the hierarchy is reinforced by internal repetitions of E♭, giving the pitch a quasi-tonic function and also serving to create expectations of the twelfth pitch A. Furthermore the E♭–A relationship is by no means arbitrary, since the A has a dominant function in relation to the overall centre of D (note, for example, the cadential preparations at bars 60 and 140 of the third movement), while E♭ is the strongest alternative centre.

Wellesz's obvious concern to integrate serialism with tonality is also apparent in later piano and chamber compositions, including the forceful *Triptychon* for piano (1966) and the Four Pieces for String Quartet (1968), where the total chromatic is kept in play without recourse to strict serial procedures. That concern is echoed in the music of Benjamin Frankel (1906–73), whose eight symphonies were all composed between 1960 and 1972. But where Wellesz was happy to abandon the method in parts of a work and indeed for complete compositions, Frankel's serial practice was altogether more rigorous, concerning itself with a dialectic between clear, audible serialism and more equivocal, though no less strict, presentations. In the Seventh Symphony, for instance, the identity of the row becomes clear only gradually, presented as a melodic form, which generates its own harmonies, only some way into the first movement (at Fig. 13). Throughout the first movement Frankel's alternation of such clear melodic presentations of the row with sections where it is lost in more complex, overlapping forms has something in common with the statement and development of sonata dialectic. The triadic formation of the Seventh Symphony's row is immediately obvious to the ear and its dominant-quality components are used by the composer in such a way that tonal affirmations at the end of the outer movements emerge naturally from earlier harmonic material. The final bars of the work demonstrate clearly Frankel's fusion of tonal and serial, a fusion that has also interested many older- and middle-generation post-war composers outside Britain, from Dallapiccola and Fortner in Europe to Copland in America.

Apart from the Third, all Frankel's symphonies were composed against a background of conventional symphonic design, expressed moreover through thematic working of a traditional kind. Another British composer who explored serial methods in the context of traditional formal design was Humphrey Searle (1915–82). The key to Searle's distinctive musical personality lies in his adaptation of orthodox serialism to a romantic sound-world owing more to the passionate, impulsive rhetoric of Liszt than to the *Angst* of Mahler. Searle himself maintained that, far from constructing rows according to elaborate pre-compositional schemes, he allowed them to arise naturally from the initial inspiration for a work. His manipulation of the series, like that of Wellesz and Frankel, was comparatively unadventurous and his music relies for its broad structural outlines on an alliance with traditional formal concepts.

The first movement of the Second Symphony (1958), for example, re-creates a conventional sonata-form design in terms of serial practice. In the introduction to the movement P_0 (Ex. 10.4a) is unfolded against a pedal D, the tonal centre of the work, before culminating on a referential chord based on the alpha hexachord (Ex. 10.4b). The first-subject material that follows is based on I_0, but it demonstrates clearly Searle's willingness to subordinate strict serial ordering to motivic features (Ex. 10.4c). The formal pattern that ensues has the almost neoclassical characteristics that we associate with serial Schoenberg. It is perhaps inevitable that with a 12-note work contrasts in melodic and harmonic material will be less immediately perceptible than in a tonal idiom, and Searle tends to accentuate formal divisions by means of abrupt character contrasts. Residual traces of tonal thinking are also an important feature of this symphony. The soaring lyricism and highly dissonant harmonic support build up at times to climaxes of shattering force, and these often resolve in a quasi-tonal manner. The main climax of the first movement (bar 112), for example, generates a colossal harmonic and rhythmic tension which is released on to a unison D. Likewise the main climax of the finale, which incidentally explores Lisztian

Ex. 10.4   Searle: Symphony no. 2, 1st movement

transformations of first-movement material, culminates in a dominant preparation for the return of the opening 'maestoso' where consonant – even triadic – elements are introduced with magical effect.

Middle-generation composers who would argue, with Searle, that 'classical forms are still usable even if tonality has disappeared, as Schoenberg showed in his last two string quartets and his Violin Concerto' (Searle 1962) include Hugh Wood (*b* 1932), David Blake (*b* 1936) and Richard Rodney Bennett (*b* 1936). Wood is a true Schoenbergian in his commitment to thematic organization of a traditional kind and in his reliance on classical genres and formal types. His 'thematic' serialism was clearly established in the First String Quartet (1962) and Three Piano Pieces (1960–63), and it was developed further in a succession of large-scale instrumental compositions including his Cello Concerto (1965), Second String Quartet (1970), Violin Concerto (1971), Chamber Concerto (1971) and Symphony (1981). Admittedly the Second String Quartet hints at a more fragmentary approach to musical structure. Wood himself refers to 'a new style of continuity', to 'the idea of making a "collection" – as of sea-shells'. Yet, despite its 39 distinct though continuous sections, the quartet remains a thematic composition in the true sense, and it preserves something of that goal-directed quality which so distinguishes Wood's music. The concertos and Symphony are among the most intensively 'thought-through' serial compositions written in Britain in recent decades.

The Cello Concerto may be taken as representative. It is a single-movement sonata structure incorporating a 'slow movement' and with a long cadenza preceding the recapitulation. A final bleak epilogue quotes briefly from Elgar's Cello Concerto. The saturation of the work's texture with motifs derived from the row ensures a density of thought comparable to Schoenberg's. But the truly impressive feature of the work (as of the Violin Concerto) is Wood's ability to build extended paragraphs where motivic working is incorporated within broader directional melodic and bass motions which give structural perspective to detailed serial manipulation. The opening is such a paragraph, and Ex. 10.5 demonstrates how the magnificent melodic span of the cello line is built from a succession of the work's basic motifs and intervals while the bass line has the dual function of outlining these motifs and intervals in augmentation and at the same time providing a strong directional momentum towards the climax. If Wood's motivic working suggests Schoenberg in its rigour, his harmony is often closer to Berg. The stepwise part movement at this climax inevitably suggests a distant tonal background, and this is reinforced by the recurrence of basic motifs at the same pitch, both in the solo line and in the bass. One of the principal tonal invariants is the tritone A–E♭ which forms part of P_0 and is strongly emphasized by the soloist before the first climax. It forms a stable pedal point against which the 'adagio' epilogue unfolds.

David Blake, in his early serial compositions, shared Wood's commitment to thematic organization of a traditional kind. But Blake, a student of Hanns Eisler, is no orthodox serialist, and his later works have engaged increasingly with a stylistic pluralism which is far removed from the tough-grained Schoenbergian qualities of the First String Quartet (1961) and the Chamber Symphony (1966), an idiom that culminated in *Metamorphoses* (1971) for large orchestra, one of several Blake works to draw upon classical mythology. After *Metamorphoses*, Blake's music became both more expansive and more relaxed in tone. The Violin Concerto of 1976 was a direct response

Ex. 10.5   Wood: Cello Concerto (summary of bars (1–31)

to Italy (specifically to the work of Michelangelo), and its indebtedness to Berg's concerto is apparent in the overall structure (two bipartite movements), the closing *cantus*, a 'setting' of Michelangelo, and the tonally evocative and at times diatonic harmonies in an atonal context. It was followed by several chamber works in a lighter vein, including *Cassation* for wind octet, which culminates in a magnificent dance movement, and *Capriccio* (1980) for septet, a kind of divertimento setting different musics against each other with no attempt at synthesis. Blake now seems able to adopt several 'tones' as a composer. The Clarinet Quintet (1980), a 'Socratic dialogue' between the clarinet and strings, and the Third String Quartet (1983) demonstrate, for instance, that he has by no means lost his taste for music of a tough, intellectually rigorous quality.

The major instrumental works of Richard Rodney Bennett have also been serial, though their spirit is closer to Bennett's teacher Lennox Berkeley than to Schoenberg. They range from the Third String Quartet, composed in 1955 when the composer was 17, to the First Symphony of 1965. The symphony is characteristic of Bennett's polished, 'Gallic' serialism, with its avoidance of profound argument, its neoclassical formal pattern and its delicate scoring. Bennett himself referred to a 'comic opera element' in the work, and the remark is especially significant in the light of his later chamber works and concertos, whose quasi-operatic conception hinges on a fully developed principle of instrumental characterization. His piano and guitar concertos are transitional in this respect. They adhere to classical formal patterns but have an implicit dramatic conception which points towards his later instrumental 'monodramas'.

Bennett's instrumental characterization will be discussed briefly in a later section, but it should be noted here that even in his later concertos the language is strictly serial. The Oboe Concerto of 1970 is a fully worked example of Schoenbergian combinatorial method, associating P_0 and I_5 through complementary hexachords (Ex. 10.6a). It seems characteristic that Bennett should have been attracted by a technique whose *raison d'être* is pragmatic – the avoidance of doubling, especially in orchestral textures. The introduction to the Oboe Concerto presents each hexachord of P_0 separately before the two principal groups establish the combinatorial relationship (Ex. 10.6b for the second group), each group accompanied by its inversionally related row-form. In these and in the third group internal repetitions in row statements contribute to a more expansive melodic line with traditional leanings. In the slow movement of the concerto Bennett reorders the hexachords, presenting the opening melody in a reordering of P_0 accompanied by a reordering of I_5, before reversing the procedure at Fig. 25.

It remains to be seen if attempts to renovate the traditional forms through serialism will prove to be of lasting significance. There can be no doubt that for many serial composers today there is an unacceptable tension between the inherent tendencies of the method and the older forms. The later music of Roberto Gerhard typifies the need felt by many such composers to allow the serial principle to generate new forms and phraseology, rather than to attempt a compromise or synthesis with those inherited from the tonal tradition (see *Tempo* 1981, and K. Potter 1972 for detailed commentaries on his music). His First Symphony of 1953, while it retains an orthodox three-movement scheme, is one of his first works to reject thematic organization of a traditional kind, though motivic links abound. From the Second Symphony (1957) onwards he concerned himself only with single-movement structures, abandoning conventional

Ex. 10.6 Bennett: Oboe Concerto, 1st movement

tonal and thematic argument in favour of a much greater reliance on the series as a form-generating principle. Milton Babbitt proved an influence in this respect. In several works, notably the Second String Quartet (1962), Gerhard employed Babbitt-inspired numerical series which enabled him to interrelate pitches and durations to create a more tightly knit texture. Yet he was never rigid about this, and he was certainly never a prisoner of his influences.

The conception of the late works is indeed quite unlike other expressions of 'advanced' serial techniques in the 1950s and 1960s. The 'sculptured' sound of the Third Symphony (1960), for instance, is closer to Edgard Varèse than to Babbitt. The work is athematic and without explicit motivic connections, and the inclusion of an electronic tape emphasizes that the primary compositional determinants are textures and timbres rather than themes and harmonies. The first two of the seven main sections present four basic types of material, characterized through texture and timbre and separated by means of clearly defined punctuations, and the essential dynamic of the music is achieved through an alternation of these strongly characterized materials. This approach was taken very much further in Gerhard's later works, including the *Concert for Eight* of 1962, scored for an unconventional ensemble of piccolo, flute, clarinet, double-bass, piano, mandolin, accordion, guitar and assorted percussion. It is appropriate that the inspiration for this work should have been the *commedia dell'arte*, underlining the characterization concepts that come to the fore in Gerhard's later music.

The affinity with late Tippett is striking, and it is reinforced by Gerhard's Concerto for Orchestra, completed in 1965, immediately before the Fourth Symphony. Gerhard himself referred to a contrast in this work between 'three types of continuity' which, in their alternation, affect our awareness of the passing of time. These 'types of continuity', and in particular the contrast between 'a high rate of eventuation' and 'static, yet pulsating' materials, anticipate in their characters features of Tippett's rather later Third Symphony. Gerhard's flurrying surface activity in the sections concerned with 'tonal configuration' usually conceals a carefully organized harmonic structure, much of it based on serial working. The opening paragraphs of the concerto demonstrate how the series unfolds beneath its surface presentation in passage-work, to build up strong underlying harmonies. In contrast pitch is of only subsidiary importance in the 'static, yet pulsating' material, where Gerhard is primarily concerned to organize duration, and in those remarkable moments of the work described by the composer as 'action in very slow motion', where 'everything casts long shadows'.

The Tippett-like formal intercutting of the Concerto for Orchestra is also a feature of the Fourth Symphony of 1967. Here the surface of the music is much more obviously mosaic-like in structure, though some commentators have detected the underlying presence of more traditional formal schemes (see Keller 1969). Certainly contrast functions as a principle of progression in this work, though the tonal and thematic contrasts of the traditional symphony have been largely replaced by contrasts of texture, timbre, rhythm and dynamics. The entire process is described by Gerhard himself with reference to *Gemini* for violin and piano (1966), the first of the three 'astrological' chamber works written at the end of his life. 'The work consists of a series of contrasting episodes, whose sequence is more like a braiding of diverse strands than a straight linear development'. In both *Libra*, which was Gerhard's zodiacal sign, and *Leo*, his wife's, he returned to an ensemble similar to that used in *Concert for Eight*. With a poignant symbolic significance, Spanish elements make a reappearance in these final works by Gerhard, notably in the guitar writing of *Libra*, and in the ostinato folk-like figure on clarinet answered by piccolo with which both works end.

INSTRUMENTAL MUSIC II

British serialists of the older generation who, like Gerhard, turned away from established constructive methods include Elisabeth Lutyens (1906–83) and Iain Hamilton (*b* 1922). Hamilton, who lived in America for many years, put the position concisely: 'As we no longer consider tonality to be the overriding power, it is no longer logical to employ these forms (sonata, rondo, fugue)' (Schafer 1963: 158). His own musical style changed direction markedly in the late 1950s, largely because of his growing interest in the music of Webern. Where earlier instrumental works, such as the first two symphonies (1949, 1951), the Clarinet Quintet (1949) and the First Violin Concerto (1952), retained close links with traditional formal types, subsequent works made every effort to forge a musical language that is no longer dependent on these. A turning-point was the Sinfonia for two orchestras of 1959. Here thematicism has been suppressed in favour of a 'pointillist' idiom whose gestures are clearly those of the post-Webern avant garde, though the serial method is in essence straightforward, modelled on Webern op. 27. Formally the work is made up of 11 instrumentally differentiated sections played continuously and arranged in an extended arch, thus *ABCD CBC DCBA*.

Two short pieces, *Arias* and *Cantos*, composed in the early 1960s, continue to explore the strict serialism of the Sinfonia, but in the works written in the next decade beginning with *Voyage* for horn and orchestra of 1970 (again there is a highly sectionalized structure), Hamilton demonstrated increasingly his interest in sonority and texture *per se*. The difficulty in achieving any real sense of progression and development in a large-scale work whose building blocks are textures and timbres rather than themes and harmonies is considerable, however, and the inevitable parallel with Gerhard's Concerto for Orchestra and Fourth Symphony serves only to underline the remarkable formal richness of the Gerhard works. Beside them Hamilton's Sinfonia and *Voyage* seem stilted and crudely sectional.

Stylistically, Hamilton's music has continued to move with the times. His instrumental music of the 1970s – such as *Amphion* (Violin Concerto no. 2) and *Aurora* (1975) – employs many of the familiar techniques of modern music, from microtonal writing to aleatory procedure. Later works such as the Third and Fourth Symphonies (both of 1981) have even taken on board the world of postmodern neo-tonality, down to the use of key signatures in both works. Elisabeth Lutyens, in contrast, was never much interested in musical fashions, and her music has an individual profile that Hamilton's lacks; indeed her arrival at a personal 12-note technique in the Chamber Concerto no. 1 for nine instruments (1939) was largely an independent achievement, following only a brief acquaintance with scores by Schoenberg and Webern. Lutyens's best work was written in response to extra-musical stimuli, most often in the form of a poetic text. Her attempts to sustain an extended musical argument without the aid of such stimuli (as in the Sixth String Quartet of 1952) were courageous in their refusal to rely on conventional methods, but were seldom wholly successful.

Her most impressive extended works are those which, like *Quincunx* of 1960, have clear textural contrast built into their formal scheme and a text to evoke the lyricism at the heart of Lutyens's music. Tutti 3 from *Quincunx* (see Ex. 10.7b) is one of the most haunting moments in her output, with the vocal solo providing a melodic nucleus around which the orchestral lyricism of the rest of the work has been grouped. The harmonic backcloth has been sketched in simply but effectively by allowing the wind to sustain notes from the Webernian string motifs. Although the serial working here is simple and audible (see Ex. 10.7a for the row), Lutyens demonstrates elsewhere in the work considerable resource in projecting it to broader structural levels.

The alternation in *Quincunx* of tutti and solo sections, each with its own instrumentation, is reminiscent of Hamilton's Sinfonia, indicating perhaps the need felt by both composers to impose clearly defined external patterns on an idiom whose melodic and harmonic material lacks an in-built differentiation. A similarly rigid formal scheme is used in Lutyens's *Novenaria* (1967), and its arch structure – *ABCDEDCBA* – again reminds us of Hamilton. Clearly such formal schemes offer little of the richness of the sonata structures of the past, but attempts by Lutyens to abandon them in favour of freely evolving forms in an athematic context have proved unsuccessful. Miniatures such as the *Five Bagatelles* for piano (1962) work well enough, but the problems are naturally more acute with extended structures. In *Music for Orchestra II* (also 1962), Lutyens presents a stream of constantly developing material in a surging, almost expressionistic flow of ideas which has no clear point of articulation until the final paragraphs. It is a remarkable work, making few concessions to traditional formal design, rhythmic continuity or thematic working, though there are recurring motivic shapes whose structure resembles Webern though their setting is

Ex. 10.7   Lutyens: *Quincunx*

quite different. Harmonically and rhythmically it is one of Lutyens's most severe compositions, pausing to take breath only at the chorale-like coda, an exquisite moment which presents four permutations of the row bound together by a single sustained G, analogous to the B♭ at the end of *Quincunx*.

It is perhaps significant that the most formally satisfying of Lutyens's purely instrumental compositions, *Music for Orchestra III* (1963) should be the one that adheres most closely to traditional formal types. Whatever the other merits of their music, neither Lutyens nor Hamilton were wholly successful in their attempts to build convincing serial structures that remain independent of the tonal forms. It remained for middle-generation composers to address themselves to this problem in a more thorough-going manner. Alexander Goehr (*b* 1932) and Jonathan Harvey (*b* 1939) have both recognized the aptness of Schoenberg's method for his own needs – a means of renovating rather than replacing the forms and procedures of the tonal tradition – but both have demonstrated their dissatisfaction with it for their creative purposes. Like many of their contemporaries, they see its potential for building large-scale forms and also for generating logical harmonic structures as limited. Yet the alternatives provided by both composers have been very different.

Goehr's early serial music – the Piano Sonata (1952), *Fantasias* for clarinet and piano (1954) and First String Quartet (1956–7) – describes the gradual emergence of a personal musical voice from a close involvement with the post-Webern avant garde. The marks of that involvement are still perceptible in his orchestral *Hecuba's Lament* of 1961, but in the Violin Concerto of the following year there are indications of a new maturity. The longer-spanning lines of the concerto provide one of several signs that in this work Goehr was consciously attempting to come to terms with more traditional ways of using the orchestra. Moreover, the formal organization of this work reveals a more searching originality – an avoidance of easy solutions. The first of the concerto's two movements is a set of chorale variations, exploiting the *cantus firmus* technique which was to grow in importance in Goehr's music. Although the movement is not completely serial, the hexachordal structure of the *cantus*, retrogradably related, is clearly indebted to serial thought, and it is subjected to simple kinds of serial manipulation. The opening of the second movement is a further instance of Goehr's lucid serial polyphony which, unlike much of Schoenberg's, keeps the identity of each line clear and distinct (Ex. 10.8). The passage also demonstrates his obvious concern to create a harmonic language that has affinities with traditional tonality.

This question of harmonic quality proved a crucial consideration in the particular application of serialism that Goehr devised after the Violin Concerto. He was not of course the only composer to have felt the need to modify Schoenberg's method in order to make more sense of the vertical dimension of serialism. Stravinsky's trans-

Ex. 10.8   Goehr: Violin Concerto, 2nd movement

position-rotation was partly directed towards this end, and so too was the special use of serialism devised by George Perle. In essence Goehr's system enabled him to create new rows and harmonies by superimposing statements of a row at the varying degrees of a modal scale (see Goehr 1973). The transformed rows and the harmonies that resulted from these superimpositions (like Stravinsky, Goehr would read off 'verticals') are characterized by note repetitions, and the pitch-class collections have as much in common with the modes of Messiaen (with whom he studied for a time) as with the rows of his father's teacher Schoenberg. Indeed Goehr's system was in some respects a personal synthesis of the methods used by the two composers who have influenced him most.

The opening chorale of the *Little Symphony* (1963), with its characteristically distorted triads, indicates the reintegrated consonance–dissonance relationship that results from the new method (Ex. 10.9). This reinstatement of the triad as a harmonic reference point, against which dissonance is measured, is also apparent in the second movement, another of Goehr's *cantus*-variation forms. The fourth and seventh variations, for instance, present triadic distortions similar to the opening chorale, while the final variation culminates in a distorted E♭ major which makes explicit a tonal implication of the introductory material. The influence of Messiaen is registered not only in the filigree writing of the third and fifth variations, but also

Ex. 10.9   Goehr: *Little Symphony*, 1st movement

in the scherzo of the *Little Symphony*, where scalar melodic patterns, of a kind that would have been inconceivable in *Hecuba's Lament* or the Violin Concerto, remind us of Messiaen's modes. The strong, pulsed music of the finale demonstrates, moreover, the cleaner rhythmic definition that accompanied Goehr's new-found harmonic simplicity in this work. Its combination of slow movement and finale is typical of the kind of formal fusion common in Goehr's music; the second movement of the Piano Concerto (1972) is similar.

That Goehr's new 'serial modality' was an inspired answer to his compositional needs is clearly indicated by the technical mastery and formal cohesion of the *Little Symphony*, far in advance of anything in his earlier music. A version of the method was used again in the first of his Three Pieces for piano (1965), his strongly individual Piano Trio (1966) and his Second String Quartet (1967). Characteristically, all three movements of the quartet are based on a variation principle, though Goehr engages in various strategies of concealment. The double variations of the first movement are welded into a single through-composed flow of ideas, for example, while the finale has something of the character of a long, introverted and intense 'endless melody'.

Variation form is less conspicuous in two works composed in the late 1960s, the *Romanza* for cello and orchestra (1968) and the *Konzertstück* for piano and orchestra (1969). They are sharply contrasted in character, the former a contemporary exploration of 'the spirit of romantic performance' and the latter a rhythmically taut, almost neoclassical conception, close at times to Stravinsky. Yet, despite the contrast, the two works have several technical features in common, and especially a shared attempt to establish organic connections between successive episodes based on a small repertoire of serially derived cells which are clearly audible in performance. There are two such cells in the *Romanza*, while in the *Konzertstück* the separate paragraphs are each closely related to the 12-note *cantus*, presented in single bell-like notes by the soloist, and to the opening horn duet. The formal organization of the *Konzertstück* in particular appears to reconcile on yet another level aspects of the music of Messiaen and Schoenberg; the short-breathed formal units, episodic in external pattern, are underpinned by a motivic working that is developmental and goal-directed.

Variations come to the fore again in the Symphony in One Movement, composed in 1970 and one of Goehr's most ambitious instrumental compositions. The opening viola melody and its harmonic support form the serial nucleus of the work, creating at the outset a melodic and harmonic framework that forms the basis of succeeding variations. As in so many Goehr movements the 12-note shape functions as a *cantus* underpinning the variations, rather as in Schoenberg op. 31. The climactic point of the work, brilliantly prepared and paced, is succeeded by a massive descent through the entire orchestra with a regularly patterned rhythmic *accelerando* – apparently the initial inspiration for the work. A gradual ascent follows the ensuing silence, forming a ternary, scherzo-like section (Goehr himself has referred to an affinity with Beethoven's Fifth) which culminates in a chorale on divided strings. The simultaneous presentation of this chorale (in 2/2 time) and a distorted 7/8 march – they overlap but never meet – is as close to Ives and late Tippett as Goehr ever comes. As the chorale ends, the 7/8 tempo becomes the principal one and the thunderous Beethovenian climax modulates rhythmically to accommodate the return of the opening variations.

Following his classically conceived Piano Concerto of 1972, Goehr turned his attention rather more to vocal and dramatic works, though major instrumental works such as the Third String Quartet (1975–6) and Sinfonia (1979) did appear. Then, in the 1980s, the serial basis of his musical language began to recede in importance, replaced by a deeply thoughtful and challenging reinvestigation of more traditional tonal methods, certainly one of the most individual – and least modish – expressions of a postmodern aesthetic in British music. Goehr became increasingly involved with the 'common materials' of Western music, including characteristic modes and basic melodic shapes. Works such as the four-movement Symphony with Chaconne (1986) are both more tonal in technique and more obviously neo-baroque in style than his music of the 1960s and 1970s. That work represents a culmination not only of Goehr's long-standing interest in a synthesis of sonata and variation forms, but also of his preoccupation with the idea of the symphony, a genre he has approached from several angles during his creative life. There is indeed a change of tone in Goehr's later music, but it could easily be exaggerated. Several recent compositions, such as the Cello Sonata and Fourth String Quartet, suggest that serial concerns are re-emerging in a new way.

Jonathan Harvey's early serial compositions had a similar starting-point to Goehr's. Like Goehr's *Little Symphony*, his Symphony of 1966 makes clear its indebtedness to both Schoenberg and Messiaen. The first movement is akin to the Schoenberg of *Erwartung* and the Five Orchestral Pieces in the impassioned lyricism of its lines, exploring above all the extreme tensions that can be generated by high-tessitura violin writing. It is difficult in a way to square this with the static, Messiaenic calm of the finale, its crystalline piano writing so obviously inspired by the French composer. Again like Goehr, Harvey demonstrated in this work a concern for harmonic quality that led him to his own modification of serial practice. Essentially he created sub-sets from a 12-note row by 'filtering' fixed pitches from different transpositions in order to achieve a quasi-tonal feeling. The opening of the second movement, for example, suppresses the pitches D♭, F and A♭ to suggests a G major–minor tonality.

The works that followed this symphony reveal the impact of techniques and ideas far removed from such a tonal–serial synthesis. The *cantus firmus* construction of *Chaconne on Iam dulcis amica* and the parody techniques of *Benedictus* indicate a sympathy with Peter Maxwell Davies shared by several younger British composers in the late 1960s, but this line of thought proved to be of only passing importance for Harvey. His contact with the ideas of Milton Babbitt during a year in Princeton (1969–70) led him to a view of serialism as an all-embracing system of composition where the set would have primary responsibility for structure. Numerical series relating pitches and durations in the manner of Babbitt were used in a number of works of the early 1970s, among them the cantata *On Vision*. But Harvey did not remain satisfied with this approach either. His study of Heinrich Schenker's analyses of tonal music led him increasingly to the conviction that the central question for music today is 'how to compose multi-dimensional structures as rich in meanings as those within the tonal system' (Harvey 1975: 31). The theories of Stockhausen proved of great significance to Harvey in his search for such multi-dimensional structures, for Stockhausen was concerned not with an arbitrary connection of pitch and duration via a numerical series, but with an organic connection based in acoustical realities.

In a sense Harvey's mature music has drawn from both Babbitt and Stockhausen without imitating either. The symphonic poem *Persephone Dream* (1972) creates a numerical correspondence between pitch and duration series. But in addition Harvey takes each interval of the basic series in turn to build vertical aggregates (12 all together) which act as filters, suppressing notes other than their own and governing the long-range harmonic movement of the work in a succession of 'serial spaces', to use the composer's own term (Northcott 1973). The result is a multi-levelled concept of form and progression, especially clear in the first part of the work where the serial spaces underpin more rapidly changing string harmonies which in turn support wind and percussion figurations. It is difficult to avoid the parallel with Stockhausen's *Gruppen*, where a similar correspondence of foreground and background is achieved by serial means. Like *Gruppen*, *Persephone Dream* benefits from a clearly perceptible macro-structure, a bipartite scheme where the final section mirrors and transforms earlier material. Again like *Gruppen*, the power of the work in terms of sheer sonority ensures an immediacy of impact that belies its complex, subtle organization.

In a later series of pieces called *Inner Light*, Harvey extended his exploration into serial structure, again fusing technical ideas from Babbitt – above all the gradual arrival at a series through exhaustive working of each interval in turn – and Stockhausen. From Stockhausen comes the general preoccupation in these pieces with a progression from disorder to order, from darkness to light. There is a close parallel between the eventual emergence of three clear chords out of earlier sonic exploration in *Inner Light I* and the affirmative 'Hymn of Pluramon' from the diverse, 'meaningless' opening of Stockhausen's *Hymnen*. Stockhausen also lies behind Harvey's investigation of electronic resources as a means of mediating between timbre and harmony, building chords from the acoustic nature (combination of partials) of particular instrumental sounds. The resulting harmonies are treated rather like the serial spaces in *Persephone Dream* – as vertical areas within which diverse activities will take place.

Harvey is one of several British composers whose interest in electronic and computer resources has proved enduring, and it will be worth saying something about this development in parenthesis before concluding our discussion of Harvey's own music. Two Australian-born composers have played a part in it: Don Banks (1923–80), who was resident in Britain in the 1950s and 1960s, and David Lumsdaine (*b* 1931), who has lived here for many years. Other composers of electro-acoustic music include Tristram Cary (*b* 1925), Tim Souster (1942–94), Trevor Wishart (*b* 1946), Simon Emmerson (*b* 1950), Denis Smalley (*b* 1946), and Jonty Harrison (*b* 1952). It may be possible to give some hint of the diversity of aims and traditions in British electro-acoustic music by referring to just one issue – the very different approaches composers have adopted to the combination of electronic tape and live instrumental forces. Like Gerhard in his Third Symphony, Don Banks – in *Intersections* – exploited the dramatic possibilities of a contact between live and electronic resources. Harvey's *Inner Light III*, on the other hand, is concerned more with the capacity of electronics to strengthen structural unity by mediating between discrete dimensions of sound. *Song of an Average City* by Tim Souster is really an essay in *musique concrète*, while *Fusions* by Paul Patterson (*b* 1947) attempts to merge both media in a mutually supportive exploration of a sound-world dominated by shifting textures and constantly changing timbres. Different again is Lumsdaine's powerful *Hagoromo*, where a low rate of surface activity or information in both tape and instrumental parts characteristically conceals a high degree of organization, including the use of a 'matrix method' to control both the pitch content of the work and its complex pulse patterns.

Several British electro-acoustic composers – notably Trevor Wishart in an output of mainly tape works – have benefited greatly from the facilities of Boulez's Research Institute, IRCAM, in Paris. But none has been so intimately connected with IRCAM as Jonathan Harvey, much of whose recent music would have been inconceivable without the impetus provided by its technology. Following Harvey's highly successful tape work *Mortuos plango, vivis voco* (1980), IRCAM commissioned the 12-movement *Blakti* (1982), where the tape uses sounds drawn from the instrumental ensemble, transformed and mixed by the computer. It was also at IRCAM that Harvey realized the tape part for his later orchestral work, *The Madonna of Winter and Spring* (1987). Here again the electronics extend the sound-world of the orchestra, though in a formal context in which some links with traditional archetypes are reforged – even down to the thematic working of the opening section. Harvey's project as a composer has involved a spiritual search for a 'new type of music', which might in turn promote a 'change of consciousness' (Griffiths 1985: 52). In view of other recent developments, not least in the music of Goehr, it is perhaps significant that this search has led him – in some works at least – to a creative reinvestigation of traditional resources.

IV: New Freedoms

The once widely held view that serialism represented the only path to the future can clearly carry little conviction today. At the same time it is demonstrably one path to the future, having proved itself capable of adaptation to traditional tonal forms and phraseology, and at the same time of generating new structural methods. The impact of the method could scarcely be overestimated, for it has created a world of sound that has been explored by serialist and non-serialist alike. For many composers contact with serial techniques proved the crucial liberating influence that helped them shake off the cramping attitudes of a conservative training, and often when it had served that purpose it could be freely dispensed with. Thea Musgrave (*b* 1928) is a case in point (see Bradshaw 1963; Kay 1969; East 1975). Her exploration of strict serialism in works such as *Obliques* (1958) followed a substantial corpus of tonal music. Like the later Sinfonia, *Obliques* couches its serial working (the seven variations are based on a seven-note row) in traditional gestures that seem curiously faceless when compared with the composer's later, more characteristic 'dramatic abstracts'.

The turning-point in Musgrave's work was her Second Chamber Concerto of 1966. It is significant that the work was dedicated to the memory of Charles Ives, and that its course should be interrupted at three points by Ives's infamous 'Rollo' with tunes such as 'Swanee

River' and 'Keel Row'. The notion of dramatic characterization in instrumental terms is clearly far from new in music, but it has assumed considerable importance in our century, perhaps partly in deference to acknowledged problems in the communication of difficult musical styles. Musgrave's series of 'dramatic abstract' concertos should be viewed in the context of a growing interest in such instrumental characterization, from Ives and Stravinsky in the early years of the century to Tippett, Gerhard and Elliott Carter in more recent years.

The Concerto for Orchestra of 1967 is the first of these 'dramatic abstracts' and the later works build upon procedures found here. The first of the concerto's five (progressively faster) sections is restrained in its character contrasts, presenting a stable harmonic background against which four principal characters interact in different ways. By the third section the drama has been heightened considerably. The opening sustained string passage with superimposed staccato quavers on woodwind immediately suggests the multi-layered textures of Ives, but it is also similar to procedures in Elliott Carter, and its continuation is closer to the younger American. The string passage forms a backcloth for a capricious solo violin part, marked 'fantastico', which influences other soloists from the string section in turn. Superimposed on this drama and phasing in and out of the texture are the measured woodwind patterns which are themselves superimposed on each other at different speeds. At the climax of the drama the clarinet rebels against the orchestral body and gathers around itself a small concertante group of sympathizers, which leads to a major confrontation during which the brass group in the orchestra stands up in protest and the concertante group is gradually 'shouted down'.

The Clarinet Concerto of 1968 developed directly out of this theatrical element in the Concerto for Orchestra, with the soloist again leading and influencing a small concertante group whose episodes alternate and interact with the orchestral tuttis. In the later Horn Concerto (1971) a brass group mediates between the soloist and orchestra in a simplified (and for that reason more easily perceptible) version of the three-layer conception of Carter's Piano Concerto. Musgrave heightens the drama in these works and in her *Night Music* by requiring the performers to move about on the stage.

Such characterization methods have evoked a sympathetic response from several middle-generation composers. The dramatic scenario of Richard Rodney Bennett's Oboe Concerto is more immediately perceptible than its serial working (see pp. 300–301), and it suggests a parallel with Musgrave which is strengthened by Bennett's later music. His exploration of instrumental characterization in his *Commedia* pieces is indeed directly analogous to Musgrave's in her chamber concertos, while orchestral works such as *Zodiac* (1975–6) and *Actaeon* for horn and orchestra (1977) extended the technique to explicitly programmatic ends. It may well be that Bennett needs this kind of stimulus to infuse his instrumental music with dramatic life. Like Lennox Berkeley's, his music is always highly professional in realization, but at times anonymous in character. He is the ideal composer of background music, and there is irony in the fact that it was a pair of sympathetic commentators who remarked that the 'real Bennett' may well be found in his film and jazz scores (see Palmer and Foreman 1975).

Gordon Crosse (*b* 1937), too, in his *Ceremony* for cello and orchestra (1966), suggests a concern for instrumental characterization that has been extended in later works, notably his *Ariadne* for oboe and 11 players (1972). The conceptual parallel with Musgrave and Bennett is clear enough (compare Bennett's *Actaeon*), but in some works the parallel with Musgrave, and also with Tippett, is of a more specific technical kind. Crosse's *Some Marches on a Ground* (1970), for example, superimposes a series of marches – variations on a national-anthem-type theme – on a groundswell of string colour which keeps up, in the composer's words, 'a constant thrum and patter'. The middle section is an almost Ivesian battle symphony. Such multi-layered textures are echoed in instrumental works by other middle-generation British composers. *Antiphonies* by Justin Connolly (*b* 1933), for example, explores the interaction of five separate instrumental groups in complex polyrhythmic layers of sound. *Waves* by John Lambert (1926–95) is similarly concerned with a restrained interplay of three clearly separated streams of sound, while *Mésalliance* for piano and orchestra by Bernard Rands (*b* 1935) creates a 'polyphony of groups' in an explicitly dramatic conception. Rands, who now lives in America, is a major creative figure, and his music certainly cannot be pigeonholed in relation to a single technical feature. He initially explored a world close to Berio in some respects and to Birtwistle in others (notably in his *Wildtrack* series), but more recently he has cultivated a kind of neo-Debussian soundscape of more traditional hue. Works such as . . . *in the receding mist* (1988) for flute, harp and string trio are far removed from the aggressive oppositions of *Mésalliance*.

Thea Musgrave's concertos have yet another claim on our attention. The later works make increasing use of an aleatory technique that, in Witold Lutosławski's phrase, 'loosens the time connections between sounds'. By means of proportional notation and a system of internal cues, Musgrave succeeds in activating exciting sonorities which are at the same time carefully controlled and calculated. In the Viola Concerto (1973), and even more in *Orfeo II* for flute and orchestra (1975), conventional notation has been reduced to a minimum and more and more responsibility given to the performer. There are passages in both works where sections of the orchestra are required to improvise slow expressive melodies on a given series of notes.

An interest in various kinds of aleatory procedure spread quickly among British composers in the 1960s and 1970s, and several made such procedures an essential ingredient of their musical thought, at least for a time. Like Musgrave, Martin Dalby (*b* 1942) travelled from an early tonal style, by way of serialism, to a musical language making use of controlled improvisation. After a transitional Symphony (1970), his closest approach to post-Webern serialism, he established this new idiom in the *Concerto Martin Pescatore* of 1971, an essay in string textures owing much to modern Polish techniques. For the most part the work is a succession of fascinating surface textures, and, like many such pieces, it lacks staying-power.

There seems little doubt that the dissemination of aleatory procedures encouraged many composers to explore sonority at the expense of structure, rather as in the 1950s a commitment to post-Webern serialism resulted in a preoccupation with structure at the expense of sonority. Dalby's Viola Concerto (1974) suggests that he quickly became aware of this danger. The work certainly benefited from the exploration of sonority found in *Concerto Martin Pescatore* and *The Tower of Victory* (1973), but the sensitivity to sonority is no longer an end in itself. The Viola Concerto is in fact conventionally notated, and its confidence and certainty of purpose, apparent as much in the aggressive opening paragraphs as in the lyrical duet of the middle section, suggest that for Dalby *alea* was a necessary catalyst to his emerging musical style, but not in the end the most suitable channel for its expression.

For other composers the undoubted fascination of aleatory textures proved all too seductive. Paul Patterson, for example, rejected the polished neoclassicism of his early style in favour of an exploration of new aleatory sonorities. *Sonors* (1973) was an important work in this change of style, and the new direction was confirmed by *Fusions* for tape and orchestra (1974), *The Circular Ruins* (1976) and *Cracowian Counterpoints* (1977) for 14 instruments. More recently, however, Patterson, like Dalby, has returned to fully notated music, following his mentor Penderecki into the world of postmodern 'new tonalities' with his Concerto for Orchestra (1981) and Sinfonia for Strings (1985).

At its worst *alea* opened the doors to a rather easy, not to say modish, way of composing – often little more than a kind of doodling with sound. Even some of the better works were tainted by an over-facile adoption of notational devices that were for a time *en vogue*. The beehive sonorities of works such as *Gastrula* (1968) by David Bedford (*b* 1937) or *Montage* (1977) by Edwin Roxburgh (*b* 1937), for example, became part of the anonymous sounds of their respective decades. At the same time the sheer simplicity of works such as Bedford's *Gastrula* – their reduction to a kind of minimal musical argument – suggests points of contact with some areas of popular music which have proved fruitful. Like Terry Riley and Steve Reich in America, Bedford values these contacts, and he has collaborated with the pop composer and performer Mike Oldfield in several ventures, notably *Star's End* (1974), an attempted fusion of two streams of music in our century. The distance between the aleatory textures of the earlier part of *Star's End* and Oldfield's electric guitar in its later stages is skilfully bridged by Bedford by means of carefully plotted triadic elements and the gradual emergence of pulsed rhythm.

Other British composers have explored similar common ground between serious and popular cultures. The concertos of Peter Dickinson (*b* 1934), and especially his Piano Concerto (1984), exemplify this, though they have larger claims on our attention, often using a deliberately simple idiom rather in the manner of Satie. Roger Smalley (*b* 1943) arrived at such interests only gradually. Earlier works investigated strict serialism (Variations for Strings, 1964) and the parodistic techniques of Maxwell Davies (*Gloria tibi Trinitas*, 1965), but with *Transformation I* and *Pulses for 5 × 4*, Smalley, a pupil of Stockhausen, affirmed his commitment to improvisation as a path forwards, founding (with Tim Souster) the group Intermodulation. Richard Orton (*b* 1940) traversed a similar path, from his early orchestral *Divisions* to his improvisations for the group The Gentle Fire. Inevitably such composers have tended to avoid the traditional instrumental media, at least until Smalley's recent conversion to a neo-tonal idiom. Souster's *Triple Music II* might legitimately be described as a special case – in effect a '"composed-out" realization for full symphony orchestra which is intended to function as data for the aural tradition', an aural tradition that will 'contribute towards the transformation not only of the symphony orchestra but of all kinds of composer–performer–listener and composition–realization–improvisation relationships' (Souster 1970).

Even more radical and experimental was the work of Cornelius Cardew (1936–81) and his 'school'. Here the establishment of experimental ensembles such as the AMM free improvisation group and especially the Scratch Orchestra was inseparable from a specific view of the social role that 'free' music-making might play in society, a view heavily influenced by a political engagement with the extreme left. In the end politics split the Scratch Orchestra, as Cardew, John Tilbury and others adopted Maoist positions which proved unacceptable to some members of the group (see the contemporary music magazine *Contact, passim,* for extensive discussion of British experimental music, including that of the Cardew 'school'). The music written by Cardew himself at the end of his life replaced free improvisation with pieces in the manner of the Peking Opera. Other members of the original Cardew circle, notably Gavin Bryars (*b* 1943) and Dave Smith (*b* 1949), have produced music of considerable substance in recent years. Until the mid-1970s Bryars was much involved in Satie-inspired 'conceptual pieces', but since then he has composed operas and instrumental music, including *The Vespertine Park* (1980) and the delicately painted *Homage to Vivier* (1985). The *Piano Concerts* by Smith, dismissed by many because of their ideological motivation, are remarkable compendiums of skilfully crafted miniatures, stylistically plural in their inclusion of virtuoso studies, stylized folksong elements (especially from Ireland and Albania) and spoken pieces involving revolutionary texts. Other composers who have been associated with this group include John White (*b* 1936), Chris Hobbs (*b* 1950), Howard Skempton (*b* 1947) and Andrew Hugill (*b* 1957). Benedict Mason (*b* 1954) was also part of the fold at one time, but works such as *Lighthouses of Britain and Wales*, a kind of present-day *La mer*, suggest that he has since responded to a much wider range of influences.

INSTRUMENTAL MUSIC II

V: *Twin Peaks*

The categorization of composers in this chapter is inevitably crude, though some such attempt to find an order in the empirical variety of recent British music is clearly necessary in a survey such as this. Terms such as 'tonal', 'serial' and 'aleatory' can offer no more than a starting-point for the investigation of a composer's work, and there is always the attendant danger that the label will function as a substitute for a genuine understanding. The music of Peter Maxwell Davies (*b* 1934) and Harrison Birtwistle (*b* 1934), arguably the most highly valued British composers of the middle generation, proves especially resistant to categorization, though it reveals many points of contact with developments that have already been examined. (The major monographs on these composers are Griffiths 1982, and M. Hall 1984.)

Like Alexander Goehr and Jonathan Harvey, Maxwell Davies turned initially to both Schoenberg and Messiaen, especially in pieces such as the Sonata for trumpet and piano (1955) and the Five Pieces for piano (1956). Again like Goehr and Harvey, he responded in his own way to the challenge of post-Webern experiments in serial structure. His first acknowledged orchestral piece, *Prolation* (1958), is one of several British works of the late 1950s to 'react' to Messiaen, Boulez and Stockhausen. (One thinks here not only of Hamilton and Goehr, but of the Boulez-influenced early music of Anthony Gilbert (*b* 1934)). *Prolation* makes use of a pitch series and a duration series, each numbering five, though there has been no attempt to interrelate these in the manner of the Europeans. Maxwell Davies was never again to explore these techniques in such an uncompromising fashion, but there are, none the less, important ways in which *Prolation* looks ahead to his later music. The duration series of the work influences not only its detailed rhythmic organization, but also its large-scale proportions. In later extended works the overall proportions are similarly dictated by number working, often using a 'magic square' principle to relate the smaller sections to each other and to the whole. This is especially clear in *Ave maris stella* of 1975, where the plainsong is 'disguised' by projection through the Magic Square of the Moon, which gives the following matrix of pitch-classes and durations (Table 10.2).

For each section of *Ave maris stella* (there are nine altogether, plus a coda), a different pathway is traced through this matrix. For instance, the first section consists of a straightforward line-by-line exposition of the material with the durational unit as the quaver; for

Table 10.2 Maxwell Davies: *Ave maris stella*, pitch-class and duration matrix from Magic Square of the Moon

C♯	F	C	E	B	G♯	A	F♯	D
1	6	2	7	3	8	4	9	5
A	G♯	C	G	B	F♯	D♯	E	C♯
6	2	7	3	8	4	9	5	1
D♯	B	A♯	D	A	C♯	G♯	F	F♯
2	7	3	8	4	9	5	1	6
G	E	C	B	D♯	A♯	D	A	F♯
7	3	8	4	9	5	1	6	2
G	G♯	F	C♯	C	E	B	D♯	A♯
3	8	4	9	5	1	6	2	7
D♯	C	C♯	A♯	F♯	F	A	E	G♯
8	4	9	5	1	6	2	7	3
A♯	F	D	D♯	C	G♯	G	B	F♯
4	9	5	1	6	2	7	3	8
D	F♯	C♯	A♯	B	G♯	E	D♯	G
9	5	1	6	2	7	3	8	4
G♯	D♯	G	D	B	C	A	F	E
5	1	6	2	7	3	8	4	9

the second section, diagonals are used; for the third, the path leads from the centre of the matrix in gradually expanding squares to the outside; and so on. This provides each section with a *cantus firmus* which is then elaborated with material taken from the matrix either strictly or in somewhat freer configuration (for the ingenious derivation of this matrix from the plainsong see Roberts 1978: 28–9).

Maxwell Davies's architectural mastery is indeed one of his strengths as a composer, apparent even in his most expressionistic works. The rigid rhythmic organization of *Prolation* (and of the coeval *St Michael Sonata*) finds a place in his later music where it is deemed a structural necessity. And in certain instances (for example the isorhythmic section of the chamber work *Hymn to St Magnus*, where a special grid is used to notate the 3 : 2 proportions) this results in performer difficulties as great as those posed by Boulez and Stockhausen in the early 1950s.

INSTRUMENTAL MUSIC II

More crucially, the serial thought that underlies *Prolation* remained an active force in Maxwell Davies's music for many years. Of the many different extensions of serial technique in Britain, few are more individual than his. Maxwell Davies's special uses of serialism are in some ways closer to Berg than to Schoenberg. Like Berg he is concerned above all with the transformation of rows. Methods of transformation vary in detail from work to work, from simple permutation to the application of a 'modulator' to transform the interval content of a row, as in the second of the *Seven In Nomine*, the chamber work *Antechrist* or the orchestral *Worldes Blis*, whose transforming agent is the thirteenth-century melody of that name. These transformation processes reflect technically some of the underlying themes of Maxwell Davies's work, in particular his concern with 'things which are not quite what they seem' – the interplay of the false and the real which is symbolized for him by the figure of the Antichrist. It is entirely typical that in his opera *Taverner* sets are transformed into their own inversions and that in some works the initial form of a set may never return.

Transformation methods, then, were ideally suited to Maxwell Davies's philosophical, as well as his purely musical, preoccupations. Yet his interest in such methods has been cultivated in close alliance with more traditional symphonic concepts. His five symphonies remind us that the symphonic tradition remains an influential force in British music today. The historical archetype of the classical symphony is still respected by many British symphonists today, and not always in *neo*classical vein. Ultimately, however, it seems likely that the development and refashioning of symphonic thought in the hands of Tippett, Gerhard and Goehr will prove of more lasting significance, and it is this renovative attitude which Maxwell Davies too has adopted. Two earlier works pointed the way. His Second Taverner Fantasia (1964) has formal outlines described by the composer in terms of traditional symphonic movements – sonata form, scherzo and slow movement – while *Worldes Blis* (1966–9) adopts a formal scheme which is deliberately counterpointed against that of the Fantasia, with ironic intention.

Unlike Tippett and Gerhard, who have restated the polarities – the contrasts – of the traditional symphony in a contemporary way, Maxwell Davies has emphasized the 'developing variation' and transformation procedures which Schoenberg regarded as the most progressive aspect of nineteenth-century thematicism. In the Second Taverner Fantasia and in *Worldes Blis*, he employs a number of

Ex. 10.10   Maxwell Davies: Second Taverner Fantasia

intervallic cells which are subject to continuous transformation. The opening 'frame' of the Fantasia, for example, sets out a nucleus of three cells which generate virtually all the melodic and harmonic material of the work (Ex. 10.10). The succeeding material is based principally on the first two cells, building two huge parallel progressions towards a major climax, while the third cell forms a link into the main 'Allegro' section. Derivations here are equally clear, with the timpani using the third cell and the 'first subject' growing out of an interversion of the second cell before it is transformed into a secondary group. At the beginning of the 'development section' (bar 267) the harmony crystallizes into three referential areas, the tritone A–E♭ on harp, the whole-tone chord on horns and a verticalization of the first three notes of cell 2 on tuba and harp. This tendency for the harmony to be clarified at major structural points in the work is continued throughout and acts as a major stabilizing influence.

INSTRUMENTAL MUSIC II

Both the Second Taverner Fantasia and *Worldes Blis* are based on material borrowed from early music; indeed the end of the later work comes close to a literal quotation of its source in the manner of the First Taverner Fantasia and *St Thomas Wake*. Maxwell Davies's preoccupation with medieval and renaissance music is well known, and there can be no doubt of its importance for his musical thought, just as the medieval church and social order have acted as powerful symbols for his work, capable of multiple interpretations. Already in his *Alma Redemptoris mater* for wind instruments (1957) he used a medieval source, together with *cantus firmus* techniques and decorative melismata derived from medieval music. Other chamber works based on early music include the *Ricercar and Doubles* (1959), the String Quartet (1961) and the *Seven In Nomine* (1964–5).

His interest in medieval music is not simply parodistic, but extends to a deliberate use of medieval musical techniques such as the *cantus firmus*, mensural canons and isorhythmic patterns of the Second Taverner Fantasia and First Symphony. Such techniques are intended to function as positive unifying methods which might compensate for 'the lack of form-building elements in post-tonal music' (Schafer 1963: 175). But they may also combine with transformation processes to highlight Maxwell Davies's mocking, often violent and destructive, attitude to his models. Irony is part and parcel of his musical technique, as it is of Mahler's, and in some works – notably *Revelation and Fall* (1965), *Hymnos* (1967) and *St Thomas Wake* (1969) – it results in a highly dramatic, expressionistic, tortured style, often assaulting the listener with passages of concentrated ferocity.

In *St Thomas Wake* the ironic play on different levels of musical meaning is characteristically overt and violent. The work grew out of the second of Maxwell Davies's Purcell realizations, the Two Pavans, where the original dances are reinterpreted in terms of the twentieth-century foxtrot. In *St Thomas Wake*, based on a John Bull pavan, the foxtrots, evocative of the 'heedless society' of the 1930s, are played by a nine-piece dance band. This is pitted against the full resources of a large symphony orchestra, whose material is itself a parody of the gestures of *Worldes Blis* and which seems determined to destroy the foxtrots and the world they represent. As in most of Maxwell Davies's parody works the 'middle ground' between the idea and its distortion or corruption is purposefully ambivalent, in the precise technical sense that transformation procedures are built into the main pitch argument of the work. Yet this is not to imply that there is a synthesis of the opposing forces. As in Ives, the styles comment upon each other and their separateness is an integral part of the conception.

In retrospect, it now seems possible to identify particular phases in the development of Maxwell Davies's musical style. The Second Taverner Fantasia, composed in 1964, might be regarded as the culmination of an early period, during which he acquired and consolidated a distinctive musical language. The works of the later 1960s seem in a sense to have deconstructed that musical language, smashing it to pieces, and against that background *Worldes Blis* emerges as an important attempt at reintegration. Significantly, Maxwell Davies composed little of substance during 1970, and he withdrew several of the works that he did compose. The 1970s form a third period, during which there was a synthesis of the meditative and expressionistic elements of his art. Works such as the *Hymn to St Magnus* (1972) are characteristic of this synthesis, its eruptive third movement 'placed' and controlled by the tranquil surroundings. Also characteristic are *Psalm 124* (1974), *Ave maris stella* and its later sister work *Image, Reflection, Shadow* (1982).

The meditative quality of much of this music no doubt reflects the change in outlook that accompanied Maxwell Davies's move to Orkney in the early 1970s. Orkney gave him a landscape through which to re-create aspects of a British 'pastoral' tradition. It also gave him a community for which to compose and fostered a sense of the social responsibility of the composer which had played some part in Maxwell Davies's vision from the earliest days. His period as a schoolmaster at Cirencester offered the first hints of this enthusiasm for a Kapellmeister spirit. That enthusiasm clearly waned, or was suppressed, during the later 1960s, but it came to the fore again in Orkney, not only in works for children (the parallel with Britten at Aldeburgh is inescapable), but in music written for professional Scottish ensembles. The 1980s were years of mastery, during which he composed prolifically, taking his compositional models more from classical than from medieval or renaissance sources. In some cases – as in some of the 'Strathclyde Concertos' – the results have been less than memorable. But at its best, as in the magnificent Trumpet Concerto of 1988, Maxwell Davies's music has found a new assurance with no loss of strength.

Harrison Birtwistle's remark about his own music that he could rewrite it with different pitches without doing damage (Nyman 1969: 50) can scarcely be taken literally, but it does emphasize his affinities with the texture-based structures of Varèse and the later

INSTRUMENTAL MUSIC II

Gerhard. The orchestral style of his Chorales (1963) already suggested a connection with these composers, but it was *Tragoedia* for ten players (1965) that marked his stylistic maturity and at the same time spelt out his allegiance to a non-German line of development in our century. This is apparent in the verse form of the work (a feature of Birtwistle's earliest music, as in *Refrains and Choruses* of 1957), and also in its repetitions, symmetries and multi-layered textures (Ex.10.11).

Ex. 10.11 Birtwistle: *Tragoedia*

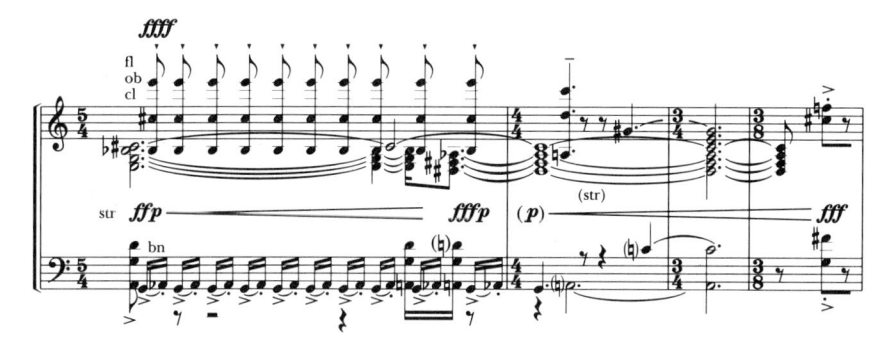

Many of these features have continued to play an important part in Birtwistle's later music, taking their place alongside ideas of more recent formulation. The verse forms of *Tragoedia* reappear in *Verses* for clarinet and piano (1968), while the multi-layered textures are prominent in *Grimethorpe Aria* for brass band (1973). Separate character-continuities are established in *Grimethorpe Aria* – sustained dissonant chords, *cantabile* solo lines and angry stabbing chords. The resemblance to *Tragoedia* can be misleading, however, for the static symmetries of the earlier work have now been replaced by a cumulative, goal-directed musical motion which reaches a multi-layered climax in sections 6 and 7 of the ten-part structure.

Already in *Nomos* (1968) and *An Imaginary Landscape* (1971), both through-composed works, Birtwistle had indicated that he was moving away from the formal symmetries of *Tragoedia* towards a different conception of form and progression. Multi-layered textures remain important in both works, however. In the later stages of *Nomos* the amplified wind quartet, which had provided a *cantus* throughout, assumes a more prominent role, creating an unbroken layer of sound against which other material is counterpointed.

Equally in *An Imaginary Landscape* the brass, percussion and basses establish separate character-continuities which interrupt, overlap and combine with each other in many different ways. The interplay of such character-continuities, defined essentially through texture, timbre and rhythm, is ultimately a more telling key to Birtwistle's musical thought in these pieces than precise pitch content.

It was above all in *The Triumph of Time* (1972) and *Melencolia I* (1976) that Birtwistle's changing approach to form and progression crystallized. In these works he demonstrated a masterly control over the large-scale, sustained unfolding of ideas in a series of progressive and recessive textures which have no real psychological break and which culminate in climaxes of shattering proportions. Yet despite the through-composed character of these works, they still rely on formal methods derived from the character-continuity principle operating in *Tragoedia*. The notion of a slow procession of essentially unrelated ideas lies at the heart of *The Triumph of Time*, derived perhaps from the Bruegel painting that gave it its title. Birtwistle's own phrase is 'a linked chain of material objects which have no necessary connection with each other', or again 'a piece of music as the sum of musical objects, unrelated to each other, apart from one's decision to juxtapose them in space and time'. Of these ideas, subject to varying degrees of transformation from unchanging to permanently changing, each comes directly into focus at some stage in the work before receding into silence.

The 'adagio' pace of *The Triumph of Time* is again a feature of *Melencolia I* for clarinet, harp and two string orchestras, though in this work the sense of forward motion is even slower. As in *Tragoedia*, the harp functions as a mediator between the antagonists in an implicitly dramatic conception which in part defines the three main sections of the work. The opening bars reveal an interplay of several characters, distinguished by different tempi, against which the solo clarinet gradually unfolds its material. (As so often in Birtwistle everything grows from a single pitch, before gradually diverging from there to form a large, complex structure). The final section makes the restrained dramatic element of the work explicit. At the multi-layered climax the two string orchestras play 'out of phase', while the clarinet shrieks its independence before the music disintegrates in an aleatory section.

Birtwistle has since distanced himself from the goal-directed qualities of these works, while preserving something of their sense of 'placing' musical objects within an imaginary landscape – viewing them from many different angles. *Silbury Air* (1977), composed for the London Sinfonietta, is a piece of this order. Here the musical objects (including brass fanfares) take their place in a landscape derived from four pulse labyrinths (Ex. 10.12), where the vertical columns co-ordinate the units of duration, arranging them into groups (bars), and the horizontal lines co-ordinate the metronome marks. But instead of processing forwards, as in *The Triumph of Time*, the music circles back constantly to its starting-point, the middle E which plays such an important role in all Birtwistle's Orpheus-related works. We have a sense of traversing a landscape many times and seeing the same objects from different perspectives. There are similar concerns in *Carmen Arcadiae Mechanicae Perpetuum* (1977), where six musical objects are juxtaposed in many different ways, and also in *Secret Theatre* (1984), which seems to draw together several themes from Birtwistle's earlier music, including the use of a *cantus* (as in *Nomos*) and of ostinato-like accompaniments (as in *Verses*).

Yet this is less a matter of synthesizing earlier developments than of recycling (in the best sense) the same techniques and concepts in each new piece. There is a real sense in which Birtwistle composes the same piece again and again in many different manifestations. *Earth Dances* (1986), for instance, returns to issues that were already well rehearsed in *The Triumph of Time*. It also returns to the full orchestral forces of that work, following numerous instrumental works written for the smaller forces of the London Sinfonietta. *Earth Dances* is conceived almost in archaeological layers, with the music passing through these layers, so that objects emerge and recede between background and foreground, exactly as in *The Triumph of Time*, but without the goal orientation of that work. If there is a close parallel with any other composer and work, it is with the Concerto for Orchestra by Elliott Carter.

Birtwistle's more recent instrumental works, *Endless Parade* (1987) for trumpet, strings and vibraphone, and *Antiphonies* (1993) for piano and orchestra, continue earlier concerns (compare *Melencolia I*) in presenting solo protagonists in contexts that eschew the traditional concerto genre.

VI: Panorama

The concept of a musical landscape is clearly of the utmost importance for Birtwistle, as it is also – though in different, more traditionally evocative, ways – for Maxwell Davies. It is perhaps not far-fetched to

Pulse Labyrinth

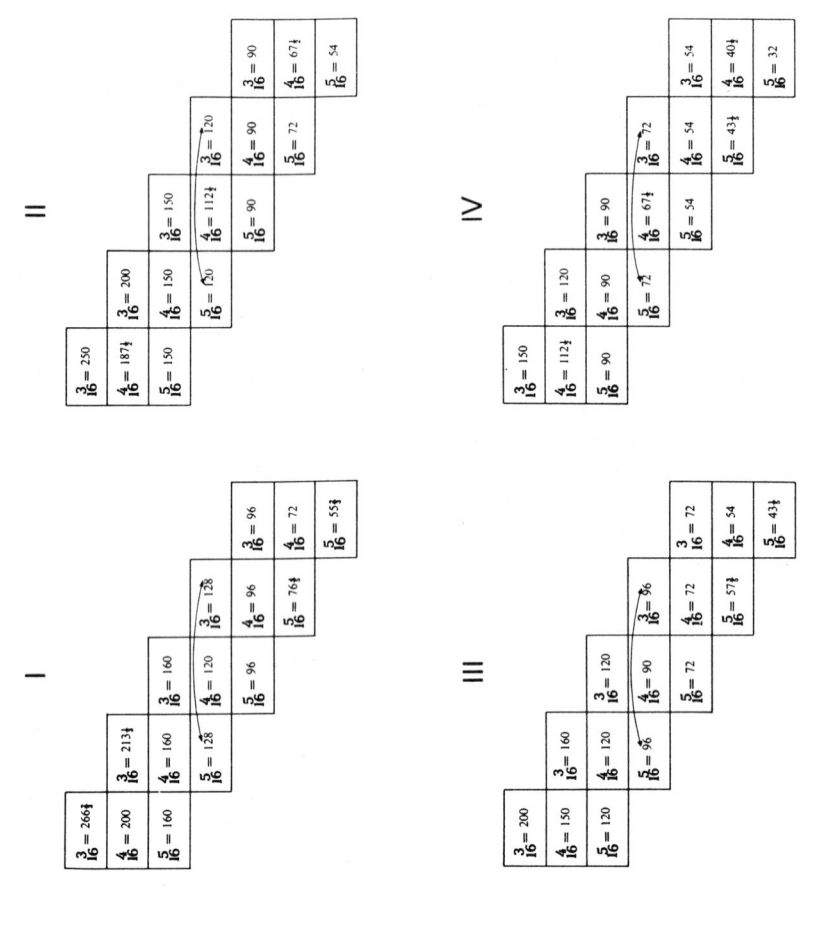

Ex. 10.12 Birtwistle: *Silbury Air*

see in this aspect of their work some kind of refashioning of a British pastoral tradition, though not of course a return to the pastoral modality of Vaughan Williams. Indeed if there is any specific early twentieth-century model, it is rather the Holst of *Egdon Heath*. Other middle-generation composers have been even more explicit in their blend of British pastoralism and a constructivism derived from European traditions. Of these, Anthony Payne (*b* 1936) is arguably the most persuasive. The intercutting devices of his Concerto for Orchestra (1974) and the Schoenbergian 'splitting of formal functions' in his String Quartet (1978) represent the outward-looking, European side of Payne's work. But beneath the surface there were other less obvious influences at work, and they came to the fore in his music of the 1980s. Somehow his music of this period manages to register a love of Delius on the one hand and of Schoenberg on the other, with Delius especially apparent in works such as *Songs and Seascapes* (1984). There is a sense in which Payne's recent music has been an attempt to rediscover, and come to terms with, his own musical roots in an early twentieth-century British style. He is far from prolific (most of his output is vocal), but works such as *The Spirit's Harvest* (1985) and *Time's Arrow* (1990) suggest that his highly personal voice grows stronger.

There is a similar concern with landscape and image among several younger British composers. Landscape may be a literal, concrete inspiration, or it may be a metaphor – an abstraction, where the piece is laid out almost like a map, inviting inspection from many angles. Either way it is a central theme of modern British music, and it will form the starting-point for a survey, necessarily superficial, of composers born in the 1940s. A sense of place – of visual imagery conveyed through music – is a marked characteristic of the music of both Edward Cowie (*b* 1943) and Nicola LeFanu (*b* 1947) (compare Cowie's Concerto for Orchestra, inspired by the Lancashire coast, and LeFanu's *Columbia Falls*). But both have been influenced in more subtle ways by the notion of a 'landscape'. Cowie, a painter and naturalist as well as a composer, has based much of his music, from *Leviathan* (1975) onwards, on the sights, sounds and structures of the natural world, and the interest continues through to recent, more tonally based works such as the Second Clarinet Concerto. LeFanu, likewise, has used a landscape metaphor to describe both the layering of formal perspectives in *A Hidden Landscape* (1973) and the relation between soloist and ensemble in her 'cello concerto', *Deva* (1979).

ART MUSIC

John Casken (*b* 1949) has also been inspired by landscape in these two senses – literally in *Orion over Farne* (1984), and metaphorically in his Cello Concerto (1991), which sets 'an individual figure in a particular place or landscape'. Nature was also the inspiration for his *Salamandra* for two pianos (1986), where the composer 'represents' the two meanings of the Greek term: a lizard-like creature and an elemental spirit which is supposed to live in fire. There is, of course, much more to Casken's music than this. His stylistic starting-point was established partly by his studies in Poland, and the Polish influence is still apparent in works written in his late twenties such as *Tableaux des trois ages* (1977) and *Amarantos* (1977–8). His later music combines an attractive surface texture, characteristic of much modern Polish music, with highly rigorous technical working, as in the beautifully wrought *Maharal Dreaming* (1989), based on material from his opera *Golem*. Poland was also the crucible for the distinctive musical style developed by Nigel Osborne (*b* 1948), though – unlike Casken's – Osborne's works often have strong socio-political overtones. His instrumental music, much of it written for the London Sinfonietta, includes skilfully crafted flute, cello and violin concertos, a Sinfonia (which uses the Gaelic folksong *An Roisin Dubh*) and a work for chamber orchestra *In camera* (1980: really a set of three linked 'nocturnes'). Osborne has branched out in many directions in recent years, from *Zansa* (1985), which draws deep structures from ethnic musics from all over the world, to *Zone* (1989), based partly on transcriptions of soundtracks from Tarkowsky films.

There is much of great value in the music of this generation of composers, and in passing briefly over three other figures I do their considerable achievements scant justice. Colin Matthews (*b* 1946) emerged strongly in the early 1980s with works such as the Cello Concerto (1984), *Suns Dance* (1985) and *Two-Part Invention* (1988), the latter owing something to Tippett's formal mosaics. In 1980 Roger Marsh (*b* 1949) produced *Still*, a highly dramatic orchestral work, notable for the wild outburst of a soprano saxophone from the orchestral stillness. He followed it with the Stravinskian Music for Piano and Wind Instruments (1986) and *Stepping Out* (1990) for piano and orchestra. John Tavener (*b* 1944), not known for instrumental works, none the less composed an impressive piece for piano and orchestra, *Palintropes*, in 1978, and went on to write the massive *Mandelion* for organ (1981) and *Towards the Sun* for orchestra (1982).

There are good reasons to focus in rather more detail on two composers of this generation, Brian Ferneyhough (*b* 1943) and

INSTRUMENTAL MUSIC II

Robin Holloway (*b* 1943) (see the chapters on both composers in Griffiths 1985; Harvey 1979 and Toop 1985 on Ferneyhough; Northcott 1974 and *Tempo* 1979 on Holloway). They are of interest not only in their own right, but because their polarized positions will form a useful framework within which to 'place' some members of the next generation of British composers, those born in the 1950s and 1960s. We may begin by glancing at the multi-layered complexity of the closing bars of Ferneyhough's Second String Quartet (1979–80) (Ex. 10.13). The enormous technical difficulty of this music arises in part from an elevation of the concept of virtuosity to a metaphysical plane, raising issues about performer and listener difficulties which have a larger resonance in contemporary music. An early Sonatina for three clarinets and bassoon or bass clarinet (1963), written in a neoclassical idiom, offers little hint of these concerns. Yet already in his next work, *Four Miniatures* for flute and piano (1965), Ferneyhough moulded techniques drawn from Webern, Stockhausen and Boulez (the Second Piano Sonata) into a powerful musical language, and one that would soon be consolidated in his *Sonatas* for string quartet of 1967. Since then Ferneyhough has developed an idiom of formidable complexity in works such as *Firecycle Beta* (1969–71), which superimposes two separate orchestral groups, one using strict notation and the other rhythmically free; *Transit* for chamber orchestra and six solo voices (1972–5); and *La terre est un homme* for large orchestra (1976–9); and the remarkable cycle of *Carceri d'invenzione* (after Piranesi), which occupied him through much of the 1980s. He has also made formidable demands on performers in a range of pieces for solo instruments – *Cassandra's Dream Song* (1971) and *Unity Capsule* (1975–6) for flute, and *Time and Motion Study I* (1971–7) for bass clarinet. These works have scored considerable successes for their composer on the European Continent and in America (he spent his early professional life in Germany and is living in America at the time of writing), but they have as yet failed to make major headway in Britain, at least beyond a circle of initiates. Like the prose of Adorno, the music of Ferneyhough refuses to compromise – to conceal its formidable difficulties in the interests of accessibility or a superficially more 'polished' end-product.

Robin Holloway, in contrast, is an eclectic, firmly committed to a pluralist approach which involves adapting his musical style to the nature of the commission, directing different styles to different performers and audiences, and even 're-composing' music with

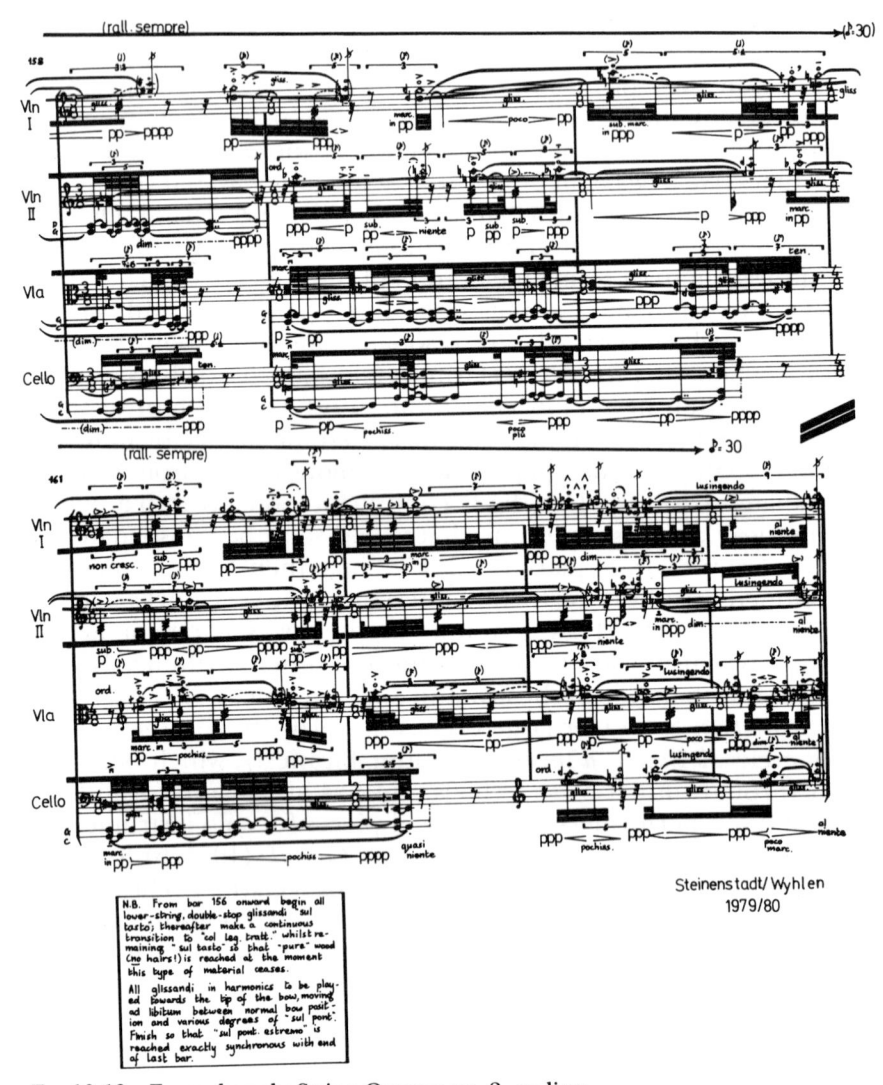

Ex. 10.13 Ferneyhough: String Quartet no. 2, ending

which his listeners already have a strong emotional identification. In his Concerto for Orchestra of 1969 the quotations from Brahms signalled his enduring dialogue with the music of the past, a dialogue that became totally explicit in *Scenes from Schumann* the following year. Here Holloway effectively recomposed a group of

INSTRUMENTAL MUSIC II

Schumann songs, juxtaposing nineteenth- and twentieth-century styles in a manner that deliberately eschews synthesis. This allusive quality, working on several levels, has been central to his work, and it involves an unashamed exploration of the resources of tonality. It is there explicitly in *Domination of Black* (1974), where Wagner and Mahler enter the dialogue, and again – though more discreetly – in the compelling, and stylistically much 'tougher', Second Concerto for Orchestra (1979), where the rich neo-romantic gestures of some earlier works are less conspicuous. They return clearly in *Seascape and Harvest* (1985–6). Echoes of Mahler, Elgar and Richard Strauss are unmistakable in this work, as Ex. 10.14, an extract from the 'Harvest' section, indicates. Holloway's technique of re-composition

Ex. 10.14   Holloway: *Seascape and Harvest*

reached its *ne plus ultra* in *Wagner Nights* (1989), where themes from *Parsifal* are transformed and recontextualized into the startlingly incongruous genre of a suite of waltzes.

Ferneyhough has proved an important inspiration to a group of younger British composers, whose style has been described collectively as the 'new complexity', though they frequently bemoan the label (see Toop 1988). Significantly they have more performances abroad than in Britain. They include the Ferneyhough pupil Roger Redgate (*b* 1958), who has written music inspired by the post-structuralist thought of Derrida – *Eidos* for piano, *mais en étoile* for ensemble and *Eperons* for oboe and percussion, all of the late 1980s; Chris Dench (*b* 1953), whose *Tilt* (1985) sets blocks of hyperactive percussion sonority against each other in a contest of 'furious objectivity'; Richard Barrett (*b* 1959), whose series of 'Fictions' includes *Earth* (1987–8) for trombone and percussion, where a complex totality is gradually dismantled into basic 'naked' processes; and Andrew Toovey (*b* 1962), whose *Adam* (1990) pits three duos against each other in a climate of terrifying aggression. James Dillon (*b* 1950) is also part of the group, though his exceptional talent and individuality place him a little apart from the others. The violent intensity of Dillon's early music – works such as *Once upon a time* – seemed to retreat somewhat in the mid-1980s, but it has returned with renewed vengeance in *Überschreiten* (Ex. 10.15) and subsequent works such as *Ignis noster*.

Michael Finnissy (*b* 1946) has also been strongly associated with the 'new complexity' school, and as a pianist he often plays their music. Yet although there are significant overlaps of texture and technique, the sources of Finnissy's music are quite different. Folk and ethnic cultures inform much of his work, and so too does the music of composers who remain somewhat apart from Western mainstreams, notably Ives and Grainger. These diverse influences somehow fuse with a Boulez-like filigree texture in one of Finnissy's first fully mature works, *World* (1976). Other works of the late 1970s reflect more obviously Finnissy's interest in the multi-levelled structures of Elliott Carter, notably *Pathway to the Sun and Stars* (1976), *Sea and Sky* (1980) and *Alongside* (1979) for chamber orchestra. Since then his musical language has become more cogent and integrated, notably in the chamber works *Banumbirr* (1982) (Ex. 10.16) and the String Trio (1986), and in the powerful, Australian-influenced orchestral work *Red Earth* (1986), where again landscape emerges as a prominent source of inspiration.

Ex. 10.15

Ex. 10.16 Finnissy: *Banumbirr*, opening

INSTRUMENTAL MUSIC II

At the other extreme to Ferneyhough, Finnissy and the 'new complexity', we may identify a group of composers who follow Holloway in their adherence to a broadly postmodern aesthetic. They include Dominic Muldowney (*b* 1952), who has worked extensively in the National Theatre (where he succeeded Birtwistle as musical director), and whose eclectic idiom has drawn heavily upon Kurt Weill and jazz styles. Like Holloway, he tailors his product to the commission, happily producing film scores on the one hand and tougher works like Sinfonietta (1986), written for the London Sinfonietta, on the other. James MacMillan (*b* 1959) also relates to this aesthetic. His music has strong socio-political overtones, often related to his native Scotland, as in his Piano Concerto *The Berserking* and *The Confession of Isobel Gowdie*, both of 1990. (Part of *The Confession of Isobel Gowdie* is presented as Ex. 10.17.)

MacMillan's strong ideals about the composer in the community, reflected in his close association with Maxwell Davies in the St Magnus Festival in Orkney, has resulted in works such as the Clarinet Quintet (*Tuireadh*) of 1991, dedicated to the victims of the Piper Alpha disaster and their families.

The Berserking was dedicated to Steve Martland (*b* 1958), another postmodernist inclined to forceful political statements, as in the orchestral piece *Babi Yar* (1985), which first brought him to national and international attention. The tripartite division of the orchestra, together with the use of electric and bass guitars and synthesizer, is illustrated in Ex. 10.18. His studies with the Dutch composer Louis Andriessen left a mark in two specific ways. First he attempted to promote interactions or crossovers with popular music (he has worked closely with the jazz orchestra Loose Tubes), notably in multi-media projects such as *Albion* (1988) and *Terra firma* (1989). And secondly he has explored minimalist or 'repetitive' techniques, especially in *Drill* for two pianos (1987). These two themes have been echoed by other British composers of the younger generation. Intersections with popular music are a feature of the music of Mark-Anthony Turnage (*b* 1958), for instance, as in his early jazz-inspired orchestral work *Night Dances* (1980–81), in his gospel-influenced *Entranced* (1982) for solo piano, and in the saxophone writing of his better-known *Three Screaming Popes* (1989). Equally, repetitive techniques cultivated by American composers such as John Adams underlie many of the scores of Michael Nyman (*b* 1944) and the colourful, rather glittery music produced by Martin Butler (*b* 1960), as in his Concertino for 14 instruments (1983), his *Bluegrass Variations* (1989)

Ex. 10.17 MacMillan: *The Confession of Isobel Gowdie*

Ex. 10.18 Martland: *Babi Yar*

ART MUSIC

and his 'river' piece with Latin American resonance, *O, Rio* of 1991.

The polarity of 'new complexity' and postmodernism focuses major issues in contemporary British music, and it will be examined again at the end of this chapter. But some of the most highly valued of the younger British composers cannot easily be related to either pole, and some brief mention of their achievements should be made at this stage. Oliver Knussen (*b* 1952) had already formed an astonishingly individual and mature musical style by his mid-twenties, merging influences from both sides of the Atlantic in his Third Symphony (1973–9), centred around a Birtwistle-like processional; *Coursing* (1978–81), a 'landscape' piece inspired by the Niagara Falls; and *Ophelia Dances*, for chamber ensemble (1975). Another child prodigy is George Benjamin (*b* 1960), a student of Messiaen as well as of Alexander Goehr (during his years at Cambridge). Benjamin's reputation was secured at an early stage by *Ringed by the Flat Horizon*, composed for a student orchestra at Cambridge when he was 19, and since performed all over the world. He is a slow worker who produces meticulously crafted compositions, which in recent years have involved electronic resources, as with the IRCAM piece *Antara*.

Two further Cambridge products might be mentioned here. Robert Saxton (*b* 1953) has gradually learnt to anchor his profuse ornamental style with strong, harmonically based structures, resulting in the 1980s in an astonishing succession of masterly orchestral pieces, many with apocalyptic programmes, and an orchestration of brilliant luminosity to match. They include the Concerto for Orchestra (1984), the Dante-inspired *Circles of Light* (1985–6), a fireworks display of brilliant textures, the Viola Concerto (1986), *In the Beginning* (1987) and the Violin Concerto (1989). Judith Weir (*b* 1952), one of the most individual of the younger generation of composers, has gained a major international reputation for opera, and her output of purely instrumental works is relatively small. Her strength has been in exquisitely finished miniatures, but there are some impressive, (relatively) longer orchestral works, such as *Isti mirant stella* (1981) and *The Ride over Lake Constance* (1984). Her lively sense of wit, established at an early stage with the opera for solo voice *King Harald's Saga* (1979) and in *King Harald Sails to Byzantium* of the same year (a Fires of London commission), has been continued in instrumental works such as *A Serbian Cabaret* (1984) for piano quartet and *The Bagpiper's String Trio* (1985).

Simon Bainbridge (*b* 1952) and Simon Holt (*b* 1958) also resist easy classification. Bainbridge's music, similar at times to Ligeti in its finely wrought textures, came to public attention when his Viola Concerto of 1976 was given its first performance two years later. The spatial concept of that work, where the orchestra expands and projects the sounds and textures of the soloist in 'layers', has remained important to Bainbridge. A visit to New York in 1978 resulted in some highly individual Reich-influenced works (*Voicing* of 1982, and, the following year, *Concertante in moto perpetuo* for oboe and ensemble, but in later works the spatial layering of the Viola Concerto has come to the fore, notably in the Fantasia for Double Orchestra (1983–4), and the String Sextet (1988), where individually profiled instrumental lines emerge from and recede into a background harmonic field. Simon Holt came to prominence in the early 1980s with works such as *Kites* (1983) and *Era Madrugada* (1984), both written for the London Sinfonietta and heavily influenced by Birtwistle. More recent works such as the orchestral *Syrensong* and *Capriccio spettrale* show Holt attempting to expand his musical thought, creating larger and more closely argued structures.

Other composers of substance include Anthony Powers (*b* 1953) and Philip Grange (*b* 1956). Powers has been concerned with special kinds of fusions in his music – notably between tonal and atonal techniques and between French and German styles. His musical language, atmospheric yet rigorously constructed, is at its best in the orchestral evocation of Venice, *Stones, Water, Stars*, and in the String Quartet, both of 1987. Grange's music, from *Cimmerian Nocturne* of 1979 to *Variations* of 1986 and beyond, has combined techniques learnt from his teacher Maxwell Davies with 'layered' structures and a large-scale rhythmic organization inspired by Elliott Carter, while remaining essentially independent of both.

The list could be extended almost indefinitely. A more comprehensive survey would find room for, among others, Brian Elias (*b* 1948), Vic Hoyland (*b* 1945), Geoffrey Poole (*b* 1949), David Matthews (*b* 1943), Jonathan Lloyd (*b* 1948) and Giles Swayne (*b* 1946). But it is perhaps of more value to conclude this chapter with some reflections on the deeper cultural significance of the diversity of styles and techniques available to younger British composers today. It is not necessary to become involved in a surface polemic of 'new complexity' and postmodernism in order to recognize that our present culture is postmodern in a much deeper sense than the adoption of tonal harmonies and pulsed rhythms proscribed by post-war modernism. The 1960s was indeed an exciting decade of experimentation in British music, echoing and also transforming the achievements of European experimental music of some ten years earlier. At the same time it is obvious that the 'official' modern art of those post-war years – thrilling and exploratory as it often was – had little in common with the explosive, dissenting modernism of the early years of the century, when the bourgeois–romantic project of greatness reached its apotheosis. Paradoxically, the notion of an avant garde, spearheading us into the future, has become itself a conservative – even an anachronistic – idea, an idea predicated on the assumption, illusory but immensely powerful, of a single culture.

For postmodernists such as James MacMillan, Boulez is the arch-conservative of our time. For them, the 'failure' of the avant garde has been an opportunity, accompanied by a cathartic sense of release from the prohibitions of post-war modernism. Yet in condemning Boulez, and with him those British composers who have perpetuated modernism into the 1990s, the 'postmodernists' court a rather glib interpretation of recent cultural history. In the first place, it is trivial to discount the conservative voice, however we formulate 'conservative' and 'radical' in today's world. And in the second place, the critique of modernism fails to grasp that the continuing modernist project has in reality few remaining points of contact with any concept of an avant garde, and need not be assessed in these terms. Far from clearing a path for the rest of our (notionally unified) culture to follow as best it can, today's modernist works in one corner of a (plural) cultural field. The classical repertoire occupies another corner of the field, and popular culture yet another, which it partly shares with the postmodernist. Arguably it is no longer helpful to view these different repertoires as sets of antinomies generating massive force-fields within a single bourgeois culture, as Adorno did in his powerful and challenging commentaries on contemporary music. In a postmodern world each finds its own public. Contemporary modernism is an *ars nova* and an *ars subtilior*. It is no longer an avant garde.

Chapter 11

MUSIC AND DRAMA

MATTHEW RYE

I: Opera: Introduction and Retrospect

British opera has had a fraught history. It thrived for a short while at the end of the seventeenth century, before Italian opera forced it out of popular taste, and then for nearly 250 years struggled to gain a foothold both at home and abroad. Few countries can have witnessed so many vain attempts. This was partly due to the cultural position of the genre: where Germany and Italy developed a dense network of provincial opera houses, Britain made do for years with few regional outlets and not even a particularly thriving culture in London. This largely accounts for the vast number of operas written over the last century or so that were given an initial production and have rarely, if at all, been seen or heard again, and for the fact that in the nineteenth century Britain produced nothing to match the output of Donizetti or Meyerbeer, let alone Wagner or Verdi, and in the twentieth only a handful of composers, Britten, Tippett and Maxwell Davies among them, who have made any lasting impression internationally. Thus the story of British opera is one of many hopeful false starts. The breakthrough made by Britten from 1945 was all the more a personal triumph for being achieved through musical and dramatic talent against those same odds to which so many before him had come to grief. Although the climate for new opera vastly improved after the Second World War, with the establishment of permanent opera companies in strategic areas of Britain and a growth in public arts funding, few if any composers have since managed to equal Britten's output in terms of quality and national, still less international, acceptance.

One of these anticipatory new beginnings occurred in 1914: the year witnessed both Thomas Beecham's first wholehearted attempt at founding a permanent opera company devoted to British opera and foreign opera sung in English, the Beecham Opera Company

ART MUSIC

(later reconstituted outside Beecham's direct control as the British National Opera Company), and the first of Rutland Boughton's Glastonbury festivals with its intended rebirth of British opera.

Older presences lingered for a few years after this: Stanford's Sheridan-based *The Critic, or, An Opera Rehearsed* (1915) and romantic fairytale opera *The Travelling Companion* (1916) are in fact the most worthy of survival among his ten operas, and Mackenzie's *The Eve of St John* (1919) was the first of a significant number of 'midsummer' operas to appear during the ensuing years (see Banfield 1986). Only Stanford's pupil Charles Wood (1866–1926) among these figures produced operas (both comedies based on Dickens: *A Scene from Pickwick* of 1921 – also referred to as *Pickwick Papers* – and *The Family Party* of 1923 from *Martin Chuzzlewit*) which began to indicate a general trend away from the romantic subjects prevalent in the previous century to a more recognizably twentieth-century interest in dramatic realism. Elgar's single and abortive foray into opera was an adaptation of Ben Jonson's *The Devil Is an Ass*, which he set as *The Spanish Lady*, with music compiled from passages of earlier works dating from the 1880s to the 1930s (listed in Young 1955, R/1973: 360–75), but which never reached a satisfactorily performable state.

One of the first obviously twentieth-century opera composers was Ethel Smyth (1858–1944). Her struggle for justice through her political activities as a suffragette was reflected in the new sense of realism she brought to operatic writing. *The Wreckers* (1904), with its prescient, Britten-like theme of the struggle between individuals and a bigoted, self-righteous community, immediately turned away from the mythical, historical dramas that had dominated Victorian opera, to concentrate on the sensitively and realistically portrayed oppressed lives of common people, something English literature had been doing for a century but to which British opera had yet to wake up. Like the operas of Delius (for a discussion of which see Burton 1981: 352–5), her earlier works had gained more attention in Germany and *The Wreckers* (originally written to a French libretto as *Les naufrageurs*) was first performed in Leipzig after both Bruno Walter and Gustav Mahler in Vienna had expressed interest. Smyth's music manages to sound convincing, despite its occasionally undistinguished nature, and her dramatic gifts, the spaciousness of the scale and her ear for orchestration tend to hide any feeling of the commonplace in her harmonic and melodic ideas.

For all Smyth's devotion to causes, there was no lack of humour in her make-up, as her next opera, *The Boatswain's Mate*, proved. This

Cornish comedy to her own libretto based on W. W. Jacobs was premièred in London by Beecham's company in 1916. Indeed, it was the first of her operas to gain its success largely in her own country. Unusually, its two parts are constructed differently: the first alternates music and spoken dialogue, the second is through-composed.

Smyth's last two operas, *Fête galante* (1923) and *Entente cordiale* (1925), were both comedies. The music of the former has a certain charm and wit, but the work's feyness is not up to Smyth's usual dramatic standards and would hardly survive modern-day revival.

Another composer who achieved more success in Germany than his homeland was Joseph Holbrooke, whose interest in Celtic mythology and legend showed him trying to find his own equivalent to Wagner's Teutonic preoccupations, something even more overt in the work of Rutland Boughton (see below). Now virtually forgotten except for the odd piece of chamber music, Holbrooke made a name for himself in the second decade of the century through his operatic trilogy *The Cauldron of Anwen* (from the Welsh *Mabinogion* epic): *The Children of Don* (1911), *Dylan* (1909) and *Bronwen* (1920). It is perhaps their vastness that has prevented them from gaining greater currency: *Dylan*, for example, is scored for a Strauss-sized orchestra, with the addition of saxophones, saxhorns (perhaps Holbrooke's equivalent of Wagner tubas) and 'unlimited' concertinas. The scoring is skilled if sometimes overblown and the vocal writing somewhat strenuous, but it is his melodic writing that lets him down most: outwardly Wagnerian in outline, the themes are often unmemorable and short-winded and Holbrooke seems to find it difficult to maintain a line for more than a few bars. Similarly, the harmonies tend to plod between the Wagnerian and the Debussian.

II: Boughton, Holst, Vaughan Williams and Brian

Of all British opera's 'new beginnings' none seemed, at the time at least, as promising as the case of Rutland Boughton (1878–1960). In 1911 he wrote an *Essay on Choral Drama* as an appendix to the published libretto by Reginald Buckley for a proposed opera, *Uther and Igraine*. Here he ambitiously and arrogantly set out his arguments for a new kind of English music drama where the chorus was to take a leading dramatic role. Boughton had completed *Uther*, now renamed *The Birth of Arthur*, in 1909, but the first major dramatic work of his to reach the stage was *The Immortal Hour* (1913).

ART MUSIC

Although standing apart from the Arthurian cycle of music dramas for which the earlier work was planned as the first of five, it was nevertheless the work he chose to launch his scheme for a kind of 'English Bayreuth' crossed with a summer school for amateur and semi-professional musicians. The Somerset town of Glastonbury, appropriately associated in popular mythology with the Arthurian legends, became the venue, but a proposed National Festival Theatre there never got beyond the planning stage and the village's Assembly Rooms served as inadequate host to the festivals. *The Immortal Hour* was first performed in August 1914 with piano and had to wait until the following spring to appear at Bournemouth in its full orchestral guise.

Although not part of his Arthurian scheme, *The Immortal Hour* was an appropriate début for his dramatic ideas. The chorus is indeed given an important role, less in the sense of being dramatic protagonists than in being used to create atmosphere, both aural and scenic: in the first scene it provides 'dancing scenery' to conjure up a spirit-ridden forest. The libretto is based on a play by Fiona Macleod (the pen-name of William Sharp), set in an invented Celtic world of spirits and kings. Boughton apparently began writing in a manner reminiscent of Debussy (there is a certain similarity between Macleod's world and Maeterlinck's imaginary kingdom in *Pelléas et Mélisande*), but then started again in a more personal idiom, one slightly closer to the harmonies of Delius and the pentatonic melodies of Hebridean folksong. Yet the music is constructed in such a way that it lacks a feeling both of momentum and of any true dramatic or symphonic development of ideas. Some of the writing is undoubtedly beautiful and original, and the scoring appropriately atmospheric, but the pace is slow and often undramatic, while the pentatonicism can seem tiresome, as in the melody associated with Etain (Ex. 11.1).

The music has undoubtedly dated more than that of some of his contemporaries, as witness the work's present-day lack of stage interest. In the mid-1920s, however, it ran for over 500 performances in London alone, making it still the record-holder of the longest continuous run of a serious operatic work in the history of the genre, and comparable with the late twentieth-century phenomenon of musicals running for years in the West End, out of all proportion to their musical merit.

The Glastonbury festivals occurred annually (except for 1917–18) until 1926. The second, in 1915, saw the first production of *Bethlehem*, Boughton's setting of the Coventry Nativity Play, which has remained

Ex. 11.1 Boughton: *The Immortal Hour*, Act I, sc.ii

[Slow]

ETAIN: Fair is the moon-light, And fair the wood But not so fair as the place I come from

orch *pp*

one of his most successful works, though it was a scandal over a production during the General Strike of 1926 in Church House, Westminster, given a contemporary setting with Christ born in a miner's cottage, that finally brought his Glastonbury dream to an end.

The first of the Arthurian cycle to be performed in full (though with piano accompaniment) was *The Round Table* in 1916, followed by *The Birth of Arthur* in 1920 (again with piano accompaniment – the orchestration was never completed) and *The Lily Maid* in Stroud in 1934. The two final instalments of the cycle, *Galahad* (1944) and *Avalon* (1945), remain unperformed. As an attempt to provide an English counterpart to Wagner's *Ring* tetralogy, it was an ambitious undertaking and took nearly twice as long as Wagner's to complete. It is also very uneven: Buckley died before he could complete more than the librettos for the first two works and Boughton's less confident texts for the later three (particularly *Galahad*) tend to give the legend a political gloss in keeping with his socialist-turned-Stalinist views. The advice Boughton received from Shaw on the libretto for

The Lily Maid could well apply to many librettos from the first half of the century (and indeed beyond), another reason for lack of interest today, where translation can hide deficiencies in the texts of comparable foreign works:

> From the literary point of view the poem is out of fashion. It is written in that curious language faked by Sir Walter Scott out of Chaucerian English, Euphuism and the old ballads, and never spoken by mortal man at any period of earth's history. Wardour Street English it came at last to be known. (January 1919, quoted in Hurd 1962, R/1993: 208)

Three other operas date from the years of work on the Arthurian cycle. *Alkestis* (Glastonbury 1922) is a setting of Gilbert Murray's 'Englished' version of Euripides and again described as a 'choral drama', with a small orchestra for accompaniment. Musically it is less distinctive than *The Immortal Hour* and is also dogged by that work's pentatonicism. More distinctive is *The Queen of Cornwall*, a setting of Thomas Hardy's verse-drama of Tristram and the two Iseults (Boughton sometimes referred to it as part of the Arthurian cycle), but it is in fact Hardy's quaint, pseudo-Gothic text that is its greatest drawback. The music, however, though sometimes too relentlessly four-square, has a certain harmonic homogeneity and motivic rigour, with only the occasional hint in the chordal writing of Wagner's *Tristan und Isolde*, a work that must have always been in the back of Boughton's mind. The last of these three operas, completed in 1929, and first performed in Bath in 1935, is *The Ever Young*, a vain attempt to follow up the success of *The Immortal Hour*.

Boughton's operatic output may have had little impact on British opera as a whole – his influence was more localized and his laudable vision for a new future of English opera impaired ultimately by a lack of the sheer musical talent needed to carry it off. His Glastonbury festivals gave several young composers a much-needed forum for performances and were of undoubted educational benefit for those who took part. But it was probably its amateurism that was its undoing, and operatic life outside the musical magnet of London had to wait several decades before fully professional operatic traditions were to become established outside the capital.

His followers fared no better. Although of a somewhat later generation, George Lloyd's first two (of his three) operas date from the 1930s and, like Boughton's, all three are set in legendary or medieval Britain: *Iernin* (1934, Lyceum 1935), *The Serf* (Covent Garden 1938) and *John Socman* (1951). All three also demonstrate the composer's

MUSIC AND DRAMA

musical conservatism. *The Serf* seems both musically and dramatically to have drifted in from the world of 1930s Robin Hood films, with its rather precious neo-Gothic text (all three libretti are by his father), harmonic naivety and overemphasis on rabble-rousing choruses. Bantock, although Boughton's senior by ten years, was undoubtedly influenced by his protégé's ideas. The last of his three operas, *The Seal-Woman* (1924), is based on a Celtic folk tale and uses 20 Hebridean folksongs as the musical basis for the work. Indeed, Trevor Bray (1975) goes as far as to say that 'the plot is there only to support the many Hebridean folksongs'.

Folksong played an important part too in the operatic writing of Holst and Vaughan Williams. Holst never matched the integrity, perfection and power of *Sāvitri* (1909, performed 1916), his first fully mature work for the operatic stage. A chamber opera (the first in English since the seventeenth century) based on an episode in the Sanskrit *Mahabharata*, *Sāvitri* uses three singers, eleven instrumentalists and offstage women's chorus to great effect in conveying a spiritual yet very human theme (a woman's triumph over Death's attempt to take her husband from her), with music combining a post-Wagnerian ardour and spare folksong modality.

His next foray into the operatic field, *The Perfect Fool* (1922, first performed a year later by Beecham's company at Covent Garden), was not so successful. 'It sins many times against the theatrical decalogue,' wrote Edwin Evans, 'from its initial ballet to its final anticlimax' (1923a). Holst indeed took great risks with this work, from its perverse plot to the use of musical satire with the appearance of two rivals for a Princess's affections: a Verdian tenor (Troubadour) and a Wagnerian bass (Wanderer) (see Ex. 11.2a and b). The opera's title has at least lived on through the popularity of its opening ballet sequence, music that finds Holst at his most characteristically brilliant and inventive.

Even more of an experiment was *At the Boar's Head* (1924). This 'musical interlude in one act' came about when Holst chanced upon the way lines from Shakespeare's *Henry IV* aptly fitted some morris and other country dance tunes. The vocal writing of the whole one-act opera is constructed from some 38 such tunes, largely from William Chappell's and Cecil Sharp's collections (the latter taken mostly from John Playford's *English Dancing Master* of 1651) and including three of Holst's own invention. They are welded together seamlessly and, given Holst's characteristic harmonic and orchestral setting, are made totally his own and stylistically all of a

Ex. 11.2a Holst: *The Perfect Fool*

Allegretto
THE TROUBADOUR: *mp*
From far-off land I come, A land of vine and o-live tree: A land where men are sing-ing songs of love all day.

piece. In Ex. 11.3, for instance, the tune 'Rufty tufty', from Sharp's third set of *Country Dance Tunes*, is given a typically quasi-bitonal accompaniment – a B♭ minor ostinato bass beneath a more D♭ major-orientated harmonization of the tune. The result is as personal as anything he wrote, though in his review of the première, Ernest Newman complained that 'there are not enough doors and windows in the score . . . The texture is all good, but it is too continuous' (1925c). Indeed, it is probably its unrelenting, chattery style and overt 'cleverness' that have kept it from the stage for much of its life.

For his last opera, *The Wandering Scholar* (1930, performed 1934), Holst returned to chamber opera, with a bawdy, 25-minute one-acter. Its fast-moving, syllabic word-setting sometimes resembles the manner of *At the Boar's Head*, but this time the music is all Holst's own, albeit with a folk-tune flavour to some of the vocal lines.

Vaughan Williams, although drawing upon folksong in much of his vocal music, never went to the extreme of Holst in basing a whole opera on found material. Yet the style of his 'romantic ballad opera' *Hugh the Drover* (1914, not performed until 1924) is so fully

MUSIC AND DRAMA

Ex. 11.2b   Holst: *The Perfect Fool*

founded on English folk melody that the traditional tunes he does include go virtually undetected. The most successful of Vaughan Williams's six operas, *Hugh the Drover* nevertheless suffers from the same short-windedness of *At the Boar's Head*, perhaps an inevitable outcome of using folksong phraseology.

Sir John in Love (1928) was in a way Vaughan Williams's response to Holst's Shakespearean scene (though their composition virtually coincides). He took his plot and text from *The Merry Wives of Windsor* and thus set himself up against the examples of Verdi and Nicolai. Yet he has made the work his own and what the opera lacks in dramatic succinctness it gains in musical invention. Part of its lyricism comes from his use of folksong. The tunes are largely subsidiary to the musical flow, unlike in the Holst, but one tune in particular, the suitably titled 'John, come kiss me now' (Ex. 11.4a), is subjected to limited variation treatment in the first scene and in a later manifestation in the second act even seems to pay homage to Holst, with melody and words (Ex. 11.4b) recalling those of Ex. 11.3.

ART MUSIC

However delightful his Shakespearean comedy, Vaughan Williams's dramatic peak came with his next opera, *Riders to the Sea* (1932, RCM 1937). A virtual word-for-word setting of the play by J. M. Synge, in it Vaughan Williams for once tempered his folksong style and composed the whole work in arioso-recitative with the orchestra painting an

Ex. 11.3 Holst: *At the Boar's Head*
('Rufty tufty' from ed. C. Sharp: *Country Dance Tunes*, Set 3)

Ex. 11.4   Vaughan Williams: *Sir John in Love*

(a) Act I

[musical example: Allegretto, pp +8va]

(b) Act II

[musical example: Andante, FALSTAFF: "Go thy ways, go thy ways, old Jack. I'll make more of thy old body than I have done."]

authentic portrait of the merciless sea to which a stoical old Irishwoman loses the last of her six sons. It can be only the opera's brevity (35 minutes) that has prevented it becoming more established: its musico-dramatic qualities, achieved as much as anything by restraint, are as powerful as those of *Sāvitri* or Vaughan Williams's own mid-period symphonies. Indeed, it shares the latter's musical world in its mode-based harmonies and melodies. The opera's reliance upon limited-transposition modes, particularly the octatonic scale, looks forward to the *Sinfonia antartica* (1949), not inaptly, with the common theme of man versus nature (and, indeed, an evocative use of wordless choral melismas). His use of modality and tonality is particularly

ART MUSIC

pointed towards the end of the work, where the foreboding expressed by incessant minor 3rds in the melodies gives way to the solace of the pure major mode as Maurya accepts the tragedy in her new peace of mind (see Ex. 11.5).

Ex. 11.5 Vaughan Williams: *Riders to the Sea*

An unsuccessful comedy, *The Poisoned Kiss* (1929, performed 1936), followed and can be dismissed, but not even his most ambitious dramatic work, *The Pilgrim's Progress*, goes far enough in fulfilling the promise of *Riders to the Sea*. Its origins go back to (and beyond) a pastoral scene composed in 1922, *The Shepherds of the Delectable Mountains*, which ultimately formed the final act's second scene. Further episodes were composed over the following 14 years, but the music was diverted into his Fifth Symphony (1943). In 1942 he composed incidental music for a BBC radio adaptation of Bunyan's work, some of which found its way into the opera that finally occupied him until 1949. This 'Morality', as he preferred to call it, was first performed at Covent Garden in 1951 as part of the Festival of Britain, but the production failed to get to grips with the unconventionality of its dramatic pace – Michael Kennedy described it as 'a series of *tableaux vivants* "in the similitude of a dream"' (1972: a comparison might be made with Olivier Messiaen's *Saint François d'Assise*). But it is the fact that he never repeated the artistic success of *Riders to the Sea* that deprived Vaughan Williams of a stronger role in Britain's operatic renaissance, despite the appreciable musical assets of his less dramatically successful works.

Nor were his contemporaries to get any closer to founding an operatic tradition, with a varied range of works no longer remembered beyond their titles, such as Tovey's *The Bride of Dionysus* (performed 1929) and Cyril Rootham's *The Two Sisters* (1920), a period piece from the folksong school. Frank Bridge's 'little opera in three scenes' *The Christmas Rose* (in the words of Anthony Payne (1984: 53): 'a musical nativity play rather than a conventional opera') was composed between 1919 and 1929 and has at least been recorded. The musical style maintains the harmonically richer manner that had dominated his earlier work before he turned to a terser language in his instrumental music of the 1920s.

ART MUSIC

One other figure from this generation made a highly original if unfulfilled contribution to British opera. In 1916, in the midst of the First World War, Havergal Brian started work on one of the strangest, most ambitious operatic works of the century. Completed in 1929 and yet to reach the stage (it has been broadcast complete and orchestral excerpts have been recorded commercially), *The Tigers* is a bold satire on virtually every area of English society, from the church to the police and the army (hence the Tigers regiment of the title). Thorough-going plot is minimal – in a sense, each scene satirizes a different group, with only the musical material bringing any coherence to the dramatic structure. It contains some fine, original music (the satire does not descend into musical parody) and an important part is given to the orchestra in the extended ballets and interludes. Brian wrote no more operas until the 1950s, when he worked on four typically ambitious dramas based on well-known mythological subjects.

III: Opera between the Wars

As a kind of antithesis to the Holst/Vaughan Williams generation, the composers who emerged in the 1920s and 1930s shared a rebellious streak. It was the age of the Sitwells, when young artists such as Walton, Bliss and Lord Berners set out to shock, or at least unsettle, their elders, with their irreverence and artistic horseplay. Only the last of these three ventured into opera at this time, with a work in French, *Le carrosse du Saint-Sacrement*, performed in Paris in 1923. It is a one-act comedy based on Prosper Mérimée, with the text set to a rather gabbling recitative and with the musical interest largely confined to the orchestra. The style reflects the perky, often humorous manner of his ballets and the opera would merit revival. Van Dieren wrote a single opera, a three-act *buffa The Tailor* (1916–30) that has never reached the stage, while the same fate has befallen the three operas of the composer and critic Cecil Gray (1895–1951), who at least attempted to give thought to new ideas of musical and dramatic construction.

In *Deirdre* (1937) Gray attempted to resolve the apparent dichotomy between the number opera, with its promiscuity of musical material, and the motivically tight Wagnerian, through-composed form, by making each act thematically exclusive, with the final scene as a kind of musical recapitulation to match Deirdre's recollections of her life.

The Temptation of Saint Anthony (1937) goes virtually to the opposite extreme and attempts to construct a musical continuity of two and a half hours, 'constituting a unified organism from first note to last, and evolving in its entirety from one thematic germ as the oak tree does from the acorn' (Gray 1948: 304). The whole of *The Women of Troy* (1939) is a passacaglia, lasting for an hour and a half.

Three composer–conductors also made a certain mark. *Samuel Pepys* by Albert Coates (1882–1953) dates from 1929 and was first performed in Munich, while his *Pickwick* (1936) has the distinction of being the first opera to appear on television when, in the early months of BBC television transmission and a few weeks before the opera's Covent Garden première in 1936, four scenes were specially staged and broadcast from Alexandra Palace. Despite Coates's conducting experience (he had been principal conductor at the Mariinsky Theatre in St Petersburg), this not un-Russian-sounding work was a failure and he did not venture into opera again until 1952, when *Von Hunks and His Devil* was given in Cape Town. Coates's assistant in St Petersburg, Lawrance Collingwood (1887–1982), became musical director of Sadler's Wells during the war years, but the theatre had earlier seen performances of his *Macbeth* (1934) and, later (1950), mounted a concert performance of *The Death of Tintagiles* (after Maeterlinck). Goossens adopted a more Germanic musical style than many of his contemporaries. *Judith* (1929), the first of his two operas (the other is *Don Juan de Mañara* of 1935 and both are to librettos by Arnold Bennett, based on his plays), utilizes a biblical story revolving around lust and beheading, and draws inevitable comparisons with *Salome* (something the composer disputed at the time of the première). Yet the musical language, while Straussian to a degree, has a distinctive sound-world of its own, though its motivic interest is perhaps too limited for the opera's 70-minute length.

Arthur Benjamin (1893–1960) wrote four operas for the stage. The first is a moral comedy *The Devil Take Her* (1931), a variant of the 'dumb wife' tale that has pervaded literature from the days of Rabelais and Jonson (and thus comparable to Strauss's *Die schweigsame Frau* of 1935). The musical language is tonal, and its 50 minutes are bound together with a strong sense of motivic cohesion. Benjamin's second opera *Prima Donna* (1933, performed 1949) was another one-act comedy, this time about the mayhem caused when two rival eighteenth-century Venetian prima donnas are accidentally invited to perform at the same soirée. The style is again straightforward, with some opportunities for pastiche (particularly in the recitative and coloratura duet for the two singers), and has several set pieces within its otherwise through-composed structure. In the 1950s Benjamin again turned to opera, setting Dickens's *A Tale of Two Cities* (1950, Sadler's Wells 1957) and Molière's moral farce *Tartuffe* (first performed posthumously in 1964). *Mañana* (1956) has the distinction of being the first opera to be commissioned for television production, but reviews of its first broadcast suggest the medium had yet to make the most of its potential and pull itself away from set-bound, 'costume drama' production values. It nevertheless sparked off a whole run of BBC commissions (as well as a few from the newly formed independent network) from such barely remembered works as Joan Trimble's *Blind Raftery* (1957), Richard Arnell's puppet opera *The Petrified Princess* (1958) and Edwin Coleman's *A Christmas Carol* (1962) to more distinguished efforts by Bliss (*Tobias and the Angel*), Britten (*Owen Wingrave*) and Tippett (*New Year*).

IV: Britten

During the Second World War, operatic activity was curtailed more in Britain than elsewhere in Europe (including Germany, Italy and France), where premières of new works continued unabated. In Britain, however, performances in London were virtually brought to a halt and touring, by the Carl Rosa and Sadler's Wells companies, became the order of the day. As soon as the war was over, the latter company returned to its home and a new attempt was begun to establish a national opera company from scratch at the Royal Opera House. The Covent Garden Opera under Karl Rankl's direction soon became the major force in London's operatic life, at that early stage still based around a company of homegrown talent and only occasionally performing operas in the original Italian or German to attract foreign performers in roles (such as the Wagnerian) where British achievement was weaker. The emphasis on sung English and a company ensemble had a fruitful impact on British opera: nine new works were presented in the company's first eight seasons, while activity was still strong at Sadler's Wells, the English Opera Group had been founded to present chamber opera and the Intimate Opera Company began a new policy of developing opera specifically written with piano accompaniment.

But it was the Sadler's Wells company that was to set British opera on a new, confident course. On 7 June 1945, exactly a month after

Germany's surrender, the London theatre reopened with the first performance of Benjamin Britten's *Peter Grimes*. It was an overnight success. Why it was that this single work – a first opera, what is more (discounting his 1941 American operetta collaboration with W. H. Auden, *Paul Bunyan*) – initiated the rebirth of British opera that had defied composers of stature for decades has occupied critics for nearly half a century. It was written in an approachable, tonal idiom (but so was virtually every other British opera before it) and said nothing particularly new in its dramaturgy (following in a direct line of *verismo* from Puccini and in its portrayal of character from Berg). Yet its combination of music and drama and the authority of its stageworthiness were of a quality never before seen in a British opera. While some critics were put off by what they saw as mere 'cleverness' and a too ill-defined central characterization, Desmond Shawe-Taylor's review was fairly typical:

> One can scarcely avoid seeing in Benjamin Britten a fresh hope, not only for English, but for European opera. Constantly, during this past week, audiences at Sadler's Wells have been saying to themselves: 'At last! After so many amateurs, a professional composer of operas!' . . . [The opera's] vigour, audacity and mastery of dramatic movement place it in a different category from the tentative affairs which we have hitherto known . . . In the first ten minutes, before any set pieces bring up the question of 'inspiration', we are convinced that the composer is a born opera-writer. In the light of all that follows, this impression of naturalness, ease and sheer competence may seem a slight virtue to insist on, but it is not. It is the pre-condition which makes all the later flights of imagination possible; it is that quality, the lack of which has strewn the history of English opera with so many distinguished corpses. (*New Statesman*, 16 June 1945, quoted in Brett 1983: 155–6)

Apart from a lull in the 1950s, the opera has held the world-wide stage ever since, and as early as 1948 had reached places as far afield as Stockholm, Los Angeles, Milan and Budapest. One of its strengths is its openness to a diversity of interpretations, most controversially Philip Brett's suggestion that, with its plot of a man at odds with and rejected by an unsympathetic community, it is an allegory based on Britten's own experiences as a homosexual and pacifist in an intolerant British society (1977; he provides further evidence in 1983: 190–96).

The opera's sources in George Crabbe's poem *The Borough* and its composition have been well documented (see in particular Brett 1983), but the quality of its stagecraft, what Ernest Newman described as Britten's conception of the 'drama so entirely in terms of music, and the music so entirely in terms of the drama, that there is no drawing a dividing line between the two' (*The Times*, 24 March 1946, quoted in Brett 1983: 91), is worth reiterating. Two of its most successful scenes are the first and the last. In a manner often compared with the opening of Verdi's *Falstaff*, we are immediately thrown into the bustle and tension of the coroner's inquest and within a few bars musical adjuncts to the characters are evident: Swallow's pompous woodwind phrase, Grimes's pensive, dreamlike chords. As a plausible means of introduction to the characters, each is brought one by one into the courtroom dialogue. For the very last scene, Britten's economy of means comes into its own. Grimes, driven on to the misty beach by the massed people of the Borough, is now close to mental collapse. Accompanied by only a distant fog-horn (tuba) and the offstage reiteration of his name by the populace, the drama is held by Grimes's vocal line, recalling earlier phrases, distorting them and ultimately dissolving into speech when Balstrode advises him to take his boat out to sea and sink it (Ex. 11.6). Between these two scenes all manner of dramatic and operatic devices are brought into play. Atmospheric interludes cover scene changes (for which the obvious precedents are Berg's *Wozzeck* and Shostakovich's *Lady Macbeth of Mtsensk*, both of which Britten admired). A quasi-leitmotivic phrase, first set to the words 'And God have mercy upon me', becomes the theme of the passacaglia interlude. Brief set pieces, including arias as well as choruses – Grimes's 'Now the Great Bear and Pleiades' (in effect a miniature for tenor and strings redolent of his song cycles) and the ensemble 'Old Joe has gone fishing' among them – blend subtly within the general dramatic flow, the overall tension losing nothing from such moments of reflection and colour.

For his next opera Britten scaled down his forces to a mere eight singers and twelve instrumentalists (plus accompanist/conductor). *The Rape of Lucretia* (1946) was commissioned for the post-war reopening of Glyndebourne's opera house. It began not only a stream of chamber operas in the years to come (though of course Holst's *Sāvitri* dated from as far back as 1908) but also ultimately resulted in the formation of the English Opera Group, which gave the genre a considerable boost, performing not only Britten's operas, but also commissioning works from composers as diverse as Walton and Musgrave (see below). *Lucretia* amply showed what was possible with restricted forces; Britten's ingenuity with the scoring, for example, is just as effective in creating atmosphere as was the full symphony orchestra in *Grimes*. Ronald Duncan's libretto has suffered criticism

Ex. 11.6 Britten: *Peter Grimes*, Act III, sc.ii

in its time and indeed its rather pompous versification tends to distract from the immediacy of the dialogue. A commenting chorus (a soprano and tenor) is amply used to set scene and character, but its over-use lends a distancing effect (deliberate, but perhaps ultimately unfortunate) to an involvement in the tragedy, while the Christian gloss (derived from Duncan's source in André Obey's play *Le viol de Lucrèce*) can have a similar effect.

From tragedy, Britten turned to comedy. But *Albert Herring* (1947) has a related theme, one which, like that of the individual versus the community in *Grimes*, it was now becoming clear would be a leitmotif running through all his operatic work: the loss or violation of innocence. In *Grimes* this could be said to be represented by the young apprentice's harsh treatment at Peter's hands. In the comedy, based on a Maupassant story, a Suffolk village boy is elected King of the May (in the absence of a suitable Queen), has his drink at his 'coronation' ceremony laced with alcohol and goes off on an adventure of self-discovery. After the broad sweep of *Grimes*, *Albert Herring* is a particularly detailed work, with a witty libretto by Eric Crozier and an emphasis on the minutiae of characterization and social comedy in the words and music that tend to make the working out of the plot itself seem slow-moving.

Even *The Little Sweep*, at the heart of his children's entertainment *Let's Make an Opera* (1949), shares Britten's theme of corruption, centred as it is around the practice of sending young boys up chimneys. The first half of the work consists of the preparations for putting on an opera, including rehearsals and constructing scenery. *The Little Sweep* itself is then performed as this opera, Britten's first masterpiece for child performers, one that involves the adults as well through some of the older roles and audience participation in the choruses that form the interludes between scenes.

With *Billy Budd*, composed for Covent Garden's contribution to the 1951 Festival of Britain, Britten returned to the scale of grand opera. It began as a work in four acts, but for a broadcast in 1960 and its stage revival in 1964 he contracted it into two, and in this form it is arguably the finest of his operas. Setting a prose text by E. M. Forster and Eric Crozier (apart from the condensed Shakespeare of *A Midsummer Night's Dream*, the best libretto he was ever given), its drama, characterization and musical power exceed even *Grimes*. Not only is the libretto detailed in its evocation of life on a man o'war, but the music too ranges through the whole gamut of atmosphere from impenetrable mist to sunlit preparations for battle. In the same

MUSIC AND DRAMA

way that the true dramatic climax of *Grimes* is effectively reached through the most minimal of musical means, so the crux of *Budd* (when Captain Vere informs the young man of his death sentence) is on paper nothing more than a sequence of variously scored, equal-length triadic chords. Elsewhere too there is an economy of musical material that yet manages to express volumes. In the same way that the passacaglia motif pervades *Grimes*, here a short note pattern (Ex. 11.7a) is again used in a quasi-leitmotivic way to mark crucial points in the libretto, usually in the context of talk of mutiny, but also as a kind of 'calling-card' for Billy himself. Ex. 11.7 illustrates Britten's use of musical motif in his operas, though it is more prevalent in *Billy Budd* than elsewhere, and in none of his operas does the leitmotivic element dominate the musical argument in a Wagnerian way, usually being limited to one salient motif per work.

The next opera was also a special commission for a national occasion, this time for Elizabeth II's coronation in 1953. One of Britten's least appreciated operas (perhaps partly as a legacy of its early cool reception), *Gloriana* centres around the relationship between the first Elizabeth and Essex (hence the thought at its Covent Garden première that this was unsuitable material to mark a coronation). By the nature of its subject, there is more ceremonial than in the earlier operas, but ultimately this has the dramatic effect of counterpointing the public Elizabeth with her private, emotional turmoil over Essex's apparent treachery.

Britten returned to the chamber medium for *The Turn of the Screw* (1954). As *Billy Budd* represents the peak of his achievement in grand opera, so this adaptation of Henry James's ghost story is his most successful chamber opera. Again picking up on his favourite theme, here the innocence of two children is undermined by the ghosts of their former valet and governess. The turning of this screw is represented musically by a twisting 12-note idea (essentially an alternation of 4ths and 3rds) that is subjected to a set of variations, one forming each of the interludes between the almost cinematic succession of scenes. Despite being Britten's most highly organized score (the 12-note theme is rooted in tonality, incidentally) it is also one of his most dramatically effective, with the same instrumental ensemble used in *Lucretia* and *Albert Herring* here employed to conjure up a totally different world of ghostly atmosphere, ambiguity and emotion.

The sea returned in Britten's next stage work. *Noye's Fludde* (1957) is a setting of the Chester Mystery Play and perhaps his most successful marrying of professional and amateur forces. The score calls for two

ART MUSIC

Ex. 11.7   Britten: *Billy Budd*

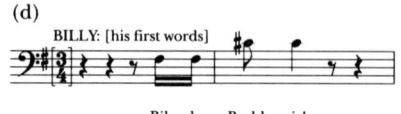

(a) Prologue

VERE: O what have I done?

(b) Act I, sc.i

CHORUS: O heave! O heave a-way, heave! O heave!

(c)

MAINTOP: Boat a-hoy!

(d)

BILLY: [his first words] Bil-ly Budd, sir!

(e)

BILLY: Fare-well to you for ev-er! Fare-well, Rights o' Man.

(f) Act I, sc.ii
[*senza misura*]

SAILING MASTER: Spit-head, the Nore, the float-ing re-pub-lic.

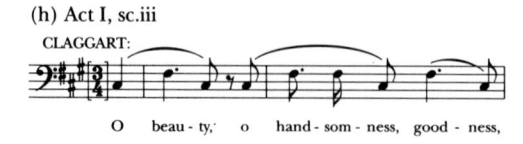

(g)

VERE: Oh, that's noth-ing.

(h) Act I, sc.iii

CLAGGART: O beau-ty, o hand-som-ness, good-ness,

(i) NOVICE: And it's gone too far,

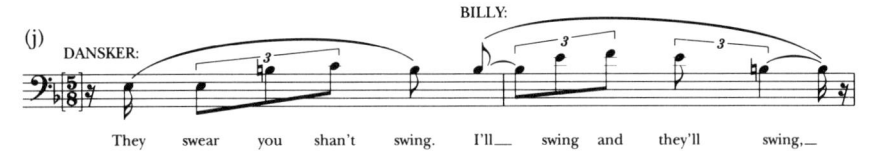

(j) DANSKER: They swear you shan't swing. BILLY: I'll swing and they'll swing,

(k) Act II, sc.iv
CHORUS:
(wordless)

(l) Epilogue
VERE: O what have I done?

adult singers (Mr and Mrs Noye), six solo child voices, a chorus of children as the animals and an instrumental ensemble combining professional players with string and percussion parts (including an infamous set of tuned tea-cups) suitable for schoolchildren. As in *The Little Sweep*, the audience (or rather 'congregation' in this case) is again involved, this time in three hymns that punctuate the telling of the story, culminating in Addison's 'The spacious firmament' to Tallis's magnificent canon.

For *A Midsummer Night's Dream* (1960), Britten and Peter Pears condensed Shakespeare's play into what is undoubtedly the most successful Shakespearean opera since Verdi. The subject matter calls for an ear for atmosphere and this Britten provides with his most magical and glittering score. The three worlds of fairies, mechanicals (here called the rustics) and lovers are each musically differentiated by instrumentation (generally speaking strings, brass and woodwind, respectively) and vocal assignment – Oberon, for example, is a countertenor. Together with a mastery of atmosphere, from the glissandi strings' opening to the Mendelssohnian chord sequence that frames the scenes in Act II, Britten also reveals a brilliance in broad comedy hardly felt since the days of *Paul Bunyan*, with the rustics' play in the last act stealing the show through its parodies of Verdian arias.

Music from the Far East had already influenced the score of the ballet *The Prince of the Pagodas* (see below) and in particular his writing for percussion, but Britten's visit to Japan in the mid-1950s also inspired in him the idea for a new kind of operatic treatment, the church parable. The Japanese influence came from the ritualistic noh dramas he had seen in Tokyo and the story of the best known of these, *Sumidagawa* (which had already inspired a work 40 years before by the conductor Clarence Raybould), was translated to an East Anglian setting as *Curlew River* (1964). Like the noh play, the drama is performed in masks by monks who process in, take on their dramatic roles and enact the story of a madwoman who finds redemption in her search for her dead son. Musically, Britten's instrumental writing had never been so sparse and there is also a harshening (especially after the richly endowed gestures of *A Midsummer Night's Dream* and the *War Requiem*) of his harmonic and melodic language. Two more church parables followed, *The Burning Fiery Furnace* (1966) and *The Prodigal Son* (1968), of which the former, with the same ensemble exploited for a greater richness of instrumental and harmonic colour, is the finer.

Owen Wingrave (1970) has suffered something of the fate of *Gloriana*, though more this time as a result of its origins as a work specially commissioned for a studio-based television recording. It was reworked for the stage, but its cross-weaving of scenes remains somewhat detrimental to its effectiveness away from the context of television. Based on another ghost story by Henry James, in this case about a pacifist who tries to rebel against his militarily obsessed family (and ancestors), it restores several of Britten's favourite themes and ideas. If *Grimes* has been identified as an allegory on the state of alienation from society for his pacifism and homosexuality, Owen is the personification of the pacifist in Britten, while his next and last opera, *Death in Venice* (1973), might be said to bring out into the open the homosexuality (though in Mann's original novella the emphasis is more on the fact of an ageing writer coming face to face with beauty, than that that object of beauty happens to be male). The opera is virtually a monologue for Aschenbach, with the various guises of the 'messenger of death', from the mysterious traveller who inspires the writer with the idea to go south of the Alps to the tempting, symbolic voice of Dionysus, taken by a single baritone. Mann's novella throws more than the usual problems for the operatic adaptor, which Britten and his librettist Myfanwy Piper (who also wrote the texts for the two James operas) overcome with characteristic ingenuity. Tadzio is portrayed by a silent dancer, making him more distant and intangible than if he were to sing, while the trap of dramatic monotony is avoided by a swift, cinematic flow of scenes charting Aschenbach's inexorable decline. Musically the whole is held together by a typical brief leitmotivic phrase (compare *Grimes*, *Lucretia* and *Budd*) representing *la serenissima* and an almost gamelan-inspired use of tuned percussion as an adjunct to Tadzio and his companions.

V: Opera in the Wake of Britten

Given Britten's success in the 1940s, it is not surprising to find many other composers, particularly of his own and earlier generations, deciding to give opera a try. Composers such as Walton, Bliss and Berkeley, all well established for a decade or two, only now took up the challenge. But almost without exception, none of their often valiant attempts has survived in the repertoire, as if Britten's presence and hold on the operatic stage was so strong that it stifled the chances of others.

Of Britten's contemporaries, Arthur Bliss was one of the first after *Peter Grimes* to get an opera on to the stage. He collaborated with J. B. Priestley on *The Olympians*, which was performed at Covent Garden in 1949 and has never been seen on the professional stage since. A couple of concert performances have revived faith in its musical qualities, among them the strong characterization and his usual skill in orchestration. Despite his experiences in films and ballet, however, Bliss's dramatic talents were ultimately not up to the challenge of turning an unconvincing plot and unoperatic libretto into a viable piece of comic theatre. But the two worlds of reality and the supernatural do not interact with the skill of the two better-known 'midsummer' operas by Britten and Tippett (see below). Bliss's second opera, *Tobias and the Angel*, was commissioned by BBC television and produced and transmitted in 1960. Published in a form for stage presentation it is musically less distinctive but more of a piece dramatically than its predecessor.

William Walton recalled that in the late 1940s,

opera was very much in the air in London . . . Ben had written *Peter Grimes* for the Sadler's Wells Theatre in Islington, and I thought it was not a good thing for British opera to have only one opera by one composer. I thought it my duty to try and write an opera. (quoted in Walton 1988: 133)

ART MUSIC

With his librettist Christopher Hassall he turned to the Chaucerian/Boccaccian sources of the *Troilus and Cressida* story (rather than the Shakespeare, which they both felt dealt too unkindly with Cressida). Despite its perceived shortcomings of libretto and dramatic prowess, *Troilus and Cressida* (1954) was by no means an outright failure in terms of audience and critical appreciation, and its 1976 revision tightened the structure, improving its stageworthiness. Yet its romantic idiom, though assured and not uninteresting in its own way, was even then dated and said nothing new musically beyond the bittersweet style that had been Walton's trademark since the 1930s. Not put off by his experiences, however, Walton leapt at Peter Pears's suggestion to write a short chamber opera based on Chekhov for the English Opera Group to perform in Aldeburgh. *The Bear* (1967) succeeds where *Troilus* did not: its libretto (by Paul Dehn) is ideally suited to its subject matter and the music finds Walton revelling in the witty manner of his *Façade* and *Scapino*, with parody and deft orchestration abounding.

Berkeley's *Nelson* was another attempt to respond to Britten, though with a historico-realist drama rather in the manner of *Budd* and *Gloriana* than of Walton's Italianate romantic tragedy. With *Budd*, of course, there is the similarity of a naval setting, though in *Nelson* the sea is more incidental to the working out of the relationships between the Admiral, his wife and Emma Hamilton than an elemental force in its own right. It was well received in 1954, but has not seen the professional stage again, perhaps unjustifiably since, for all its faults, its sophistication and sheer musical value merit revival. Concurrently with work on *Nelson* Berkeley composed a one-act comedy to a text by Dehn, *A Dinner Engagement* (1954), about an impoverished aristocratic couple faced with entertaining a visiting Grand Duchess and her son. As a comic entertainment it is a delight, allowing Berkeley to exploit the Gallic side of his musical make-up and revealing a mastery of characterization and ingenuity in his use of chamber forces (it was another English Opera Group commission for Aldeburgh).

Ruth (1956), based on the Old Testament story to a libretto by Eric Crozier, has been criticized for its static, tableau-like nature. But this is not so out of place for its subject matter (compare Poulenc and Messiaen). Peter Dickinson compares it musically with early Tippett:

When the dance element comes in . . . there is a suggestion of the Tippett of *The Midsummer Marriage*. . . The choruses in *Ruth* use Tippett's type of varied metres, without his sense of unbarred sprung rhythm, and a kind of diatonic polyphony where a rough voice-leading effect may be more important than the actual notes. (1988: 182)

For his last completed opera he turned again to Paul Dehn. A companion to *A Dinner Engagement*, *Castaway* (1967) is based on an episode in the sixth book of Homer's *Odyssey* and constitutes a single act of four scenes connected by interludes, with a musical style that seems to consolidate his later harmonic astringency together with his earlier French-inspired lyricism.

But Berkeley's style seems positively modernist beside that of some of his younger contemporaries, such as William Alwyn, Malcolm Arnold and Wilfred Josephs, who continued to work in what might be described as the traditional medium of operatic writing, using typically epic, romantic and/or historical subjects in the Verdian and Puccinian mould (some with little apparent musical advance on that age). Alwyn's most substantial operatic work was *Miss Julie*. He fashioned his own text, based on the Strindberg play, and composed the music between 1974 and 1977. The musical style is not especially original, though Alwyn uses this accepted late-romantic language to good effect: 'Miss Julie's vocal line creeps questioningly around chromatic intervals as though trying to find the tonal centre – a perfect musical representation of her character' (Milnes 1983). Arnold wrote operas that have made little headway despite his idiomatic approachability. *Henri Christophe* was abandoned after only 25 pages of full score. His librettist Joe Mendoza also contributed the text for *The Dancing Master* (1951), a one-act comic opera that still awaits a professional stage performance. *The Open Window* (1956), based on a short story by Saki making for a better libretto (by Sidney Gilliat), is a 20-minute miniature with chamber orchestra. Josephs, however, has fared differently. He chose a romantic subject for his most successful opera, *Rebecca* (Leeds 1983), based on Daphne du Maurier's novel and already the subject of a well-known film. Despite its innate musical conservatism – 'Poulencian Palm Court in the Riviera rubbing shoulders with Brittenesque chiaroscuro in Cornwall', in the words of Martin Dreyer (1983) – it proved highly stageworthy and a successful work with audiences. Dreyer went on to describe it as the first 'musical soap-opera', an apt description for its easily digestible music and romanticism.

Of composers who worked in a generally traditional language but began to make more of the varied possibilities of operatic form and substance, Elizabeth Maconchy, Denis ApIvor (*b* 1916), Philip Cannon (*b* 1929) and Phyllis Tate (*b* 1911) each made moderate experiments. Although of an earlier generation, Maconchy's first work in this field dates from the mid-1950s, but her best comes from more than a decade later with such works as *The Birds* (1968), a comedy after Aristophanes, and the ambitious children's opera after Ruskin, *The King of the Golden River* (1975). Interspersed with these is a trilogy of one-acters (first performed as such in 1977), *The Sofa* (1957), *The Departure* (1961) and *The Three Strangers* (1958–67). In all these works, Maconchy's music remains approachable, lacking the more acerbic style prevalent in her chamber music.

ApIvor's operas have ranged widely in their stylistic explorations. *She Stoops to Conquer* (1947) is a neoclassical *opera buffa* not far from being a pastiche of Donizetti, while *Yerma* (1958), commissioned by Sadler's Wells (who subsequently refused to perform it) to a libretto by Montagu Slater, makes use of a 12-note row, though treated tonally. *Ubu Roi* (1966), on the other hand, anticipates Toovey's *Ubu* in its source and Birtwistle's *Punch and Judy* with its anarchic sense of farce.

Cannon's first opera, *Morvoren* (RCM 1964), harks back to Smyth's *The Wreckers* with its Cornish setting and its expression of 'the eternal struggle of land people against the elemental sea' (Cannon 1964), as well as the strong role the village's religious community plays in the story of a mermaid who lures a young man to his death in the sea. The music's fluency was well appreciated and resulted in two commissions which were realized over the ensuing decade: *Dr Jekyll and Mr Hyde* (1973) for television and *The Man from Venus* (1967).

Tate's *The Lodger* (1960) was described by Harold Rosenthal as 'other than *Peter Grimes* ... probably the most successful "first opera" by a native composer since the war' when first performed at the RAM. Based on a novel about Jack the Ripper (the lodger of the title) it is a rather effective psycho-drama, with plenty of apt characterization in the music and a strong dramatic flow. It has not, however, lived up to Rosenthal's expectations and gained a foothold in the regular operatic repertoire.

Nor has the short chamber work based on Molière's *Les précieuses ridicules*, *If the Cap Fits* (1956) by Geoffrey Bush, its failings summed up by Raymond Leppard as 'a poor plot, a totally inadequate libretto and derivative music' (1965). This was written for the Intimate Opera Company, founded by Antony Hopkins (*b* 1921) and Joseph Horovitz (*b* 1926) in 1952 to foster a repertoire of piano-accompanied works for small venues. Hopkins's own operas from the time were similarly traditional in their tonal language and lack of dramatic ambition. *Ten O'Clock Call* (1956), for example, is a rather feeble satire on an operatic rehearsal and less successful than the earlier Intimate Opera vehicle *Three's Company* (1954). Hopkins has ventured into other realms of opera: *Lady Rohesia* is a full-length work given at Sadler's Wells in 1948, *The Man from Tuscany* a dramatic work for the choristers of Canterbury Cathedral and *Rich Man, Poor Man, Beggar Man, Saint* a choral opera on the life of St Francis. All are dogged by a musical style that is more pastiche than originality. The same might be said of the two very approachable one-act operas by Horovitz, *The Dumb Wife* and *Gentleman's Island*.

Musical conservatism found a partner in political radicalism in, to varying degrees, the operas of Alan Bush, Inglis Gundry and Arnold Cooke. Politics and social comment had been no strangers to opera in the first half of the century, but politically radical composers such as Smyth and Holbrooke kept their music free of polemic. With Alan Bush, however, left-wing thought first became overt in operatic writing. As a committed Communist he allied himself with the pronouncements of the so-called Zhdanov decrees that emerged from the Soviet Union's 1948 Conference of Russian Composers and Musicologists, calling for a greater simplicity and nationalism in music. This influence was most evident in his four operas, all on political subjects and dominated, for the same reasons as with Boughton (for a time Bush's colleague as a choral conductor), by the chorus. *Wat Tyler* (1950), about the 1388 Peasants' Revolt, set the pattern for his other operas in the way it achieved its greatest popularity to the east of the Iron Curtain, particularly the former East Germany (the première was in 1953 in Leipzig). *Men of Blackmoor* (1955, Weimar 1956) is set during a miners' strike in the 1820s, *The Sugar Reapers* (1964, Leipzig 1966) is about the black workers' rights movement in the USA, and *Joe Hill: the Man Who Never Died* (1967, East Berlin 1970) about the composer of workers' songs (for synopses of all four operas see Stevenson 1980).

Similarly, Inglis Gundry (*b* 1905), whose teaching career has included lecturing for the Workers' Educational Association, has taken socially and politically aware subjects for his operas. *The Partisans* (1946), for example, has a plot set among the anti-Fascist resistance fighters in the Balkans during the then recently concluded Second World War. But his prolific output of some dozen operatic works (the earliest going back before the war to *Naaman: the Leprosy of War* of 1937, and *The Return of Odysseus* of 1938) also includes a pair of church operas, *The Three Wise Men* (1967) and *The Prisoner Paul* (1970) and a comic chamber opera with an Arthurian setting, *A Will of Her Own* (1973). Their generally simple, uncomplicated style has made them suitable for amateur performers, with the result that they have rarely broken out beyond the fringe and semi-professional performing scene.

Arnold Cooke studied with Hindemith in Berlin and shared his penchant for *Gebrauchsmusik*, which was reflected in a rather simple, even naive, style. Though not as politically active as Bush, he took a socially apposite story for his first opera, *Mary Barton* (1954), about the Chartist movement in industrial Lancashire during the 1840s. It suffers from being too melodramatic and has too obvious an opposition between good and bad – 'the idle frivolities of the rich versus the agonized struggle of the poor', in the words of Francis Routh (1972: 87).

Politics have not only had an ideological impact on composers. The rise of fascism in Europe in the 1930s and 1940s led many musicians to emigrate from the personal and artistic restrictions of their home countries, and a number found refuge in Britain. Among them were the composers Roberto Gerhard (from Franco's Spain in 1939), Franz Reizenstein (1911–68), Berthold Goldschmidt (*b* 1903) (both from Berlin, in 1934 and 1935 respectively), and, from Vienna in 1938, Egon Wellesz. Gerhard, who had studied with both Granados and Schoenberg before settling in Britain, wrote a single opera, *The Duenna* (1945–7); based like Prokofiev's slightly earlier *Betrothal in a Monastery* on Sheridan's comedy, it shows little influence of the music of his new home. It is an unusual amalgam of several styles: the Spanish idiom of his fellow countrymen, Schoenbergian dodecaphony and a neoclassicism that remarkably anticipates Stravinsky's *The Rake's Progress* of only two years later. Although broadcast as early as 1949, it reached the stage for the first time only in 1992 in Madrid. Although Goldschmidt, Reizenstein and Wellesz all brought with them elements of the central Austro-German musical tradition, each in turn attempted an opera in English. The first was Goldschmidt, whose *Beatrice Cenci* (1950), after Shelley, won one of the Arts Council's four special Festival of Britain opera awards in 1951. In that year, Wellesz's *Incognita* was given in Oxford, a Straussian comedy somewhat at odds with the Schoenbergian, classically inspired operas of his Vienna years. Finally, Reizenstein wrote a couple of radio operas, of which the first, *Anna Kraus*, was heard in 1952. The next, post-war influx of musicians was from countries with historical, often colonial links with Britain, such as Australia and South Africa.

MUSIC AND DRAMA

While both countries had established musical traditions of their own, neither seemed to offer the quality of education or the wealth of culture to be found in London. The operas of John Joubert (*b* 1927), who arrived from South Africa in the 1950s, follow closely in the Britten tradition, both in their choice of subjects and in the proportion of works written for children to perform (such as the school opera *The Wayfarers*). *Antigone* was composed as a radio opera for the BBC in 1954, while *In the Drought* (1956) was one of the few works from his early years in Britain to draw on his South African origins. The three-act *Silas Marner* (1961) is based on the story by George Eliot about 'an outcast redeemed by human love' (Chisholm 1961). His next three-act opera, *Under Western Eyes* (1969), after Conrad's novel of a man caught up in political and revolutionary activities, shares the same overall theme. Both are 'number' operas, with a musical language firmly rooted in tonality and (again like Britten) cleverly carved out of often the most basic material. Joubert's own words (1969) show his Brittenesque techniques: '*Under Western Eyes* is also pre-eminently a singers' opera . . . the characters reveal and express themselves through what they sing (as in Verdi) rather than let the orchestra do it for them (as in Wagner).'

As first operas go, *Our Man in Havana* (1963) by Malcolm Williamson (who arrived from Australia in 1953) achieved some success with its première at Sadler's Wells, gaining a revival a season later. An adaptation of Graham Greene's thriller set in Cuba, it was one of the first British operas to have a truly contemporary and realistic setting. It is cast essentially in number form, though there are few pauses in the music. It was followed by a totally different kind of opera, *The English Eccentrics* (Aldeburgh 1964); indeed, it is less a true opera than an entertainment and sequence of character studies in the tradition of Edith Sitwell, whose book of the same title, relating accounts of real eccentrics, provided the source. Two children's operas followed, *The Happy Prince* (1965) and *Julius Caesar Jones* (1966), which showed a musical debt to Britten.

For *The Violins of Saint-Jacques* (1966), Williamson made the controversial move of toning down any modernisms in his musical style to produce a romantic melodrama with music to match the luxuriant decadence of its Caribbean setting. Stephen Walsh described this idiom as 'modern–romantic, with simple tunes spiced by bitonal harmonies . . . Williamson thus restores the grand operatic conventions of the solo aria and the concerted ensemble, and reinstates accompanied melody as the crucial factor in his musical scheme'

(1966). Next came another children's opera, *Dunstan and the Devil* (1967), a somewhat sub-Brittenesque work, then two works based on Strindberg (compare Alwyn), the chamber opera *The Growing Castle* (1968) and the pantomime-like *Lucky-Peter's Journey* (1969). His most recent full-scale opera, *The Red Sea*, dates from 1972, his rate of composition having slowed considerably since the facility shown in the 1960s. These last works were joined by his exploration of short operas with audience participation he named 'cassations': *The Moonrakers* (1967), *Knights in Shining Armour*, *The Snow Wolf* (both 1968), *Genesis*, *The Stone Wall* (both 1971) and *The Winter Star* (1973).

From immigrants to British-born composers who have spent much of their working lives in America: Thea Musgrave, Richard Rodney Bennett, Iain Hamilton and Nicholas Maw. Musgrave's first chamber opera *The Abbot of Drimock* (1955) reflects the influence of the Second Viennese School and includes passages of *Sprechstimme*. Her second, *The Voice of Ariadne* (1973), is loosely based on a short story by Henry James, *The Last of the Valerii*, and was composed for the English Opera Group to perform at the 1974 Aldeburgh Festival. These facts invite comparison with Britten's James operas, yet, as Stephen Walsh has written, it is 'not a ghost opera but a psychological drama and a fable, about the reconciliation of the quest for an ideal love with the need, in real life, to find love where we can' (1974a). Such overt romanticism sets it apart from Britten (the nearest comparison might be *Gloriana*), as does the musical treatment, where gesture and cumulative drama prevail. Notable too is the use of a pre-recorded tape carrying the disembodied voice of Ariadne. The librettist of *Ariadne*, Amalia Elguera, also provided in her play *Moray* the source of Musgrave's next opera, *Mary, Queen of Scots* (1976). It makes much use of the pageantry of its historical setting and includes a number of sixteenth-century musical touches. Musgrave's own style matured further with this opera, with expressive writing of an emotionalism perhaps a little out of tune with the times, not least in *A Christmas Carol* (1979), her first opera for her adopted home of Norfolk, Virginia. Bennett's operatic career began with *The Ledge* (1961), a highly effective 35-minute one-acter. He had already gained a reputation as a composer of film music, a fact that Cornelius Cardew, reviewing the first performance, thought 'relevant as follows: too often he has subordinated his musical ideas to the drama. Thus, the music does not represent the drama, nor transcend the words; it backs up the drama and articulates the words' (1961). A similar characteristic dogged his later operas. *The Mines of Sulphur*

(1965) has a more assured sense of dramatic pacing than the earlier work, but here, as in *Victory* (1969), based on Conrad, there is still the sense that he has tried unsuccessfully to impose his film experience's emphasis on carefully calculated small-term effect on to a grander dramatic design. Separating these two works is the comedy *A Penny for a Song* (1967), a rather successful adaptation of John Whiting's satirical play about English soldiery.

Hamilton (a pupil of Alwyn) became an advocate of serialism, until his move into opera brought a gradual tempering towards a more overtly romantic style. In the composer's own words, his first successful opera, *The Royal Hunt of the Sun* (1968), is 'basically tonal though not in a classical sense' (1977). An adaptation of Peter Shaffer's play about the Spanish conquest of the Incas in Peru, it musically failed to live up to the theatricality of its libretto. *The Cataline Conspiracy* (1973), a well-received neo-Verdian work commissioned by Scottish Opera (see Besch 1974), returned to an atonal language, though one that was no longer serial. The 'lyric drama' after Marlowe, *Tamburlaine* (1976), was commissioned as a radio opera by the BBC and made the most of the lack of visual and physical restraints to create a fast-flowing drama of some 24 scenes over a 90-minute span. But this very density of incident and lack of visual stimulus to aid the appreciation of the drama led critics to wonder whether the concept of radio opera might indeed be a contradiction in terms. One of Hamilton's most conspicuous successes was his adaptation of Tolstoy's *Anna Karenina* (1978), for which his musical language appropriately reached its most lyrical and romantic state, with a score that even drifts towards a mixture of Ravel and Strauss (Richard and Johann) for a sumptuous ballroom scene. Maw's first opera, the comedy *One Man Show* (1964), commissioned by the London County Council (the first local authority commission of an opera), ultimately failed to live up to the hopes sown by his acclaimed proto-operatic *Scenes and Arias* in 1962. *The Rising of the Moon* (1970) fared better. Another comedy, it was first performed at Glyndebourne, but has only more recently received further productions (Guildhall School; Wexford).

Gordon Crosse's first opera, the one-act *Purgatory* (1966), was commissioned for the Cheltenham Festival and is a virtually intact setting of Yeats's play. Crosse consciously modelled it on *The Turn of the Screw* with tonal treatment of a 12-note row, though there the similarity ends. *The Grace of Todd* (1968) was composed as a companion piece but is less skilfully put together. *The Story of Vasco*

(1968–73, Sadler's Wells 1974) is a motivically taut number opera to a libretto by Ted Hughes based on a French play by Georges Schehadé, and was described by Leslie East as 'rather over-indulgent, weak in dramatic tension but full of warm lyricism' (1975).

David Blake's two operas lie roughly a decade apart. *Toussaint* (ENO 1977) expresses the struggle for power in the Caribbean island of Haiti in an epic but dramatically cluttered manner in which the political message of the moral dangers of racism overrides any subtlety in the characterization. *The Plumber's Gift* (ENO 1989) is less easy to classify. Its combination of comedy, surrealism and a mythic gloss on the relationships of its down-to-earth characters owes a certain debt to Tippett, but the music is more overtly late romantic and the drama more straightforwardly theatrical.

Despite the establishment of Welsh National Opera in 1946, there was little attempt to establish an operatic tradition in the Welsh language. Between the wars, David de Lloyd (1883–1948) had composed a pair of operas in Welsh, *Gwellian* (1924) and *Tir na n-og* (1930), the latter a ballad-style opera on an Ossianic theme. Yet, in later years, more or less the sole adventurer was Arwel Hughes (1909–88), whose *Menna* (1951, based on a Welsh folk legend) and *Serch yw'r Doctor* (1960, after Molière's *Le docteur amoureux*) were both premièred by WNO (the latter at the National Eisteddfod). The single operatic attempt by Grace Williams (1906–77), *The Parlour* (1966) (see Boyd 1980), was in English; like Britten's *Albert Herring* it adapts a de Maupassant story (*En famille*) to an English setting (here a Victorian seaside town), and does not escape comparison with Britten's Suffolk comedy in terms of character delineation and (to a lesser extent) musical content.

It was another eight years before Wales saw the première of another full-length, homegrown opera, Alun Hoddinott's *The Beach of Falesá* (1974), no more Welsh in setting than *The Parlour*. It is an adaptation of Stevenson's tale of voodoo and corruption in the South Seas given, like Williamson's *The Violins of Saint-Jacques*, a suitably luxuriant orchestral setting. It uses a 12-note row, but, as so often, in a far from atonal context and a language that does nothing to hide its dramatic shortcomings. Three more operas followed in quick succession, two of them, *The Magician* (1976) and *The Rajah's Diamond* (1979), for television, the third, *What the Old Man Does Is Always Right* (1977), an adaptation of Hans Christian Andersen by Britten's librettist Myfanwy Piper. Similarly, William Mathias avoided the Welsh language and folklore in his only theatre opera *The Servants* (WNO 1980), based on the novel by Iris Murdoch.

Scottish opera took even longer to establish itself, partly owing to the fact that a permanent company came into existence only in 1962; soon afterwards it instituted a positive commissioning policy. One of the first fruits was *Full Circle* (1967) by Robin Orr (*b* 1909), a Bergian (in the sense of musical style as well as subject matter), 35-minute chamber opera set in the Glaswegian slums during the 1930s Depression and with a libretto in Glaswegian dialect (the score provides a 'translation'). Other Scottish composers, such as Iain Hamilton and Thea Musgrave, have largely sought their success south of the border or in America, though the latter has used explicitly Scottish subject matter in her *Mary, Queen of Scots* (see above). Only in more recent years have composers such as Judith Weir actively turned, for the first time since the nineteenth century, to the wealth of Scottish folklore and history (see below).

VI: New Paths

If Britten and some of his contemporaries and successors might be said to represent the Verdian, *verismo* manner of operatic writing, Michael Tippett in a generalized way returned British opera to the more Wagnerian mythic form of drama, though bypassing the merely pictorial presentations of myth of Boughton's generation. Tippett was one of the first composers in the twentieth century to make the mythic archetype his subject matter for the expression and illumination of concepts rather than 'mere' stories, something at the heart of all five of his stage works.

For *The Midsummer Marriage* (1946–52) he created his own myth, perceivably drawn from the same line as *Die Zauberflöte* and *Die Frau ohne Schatten*, in broad terms about the trials and spiritual maturation undergone by a young couple before they are ready to marry. Such a theme grew from his extensive studies of Jung and his ideas of the interaction between the different facets of the personality to achieve a balance between the feminine *anima* (in every man) and the masculine *animus* (in every woman). Thus in Tippett's opera, Mark and Jenifer (their royal Cornish names a deliberate choice) are at first rebuffed by the immature, incomplete personalities within themselves and in each other, and through a series of stylized spiritual experiences (including a series of Ritual Dances in which they are represented by dancers enacting a female hunting a male in various animal guises) are brought to an ecstatic reunion – a union of the *anima* and *animus* within each of them as well as on the level of the *animus* (= Mark) with the *anima* (= Jenifer).

In the light of this, Ian Kemp sees the work as less an opera than 'a dramatic allegory' (Tippett's earliest plans were for a 'masque') where the 'drama is precipitated not by human interaction or the obvious laws of cause and effect but by the inner impulses of individuals' (1984: 210 – Kemp deals at length with both the Jungian and the Greek dramatic theory basis to the plot, while John Lloyd Davies (1985: 55) provides annotations to the complete libretto of sources and allusions). For an opera audience used to a more conventional plot and characters (Wieland Wagner's Jungian interpretations of his grandfather's works at Bayreuth had yet to penetrate further afield), much of this went over its head at the time of the première in 1955, and it took another decade or more for *The Midsummer Marriage* to be recognized as the original masterpiece it is. The composer's own libretto was a major stumbling-block, and it certainly has its weaknesses in its obtusenesses and idiosyncrasies; but the music was appreciated from an early date, though there were those disappointed by its lack of true modernity.

Like Britten, Tippett proved there was still life in tonality if the composer was possessed of the originality to achieve new ends. *The Midsummer Marriage* marks the summation of Tippett's first-period compositional style where counterpoint reigns supreme and rules the harmonic sequences, as much in the obviously contrapuntal string quartets as in the full orchestral forces at play in the opera. Tippett makes significant use of the cycle of 5ths in progressions between areas of 'light' and 'shadow', while different kinds of music underlie the worlds of reality and magic: flutes, celesta, muted horns and trumpets delineate the latter (compare the flutes and bells of *Die Zauberflöte*), and its sense of 'unchanging ritual' (symbolized by the Ancients) is given a pseudo-antique, or baroque, style. Melodically, the opera bursts with lyrical profusion, and its 'semi-concealed' number structure allows for many points of repose in arias and choruses, which are all united in a music of boundless energy and ecstasy.

As if Tippett had used up his capacity for such expression in his first opera, for his second, *King Priam* (1958–61), the energy remained, but the musical and dramatic language underwent quite a drastic transformation, comparable (and not unrelated stylistically) to that between the Stravinsky of *The Firebird* and, say, *Les noces*. The sound-world is drier, sparer, indeed more Stravinskian and less tonally based, with wind and percussion dominating the orchestral sounds and vocal lines of greater angularity and extremes of expression. The large-scale tonal plan and 'symphonic' development of his first opera are replaced by a mosaic structure of alternating and intermingling blocks of music. Also of significance is Tippett's turning away from a self-created myth to one of more general familiarity, though the drama still remains as important beyond its immediate storytelling, a parable about choice and its relationship to unchangeable fate.

The Knot Garden (1966–9) returned again to an invented plot and another in which the 'theme' might be said to be the spiritual enlightenment of its protagonists: a psychoanalyst employed by a couple (whose marriage is in shreds) to help their intractable ward uses play-acting (scenes from *The Tempest*) to enable all the characters to come to terms with their emotional and psychological problems. Very much a work of the flower-power 1960s (its characters include a freedom fighter and a mixed-colour gay couple), its text and even its dramatic presentation may have dated, but its ideas and music contain a richness to match the earlier works.

The Ice Break (1973–6) is another matter: a story of conflict between East and West, black and white, young and old and subsequent rebirth (compare *The Midsummer Marriage*), it rarely manages to reach beyond the stereotypical images of its confrontations and characters, and the music lacks the distinction and memorability of its predecessors.

Tippett's last theatrical work, *New Year* (1985–8), on the other hand, continues the almost cyclical return to the lyricism of his first opera that began to emerge in his non-operatic works from the Fourth Quartet (1978) onwards. Yet this is no mere recapitulation of an earlier style: it is more the youthful vigour to which he has returned, added to a far wider range of musical idioms than before, including rap (Ex. 11.8), modern jazz and rock. Its plot, however, is yet another instance of 'rebirth' and spiritual renewal, symbolized by the rituals of New Year celebrations, of throwing out the old and welcoming in the new. It sums up many of Tippett's operatic preoccupations: Jungian self-renewal; the mixture of real and imaginary worlds to represent the conscious and unconscious sides of his protagonists; a level of symbolism and conceptualization of the drama; and an unbounded optimism in the human capacity to improve itself.

ART MUSIC

Ex. 11.8   Tippett: *New Year*, Act II

It seemed to take British music several decades to wake up to the experience of the Second Viennese School and the post-war modernist movement in Continental Europe and America. One of the first to respond positively to serialism was Elisabeth Lutyens, who proved, like Berg and Schoenberg before her, that tonality was not a necessity in creating musical drama. Her first attempt was a 'dramatic scena', *The Pit* (1947), which used a series in an expressionist way to help convey the horror of the people caught up in a mining accident. *Infidelio* (1954) was more radical. It virtually dispensed with action to tell the story of a failed love affair in reverse, from suicide and breakdown back to the seduction. It is arguably one of the first instances of music theatre, as opposed to narrative opera (see below, p. 389). Lutyens's next operatic project was an ambitious four-acter based on Elias Canetti's play *The Numbered* (1967), but its vast forces (and two-hour length) have always precluded the chance of performance. As if in response to this, her 'charade in four scenes with three interruptions' *Time Off? Not a Ghost of a Chance!* (1968) was more practicably written for a few singers and instrumental ensemble of ten. During its 80-minute length it ventures into music-theatre territory and at times suggests revue in its use of humour and dramatic deflation. *Isis and Osiris* (1970) approached the scale of *The Numbered*, but its means were not up to the task of supporting her inadequate libretto, nor were her dramatic skills developed enough to create sufficient interest in ritual repetition (compare Birtwistle). Lutyens's operatic legacy may not have been all that influential, but her general attitude to dramatic composition, its ambition and experimentalism, surely rubbed off on many of her younger contemporaries, particularly Maxwell Davies and Birtwistle.

Humphrey Searle remained one of the most dogged serialists. His one-acter *The Diary of a Madman* (1958, first performed in Berlin), based on Gogol's short black comedy, sticks rigidly to the note row stated in the opening bars, together with its attendant retrogrades and inversions (Ex. 11.9). As a language with which to chart the man's progress from relative sanity to total megalomaniac madness, dodecaphony might by some be deemed to be starting from that point already, but Searle in fact manages this dramatic transition with other means, differing degrees of textural and harmonic complexity, for example, with a massive 12-note chord to mark the point at which the man's madness seems irrevocably to turn from quaint eccentricity to manic paranoia. *The Photo of the Colonel* (1964), a comedy based on Ionesco, commissioned by BBC radio, is similarly marked by the complete avoidance of key, and has a vocal line largely restricted to *parlando*. Madness also has a role to play in the subject of his final opera, *Hamlet*, a work that, after a first production in Hamburg in 1968, survived only a few performances at Covent Garden. Again dodecaphony dominates, with a single row providing

ART MUSIC

Ex. 11.9 Searle: *The Diary of a Madman*

several identifying, leitmotivic themes, though the play scene stands out for being set in a late-romantic idiom.

British music had seen few real 'schools' of music develop in the manner of, for example, Schoenberg and his pupils or 'Les Six' in France, until a group of students identifiable through their common mentor and teacher Richard Hall and familiarly known as the Manchester School assembled at the Royal Manchester College of Music in the mid-1950s. At a time when Stockhausen in Germany and Boulez in France were forging new languages for music, three composers seemed to offer the same modernist hope to music in Britain: Alexander Goehr, Harrison Birtwistle and Peter Maxwell Davies, together with the composer–pianist John Ogdon and the trumpeter–conductor Elgar Howarth. Beyond their position as fellow-students, another claim to their being termed a 'school' might be their almost simultaneous discovery of music theatre as an adjunct or alternative to opera in the late 1960s (see below), yet all three independently first turned to opera in its conventional sense.

Goehr's *Arden Must Die* (1966) was first written for performance in German. It suffers from cardboard, unsympathetic characterization and, in the words of Guy Protheroe (1975), 'some rather wooden wordsetting'. More promising is *Behold the Sun* (1984), also first performed in Germany, and set during the Anabaptist uprising in Münster in 1543.

Taverner occupied Maxwell Davies from 1956 to 1970. Based on the supposed life of the sixteenth-century English composer John Taverner (since disputed) it shows how an artist gave up his craft to pursue a religious fanaticism. The composer, at one stage accused of heresy for his alleged Lutheran sympathies, becomes the persecutor following the Reformation. By no means the first opera to be based on the life of a real creator (Pfitzner's *Palestrina* and Hindemith's *Mathis der Maler* are obvious antecedents), few have so absorbed their subject's art itself into the latter-day operatic fabric. Much of Maxwell Davies's music is ultimately derived from Taverner's (in particular an In Nomine melody), despite the seeming dissonance of the result. There are sequences of renaissance dances and music for viols and recorders, yet there is little sense in the music of the sardonic humour of his pastiches elsewhere in his output. Structurally each scene is cast in a different closed form and the opera as a whole neatly counterpoints Taverner's original persecution with his ultimate role as persecutor, with the second act a kind of dramatic parody of the first: for example, the opera opens with a courtroom scene in which the White Abbot sentences Taverner to burning at the stake for his heresy (until the intercession of the Cardinal); in the first scene of Act 2, the position is reversed, with Taverner accusing the White Abbot of papism. The opera survives this seeming over-organization as well as do Berg's operas, with a wealth of characterization (from the pompous abbot to the drunken Priest–Confessor) and instrumental variety provided by the generous use of onstage ensembles.

With Maxwell Davies's move to Orkney in 1970, his music changed to a certain extent. As if influenced by the sparseness of the landscape, his style underwent a kind of purification, a whittling down to essentials, something seen to good effect in his first Orkney opera, *The Martyrdom of St Magnus* (1976). The sacrifice for his pacifist beliefs of the twelfth-century Earl of Orkney by the rival Earl of Hakon is given a part-contemporary setting – the scene of the murder is set in a present-day police state. Yet musically and dramatically it owes much to Britten's church parables of a decade earlier, with its use of plainsong, an overtly Christian moral, the almost ritualistic presentation of the story and restricted forces of five singers and eleven instrumentalists. The musical range is wider, however, with Maxwell Davies's typical freely flowing contrapuntal lines and little use of true tonality (except in the seventh scene which takes the music stylistically step by step from the twelfth to the twentieth centuries through a variety of brief snatches of dances, a process seen earlier in a more restricted time progression in *Taverner*). Maxwell Davies followed up the success of *St Magnus* with another chamber opera, *The Lighthouse* (1979), a rather open-ended dramatization of the strange disappearance of a group of lighthouse keepers.

Arguably the most potent contribution to this repertoire by the Manchester School has been the operatic works by Birtwistle (the music theatre pieces are dealt with below). Although covering a compositional span of over 25 years, they display many unifying characteristics and preoccupations. The most fundamental is their basis in myth. *Punch and Judy* (1967) relates indirectly back to Tippett's self-created myth in *The Midsummer Marriage*, with a libretto by Stephen Pruslin that merges Jungian archetypes with the ageless folk drama of Mr Punch, also drawing in, as Michael Hall has expounded (1984: 62), elements of Greek drama, Arthurian romance and the medieval morality play. The plot emerges as an intertwining of the Jungian opposition between ego (Punch) and collective unconscious (the Greek-chorus-style Choregos) and Punch's 'romantic' quest for Pretty Polly, who thrice rejects him until he has killed the devil within him. The ritualization of this scheme is endemic to Birtwistle's operas, where a given situation, be it violent murder (*Punch and Judy*) or seduction (*Gawain*), is subjected to repetition. Birtwistle and Pruslin envisaged *Punch and Judy* as 'an opera *about* opera. It is an opera in quotation marks. The characters are stock-characters raised to a principle. . . Our aim was the collective generalization of known operas into a "source-opera" which, though written after them, would give the illusion of having been written before them' (Pruslin 1980).

How suitable, then, that for his next opera (1973–84), this time in collaboration with the composer Peter Zinovieff, Birtwistle should turn to that *Ur*-operatic theme, Orpheus. But what emerges is more than an opera, as its title, *The Mask of Orpheus*, suggests. It is perhaps as near any work has come to the Wagnerian ideal of the *Gesamtkunstwerk*, with each principal character represented not only by a singer, but also by a mime artist and a puppet. Thus the visual becomes every bit as important as the aural. As with *Punch and Judy*, the presentation is deliberately stylized, with the drama expressed simultaneously on more than one plane. Musically, the opera is scored for a large wind-dominated orchestra (there are no bowed string instruments) with an all-pervasive electronic tape part.

While *Gawain* (1991, revised 1994), draws on many of Birtwistle's earlier operatic preoccupations, it departs from them in that for once the narrative element is relatively straightforward. The ritual elements are still there, such as in the extended ceremony of the Turning of the Seasons and the thrice-attempted seduction of Gawain by Lady de Hautdesert, but the action moves in a recognizably traditional manner, if often in a somewhat drawn-out fashion. As *Orpheus* drew on the Greek element in *Punch and Judy*, so *Gawain* expands that of the Arthurian quest. The Green Knight or Man is another recurring symbol in Birtwistle's dramatic work, from his appearance in *Down by the Greenwood Side* (see 'Music Theatre' below) and his suggestion in the maypole apotheosis of *Punch and Judy*. So too is the idea of seeking self-knowledge, the outcome of Gawain's test set by the Green Knight and even that for the almost anti-human Punch with his final winning of Pretty Polly. Unlike *Orpheus*, the orchestra used is largely conventional and is more pervasive than in the earlier works, to the extent that in performance the words (sung to vocal lines that are perhaps more grateful than before) are often swamped. The style is monumental, on an epic scale to match the subject matter, yet as ever with Birtwistle, this broad palette is formed from a minutely detailed degree of musical organization and colour.

In one sense twentieth-century British opera has come full circle with *Gawain*, returning to the Arthurian and Celtic myths that dominated the efforts of the Boughton–Holbrooke generation, but while British music was then still way behind the modernist developments of the Continent, by the end of the century the most successful operas are proving to be those at the forefront of international musical developments, even if to some extent they are stylistically retrogressive and postmodernist. Two of the most promising 'first operas' for many a year, written during the late 1980s, Mark-Anthony Turnage's *Greek* (1988) and John Casken's

ART MUSIC

Golem (1989) not only reinforce the return to myth as the basis for operatic subjects, but are both representative of the way the broad church of British music is moving.

Greek is a setting of Steven Berkoff's play of the same name, which updates the Oedipus myth to the contemporary East End of London. There is something of the old Brecht–Weill collaborations in this work, in which allusions to vaudeville and popular music are threaded through a score of wit and distinction. Despite the violence of the story (and particularly of Berkoff's libretto) the music is often highly lyrical, with love duets for Eddy and his wife, but the overall impression is of musical and dramatic energy, not dissimilar to that of Tippett.

Golem is more traditional in its retelling of the old Central European legend of a man of clay built to protect a threatened community, who sows the seeds of his own destruction when his brutality and innocence lead to death. The music is more individual than Turnage's, with less reliance on tonality (except in brief moments of parody – see Ex. 11.10), and a manner that hovers between expressionism and realism.

Ex. 11.10 Casken: *Golem*, sc.v

MUSIC AND DRAMA

ART MUSIC

Another composer whose first operatic works have shown great originality is Judith Weir. After experimenting with short music theatre pieces, including *King Harald's Saga*, a ten-minute, three-act opera for a solo soprano, *A Night at the Chinese Opera* (Kent Opera 1987) showed her to have a vivid theatrical imagination, and was followed in 1990 by *The Vanishing Bridegroom* (Scottish Opera), a tripartite setting of old Scottish tales, and a highly effective drama for ENO, *Blond Eckbert* (1994).

Nigel Osborne's first opera *Hell's Angels* (Opera Factory 1986) was not a success, though *The Electrification of the Soviet Union*, based on Pasternak, brought a new sense of adventure and daring to otherwise musically conservative Glyndebourne. But despite some involving music, combining Stravinskian vigour with Bergian lyricism, its convoluted plot baffled early audiences.

Now based in Canada, John Metcalf (*b* 1946) has written two operas for Welsh National Opera. The first, *The Journey*, was followed in 1990 by *Tornrak*, an adventurous recounting of the tale of an Inuit from Canada brought to Britain in the 1850s, with a score complete with Inuit throat-singing and extended voice technique.

Robin Holloway's adaptation of English literature's longest novel, Samuel Richardson's *Clarissa*, was completed in 1975 but had to wait 15 years for its stage (at ENO). As is typical with this eclectic composer, the music is lush in a rather overblown late-romantic idiom – not out of keeping with the subject matter – but its sheer datedness is bound to preclude further productions.

Holloway's contemporary Oliver Knussen has been similarly self-indulgent in his operatic writing. His two works based on Maurice Sendak, *Where the Wild Things Are* (1983) and *Higglety Pigglety Pop!* (1990), gave him the chance to draw upon all his favourite music from the past century or more. The music for *Where the Wild Things Are*, for example, is infused with the quadruple dominant 7th chord sequence of the Coronation Scene in Musorgsky's *Boris Godunov*, while both scores are rich in allusions to Ravel (his *L'enfant et les sortilèges* being an obvious precedent in aim and scope) and Stravinsky, making them acceptable fare even for a Glyndebourne audience.

Stephen Oliver (1950–92) was an operatic phenomenon on a par with the Italians of the early nineteenth century in terms of his prolific output, numbering some 40 works. Their range is wide. Of his full-length operas, the first to achieve widespread notice, *The Duchess of Malfi* (Oxford 1971, revised 1978) was followed five years later by *Tom Jones*, a commission for the first season of the English

Music Theatre Company (the reconstituted English Opera Group), then in 1982 by *Sasha*, a chamber opera for Banff Music Centre in Canada (a company later directed by John Metcalf) and in 1984 by *Beauty and the Beast* for the Batignano Festival in Italy, where many of Oliver's later works were staged.

Yet many of his operas are at the opposite extreme of scale, both in terms of length and in terms of forces used, right down to *The Waiter's Revenge* (1976, for six singers, a couple of metronomes and a libretto made up of nonsense syllables) and *Cadenus Observ'd*, an eight-minute 'dramatic sketch' for unaccompanied solo baritone (1974). Economy was always Oliver's binding principle, something he did not wholly leave behind, despite his rare chance to use a large orchestra, in his last full-length opera, *Timon of Athens* (ENO 1991). Based on Shakespeare's unfinished play about blind generosity leading to rejection and misanthropy, the result is a rather uninvolving drama, although with a clever telescoping of Shakespeare's five acts into two. The music has a certain epic sweep to it but lacks the melodic or harmonic distinction needed to give the work a chance of longevity.

Other operas of the early 1990s have similarly shown little scope for endurance. John Buller's *The Bacchae* (ENO 1992), for example, foundered because of the composer's decision to set Euripides' text in the original Greek, making it unintelligible to 99 per cent of his audience. Its music is crafted well enough, and in a modernist style beyond that of most of his contemporaries, with its reliance on chord clusters and dramatic gestures in the early Penderecki or Aribert Reimann mould, but any opera that ignores its onus to communicate (despite the supposed help of a spoken introductory narration) is bound to be consigned to history, along with so many of its predecessors in British opera.

VII: Music Theatre

By the mid-1960s there had already been many examples of operas that had broken away from some or many of the conventions of the medium, from composers as diverse as Lutyens (*Infidelio*) to Williamson (*The English Eccentrics*) in Britain and with even more precedents, from Stravinsky to Kagel, abroad. But what emerged towards the end of the decade was a recognizably wide enthusiasm for a musico-dramatic art form dubbed music theatre (not to be confused with American musical theatre, nor, indeed, with the German *Musiktheater* of Felsenstein, which was more an approach to presenting conventional opera than creating a new medium).

The term is open to a variety of definitions, and to a certain extent, each composer who has used it has defined it for his or her own purpose (Michael Bawtree (1991) prefers the term 'new singing theatre', while Bayan Northcott (quoted by Rodney Milnes: 1972) has described it as 'anything you can do with an acting space and a handful of musicians'). In general, though, music theatre implies drama where the theatricality is often an end in itself and which may be performed using the restricted facilities of the concert hall as effectively as in the theatre; where narrative might give way to a complete lack of conventional plot or storyline; and where a limitless range of vocal and instrumental techniques can be explored away from the traditions and restrictions of the opera house: in short, music theatre is an event where music, and in particular singing, become the theatre. (Rodney Milnes (1972), reporting on a music theatre workshop at London's South Bank, warned that 'composers seeking a new name for the medium and jettisoning the excesses of duration, orchestral and choral forces, diversification and diffuseness associated with late-romantic opera' were in danger of 'stealing the emperor's clothes while pretending that they do not exist').

Music theatre has remained, even after three decades, largely a fringe activity, at least compared with the relativity generous resources and audience for new opera. Yet music theatre companies have been formed specifically to concentrate on a medium whose inherent economy of means gives many composers theatrical opportunities denied by the greater financial and logistic demands of conventional opera.

The credit for its consolidation in Britain can be fairly equally divided among the three composers of the so-called Manchester School, Goehr, Birtwistle and Maxwell Davies. In 1967 Maxwell Davies and Birtwistle founded the Pierrot Players, an ensemble designed around the instrumentation of Schoenberg's *Pierrot lunaire*, for which they began writing their own works. The first with any theatrical pretensions was Birtwistle's *Monodrama*, since withdrawn, but it was Maxwell Davies's *Eight Songs for a Mad King* (1969) that, along with the earlier *Revelation and Fall* (1966), truly launched music theatre as a viable alternative to operatic narrative. With *Revelation and Fall*, dramatic presentation came more as an afterthought, when it occurred to the composer how much better the rage and emotion of Trakl's sentiments might come across to the audience if the singer were costumed and encouraged to act out the text to a greater degree than might a Lieder singer. This idea reached fulfilment with the *Eight Songs*, in which the instrumentalists themselves become protagonists in a surreal drama by taking the roles of the caged birds which the baritone actor–singer, as the mad George III, is trying to teach to sing. This work was joined in 1974 by a companion study of madness, *Miss Donnithorne's Maggot*, in which the character who provided the source for Dickens's Miss Havisham, a real-life woman who was stood up on her wedding day, has spent her remaining life going into terminal decline. Like the *Eight Songs*, this work again provides an actor–singer with the challenge of elaborate vocal lines, eccentricities of vocal production and the need for a very theatrical command of the stage.

Goehr had also developed an interest in music theatre with a trilogy of works written between 1968 and 1970, *Naboth's Vineyard*, *Shadowplay* and *Sonata about Jerusalem*. The distance from conventional opera is here perhaps not so far: the works qualify for their music theatre status more by their brevity, detached emotions and stylized presentation than by any abandonment to surrealism.

Following the suppressed *Monodrama*, Birtwistle's first significant contribution to the genre was *Down by the Greenwood Side* (1969), a 'dramatic pastoral' to a text by Michael Nyman based on the traditional mummers' play. It in fact combines this allegory of fertility and regeneration with the ballad of 'The cruel mother'. In Birtwistle's usual manner the plot is replete with ritual repetition: St George is twice killed and twice revived, the second time by the figure of the Green Man, Jack Finney. Interspersed with this, Mrs Green sings of how she killed her illegitimate children. The two dramatic worlds (differentiated musically by the fact that Mrs Green is the only singer – the mummers either speak or mime their roles) converge only at the end when Father Christmas from the allegory carts the murderess off to prison. Birtwistle's preface to the score (1971) instructs that the acting style 'should be stylized and non-realistic; strongly gestured pantomime', a major pointer to its claims to being music theatre rather than opera.

The 1970s saw many composers trying their hand at music theatre, though it is fair to say that none has made quite the long-term impact of the Manchester School works just discussed, which have now established for themselves classic status. From the beginning the genre attracted composers already at the modernist and more adventurous end of the musical spectrum.

ART MUSIC

Nicola LeFanu's first music-theatre works attempted to unite a number of dramatic styles. *Anti-World* (1972) sets Russian poetry in English and in the original language for a pair of singers, a dancer and a small instrumental group of two woodwind and percussion. *Dawnpath* (1977) gets even closer to this *Gesamtkunstwerk* idea in combining music, word and dance in a representation of American Indian creation myths. The music-theatre works of her contemporary Michael Finnissy are in a much less serious vein and include such mouthfuls as *Commedia dell'incomprensibile potere che alcune donne hanno sugli uomini* (1975) together with more sober works, including the biblical *Five Mysteries* (1972–6).

Almost as much a school of composers as those who studied in Manchester in the 1950s were those gathered around the University of York in the 1970s and in particular the pupils of the avant-gardist Bernard Rands, who brought with him the legacy of having studied with Boulez and the Italians Dallapiccola, Maderna and, most significantly in the present context, Berio. Following the composition of *Serena* (1972) for singing actress, two mimes and ensemble, he and his pupil Roger Marsh founded the music theatre group CLAP. Marsh's own works from the period include *Cass* (1970, based on Aeschylus), *Calypso* (1973, after *The Odyssey*), and *Scènes de ballet* (1974), all with their gestural rhetoric showing the influences of Japanese noh drama and the experimental theatre of Samuel Beckett which, together with the extended vocal techniques of Berio, came to be seen as the main points of contact between the York school of music theatre and international trends. Marsh's later *The Big Bang* (1989) is an eccentric intertwining of creation theories and the story of King David (linked by the 'big bang' on the head Goliath received at his hands) for a variety of actors and singers with large instrumental ensemble. As a whole evening's presentation it lacks enough musical variety (despite some amusing moments of parody and quotation) to maintain interest.

In 1981 Graham Treacher and Vic Hoyland founded Northern Music Theatre in York and this became a new focus for composers and developments in the medium. Hoyland's own *Michelagniolo* (1981) was one of the first works to be staged by the company and is a portrait in various dramatic media, in effect 'scenes in the life' of Michelangelo. His theatre works show an eclectic mixture of linguistic and literary sources redolent of Berio's quasi-dramatic vocal pieces. The Chaucerian *Head and Two Tails* (1984) is a tripartite work using old and middle English texts, while *Crazy Rosa – La madre* (1988) is based on Dario Fo.

Another composer in the York orbit of influence is Philip Grange, whose *The Kingdom of Bones* was first given by Northern Music Theatre in 1983. This Schoenbergian monologue (reminiscent of *Erwartung*), with a text in Russian, relates a woman's unsuccessful attempt to keep her baby sheltered in the forest away from the plague. Its high degree of rhythmic organization does not detract from what is musically and dramatically a successful work.

There is continued interest in music theatre among the younger generation of composers, though increasing provision for new opera in recent years has perhaps led many through projects such as the Royal Opera's Garden Venture into genres that are more truly chamber opera. Nevertheless, David Sawer (*b* 1961), for example, studied in Cologne with the father of Continental musico-theatrical experiment Mauricio Kagel and produced his own music-theatre works in the 1980s, *Etudes* (1984) and *Food of Love* (1988), but his dramatic skills have perhaps best been used so far in the medium of radio (see below).

VIII: Ballet

While the operatic infrastructure in Britain took several decades to mature after the First World War, that of ballet, although starting from a less substantial national base, stabilized relatively soon. Ballet music also distinguished itself from opera written over the same period by its relatively restricted quantity. Two reasons account for this: the fact that a large proportion of music used by ballet companies is borrowed or adapted from other areas of music (symphonic or compilations and orchestrations of piano miniatures, for example), and because, unlike an opera which may often be written to satisfy a composer's inner need rather than a commission, ballets are rarely written speculatively.

During the early decades of the century, most of the balletic activity in Britain was imported from abroad, principally Diaghilev's Monte Carlo-based *Ballets russes*. Although its musical repertoire was Russian and mostly French in origin, Diaghilev was quick to commission works from British composers, namely Constant Lambert and Lord Berners. The commission from Lambert was for a full-length ballet based on a scenario for Adam and Eve, which soon became adapted as *Romeo and Juliet* (1925), but with the twist that the ballet presented the story as if it were a rehearsal of the Shakespeare.

Lambert's music, much of it pastiche Italian baroque (particularly Domenico Scarlatti), was soon to be superseded in the repertoire by Prokofiev's superior score. Diaghilev's other British commission was Lord Berners's *The Triumph of Neptune* (London 1926), an 'English Pantomime in Twelve Tableaux' to a scenario by Sacheverell Sitwell. The music is more obviously English than Berners's other, more French-inspired work of the period, but the effect is at best witty and lively, at its worst unmemorable and ephemeral.

The influence of the Ballets russes in Britain also had a wider effect than simply its performances and Diaghilev's commissions. In 1919, Arnold Bax collaborated with the playwright J. M. Barrie on a play with dance called *The Truth about the Russian Dancers* (subtitled 'showing how they love, how they marry, how they are made, how they die and live happily ever afterwards'). Less a ballet than 'incidental dance' comparable to incidental music to a play, Bax's score largely consists of short numbers and is written in his characteristic warm, romantic style, with a definite nod towards the Russian. Bax's other ballet score, *From Dusk till Dawn* of 1917, is in a more personal idiom.

Diaghilev's influence on British balletic life was to remain even after his death in 1929, owing to the fact that three of his principal ballerinas, Ninette de Valois, Marie Rambert and Alicia Markova, settled in London. Between them they established permanent native British companies for the first time. The first step was the setting up of training establishments and both Rambert's Marie Rambert Dancers and de Valois's Academy of Choreographic Art were founded in 1926. Independent from this, the Camargo Society was set up in 1930 to promote evenings of ballet in London's West End and presented the first performances of Vaughan Williams's *Job* and Walton's *Façade* ballet in 1931. But also of significance that year was Lilian Baylis's invitation to de Valois to form a permanent company for her twin London theatres, the rebuilt Sadler's Wells in Islington and the Old Vic in Waterloo. At first the intention was to provide the ballet requirements for her operatic activities, but the company soon gained a life of its own, giving regular full evenings of ballet. Alicia Markova became for a while its principal ballerina, Constant Lambert was appointed its music director and Frederick Ashton joined as chief choreographer in 1935.

Job, described as a 'masque for dancing' rather than a ballet, is based on William Blake's *Illustrations to the Book of Job*, the scenario incorporating stage pictures to match Blake's images. The music combines Vaughan Williams's characteristic 'pastoral' style with an ironic humour associated with Job's comforters and an epic grandeur marking the powers of good and evil.

A string of new works followed and though overall their musical pretentions may not have been over-ambitious on a contemporary European scale, the 1930s might with justification be described as the golden age of British ballet music. Principal among its exponents were Lambert, Berners, Walton and Bliss.

Lambert's *Pomona* (1926) entered the Vic–Wells repertoire in 1933, but was overshadowed by his best-known ballet score, *Horoscope* (1937). Musically, this work ranges from a jazzy, *Rio Grande*-like syncopated style, through graceful Gallic dances ('Sarabande for the followers of Virgo' and 'Valse for the Gemini'), to a full-blooded romanticism in the final 'Invocation to the Moon'. Lambert's last ballet, *Tiresias* (1951), however, which more or less led to his final illness, suffered criticism that it was too long and that the plot's concentration on sexuality was both immoderate (particularly for a Royal Gala première) and balletically unsuitable (Ashton later admitted the impossibility of his task to represent in dance the relative sexual pleasure gained by men and women). After a more successful American production in 1953, two years after Lambert's death, the work disappeared from the repertoire and the score was lost for many years.

Berners followed up *The Triumph of Neptune* with *A Wedding Bouquet* (1936), an idiosyncratic setting of a text from Gertrude Stein's play *They Must be Wedded to Their Wife*, with a narrator (a role taken on occasion by Lambert) delivering the often nonsensical text from a seat on the stage. The music is in Berners's typical light-hearted, parody style and, though wittily scored and designed, adds up to less than the sum of its parts. *Cupid and Psyche* followed in 1939 and *Les sirènes* in 1946.

Apart from the ten-minute revue item *The First Shoot* (1935) – if we discount the *Façade* adaptation and *The Wise Virgins* (his 1940 arrangement of movements from Bach cantatas) – Walton's only true ballet was *The Quest* (1943), based on part of the life of St George and a patriotic wartime contribution to the Sadler's Wells repertoire. Despite its distinguished choreographer (Ashton), cast (including Fonteyn and Helpmann) and designer (John Piper), the ballet was never revived and the score even disappeared for some 15 years. Vilem Tausky compiled a suite in 1961 and the whole work was finally recorded complete in 1990 (its full history is related by Christopher Palmer: 1990). The speed of composition ('45 mins music in less than 5 weeks', the composer admitted (p. 4)) is felt in the variable success of the music, which ranges from seductive waltzes and an enjoyable set of theme and variations for the seven deadly sins to film-music bombast.

Arthur Bliss's first ballet, *Checkmate*, dates from 1937 and is arguably the most worthy survivor of all the scores from this period, containing some of his most colourful and memorable music in which his muscular rhythmic instinct and sometimes bitter-sweet romanticism seem ideally matched to the demands of dance. *Miracle in the Gorbals* (1944) is more symphonically organized than the more usual pot-pourri structure prevalent at the time, with a strong sense of dramatic progression (though divided into 15 separate dances) from the atmospheric, scene-setting overture, to the ecstatic 'Dance of deliverance' and the tragic, almost graphically delineated finale. A year later he began work on his last ballet, *Adam Zero*, an allegory of a man's life-cycle reflected in the passing seasons of the year and set in the world of ballet itself.

Other works from the 1930s that were popular in their time but are rarely revived today include *The Haunted Ballroom*, a de Valois/Markova/Helpmann collaboration for Sadler's Wells in 1934 with a nostalgically romantic score by Geoffrey Toye (1889–1942). Gavin Gordon's *The Rake's Progress* from a year later is largely eighteenth-century pastiche in the manner of Strauss's *Le bourgeois gentilhomme* (the Hogarth prints were used as the basis for the designs) though with an orgy scene that ranges musically from subtle allusions to Wagner's Venusberg music to an Eric Coates-style banality.

The ending of the war saw a major restructuring of the ballet establishment. The Sadler's Wells company was lured to Covent Garden to become the Royal Ballet (its first new work in this guise was Bliss's *Adam Zero* in April 1946) and a second company was soon set up back at Sadler's Wells – the Sadler's Wells Theatre Ballet – as the Royal Ballet's touring arm; it was renamed the Sadler's Wells Royal Ballet in 1976 and in 1990 moved permanently to Birmingham to become the Birmingham Royal Ballet. Meanwhile the Ballet Rambert developed a wider repertoire and a less strictly 'classical' approach to dance. This was further emphasized in 1966 when it was reorganized into a body of 17 solo dancers, dropped the classics from the repertoire and concentrated on more progressive styles of choreography and diversity of musical input.

MUSIC AND DRAMA

The regular commissioning of new ballet scores continued after the war, but with the result that even fewer of real distinction were written than in the 1930s. From 1947 comes the first full-length ballet by a British composer (if one discounts Lambert's *Romeo and Juliet* for Paris), Arthur Oldham's *The Sailor's Return* for Ballet Rambert. From the 1950s come Denis ApIvor's *A Mirror for Witches* (1952), with a bold use of 12-note music in a dramatic and colourful score to a plot about witch-hunting in New England; this was followed a year later by a work based on Lorca's *Blood Wedding*. Also on a Spanish theme was Roberto Gerhard's *Don Quixote*, given in 1950, and, as in his opera *The Duenna* (see above), making full use of Spanish idioms. Immediately forgettable comedies from the same period included Oldham's *Bonne bouche* (1952), John Addison's *Carte blanche* (SW 1953) and Antony Hopkins's *Café des sports* (SW 1954). In a more serious vein, Malcolm Arnold's *Homage to the Queen* (1953, a coronation divertissement) and *Rinaldo and Armida* (1955), as well as Alan Rawsthorne's *Madame Chrysanthème* (1955, from the same source as Puccini's *Madama Butterfly*), have made little long-term impact. Another major provider of ballet scores from the 1940s to the 1970s was Leonard Salzedo (*b* 1921), an English composer of Portuguese origin who was both an orchestral violinist and a conductor, and who was at different times in charge of the Ballet Rambert and Scottish Theatre Ballet. His works include *The Fugitive* (1944), *Witch Boy* (1956) and *Hazard* (1967).

Musically the single most significant ballet from the period, and indeed since *Job* and *Checkmate*, was Britten's *The Prince of the Pagodas* (CG 1957). It may represent a byway in the composer's musical output, but it reveals to the full his orchestral expertise and ability to characterize in memorable music even the cardboard figures of a fairytale plot. Of most significance to his own musical development is the oriental aspect of the music. In the midst of its composition (one of the most protracted and difficult jobs in the usually fluent composer's experience) he went on his world tour, during which he not only encountered the Japanese noh dramas that were to influence his operatic direction, but also, at first hand, Balinese gamelan. With great mastery he managed to turn the conventional instruments of the Western orchestra (including standard percussion) into a convincing imitation of a gamelan orchestra for a scene in the second act of his ballet in which the pagodas aptly revolve to the music (this scene also looks forward to the percussion writing in *Death in Venice*).

The Prince of the Pagodas is really the only ballet score since the war to have gained any significance beyond its role as accompaniment to dance. The rate of new commissions has notably dropped since the 1960s. More newly created ballets have made use of pre-existing music (often with storylines imposed on seemingly unsuitable, abstract musical works), while choreographic and musical styles have broadened to such an extent, particularly with exponents of 'contemporary dance', that a new work is as likely to be abstract, modern dance technique allied to a rock score as it is to be a traditional 'classical' ballet with a musically undemanding orchestral score.

There have been limited exceptions, with works such as Malcolm Williamson's theatrical *Sun into Darkness*, written during his most prolific period in the mid-1960s for the Bristol-based Western Ballet Theatre, or Thea Musgrave's *Beauty and the Beast* (1969) for the same company, re-formed as Scottish Theatre Ballet. More recently, Wilfred Joseph's *Cyrano* (1991) has proved a successful if musically undistinguished addition to the Royal Ballet's repertoire, joined in 1992 by Brian Elias's *The Judas Tree*, a gritty latter-day *Rite of Spring* and a consummately constructed symphonic score.

IX: Radio

'There is no such thing as radio music,' wrote Lance Sieveking (1934). 'Composers go on composing music just as if wireless had not been invented.' Sieveking's aim was to assert that broadcasting had not changed the way composers in writing for the new medium approached their music. This may well apply to standard concert and recital repertoire, where the effect of radio on music was no advance on the already thriving phonographic reproduction (though without the need for works to be cut into short spans to fit on sides of records). But Sieveking's remark ignores the fact that even then composers were beginning to look upon radio as a new medium, offering new forms and opportunities, though in these early days before the general adoption of magnetic tape, much that was broadcast was live.

From its foundation in 1922, the BBC took the lead in the development of new music in Britain. While this was more often through the commission of concert works and broadcasts of music from all over the world, it also included the experimentation of new art forms in which radio became the venue in the same way that a

MUSIC AND DRAMA

theatre was for opera, or the concert hall for the symphony. These can be divided into three broad areas, by no means exclusive or devoid of interrelation, and it is indeed often difficult to pigeonhole a given work into one of them: radio operas and music theatre, comprising musico-dramatic works conceived specifically for a sound-only medium; radio features – sometimes a music-based documentary or a work of a more cantata-like nature which may draw together a variety of aural elements, such as song and spoken poetry; and incidental music for radio dramas and documentaries (performing much the same function as incidental music in the theatre or on film).

Radio operas have already been dealt with individually above. The medium is inevitably one fraught with problems, more so than radio spoken drama, simply because intelligibility of words is of prime importance when the listener has to create his or her own visual picture for the action and staging.

Given Britten's dominance of the operatic stage for over a quarter of a century, it is perhaps surprising that this is one radio medium in which he never worked. But for seven or eight years or so before the première of *Peter Grimes*, however, he contributed to a significant number of BBC and American radio productions in the fields of drama and the feature, a logical progression from his work with the GPO Film Unit. His first, in 1937, was music for *King Arthur*, a drama put together by the Australian-born producer D. Geoffrey Bridson, and boasting a moderate-sized orchestra and chorus.

There then followed the first of two cantatas, *The Company of Heaven* (1937), the only one of these early works to be revived in recent times and to be published and recorded. This Michaelmas programme devised by Richard Ellis Roberts featured readings of poetic and scriptural texts interspersed with vocal settings for soloists and chorus by Britten. Although since performed in concert, the work needs the concentration provided by radio listening to appreciate the readings, though the music, contemporary with the *Bridge Variations*, already shows many of Britten's tell-tale musical and dramatic signs, from the confident choral writing to the economy of the solo numbers, such as the setting of Emily Brontë's 'A day dream' – 'A thousand thousand gleaming fires', his first piece written for Peter Pears. The success of the original enterprise led to a second radio cantata for Whitsuntide, *The World of the Spirit* (1938), an oratorio in all but name.

Other BBC projects from the period include collaborations with W. H. Auden (*Hadrian's Wall*, 1937); incidental music for a documentary series about national and international communication, *Lines on the Map* (1938); music for a six-part adaptation of T. H. White's *The Sword in the Stone* (1939); a large-scale, fully developed score (amounting to some 70 minutes of music) to Edward Sackville-West's Homeric epic *The Rescue* (1943, see Foreman 1988); incidental music for Louis MacNeice's radio play *The Dark Tower* (1946); and, in 1947, a set of orchestral variations on the carol 'God rest ye merry, gentlemen' for a Christmas feature *Men of Goodwill*. The more than purely historical value of much of this music has been shown by the number of subsequent revivals several of the dramatic productions have received, partnered with newly recorded versions of the scores.

Britten rarely found the time again to work in radio once his operatic career began to bring greater rewards, leaving his contemporaries room to make their own mark over the airwaves. In 1942, for example, Vaughan Williams was invited to contribute music for a presentation of Bunyan's *The Pilgrim's Progress* (a version now recorded), some of which found its way into his opera on the same subject (see above). The same year, Walton wrote a score to accompany a production of Louis MacNeice's epic verse drama *Christopher Columbus*.

After the war, music for drama and features continued to be produced at a prolific rate. Bridson alone commissioned scores from composers as diverse as Seiber, Walter Goehr and Gerhard (the BBC seems to have provided a much-needed home to expatriate composers in the 1940s and 1950s). Gerhard's contributions ranged from incidental music to Archibald MacLeish's *Conquistador* (1953) to an electronic score accompanying a reading of Lorca's poem *Llanto por Ignacio Sanchez Mejas* (Lament for the Death of a Bullfighter, 1959), both drawing upon his Spanish musical heritage.

This last enterprise was carried out in the BBC Radiophonic Workshop, an experimental studio founded in 1958 to provide sound and music for both television and radio. It began as an effort to emulate the *musique concrète* developments in Paris and Cologne and with the initial purpose of simplifying the production of sound effects as magnetic tape grew in fidelity and sophistication. But as time went on, 'radiophonic music' began to come into its own as a medium, but a medium with as many forms as there were radio programmes, from simple incidental scores to whole programmes justifiably termed 'radiophonic poems'. As in electro-acoustic music intended for the concert hall, the boundary between music and creativity with sound became blurred, but with the lack of visible performance paraphernalia (despite attempts in concert to make up for a 'performance' element with lighting and sound diffusion), the radio perhaps provided the ideal home for electro-acoustic music.

Aside from the purely electro-acoustic medium, more conventional music has continued to be written for radio. Richard Rodney Bennett, for example, with his long experience in writing music for films, was an inevitable choice for scores to radio dramas and contributed to *The Long Distance Piano Player* (1962) and *The Diary of Nijinsky* (1965). Despite more pressure these days on commissioning and performing funds, ambitious projects are still forthcoming, such as David Ward's 1984 radio opera, an adult fairytale version of *The Snow Queen*, or, particularly successfully, David Sawer's *Swansong* (1989), a 'radio fantasy' setting Berlioz's creation of his utopian country of Euphonia in a highly effective mixed-media musical context.

Chapter 12

VOCAL MUSIC

STEPHEN BANFIELD

I: The Rise and Fall of Genres

Referring to the earlier twentieth century, Brian Ferneyhough has said, 'Sometimes I envy the composer living in a period in which speech inflection and musical gesture were so intimately related . . . nowadays there is no tradition of heightened melodramatic oration . . . so that a chasm has opened up between musical and verbal pattern-making' (1989: 157). What he does not say is that the counterpart to this loss of direct expression in vocal art music has been its rise in folk, jazz, pop, commercial and ethnic musics. From the jingle to rap, from the pop or stage ballad to the soul, funk, disco or blues chorus, most twentieth-century popular music is vocal, its communicative partnership – not just between voice and audience but between voice and microphone, voice and guitar, voice and saxophone or voice and voice – as intimate, direct and rhetorical as one could wish. It is art music, not all music, that has taken its custom elsewhere. And while this would seem to be true of the Western tradition as a whole, the hegemony of the English language in so many popular genres, from rock and jazz to the musical, may render it particularly noticeable in Britain and America. Also implicit in Ferneyhough's remarks is the modern reluctance towards, or plain suspicion of, massed exhortatory expression, perhaps a paradoxical inhibition in democratic societies but a pervasive one none the less, particularly after the Second World War when popular and choral expression in working-class music went their separate ways (or as Boyes (1993: 214) observes: 'Massed voices suddenly seemed "rather out of place in the post-war world"'). The 'we' in vocal music becomes increasingly difficult as does the 'you' or 'thou' to whom it may be addressed. Without this choric persona, the vocal soloist becomes more and more isolated or dramatized in a world of

VOCAL MUSIC

instruments or objects, in an ensemble or (in opera and music theatre) on stage.

On the face of it, then, a wholesale shift from vocal to instrumental culture may be sensed in the history of British art music in the twentieth century. The 1870 Education Act, albeit with some tardiness, made provision for the reward to any school of one shilling for every child who was taught to sight-sing (see Scholes 1947: 617–18); and the growth of the mass choral movement as a social phenomenon in the nineteenth century is a well-appreciated facet of Britain's past. It can be argued that the decline of vocal music in the twentieth century, already discussed in Chapter 8 as it has affected amateurs, has become as obvious a historical fact as these.

There are separate trajectories for each vocal genre, of course. Choral music is difficult to compartmentalize, and even the broad category of partsong needs breaking down into at least two traditions: the madrigalian use of vocal harmony and polyphony, with or without accompaniment, for the creation of anything from melopoetic miniatures to quasi-symphonic structures; and the use of massed voices, often children's in an educational context and in unison or two or three parts with piano, for some kind of team exercise in tune, descant and musical recitation. (See pp. 431ff for further distinctions.) The first of these has in general become less and less the province of large, often municipal choral societies expressing feats of quasi-military mass discipline (crack choirs such as Henry Leslie's in the nineteenth century were often surprisingly large) and has latterly often taken performances to a very high and presumably more flexible standard in chamber choirs of, say, 12 to 40 voices, be they amateur, from a village, school, college or place of work, or professional (such as the John Alldis Choir, the BBC Singers and crossover groups like the King's Singers). The second has probably declined as both the piano and Cecil Sharp's disciplined vision of a national folk heritage have lost their authority (see Boyes 1993), and the singing class has given way to other forms of group activity, instrumental or dramatic, and to individual instrumental or vocal tuition in the educational and social curriculum.

This last set of changes itself complements the demise of elocution training and of the recitation of narrative poetry in school, in the home and in public (and here, for reasons doubtless connected with the rise of the electronic media, we are back with Ferneyhough's point about rhetoric), a phenomenon that has affected large-scale choral music as well, the narrative ballad or dramatic cantata being thought of as a Victorian genre (Stanford's *The Revenge* one of its classics) more or less extinct in the twentieth century. Celluloid (though still with music) replaced verse as the vehicle for fast-paced adventure, and it is probably also true that with superficial literacy and rehearsal time at a premium latter-day choirs seldom attain the requisite level of disciplined response for corporate storytelling. Britten's choral ballads (*The Ballad of Little Musgrave and Lady Barnard*, *Children's Crusade* and *The Golden Vanity*) may not suffice to gainsay Nigel Burton's assertion that Coleridge-Taylor's *Scenes from the Song of Hiawatha* was 'the last really successful English secular cantata ever written' (1981a: 233). On the other hand, it seems to have been the secularity, not the narrativity, that finished the genre off: colourful, even hilarious feats have continued to be recounted in the name of religion, witness Britten's *Saint Nicolas* (the saint in his bath) and the pop cantatas mentioned below; nor should this appear unduly curious when we recall the vividness of Jesus's own storytelling, something that Britten again conveys without inhibition in his *Cantata misericordium*.

English solo song, more or less in parallel with and as a response to the German *Lied* and French *mélodie*, rose from a salon activity to a concert genre at the end of the nineteenth century. Its flowering and subsequent mutation will be traced in more detail below. Anglican church music and to a certain extent that of other denominations has suffered the decline of the boy treble and the rise of the often clerically led music group at the expense of the organist/choirmaster. This affects the cathedral as much as the parish church and is thus a professional as well as an amateur factor (the latter having been discussed in Chapter 8) – Simon Preston resigned as Organist and Master of the Choristers from Westminster Abbey in 1987 to become a freelance recitalist partly because of these changing patterns of musical authority. Probably more choral art music is being sung in churches that ever before, but less of it takes place in worship, more in concerts. The late twentieth-century specialist choirs and vocal ensembles such as the Tallis Scholars, the New London Chamber Choir, and Singcircle, whether they perform old repertoire (see Chapter 14) or new, keep vocal music in the forefront of things strikingly enough, as do some local authority composers in residence and civic festivals on the one hand, and competitions such as Sainsbury's Choir of the Year on the other. But it remains to be seen whether the professional groups emulated by the amateurs will recruit new generations of voices (largely via the universities,

VOCAL MUSIC

particularly through the Oxbridge choral establishment) if the stream of professionally apprenticed choristers and organists dries up (see, again, Chapter 8 on the shortage of the latter). And choral singing in schools continues to take second place to instrumental prowess.

Yet it would be difficult to demonstrate a drying-up of repertoire. Even Bliss's confident assertion in 1921 that the Stravinsky revolution had killed off 'the oratorio composed especially for the provincial festival on the lines laid down by the Canon and Chapter' (Roscow 1991: 18) was premature, though indeed the genre has sometimes found itself in dubious company if one thinks of Horovitz's *Horrortorio* (for the 1959 Hoffnung festival) or Roger Marsh's *Samson* (1983), one of a series of music theatre and other vocal pieces in which Old Testament characters take on the manners of fishwives and heavy metal thugs. And it is surely indicative of some continuing, deep-seated need in the British psyche for togetherness and transcendence that two of the century's most successful popular composers have attempted large-scale choral works, Andrew Lloyd Webber a Requiem (1985) and Paul McCartney his *Liverpool Oratorio* (1991), and had them accepted in one sense or another, despite the former's unnecessarily difficult choral writing and perplexing stylistic range (encompassing Verdi, Janáček, Britten, Prokofiev and rock) and the latter's bizarre and unintentionally forged link between Fauré and Monty Python. Death, rather strangely, has remained fashionable in choral music – 'Think of all those requiems, with little musical equivalent celebrating birth. Think of all those painted and sculpted madonnas and child, with little musical equivalent' (Walter 1992: 280, paraphrasing Bayan Northcott). Another popular Requiem, simplistic where Lloyd Webber's is complicated, is Rutter's (1985); and Geoffrey Burgon (*b* 1941) wrote one (1976) prior to commercial success with a sacred choral piece, the *Nunc Dimittis* used in the television series *Tinker, Tailor, Soldier, Spy* (1979).

Part of McCartney's problem is his religious sincerity, just as a key to Walton's success in *Belshazzar's Feast* is his lack of it, as implied in the criticism that the jubilation of the Jews and the Babylonians cannot be told apart. (*Belshazzar's Feast* sits ill with the clergy, references to concubines and eunuchs in the text having prevented its performance at the Three Choirs Festival until 1975 – see Boden 1992: 199.) The pop cantata, another fashionable vocal genre, has flourished on Walton's premise, that a lively Old Testament story works best in narrative rather than reflective musical setting and can afford to be witty, even cartoon-like, given such familiar, everyday figures as

ART MUSIC

Noah and Joseph. Herbert Chappell's *The Daniel Jazz* (Vachel Lindsay; 1963) started the trend. Michael Hurd's *Jonah-Man Jazz* (1966) and his many other similar works lack something of Chappell's raw edge, but their lyrics more than compensate for this ('For I will smite 'em, / Ad infinitum'), snugly fitted to knowingly idiomatic and ironic pastiches that stop just short of camp. Horovitz's *Captain Noah and His Floating Zoo* (Michael Flanders; 1973) again trades well in lyric wit ('male and female spotted cheetahs, armadillos and anteaters and mosqui*ters* and two lions from their den'), and the score's Preface is at pains to point out that 'The work is not intended as a contribution to "pop" religion.'

There was humour in the medieval mystery plays, and Britten reflected it in *Noye's Fludde*, which pre-dated pop cantatas and is very different (see Chapter 11), embracing a far broader range of musical involvement than most of them, in terms of children of different ages and abilities, professional and perhaps amateur adult performers, and a singing congregation. Britten was the first and the best in this field, but he was soon joined by Maxwell Davies, whose carol sequence *O magnum mysterium* (1960), written for Cirencester Grammar School, showed how astonishingly high sights could be set where music in state education was concerned, post-Webernite instrumental interludes and all. In retrospect, it was a golden moment.

Music for young performers (as it is currently described by publishers) surely represents one area of huge overall growth in vocal music, financed largely by the educational system; and though it has become customary (for instance, in publishers' composer catalogues) to place instrumental above vocal music, composers appear to have been writing as much vocal music as ever, albeit again, as this chapter will discuss, with differing emphases and patterns of production. What probably has changed is the amount of money, relatively speaking, they earn from it. Smaller secular and school choirs and fewer church ones mean fewer copies sold or performances given; royalties give way to commission fees as a source of income, and in fact more has to be written to keep the money coming in.

II: *Oratorios, Cantatas and Large-Scale Masses*

The major commissioners of large-scale British choral works since the death of Handel have been the cathedral and triennial civic festivals (see Burton 1981a for details of nineteenth-century works), and their main task since 1900 has been to find a successor to Elgar's *The Dream of Gerontius*. Elgar himself failed to do this. In *The Apostles* and *The Kingdom* he provided full-length narrative works of Wagnerian flux and continuity, thus reaffirming for his own time oratorio's original analogy with opera, but at the considerable expense of imagination: quadruple metre and a moderate harmonic pace provide the all too unvarying framework for thematic motif, solo narration and choral part-writing in ways which influenced and restricted many another composer's contribution (for example, Vaughan Williams's *A Sea Symphony* and Finzi's *Intimations of Immortality*) for the next 50 years. In *The Music Makers* (1912) he retreated further, to a structural match of the poetic ode in scale and unity, but with limited length: the restricting principle is that of the single span, signalled here by a refrain ('We are the music makers' returns at the end, as does, for instance, 'Say, heart, what will the future bring?' in Ireland's *These Things Shall Be* (1937) and the 'intimations' motif in Finzi's ode) and by the overall kinetic scope of poetic stanzas or sections, their shape and size, and the links or pivots between them. Many twentieth-century choral works are for this reason of little greater length than a symphonic poem, though admittedly this had long been a popular option in the choral ballad with initial stanza or stanzas repeated at the end (see Armstrong Gibbs's 1932 cantata *The Highwayman* for a late example). Or they echo baroque articulations such as the cantata with arioso and aria or even the prelude and fugue (Walton's *Belshazzar's Feast* operates on this level, pivoting on the king's death). And most masses are nearer the scale of Palestrina than that of Bach and Beethoven. (The 1948 Mass by Julius Harrison (1885–1963) is an exception to this, but at the expense of style.)

As for the festivals, Birmingham's scarcely survived the First World War, though it produced one enterprising work in 1919, William Harris's setting of Francis Thompson's poem *The Hound of Heaven*. The Norwich Festival, operating fitfully, managed only one front-rank choral commission, Vaughan Williams's *Five Tudor Portraits* (1936), in its days of triennial distinction, and eventually became a common annual. The Leeds Festival, flourishing between the wars, notably with *Belshazzar's Feast* (1931), withered in the 1980s; now the musical public turns triennially to the city for new pianists, not new choral works. The most consistent British choral (and sometimes solo vocal) patron throughout the twentieth century has been the Three Choirs Festival, its substantial commissions and first performances including Howells's *Missa sabrinensis* (Worcester 1954), his *Hymnus paradisi* and Finzi's *Intimations of Immortality* (both Gloucester 1950), Dyson's *Quo vadis?* and Finzi's *Dies natalis* (both for Hereford 1939 but postponed because of war), Vaughan Williams's *Hodie* (Worcester 1954), *The Water and the Fire* (Hereford 1964) by Anthony Milner (*b* 1925), Crosse's *Changes* (Worcester 1966), Bennett's *Spells* (Worcester 1975), Burgon's Requiem (Hereford 1976), Harvey's *Ludus amoris* and *Resurrection* (Worcester 1969 and 1981), Mathias's *Lux aeterna* (Hereford 1982) and Patterson's *Mass of the Sea* (Gloucester 1983). Yet the festival has failed to host any major new work by Britten, Tippett or Maxwell Davies; Holst would be excluded from this stricture only by virtue of his Choral Fantasia (Gloucester 1931), an austere but satisfying compensation for his disappointing Choral Symphony, in which he set parts of the Robert Bridges text originally written for Parry's *Invocation to Music*. Other cathedral cities have more or less copied the Three Choirs' patronage, from Winchester (Dyson's *The Canterbury Pilgrims*, 1931) to Chester (Tavener's *We Shall See Him as He Is*, 1992), with many titular echoes of Chichester Cathedral's celebrated commissioning of Bernstein's *Chichester Psalms* (1965), for instance Joubert's *Herefordshire Canticles* and the *Chester Mass* by Edward Harper (*b* 1941), both 1979, Patterson's *The Canterbury Psalms* (1981), and *Lichfield Canticle* (1972) by John Rutter (*b* 1945).

Bantock's *Omar Khayyám* (1906–9), a work of greatness after its fashion and one whose day may yet come, is gloriously unrelated to these conditions and imperatives. In three parts lasting three hours, it was published in Leipzig and performed in Vienna in 1912, uses a double orchestra, has no temporal narrative (the soloists are the Beloved, the Poet and the Philosopher) and could hardly be further from Anglican eschatology. Beginning with 'Allahu Akbar!', the muezzin's call to prayer, its agnostic sentiments culminate at the end of Part II in FitzGerald's celebrated apostrophe to a guilty God:

> Oh, Thou, who Man of baser Earth didst make,
> And ev'n with Paradise devise the Snake:
> For all the Sin wherewith the Face of Man
> Is blacken'd, Man's forgiveness give – and take!

Yet the defiance is still wholeheartedly romantic, the two concluding *fortissimo* words and their daring chords ($\flat\text{VI}^7\text{d}-\text{I}$ the first time, [$\flat\text{II}-\text{II}-\sharp\text{II}-$]$\text{III}-\text{I}^{\text{maj}7}$ under an inverted tonic pedal triad the second) no less thrilling in intent than the opening call to transcendence of Vaughan Williams's *A Sea Symphony* (Leeds 1910; see Chapter 9)

VOCAL MUSIC

whose context the British preferred. Choral settings of Whitman abounded at this period; in addition to the *Sea Symphony* there were Charles Wood's and Holst's settings of the *Dirge for Two Veterans* (the former Leeds 1901, the latter 1914), Vaughan Williams's *Toward the Unknown Region* (Leeds 1907), *The Mystic Trumpeter* (Leeds 1913) by Hamilton Harty (1879–1941) and Holst's *Ode to Death* (Leeds 1922). But why were they all written for Leeds?

Whitman's positivistic humanism and voicing of collective consciousness with apostrophes to the soul stuck in the throat with the First World War, and the timing of Harty's *The Mystic Trumpeter* could scarcely have been worse, with its bacchanalian finale lauding 'A reborn race . . . a perfect World . . . War, sorrow, suff'ring gone'. However, Whitman's experience of the American Civil War could still strike home. In *Dona nobis pacem* (1936) Vaughan Williams as usual showed himself capable of rising to the long view, the 'Reconciliation' movement setting Whitman's words 'Beautiful that war and all its deeds of carnage must in time be utterly lost' with extraordinary sympathy and simplicity. *Morning Heroes* (1930), which likewise included Whitman in its textual anthology, was Bliss's exorcism of the nightmares of the First World War; probably only Vaughan Williams had the stature to combine something of this function, in *Dona nobis pacem*, with a warning about the impending Second. His structural corollary to this was the use of a soprano solo to sing the Agnus Dei and link the movements with its final phrase, the work's title, pivoting between benediction and supplication, cadential repose and motivic apprehension (in Ex. 12.1 the soprano's A–E cadence is picked up by the bass at the start of the following movement, but only after the interim G♯–F♮ transformation has unsettled it, rhythmically by its offbeat repetition as well as pitchwise).

Bliss also made what was probably the first setting of Wilfred Owen in *Morning Heroes*. Owen's was a voice more appropriate than Whitman's to the twentieth-century experience of war, but it was co-opted into the effort of choral catharsis with a far slimmer belief in the conciliatory capacities of rhetoric. *Morning Heroes* does without singing soloists; Britten's *War Requiem* was to go further and directly oppose Owen's texts and their music to the choral observance of the Mass. Moreover, both *Dona nobis pacem* and *Morning Heroes* anthologize the texts of several authors (as does Bliss's other cantata of the period, the *Pastoral: Lie Strewn the White Flocks* of 1928); it is as though the sustained single voice can no longer muster the requisite authority or is no longer to be trusted.

ART MUSIC

Ex. 12.1   Vaughan Williams: *Dona nobis pacem*

[musical score excerpt, Andantino, Soprano Solo and Chorus: "Dona, dona nobis pacem... Dona, dona nobis pacem, pacem", with text "-gain ev- er a - gain ... this soiled world." and "IV Dirge for two veterans, Moderato alla marcia", Orchestra]

One could go so far as to say that British confidence in choral expression has never been entirely regained since the First World War. Some composers made only minor contributions. Frank Bridge wrote *A Prayer* (à Kempis; 1916), Moeran a *Nocturne* (Nichols; 1934), Goossens *Silence* (de la Mare; Gloucester 1922 – his huge cantata *The Apocalypse* dates from his Australian years), Quilter *The Sailor and His Lass* (Rodney Bennett; 1945). Lennox Berkeley produced a full-length biblical oratorio in conventional format, *Jonah* (Leeds 1937), that was savaged and withdrawn, though it probably deserved better and was 'a link between *Belshazzar's Feast* and Tippett's *A Child of Our Time*' (P. Dickinson 1988: 43) that may even have influenced the latter. Others who did sustain personal expression in choral music have not always received their due. *April* (1913) and *Philomela* (1923) by

VOCAL MUSIC

Henry Balfour Gardiner (1877–1950) are charming, Bax's *Enchanted Summer* (1910), *To the Name Above Every Name* (1923) and *Walsinghame* (1926) egregious for their respective refulgence, ceremony and desolation. Patrick Hadley (1899–1973) contributed *The Trees So High* (1931), a fine set of orchestral variations culminating rather like Delius's *Appalachia* in a vocal statement of the ballad (and a choral finale); *The Hills* (1944), again suggesting a Delian parallel, with his *Song of the High Hills*; and *Fen and Flood* (1954). Hadley also made a choral setting of Keats's *La belle dame sans merci* (1935), as did Cyril Scott (1879–1970) in 1916. Ferguson twice approached medieval poetry in *Amore langueo* (1956), an intense essay in erotic yearning, and *Dream of the Rood* (1959); Rawsthorne did so rather differently in *Carmen vitale* (1963), a substantial suite with settings of the hexachord mnemonic 'Ut queant laxis' as a clever binding element, and in *Medieval Diptych* (1962).

It is also notable that Vaughan Williams, for all his servicing of the various choral genres (and an Oxford University Press list of 'Modern [British] Choral Works' puts him in a special category by 'not including works by R. Vaughan Williams'), never made another choral statement with the scope of *A Sea Symphony*, itself not quite a full evening's programme. (*Hodie* lasts nearly an hour, but is a relatively unconstrained work, despite some striking motivic usage in the narrations. *Five Tudor Portraits* is somewhat shorter.) Rather, he aimed his representation of the transcendent, of the moral quest and struggle, even of the pastoral, at instrumental symphonies, at dance (in *Job*) and ultimately at the lyric stage in *The Pilgrim's Progress*; *Sancta civitas* (1925), though apocalyptic in subject, is only a step on that road. Meanwhile, the modal platitudes of the *World Requiem* by John Foulds (1880–1939), unique in its mass popularity as part of the Armistice commemoration in the Albert Hall for several years from 1923, were not seen as the answer by a suspicious, critical establishment (see Swann 1994). Nor, to a war-weary world, were the hard sentiments of Delius's atheistic Requiem (1914–16, performed 1922), to a Nietzschean text of his own and dedicated 'to the memory of all young artists fallen in the war', though a comparison of its final section ('The snow lingers yet on the mountains, but yonder in the valleys the buds are breaking') with Janáček's ecstatic honouring of nature (for instance, at the end of *The Cunning Little Vixen*), and steely performances to match, might rescue the work from assumptions of decadence.

No one in the decade after the war fully took up the challenge originally laid down in Britain by Handel's *Messiah* and Mendelssohn's

Elijah, and it may be significant that it was with two choral works of 1924–5, *Flos campi* and the Choral Symphony (Leeds 1925), that Vaughan Williams and Holst for the first time puzzled and disappointed each other. Vaughan Williams felt only 'cold admiration' for Holst's apparently disengaged settings of Keats in the latter; and Holst must not have understood *Flos campi*'s realignment of erotic, oriental, biblical, primitive and pastoral strands, indeed of genres (suite, cantata and concerto are fused, choral and verbal – the choir is wordless – are prised apart), which we can now see was a timely avenue out of the assumptions of the choral tradition. Before this, Holst's *The Hymn of Jesus* (1917) had seemed for a while to carry that tradition's flame, and one can see why Vaughan Williams said it made him 'want to get up and embrace everyone and then get drunk' (U. Vaughan Williams 1964: 137). Its aggregation of monodic chant, polychoral masses of sound (with the famous sliding of triads away from one another – see the 12-part passages before cue 15), irregular metres, liberated part-writing, sacred poetry (from the Apocrypha, not the Bible) and dance, hinting at a 'natural' alliance of folkdance and plainsong in ex. 12.2, must have seemed a highly refreshing recipe, possibly a new national one, after the war; but without anything comparable following from Holst's pen the vision remained modest, difficult to enlarge, and pale beside Stravinsky's reordering of resources.

Incompatible with *The Hymn of Jesus* in almost every way, Constant Lambert's *The Rio Grande* (1927) was hailed as another kind of breakthrough, a cantata for the jazz age. The poem, by Sacheverell Sitwell, already suggested an iconoclastic tone since it borrowed the hallowed technique of conjuring up a list of objects or properties, an 'image procession' (often about music itself), but reversed the point with negatives:

> By the Rio Grande
> They dance no sarabande
> On level banks like lawns about the glassy, lolling tide;
> Nor sing they forlorn madrigals
> Whose sad note stirs the sleeping gales
> Till they wake among the trees and shake the boughs,
> And fright the nightingales

In the music, a moment of 'forlorn' madrigalian imitation, such as would still be the choral stock-in-trade for Finzi and others 25 years later, passes and leaves the nightingales to be depicted by a blues phrase on muted trumpet and corresponding solo contralto. The

Ex. 12.2 Holst: *The Hymn of Jesus*

work is an exhilarating amalgam of Latin American rhythms (and percussion), ragtime, Debussian cakewalk, novelty piano, blues and gospel harmonies craftily combined with the continuing influence of the symphonic poem in its suggestion of being also a miniature piano concerto (with a fast–slow–fast–coda sequence of sections); Lambert even quotes Liszt (see Shead 1973: 73). But it did not represent sustainable development, and Lambert's other choral work of consequence, *Summer's Last Will and Testament* (Nashe; 1936), was to be very different, an extraordinarily powerful masque of death which is utterly *sui generis* – cosmopolitan, yet in some respects fitting the English choral tradition uncannily well (one senses that Finzi in particular must have been influenced by it). The metamorphic association of the Elizabethan tune 'Watkins ale' with the *Dies irae* in the 'King Pest' scherzo is emblematic of this.

The greatest contributions to large-scale choral music in Britain between the wars were made by William Walton and George Dyson

(1883–1964). Thirty years ago Ernest Bradbury (1963: 339–43), in an essay on the period, chose for his first musical examples a comparison of their settings of Dunbar's poem *In Honour of the City of London*, Dyson's from 1928, Walton's from 1937. There are other parallels. Both produced their choral masterpiece in 1931; Dyson's is *The Canterbury Pilgrims*, a full-length work based on Chaucer's *Prologue*, and Walton's – *Belshazzar's Feast* – was followed by Dyson's *Nebuchadnezzar* (Worcester 1935). Both later went to the heart of English patriotic self-representation with Henry V's 'St Crispin's Day' speech, Dyson in his late choral work *Agincourt* (Petersfield 1956), Walton in his music for Olivier's *Henry V* film (both composers bring in the fifteenth-century 'Agincourt song' at the end). Both understood the value of carnivalesque plenitude in choral contexts, Dyson for example in his (and Dunbar's) recapitulatory celebration of the City of London's 'wallès', 'river', 'churches', 'merchants', 'wives' and 'virgins', to the characteristic English stateliness and flexibility of slow triple, not quadruple time, at the end of *In Honour of the City*, Walton from beginning to end of *Belshazzar's Feast* but especially where the king's march depicts the gods of various hard materials, an image procession riotously mimicked by the percussion.

Dyson's geniality in *The Canterbury Pilgrims* is no match for Walton's tonal wit and wizardry, but neither is it parochial nor a stranger to Franco-Russian colour, and in passages such as Ex. 12.3, from 'The squire', the naive vitality reminds us of craftsmanly achievements in film and light music of the period and bids generic distinctions be forgotten. With its appropriation of Chaucer and its wholehearted purveyance of the 'merrie England' myth (and, touchingly, its reminder of the deeper, figurative meaning of the word 'pastoral' in its portrayal of the Parson), *The Canterbury Pilgrims* is very much a work 'of the school of Vaughan Williams'. Curiously, though, the master had provided no obvious model and if anything followed Dyson's example with his settings of a classic British pastoral text (from Shakespeare's *The Merchant of Venice*) in the *Serenade to Music* (1938) and pre-Elizabethan ones in the Skelton *Five Tudor Portraits*, the former on a small scale and both works straightforward, even rough, perhaps deliberately so, in their effects, avoiding the cosiness which is Dyson's limitation. It is difficult to put one's finger on why, as with *Summer's Last Will and Testament*, *Five Tudor Portraits* has not become a staple, with its deeply impressive first movement, crosscurrents with Orff and Shostakovich as well as Lambert, and its apostolic claim – Elgar had said to Vaughan Williams at the 1932

Three Choirs Festival that 'he had always wanted to make an oratorio out of "Elinor Rumming" but now passed on the idea to V.W., adding that the Skelton metres were "pure jazz"'(Kennedy 1977: 11).

Ex. 12.3   Dyson: 'The squire' (*The Canterbury Pilgrims*)

Dyson himself sharpened his musical language in *Nebuchadnezzar*, doubtless with the sample of *Belshazzar's Feast* to hand. (The same applied to Finzi when he first worked on a large scale in his *Intimations*.) Both Dyson and Walton knew how to tell a pagan story with energy, sweep and barbaric excitement, and Dyson's choral characterization in *Nebuchadnezzar*, whose wheedling bass trio of Chaldeans in chromatic polyphony is foiled by the homophonic modal triads of Shadrach, Meschach and Abednego, tenors to a man, is very much in the tradition of concerted contrasts stretching back to Schütz's *Weihnachtshistorie*. Walton also draws on this tradition, scoring his opening prophecy as it were for a quartet of elders in a way that also echoes the initial *coup de théâtre* of Mendelssohn's

Elijah, as does the people's reaction to its fulfilment, frantic in Mendelssohn, grieving in Walton (Ex. 12.4).

Ex. 12.4   Walton: *Belshazzar's Feast*

As stated earlier, Dyson's biggest choral work, *Quo vadis?*, remained unperformed until after the Second World War, and it was one of a number of similar instances. Finzi's *Intimations of Immortality*, Howells's *Hymnus paradisi* and Armstrong Gibbs's choral symphony *Odysseus*

VOCAL MUSIC

were all conceived or completed by 1939 but not performed for a decade or more; additionally, like Vaughan Williams's *The Pilgrim's Progress*, they were all humanistic 'quest' works of one kind or another, and as such seemed old-fashioned or too liberally individualistic in ethos for the spirit of post-war reconstruction with its hard-edged corporate dogmas and authorities, be they of science, state or organized religion. Finzi's *Intimations* has since made its mark, not necessarily his best work (it is his biggest) but neither the impertinence it was once deemed as an attempt to set Wordsworth's philosophy to music. Finzi also revived the collaborative ode with Edmund Blunden in 1947 when they wrote *For St Cecilia*; but his most perfect choral work is *In terra pax* (1954), a miniature blend of nativity and pastoral, sacred and secular (its text a poem by Bridges that quotes St Luke), solo narration and choral response. Gibbs has never consolidated a position in the larger choral repertoire and he probably deserves better; *Odysseus* and a number of other works await more than the occasional amateur performance. Gibbs's colleague Howells, equally involved by way of a living with small-scale choral composition and adjudicating, stands higher through having produced the work that, though flawed by the aesthetic limitations of the English musical renaissance, represents its choral culmination: *Hymnus paradisi*. He had produced earlier, smaller choral works – the ballad *Sir Patrick Spens* (1918), *Sine nomine* (1922, wordless) and *A Kent Yeoman's Wooing Song* (1933, wittily juxtaposing Ravenscroft's text with that of Vautor's 'Mother, I will have a husband') – which are now beginning to enjoy habilitation, and he later matched *Hymnus* in scale with the *Missa sabrinensis* and eventually the *Stabat mater* (1963); but he never matched it in quality.

Like Britten's later *War Requiem* and perhaps influenced by the use of the title phrase in *Dona nobis pacem*, *Hymnus paradisi* intermingles the texts of the Requiem with others, in this case sacred. The vision at its height attains a romantic ecstasy rarely surpassed even by Delius, whom Howells honours (see Ex. 12.5), and when, slightly earlier in the cathartic last movement, he breaks into one of those English sarabandes, the image of the dance (evoking his earlier song 'Come sing and dance') is carried with such natural inspiration as to make it seem as universal as in Botticelli's *Mystic Nativity* or Signorelli's resurrection frescoes in Orvieto Cathedral. But such transcendence is not easily or permanently won: the death of Howells's son at the age of nine, which occasioned the work, gives rise through the textual plan and musical interpretation to poignant analogues and conflicts, between institutional and private grief, the church and the hills, the vision and the reality. And after the splendour of Ex. 12.5 has faded, its residual chord of A♭ is returned to a lower plane of existence with the superimposition of G major/B minor sonorities and their chant-like melody which opened the work, the two tending to fuse into an octatonic segment, a sound-world upon which Howells relies here and elsewhere (for example in his characteristic major scale with sharp 4th and flat 7th) and whose intervallic properties betoken dissolution rather than affirmation.

Angelic symbolism permeates the choral semiotics of Christian cultures, so the choral work as dream should not surprise us with its conceptual durability (and once again there are links with the symphonic poem). Ireland's *These Things Shall Be* confirms its vision with a secret quotation of the 'Internationale' and then dissolves it – while protesting that the utopian image procession has been 'no dream' – with a gesture similar to Howells's, again octatonic (except for the tonic pedal – see bars 289–95). But it seems strange that this relatively modest and naively apolitical work (see Longmire 1969: 92–3, 151), dedicated to and orchestrated by Ireland's friend Alan Bush, should be virtually the only choral reminder in the current repertoire of the left-wing aspirations of the 1930s. Bush's own larger-scale choral music, including *The Winter Journey* (Swingler; 1946), *Ballad of Aldermaston* (1958) and *The Byron Symphony* and Piano Concerto (1960 and 1937 respectively, both with baritone solo and chorus in the finale), is

Ex. 12.5 Howells: 'Holy is the true light' (*Hymnus paradisi*)

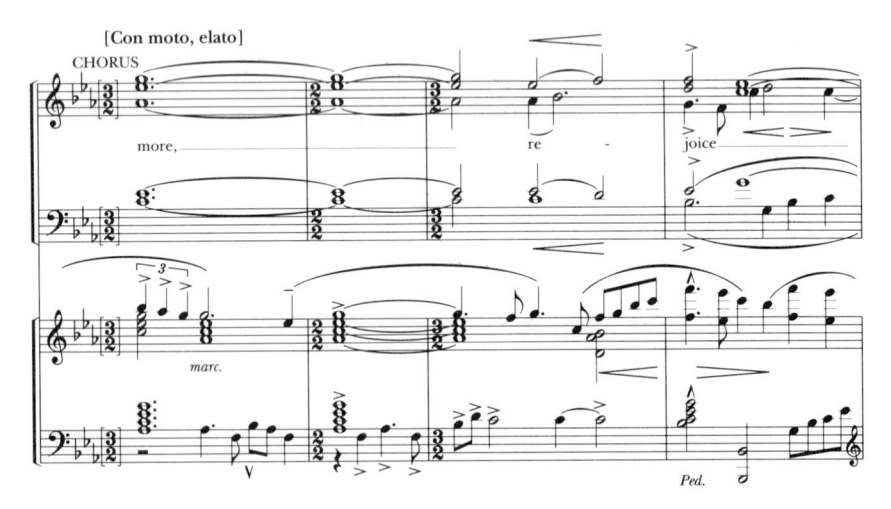

mostly later and scarcely known; Boughton's comprises only *Pioneers* (1925), a Whitman setting. Britten produced little more than the *Ballad of Heroes* (1939) before his career reached the point at which protest was constrained within an establishment overview, which is the root condition of the *War Requiem* (commissioned for the opening of Coventry Cathedral in 1962) and one possible reason why he waited so long before writing anything of its oratorical scope. He also had to make his peace with the English choral tradition, something for which he shows little inclination in *Saint Nicolas* (1948), with its petitionary prayer to the saint to 'strip off your glory', the *Spring*

Symphony (1949) and the splendidly mock-pompous *Cantata academica* (1959), and which he did not demonstratively do until a decade after the *War Requiem* when, with his partner Peter Pears (1910–86) in the title role, he made a magisterial recording of *The Dream of Gerontius*.

In the meantime, Tippett became the exemplar of the 'committed' British composer with *A Child of Our Time* (1939–41). Here, for the first time, oppressed minorities are represented not aesthetically for purposes of dramatic characterization and struggle, as on the romantic and nationalist operatic stage, or theologically, with the justification of faith accomplished by the *deus ex machina* as in Dyson's and Walton's oratorios, but with the imperative of political alliance and action. The intention of the interspersed choral arrangements of negro spirituals is collective, and implicitly congregational as with the chorales in Bach's Passions: while not actually singing them, the audience identifies with them through familiarity, with the blacks whose music they are and hence with the persecuted Jews of the narrative. This use of 'people's' music as a correlative to the power of the democratic bloc has become a commonplace with the dissemination of jazz and a wide variety of popular and world musics, but it was a new thing for English oratorio in 1941 and a timely counter to the folksong panacea.

The line of committed oratorio, from *A Child of Our Time* to Michael Berkeley's *Or Shall We Die?* (1983), is not a broad one, though if the *War Requiem* is included it passes at least one high point. Tippett himself has not returned to it, writing his sense of social solidarity instead into his later operas and the Third Symphony, though he has, almost uniquely among front-rank British composers, kept faith with oratorio as a metasymphonic genre, in both *The Vision of St Augustine* (1965) and *The Mask of Time* (1982). *Or Shall We Die?* is the oratorical response to Hiroshima that Britten considered but never wrote (see Duncan 1981: 54–6; Carpenter 1992: 405). Musically undistinguished, it none the less has an excellent text by the novelist Ian McEwan, written especially and including an anthology element in the quotation of Blake and the use of fabricated 'extracts' from non-literary modes of writing and speaking – the diary entry, the personal memory – like a latter-day version of *Dona nobis pacem*. McEwan found that oratorio offered much to his purpose: a novel about the nuclear threat, which he took the opportunity to abandon, was banal, a libretto was not. 'I had a moral argument to make of which I was not ashamed, and in words that were to be set to music I could carry that argument without embarrassment' (McEwan 1989: 5).

VOCAL MUSIC

Yet to preach, which was exactly what oratorio was originally supposed to do, has become a pejorative idea. This is a pity when it can be as persuasive as in the voice of Eric Crozier's and Britten's *Saint Nicolas*: one of their cantata's greatest strengths is its juxtaposition of gaudy stained-glass narrative with the passionate prayers and confessions of the saint himself, in his solo arias ('Heartsick' and 'O man!') but above all in the bare yet heart-moving E major monologue after the storm scene. Conversely, a return to straightforwardly biblical or liturgical texts has been a striking trend on the part of other British composers, one gathering pace since the war seemingly as a matter of impersonality. There are, for instance, large-scale masses by Grace Williams (*Missa cambrensis*, 1971) and Williamson (*Mass of Christ the King*, 1977), many smaller ones, *a cappella* or organ-accompanied (Berkeley, Cannon, Hamilton, several by Leighton and Rubbra), and a host of *missa brevis* settings (Berkeley, Burgon, Ferneyhough, Leighton, Mathias, Rubbra, Smalley, Walton), though admittedly some of these shade over into church music, as do Britten's Festival *Te Deum* and comparable settings by Cannon, Joubert, Mathias and Walton. There are settings of the Requiem by Harrison (1957), Josephs (1963), Patrick Standford (*b* 1939) and Patterson (1975) in addition to those noted earlier; settings of the *Stabat mater* by Berkeley (1947), McCabe (1976) and Patterson (1986); and works such as Bliss's *The Beatitudes* (1961), Hoddinott's *Job* and Raymond Warren's *The Passion* (both 1962), Christopher Brown's *David* (1970), Howard Blake's *Benedictus* (1979), Mathias's numerous Latin-texted motets and antiphons and Burgon's *Revelations* (1984).

This is not the whole story, however. Both the Brown and Blake works referred to above include English poetry settings (of Smart and Francis Thompson respectively), as does Burgon's Requiem of St John of the Cross (/); Fricker's *The Vision of Judgement* (1958) intersperses Cynewulf with Latin, just as Reizenstein's *Genesis* from the same year intersperses biblical passages with poems by various English authors. Further, Michael John White has astutely pinpointed in *Revelations* and a danced Mass by Burgon (1985) a 'Blakeian spirituality, in taking ecclesiastical, sometimes strictly liturgical texts out of their normal context' (White 1985), and we shall see with the example of Britten's *War Requiem* where else this has led. Nevertheless, the renewed ascendancy of liturgical Latin is evident (though *Job* is in Welsh), and while it would be wrong to view such a preference cynically as a convenient peg on which to hang musical concerns and doubtless right to applaud the impulse towards universality or at least internationalism, it does underline Ferneyhough's point about the retreat from vernacular rhetoric and persuasive exegesis. Indeed, Rubbra's *Missa a 3* (1958) is an early example of retreating further than the usual sixteenth-century stylistic concomitant of such an ethos as perceived in the British mainstream, for it includes Landini cadences and differentiated key signatures.

On the other hand, there has been a notable survival of the choral symphony, with post-war examples by Rubbra, Williamson and Patric Standford (respectively, nos 9, 3 and 2, all 1972), Milner (no. 2, 1978), Mathias (*World's Fire*, 1989) and Joubert (*The Choir Invisible*, 1968, *Gong-Tormented Sea*, 1981, and *For the Beauty of the Earth*, 1989) in addition to pre-war ones by van Dieren (*Chinese Symphony*, 1914), Smyth (*The Prison*, 1930) and Cyril Rootham (no. 2, *Revelation*, 1938) as well as those already mentioned. This becomes a personal form *par excellence* at the hands of Joubert and some of its other exponents. Rubbra's Ninth Symphony (*Sinfonia Sacra: The Resurrection*) need not tempt parallels with Beethoven's, or with Mahler's Second, but it is a radiant and deeply impressive work, very much in the Passion tradition with its striking use of chorales whose arrangements, like the spirituals in Tippett's *A Child of Our Time*, are blended expertly with Rubbra's own material. It is perhaps too religious for non-seasonal use and would probably not sit comfortably on the concert platform with other works; this seems to have excluded it from the repertoire, which is a pity, for it is both genuinely symphonic and the only full-scale oratorical contribution from a composer who wrote many smaller choral pieces, the medium being 'natural . . . for [one] whose polyphonic sense is closely allied to a feeling for subtly inflected conjunct melody' (Ottaway 1980: 293). There is also, of course, Brian's *Gothic* (Symphony no. 1, 1919–27) with its *Te Deum* setting in Part II, presumably emulating both the scale and the devotional aspects of Mahler's Eighth, though its orchestral imaginings, especially when they incline to scherzo, blend less of the motet in with symphony than do Mahler's.

Britten too wrote a choral symphony, the *Spring Symphony*, but like the *War Requiem* it stands apart from these representatives of older genres. If the problem with many a vocal symphony is the provision of large-scale contrast and segmental balance within a movement (often raised by searching for them within a single poem), Britten solves it and appeases the twentieth-century distaste for structural redundancy by casting each movement as a set of poems. One can play cognitive games relating each of these sets to sonata form or whatever, but what matters is that a 'moment' comes and goes and takes its place in a larger whole; were this not the case, the 'Poland' outburst at the end of the slow movement, to take the most striking instance, would musically and conceptually overbalance Auden's poem in which it is situated and which is at the centre of the symphony. And if the *Spring Symphony* has remained somewhat outside the repertorial mainstream, it had one obvious and perhaps more accessible offspring in Crosse's *Changes*, where again short poems are concatenated to form a four-part whole. Again a boys' chorus is used for specific symphonic 'moments', but Crosse risks less than Britten by way of self-standing diversity, for he underlines his theme of bells and spells exhaustively with a musical representation of the work's title, an initially Stravinskian peal that in its later composings-out of the scale motif 0 2 3 5 6 accounts for about 80 per cent of the material on the composer's own reckoning (Crosse 1970).

As for the *War Requiem*, from the beginning its conception of both the sacred and the secular texts is theatrical. Its presentation of the liturgy is more akin to Verdi's (or even Puccini's in *Tosca*) than to Beethoven's or Brahms's, and this is not just in the spatial effect of the distant boys' choir with its chant and shō-like organ accompaniment (much imitated by later composers, for instance Rutter in *The Falcon*, 1969) and in the dramatic use of brass fanfare, choral outcry and soprano lament. Concerning the main choir and orchestra our standpoint is that of observation rather than observance – of some ritual of old, shuffling bodies and muttering, ungraceful voices in the shadowy opening phrases. It is not a partaking of divine celebration in structures of sound (there is little counterpoint or fugal imitation in the work, except in 'Quam olim Abrahae'), and this picturing from the outside – ominous from the start, with the dragging quintuplet motif in the strings already suggesting some weary, punishing ritual activity other than worship – acts as effective mediation between the rite and the Owen poems, where the images become confrontative in the manner of newspaper or film and we are drawn in. The cross-cutting between massed and ensemble music, longshot and close-up, is particularly filmic, most strikingly prior to the repeat of the 'Quam olim Abrahae' fugue, and the chamber music to Owen's poems takes its place in the twentieth-century art-music tradition of parody minstrel ensemble that stems from Stravinsky, Schoenberg and Weill (see below), offering a foretaste of Maxwell Davies's expressionism, its coarse rhythms, counterpoint and instrumental registers suggesting the jerky puppet

ART MUSIC

movements of characters caught in some painful action they themselves do not control (see Ex. 12.6a). Yet these highly visual analogues are ultimately subservient to naked, direct rhetoric. As

Ex. 12.6a (a) Britten: 'Requiem aeternam' (*War Requiem*)

VOCAL MUSIC

has recently been observed (Shaw 1993), Britten's techniques of vocal rhetoric deserve further study; and as Owen's persuasion becomes most eloquent of 'the pity of war', so do Britten's declamatory devices, artifices of vocal statement and instrumental reflection, take on a monodic simplicity which is not the stout, socially bastioned plain speaking of British manners, more to do with the melopoetic transparency of classical Greece (Ex. 12.6b).

As we have seen, the *War Requiem* was not the first work to intersperse texts of the mass with others, but it was the seminal one. When David Fanshawe (*b* 1942) subsequently came along with his *African Sanctus* (1972), as jubilant as the *War Requiem* is severe and combining field recordings of African musics with his own mass settings, it felt natural and inevitable, if essentially unrepeatable. Someone was bound to take advantage of recording technology, crossover aesthetics from the 1960s, ethnomusicological trends and postcolonial travels and mix these impulses together, though the freshness and discipline of Fanshawe's own compositional powers are what make the piece work so well. Nevertheless, twenty years on, the seductive appropriation of folk material when Fanshawe's own is superimposed on it can feel imperialist rather than celebratory.

Staying at home, others have sought new perspectives on the mass but have seldom been rewarded with such vividness. Four may be mentioned; Paul Patterson, John Gardner (*b* 1917), Judith Weir and Peter Dickinson. The ploy of Patterson's *Mass of the Sea* (1983) is an admixture of texts about the sea, based on biblical ones, by Tim Rose Price, and the substitute of a 'Flood' movement for the Credo feels subtly ecological. Gardner, in his Mass in D (1984),

Ex. 12.6b (b) Britten: 'Libera me' (*War Requiem*)

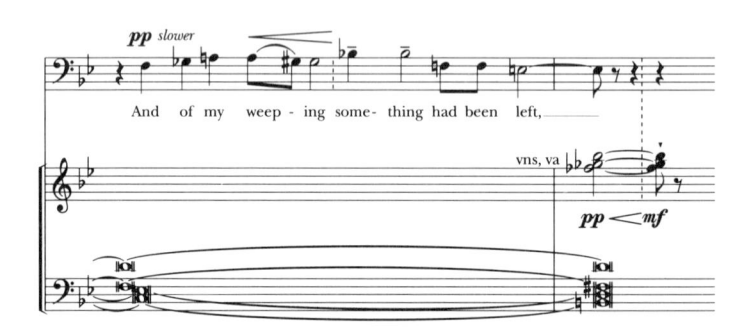

restricts himself to the mass text but accomplishes an unusually forceful dynamic curve to the work by setting some of it in English, for example the Creed, which is monotonally chanted with all the musical interest in the orchestra. His other strategy is the use of both an *incipit* from Chopin's op. 18 *Valse* (curious but effective) as motif, and a solo saxophone to complement the contralto soloist. Weir's *Missa del Cid* (1988) is the epitome of mass deconstruction, its text the composer's mixture of the ordinary and a medieval battle epic. Dickinson's *Mass of the Apocalypse* (1984) intersperses spoken texts from Revelation with the sung Anglican ordinary, minus Creed but with a vocalized 'Ite missa est', accompanied like the rest of the work by two percussionists and piano. More intriguing, however, is his *Outcry* (1969), an anthology of poems about our (in)human treatment of animals set for mezzo-soprano, choir and orchestra; as Dickinson (1989) points out: 'It was written at the same time as a setting of the mass for voices and organ and, although the poems do not exactly correspond, there are deliberate connections and some musical overlapping.' The ritual participation in slaughter depicted in Clare's shocking poem 'Badger' is underlined with the blowing of referee's whistles by four members of the chorus in this movement and by the finale's parodying of a congregational chorale in its setting of 'Nature's hymn to the Deity' (Clare again). The contrast between this and Bantock's apostrophe in *Omar Khayyám* sixty years earlier is striking: choral acclamation still carries a moral or philosophical charge, but now the finger is pointed at humanity rather than God:

> All nature owns with one accord
> The great and universal Lord:
> Insect and bird and tree and flower –
> The witnesses of every hour –
> Are pregnant with his prophecy
> And 'God is with us' all reply.
> The first link in the mighty plan
> Is still – and all upbraideth man.

Was Clare consciously parodying Addison's 'The spacious firmament on high'? Dickinson certainly echoes its use, and the din, at the end of *Noye's Fludde*.

Several composers spring to mind who, like Patterson, have continued to serve the choral tradition (and have taken it with them on their stylistic journeyings, in Patterson's case from an affinity with the Polish avant garde to a rather dull latter-day British modalism). Harvey is one. Mathias, whose *This Worldes Joie* (1974) should be added to his works mentioned earlier, was another, nearer the opposite end of the spectrum of stylistic challenge. However, the most intriguingly durable figure in British choral music in the last third of the twentieth century is John Tavener. He came to notice early and notoriously with *The Whale* (1966), where the anthology principle was taken to the initial length of a spoken encyclopedia entry on the creature; this and further mobile accretions threatened to 'swallow' musically the biblical narrative of Jonah (Composer's note, 1983) and was part of his collage approach, also touchingly evident in the children's songs and games included in his *Celtic Requiem* (1969). *Cain and Abel* (1965) had preceded *The Whale* and many other works followed it, increasingly devotional in intent as well as sacred in material (though not all with chorus) and including *In alium* (1968),

ART MUSIC

Ultimos ritos and *Little Requiem for Father Malachy Lynch* (both 1972), *Requiem for Father Malachy* (1973), *Akhmatova Requiem* (1980), *Risen!* (1981), *Akathist of Thanksgiving* (1987), *Ikon of St Seraphim* (1988), *Resurrection* (1989) and *We Shall See Him as He Is* (1990). His spiritual journey has taken him from the Presbyterian to the Russian Orthodox Church via Roman Catholicism, his musical one from the aleatoric freedoms of the 1960s, as with Bedford's not untinged with pop, to a rediscovery of simple triadic formations, beginning to emerge like a continuation of Vaughan Williams's aesthetic in certain sections of the *Akhmatova Requiem* and fully taking on 'holy minimalism' in *We Shall See Him as He Is*.

Now he has (last) trumped everything with *The Apocalypse* (Proms 1994), a two-hour representation of the Book of Revelation. Others have been there before him: Goossens, like Tavener, uses a consort of recorders, much of the same scenario and text and an amplified baritone for the voice of God; Tippett, again like him, casts his choral magnum opus (see below) in a ninefold form; Holst perhaps deserves pioneer status for his response to the monotonal beauty of Indian melody and his re-ritualizing of Christian chant in concert music. Still, *The Apocalypse* is impressive, though it should remind us how much has remained constant in Tavener's purely musical technique over the years in which his spirituality has moved on – monotonality (the embattled yet ever-present E♭ and E♮ respectively of the *Celtic Requiem* and *In alium* presaging the continual D of *The Apocalypse*); consonant harmony (Victorian hymns in the early works, modal homophony or tonal fanfares in the recent ones); naive pseudo-serial dislocations of line; plain declamation (ritual, Stravinskian Latin in *The Whale*, biblical English in the recent oratorios); and a continuum of great slowness or timelessness punctuated by outbursts of intense activity. What seems to have been lost along the way is the surrealist sense of humour, as when his baritone in *The Whale* shouted echoingly into the whale's belly (alias a gaping black piano with silently depressed note cluster) – and, indeed, when his streetwise girls with their gruesome rhymes in the *Celtic Requiem* routed Britten's choirboys at a stroke.

Is *The Apocalypse* the second coming of English oratorio? Time and the millennium will no doubt tell, though they will probably also show Tavener's marshalling of gestures and resources in space and time to be much more obviously in the Britten tradition than it appears at close range. Other composers, meanwhile, are still searching for a representative choral identity. Some believe in keeping the frontiers open and modernist passports valid, though choral citizenship in such territory can still be problematic (see D. Clarke 1994 for a review of the first performance of Geoffrey Poole's *Blackbird*). Others have retreated behind older or redrawn boundaries. Goehr was asked for a work to fit the British choral tradition with his 1992 Prom commission and wrote *The Death of Moses*, a cantata whose scoring may still reflect the century's cosmopolitan watchwords – Stravinsky, Monteverdi – but whose simple neotonality is Brittenesque and whose clear word-setting even recalls Finzi. Gavin Bryars's *The War in Heaven* (1993) revels in a harmonic kaleidoscope such as Howells might have enjoyed; and Turnage's *Leaving* (1990, revised 1992), an anthology cantata for soprano, tenor, chorus and large ensemble, while still setting 'alienated' poets such as Smith and Plath, does so in a manner suggesting an exploration of the choral persona that has taken the composer within earshot of Bliss or even Elgar.

Finally, there is Tippett, somewhat skated over earlier. *The Vision of St Augustine* has never become popular, probably because its transcendentalism operates in too austerely difficult musical terms, particularly for the choral singer. *The Mask of Time* is a different matter. Here, if anywhere and if with characteristic naivety, is the full-length work that reaffirms the British oratorio tradition for the end of the century – not for him the need to blow it away as a 'fog' of 'insufferable moral earnestness' (Crosse 1970). From its first sonorous bars – to the word 'sound' – the choral writing is warm, surprisingly comfortable in performance, accepting of traditional textures. In the 'Dream of the paradise garden' even the English partsong is lovingly evoked – both text and music of the passages 'Evening shadows bring surcease' and 'It was a sweet communion', with their chords hovering artfully on the brink of dominant 7ths, almost suggest the Sullivan of 'The long day closes'. There are also faint echoes of FitzGerald and Bantock when God speaks as Allah ('The heaven and the Earth and all between; thinkest thou I made them in jest?'). No inhibitions about the choral 'we' beset Tippett, for he will settle for no less than the collective meaning of humanity as his subject; and he remembers Vaughan Williams and Holst (there is a quotation from 'Uranus') in making choral sound the final representative of human destiny, though where they cause their voices to fade into infinity at the end of the *Sea Symphony* and *The Planets* he cuts them off suddenly. At the other chronological pole he joins his juniors such as Swayne and Wishart (to be discussed below) in essaying vocal continuity between the human and animal kingdoms, such as in the frog episode. Here too, and again, is the oratorical response to the century's great pivot of Hiroshima (like Tavener he uses Akhmatova poems). Then he joins Birtwistle in using the Orpheus legend once more to depict the essence of music, which lies after all not in oratory but in song (the work ends with 'Three songs'). And if Tippett's inclusiveness of verbal and conceptual reference (to his own text anthologizing many sources) has never quite risen above the 'fog' of theosophy that alienates some of his hearers, the staging of scenes and presentation of images – such as the witty, Shavian conversation with Ancestor and Dragon – keeps imprecision or cliché at bay. Most of all, the music remains rock-hard, crystal clear as Stravinsky; there is nothing foggy about this.

III: Smaller Choral Works

At the beginning of the century, Bantock made unaccompanied voices aspire to the condition of symphony in *Atalanta in Calydon* (1911), *Vanity of Vanities* (1913) and *A Pageant of Human Life* (1913). Encouraged by the scope for massed sound, breadth and contrast in the madrigals of Weelkes and Wilbye and the motets of Byrd, and by the twentieth-century secular choirs that still sang them (such as Charles Kennedy Scott's Oriana Madrigal Society, the English Singers and, to the present day, the BBC Singers), other composers followed suit, though not on such a large scale. Bax offers an ambitious interchangeability of means and genres in 'Mater ora filium' (1921); his scoring is for double choir with further subdivisions using 'many tricks that one also finds in the orchestral scores (3 solo sopranos, running thirds and sixths)' (Foreman 1983), and, like Vaughan Williams in the *Pastoral Symphony*, is unafraid to explore the effects not just of static against moving lines of sound but of triads conceived simply as thickened lines, as though he were dealing with triple woodwind or brass or *divisi* strings. This ethos survives much later in the century in a work such as Joubert's *Rorate coeli* (1985), an unaccompanied cycle of four motets cast symphonically (the scherzo second) with much triadic working of vocal subdivisions against held lines and with a recurrent title motif. Bax's 'This worldes joie' (1922) is a shorter, less muscular piece than 'Mater ora filium', but its formal urgency is equally symphonic, the driving ostinato (Ex. 12.7, *x*) – couched astutely as an entirely upbeat tetrameter – combining with the initial modal theme (*y*), and a countersubject (*z*) which displaces any hope of an 'Amen', to form an impassioned contrapuntal argument thrown into greater relief by the drama of the homophonic surroundings. The sense of huddled and fleeing groups of souls is as powerful and dynamic a schema as in a medieval wall painting.

Bach's motets may have been another inspiration for Bax and perhaps for the young Britten when he came to use instrumental forms on vocal occasions, as in the variation structure of *A Boy Was Born* (1933). The SSATB disposition of Britten's *Hymn to St Cecilia* (1942) may also have been influenced by Bach – and Britten executes his richly textured canvas of mass and line, even in the solo passages, with no further voice divisions until the very end of the work – but his concept of a vocal scherzo in the second movement is, as in his other vocal music (including the operas), very much his own, one almost as innocent of contrapuntal interaction as it is of harmony. Auden's poem then invokes ode conventions in the last movement with an image procession of musical instruments (violin, drum, flute, trumpet); Britten spotlights them in his choral 'orchestra' with solo imitations in a sequence of accompanied cadenzas, almost as though *The Young Person's Guide to the Orchestra* were already in his thoughts.

Britten's virtuosity may seem like another example of the neoclassicist's or cubist's distortion of nature, but to determine exactly what is natural to voices in combination in twentieth-century terms has been no easy matter. For example, is the practicability of the clustering in Ex. 12.8, from Patric Standford's *Stabat mater* (itself part of his Second Symphony, the *Christus-Requiem*), hostage to the diatonic reference points marked *x* or shrewdly assisted by them?

The rehabilitation of modal and polyphonic traditions is one prominent doctrine, and it links the beginning of the century with its end, but there are many who feel as uneasy about what Vaughan Williams was attempting in the Mass in G minor (1921) – part of the legacy of Richard Terry's 'brilliant developments' at Westminster Cathedral that were none the less 'not particularly conducive to contemporary composition' (Temperley 1981: 212–13) – as about Tavener's 'contracting-out' ethos (D. Clarke 1994).

Yet the partsong and motet traditions had retained no obvious anchors other than the *stile antico*, which at least allowed for the inbuilt contrasts of madrigal textures and topics, and short-breathed strophic models (essentially accompanied top-voice melodies), or

ART MUSIC

Ex. 12.7   Bax: 'This worldes joie'

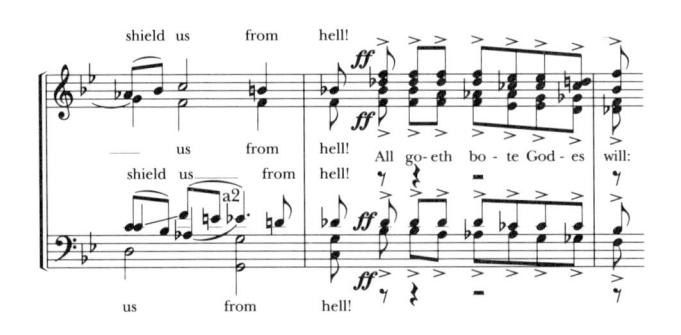

VOCAL MUSIC

Ex. 12.8 Standford: *Stabat mater*

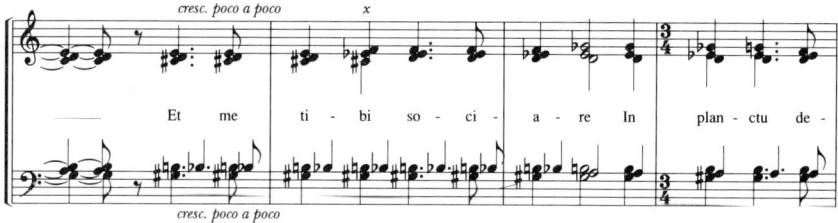

any mixture of the two; multi-sectional glees were perhaps too ingenuously classical to have been perpetuated as structural blueprints. This active inheritance hardly made for tonal discourse and, until Britten, tended to shut other kinds of dialectical or structural devices, especially rhythmic and textural propositions. Moeran's seven *Songs of Springtime* (Elizabethan poems; 1930), for instance, contain a great deal of chromatic colouring, whose flavour is a mixture of archaic and late-romantic, and whose effect is not always directly proportional to its difficulty, but which only accompanies or occasionally tropes what are essentially quadratic tunes, stated once or repeated with variation for two or three strophes. According to some definitions (Apel 1944: 556; Kemp 1984: 179; but not Westrup 1980) this is exactly what a partsong (as opposed to a madrigal) should be, and Ex. 12.9a shows one such frame and its elaboration: the proposed notional F♯ of the quadratic skeleton is realized and prolonged as G♭ within a chromatic context typical of Moeran. Imitation is most apt to occur in the final refrain phrases of these tunes, a distant echo of eighteenth-century fuguing procedure, but it remains incidental. Moeran's texture is otherwise of unrelieved four-part harmonization much indebted to Warlock's solo songs in the 5/8 melody of 'Sigh no more, ladies' and the 2/4 jog-trot of 'Good wine'. Warlock's choral music, however, which is all too often passed over (see Copley 1979: 183), includes convivial folksong and other arrangements with piano such as 'One more river' (1925) on the one hand, intense *a cappella* carols and essays such as the *Three Dirges of Webster* (1923–5) on the other, and tends to interpret the partsong brief less fastidiously than Moeran, risking bold conceptions in passages like the moaning coda to the word 'wind' in 'All the flowers of the spring', the first of the Webster dirges.

Ex. 12.9a   Moeran: 'Love is a sickness' (*Songs of Springtime*)

VOCAL MUSIC

Ex. 12.9b   Britten: 'To daffodils' (*Five Flower Songs*)

Moeran's last poem in *Songs of Springtime* is 'To daffodils', and here the idea of a strophic melody (it comes twice) and the use of madrigal topics (imitation, white-note homophony, momentary silence) are more seriously blended. Nevertheless, one has only to look at Britten's setting of the same poem, as the first of his *Five Flower Songs* (1950), to see how pointedly he relished starting where Moeran left off. Britten still has a complete top-voice melody for the first stanza, but it is more abstractly structured, from stepping 3rds, than a vernacular or classical tune would be. In the very first bar, moreover, he is out to affront both conventional harmonizing and imitation: there is no real bass, for the outer parts have the tune in octaves, while the tenor and the bass imitate in pairs (Ex. 12.9b). Convention would have played both pairs off in 3rds or 6ths, most likely the upper parts against the lower. Britten's second stanza involves 'symphonic' contrast and development in that the top three parts have a completely new, contrasting motif (homophonic chords focusing on close position) while the bass fashions an ostinato out of the opening notes (and words) of the first stanza; strophic paraphrase is reserved for the final line. The second song, 'The succession of the four sweet months', does the obvious, but does it boldly: the four parts enter one by one in a broad fugue – no incidental imitation here – as the four months are described. For the third poem, Crabbe's 'Marsh flowers', Britten does without four-part harmony altogether for the first sestet and final couplet of what is a sort of sonnet, setting them in sparse two-part counterpoint or even just octaves. 'The evening primrose' is closer to Moeran's conventions – though even here Britten feels no compunction to restrict textural contrast and counterpoint by insisting that every voice sings every line of text – but the final song, 'Ballad of green broom', is one of Britten's vocal scherzos, and a *tour de force* of simple and witty logic. The first four stanzas are given one to each part in turn while the other parts have increasingly intricate (and tongue-twisting) ostinatos; stanza 5 pairs the two sets of adjacent parts in imitation, first the men, then the women for the Lady's question; stanza 6 first pairs two non-adjacent parts then uses all four for one of the few pillars of four-part homophony in the cycle.

Perhaps this comparison exaggerates the differences between generations. Moeran's near contemporary Finzi has a subtler range of procedures than he, and Vaughan Williams's *Three Shakespeare Songs* (1951), while of a fatter sonority than would have appealed to Britten, are adroit essays in timbral imagination. Nor does Peter Evans find the *Five Flower Songs* particularly distinctive by the standards of Britten, who had moved beyond partsong decorum as early as *A Boy Was Born* (1933) (see P. Evans 1979: 430), in the process perhaps helping to patent a new set of stock choral devices – octave doubling of two-part writing, harmonies fanning out from a unison opening, chromatic upward shifts towards the top of a voice range, and so on (see the theme of *A Boy was Born*).

Finzi's *Seven Poems of Robert Bridges* (1934–7) can be taken to represent the last flowering in English choral music of Parry's lyric ideal, its restrictions doubtless observed all the more carefully in setting a poet and formidable prosodist with whom Parry had worked so closely. With odd exceptions (most notably the very first phrase of 'Wherefore to-night so full of care'), every voice enunciates the whole text, and does so to rhythms of 'just declamation'. No word or verbal phrase is ever repeated in an individual voice, there is not a single melisma, and feeling comes from the effect and underlining (with melodic contour, rhythmic stress or quantity, and harmonic depth) of the text on its syntactic axis, rather than from musical structures, ideas or images. The results heavily privilege the singer over the listener as recipient and render musical form and expression now refined, now dull. The refinement is to be found in strophic variation when Finzi lets little more than an initial head-motif stand for equivalence. See, for example, 'I praise the tender flower', in which the 'binding' self-referential conceit of the poem – one stanza each for flower, maid and song – is matched with a strophic head-motif that is differently contoured for each stanza, as are the three none the less matching final cadences. Between these reference points, melodic and harmonic flux are deliberately not kept parallel, so that every verbal phrase has a different musical nuance, rhetorically graded for instance by pitch contour (the melodic peaks are progressively d", e", f", g" and a", across the three stanzas). The dullness results from unvarying pace, watery diatonics and a generally unrelieved texture whose points of imitation are just points of decorum (counteracting cadence and stress in an individual voice) and can appear fatuously ruminative; there is no real role differentiation between voices, a severe limitation not encountered so obviously in Finzi's solo songs, where the piano can add a persona and thus a viewpoint.

Finzi's 'White-flowering days' (Blunden) is larger than this in scale but not, on the whole, in scope (though the rule against repetition has been relaxed). It was his contribution to *A Garland for the Queen*, the 1953 Coronation anthology of new British 'madrigals' (new poems as well as music) paralleling *The Triumphs of Oriana* that, given what we have been saying, rather spelt the obsolescence of such modelling than its renaissance. None of the ten composers commissioned by the Arts Council was much under 50 – Rawsthorne and Tippett were the youngest; Walton and Britten were missing – and no one wrote anything striking enough to overcome the sense of anachronism. Ireland, in 'The hills' (James Kirkup), achieved a nostalgic opening phrase worthy of Elgar but failed to follow it up; Bax yearned outrightly in 'What is it like to be young and fair?' (Clifford Bax); Vaughan Williams dedicated his slightly mawkish 'Silence and music' (Ursula Wood) to the memory of Stanford and his 'Blue bird'. Bliss ('Aubade'; Henry Reed) at least attacked a broad canvas with a strong sense of colour and shape, while Tippett glossed the Monteverdian rather than the English madrigal with his vocal gymnastics and echoes in 'Dance, clarion air' (Christopher Fry). If Tippett's contribution was 'the most enduring in the collection' (Kemp 1984: 292), Rawsthorne's ('Canzonet'; Louis MacNeice) was perhaps the simplest and most memorable, angular and insistent like a medieval carol rather than undifferentiated like some of the other settings. The *Times* reviewer (3 June 1953: 4), aware of 'the cruel difficulties of modern choral writing' and of the danger of 'borrow[ing] dissonances from string writing that will sound dull instead of bright on voices', questioned the value of the whole enterprise.

Since then, few works resting on the unaccompanied partsong tradition have hit home in their setting of poetry or found any new vocal authenticity. Nevertheless, until 1979 Novello continued the time-honoured practice of promoting the partsong as a periodical free supplement, with the *Musical Times*. A cross-section of what was offered in the last ten years summarizes the repertoire as far as it went, perhaps as far as it could go, and affords some measurement of the tidal range in what one might characterize as Arts-Council Britain, given that many of the partsongs listed below will have been commissioned in its heyday.

Any continuing norm was represented by the common-currency style (somewhere in the vicinity of Walton's) of such pieces as Mathias's 'A refusal to mourn the death, by fire, of a child in London' (Dylan Thomas; 1969), Geoffrey Bush's 'Ozymandias' (Shelley; 1967) and Anthony Hedges's 'Epitaph' (anon; 1972). Neo-diatonicism was a more dogged ploy, with a conventional tune (David Gow, 'To an isle in the water', Yeats; 1977), or without (Brian, 'O happiness celestial fair', Hannah More; 1969 – set as a very strange pseudo-canon four-in-one), or with Stravinskian astringencies (Richard Stoker, 'Visits of truth', Emerson; 1968). Rhythms and melodic contours either continued within more or less madrigalian restrictions while harmonies were looser or downright cryptic, as in Alan Bush's 'Earth has grain to grow' (Day Lewis; 1972) and Holloway's 'Ah fading joy' (Dryden; 1974) respectively; or they sharpened themselves up to match the knotted energy of much twentieth-century verse, as in Lennox Berkeley's setting of Hopkins's 'The windhover' (1968), a tough piece in every respect (compare Tippett's 1942 setting of it and see P. Dickinson 1988: 182; Kemp 1984: 179). A further setting of 'The windhover', also published in the *Musical Times*, was Smith Brindle's (1971). He weighed Hopkins's words by a graded spectrum of devices, all within conventionally precise rhythms and dynamics: fully notated yet 'approximate' solo melodic pitch; individually chosen melodic pitches simply indicated as low, medium or high; clusters of sung pitches filled out evenly by prearrangement; notated chords in up to eight parts; and 'sung-spoken', spoken and whispered syllables. Dickinson's comparable concern for choral massing of individual words and syllables in 'Late afternoon in November' (1975) was to add upper-voice chords rather like overtones on selected ones. On the whole, though, extended choral sounds and notation, as in Naresh Sohal's 'Poets to come' (Whitman; 1975), were not common; nor was aleatoricism, as in John White's 'Humming and ah-ing machine' (1971). Many composers bluntly posed the difficulties of unaccompanied dodecaphony without giving any indication that tonally freed pitches might shade legitimately into freely pitched declamation; one senses that it was the structural containment of a partsong that appealed most to the 12-note mind. Such essays included Searle's 'I have a new garden' (anon; 1969) and 'From *The Divine Narcissus*' (Sor Juana Inés de la Cruz; 1969), Nieman's *Catalogue of Flowers* (1968), David Blake's *The Almanack* (John Hatfield; 1967), Hugh Wood's 'To a child dancing in the wind' (Yeats; 1973), Don Banks's *Findings Keepings (I)* (1968) and Lutyens's 'Verses of love' (Jonson; 1970). Finally there were those who came out the other side of the total chromatic, Smalley with an ambitious and challenging but skilfully idiomatic partsong, 'The crystal cabinet' (Blake), Musgrave and Douglas Young with the refulgent harmonies of 'O caro m'è il sonno' (Michelangelo; 1978) and 'Canticle' (Auden; 1971) respectively. The pairing of voices in the Smalley (Ex. 12.10) reflects the contrapuntal parody techniques, similar to Maxwell Davies's, used in Smalley's slightly earlier *Missa brevis* for 16 solo voices (a work that is based on a 'Gloria tibi Trinitas' by Blitheman).

Several of these partsongs (those by Stoker, Blake, Nieman and Banks) extended the principle of small-scale apposition to become miniature poetic triptychs, setting three short poems in succession, an idea also seen on a slightly larger scale, beyond the magazine supplement, in McCabe's *Visions*, which fuses two poems, and Holloway's *He-She-Together* (Joyce; 1978). But aphorism within the bounds of the *Musical Times* rarely became lightly worn wit, and *Findings Keepings* was an exception when it set to music, more or less serially, a description of limb severance 'at or above the wrist or ankle' from a car insurance policy.

Choral suites, in spans preferable to single partsongs for the professional concert programme, have allowed freer range to moods and techniques. Transformations between choral harmonies and choric effects occur in Richard Rodney Bennett's cycle of four songs, *Sea Change* (1984); the vertical world ranges from octatonic murmurings in the first, through pure triads in the second and approximately notated though still sung pitches in the third to Bennett's beloved jazz harmonies in the fourth. Poole's *Because It's Spring* (cummings) similarly explores different idioms in the different movements, including mock-barbershop in the third.

Bliss's later partsong assignments, done as Master of the Queen's Musick and including 'Mar Portugues' (Fernando Pessoa), sung to Edward Heath and the Prime Minister of Portugal at a banquet in 1973, and 'Birthday song for a royal child' (Day Lewis), celebrating the birth of Prince Andrew in 1959 and broadcast after the nine o'clock news, merely added to the genre's quaintness; but he was a striking

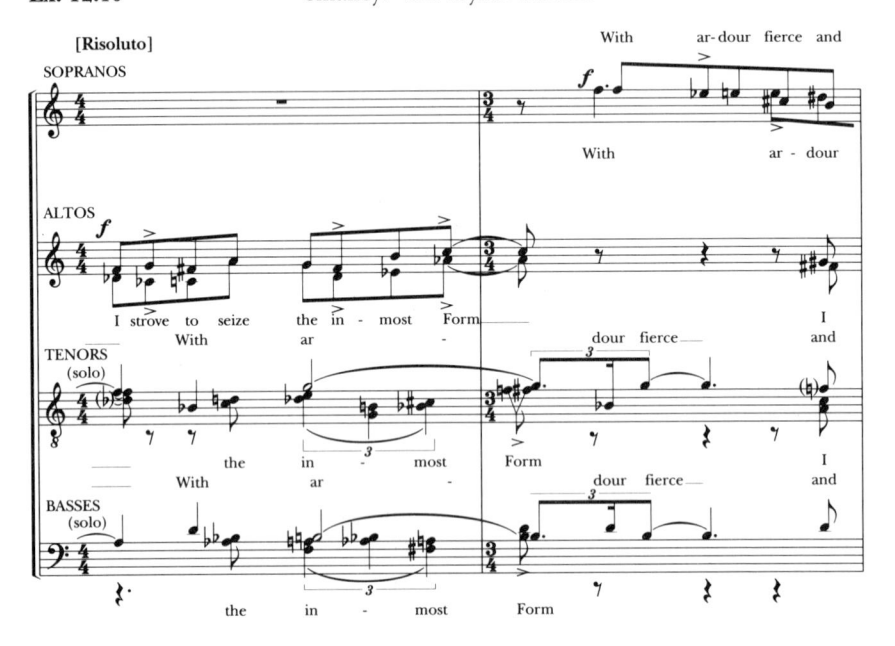

Ex. 12.10   Smalley: 'The crystal cabinet'

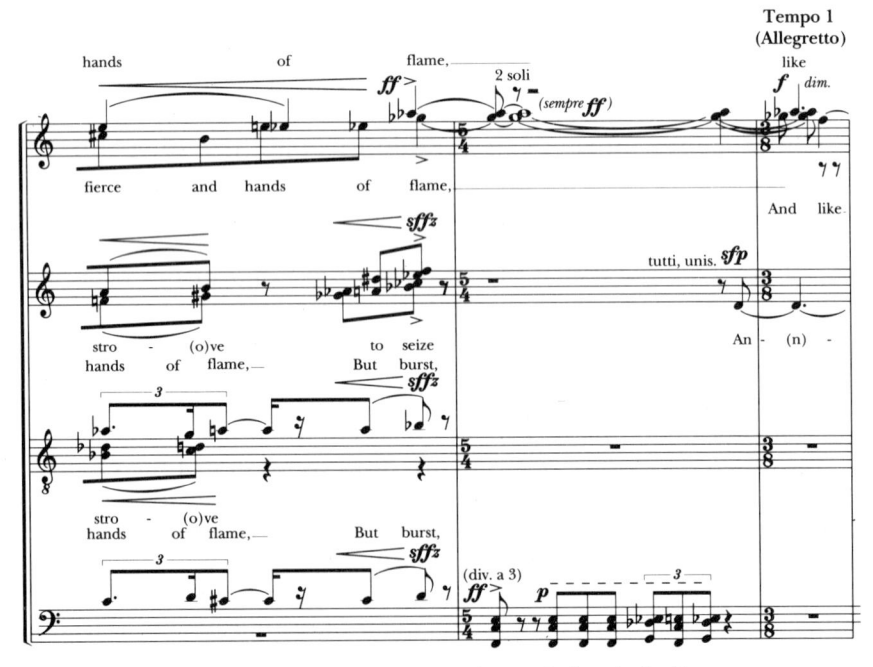

and perhaps surprising late contributor to two other small- or medium-scale choral genres, as we shall see, and these were less problematic to him, for alongside the *a cappella* motet, mass and madrigal one can detect several other distinct and not unfertile models in the twentieth-century British repertoire. The cantata with instruments, particularly the Bach cantata, was one; the multi-sectional anthem or cantata with symphonic organ part, surprisingly undeveloped before S. S. Wesley, surprisingly indigenous, and surprisingly distinctive in, say, Stainer's *Crucifixion*, another (we shall see Finzi and others servicing it well in their church music); the Gabrieli or Schütz *concertato* with various instrumental groupings a third. Vaughan Williams's 'The Hundredth Psalm', written for his Leith Hill Festival of 1930, triadically jubilant in its ritornelli like the Bach *Magnificat* and elsewhere serenely pastoral like many of Bach's solo and chorale arias, is an obvious example of the first, and one notices similar ritornello energy in the last section of his *Benedicite* (1929). Leighton's almost unbearably penitential *Crucifixus pro nobis* (Patrick Carey and Phineas Fletcher; 1961), although scored for organ, is another, in its use of florid and emotionally intense *obbligato* lines and trio-sonata counterpoint (alongside a desperation and urgency, especially in the second movement, that suggest Shostakovich). Two fine but little-known works for chorus and brass, Rubbra's *Veni,*

Creator Spiritus (1966) and Bliss's *The World Is Charged with the Grandeur of God* (Hopkins; 1969), demonstrate the wisdom of the third model, for the combination of sung and mouthpiece-blown breath is a natural and unprejudicial one (Bliss's central movement of the three, a setting of 'Heaven-haven', furthers the *concertato* idea by changing the scoring to female voices with two flutes). Others who wrote for this combination include Payne (*Phoenix Mass*, 1972) and Maconchy (*And Death Shall Have No Dominion*, Worcester 1969). Holst created a special kind of accompanied partsong in his *Choral Hymns from the Rig Veda* (four groups; 1908–12), *Seven Partsongs* (Bridges; 1926) and *Six Choruses* (medieval; 1932); but since nearly all of these, fine works that they are, employ only female or male voices and orchestra (mostly strings alone), they are difficult to programme and have tended to be overlooked.

As for the cantata with organ, one might broaden it to include Dickinson's effective *Martin of Tours* (Thomas Blackburn; 1966), scored with chamber organ and piano duet. Bliss's own contribution was almost his last work, *Shield of Faith* (1974), an anthology of spiritual poetry with a virtuoso and highly imaginative organ part, one perhaps reminiscent of Finzi's 'Lo, the full, final sacrifice' in the beautiful introduction to the third movement ('Love bad me welcome'; Herbert) or of a French toccata in its sequel, taken from Pope's *An Essay on Man*. Only in the final movement, to parts of Eliot's 'Little Gidding', does the scope of the anthology seem rashly ambitious.

Two choral genres remain to be mentioned rather than covered: folksong arrangements and the unison and two- or three-part songs with accompaniment referred to on p. 403 and bunched under the description of choral songs. Folksong arrangements have continued to be popular with much the same clientele as carols, and there are now accordingly two volumes of *Folk-Songs for Choirs* (1983) which incorporate several of Rutter's and Willcocks's arrangements as well as older ones, for instance by Vaughan Williams and Holst, that were as much a part of the folksong revival as solo settings (see below, p. 468; and 'Greensleeves' is not omitted (see Howkins 1989). These unaccompanied arrangements, like many others in circulation, are sometimes twee, rarely matching the power and invention of those by Percy Grainger (1882–1961), which are difficult and not made easier to rehearse and programme when they include heterodox combinations of instruments, as in 'The three ravens' of 1902. Nor has the earthy impetus gained from contact (and international competition) with Eastern European choirs and their repertoire of

VOCAL MUSIC

arrangements by Kodály, Bartók and others been fully incorporated, though Seiber's *Three Hungarian Folk-Songs* (1955, published to English words) remain popular. Perhaps the English tunes themselves have inbuilt limitations of character. Nevertheless, Tippett found a meaningful agenda and a co-operative style in his *Four Songs from the British Isles* (1956), one movement of a 'suite-like' (Kemp 1984: 291) or symphonic whole for each principality; and Finnissy has recently blown more dust off the choral folksong in his unassuming but shrewd *Australian Sea Shanties* (1984).

Choral songs are difficult to pin down. They may be national tunes – secular hymns, effectively – that have had words added or went from solo to choral, audience or even congregational constituency as their popularity, whether or not engineered or envisaged by the composer, grew. Elgar's 'Land of hope and glory' was written as the trio of his first *Pomp and Circumstance* march (1901), A. C. Benson's words being added, against Jaeger's judgement, for its incorporation into the *Coronation Ode* and afterlife as a song (see Kennedy 1968, R/1982: 168–72). Holst added Cecil Spring-Rice's words to the big tune from 'Jupiter' in *The Planets* when he made it into the unison song with orchestra, 'I vow to thee, my country', in 1921. Parry's 'Jerusalem' (Blake) was composed in 1916 for mass singing at a meeting of 'Fight for Right', a wartime propaganda organization, and was later taken up by the women's movement (it is the national song for the WI) – see Dibble 1992: 483–5. Many other contributions lie behind these all-obscuring peaks, and their origins, stance and texts would make a fascinating study, illuminating the history of national myth. Vaughan Williams's 'The new commonwealth' (Harold Child; 1943) must be one of the last of such songs – how many does a nation need? – and again owed its origin to wartime propaganda, in this case the film *49th Parallel*, for which he wrote the score and from whose Prelude he extracted the tune. However, Ireland's 'Man in his labour rejoiceth' (Bridges; 1947), dedicated 'to the mineworkers of Britain', was still to come, as was Dyson's 'Song for a festival' (Day Lewis; 1951), commissioned by the Arts Council for the Festival of Britain. 'Jerusalem' above all set the stylistic pattern – see Geoffrey Shaw's 'Worship' (Whittier; 1927) as a hoary offshoot – though even Parry's attempt at a sequel, 'England' (John o'Gaunt's speech from Shakespeare's *Richard II*; 1918), could not match it. Later additions to the communally sung repertoire have tended to come from the West End or Broadway, or from pop, or both ('You'll never walk alone'), and Britten was wise not to attempt self-conscious hymning; had he done so, no doubt the result would have been as curious as Ronald Stevenson's 'No coward soul is mine' (Emily Brontë; 1969) for female voices and harp. Nevertheless, unison songs have continued to be written – witness Tippett's 'Music' (Shelley; 1960), provided for a festival of rural choirs. Convivial or drinking songs with chorus are a slightly different breed, shading into both solo songs and partsongs (Warlock's, for instance) or even the cantata (Stanford's *Songs of the Sea* and *Songs of the Fleet*). And if these tend to be male-voice orientated, it is obvious that songs written for school commissions, affiliations or markets are predominantly for treble voices. What is remarkable is how far Britten serviced and shaped the latter repertoire and how at his hands it ranged naturally between the small- and large-scale and the sacred and secular. One believed-in impulse, to sing a tune, tell a story, take a part, make a sound or pattern, interact with a professional or adult, render a community or an institution or just spare time creative, underlies the scope of this considerable portion of his output, from the twelve classroom songs of *Friday Afternoons* (1933–5) to the *Children's Crusade* (1968) and other narrative ballads mentioned earlier, and from the setting of *Psalm 150* (1962) and the myriad works mentioned elsewhere (such as *A Ceremony of Carols*) to his last composition, the *Welcome Ode* (1976). Tippett's equivalent contribution to the larger among these was the cantata *Crown of the Year* (Christopher Fry; 1958) for treble voices and instruments.

We have seen that in cantatas and other smaller-scale works combined voices with all their problems of corporate identity have continued to thrive in apposition to instruments with all their concreteness and powers of symbolism. On the other hand, to allow human voices to be themselves, a major incentive for composers for chorus and vocal ensemble in the second half of the twentieth century, one must include their powers of imitative representation as well as their verbal and other non-verbal sign systems. Where the morphology of musical sound in general is concerned, voices have taken their place alongside other sources for the purposes of electro-acoustic transformation; but the electronic revolution has been of particular assistance to vocal music for two reasons. One is that the microphone has been able to capture the flexibilities of intimate vocal expression in direct and infinitesimal ways which the unamplified, classically trained voice had abandoned as early as the initial rise of the opera stage and concert platform. The other is that the spectrum of vocal sounds and meanings, all the way from primal

VOCAL MUSIC

phonic utterance to the elaborate concatenation of phonemes and syllables that make up words and sentences, can be explored within a technical framework that poets, novelists and other performance artists might envy, if one thinks above all of the aesthetic aspirations of Joyce and Beckett.

Sound sources can now be manipulated digitally to an extent that obliterates, or if the composer desires, reconstitutes all distinctions between poem and music, voice and instrument, abstraction and image. Some have accordingly pursued the purely electro-acoustic medium, word and 'song' featuring prominently in the work of Joseph Hyde, for instance. Others prefer to stay on more tangible planes. Harvey is highly conscious of the new morphological dimensions in his *Inner Light II*, the only piece in the *Inner Light* trilogy (1973–7) to include voices (it is scored for SSATB soli, large chamber ensemble and tape), for he applies them not only to the transformation of sounds but to the human condition itself: the work and the chosen texts from Eliot, Kipling, Blake, the Bible and Rudolf Steiner are about 'the difficulty of connection' which Harvey, in his introduction to the score, goes on to parse in terms that are virtually a creed for the later twentieth-century composer:

The vocal writing covers a wide range of possibilities (twelve in all) ranging from the pure expression of feeling in sung vowel sounds, through objectification in formations of consonants, passages in which instruments supply the missing vowels or consonants in the singers' words (as if matter itself is trying to speak), different kinds of vocal gesture with varying degrees of 'meaning', jumbled language, speech in an unknown language, as if from another world (actually invented by the composer), struggles to form communicating language, to straight speech, and at the extreme, to a simply understood story (though paradoxically a story about struggling to communicate). All these, and the various degrees of singing, are assembled and shuffled in a quasi-structuralist network with serially ordered proportions, as in the pitch and rhythm domains.

The tape, as well as adding to the dramatic quality of the images, makes 'bridges' (as in the other Inner Light works), and here changes sung vowel sounds (each vowel has three characteristic formant areas above its fundamental – that makes four pitches) into four-part chords related to the harmonic structure of the piece. By this means, instrumental tones and what they play are translated into the domain of the human voice.

If we seem to have come a long way from Walton's and Bliss's naive experiments with text and music of the 1920s (see below, p. 487), it is even further from the conventional rhetoric of earlier centuries whose passing Ferneyhough noted.

Ferneyhough's own sense of 'making bridges' with voices is more severe. In his *Missa brevis* (1969) he sees his text as a 'culturally integral monument' and his extremely difficult 12-voice writing as involving 'overwhelmingly traditional . . . techniques' (1989: 166–8). *Time and Motion Study III* (1974) takes more phonemic, phonetic and extended approaches to vocal material, though still with some sense of the conventions of choral discipline. *Transit* (1975), a 45-minute work, amplifies six solo voices and includes performer freedom but pitches it against his instrumental demands. These scores may be formidable, yet *Transit* is simple in its symphonic effect, and one accepts the voices in the orchestra quite naturally.

At well over an hour in length, Giles Swayne's *Cry* for 28 amplified voices (1979) is larger still and may be thought a further candidate for the looked-for status of latter-day British choral masterpiece. The title makes its own late twentieth-century point – that voices come first after all – and *Cry*'s concerns are universal enough: each of the seven movements represents a day in the Genesis creation myth (the seventh, 'Rest', facilitating an almost traditionally cyclic process of fragmentary recapitulation); and the text consists of syllables rather than words, with the arguable exception of 'anima' in the last movement. Swayne's reappraisal of his musical language in *Cry* was to make everything as primal as possible, and the effects of counterpoised blocks of sound are wonderfully grand and simple, at the same time crossing and re-crossing the whole continuum between noise and harmony. Those blocks with simple modal parameters function as a succession of contrasts or are simultaneously set against percussive shouts and other non-melodic techniques; or they may be chords ('light' in the first movement, 'song of the moon' in the fourth), African syllabic rhythms (6: 'Creatures of the dry land'), heterophonic fugues, or long single notes (5: 'Creatures of the air and water'). Swayne disclaims any emulation of the English choral tradition; though if we are none the less reminded not just of Tallis's *Spem in Alium* but, repeatedly, of 'Neptune' in *The Planets* and the broad-brush directness of Vaughan Williams's choral effects in works such as *Flos campi* and *Dona nobis pacem*, it is a tribute to their originality as much as to his unconscious affinities.

Whether or not in response to *Cry*, Trevor Wishart's *Vox* (1979–86) succeeded it as another large-scale, multi-movement vocal interpretation of primal myths and impulses – a symphony, one might argue, since it explores 'many different aspects of what it means to be

VOCAL MUSIC

"human"' (Wishart 1990). Wishart has made other major statements at the meeting-point of electronics and voices, such as *Red Bird* (1977), a 40-minute electro-acoustic piece using the basic 'sound-symbols' of birds, machines, animals/bodies and words, and *Anticredos* for amplified SSTBBB solo voices, written for Singcircle in 1979 and consisting of transformations of the phonemic constituents of the word 'credos'. But *Vox* caps these works. For four amplified voices and tape with delay and spatial projection systems, it triumphantly demonstrates that with microphones and, in Electric Phoenix, a vocal quartet specializing in their use, partsong and *musique concrète*, diminished-7th harmony and extended vocal techniques can live side by side. And if *Vox* and Electric Phoenix were both made possible by preceding works and performers such as, respectively, Stockhausen's *Stimmung* and the San Diego Extended Vocal Techniques Ensemble (for which Roger Marsh's *'Not a soul but ourselves . . .'*, discussed below, was composed in 1977), their affinities and characteristics are none the less a proud new manifestation of British choral adaptabilities. Many of the new music vocalists – and even some pop singers – were schooled in English cathedral choirs and have made and sustained easy transitions between art music and commercial, sacred and secular, old and new repertoires, groups such as the King's Singers tackling all these. Similarly, Wishart's universalist aspirations have taken him, in *Vox*, all the way from abstraction of sound (*Vox 5* is entirely electro-acoustic) through various transformations between the natural and cultural (such as with the call of the great northern diver and its metamorphoses in *Vox 2*) and the aesthetic and the psychological (sound constituents in *Vox 4* range from syllabic or other 'non-note' particles to sound images such as interrogators hammering on a door) to the blatant disco finale, admittedly a 'provisional' one, which is *Vox 6* and which, along with its 3000 occurrences of the word 'dance' (with American pronunciation), even acknowledges the musicological and British choral establishments with rap references to Schenker and Belshazzar and his feast. Ex. 12.11 gives some idea of the precision, amplitude and suggestiveness of detail at Wishart's command. But what makes *Vox* so impressive is less its technical scope than its monumental sense of dramatic shape, particularly in the *crescendo* of an erupting riot in *Vox 4* – the four singers seem to be huddling together against this background – which leads to a single culminating sound like breaking windows whose aftermath is the solitude of deep sighs that then gather themselves into the 'one all-enveloping vocal utterance' of *Vox 5* (Wishart 1990), itself dispelled

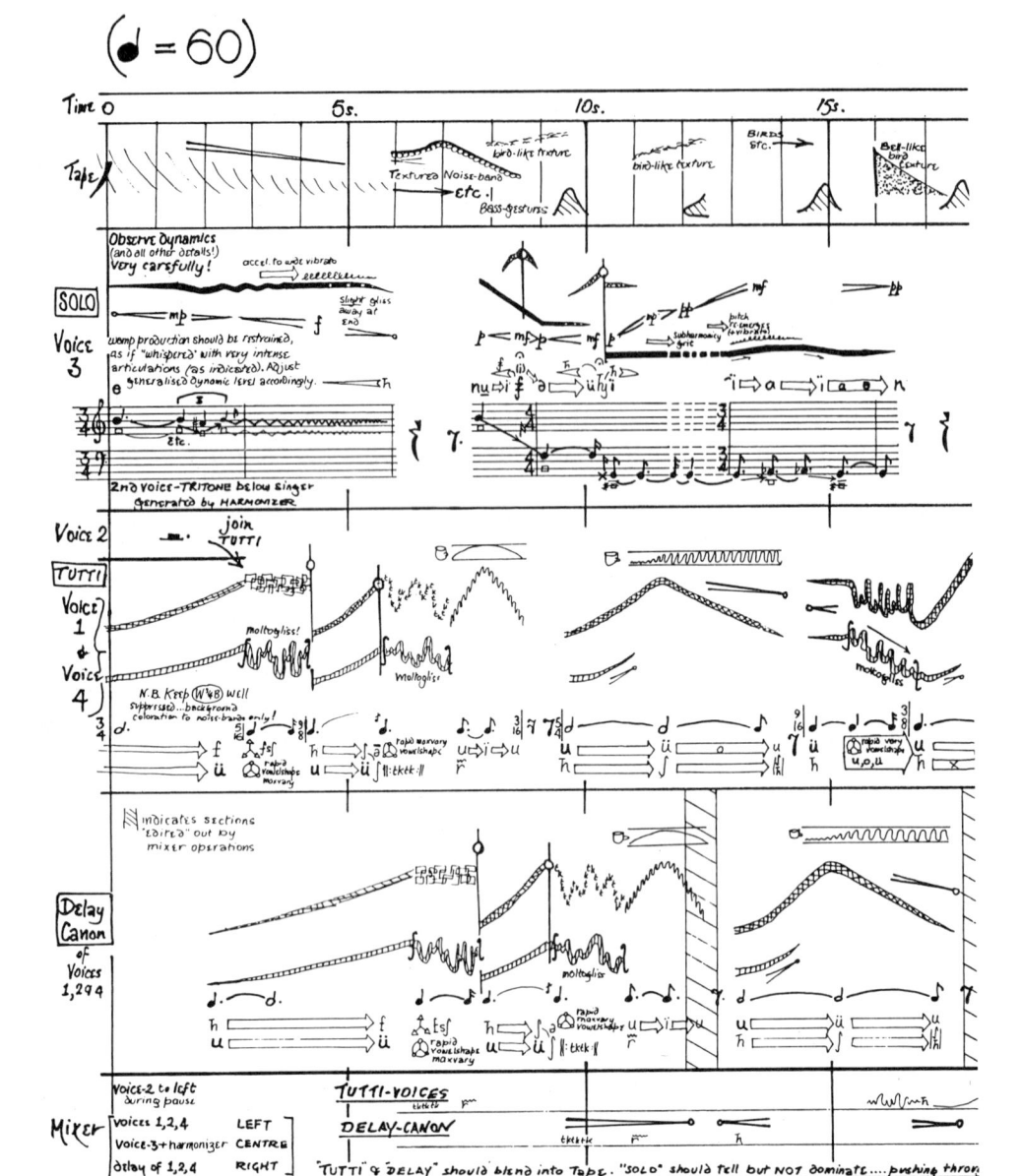

Ex. 12.11 Wishart: *Vox 2*

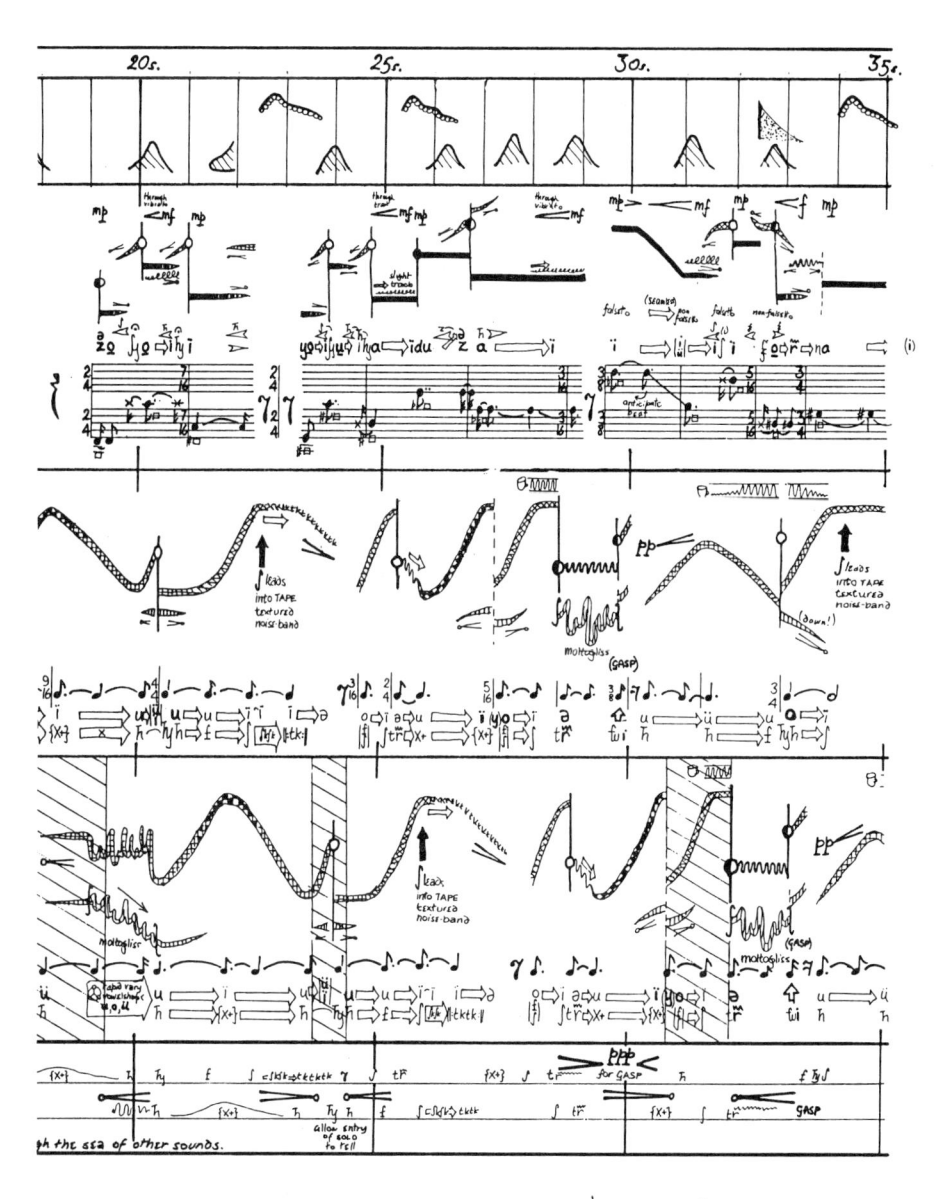

Vox II   Trevor Wishart   Page 8

in images of thunder and rain and followed by the dance finale. Such crass description can give no idea of the poetic power of the sequence.

Vox heads a classic repertoire in the making. Patterson's *Brain Storm* (1978) was an early Electric Phoenix commission and internalized the amplified voice and its effects to something that was 'all in the mind', as the refrain put it in this piece about a nervous breakdown. More recent and much more extrovert is Stephen Montague's *Tigida pipa* of 1983, written for Singcircle, and basically a vocal toccata. Another Singcircle commission is *Son entero* (1989) by Alejandro Viñao (*b* 1951), redolent of Latin American rhythms and harmonies and wholeness (the title can mean 'the complete sound' or 'the entire story'). And like *Vox*, Marsh's '*Not a soul but ourselves...*', a much smaller-scale work notwithstanding a text taken from Joyce's *Finnegans Wake*, demonstrates the fertility of a crossover with pop, not in rhythmic or harmonic vocabulary but in vocal tessitura: the four voices (two male, two female) occupy the close, harmonically clean, youthful range patented by groups such as the Beatles and Abba, its male falsetto component directly dependent upon the separate and intimate miking specified by the composer. The spectrum between syllabic music and musical prose runs from Joyce's repetitive washerwoman's gossip (spoken 'sing-song' by Anna) to the chimingly consonant, homophonic singing of Joyce's restricted, musically congruent range of vowels and consonants that constitute his heroine's name, 'Anna Livia Plurabela', and, together with 'tell me', form the only sung text (Ex. 12.12a). Both these items act as formal refrains, generating interspersed material that privileges

Ex. 12.12a   Marsh: 'Not a soul but ourselves...'

VOCAL MUSIC

Joyce's verbal puns and transformations and explores further points on the phonic spectrum (syllables and phrases unvoiced or half voiced, along with inhalations and exhalations). But the baroque, concerto-like feeling of the piece with its almost Vivaldian joyousness is enhanced by keeping these refrains as separate layers, and with Stravinsky or even Britten sensed in the abstraction of Ex. 12.12a there is never any doubt about this being above all a formal piece of music, though it has been effectively staged as music theatre. The long, haunting coda even suggests Sibelius as well as American minimalism (Ex. 12.12b). If voices can draw together such diverse strands they may yet hold the key to our musical future.

Ex. 12.12b Marsh: 'Not a soul but ourselves . . .'

ART MUSIC
IV: Church Music

Emerson, on a visit to England in 1848 and witnessing the enthronement of a new Archbishop of York, had enjoyed the reading of an Old Testament story from 'the morning of the world' to 'the decorous English audience, just fresh from the Times newspaper and their wine . . . That was binding old and new to some purpose . . . Here in England every day a chapter of Genesis, and a leader in the Times' (1856: 129). The unbroken use and setting to music of seventeenth-century biblical prose and verse have given English church music in the twentieth century a curious profile, oblique and often archaic in its usage of musical forms, tonalities and periodic structures – the lyrical norms underlying so much of the classical development of secular music scarcely apply – yet not entirely unresponsive to modern developments. The genius for accommodation sensed by Emerson has continued to apply, and to demonstrate it a good place to begin is with one of the century's best-known anthems, a piece already mentioned in Volume V of this series (Temperley 1981: 210) but exacting analysis here: 'Greater love hath no man' (1912) by John Ireland, a composer who met Emerson as a child.

The lack of a lyrical blueprint makes it surprisingly complex for a small-scale composition (see Table 12.1). The words, a miniature sermon on love and its imperatives, have been compiled from various parts of the Bible and are used flexibly, laid out with an unequal amount of repetition. The title phrase, not repeated and the only saying of Christ to be used, is like the preacher's text, preceded by an introduction and set within an overall progression from the Old Testament through the Gospel to St Paul's exegeses. The age-old technique of scholarly concordance comes into its own in the juxtaposition of text sections 4 and 5, and Ireland's music runs straight on between them.

There are comparable uses of musical concordance: all the main melodic material is based on the opening vocal motif whose changing-note shape and subsequent scale with the pair of quavers are subjected to developing variation (such as by inversion) and interpenetration (see the distributional analysis in Ex. 12.13, in which all the material has been transposed to A major or F♯ minor for maximum congruence). Ireland would have learnt this metamorphic habit of mind from Stanford, who was well aware of it in Beethoven, Schubert and Brahms (see Stanford 1911: 39–41, 70–72, 89) and used head-motifs in his own church music (for example, the *Te Deum* in B♭). As

VOCAL MUSIC

Table 12.1   John Ireland: 'Greater love hath no man'

TEXT

1. *Song of Solomon viii/7 (part)*
   a. Many waters cannot quench love,
   b. neither can the floods drown it.
           /6 (part)
   c. Love is strong as death.
2. *John xv/13*
   Greater love hath no man than this, that a man lay down his life for his friends.
3. *I Peter iv/24 (part)*
   a. Who his own self bare our sins in his own body on the tree,
   b. that we, being dead to sins,
   c. should live unto righteousness.
4. *I Corinthians vi/11 (part)*
   (But) ye are washed, (but) ye are sanctified, (but) ye are justified in the name of the Lord Jesus.
5. *I Peter ii/9*
   a. (But) ye are a chosen generation, a royal priesthood, a holy nation, a peculiar people; that ye should shew forth the praises of him who hath called you
   b. out of darkness
   c. into his marvellous light.
6. *Romans xii/1*
   a. I beseech you (therefore), brethren, by the mercies of God, that ye present your bodies a living sacrifice,
   b. holy,
   c. acceptable unto God, which is your reasonable service.

FORM

Musical section
I			II		III			IV
A	B	C	D_1	D_2	E	F	E	G coda
choir ────────			sop solo	bar solo	choir ────────────			

Musical motifs
| i | i | ii── | [ii] | iii | iii | iv | ii────── | iv | v |

Text
1			2	3		4	5		6
ab	ab	cc a		ab bc	bcc	bcc		a	bbc	a bbc

ART MUSIC

with the subject of the verbal text, the musical motifs, particularly the recurring fanfare (ii), are what bind together a non-periodic structure and non-recapitulatory argument whose asymmetries are noteworthy in several respects. For instance, musical section II sounds like a 12-bar period with halfway pivot in the dominant (at the end of D_1), but the prose makes D_1's two phrases each five bars long, not four. Most striking is the way musical and textual segments are overlapped or counterpointed. The first period of musical section III (E, with motif iv) is an eight-bar phrase; however, not only is it recapitulated to a different section of text (its prosody now necessitating a multiple upbeat) but in both cases it arrives in the middle of a verbal passage.

Ex. 12.13   Ireland: 'Greater love hath no man'

As for the musical style, it is a rich and knowing mixture of old and new, sacred and secular. The lack of quadratics (two- or four-bar phrases and their multiples) – and this is applicable to virtually all British choral music, with its uninterrupted currency – bespeaks archaism, the legacy of renaissance motet and madrigal, as does some of the harmony (see the plagal cycle of reversed 5ths, I–V–ii–vi repeated I–v–ii–vi, accompanying the opening motif), while the motivic thinking is symphonic. The coda ('holy, acceptable') is angelically lydian, and the final words ('reasonable service') rhetorically unconstrained, yet the organ epilogue's harmonic closure, virtually that of *Tristan*, could hardly be more tonally charged; the climactic organ chord after the word 'light' is also highly Wagnerian. There is additionally an awareness of Elgar, in the march of the opening (compare the First Symphony motto) and the three-part texture of section III (E), and of Brahms (the dominant 7th pivoting

VOCAL MUSIC

as an augmented 6th at the title words). Altogether the style is far from being just 'School of Stanford' (Long 1972: 411).

Merely local harmonic thinking has been identified elsewhere in this volume as a British shortcoming (see Chapter 9), but it has been responsible for some treasured effects none the less, the moment of eschatological vision being the beloved topic of the English romantic anthem. Temperley (1981: 208–9) has dealt with Wood and Bairstow; 'And I saw a new heaven' (1928) by Edgar Bainton (1880–1956) is something of a *locus classicus*, with its succession of disembodied modal writing and all too embodied catharsis complete with slow waltz tune, climactic $\frac{6}{4}$ and IV^6–iv^6–I plagal cadence. Earlier, Edward Naylor's motet 'Vox dicenti: Clama' (1911) is virile enough, and Mervyn Cooke (1993: 4) is right to identify a Verdian spirit, but the treble solo at the lines of affirmation of utopian pastoral melt the heart with Gounod's or Massenet's sweetness. In another favourite motet, the double-choir 'Faire is the heaven' (1925) by William Harris (1883–1973), the poet, Spenser, asks, 'How then can mortall tongue hope to express / The image of such endlesse perfectness?' The answer is, after a middle section full of modal false relations, by employing no fewer than four enharmonic returns to D♭ major, the last one drawn out with sumptuous part-writing, an almost 'endlesse' appoggiatura and a $\frac{6}{4}$ sonority never finally grounded in dominant resolution. Such topics work well in choral writing and can still be found in Walton's 'Set me as a seal upon thine heart' (1938) and, if somewhat more elliptically and with the help of organ, in Berkeley's 'The Lord is my shepherd' (1975), one of the later fruits of the 'Hussey legacy' (Burn 1988) – works commissioned by Walter Hussey, first as vicar of St Matthew's, Northampton, then as Dean of Chichester, and his successors. As for the more culpable harmonic implications of *Tristan*, Balfour Gardiner draws unashamedly on them in the lead-in to the central part of his 'Evening hymn', relishing the perils of nocturnal fantasies with full Augustinian *Angst*, but cleans himself up diatonically in the outer sections with the help of organ pedal points.

Gardiner's anthem has breadth and span as well as harmonic indulgence. To see the gap that needed to be bridged by others in this respect we can compare Ireland's 'Greater love', in which despite the thematic logic most of the harmonic interest is localized, with Britten's early *Te Deum* in C, written in 1934 just after he had studied with Ireland at the RCM and similarly based on a changing-note motif. Britten sets a broad harmonic scale by making the motif suffix a G in the organ pedals, in other words as an elaboration of a $^6_4$. This both generates harmonic tension and, because its essence is melodic extension, not unitary chordal function, indefinitely defers resolution. When a C does arrive in the bass, after more than two pages, it is to a quartal sonority. Long-term connections are sustained: the middle section is in A major, thus the $^6_4$ elaboration now refers to E (completing a kind of *Bassbrechung*) complemented by A, falling again to G for a recapitulation, whence a background scale descent marks out F (against the highest soprano note, a"), E and a repeatedly reached D before rising almost two octaves – all the while with motivic elaboration – for what is virtually the first root-position C major triad in the piece (at the words 'in Thee have I trusted'). Bottom C is reached as triadic tonic for the only time at the very last chord.

When Gerald Finzi came to write a commissioned *Magnificat* – and it is a not unsuccessful one, though also not liturgical – his wife noted that 'G, having had so many years of . . . innumerable dreary automatic magnificats finds it hard to throw any new light on the words – the orange is sucked dry' (Joy Finzi, journal entry, 25 July 1952). Overriding strategies such as Britten's in the *Te Deum* were a foil to excessive textual familiarity on the one hand and, on the other, to the structure of canticle verse seeming, if not set antiphonally, all too loose and unperiodic. In the *Jubilate Deo* (1961) Britten again keeps a motif in dynamic flux throughout, this time a peal of four conjunct semiquavers followed by three pairs of disjunct quavers, on which every conceivable change is rung with almost no exact repetition. Nor are the vocal lines subservient to this: they have their own equally thorough-going dotted rhythm and melodic shape.

Simplicity, logic and vivid character are Britten's watchwords in his church music, this last attribute raising him head and shoulders above most practitioners even in such a little-known work as his 'Hymn of St Columba' (1962). Others have learnt from his management of unfolding line and pervasive motif and achieved impressive results, particularly in organ-accompanied anthems such as Leighton's chromatically austere 'Give me the wings of faith' (1962), Gardner's 'O clap your hands' (1953) and the rather similar 'O praise God in his holiness' (1968) by Joubert, whose other essays show similar qualities (for example 'All wisdom cometh from the Lord' (1969) and the popular 'O Lorde, the maker of al thing' (1952) in which an ostinato recalls Holst or perhaps Bax's 'This worldes joie'). But few risked Britten's wit.

VOCAL MUSIC

The conversational flux of harmonic syntax was more comfortable, and the influence of Elgar in particular is responsible for the modal flavour of many a passage in which a composer similarly substitutes the minor 'shadow' chords iii and vi for V and I. Bullock's 'Give us the wings of faith' (1925) is typical of the resulting flavour, which can still be heard echoing wanly in the many workaday anthems of Eric Thiman (aimed more at nonconformist than parish or cathedral choirs). In Howells's 'Gloucester' *Magnificat* and *Nunc dimittis* there is a particularly striking example of the technique: at the climax of the *Nunc dimittis* (Ex. 12.14) the dominant (at the word 'thy') is first tempered by both the C♯ in the tenor and the F♯ in the organ, which tend towards open-5th sonorities and minor-triad implications, and then taken to a submediant rather than tonic resolution, ambiguous in that with the A bass it is not as emphatic as an interrupted cadence but implies the relative minor none the less with the two downward 5ths in the soprano (the first negating the A major leading note); an austerely uninflected imperfect cadence back in the major follows, and the overall result is introverted, understated rhetoric.

Yet Howells's vision was as ecstatic as his forebears' and grounded in techniques that enabled him to sustain it through no fewer than ten settings of the *Magnificat* and *Nunc dimittis* that are very much at the heart of the twentieth-century cathedral repertoire. Some of these techniques, as found in *Hymnus paradisi*, have already been discussed, but they need glossing (see Routley 1964: 59, and Long 1972: 430 for comparable taxonomies). A distinctive and very English approach to rhythmic flux and word-setting is in evidence, whereby a marked preference for subdivisible triple time cushions a varied placing of accents and number of syllables per bar (three, four, five are common) and thus obviates gaucheness in the irregular phrase-lengths of the text. All seven settings examined are wholly or predominantly in this sarabande-like triple time, especially in the *Magnificat* and the concluding Gloria sections, and it also lends itself to winging multiple upbeats, often contrapuntally disposed in the organ part. (One of Howells's last anthems, 'The fear of the Lord', 1976, makes much of these.) Howells's harmony cannot be properly examined here, but proto-octatonic segments, as we have seen, prove highly integral and mediate spiritually between static modality and ecstatic chromaticism or bimodality. For instance, the very first sonority after the opening tonic in the 'Collegium regale' *Magnificat* (0 1 3 6) can be heard as part of a diatonic hexachord spread out

Ex. 12.14   Howells: 'Gloucester' *Nunc dimittis*

(given due cathedral resonance) over the remainder of the bar as 0 2 3 5 7 9; or it can suggest the beginnings of two minor scales a minor 3rd apart, which eventuate later on (for instance, as G minor and B♭ minor at the passage '. . . his servant Israel: as he promised . . .', to octatonic segment 0 2 3 5 6 8), and which are congruent with the blues element identified by Mervyn Cooke (1993:4) in Howells's best-known anthem, 'Like as the hart', where it is a matter of E minor plus G major with a blue 3rd. All in all, Howells created a limited but intense sound-world that has proved a durable mirror of both the restraint and the exultation of the Anglican experience; nor do his *Magnificat* settings forget their Marian origins, and most of them begin with or include passages for trebles.

It is, ultimately, a matter of stylistic icons, and one can trace these as they shift and develop in church music throughout the century, often in accordance with textual preferences. Dyson's Christianity, for instance, is of the muscular variety, carried with such sunny, bell-pealing Sunday morning confidence in the *Jubilate Deo* of the D major canticles (1924) that one is taken right back to Emerson's apprehension of complacent well-being at the heart of the English church. Finzi can be just as full-blooded – 'God is gone up' (1951) is the most extrovert of his occasional contributions – but his motivation is the corporeality of his metaphysical poets' texts, for whose intense, mystical imagery he is already more than a match on the first page of 'Lo, the full, final sacrifice' (1946), even before a word has been sung; here his understanding of the colours and discourse of the organ, lost in the orchestral version, proves outstanding.

Harper (1990) has identified the setting of seventeenth-century texts as one of three such preferences in twentieth-century English anthems, the other two being translated Latin hymns and biblical texts. Holst set Henry Vaughan in 'The evening-watch' (1924), and Harper singles out for comment his use of strikingly radiant sonorities, built on multiple 4ths, for the poet's gem-like flame of vision. In the second half of the twentieth century composers' sound-worlds have tended to match these preferences in fairly specific ways.

Biblical texts, particularly the psalms and canticles of praise, have often occasioned a return to the primitive, its recurrent signifiers being the use of parallel triads, quartal harmonies and irregular rhythms. Presumably musical primitivism has taken its cue partly from ecclesiastical art, itself particularly eager to adopt this aspect of modernism in post-imperial times (as much of the iconography of, say, Coventry Cathedral makes clear, with its rugged fonts, gaudy windows, Hebraic visages and tribally angular statuary). Parallel triads we immediately associate with Vaughan Williams, not idly when one considers a work such as 'O clap your hands' (1920, originally with brass); here he makes absolutely no bones about their use, and boldly dissociates parish praise from the niceties of voice-leading, which probably needed to be done, though elsewhere his contextualization is more subtle, as in the beautiful 'Whitsunday hymn', one of his *Three Choral Hymns* (Coverdale; 1929) or the final

ART MUSIC

cadence of 'O taste and see' (1952). Quartal harmonies and irregular rhythms, which tend to go together and probably took more from Bartók and Hindemith than from Stravinsky, arrived in earnest with Britten's church cantata setting Christopher Smart's pseudo-psalms, *Rejoice in the Lamb* (1943), the very first Hussey commission (see Ex. 12.15a). They have since become a cliché, dependable but overworked by Mathias, Rutter, Francis Jackson (for instance, 'Lift up your heads', 1974) and occasionally Leighton and others in works largely commissioned for festal occasions. In Mathias's 'Make a joyful noise', 1964, the initial vocal line (though not the organ part) might be realigned as one bar of 4/4, two of 3/8 and one of 3/4; Rutter's 'Praise ye the Lord', 1969, exhibits mannerisms he has since pulled away from. Patterson has also taken on a comparable idiom, rather late in the day, in his *Magnificat* and *Nunc dimittis* (1987). Such pandiatonicism has not stretched liturgical imaginations very far, and those bold enough to take them further have been few, notably Tippett in his 'Collegium Sancti Johannis Cantabrigiense' *Magnificat* and *Nunc dimittis* (1962), with its strident fanfares for the organ *trompettes en chamade* in the *Magnificat* and its opposing tight diatonic clusters between choir and soloist, almost filling chromatic space (Ex. 12.15b), in the *Nunc dimittis*. Thirty years ago David Lumsden adjudged this 'perhaps the most strikingly original setting of *Nunc dimittis* ever written' (Knight and Reed 1965: 211).

Britten, like Tippett, confronted church music with the total chromatic in the 1960s, marrying quartal sonorities with a 12-note row in a celebrated instance, the Sanctus of his *Missa brevis*, written for the Catholic rite (Westminster Cathedral) in 1961 (Ex. 12.15c). Less compromise between tonal and serial thinking has more recently been attempted, for instance by Payne in his expressive 'A little Passiontide cantata' (anon; 1975), but the disjunctions of writing such as Ex. 12.15d, despite their underlying lyricism, present enormous learning difficulties for choirs and perceptual ones for audiences. Nor have performer or notational freedoms or extended vocal techniques yet provided a new foundation for liturgical expression, despite their occasional take-up, for instance by LeFanu ('The little valleys', from *The Valleys Shall Sing*, 1973), Lumsdaine ('Dum medium silentium', 1976) and Oliver ('The elixir', Herbert and Skelton; 1976).

As the century draws to its close the essence of expression in church music in Britain appears to be again harmonic. Messiaen, his own church output being for organ rather than choir, has none the

VOCAL MUSIC

less been a considerable influence, perhaps above all because modes of limited transposition empower harmonic 'being' rather than 'becoming' and with it a timeless, visionary aesthetic. In retrospect Howells and perhaps even his romantic forebears can be linked with this as a central rather than peripheral strand of modern musical thought, and Harvey can be heard as a successor to Howells (as well

Ex. 12.15a　　　　　Britten: *Rejoice in the Lamb*

ART MUSIC

Ex. 12.15b Tippett: 'Collegium Sancti Johannis Cantabrigiense', *Nunc dimittis*

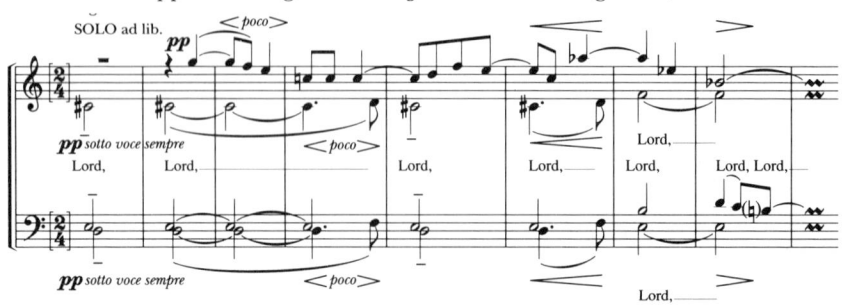

Ex. 12.15c Britten: Sanctus (*Missa brevis*)

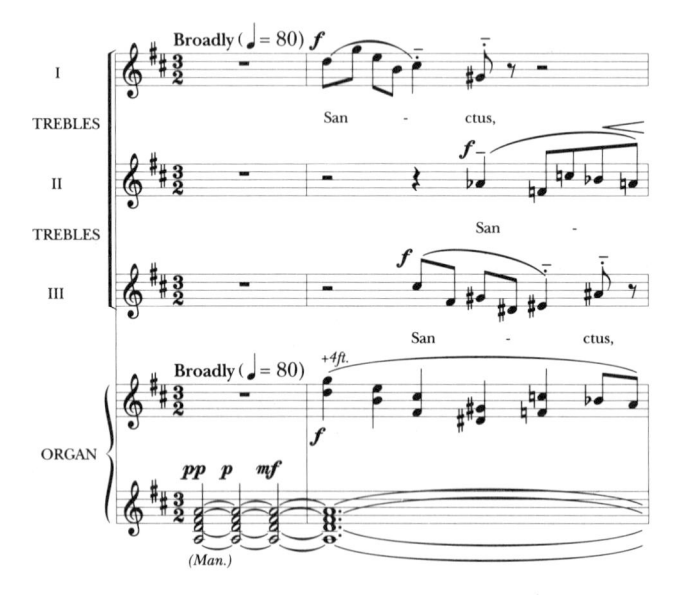

as, more obviously, Holst) when, in 'I love the Lord' (1976), he superimposes an E♭ minor triad on a G major one, thus beginning to suggest Messiaen's mode 3 (though it is not rigidly adhered to). This is a quite breathtaking piece, in no sense bound by Anglican restraints yet simple, plain in its word-setting, and chorally conceived from beginning to end. Harvey's slightly earlier 'The dove descending' (Eliot; 1975), with organ, also enjoys Messiaenic

Ex. 12.15d Payne: 'A little Passiontide cantata'

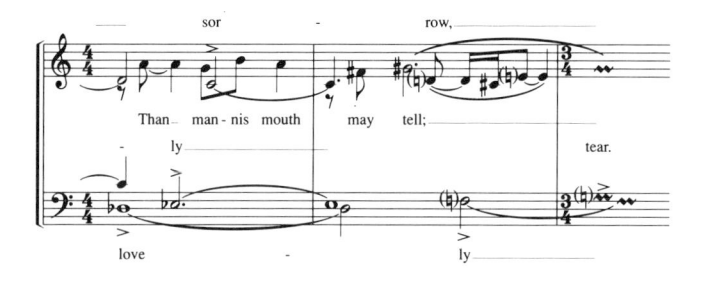

colours, as does Sebastian Forbes's 'Gracious spirit ' (1969), cast throughout in 5/8 and refreshingly song-like. But the fullest measure of acceptance of Messiaen's corporeal approach to celestial concerns comes with Judith Weir's 'Ascending into heaven' (Hildebert of Lavardin; 1983). A virtuoso organ part, lilting triple-time vocal rhythms, choral glissandi and coruscating octatonics furnish a heavenly vision of Byzantine glitter rather than Gothic gloom.

It is Weir, again, who has furnished one of the brightest and best of recent additions to the carol repertoire, 'Illuminare, Jerusalem' (Scottish; 1985), which with its unique combination of the witty and the numinous provides a much-needed fresh start to what has become a stale genre. Casken's 'A gathering' (Lancelot Andrewes; 1991) similarly partakes of the octatonic fluidity but not of the wit. Both were written for the annual Festival of Nine Lessons and Carols at King's College, Cambridge, where Stephen Cleobury has made a point of commissioning a new work each year. Little need be added to the account of the carol revival given in the preceding volume in this series (see Temperley 1981: 174, 263–5), because, like many another supposedly timeless English tradition and like the commercial Christmas itself, it laid down its capital in the nineteenth century and has been enjoying the interest ever since. One indication of this is that a surprisingly small number of new tunes has been added to the Victorian repertoire of those sung or known by all; 'The little road to Bethlehem' (1946) by Michael Head (1900–76) might be cited as an exception, and Armstrong Gibbs's 'While the shepherds were watching' from the cantata *A Saviour Born* (Benedict Ellis; 1952) deserves to have been another. However, it has to be realized what the odds are: the destiny of a really popular twentieth-century Christmas song is the charts, not the carol books. Berlin's 'White Christmas' is not unsusceptible to choral arrangement or congregational singing or any less religious than 'Here we come a-wassailing' or 'We wish you a merry Christmas', but its sentiments and language have not been hallowed by age (nor has its copyright expired). Carols that have been so hallowed are now arranged *ad infinitum* almost like jazz standards: for instance, there is a through-composed five-verse arrangement of 'Noël nouvelet' by John Rutter (1969) in *Carols for Choirs 2*, and two different arrangements of it in *The Novello Book of Carols* (1986), one a simpler affair by Ian Humphris, the other, by Stephen Jackson, a six-verse *tour de force* of harmonic design and technical finesse that takes the arranger's art as far as it can go this side of commercial routining, though its two-part canon in verse 3 pales beside the canon four-in-one achieved by Bill Tamblyn, virtually without consecutives, in his setting of the tune as 'Love is come again' (1977).

In some cases even the arrangements have become standard; this is particularly true of some of David Willcocks's in *Carols for Choirs 1*, published in 1961, and his descant and organ part to 'Hark! the herald angels sing' and 'O come, all ye faithful' are well enough known to have dissolved any distinction between congregational and choral proprietorship, rather as with the fugued passages found here and there in other carol refrains and some hymns. Elsewhere on the spectrum there are the original carols that have become popular with choirs and audiences but (so far) have stopped short of folk appropriation: 'Torches' by John Joubert (1952) is a good example, as are many of John Rutter's, for example the 'Shepherd's pipe carol' (1967), 'Star carol' (1972) and 'Donkey carol' (1976). The children's market has helped these last sail home – though like Christmas train sets they probably appeal to adults just as much – and no one would begrudge Rutter his shrewd touches of Hollywood and Broadway, even in church; but his lyrics have no pretensions beyond serving the music. A fresh Christmas poem is even rarer than a fresh tune, which is what makes Howells's 'Tryste Noel'

(Louise Imogen Guiney; 1978) so powerful. This poem had in fact been set to music as a solo song as early as 1927 by C. W. Orr, and its air of melancholy profanity is recognizable as one of the enduring strengths of the British carol tradition (though Guiney was American). Whether the mood's correlative be nature in the bleak midwinter, the lost symbolism of anonymous medieval verse, the pain of the Madonna as the Passion is foreshadowed, the hint of agnosticism, or just the sense of sadness that seems to accompany so many lullabies, it belongs to a genre with lasting appeal. Hardy's poem 'The oxen' has been set to music many times (Britten's setting, for female voices, dates from 1967); other examples might include Warlock's haunting 'Bethlehem Down' (1927), Hadley's delicate 'I sing of a maiden' (1936) and Leighton's fine setting of the words of the Coventry Carol, from his *Three Carols* (1956). Harvey's 'Carol' (1968), on the other hand, is simply too medieval a conception to have caught on when it sets four different texts simultaneously, especially since it does so to a strong static dissonance. Very much in line with the stylistic icons described earlier, British choral carols of the past 40 or 50 years have utilized a good deal of neo-medievalism in their *tempus perfectum*, austere counterpoint and quartal harmonies or confrontative dissonance; this applies to Bennett, for example, as in 'Out of your sleep' (from *Five Carols*, 1967), and more challengingly to Maxwell Davies in his various carols and motets from the 1960s, to one of which the *Musical Times* controversially nailed its colours in 1961 (see Routley 1964: 143). But the results have rarely been catchy enough to oust Victorian comfort and joy. Christmas cantatas and suites of carols more for concert than liturgical use are a rather different matter, and Vaughan Williams's *Hodie* (1954) has been taken to heart; so, rather more than his *A Boy Was Born*, has Britten's *A Ceremony of Carols* (1942), though a lesser-known sequence for treble voices and instruments, Maconchy's *Christmas Morning* (1962), might more frequently be substituted.

V: *Solo Songs*

English song flourished for the first half of the century (see Banfield 1985). The genre sustained and identified itself particularly with three interrelated movements: the upsurge of post-Victorian lyric poetry that can broadly be termed Georgian, and the Tudor and folk revivals. In so far as it represented a miniaturist, vernacular,

ART MUSIC

parochial or conservationist ethos, part of the long-term counter-capitalist swing in British culture from the later nineteenth century onwards (see Wiener 1981), the song renaissance was one of the products of what is now increasingly recognized as a highly politicized artistic period (see Boyes 1993, Stradling and Hughes 1993).

Its poetic sensibility was essentially still romantic and manifested itself in settings of Housman, Hardy, de la Mare and early Yeats, also drawing on many slightly earlier or lesser names including Arthur Symons, Ernest Dowson, John Masefield, Rupert Brooke, Robert Graves, W. H. Davies, J. C. Squire and Celtic Revival poets such as Fiona Macleod, Padraic Colum, Seumas O'Sullivan and James Stephens. Some composers found ways of conveying a poet's toughness along with lyrical ease – Finzi and Ireland did this with Hardy, Lennox Berkeley with Housman, Warlock with Yeats, Moeran with O'Sullivan and Gibbs and Howells with de la Mare. Most settings before Britten, however, did not, and must be recognized for what they are, Georgian encapsulations of nature and love idylls, often to be singled out for their ephemeral beauty. Such are Ireland's 'Spring sorrow' (Brooke; 1918), Frederick Keel's 'Trade winds' (Masefield; 1919), Christopher le Fleming's 'If it's ever spring again' (Hardy; 1942), Michael Head's 'Sweet Chance, that led my steps abroad' (W. H. Davies; 1928), Elizabeth Poston's 'Sweet Suffolk owl' (Vautor; 1925) and many others.

'Sweet Suffolk owl' is a setting of an English madrigal text; and the use of Elizabethan and Jacobean poetry was only one of the ways in which early twentieth-century British solo song modelled itself on its equivalent of 300 years earlier. Ivor Gurney (1890–1937), by his own reckoning (see Hurd 1978: 37), broke through to something individual as a young composer with a set of *Five Elizabethan Songs* (1913–14), his 'Elizas', which includes his best-known setting, 'Sleep' (Fletcher), and he must have been aware of a comparison between him and Campion as he developed his dual gift as song composer and poet (though, unlike Campion, he rarely set his own verse). Philip Heseltine (1894–1930), known as Peter Warlock, identified with renaissance figures and their work not just in his roistering lifestyle but by making scholarly editions, particularly of lute songs. As a composer he limited his output, saying, 'I should be more than happy if at the end of my days I could look back upon an achievement comparable to that of Philip Rosseter, who left behind him but one small book of twenty-one immortal lyrics' (Copley 1979: 252). He did leave some perfect miniatures and certainly knew how to

VOCAL MUSIC

work an archaic musical conceit, such as in 'The lover's maze', where the labyrinthine sentiments and strategies of courtship are mirrored in intricate motivic counterpoint full of the paradoxes and ironies of false relations (Ex. 12.16a). Other composers notable for their Elizabethan settings include Ireland (*Five XVIth Century Poems*, 1938), Finzi (the Shakespeare set *Let Us Garlands Bring*, 1942), Moeran, who additionally set *Seven Poems of James Joyce* (1929) from *Chamber Music*, Joyce's collection of lyrics avowedly modelled on Elizabethan verse (see Banfield 1985: 271), and Roger Quilter (*To Julia*, Herrick, 1905; several Shakespeare sets; *Seven Elizabethan Lyrics*, 1907). Like the others, however, Quilter also identified with the approachable verse of his own period, his *Weltschmerz* finding telling expression in his *Four Songs of Sorrow* (Dowson; 1907), where something of late Brahms supplements a French exquisiteness (Ex. 12.16b).

Ex. 12.16a Warlock: 'The lover's maze'

Ex. 12.16b   Quilter: 'In spring' (*Four Songs of Sorrow*)

Those who died young or for whatever other reason produced little are often seen as the archetypal English song composers. Their 'unfulfilled' outputs (the word was often used) suggested both the promise of the English musical renaissance and a little of the 'mute, inglorious Milton' epitomizing the vanished Folk whose songs and dances were being contemporaneously collected from barn and hedgerow by Cecil Sharp (1859–1924) – and indeed, by some of the composers themselves, including Vaughan Williams, Holst, Moeran, Grainger and Butterworth. (Sharp provided piano accompaniments for 500 of the 1100 tunes he published from the 5000 he had collected; their decorum tells us much about the movement as a whole.) Rather more mundanely, the repertoire reminds us that song was widely used in composition teaching (for instance, by Stanford – see H. P. Greene 1935: 98–9, 204, 242; Stanford 1911) and that composers needed to progress beyond it. The catalogue of

VOCAL MUSIC

limitation might include Quilter's hypersensitivity, the character instability of Moeran, Hadley and Warlock (and Warlock's suicide), Gurney's insanity, the ill-health of C. W. Orr (1893–1976), le Fleming, William Baines (1899–1922) and Geoffrey Molyneux Palmer (whose *Chamber Music*, a cycle of 32 of Joyce's 36 poems, recently came to light and has been published – see Russel 1993), the gender of Morfydd Owen and Poston, the fastidiousness of Ferguson and Finzi, the *Liederjahr* of the lovesick Benjamin Burrows (1891–1966) – see Daubney 1979 – and above all the deaths in the First World War of Butterworth, Denis Browne and lesser lights such as Frederick Kelly, (1881–1916), Ernest Farrar (1885–1918) and George Jerrard Wilkinson.

George Butterworth (1885–1916) fitted all the requirements for fragile immortality: a slender tally of songs, all written between 1909 and 1912 (eleven Housman settings, published as *Six Songs from 'A Shropshire Lad'* and *'Bredon Hill' and Other Songs*, the W. H. Henley cycle *Love Blows as the Wind Blows* with string quartet, and little else); a polished, understated style with flashes of passion (presaged by the wistful accumulation of a secondary 7th in Ex. 12.17, from 'Loveliest of trees', as the cherry blossom falls to earth); and a gallant death at the Somme. As a folksong collector he also published *Eleven Folksongs from Sussex* at the height of the revival in 1913; and the distinction between *trouvé* and artefact, in any case problematic where arrangement and publication were concerned, is slight indeed in some of his songs, as in 'With rue my heart is laden' (the modal melody of which later became his rustic epitaph when quoted both by himself at the end of his *Shropshire Lad* orchestral rhapsody and in 1924 by the young Finzi as a suffix to the manuscript score of his war elegy, *Requiem da camera*). William Denis Browne (1888–1915), Cambridge protégé of E. J. Dent, pupil of Busoni and friend of Rupert Brooke, wrote even less (11 songs), but perhaps with greater promise, showing a bolder imagination than most of his contemporaries in 'To Gratiana dancing and singing' (Lovelace; 1913) and 'Arabia' (de la Mare; 1914).

Something more substantial is not always sought from this period, but it can be found. Bax, for whom songs were not a central concern, none the less wrote a good many of them and went refreshingly beyond the British miniaturist predilection, for instance in 'The fairies' (Allingham; 1905) and 'Glamour' (1921; text by himself as Dermot O'Byrne), both cast as broad and colourful scherzo-and-trio structures. Rebecca Clarke wrote a number of striking songs, with a penchant for the macabre or revelatory in narrative, as in 'The seal

Ex. 12.17   Butterworth: 'Loveliest of trees' (*Six Songs from 'A Shropshire Lad'*)

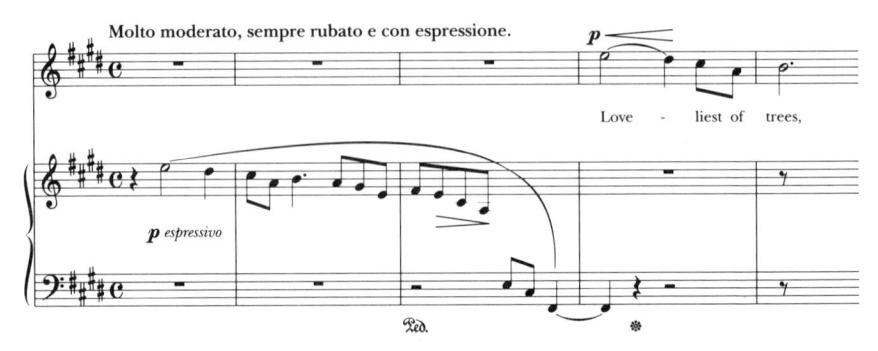

man' (Masefield; 1922). Bridge at least touched on his new, existentially probing musical language in song prior to the late concentration on instrumental works, to notable emotional effect in the three Tagore settings with orchestra (1922–5) and 'Journey's end' (1925 – compare Holst's cooler approach in his setting of 1929 from the *Twelve Songs* of Humbert Wolfe). A more sustained achievement with similar chromatic depths of feeling is Warlock's cycle of four Yeats poems about lost love, *The Curlew* (1915–22), for tenor, flute, cor anglais and string quartet, in which the romantically imprisoned language of van Dieren and Delius seems to meet that of Bartók for the moment on wholly natural (though extremely desolate) terms; it is a uniquely powerful work. Something of its disciplined melancholy can also be found in Moeran's *Six Songs of Seumas O'Sullivan* (1944), particularly the last, 'The herdsman', with its deathly ending.

Vaughan Williams gave English song a tremendous boost with his early achievements, an admirably plain antidote to the preciousness of others even in the very popular 'Linden Lea' (Barnes; *ca* 1901) and all the more so in the Dante Gabriel Rossetti sonnet sequence *The House of Life* (*ca* 1903, including 'Silent noon') and the Stevenson cycle *Songs of Travel* (*ca* 1904). While others were content to follow, however, he himself moved on, opening out the genre first with varied forces and their dramatic impressionism in the influential Housman cycle *On Wenlock Edge* for tenor, string quartet and piano of 1908–9 (Gurney's Housman cycles for similar combinations, *Ludlow and Teme* and *The Western Playland*, followed after the war), then towards sacred contexts and metaphysical poetry in *Five Mystical Songs* (Herbert; 1905–11) and *Four Hymns* (various; 1913–14). The *Four Hymns*, like *Flos campi*, include solo viola, and later still he explored unaccompanied song (*Two Poems by Seumas O'Sullivan*, 1925), and other combinations in *Along the Field* (Housman; ca 1927) for voice and violin (compare Holst's *Four Songs for Voice and Violin*, 1917) and *Ten Blake Songs* for voice and oboe (1957). Vaughan Williams's determination always to pare, highlight and question basic resources aligns him in these later works with younger generations, though probably without actual influence on them.

The best composers were those who managed to build musical structure and motivic and harmonic characterization – melodic characterization was often another matter – into an entity with poetic image. Gurney, for all his haunting openings and endings – see, for example, the wayside beauty of piano introduction and coda and mixolydian melodic opening of 'Desire in spring' (Ledwidge; 1918) – rarely sustained this in his outpouring of nearly 200 songs between his release from active service in France in 1917 and his confinement in October 1922. His friend Howells, on the other hand, did, notably in 'King David' (de la Mare; 1919), its sarabande rhythm, richly textured harmonies, yearning modulations and melodic arabesques all of a part with both his abstract personal style and the concrete image of the melancholy king in the garden with the nightingale. So did Gibbs, in another de la Mare setting, 'Silver' (1920), its impressionist means simple (slow oscillating chords, ostinato pedal, semi-*parlando* voice part floating on these), its effect sure. Gibbs has been neglected, but his modestly adept handling of image and mood has something of Wolf about its often whimsical variety.

Ireland and Finzi achieved the best rapport with serious verse. Both of them tackled Hardy at his most pregnant: in Ireland's *Five Poems by Thomas Hardy* (1926), a rich, almost inarticulate intricacy of harmonic figuration supports the depth of emotional tragedy and catharsis in poems such as 'In my sage moments'; in many of the songs Finzi wrote between 1926 and 1956 and compiled as *A Young Man's Exhortation, Earth and Air and Rain, Before and After Summer, I Said to Love* and *Till Earth Outwears*, he does not hesitate to express the breadth of Hardy's fatalistic philosophy, often in unorthodox musical forms. Finzi's 'Channel firing' combines rondo, scherzo and sectional toccata elements; 'He abjures love' is in a kind of sonata form; 'I said to Love' includes a piano cadenza and 'Proud songsters' an entire piano 'verse'. 'At a lunar eclipse' is a fugue, and 'The clock of the years' is as much a miniature dramatic scena (with striking use of reverse cycles of 5ths for the winding back of time) as some of the others are miniature cantatas with their baroque indicators of recitative, aria and the like. Hardy the 'man who used to notice such things' is also well served by Finzi's genius for affectionate detail, as with his drooling cow (Ex. 12.18a). Above all the two composers know how to convey the power of attraction and capacity for suffering of Hardy's women, Ireland in the haunting 'Her song', Finzi in the wistful 'The sigh', 'To Lizbie Browne' and 'Amabel' as well as in 'The phantom', where the exhilaration of memory is as potent as the original passion and the contrapuntal detail is as sharp and exact as the mind's eye. Both composers were also literary connoisseurs who mapped their own inner experience on to a wide range of verse. Finzi sought out Traherne in the solo cantata *Dies natalis*. Ireland deployed a consistent personal vocabulary of musical symbols across different songs and poets (Banfield 1985:163–78) – see Ex. 12.18b and c for his musical correlatives to impressionistic *ecstasis* and erotic passion as found in 'The trellis' (Huxley; 1920), a poem whose title provides the image for the secrets of love much as do Ireland's musical symbols (and Ireland needed the secrecy; his love was homosexual).

English song before the Second World War demanded syllabic voice parts and highly interventionist accompaniments, to the extent that in much of the repertoire it is the piano, paradoxically, that acts as the poet's 'voice', with its rhetorical duties of harmony and motif. Britten changed all that, and, as we have already seen in the partsong, made a point of overturning the English declamatory manners of Finzi and Ireland and their contemporaries. He set no fewer Scottish and foreign-language texts than English ones, all from a wide range of periods and traditions, notably Hugo and Verlaine (*Quatre chansons françaises*, 1928), de la Mare (*Tit for Tat*, 1928–31, revised 1968), Auden (*Our Hunting Fathers*, 1936; *On This Island*, 1937), Rimbaud (*Les illuminations*, 1939), *Seven Sonnets of Michelangelo* (1940), *The Holy Sonnets of John Donne* (1945), Hardy (*Winter Words*, 1953), *Songs from the Chinese* (1957), Hölderlin (*Sechs Hölderlin-Fragmente*, 1958), *Songs and Proverbs of William Blake* (1965), Pushkin (*The Poet's Echo*, 1965), Soutar (*Who Are These Children?*, 1969), and Burns (*A Birthday Hansel*, 1975). He also compiled deftly thematic anthologies on subjects that for some reason preoccupied him: evening (*Serenade*, 1943), night (*Nocturne*, 1958) and slumber (*A Charm of Lullabies*, 1947). He wrote for specific singers, the first British composer since the days of the royalty ballad who could rely on a real market partnership with them in concert and (thanks to improving technology) on record. Most of the songs, again unlike

VOCAL MUSIC

Ex. 12.18a   Finzi: 'Channel firing' (*Before and After Summer*)

Ex. 12.18b   Ireland: 'The trellis'

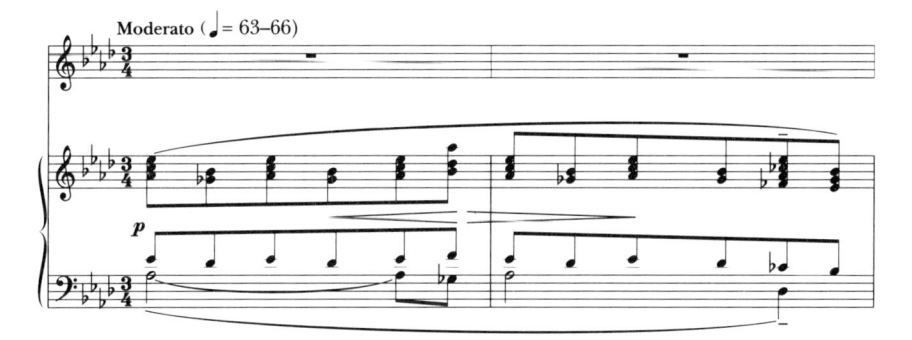

Ex. 12.18c   Ireland: 'The trellis'

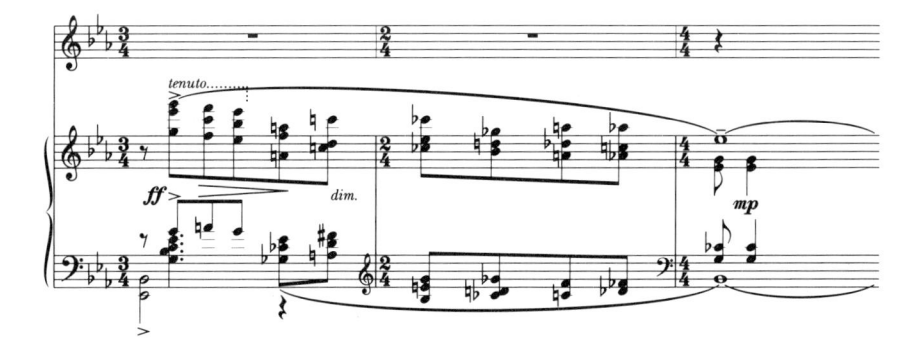

Finzi's, commanded the brilliance of a high voice, the earlier cycles inspired by Sophie Wyss, the later by Peter Pears; the Blake songs were written for the world's greatest post-war *Lieder* baritone, Dietrich Fischer-Dieskau.

Britten's voice parts accordingly keep uppermost the singer's desire to convey a melodic line, whose job of rhetorical or aesthetic persuasion he does not encourage the accompaniment to colonize, thus avoiding redundancy of information between the two. His folksong arrangements, of which there are seven volumes published between 1943 and 1976, five of them for voice and piano, demonstrate this clearly. In 'Early one morning' (1961), for instance, the fact that the second bar of the voice part outlines tonic harmony becomes a reason not to duplicate it in the piano (except in motivic shadow an octave – or two – higher; see Ex. 12.19a). This is not simply a neoclassical matter of multiple perspective, the dominant arriving in the accompaniment at this point because it operates on a one-bar harmonic rhythm, whereas in the melody the implied tonic–dominant shifts occur every two bars; it also allows the voice to set up its own *legato* triadic resonance without masking from the piano, something Pears's voice could do with unusual richness. Again, Britten is happy to colour individual chords much as a singer will colour individual notes and words, as with the flat 7th on 'leave' (Ex. 12.19b); the emotional meaning of this note is perfectly clear without its being 'correctly' resolved, and in fact to have done so would have involved pedantically complex grammar, as the context for a comparable nuance in Grainger's setting (1901–40 [*sic*]), a version in its own way powerful and original, demonstrates (Ex. 12.19c).

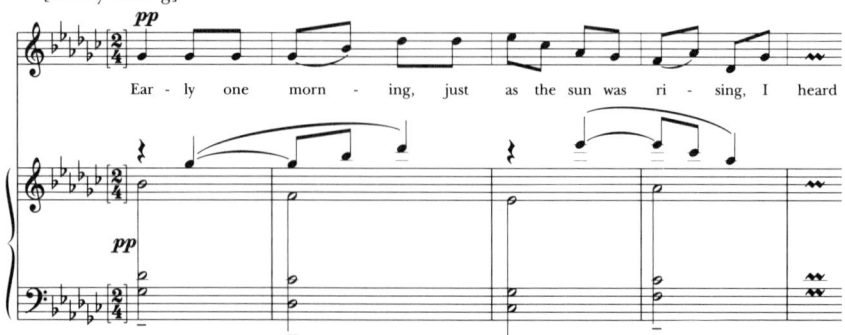

Ex. 12.19a   Britten: 'Early one morning'

VOCAL MUSIC

Ex. 12.19b   Britten: 'Early one morning'

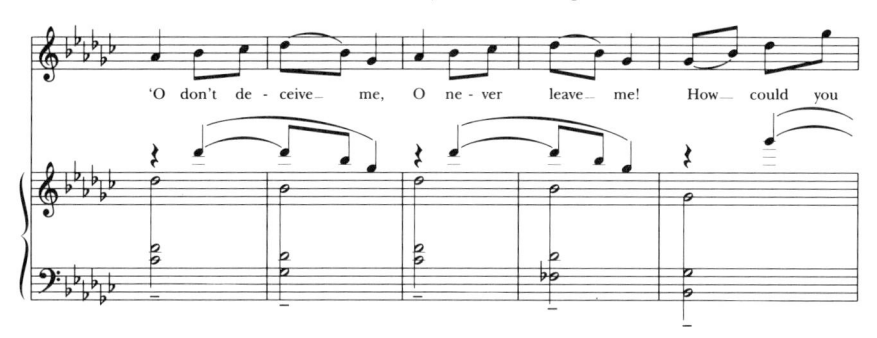

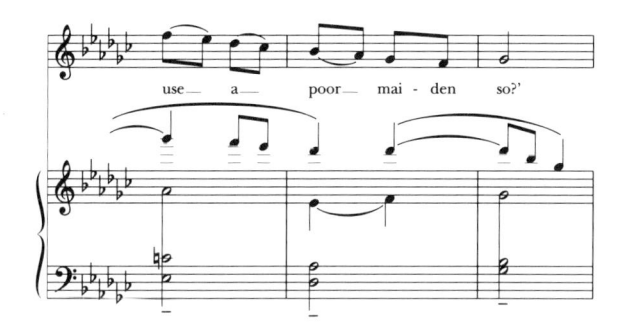

'O don't deceive me, O never leave me! How could you use a poor maiden so?'

Ex. 12.19c   Grainger: 'Early one morning'

[Slowly, anguished]

'O don't deceive me, O never leave me! How could you use a—'

Ex. 12.19d Britten: 'Early one morning'

VOCAL MUSIC

Britten even makes a point of showing us in 'Early one morning' how the very idea of 'implied' harmony in a tune can be fallacious, for the tonic anacrusis (at 'I heard', Ex. 12.19a) is perfectly logical melodically and only sullies the dominant harmony if the latter is still sounding instrumentally; having ignored the quibble in his first stanza he wittily builds the whole of his second and third on it (see Ex. 12.9d). Finally it is worth noting how this enhanced vocal independence in Britten more or less coincided with the shift towards unaccompanied singing, or away from the piano towards the less dominating guitar as accompaniment, in the folk revival – it was in 1952 that the English Folk Dance and Song Society sponsored unaccompanied recordings of Ewan MacColl (see Boyes 1993: 216). Britten (*Songs from the Chinese* and a folksong set), Berkeley (*Songs of the Half-Light*), Walton (*Anon. in Love*, 1959) and others all wrote song cycles for voice and guitar, most often for Julian Bream (*b* 1933). Voice and harp appeared as another fresh combination (Britten's *A Birthday Hansel, Canticle V* (1974) and his final folksong set; Maconchy's *Three Songs*, 1974); this time the catalyst was Osian Ellis (*b* 1928), though other composers had already explored the medium, for example Rubbra in various religious songs from the 1920s (including 'Jesukin' and 'A hymn to the virgin'), Cannon in *Cinq chansons de femme* (1952) and 'Cecilia' (1953) and Hadley in *Crazy Jane* (Yeats; 1958).

The vividness of both vocal and instrumental personae and the potentially brilliant flexibility (in the hands of virtuoso performers) of their mutual relationship are the cardinal elements in Britten's songs. Examples might include the 'florid music' of a baroque aria (without *da capo* but with trumpet fanfare and violin *bariolage* imitations) in the first song of *On This Island*; the naive, waterborne Venetian guitar serenading of Michelangelo's Sonnet XXX; the interplay of registers, agilities and imitations between tenor and horn in the *Serenade* and tenor and various instruments in *Nocturne*; the release of the long triplet melisma at the final words 'I shake with feare', and at a new extremity of register for voice and both hands of the piano, in 'Oh, to vex me' (*Donne Sonnets*); the heterophony between voice and piano for the songbirds of 'Proud songsters' (*Winter Words*), which could hardly be farther from Finzi's setting; the chorale-like, 'innocent' quantitative syllabification and short-lined contours of most of the vocal melodies in the Blake songs, while the piano stalks and probes and mimes with mock and mow; and the schematic distinction between the children's rhymes in Scots dialect and the poems in English in *Who Are These Children?*, the piano in the former partaking of the corporate games (and, as it were, of the accent when it has skipping Scots rhythms), in the latter setting up a more dialectical persona.

Two facets of Britten's approach to song are also found in others. The often vehement flashes of beauty and humour in Scottish poetry, with its triumphantly 'classless' lack of dissociation between language and thought (rather as in Blake), suited Britten's fusion of instrument and material and also permeate the substantial achievement of the six sets of *Scottish Lyrics* and many other songs of Francis George Scott (1880–1958), a number to poems by Burns and Hugh MacDiarmid. Musorgsky's directness of address is probably a fair comparison for some of Scott's moods of inspiration, expressionist Schoenberg for others – see, for instance, the lullaby-like erotic simplicity of 'The tryst' (Soutar; 1944) and the daemonic abandon of 'Crowdieknowe' (MacDiarmid; 1924); or the gnomic sternness of 'An apprentice angel' (MacDiarmid; 1933) and eeriness of 'Moonstruck' (MacDiarmid; 1927). Tippett's two substantial essays in song, the cantata *Boyhood's End* (W. H. Hudson; 1943) and the cycle *The Heart's Assurance* (Sidney Keyes and Alun Lewis), both written for Britten and Pears to perform, mirror Britten's Beethovenian energy and openness of piano writing and Italianate emotional directness of vocal melody (see Ex. 12.20, where the vocal assonances – 'meadows', 'lovers', 'flowers' – seem to seek Italian terminal vowels). *Boyhood's End* provides an obvious parallel to *Dies natalis* in subject matter, though not in technique, and both works share their fresh, candid address with Alan Bush's *Voices of the Prophets* (1952), politically inspired but no less radiant for that. A more recent example of what seems to be a British *Bildungskantate* tradition would be Leighton's *Earth, Sweet Earth* for tenor and piano (1986); here the preludial fine prose, difficult to resist, is Ruskin's.

Much more contained within conventional parameters of texture, accompaniment figure and cadence were the emotional pace and tone of Lennox Berkeley, the only other major British composer of Britten's generation to foreground the recital song consistently in his output. (This is to acknowledge that Walton's only approaches to the genre were *Anon. in Love* and the splendid *Song for the Lord Mayor's Table* (1962) and that Lutyens's vocal music belongs largely in another category.) 'Tant que mes yeux (A memory)' (Louise Labé; 1940) testifies both to Berkeley's French training and sensibility (he was a Boulanger pupil) and the plainness of his approach: he sets the octave of the sonnet on the plan of the first half of a

VOCAL MUSIC

Ex. 12.20 Tippett: 'Remember your lovers' (*The Heart's Assurance*)

ART MUSIC

32-bar song, two bars to a line. Keeping this pace for the remaining sestet involves skilful compression of the second 'half' of the music, but the simple control pays off, for the poem is a searing, wounded cry for lost love disguised as a rational benediction, just as the chromatics and harmonic expansion of Berkeley's accompanimental building block give the emotional game away while keeping the musical argument moving. It was this same combination of cold lyric ease and burning emotion that enabled Berkeley to set Housman so well, in the same year, in his *Five Housman Songs*. C. W. Orr (1893–1976) may have responded to Housman most frequently among British composers (there are 24 settings, some of the best being of the less popular poems such as 'The carpenter's son', 'Along the field', 'Farewell to barn and stack and tree' and 'Oh see how thick'), but Berkeley's settings are surely among the finest we have. Even the unmusical Housman might have appreciated the stiffness of his soldier's upper lip (mustachioed, no doubt) in the third song and, in the final one, the image of 'the heart no longer stirred' as its dactylic rhythm finally takes its own life, passionate to the end under (or rather over) its apparent equanimity with the dominant 13th on the last note of the voice part (Ex. 12.21). Elsewhere Berkeley, the older man, followed Britten in making a thematic anthology (*Autumn's Legacy*, 1962) and in setting de la Mare (*Five Songs*, 1946; *Songs of the Half-Light*, 1964; *Another Spring*, 1977), Auden (*Five Poems*, 1958), Chinese and other foreign poetry (*Three Greek Songs*, 1953, and *Five Chinese Songs*, 1975, though both in translation), French poetry for voice and orchestra (his second set of *Ronsard Sonnets*, 1963) and ecstatic poetry for voice and strings (*Four Poems of St Teresa of Avila*, 1947), and preceded Britten with a work for voice and harp (*Herrick Songs*, 1974). However, in most of these works his more modest understanding of song techniques is no bar to exquisite and sometimes profound lyricism, though it can become clogged.

There has been little that is really new in British recital song (as opposed to chamber song, discussed below) since Britten. A truly vernacular genre is out of the question, at least in England, and in so far as song recitals survive at all in concert series they are in the 1990s as likely to include a sequence of American popular numbers (for instance, Gershwin) as part of the programming formula as, 30 years ago, an English folksong group. Few composers have been in a position to compete with this kind of novelty appeal. Those who have persevered with songs with piano or orchestra have tended to do so with a preference for, or mixture of, one or more of the following

Ex. 12.21 Berkeley: 'Because I liked you better' (*Five Housman Songs*)

aesthetics: neoclassical, modernist, serial, surreal, English pastoral, humorous, popular or postmodernist. Withal, expression becomes habitually a matter of *Angst*, distancing or presentation in quotation marks, and it is notable that composers who, as exceptions, still find something immediate and 'sincere' in song tend to be those in the margins. The folksong aesthetic has survived best on the Celtic fringes (see, for instance, the many Scottish arrangements by Cedric Thorpe Davie, Hoddinott's *Six Welsh Folk-Songs* of 1984, and, outstandingly – though by way of folk inflection rather than arrangement – Weir's *Scotch Minstrelsy*, 1982); a gay perspective has occasionally contributed something distinctive (Ferguson's 1951 cycle *Discovery*, to poems by Denton Welch), as has a woman's (see the settings of May Sarton and Emily Dickinson by Rhian Samuel, *b* 1944).

Nevertheless, Geoffrey Bush has perpetuated the English 'sensibility' song effectively and prolifically. Like Quilter's, many of his sets, including *Three Elizabethan Songs* (1948, ending with the popular

'Sigh no more, ladies'), *Four Songs from Herrick's 'Hesperides'* (1951), *Five Spring Songs* (1953) and *Three Songs of Ben Jonson* (1959) are to Elizabethan texts. He has also ranged more widely, with Kathleen Raine settings in *The End of Love* (1954), 'The wonder of wonders', a song with real panache from *Songs of Wonder* (1959, with strings), *A Little Love-Music* (1976) for unaccompanied soprano and tenor, and 'Cuisine provençale' (1982), commissioned by those saviours of the song recital, the Songmakers' Almanac, to a passage from Virginia Woolf's *To the Lighthouse* that takes him to the borders of the surreal. Trevor Hold, of a younger generation and less genial style, is one of a great many minor, sometimes amateur, often rurally affiliated British composers who continue to explore lyrical poetry through the art song (Hold lives in Northamptonshire and has set John Clare). Like Bush he has also worked with song as a musicologist, and some of his cycles (for instance, *The Image Stays*, 1974) are to his own poems.

Holloway, more prolific still in sets of songs written between the mid-1960s and 1980, is a quite different case. He too has continued to respond to the well-tried lyrical poets – Edward Thomas in *Lights Out* (1974), even Housman (*inter alia*) in *Georgian Songs* (1972) – as well as Larkin, Wallace Stevens, William Empson and others, but his generally staid textures, motifs and phrasing, and a repertoire superficially similar in range to, say, Lennox Berkeley's though more reliant on German romantic seriousness, serve a complex, seldom ingratiating syntax. One might compare this with the Graves poems he sets to music in *Wherever We May Be* (1980–81). Poetic functions and vocabulary are traditional – lines scan, words rhyme, rhetoric builds – just as in Holloway's music voice-leading connects, cadences resolve and contours grow. But this is in no sense comforting or populist: there are no cars or fridges in Graves, and words and phrases such as 'tilth', 'pilgrim', 'serpent' and 'stroke of midnight' can sound as disturbingly lost in the past as can the triads and appoggiaturas in Holloway's music. It is all very *innig*, a sensibility difficult to share in the late twentieth century in songs where no overriding colour or pace or textural proposition eases the argument. Yet its yield is rich when privately savoured.

If the *Robert Graves Songs* (fifteen in three sets, 1966–83) of Holloway's Cambridge University colleague Hugh Wood communicate more easily, it is within the supposedly difficult tenets of modernism. Kennedy (1991) speaks of Wood 'unerringly captur[ing] the ironic detachment at the heart of Graves's love poetry', but his direct word-setting and its imitative reflections in the piano part (see Ex. 12.22) –

Ex. 12.22   Hugh Wood: 'The foreboding' (*Robert Graves Songs*, Set I)

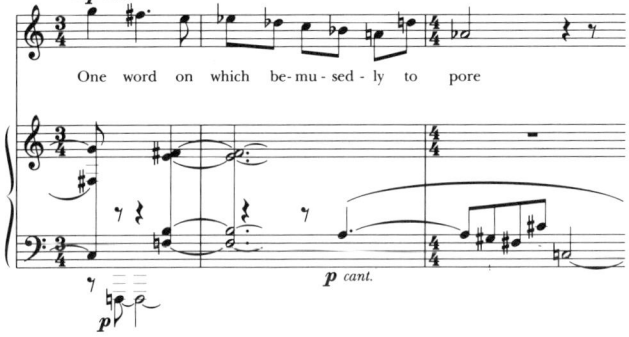

fitting enough in this song with the Schubertian resonance of a man viewing himself from outside a window – could also be read as the lucidity of naive involvement: an honestly Schoenbergian quality, however little it is what we expect of the serial tradition. The notes may be different, but the contrapuntal rumination is not that far from Finzi. Similar qualities were in evidence as early as Wood's *Four Logue Songs*, op. 2 (1961, revised 1963), for contralto, clarinet, violin and cello, despite their tough credentials as serial chamber music.

   As for Holloway's unaccompanied settings, it is perhaps significant that the first song of the Stevie Smith set *Five Little Songs About Death* (1973) is marked 'semplice: characterized', in a medium that allows the voice and the poem to do their work in this respect without more than melody getting in the way. Yet to reassert the freedom as well as the simplicity of monodic song traditions using the full syntax and notation of modernism (which is what Nicola LeFanu, for instance, is evidently doing in the 1972 *Rondeaux* for tenor and horn on French medieval love poems) can become self-defeating in its intricacy and decorum, as it has been for a number of her contemporaries when they present comparable source material. What is it in a lyrical poem that the song composer is trying to capture? Peter Dickinson offers one response when, in *Stevie's Tunes* (1984), he chooses poems by Smith that were based on well-known melodies (mostly Anglican hymns) and demonstrates the fact, with neoclassical insouciance in the accompaniments and an intermittent linking refrain based on Tchaikovsky's *Pathétique* Symphony. Perhaps, therefore, the best that the lyrical art song can do in the aftermath of modernism is, like the poetry of Smith and Betjeman and even Auden, to catch some of the flavour of the parochial, the suburban, the bygone, the vernacular, as though in a junk shop display; it can create another kind of image procession, affectionate, lonely, slightly surreal, but still ringing with rhyme and cadence. Lutyens's *Stevie Smith Songs* did this as early as 1948. Madeleine Dring's *Five Betjeman Songs* (1980, posthumous) have become classics, trading in a mellifluence that may suggest English hymns even when unoccasioned by poetic reference to them (see 'Business girls' and 'Upper Lambourne'), and in jazzy sleaze in 'Song of a nightclub proprietress'. The hymn-like takes on surrealism in Dickinson's *Surrealist Landscape* (1973), which as with the second of Tavener's *Three Surrealist Songs* (1968) superimposes live fragments from a song on a ghostly recording of it. (Dickinson's work is a setting of a surrealist poem by Berners dedicated to Dali; Tavener's three songs, to poems by Edward Lucie-Smith, are dedicated to Magritte, Ernst and Dali.)

Bennett's case is also indicative. Given his abilities, it may seem a pity that he has not invested more of his creativity in song. He has found no difficulty in wedding 12-note techniques with easy lyricism in the genre, and a late example, the cummings setting 'this is the garden' (commissioned for the 1985 English Song Award, although suffixed 'New York City, Sept. 15–17 1984'), breathes the English tradition so relaxedly as to suggest that dodecaphony was the natural destiny of Moeran's or Bridge's harmonic world; and there is at least one substantial utterance, *The Music that Her Echo Is* for tenor and piano (1967). But his occasional meetings with some of the aesthetic topics mentioned above have proved more attractive, for example the parabolic detachment of his little four-song cycle *The Insect World* (John Clare *et al.*; 1966), and above all the affectionate humour of *A Garland for Marjory Fleming* (1969), settings of poems by an early nineteenth-century girl who died at the age of eight which make us realize that song and its verse will survive so long as they can be as funny and innocent as this.

VI. Beyond Song and Back to It

As song shades over into aria, dramatic scena or vocal symphony, the picture has latterly been one of greater confidence than the above comments might suggest. British composers since the Second World War have not been frightened to explore vocal sensuousness and breadth, possibly as a result of realigning the primacy of these qualities in opera with their own expressive aspirations. Nor should Viennese exemplars be underestimated, coming from Berg and Schoenberg but also from Mahler (Bruno Walter's 1952 recording of *Das Lied von der Erde* with Kathleen Ferrier (1912–53) was certainly influential). There are some striking essays for solo voice(s) and orchestra from the last thirty years, and particularly from the 1960s and early 1970s: Maw's *Scenes and Arias* (1962, revised 1966); McCabe's *Notturni ed alba* (Hereford 1970); Crosse's monodrama *Memories of Morning: Night* and the 19-year-old Knussen's outstanding Second Symphony with soprano to texts by Trakl and Plath (both 1971); Britten's *Phaedra* (1975); and, pre-eminent perhaps, Hugh Wood's *Scenes from Comus* (1965). Whether Dickinson's *The Unicorns* (John Heath Stubbs), written in 1982 for Elisabeth Söderström and unusually scored (complete with a lullaby) for soprano and brass band, should be placed within this tradition would be difficult to say. More recently, David Matthews's *Cantiga* (1988), a lush song-cycle for soprano and chamber orchestra to macabre poems by Maggie Hemingway, has proved appealing; and Goehr's concert aria *Behold the Sun* (1981), a virtuoso work for coloratura soprano and large ensemble and cast in one floating span by no means interrupted by the refrain structure, was actually incorporated into his opera of that title. Tippett's *Byzantium* for soprano and orchestra (Yeats; 1989) is less dramatic but even broader, offering a rare match of poetic and musical depth; and Birtwistle's *Meridian* (1971) might be added to this list of wide-arching structures.

The Wood, Maw, Crosse and McCabe pieces conveniently form a group for discussion. They range from orchestral song cycle (McCabe) – commissioned as 'a *Dies natalis* of the 70s' (Boden 1992: 217, quoting Richard Lloyd) – to expressionist monodrama (Crosse), and an earlier composer would almost certainly have made Wood's text (from Milton) into a choral cantata or ode. Yet they have a lot, significantly, in common. All four works are in one continuous span of some substance and employ the female voice with orchestra (Wood adds a tenor, Maw writes for soprano, mezzo and contralto, often very much as a trio). All four view a sophisticated post-tonal language with 12-note propensities as a gateway rather than a barrier to triumphant lyricism, though Crosse's over-extended psychological monologue with its tune fragments and internalized narrative (his text from Jean Rhys's *Wide Sargasso Sea*, his protagonist the first Mrs Rochester in *Jane Eyre*) now seems rather dated and under-composed. However, despite the command of vocal expression, the triumph in all four works is as much the orchestra's as the voice's. Wood's central event is a thrilling orchestral dance, Comus's 'light fantastick round'. Maw's is the lover's yearning cantilena on the violins (second of four orchestral interludes) separating the two medieval poems that he sets in his bipartite structure. McCabe's is an orchestral scherzo prefacing the third of his four medieval lyrics about night and dawn (the one about dreams and nightmares). Crosse's musical culmination comes near the end, as a 12-note row is clarified on the horn, at the passage 'Then I woke up' (and compare McCabe's orchestral 'alba' after his last song). All four works use these sections to represent the inner reality and intensity of desire, separation, dream, enactment, illusion, awakening.

On a smaller scale and with piano rather than orchestra, but with an impressionist richness of colour, figuration and line none the less, two 1970s works to French texts might be singled out for their refulgence: Colin Matthews's *Un colloque sentimental* (1971–8) and Casken's *Ia Orana, Gauguin* (1979). In the former, the framing title poem by Verlaine takes us all the way back to early Yeats and *The Curlew*, though it is the rare ecstasy of Warlock's 'Consider' or some of Ireland's songs that might suggest a continuing tradition of Anglicized symbolism – if such were sought – flowing through the expansive Baudelaire setting 'Le jet d'eau'. Casken's harmonies glow even more, while his critique of post-impressionism is structural: his title indicates the suggestive connections between vowel, syllable, word, phrase and name that make his (own) verbal text an aspect of the music rather than an adjunct to it.

Sensibilities have, by and large, not remained so pleasurable. In 1921 Arthur Bliss gave a paper to the Society of Women Musicians on 'What modern composition is aiming at' and, announcing his 'distrust of all existing sound combinations', explained:

The idea of the instrumental groups in the classical orchestra is done away with, and the composer uses instruments that are widely incongruous in quality and dynamic value, just as Wyndham Lewis, Wadsworth, or the Nash Brothers create a picture with tones that are varying in density. (Roscow 1991: 21–3)

This 'preoccupation with the timbre of instruments and the resulting mass sonority obtained by the combination of them' was, as Bliss's manifesto makes clear, very much in line with iconoclasms such as Wyndham Lewis's in art and literature, and indeed is illustrated in countless pictures by Picasso and his contemporaries: a group of musicians or *minstrels*, raw and popular in costume and sound, becomes the subject matter, perhaps with a singer or an actor or reciter at the centre, and with cabaret stage or street pavement as the platform. As the century unfolds, jazz combinations soon strengthen the image of instruments other than the piano as foil to the individual voice, and eventually the popular concert stage is occupied by rock and folk groups.

Art music has reflected these developments in popular culture by abstracting them rather than joining the party. Schoenberg's *Pierrot lunaire*, the *locus classicus* of expressionist minstrelsy, was parodied by Walton in *Façade* for speaker and six instruments (Edith Sitwell; 1921–8), but while being subtitled *an entertainment*, *Façade* had avant-garde pretensions too, seized upon by critics and audience in its initial concert guise with Futurist megaphone and screen (the screen for one performance being painted by Severini). Bliss, as is clear above, was serious about his modernism, though the geniality of his works for voice and ensemble of the 1920s belies the fact, and in any case 'Madam Noy' (E. H. W. Meyerstein; 1918), the wordless 'Rhapsody' (with two voices; 1919) and nonsense-syllabled 'Rout' (1920), *The Women of Yueh* (Li Po; 1923) and the *Two Nursery Rhymes* with clarinet (1921) and *Four Songs* with violin (*ca* 1927) gave way to more conventionally lyrical works such as *Serenade* for orchestra and baritone (1929) and *Seven American Poems* (Edna St Vincent Millay and Elinor Wylie; 1940) for voice and piano, though he explored a voice and ensemble aesthetic again, with texts to match its instrumental mobiles, in *A Knot of Riddles* (eighth century; 1963).

Grainger was the great natural among composers for new combinations (his version of 'Early one morning' quoted earlier was originally scored for soprano, flute, double bassoon, horn and strings), though the bulk of his folksong arrangements – there are relatively few original compositions – were made or completed after he left England in 1914. Vaughan Williams, as we have seen, questioned the resources of song in his later career. Younger British composers who made forays away from voice and piano before the Second World War included Rubbra (like Bliss, he wrote a wordless vocal 'Rhapsody' – for soprano, string septet, flute, oboe, clarinet, two horns and harp, 1927), Hadley (the charming 'Scene from [Hardy's] *The Woodlanders*', 1926) and Constant Lambert's *Two Songs* for soprano, flute and harp (Sacheverell Sitwell; 1923). Plenty of songs with string quartet and songs with orchestra also continued to be written.

The real shift in aesthetic, however, not just away from voice and piano but away from song as an accompanied lyrical entity setting compliant poetry in a manner ultimately traceable to Schubert, occurred after the war. One sees it in the vocal output of Elisabeth Lutyens, prolific and undervalued. Exchanging an insider's inheritance (her father was the famous architect) for an outsider's stance, she virtually created the musical avant garde in Britain. She courted difficulty as second nature in all her writing, choosing to set Wittgenstein (the choral Motet 'Excerpta tractatus-logico philosophici', 1952), or a poetry index, wittily selected from the 'I' and 'If' sections of *The Oxford Book of English Verse* ('The egocentric', 1968), or presenting unfamiliar verse surrounded by an instrumental ensemble, as in *The Valley of Hatsu-se* (Japanese, set in the original language; 1965) and *Akapotik Rose* (Eduardo Paolozzi; 1966), both for soprano, or *And Suddenly It's Evening* (Quasimodo; 1966) for tenor, the instrumentation of this last being particularly quirky: two trumpets, two trombones, double bass, harp, celesta, percussion, violin, horn and cello, with much of the rhetorical continuity being carried by the brass. Yet through such challenges the aim and essence of her voice are none the less the discovery of beauty, be it passionate yet neatly contained and symmetrical in *The Valley of Hatsu-se*, impassive yet heartfelt in 'Requiescat' (Blake; 1971), a memorial to Stravinsky, or compressed in the much earlier 'O saisons, ô châteaux' (Rimbaud; 1946), a tiny yet somehow extravagant, jewelled cantata.

At the time when she was finding her voice, three immigrants were among others who brought new perspectives. The first vocal works in English of Wellesz ('The leaden echo and the golden echo', 1944) and Gerhard (*The Akond of Swat*, 1954) were respectively for soprano, clarinet and piano trio and for medium voice and two percussionists, and Seiber set his *Four Medieval French Songs* (1944) for viola d'amore, viola da gamba and guitar. Indicative rather than influential, these works and composers again, like Lutyens, signalled in their choices of text (Hopkins, Lear and medieval poetry) trends away from previous staples, Seiber also making settings of Joyce's *Portrait of the Artist as a Young Man* in his *Three Fragments* (1957) with speaker and chorus. Difficult, distant (ancient or foreign), oblique, inflammatory, ritualistic or naive poets have in the second half of the century generally been preferred to lyrical, straightforward, realist or romantic ones, partly in accordance with literary and political fashion. Thus there are also numerous settings of St John of the Cross, Donne, Baudelaire, Rimbaud, Mallarmé, Trakl, Rilke, Neruda, Lorca, Eliot, Dylan Thomas, late rather than early Yeats, Beckett, MacDiarmid, Edith Sitwell, Ted Hughes, Wallace Stevens, cummings, Auden, Stevie Smith, Plath, Betjeman, Lewis Carroll, oriental lyrics and Celtic and Eastern European folk poetry, but not, despite his exceptional standing, of the direct and reactionary Larkin (Holloway's *From High Windows*, 1978, and Dickinson's *Larkin's Jazz*, 1989, being among the few). Blake seems to have been set to music most of all.

Another indicator of detachment, extremity or obliquity – we may as well call it alienation – is the use of non-standard instruments. New sounds have rarely been to the British taste (but note Frank Denyer, who, if not quite Britain's Harry Partch, has written for such forces as giant ocarinas, shakuhachi, banjo, fishing rods, eunuch flutes, tin whistles, melodica, rubbed percussion and various instruments of metal, slate and glass, with and without voices, in *After the Rain* (1983), *A Monkey's Paw* (1988) and other works). Old sounds, on the other hand, have flourished in the wake of the early music revival. Britten's *Canticle IV* – again, not song – *Journey of the Magi* (Eliot; 1971) includes countertenor, one of many parts written for James Bowman (*b* 1941), and indeed Britten had already gone further in 'strange' vocal characterization in *Canticle II: Abraham and Isaac* (Chester Miracle Play text; 1952), where the voice of God is portrayed using alto and tenor in organum-like homophony (the same ploy is adopted for Owen's parody of this story in the *War Requiem*).

Works, with or without countertenor, for baroque or renaissance instrumentation – viols, recorders, lute, harpsichord – and commissioned by early music groups, abounded after 1950. Examples include Fricker's 'The tomb of St Eulalia' (1955), McCabe's *Rain Songs* (1966) and 'Les soirs bleus' (1979), Tavener's *Canciones españolas* (1971), Bennett's 'Time's whiter series' (1974), Leighton's *Animal Heaven* (1980), Dickinson's *Four Poems of Alan Porter* (1968) and *A Memory of David Munrow* (1977) and Crosse's *Verses in memoriam David Munrow* (1979) and *A Wake Again* (1986, and like Dickinson's *A Memory of David Munrow*, employing two countertenors). Joubert has engaged a good deal with early music combinations ('Dialogue', 1970; 'Crabbed age and youth', 1974; 'The phoenix and the turtle' and 'The hour hand', 1984; 'Roundelay', 1987), and his memorial to Munrow, *Music for a Pied Piper* (1985), is scored for six voices, recorder, two violins, bass viol, violone and two lutes. Peter Wishart (1921–84) was another composer who wrote for voice with baroque forces (*Three Hymns*, 1968; *To the Holy Spirit*, 1972) as well as with guitar. It may not be accident that these last four composers were all at the University of Birmingham in the late 1950s or 1960s, at the height of the Barber Institute's baroque opera revivals. More recently, Musgrave's *Wild Winter* for vocal quartet and viol consort (1993) was written for Red Byrd and Fretwork, and Weir's *Lovers, Learners and Libations: Scenes from Thirteenth-Century Parisian Life* for three voices and medieval ensemble (1987) for the Scottish Early Music Consort. The times do not always suit such interchange of constituencies, any more than new music for gamelan seems to satisfy. Nevertheless, the traversable ground between pastiche baroque and the ritual dislocations in late Stravinsky may be wide and rich, as Crosse demonstrates in *A Wake Again*, in which he interprets his instruments' attributes boldly, through harpsichord trills and *gruppetti* to out-of-phase ostinatos, frantic figuration and (following Britten's example) countertenor organum effects. George Benjamin takes a comparably broad leap between the sound of the consort song and the tricks of the string quartet trade in his 'Upon silence' (Yeats; 1990) for mezzo soprano and five viols. Weir in *Lovers, Learners and Libations* opts for the reflexive humour of a music theatre mind (the third movement, for instance, 'A recipe', describes 'how to make strings for the harp', intestines and all).

The resource most central to later twentieth-century vocal expression, however, appears to be the solo female, especially soprano, voice. Conversely, a new work for that staple of earlier English song, solo baritone, is almost a rarity nowadays. Where voice and ensemble are concerned it is partly a matter of acoustic space – Osborne's *I Am Goya* (1977) is scored for bass-baritone with four instruments of which three, flute, oboe and violin, are upper ones, but plays with this space by having the soloist's first entry falsetto, textless, and from among the instruments – but the apotheosis of the soprano might be explained in various other ways as well. One is certainly as an image fixation of the male, be it as madonna (note the three Marys listed below), goddess, witch, madwoman, victim, siren or diva. Expressionism has certainly been a crucial precipitant. A single image by Munch cast a potent spell over the century – it is reproduced on the cover of the score of Maxwell Davies's *Revelation and Fall* – as did Wagner's female outcries (see also Friedheim 1983); thus, as seen below in Davies's *The Medium*, the scream has frequently governed a(n ir)rationale of contour, climax or dynamic (raucous clarinet in the upper register often the corollary), the high voice being to the agony of art music what the low female register is to the resignation and sultriness of blues and jazz. The female range can use height to dominate a complex texture or extremes of register to express insecurity, not unlike the violin in the nineteenth century with its appeal to everything from ecstasy to desolation. Above all, unlike male utterance, the female voice has not been generally associated with rhetorical persuasion, a factor to which we return yet again.

Once more Schoenberg led the way, in *Erwartung* as well as *Pierrot lunaire*, while Stravinsky, curiously, did not. Stockhausen's use of a boy's voice in *Gesang der Jünglinge* kept the issue in mind by standing it on its head. Berio and his wife Cathy Berberian set the most important example of all, for his works of the 1960s and early 1970s written for her, *Visage, Circles, Sequenza III* and *Recital I*, all of which incorporate theatrical elements and extended vocal techniques, were highly influential in Britain, which has produced a remarkable succession of new music sopranos in response. Jane Manning (*b* 1938) is the foremost, with Mary Thomas (*b* 1935), Mary King, Mary Wiegold, Linda Hirst and Nicola Walker Smith of comparable versatility. All are tireless in promoting and commissioning works, largely, of course, from their male colleagues, who have also, things being what they are (or were), constituted the majority of the players, thereby underlining the connotations of gender conflict common in the genre. Manning is married to Anthony Payne, and two further singers, Jane Ginsborg and Meriel Dickinson, have had performing partnerships with their husband and brother respectively, composers George Nicholson and Peter Dickinson. Compositions commissioned or first performed by Manning, to enumerate only works not simply for voice and piano and by composers not listed in her *Grove* entry ('Bennett, Birtwistle, Davies, Hopkins, Lutyens, Wood and many others'), include Michael Berkeley's *The Wild Winds* (1978), Elias's 'Peroration' (1973), Jonathan Lloyd's 'Everything returns' (1978) and *Three Songs* (1980), Marsh's 'Streim' and Saxton's

ART MUSIC

'La promenade d'automne' (both 1972), Weir's 'Don't let that horse' (1990), Knussen's *Four Late Poems and an Epigram of Rainer Maria Rilke* (1988) and Gilbert's *Long White Moonlight* (1980) and *Beastly Jingles* (1984).

Mary Thomas was the singer in the Fires of London (previously the Pierrot Players) and Maxwell Davies wrote most of his vocal chamber music for her. He was the key figure in the consolidation of this genre in Britain in the 1960s, and since it is one that is separated by no firm line from music theatre, works such as his *Revelation and Fall* are discussed in Chapter 11. Other than these, the succession for female voice and instruments included *Leopardi Fragments* (with alto as well; 1961), 'Epitaph' (German texts; *ca* 1967), *From Stone to Thorn* (Mackay Brown; 1971), *Blind Man's Buff* (a masque including a mime), 'Hymn to St Magnus' (twelfth century) and *Tenebrae super Gesualdo* (all 1972), 'Fiddlers at the wedding' (Mackay Brown; 1974), 'My Lady Lothian's lilt' (1975), 'The blind fiddler' (Mackay Brown; 1976), *Anakreontika* (Greek poems; 1976) and *Winterfold* (1986).

From Stone to Thorn conveniently demonstrates Maxwell Davies's preoccupations, pivoted as it is between his earlier, human expressionism and later, more nature-orientated abstraction (it was his first Orkney work and first setting of George Mackay Brown; see Griffiths 1982: 118–19). Mackay Brown's poem, from *An Orkney Tapestry*, consists of 14 two-line titled sections, some rather like riddles or folk incantations, others like prayers, each curt or cryptic, which trace the agricultural cycle from one winter to another and Christ's life through to burial and rebirth at Christmas. Each pair of lines is a tetrameter followed by a dimeter, the overall number of syllables varying from 10 to 16, and every second line has the same rhyme or near-rhyme. The title of Maxwell Davies's piece, summarizing the parallel imagery, occurs at the end of the seventh section, in other words in the middle, and three of Mackay Brown's sections have a marking-off function ('First Fall' etc.) Upon this highly schematic arrangement Maxwell Davies superimposes a broader one by the insertion of instrumental sections (and one wordless one). Segmentation is not absolute, but it can be argued that he adds four interludes, a cadenza and an introduction, thus making 21 sections in all, the same number as in *Pierrot lunaire* (see Table 12.2), with the title 'rune' again in the centre (in the middle of a run of three sections with the same instrumentation). Again like Schoenberg, Maxwell Davies permutates his forces with both abstract delight and symbolic resonance. All five performers are used only in the wordless section and the final one, and all five four-performer combinations are used once each before the central span. Dramatic dispositions inform the second half, with three two-performer combinations surrounding the ritual killing of the corn ('Third Fall') followed by two sections of a three-performer combination for its flailing and Christ's crucifixion; and after their death (a *fortissimo* climax reverting to four performers) comes the one lonely solo, striking in that an expressionist section for the voice is eschewed in favour of a cadenza for its erstwhile partner-in-crime, the clarinet. These two have drawn together earlier in that the clarinet reflects the voice's 'gagged' effect by fluttertonguing in the humming section, and other complementary aspects of timbre and gesture are evident. In Ex. 12.23a, voice and clarinet tend to offset each other synchronically, constantly crossing each other's paths and exploring similar registers (the clarinet tending to venture a 3rd or so lower and 4th higher than the soprano), while the plucked-string guitar and harpsichord converse with more diachronic decorum, the guitar also lending a percussive aura to the voice with frequent rhythmic unisons. Despite the directness of Mackay Brown's text, the words are unlikely to be heard because of the melismas; on the other hand, phonemic equivalences are highlighted (the hollow accented staccatos in bar 2 of the clarinet part echoed by the tenuto, detached vowels 'of ho- . . .' in bar 3, both descending disjunctly). These are classic techniques of abstract expressionism in music. So are the pitch formulations, still essentially dodecaphonic – the voice and clarinet parts set off on two more or less pure twelve-note rows, the guitar retrograding part of the clarinet's, and four- to six-pitch sonorities are kept in harmonic flux, for instance over the first three bars, these sonorities rich in 3rds and 4ths tempered by semitones, two or three pitches carrying over from one to the next. However, the curious obverse of such intricacy is Maxwell Davies's tendency towards heterophony (see the unison Ds and Fs in bar 2 of Ex. 12.23a).

Not found in *From Stone to Thorn* are three other classic ingredients of the Fires of London and their repertoire: parody, a theatrical dimension and extended vocal or instrumental techniques. Maxwell Davies had not abandoned these, as *The Medium* (1981), a 50-minute monodrama for unaccompanied soprano, exemplifies. Music theatre it may be, but it is also vocal chamber music, its drama intrinsic to the score, for performance 'with the minimum of extraneous effects' (no lighting or props beyond a chair and a

Table 12.2   Maxwell Davies: Plan of *From Stone to Thorn*

	Cl	Perc	Gui	Voice	Hpd
(Introduction)	/	/	/		/
Condemnation	/		/	/	/
Cross	/		/	/	
(Interlude)		/			/
First Fall	/	(/)	/	/	
Mother of God	/	/	/	/	
Simon		/	/	/	/
(Wordless section)	/	/	/	/	/
(Interlude)	/	/			/
Veronica	/	/		/	/
Second Fall (inc. Title)	/	/		/	/
Women of Jerusalem	/	/		/	/
(Interlude)		/	/		
Third Fall		/		/	
(Interlude)		/	/		
The Stripping		/	/	/	
The Crucifixion		/	/	/	
Death	/	/	/	/	
(Cadenza)	/				
Pietà		/		/	/
Sepulchre	/	/	/	/	/

handbell) and 'to a small audience in fairly claustrophobic circumstances' (Composer's note). But here the singer creates the opposing or accompanying 'instruments' in her deranged mind, and they form a continuum between object and mode, content and manner, which is a crucial aspect of the modernist aesthetic. Thus she can imitate or 'voice' a 'clarionet', trumpet, dog, crab, child, spirit master, religious ecstatic, gospel music, plainsong, hymn, eighteenth-century song, operatic coloratura, waltz, hum, cry, gasp, and so on. The heterogeneity of the list is justified in that as events in the score these are not just another image procession but underlying resources that can recur to create a formal mosaic, held together by transformations of pitch material (for instance, the swings between D♭ and B♭ tonalities in Ex. 12.23b), of phoneme-plus-note (the 'know'/ 'oh' shift and staccato marking-off of note, word and thought on the

Ex. 12.23a   Maxwell Davies: *From Stone to Thorn*

ART MUSIC

Ex. 12.23b   Maxwell Davies: *The Medium*

VOCAL MUSIC

last letter of 'skirt' in Ex. 12.23b), and above all, of the singer's moods and perceptions. Again it was written for Mary Thomas, a *tour de force* for both performer and composer in much the way that *Peter Grimes*'s mad scene was for Pears and Britten (see Chapter 11, Ex. 11.6).

In Birtwistle's music issues of line, melody, voice and mass work themselves out in a more monolithic way, invoking song and narrative to bind structures rather than fragment them, and as with Britten in the *War Requiem*, the ancient Greek lyrical ideal seems a conscious analogy. Hence the spotlight on Orpheus, as in *Nenia: The Death of Orpheus* (1970) and *The Fields of Sorrow* (1971). In *Nenia* he retains the soprano voice and her song as a simple linear constant throughout the piece, which is therefore essentially a melody accompanied by the sharply contrasting masses of tuned 'percussion' – prepared and pizzicato pianos (one player) and crotales – and three bass clarinets. One of the latter switches to normal clarinet at the climax of the story and joins the soprano for a classic expressionist duet (see the series of 'strident' clarinet notes prefacing the soprano's *fff /sffz* 'Blood'), though one also transfused with sensuous counterpoint based notably on perfect 5ths at the point immediately prior to the passage just mentioned. This preoccupation with line gives rise also to a kind of *style brisé* at the opening, the soprano creating two voices out of one by narrating in *Sprechstimme* while humming or singing the matter of the narration between syllables; she also presents the song of both Orpheus and Eurydice. This is certainly an extended vocal technique, but so were Monteverdi's *gorgie*, which are also employed (see Wright 1994: 430). The purity of melody is further spotlighted by restricting the sung text largely to the syllables (subjected to permutation) of the two lovers' names for the first half of the piece. This does not prevent Peter Zinovieff's poem from being treated with expansive, syllabic rhetoric, almost conservatively English in the direct contours of its intonation (see Ex. 12.24), all very different from Ex. 12.23a and a much more lyrical interpretation of the imperatives of post-serial melody, though the distinction, striking also in his *Prologue* (Aeschylus; again 1970), applies less in other Birtwistle vocal works such as *Monody for Corpus Christi* (medieval English carols; 1959 – but note the title), 'Ring a dumb carillon' (Christopher Logue; 1965), *Cantata* (Greek texts; 1969) and *Songs by Myself* (1984).

Nenia was another Manning work, skilfully adapted to her sustaining power. So were two other pieces using three clarinets (because commissioned by Alan Hacker's group Matrix), both from 1975: Knussen's 'Trumpets' (Trakl) and Bainbridge's *People of the*

Ex. 12.24 Birtwistle: *Nenia: The Death of Orpheus* (voice part only)

Dawn. Again in the Bainbridge, which like *Nenia* includes percussion, the soprano role contains indications of displacement – she moves around and eventually leaves the ensemble and at one point 'begins to look more and more frantic and distraught' – and in conjunction with the text, taken from creation myths of the Navajo Indians, this suggests some quest for or loss of primal community. Have such specifications and aesthetic topics been overworked to the point of cliché? It is impossible to represent the sheer bulk of repertoire for female voice and ensemble in this essay, and the output of younger composers suggests that its concerns have not yet worked their way out. See, for instance, Turnage's *Lament for a Hanging Man* (Jeremiah and Plath; 1983) and *Her Anxiety* (Yeats; 1991). The former once again dislocates the (mezzo) soloist – she plays percussion, mouths to the sound of the soprano saxophone whose player she stands immediately behind, and so on – and once again is scored with clarinets (two basses plus Turnage's beloved saxophone). The best of the genre will probably find its way to the top, or rather to the bottom where Knussen's *Océan de terre* (Apollinaire) with its submarine and octopus imagery is concerned. This fine, sonorous work, first performed in 1973 but not published until 1985 or recorded until 1993, reconciles modernist complexity with harmonic clarity and symphonic scope within a twelve-minute span.

Meanwhile, Knussen is not alone in having made his peace with song and with the century. He points out that whereas the *Whitman Settings* (no more rhetorical poet could have been chosen) 'constitute my eighth concert work for a soprano voice' they are 'my first in many years for voice and piano' (1993: 10–11), and adds:

> Earlier attempts having been impossibly dependent on models rather too close to home, I was very conscious of trying to re-imagine a very familiar genre with fresh ears – specifically of setting the voice in different contexts within the all-encompassing range of the piano.

This is one recent rapprochement, with American song (Copland) as much as British. On another level, Roger Marsh responds as much to the word 'love' as to the idea of song in two works clustering around '*Not a soul but ourselves . . .*': *A Psalm and a Silly Love Song* (1979) for soprano, mezzo and ensemble and 'Another silly love song' (1976) for soprano, clarinet and piano, both of which vocalize permutations of 'liva luva' syllabification as though to suggest that the way round the silliness of the words of love songs is to go beyond any meaning to the sound and feel of the word 'love', with all those soft labial consonants.

Furthermore, Manning has passionately and successfully shown in her career and taught in her book (Manning 1986, 2/1994) how new vocal music can take its place within the conventional song recital. Another rapprochement concerns a later singer than Manning, Mary Wiegold, who has been catalyst to something different again from both the 'dislocation' tradition and the renewed recital cycle. Her Composers Ensemble has performed, for example, MacMillan's 'Scots song' (Soutar; 1991), Weir's 'The romance of Count Arnaldos' (anon; 1989), Birtwistle's 'White and light' (Celan; 1989) and her partner Woolrich's 'The Turkish mouse' (1988; she also premièred most of his earlier solo vocal works), and these are contributions to an ongoing series of short commissions for *Mary Wiegold's Songbook* which had already involved nearly 80 composers, mostly British and including a few jazz figures, between 1988 and the issue of a recorded selection in 1991. The format, ranging from 'near-aphorisms to mini-cantatas' (Maycock 1991: 3), is soprano and up to five instruments (two clarinets and saxophone doublings, viola, cello, double bass), confirming the fact that the chamber song, not the recital song, is the species of our time – that is, given the group of players employed, 'in concerts, groups of songs can alternate with instrumental music' (p. 3). This consort ethos continues to parallel the early music revival and at last recognizes that 'out in the real world, modern music is songs – three-minute ones that can top the charts, whether pop or Puccini', hoping to prove that 'whatever gloomy traditionalists may say, the song can be alive and well'.

PART IV
Music and Scholarship

Chapter 13

CRITICISM AND THEORY

CHRISTIAN KENNETT

I: The Decline of the Gentleman Scholar

The history of British musicological writings since the end of the First World War is primarily a history of criticism. The growth (or rebirth) of British theory and aesthetics is largely a phenomenon of the last 35 years, due to two factors, the influx of musicians and scholars from Eastern Europe and the far-reaching changes to the structure of university degrees in music. The effects of both developments began to be felt in the late 1950s.

Until the end of the Second World War the majority of British musical scholars were dilettantes with a high level of general education, breeding, taste and wit, trained at Oxford or Cambridge or one of the London music colleges. Neither university awarded honours degrees in music before 1947, and BMus students were encouraged to have a thorough grounding either in Classics or *Literae Humaniores* at undergraduate level before attempting the degree. Against this background of the gentleman amateur, a group of musicians, sensing the need 'for the investigation and discussion of subjects connected with the art, science and history of music', had founded the Musical Association in London in 1874 (it received a royal charter in 1944). Papers on acoustics and aesthetics briefly flourished in its first 15 years, but by the 1890s the 'scientific' aspect of musical scholarship had all but disappeared, papers concentrating instead on criticism (and, to a lesser extent, history). Indeed, in the wider musical environment, there were historiographic exceptions, notably *The Oxford History of Music* (1901–5) edited by Henry Hadow, but the vast majority of writing about music at the end of the century took the form of regular criticism in a newspaper or journal. Quality varied wildly, often revealing more about the critic than the music. The apogee of this style of writing was reached with

George Bernard Shaw and his successor John Runciman (see Banfield 1981b: 469–73; Runciman 1901).

In the early years of the twentieth century, however, and especially after the First World War, some critics questioned the point of such subjectivity. As early as 1906, Percy Buck (1871–1947) was trying to lay down some objective standards for criticism since, he claimed, at the time of writing 'our musical critics . . . prefer to give personal impressions and opinions rather than to aim at reaching a valuation by means of analysis and comparison' (1905–6: 156). To Buck, criticism should be concerned with how music makes its 'purely psychological' appeal. The question of this appeal is subdivided into two classes for critical review: 'intrinsic' qualities, existing prior to performance ('grammar', 'subject matter' and 'presentation'), and 'extrinsic' qualities, arising from performance ('sensuous', 'intellectual' and 'emotional' (p. 161)). This division into 'intrinsic' and 'extrinsic' qualities implies that the latter represent the inessential, the siren temptations of aesthetic appeal, which the critic has to disregard in order to preserve objectivity. The subjective, even vague nature of these criteria for objectivity is clear, but the fact that such questions were raised at all is surprising and healthy. In any case Buck admits the limits of objectivity in his critical–analytical method: 'In analysis there is no such thing as Truth; but there are truths' (p. 171).

II: Dent, Newman, Tovey and Others

Buck was one of the first British writers to advocate analysis in the service of criticism. After the war two critics, Edward Dent (1876–1957) and Ernest Newman (1868–1959), took up Buck's banner. Dent lectured at Cambridge from 1902 and returned in 1926 as Professor, a post which he held for 15 years. For eight years before his return he worked in London as a music critic. Throughout his working life he campaigned for critics to develop 'a scientific attitude of mind':

There is a vast conspiracy among listeners, critics and even among musicians, who ought to know better, to maintain the doctrine that all music, whether composition or performance, is a matter of direct inspiration from unfathomable sources . . . and that of all the arts music is the most completely dependent upon unexplainable impulses. English people are notoriously hostile to thought. (1931: 8)

In his essay on 'The historical approach to music', Dent adds:

> There are many people who are positively frightened of any sort of analytical or historical approach to music, because they are convinced that it would destroy all their pleasure in the art . . . We must teach them young, if we can, that the intellectual appreciation of music immensely widens the powers of enjoyment. (H. Taylor 1979: 198)

Dent's ideal 'intellectual appreciation', then, is an amalgam of historiography and analysis, although he eschews 'mere excavation' (p. 190). Quite what sort of analysis Dent advocates here is not clear, but in another essay, on 'Binary and ternary form', his 'preliminary suggestion' for an analysis of the *Tristan* Prelude consists mainly of comments about large-scale form and harmony, which he does not claim to be a full analysis; but the basically descriptive nature of this 'preliminary suggestion' has resonances with the writings of Donald Tovey, below. Whatever the method, Dent can assert that 'the ultimate function of all research in music is to teach ourselves and others that intellectual understanding is the only key which will unlock the door to the innermost experience which music can bring us' (1931: 8).

Newman came from a less academic background than Dent, but was much longer-lived as a critic: his career began in 1905, and from 1920 to 1958 he was music critic for *The Sunday Times*. He shared Dent's view of the merit of analysis, but with the emphasis less on individual works than on 'a physiology of style that is the basis of [a composer's] psychology' (1956: 15). Therefore Newman's ideal criticism 'must recognize as the object of its study not the critic's own temperament but *the composer* [my italics] and the work' (p. 21). This stylistic analysis was to become the most popular analytic methodology after the Second World War, as evinced by the classic genre of English musicology, the life-and-works monograph.

Where Dent's analysis is primarily aimed at an improved emotional and intellectual perception of a performance, Newman's methodology is aimed at improving the performance itself:

> Knowledge . . . of the elements of a composer's style is not merely interesting from the scientific–analytic point of view. It is not a mere curiosity: it has a practical aesthetic value. For while on the one hand we see a certain mood always realised through a certain formula, on the other hand whenever we meet with the formula we are entitled to infer the mood. (p. 16)

In other words, statistical knowledge of the elements of a composer's style (the 'formula') should empower the critic to dictate the manner of interpretation to a conductor (the 'mood'). This is all very well provided that (a) the formula is clear and convincing enough to win over the conductor to one's opinion, and (b) the 'mood' is equally convincing. If we combine this with another Newman comment, that 'a certain school has tried to foist on us the mountebank doctrine that music must not attempt to "express anything beyond itself"' – as if the musical faculty worked in a sort of vacuum . . . It really will not do' (p. 168), we shall see that Newman's position includes many of the merits and demerits of the theories of Deryck Cooke.

The earlier comparison between Tovey and Dent would doubtless have been invidious to both. Dent was a committed academic and modernist, becoming first president of the International Society for Contemporary Music in 1923 and attaining the same rank in the International Musicological Society in 1931. Tovey (1875–1940), in spite of occupying the Reid Chair of Music at Edinburgh University from 1914, hated the company of musicologists, disliked radical contemporary music, and thought of himself as a popularizer who aimed his programme notes, later compiled and published as *Essays in Musical Analysis* (1935–9, 1944), at enlightening the 'naive listener'. However, the same sort of descriptive analysis as in Dent's sketch of the *Tristan* Prelude also obtains in Tovey's writing, and both critics share an interest in problems of structure; history too is indirectly invoked by Tovey as an aid to understanding.

A typical Tovey analysis starts with a brief biographical sketch of the events surrounding a work's composition, followed by a travelogue of the unfolding of the work's surface events, as in this example, from the *Chamber Music* volume of his *Essays*: 'The first movement opens with two broad melodies; one in the tonic and one in the relative major.' Then, later, comes 'a new figure, which closes in a great theme, whose jubilant character will eventually prove a pathetic contrast to what it becomes at the end of the movement' (1944: 185).

The main difference between Tovey and Dent is in Tovey's primary interest in the way that tonality articulates structure, with all other parameters subordinated; hence his substitution of the word 'group' for 'subject' in analyses, 'which has the merit of not necessarily implying themes at all' (1935–9, i: 2), but concentrates on harmony. This flexible and empirical approach forms the cornerstone of Tovey's analytical technique: 'My master, Parry,' he points out, 'taught me to study the classics of music from point to point according to the course of each individual work, instead of setting up classical forms *a priori* and treating the individual work as if it were compelled to fit the forms' (1935–9, vi: 139). None the less, Tovey inevitably uses the language of sonata form in his analyses, in spite of the adjustment of terminology. In addition, when viewed as a whole, Tovey's essays begin to form a 'physiology of style' for each composer in a manner akin to Newman. At the same time, however, each piece for Tovey is its own context; by exploring thoroughly the musical surface in its chronological order it is possible to describe what makes a work unique. Unfortunately, a by-product of this approach is that issues of hierarchical unity are almost entirely neglected. Thus Tovey's 'analyses' inevitably concentrate on describing what is obvious to all but the 'naive listener', and it is even likely that his hypothetical *ingenu* could make similar judgements after repeated hearings; but as short cuts to simple appreciation of unfamiliar music Tovey's essays remain a useful starting-point, and they influenced two generations of scholars.

The analytical programme note had existed in some form since the middle of the previous century, but in the inter-war years a few critics tried to swim against the Toveyan tide, writing analyses with the strong 'scientific' bias inimical to Tovey. Most notable among these writers was Edwin Evans *père* (1844–1923), who contended that a full understanding of a work can be achieved only through the medium of 'analysis reaching to the rhythmical significance of every bar; accounting for all material, whether subjects or intermediate motives; laying bare all formal proportions and developments; and fully describing all contrasts and characteristic features' (E. Evans 1935: ix). (His son, also named Edwin (1871–1945), carried on his father's analytical work both as critic of the *Daily Mail* from 1933 and with his own programme notes for London concerts, though it was as a strongly partisan advocate of Franco-Russian modernism that he made his greatest mark.)

Nevertheless, it was Tovey's influence that was strongest, in the years leading to and immediately following the Second World War, when his suspicion of *a priori* theory, such as he believed was practised by Evans, was used by the majority of critical opinion as an excuse to avoid discussing music in any scholarly way. Neville Cardus (1888–1975), music critic of the *Manchester Guardian*, was typical:

The jargon and pedantry of the present are not more edifying and are certainly less entertaining than the picturesque mode of writing which discovered moonlights in sonatas and Fate knocking at the door . . . It is a barren pedantry that insists on a technical account of the 'organisation' and the 'pattern'. (1959: 210)

Bernard van Dieren suggested that 'occupation with musical research exercises a baleful influence on the intelligence' (1935: 215). This suspicion of analytical thinking was intensified throughout the 1930s and 1940s, and more often than not went hand-in-hand with a profound dislike of the way musical composition was going. Cardus maintained:

It is to-day possible to put together a large-scale work in terms of the attraction to or repulsion from a tonal centre, jig-sawing your material into rhythmical patterns, or by working-out mathematically . . . inversions, diminutions, expansions, and so forth, of a germ-theme of new notes which anybody could pick out on the piano. (1959: 187)

Van Dieren and other composers like Sorabji and Gray had their entertaining, if prejudiced, twopennyworth in the debate of modernism versus folksong, but the composer-cum-critic who most trenchantly, though for different reasons than the above writers, sums up the feeling of composition somehow losing its way is Constant Lambert. In *Music Ho!* Lambert contends that, by the time of writing (1934), all of the revolutionary spirit has gone out of music, and composers are forced into a 'psychological cul-de-sac' (p. 235) of their own making:

Unable to progress any further in the way of modernity [the composer] has not a sufficiently sympathetic or stimulating background to enable him to start afresh or to consolidate his experiments. The stupider composers . . . escape from the situation either by an empty and wilful pastiche of an older tradition or by an equally fruitless concentration on the purely mechanical and objective sides of their arts. The more intelligent composer is forced in on himself and forced to overconcentrate on his own musical personality, a process which is inclined to be dangerous and sterilizing. (p. 242)

Often bigoted and wrong-headed, Lambert none the less expresses real concerns about the decline of individuality, often in hilariously apposite terms. However, with the above exceptions, the Continental phenomenon of the composer–critic largely bypassed inter-war Britain, highlighting the beginnings of an ideological rift between practitioner and thinker which widened as the century progressed.

CRITICISM AND THEORY

By the end of the 1950s, Tippett was virtually the only remaining British exponent of both arts.

With criticism and composition in the doldrums, there was a resurgence in interest in historiography, scholarship about a recently deceased or long-dead genius being much easier to contemplate than dissemination of new works in troubled times, especially since the criteria for judging their worth were so poorly sketched out. This is not to say that the new histories of Westrup (1943), Abraham (1938, R/1949) and many others avoided criticism of contemporary works, but their main brief was to look back on the past, especially the recent past, tracing compositional trends in the hope of finding a way out of their present malaise.

III: After the War: Keller, Cooke and Academic Scholarship

The death-knell for the gentleman amateur seemed to be the reorganization of musical activities in universities. Before the Second World War few universities outside Oxbridge employed Professors of Music (see Table 13.1), and many of these were still part-time posts. The year 1947 saw the appointment of Jack Westrup at Oxford, Arthur Hutchings at Durham, Anthony Lewis at Birmingham and Gerald Abraham at Liverpool as full-time professors (Abraham being Liverpool's first full-time incumbent). With these new appointments came new courses, first degrees in music, more rigorously academic than before, mainly concentrating on the cultivation of historiographic skills, reflecting the research interests of each establishment's professor. The immigration of Central European scholars such as Hans Redlich, Mátyás Seiber, Otto Deutsch and Erwin Stein, before and after the war, also had a profound influence on musical thought inside and outside the academy, an influence beginning with the appointment of Egon Wellesz as lecturer at Oxford in 1943.

Nowhere was this wind of change more strongly felt than in the areas of theory and aesthetics. Before the arrival of the Central Europeans, theory, such as it was, was subsumed into descriptive analytical criticism, and the word 'aesthetic' was almost always used as some sort of fuzzy adjective in a newspaper review of a concert. By the mid-1950s a new generation of students weaned on the writings of Schoenberg and Réti, or Marx and Adorno, as well as the historiography of Westrup *et al.*, was emerging, while newspaper criticism was on the decline, losing potential exponents to the

MUSIC AND SCHOLARSHIP

newer fields of aesthetics and theory. (These students went on to found strong music departments of their own throughout the country.) Study of theory emerged as the stronger thought-stream due to the influence of Hans Keller (1919–85).

Table 13.1   (i) Directors and Principals of the major colleges of music

Royal College of Music

Hubert Parry	1894–1918
Hugh Allen	1918–37
George Dyson	1938–52
Ernest Bullock	1952–60
Keith Falkner	1960–74
David Willcocks	1974–84
Michael Gough Matthews	1985–93
Janet Ritterman	1993–

Royal Academy of Music

Alexander Mackenzie	1888–1924
John McEwen	1924–36
Stanley Marchant	1936–49
Reginald Thatcher	1949–55
Thomas Armstrong	1955–68
Anthony Lewis	1968–82
David Lumsden	1982–93
Lynn Harrell	1993–95
Curtis Price	1995–

Guildhall School of Music and Drama

Landon Ronald	1910–38
Edric Cundell	1938–59
Gordon Thorne	1959–65
Allen Percival	1965–78
John Hosier	1978–88
Ian Horsbrugh	1988–

Trinity College of Music

Stanley Roper	1929–43
W. Greenhouse Allt	1944–65
Myers Foggin	1965–79
Meredith Davies	1979–88
Philip Jones	1988–94
Gavin Henderson	1994–

London College of Music

W. S. Lloyd Webber	1946–82
John McCabe	1983–90
Richard Roberts	1991–

Royal Northern College of Music
(formerly Royal Manchester College of Music)

Adolf Brodsky	1895–1929
Robert Forbes	1929–53
Frederick Cox	1953–70
J. Wray	1970–72
John Manduell	1972–

Royal Scottish Academy of Music and Drama

W. G. Whittaker	1930–41
Ernest Bullock	1941–53
Henry Havergal	1953–69
Kenneth Barritt	1969–76
David Lumsden	1976–82
Philip Ledger	1982–

Birmingham Conservatoire
(formerly Birmingham and Midland Institute School of Music)

Granville Bantock	1900–34
A. K. Blackall	1934–45
Christopher Edmunds	1945–56
Steuart Wilson	1957–60
Gordon Clinton	1960–73
Louis Carus	1973–87
Roy Wales	1987–9
Kevin Thompson	1989–93
George Caird	1993–

CRITICISM AND THEORY

(ii) Professors of university music faculties/departments most fully established before the end of the Second World War

Oxford

Hubert Parry	1900–1908
Walter Parratt	1908–18
Hugh Allen	1918–46
Jack A. Westrup	1947–71
Joseph Kerman	1971–4
Denis Arnold	1975–86
Brian Trowell	1988–

Cambridge

Charles Stanford	1887–1924
Charles Wood	1924–6
Edward Dent	1926–41
Patrick Hadley	1946–62
Thurston Dart	1962–4
Robin Orr	1965–76
Alexander Goehr	1976–

London/King's College

Frederick Bridge	1903–25
Percy Buck	1925–37
Stanley Marchant	1937–49
Herbert Howells	1950–64
Thurston Dart (first of King's)	1964–71
Howard Mayer Brown	1972–4
Brian Trowell	1974–88
Arnold Whittall (of Musical Theory and Analysis)	1982–95
Curtis Price (Edward VII)	1988–95
Harrison Birtwistle (Purcell)	1994–

Durham

Philip Armes	1897–1908
Joseph Bridge	1908–29
Edward Bairstow	1929–47
Arthur Hutchings	1947–68
Eric Taylor	1968–85
David Greer	1987–

Edinburgh

Friedrich Niecks	1891–1914
Donald Tovey	1914–40
Sidney Newman	1941–70
Kenneth Leighton (Reid)	1970–88
Michael Tilmouth (Tovey)	1971–87
Peter Williams	1982–5
David Kimbell	1990–
Nigel Osborne (Reid)	1990–

Birmingham

Edward Elgar	1905–8
Granville Bantock	1909–34
Victor Hely-Hutchinson	1934–44
Jack A. Westrup	1944–6
Anthony Lewis	1947–68
Ivor Keys	1968–86
Basil Deane	1987–92
Colin Timms (Peyton and Barber)	1992–
Stephen Banfield (Elgar)	1992–

After taking Tovey to task for his 'pleonastic description' (Keller 1956: 49), in his search for 'the *latent* elements of the unity of *manifest* contrasts' (p. 50), a search strongly informed by Schoenberg's 'developing variation' and Réti's thematicism, Keller proposed a mainly notated method of analysis, Functional Analysis (FA), to trace the development of thematic material through individual movements with an attention to detail rarely if ever witnessed before in Britain. This analytic score would then be played before and after and in between movements of the work being considered. By 1957 Keller had abandoned verbal description ('words *about* music') entirely, in order to let the 'music *behind* the music' shine out without verbal hindrance. He suggested that 'FA is merely doing what literary criticism has always been doing: it uses the art's own language' (1960: 238). The need to do this arises because:

> You cannot fix a word, a term, to any given instance of a background unity of contrasts, because any such instance, if it is any good, is unique, whereas any possible term is an abstraction applicable to more than one case. Thus, conventional analysis tends to isolate what is, from the artistic point of view, the least important aspect of any particular musical thought. (p. 237)

In the end, this stance is so subjective as to seem more critically than analytically based, not least in terms of the segmentation of the motif that is to be developed throughout the analytic score, especially in the absence of a clear 'how-to' manual so that FA could be replicated by others. In addition, there is the paradox of FA as blatant recomposition, since the centrepiece of FA is that what music communicates is fundamentally inexpressible, implying that FA is not really 'analysis' at all, since analyses are no more use than Tovey's 'pleonasms'. These and other problems ensured that FA was a relatively short-lived and localized phenomenon, being restricted to one practitioner; but Functional Analysis nevertheless had an influence that far outshone its use as a cogent methodology. Firstly, it gave rise to a large amount of scholarship on analytical and critical methodologies, albeit developing along existing lines rather than throwing up any new indigenous theory. Alan Walker produced two polemical and witty exemplars of this (1962 and 1966). Others may be seen in the periodicals *Music Review* (first published in 1940) and *Music Survey* (1947–52, a short-lived but influential journal edited by Donald Mitchell – later with Keller). Both publications challenged the belletristic bias of their main competitor, *Music and Letters*. Secondly, it breathed new life into the traditional British pursuit of the life-and-works monograph, by giving archetypal style analysis a more cogent means of tracing thematic relationships, not just through a work, as Keller had done, but through a body of work: for the first time the emphasis was on the works rather than the biography of a composer. Notable among many authors of such studies are, on British composers, Michael Kennedy (Vaughan Williams, 1964; Elgar, 1968), Peter Evans (Britten, 1979) and Ian Kemp (Tippett, 1984). Indeed, largely as a result of this change of emphasis, some British monographs on foreign composers have become standard works even in the country of their subjects' origin.

CRITICISM AND THEORY

Style analysis is at the heart of *The Language of Music* (1959) by Deryck Cooke (1919–76), but of a kind that recalls Newman's wish for music to say something cogent 'beyond itself' and for that something to be translatable into words. Cooke's theory

> tries to pinpoint the inherent emotional characters of the various notes of the major, minor, and chromatic scales, and of certain basic melodic patterns which have been used persistently throughout our musical history. It also investigates the problem of musical communication ... [and] how it may perhaps be possible to come to some objective understanding of the 'emotional content' of 'pure' music. (1959a: xii)

The theory is to be confined to tonal music:

> Since the new language [of twentieth-century non-tonal music] is unrelievedly chromatic by nature, it must be restricted to expressing ... emotions of the most painful type ... The fact that the new music shuns ... basic acoustical consonances ... suggests that it does not express the simple fundamental sense of being at one with nature. (p. xiii)

The old music is at one with nature because of the basic sonority of the triad: the major 3rd, 'present ... early on in the harmonic series', is 'nature's own basic harmony' (p. 51), therefore major-mode music is basically happy, and so on.

It is easy to ridicule the way Cooke's theory stumbles from unprovable 'fact' through non-sequitur to downright error; but what is most tiresome about *The Language of Music* is that, as a work of subjective criticism informed by a deep knowledge and love of a wide variety of tonal musics, it is excellent; as a Toveyan travelogue through the tonal repertoire, splendid; only as a work of theory does its naive positivism let it down. The first two aspects of Cooke's thesis endeared it to the developing aestheticians as a theory of meaning untainted by 'scientism'.

The development of historiography in the 1930s and 1940s was at the heart of a renewed interest in lexicography. The third and fourth editions of *Grove* (1927–8 and 1940), edited by Henry Colles (1879–1943), were mainly updated versions of the original edition, still imbued with George Grove's self-made amateur spirit. Even the fifth edition (1954, supplement 1961), edited by Eric Blom (1888–1959), was sometimes eccentric in its relative length of articles, and was certainly insular, the vast majority of its contributors being British. It did, however, encompass a considerably broader

MUSIC AND SCHOLARSHIP

range of subject entries, including articles on 'Analysis', 'Gestalt' and 'Criticism', though neither 'Theory' nor 'Aesthetics' received separate treatment and the article on criticism was, perhaps predictably, over 20 times as long as the entry for analysis, and was used largely unaltered in the sixth edition (1980) edited by Stanley Sadie (*b* 1930). With the exception of a few entries, this last edition was so thoroughly revised and expanded that it merited the title *New*, running to 20 volumes. A much more cosmopolitan affair, it took full advantage of the broad horizons of the European immigrants – indeed it drew on scholars throughout the world – and was also the first edition to include the work of the new wave of homegrown scholars, reaping the benefits of the changes in university education after the war.

IV: Journalism and Current Concerns

Since the turn of the century, with J. A. Fuller Maitland (1856–1936) as chief critic (see Table 13.2), *The Times* had exercised a hegemony of newspaper criticism, albeit challenged by regional papers, notably the *Manchester Guardian* and the *Birmingham Post*, but in the years when Frank Howes (1891–1974) was *The Times*'s chief critic (1943–60 – he

Table 13.2
Some twentieth-century chief music critics and editors of journals

Financial Times		*The Times*	
Andrew Porter	1955–74	J. A. Fuller Maitland	1889–1911
Ronald Crichton	1974–9	H. C. Colles	1911–43
Andrew Porter	1979–85	Frank Howes	1943–60
Max Loppert	1985–	William Mann	1960–82
		Paul Griffiths	1983–
Independent			
Bayan Northcott	1987–	*The Sunday Times*	
		Leonard Rees	1897–1920
		Ernest Newman	1920–58
Daily Telegraph		Desmond Shawe-Taylor	1959–83
Robin Legge	1906–31	David Cairns	1983–91
Herbert Hughes	1931–3	Paul Driver/Hugh Canning	1992–
Richard Capell	1933–54		
Martin Cooper	1954–76	*(Manchester) Guardian*	
Peter Stadlen	1977–86	Ernest Newman	1905–6
Robert Henderson	1986–8	Samuel Langford	1906–27
Alan Blyth	1988–90	Neville Cardus	1927–39
Robert Henderson	1990–	Granville Hill	1939–51

CRITICISM AND THEORY

Colin Mason	1951–64
Edward Greenfield	1964–93
Andrew Clements	1993–

Observer

George Clutsam	1909–18
Ernest Newman	1919–20
Percy Scholes	1920–25
A. H. Fox Strangways	1925–39
William Glock	1939–45
Charles Stuart	1945–9
Eric Blom	1949–59
Peter Heyworth	1955–91
Nicholas Kenyon	1992
Andrew Porter	1992–

Birmingham Post

Ernest Newman	1906–19
A. J. Sheldon	1919–31
Eric Blom	1931–46
John F. Waterhouse	1946–69
John Salding	1970–78
Barrie Grayson	1979–88
Christopher Morley	1988–

Yorkshire Post

Herbert Thompson	1886–1936
Ernest Bradbury	1948–84
Robert Cockcroft	1984–94

Early Music

John Thomson	1973–83
Nicholas Kenyon	1983–92
Tess Knighton	1992–

Music Analysis

Jonathan Dunsby	1981–7
Derrick Puffett	1987–

Musical Times

Frederick G. Edwards	1897–1909
William McNaught (*père*)	1909–18
Harvey Grace	1918–44
William McNaught (*fils*)	1944–53
Martin Cooper	1953–6
Harold Rutland	1957–60
Andrew Porter	1960–67
Stanley Sadie	1967–87
Andrew Clements	1988
Andrew Clements/ Alison Latham	1989
Eric Wen	1989–90
Basil Ramsey	1990–92
Antony Bye	1992–4
Antony Bye/ Gavin Thomas	1994–

Music and Letters

A. H. Fox Strangways	1920–37
Eric Blom	1937–50
Richard Capell	1950–54
Eric Blom	1954–9
Jack A. Westrup	1959–75
Edward Olleson	1976–87
Denis Arnold	1976–80
Nigel Fortune	1981–
John Whenham	1987–92
Tim Carter	1992–

Music Review

Geoffrey Sharp	1940–74
A. F. Leighton Thomas	1974–

Music Survey

Donald Mitchell	1947–9
Donald Mitchell/ Hans Keller	1949–52

Opera

Earl of Harewood	1950–53
Harold Rosenthal	1953–86
Rodney Milnes	1986–

Tempo

Donald Mitchell	1958–62
Colin Mason	1962–71
David Drew	1971–82
Calum MacDonald	1982–

first joined the newspaper in 1925) that hegemony was even stronger, as the regional newspapers declined. Howes was a passionate advocate of English music and used his position to fight a rearguard action against what he saw as dangerous new developments in composition. His damning verdicts on composers trying to assimilate European influences, particularly those of the Second Viennese School, often had a profoundly deleterious effect on their reputation; in *The Times* in 1926 Howes accused Bridge of 'uglify[ing] his music to keep it up to date' (the assertion was repeated in Howes 1966: 160), which dealt Bridge's reputation a blow from which it never recovered in his lifetime.

While Howes was at *The Times*, the influence of criticism elsewhere declined dramatically, mainly because of the growing availability and quality of gramophone records and the ascendancy of the BBC as a forum for criticism, especially after the launch of the Third Programme in 1946. The newspapers changed their approach to try to meet this competition. In 1955 the first regular music critic of the *Financial Times*, Andrew Porter (*b* 1928), was allowed space for long, educational articles to complement and sometimes eliminate daily concert reviews, and in the 1960s the dailies began previewing forthcoming concerts or important anniversaries; these trends have gathered momentum.

Much of the theoretical scholarship since Keller and Cooke has reflected 'the characteristic British disposition, which is to write about analysis rather than to write analyses', as Arnold Whittall commented in his gloomy 1980 survey of British post-war musicology (Blacking *et al.* 1980: 58). However, since the early 1970s, reflecting an internationalism fostered directly and indirectly (via the United States) by the wartime European diaspora, there has been a steep rise in the output of British literature of a mainly theoretical nature. Schenker studies, pitch-class set theory and semiotics have burgeoned in Britain, largely owing to the journal *Music Analysis*, founded in 1982 by Jonathan Dunsby (*b* 1953), and to the institution of a regular Music Analysis Conference in 1984, the first being held at King's College, London.

Aesthetic writing in Britain had existed prior to this, primarily represented by Ogden, Richards and Wood (1922). Howes (1948 and 1958) explored the notion of music as a knowledge-based system. But it was not until the late 1960s that the ideas of Adorno, Marx, Langer and others fully permeated British critical thought. The first result came in the provocative work of Wilfrid Mellers (*b* 1914) and

Michael Tippett. In *Caliban Reborn* (Mellers 1967), critical discussion of twentieth-century masterworks is fused with pantheism to suggest how tradition and revolution might be reconciled in today's music and a musical rebirth effected. *Moving into Aquarius* (Tippett 1974) tries to answer questions relating to the place of the composer in a culture of disintegration. Tippett's book among others led writers to consider sociological issues; how culture mediates and relates to music as a language (Shepherd *et al.* 1977) and even dilutes and distorts its message (Small 1977) is more urgent than traditional musical questions. The contributors to *Music and the Politics of Culture* go even further:

Formalism can be seen to represent in its purest, most seductive yet coercive form that version of aesthetic ideology that polices the boundary between experience and knowledge, art for the consumer and art as the realm of specialised understanding inaccessible to all but the expert. (Norris 1989: 9)

Thus they contend that writing about music, divorced from its socio-political context, serves no purpose except to reinforce or re-create the old boundaries between gentleman amateur and plebeian professional. This is perhaps predictable, coming from writers who are primarily sociologists, but, owing to the still-prevalent English mistrust of analytical theory, this view has been widely, and indeed usefully, accepted by many, including some recent theorists.

Much work remains to be done before British aestheticians and theoreticians reconcile their differences, but already Nicholas Cook's *Music, Imagination and Culture* (1990) shows one possible avenue of research, handling aspects of criticism, historiography, aesthetics and analysis. It is conceivable that an all-encompassing British theory might lie at the end of this road. It is certainly remarkable that the effects of postmodernism, long felt in all other areas of the arts, have yet to make much impression on musical scholarship, though under the recent editorship of Anthony Bye and Gavin Thomas the *Musical Times* has suddenly and confidently discovered the 'new musicology'. It is also possible that, after a brief flirtation with formalism in the 1980s, the widely perceived need for contextual approaches to musicology, highlighted in Norris 1989, might result in a return to some of the values of the newly classless (but probably still ABC1) amateur. Indeed, in a sense the amateur spirit never really died, as shown by the important work of Winton Dean, Mitchell, Sadie and others, most of it produced outside the academy. A third, less optimistic possibility is that the British will concentrate on writing excellent source material for the scholars of other nations; the fear of 'scientism', six editions of *Grove*, the writing 'about analysis rather than . . . analyses', the recent increase in the output of thematic catalogues (Craggs 1977 and Hindmarsh 1983 are examples), the success of manuals of entry into musical professions (York 1991): all may be pointers to this situation. It would closely parallel developments in British scientific research in this century, where many breakthroughs have occurred and another country has capitalized on them.

Chapter 14

THE REVIVAL OF EARLY MUSIC

HARRY HASKELL

I: *Arnold Dolmetsch*

The motley strands of England's nineteenth-century early music revival came together in the mercurial figure of Arnold Dolmetsch (1858–1940). 'A skilled craftsman, a performing musician, a bit of a composer, a scholar, and an impatient enthusiast all rolled into one person': Thurston Dart's description (1958: 400) reflects the admiration of a latter-day kindred spirit. Many of the fashionable Londoners who flocked to his concerts of 'ancient music' in the 1890s found Dolmetsch equally hard to categorize. The antiquarian scholasticism that animated his predecessors in the early music field ran counter to his essentially pragmatic and intuitive temperament. Dolmetsch's unconcealed disdain for 'les musicologues' and the musical establishment ensured that he would be regarded throughout his career as a renegade. It took a fellow iconoclast like Bernard Shaw to foresee the far-reaching impact his ideas would have on musical culture in the twentieth century.

A Frenchman by birth, Dolmetsch was apprenticed as an organ builder under his father and studied violin in Brussels with Vieuxtemps. In 1883 he enrolled at the newly opened RCM and soon made his mark in London as a teacher of genuine if unorthodox inspiration and a keen student of early music and instruments. From the beginning he found his most enthusiastic allies not among musicians but among artists, writers, dancers and theatre people. It was at the instigation of William Morris and Edward Burne-Jones that Dolmetsch built his first harpsichord, in 1896, and by the end of the decade he was famous enough to serve as the model for the heroine's father in George Moore's novel *Evelyn Innes*. Like the Pre-Raphaelite Brotherhood and the Arts and Crafts movement, the early music revival encompassed both progressive and reactionary tendencies.

Dolmetsch, the 'apostle of retrogression' (as an American critic dubbed him), thrived in the self-consciously avant-garde atmosphere of *fin de siècle* Bloomsbury. At his 'house concerts', devoted chiefly to early English instrumental music, the performers wore Elizabethan costumes and the emphasis was on intimacy and informality. In discarding the genteel conventions of the Victorian concert hall, Dolmetsch helped spawn the familiar image of the early musician as an eccentric counterculture figure.

Dolmetsch's reputation as a scholar rests largely on his one book, *The Interpretation of the Music of the XVIIth and XVIIIth Centuries*. Published in 1916, it was among the earliest attempts to survey the vast array of source material pertaining to performance practices of the late renaissance and baroque eras. It also served as a manifesto for the nascent historical performance movement. 'We can no longer allow anyone to stand between us and the composer,' Dolmetsch memorably concluded (1916: 471). How to attain that elusive goal was a question scarcely less problematic 80-odd years ago than it is today. By framing the issue in such uncompromising terms, however, Dolmetsch decisively set himself apart from the majority of his contemporaries. He believed that no music could be fully appreciated without reference to the sonorities of the instruments on which it was originally played and the stylistic conventions of the period in which it was written. Despite his increasing dogmatism in later life, Dolmetsch remained at heart a nonconformist, and it was this attitude above all that he instilled in such protégés as the musicologist Robert Donington, the lutenist Diana Poulton and the harpsichord maker John Challis.

As an instrument maker, Dolmetsch charted an equally independent course. He began repairing, restoring and eventually building keyboard instruments in the 1880s at the behest of A. J. Hipkins. Unlike the contemporary French and German revival harpsichords, with their heavy, piano-like frames, strings and bridges, Dolmetsch's instruments reflected a concern for historical fidelity in design, construction and materials. His harpsichords, clavichords, viols and lutes were immediately recognized as outstanding examples of craftsmanship. Yet Dolmetsch was not content to make historical replicas; he experimented with such modern innovations as an improved harpsichord action, a sustaining pedal and a vibrato-producing device. The period he spent in Boston as head of the department of early instruments at the Chickering piano factory (1905–12) was especially productive; his far-flung concerts and lectures laid a foundation for the early music revival in America. After returning to England, Dolmetsch established a workshop in Haslemere, Surrey, and expanded his line to include recorders and other instruments (see Donington 1932). Among the instrument makers who served their apprenticeships at Haslemere were Hugh Gough, Peter Harlan, Frank Hubbard and Robert Goble.

Lacking formal academic credentials himself, Dolmetsch looked askance at book-learning and traditional conservatoire training. Nor as an executant did he aspire to the level of virtuosity exemplified by Landowska and other leading concert artists of the day; his keyboard technique was eclipsed by that of his most successful harpsichord pupil, Violet Gordon Woodhouse. Even admirers criticized his lax performance standards and tolerance for second-rate music. The recordings he made towards the end of his life afford glimpses of the erratic brilliance described by his contemporaries. It is not, however, in any one area of his multi-faceted career that Dolmetsch's importance lies, but rather in the totality of his achievement. No early musician left a more lasting imprint on the study and performance of early music in his time (see Campbell 1975).

II: The Choral Revival

Dolmetsch's example was emulated by revivalists of early vocal music. Foremost among them was Richard Runciman Terry (1865–1938), organist and choirmaster at Westminster Cathedral from 1901 to 1924. Terry had been drawn to the Anglo-Catholic church as an organ scholar at Oxford. Transferring to King's College, Cambridge, he sang alto in the chapel choir under A. H. Mann and gradually awoke to what he called 'the possibilities of unaccompanied choral singing' (Andrews 1948: 39). His edition of Byrd's Mass for five voices was published in 1899 – not, significantly, in England but by Breitkopf & Härtel in Germany. By that time his research into pre-Reformation English music had already been noted; but it was as a practising musician, not as a scholar, that Terry came to the attention of the wider musical world. Westminster Cathedral was both his stage and his pulpit. Starting with 25 boy altos and 16 men, he built the choir into one of England's most celebrated vocal ensembles. Much of the music that Terry transcribed and edited from manuscripts in the British Museum, the Bodleian and other repositories was eventually heard at Westminster. It ranged from the

Cantiones Sacrae of Peter Philips and Byrd's *Gradualia* to masses and motets by Taverner, Tye, Sheppard, Dunstable, Power, Fayrfax and other largely forgotten composers. In 1916 the Carnegie United Kingdom Trust recognized Terry's pioneering work by appointing him editor of *Tudor Church Music*. His volatile temperament and impatience with scholarly minutiae brought him into conflict with his colleagues, however, and he withdrew from the project in 1922. He continued to exert a strong influence on British musical life as a writer, adjudicator and speaker (see Roche 1988).

England's ecclesiastical establishment provided fertile soil for the revival. Francis William Galpin organized annual concerts during his vicarate at Hatfield Broad Oak between 1893 and 1915. Most included renaissance or baroque music played on recorders, lutes, rebecs, virginals and other early instruments from Galpin's extensive collection, 'though clearly the Canon never forced his antiquarian tastes down the throats of his parishioners' (Godman 1959: 10). Another cleric who did much to promote early music, Edmund Fellowes (1870–1951), set out to raise the level of choral singing. 'It became more and more irksome to hear the services of Byrd, Gibbons, Farrant, and the rest drawled at a low pitch, with false verbal accentuation; and the same thing was true of the performance of the anthems and the madrigals' (1946: 120). The 36-volume *English Madrigal School* (1913–24), the 32-volume *English School of Lutenist Song-Writers* (1920–32) and a collected edition of Byrd's music (1937–50) testify to Fellowes's editorial industry; he also found time to write several books and to perform widely as a choir director and lutenist. His work with such groups as the English Singers, the Tudor Singers and the Fleet Street Choir helped revitalize the madrigal tradition. Mention must also be made of the Plainsong and Mediaeval Music Society, which from the 1920s sponsored performances and broadcasts under the direction of Dom Anselm Hughes and Pearce Hosken as a supplement to its publications and scholarly activities.

Among the other choral groups that made notable contributions to the revival in the early 1900s were Charles Kennedy Scott's Oriana Madrigal Society, the Choir of King's College, Cambridge, under Boris Ord, and the BBC Singers and Wireless Chorus. In 1926 Kennedy Scott and Hubert Foss founded the Bach Cantata Club, built around a choir of some 25 voices, which helped create an audience for the small-scale performances of Bach's music that were becoming increasingly popular in Germany and elsewhere on the Continent. (A. H. Mann at Cambridge and Harold Darke, conductor of the St Michael's Singers in London, had previously performed baroque music in chamber style.) At the other end of the spectrum, the Bach Choir continued to give romanticized performances of the oratorios with inflated forces. Vaughan Williams, who conducted the choir in the 1920s, when it numbered 300, defended the policy on practical grounds. 'Truly, the ideal way to give such music is by a small choir in a small building. But where are these ideal circumstances to be found? – not apparently in the concert-rooms of London' (U. Vaughan Williams 1964: 423). Both the Bach Cantata Club and the Bach Choir used orchestras of modern instruments; even a harpsichord, Vaughan Williams argued, would impart an 'antiquarian' flavour to the music that he wanted 'to avoid at all costs'.

Scholars responded to the burgeoning interest in pre-classical music by producing more editions designed to meet the needs of performers. The pragmatic editorial hands of Terry and Fellowes were evident in the *Tudor Church Music* series (1922–9). Although the ten original large-format volumes were intended principally for libraries, many of the pieces were later issued individually in cheaper octavo scores for choirs. The proliferation of performing editions by Terry, Fellowes, Dolmetsch, Dent, William Barclay Squire, Hilda Andrews, Jack Westrup, Peter Warlock and others marked the waning influence of the gentleman scholar and purely antiquarian attitudes towards early music. In Britain more than in most other countries, many prominent musicologists have also been distinguished practitioners. This overlay of scholarly and practical concerns shaped many subsequent publishing projects, notably the ambitious *Musica Britannica* series launched during the Festival of Britain in 1951, which under Anthony Lewis's editorship was conceived explicitly as a resource for both students and performers.

III: The Early Music 'Boom' of the 1920s and 1930s

The surge of early music activity in the 1920s was fuelled by nationalistic sentiment and heightened appreciation of Britain's musical past. The mechanized mayhem of the First World War inspired a widespread yearning for a nobler, more innocent world; the glory of England's 'golden age' could be recaptured in part via the technology of radio and recordings. From its inception in 1922 the BBC aired a significant amount of early music, and by the end of the decade listeners could have heard broadcasts from the Dolmetsches' Haslemere Festival, an English-language performance of Monteverdi's *Ritorno d'Ulisse in patria*, a series of programmes devoted to Bach's church cantatas, and a concert of medieval choral music commemorating the 40th anniversary of the Plainsong and Mediaeval Music Society. Columbia and HMV issued recordings by Violet Gordon Woodhouse, the English Singers, the Dolmetsch family, the Bach Cantata Club and other early musicians from Europe and America. The tercentenaries of Byrd (1923) and Gibbons (1925) prompted such a rash of live and recorded performances and broadcasts that the country was said to be in the grip of 'Elizabethan fever'. The contagion even spread to the film industry: in the early 1930s the Dolmetsches recorded soundtracks for two feature-length adventure films. There was growing interest, too, on the part of nonspecialist performers such as the pianists Harold Samuel and Harriet Cohen and the conductors Boyd Neel and Thomas Beecham, and on the part of composers like Howells, Vaughan Williams, Warlock, Lambert and Grainger (Haskell 1988: 80–84). During the 1930s the British early music scene was enriched by the arrival of Walter Goehr, Karl Haas, Walter Bergmann and other European refugees. In 1937 Carl Dolmetsch and Edgar Hunt founded the Society of Recorder Players, the forerunner of the Lute Society (1948), the Viola da Gamba Society (1956) and similar groups. Two years earlier Decca had spent a huge sum on a subscription recording of *Dido and Aeneas*, a tangible measure of early music's increasing acceptance.

Purcell's opera had enjoyed a steady resurgence since the late nineteenth century. During the bicentenary observances in 1895, the RCM performed it in a lush modern orchestration by Charles Wood. Five years later the Purcell Operatic Society mounted an avowedly modernist staging by Gordon Craig, and Rutland Boughton revived the opera at the Glastonbury Festival in 1915. In the 1920s Dent's authoritative edition gave *Dido* fresh currency, and he had a hand in the landmark productions of Purcell's *Fairy Queen* and Handel's *Semele* given by the Cambridge University Musical Society in the same decade. Dent's attitude towards the *da capo* aria is indicative of the compromises that he and his contemporaries were willing – indeed eager – to make in the cause of bringing baroque operas to the stage. In essence, he advocated shortening the arias by telescoping the three sections together and adjusting the harmonies as necessary. 'The advantage of it', he explained, 'is that it saves the whole of the music (apart from negligible cuts), avoids the loss of time spent on the *da capo*, and at the same time preserves the illusion of a *da capo* and makes the song end at the right place' (1935: 184). Yet Dent vigorously criticized the wholesale cuts, transpositions and re-orchestrations that disfigured early baroque opera revivals in Germany, France and elsewhere.

In 1925 the Oxford University Opera Club made its debut with an English-language production of Monteverdi's *Orfeo*, followed two years later by *The Coronation of Poppea*. Both editions were prepared by J. A. Westrup, then an undergraduate at Balliol, and they differed markedly from those of Vincent d'Indy which had been used in most previous modern revivals of the operas. Westrup made virtually no cuts in the scores, though as a practical matter he called for modern instruments. Among the other productions staged at Oxford before the war were Gluck's *Alceste* and *Iphigenia in Aulis*, and Rameau's *Castor and Pollux*. In 1930 the short-lived London Festival Opera Company offered a season of rarities including *Orfeo*, Handel's *Julius Caesar*, and a double bill of *Dido and Aeneas* and Locke's *Cupid and Death*, all in English. Although the venture was a box-office disaster, the 1930s saw further productions of Handel's *Rodelinda, Serse, Rinaldo* and a handful of other baroque works, setting the stage for later, more ambitious revivals.

IV: The Post-War Period

As in the 1920s, the BBC was a major catalyst of the post-war revival. The inauguration of the Third Programme (later Radio 3) in 1946, under the musical direction of Anthony Lewis, provided a new forum for early music and an important source of employment for musicologists and performers (see Stevens 1989). A 70-part survey of European art music, launched in 1948, became the basis for HMV's *History of Music in Sound*, which introduced generations of students to the pre-classical repertoire. Elizabeth Roche has calculated that in a single week in 1953, works written before 1700 accounted for nearly a third of the music broadcast on the Third Programme (1979: 823). The BBC gave valuable exposure to performers like Alfred Deller, George Malcolm and Julian Bream, and to musicologists like Fellowes, Denis Stevens and Thurston Dart. The publication of *Musica Britannica* had a similarly galvanizing effect;

once again, the aftermath of war engendered a renewed commitment to preserving Britain's musical heritage.

The spirit of the revival in the 1950s, however, was notably different from that of its previous phases. It was embodied by Dart (1921–71), a performing scholar of wide-ranging interests who was a nonconventionalist in the Dolmetsch mould, though he rejected the amateurism of the Dolmetsch circle. His short book *The Interpretation of Music*, published in 1954 and often reprinted, heralded the philosophy of historical performance that was to become the dominant musical ideology of the late twentieth century:

'Bach's music (or Purcell's or Dufay's) is an inheritance, not a lottery prize. To tarnish it is easy: to squander it, contemptible. To link one's own name to the composer's with a hyphen is to pimp on his capital; to efface his style with one's own is to erase his original inscriptions; to flout the help of the scholar is to debase the composer's coinage; to issue one's own music falsely bearing the name of a man long dead is to mint counterfeit money'. (Dart 1954: 166)

Equally distinguished as a musicologist and as a harpsichordist, Dart moved easily between the realms of theory and practice, and from medieval music to jazz. Like Dolmetsch, he was an intuitive scholar, autocratic by nature and prone to controversy. In the tradition of Dent and Westrup, he believed that the ultimate purpose of scholarship was to bring music to life in sound. His performances, including many with his own Philomusica Orchestra and Jacobean Ensemble, were exceptionally robust and imaginative. Dart was the central figure in the younger generation of musicologists, a number of whom – Lewis, Stevens, Philip Brett, Christopher Page – have been actively involved in performance as well.

The early opera revival, too, gained fresh impetus after the war. The Handel Opera Society, founded in 1955 by the conductor Charles Farncombe, gave the modern British premières of many of the composer's dramatic works. Subsequently the Unicorn Theatre Group at Abingdon (near Oxford), the Barber Institute at the University of Birmingham (where Lewis was Professor of Music) and Kent Opera restored most of Handel's operas to the repertoire. Their work had little immediate impact on the major companies: the two decades after 1955 saw a mere handful of Handel productions at Covent Garden (*Samson* in 1958, *Alcina* in 1960 and 1962), the Coliseum (*Semele*, 1970) and Glyndebourne (*Jephtha*, 1966).

THE REVIVAL OF EARLY MUSIC

Purcell's stage works fared little better. The Royal Opera mounted an opulent *Fairy Queen* in 1948, to celebrate the reopening of Covent Garden, but it was only distantly related to the original. Again, it was left to a smaller company to place Purcell in historical context: in 1951 the English Opera Group presented *Dido and Aeneas* in a new edition by Britten that was substantially closer to what Purcell wrote than any of its predecessors (Harris 1987: 148 ff).

None the less, the operatic establishment did not long remain untouched by the historical performance movement. In the 1960s and 1970s Raymond Leppard edited and conducted a notable series of Cavalli and Monteverdi operas at Glyndebourne. Although his scissors-and-paste treatment of the scores incurred criticism, the polished stagings and well-integrated ensemble work of the Glyndebourne casts set a new standard for baroque opera performances. In recent years increasing attention has been paid to historical styles of singing and playing, even when the production itself is deliberately antihistorical. The period-instrument Orchestra of the Age of Enlightenment first took part in Mozart productions at Glyndebourne in 1989. The conductor John Eliot Gardiner has worked to bring historical Mozart, Gluck and Rameau into the operatic mainstream, while Lina Lalandi and the English Bach Festival have concentrated on re-creating eighteenth-century stagecraft and choreography in the French opera–ballets. Other opera conductors prominent in the revival include Roger Norrington (Kent Opera and the Early Opera Project), Nicholas McGegan and Andrew Parrott (the Taverner Choir).

In choral music the leading figures of the immediate post-war period were Malcolm at Westminster Cathedral and Ord at Cambridge. A number of historically minded choir directors, such as David Willcocks, Philip Ledger, George Guest and Simon Preston, followed in their footsteps. Among the most successful choral ensembles in the 1950s and 1960s were the Renaissance Singers, the Ambrosian Singers, the Deller Consort and the Monteverdi Choir. It was from these and other ensembles that many of Britain's early music singers emerged. The pure, fluty, androgynous vocal timbre exemplified by Alfred Deller (1912–79) and Emma Kirkby (*b* 1949) is indebted to the sound of the modern English cathedral choirs, as is the 'suspiciously mellifluous' (Kerman 1985: 207) blend of such all-male groups as Pro Cantione Antiqua, the King's Singers and the Hilliard Ensemble.

In the 1960s two ensembles challenged the prevailing concept of early vocal sound: Musica Reservata, devoted primarily to medieval secular music, and the Clerkes of Oxenford, who emphasized sacred choral music of the renaissance. Michael Morrow, the founder of Musica Reservata, employed a principal singer, Jantina Noorman (a Dutch mezzo who studied in the United States), whose nasal, raucous tone led others to re-examine their approach to the medieval repertoire. Similarly provocative was David Wulstan's contention that modern choirs sang most Tudor music roughly a 3rd below historical pitch. The higher tessitura adopted by his Clerkes of Oxenford proved too taxing for boy sopranos, and Wulstan eventually replaced them with women. The Clerkes were a strong influence on two ensembles which came to the fore in the 1980s, the Tallis Scholars and The Sixteen (Day 1989: 35–7).

In respect of early instrumental music, the key figure of the post-war years was David Munrow (1942–76). The Early Music Consort of London, which he founded in 1967, won new and enthusiastic audiences for the pre-baroque repertoire and served as a springboard for such performers as James Tyler, James Bowman and Christopher Hogwood. (The latter's Academy of Ancient Music became perhaps the most widely known British-based early music ensemble of the 1970s and 1980s.) Munrow's virtuosity on wind instruments was incontestable, though his colourful arrangements drew rebukes from musicians of a less latitudinarian cast of mind. A child of the media age, Munrow made many recordings, performed frequently on radio and television, and composed or arranged music for several films. By temperament a popularizer rather than a scholar, he was nevertheless at work on an extended study of early instrumental music when he committed suicide in 1976. Since then British early musicians have increasingly turned towards the music of the baroque and later periods, although a few groups – the Consort of Musicke, Circa 1500, Fretwork, Gothic Voices and the New London Consort – have continued to mine the earlier repertoire.

By the 1980s several period-instrument orchestras had made their homes in London. The Academy of Ancient Music, the English Baroque Soloists, the English Concert, London Baroque and the Orchestra of the Age of Enlightenment drew from the same pool of talent (often players in the major symphony orchestras who doubled on early instruments) and subsisted largely on income derived from recording and touring. The Mozart symphony cycle that the Academy of Ancient Music recorded in the late 1970s and early 1980s opened the door to period-instrument versions of mainstream classical and romantic repertoire by orchestras like the Hanover Band and

L'Estro Armonico. Another trend of recent years is illustrated by Norrington's popular series of 'experiences' on London's South Bank, intensive weekends of lectures, workshops and performances focusing on major works by composers from Beethoven to Brahms. Other performers specializing in historical performances of late eighteenth- and nineteenth-century music include the London Classical Players, Hausmusik, the Purcell Quartet, the Music Party, and the fortepianists Richard Burnett and Melvyn Tan. More recently, the New Queen's Hall Orchestra has begun performing early twentieth-century music in period style.

The influence of the early music revival permeates British musical life. *Early Music* magazine, launched in 1973 by Oxford University Press, became the major English-language journal in the field and an influential forum for the exchange of views between scholars and performers. A conference on the future of early music in Britain held in 1977 raised the issue of institutional support and co-operation among early music groups, as well as putting forward several educational initiatives (J. M. Thomson 1978). These discussions bore fruit in the establishment of the Early Music Centre, the National Early Music Association and a regional touring network subsidized by the British Arts Council. As a result early music is now promoted in much the same way as contemporary music and similarly appeals to many as a refreshing alternative to the mainstream. (On this view, 'authentic' performance can be seen as the counterpart of the 'natural' foods craze and other social trends of recent years.) Composers as diverse as Tippett and Maxwell Davies have drawn lasting inspiration from pre-classical music. The electronic media have continued to play a significant role in the revival. Compact disc technology in particular has proved a boon to the smaller record companies, several of which specialize in early music and period-instrument performances. Courses in early music at the RCM, RAM, Guildhall and other colleges provide a continuing supply of performers for the summer festivals at York, Spitalfields, Haslemere and elsewhere. In brief, what began the century as a fringe movement has grown into a centrepiece of the British musical renaissance and a vital force in contemporary Western music.

LIST OF SOURCES

ABRAHAM, G. 1938, R/1949: *A Hundred Years of Music* (London).
ADAMS, F.E. 1929: *Bioscope*, 8 May.
ANDREWS, H. 1948: *Westminster Retrospect* (London).
ANON 1909: *Report of the Committee on the Law of Copyright* (Cd 4976).
ANON 1926: untitled article, *Musical Mirror*, vi (April): 78.
ANON 1949: *Music: a Report on Musical Life in England* (Arts Enquiry).
ANON 1951: *Music and the Amateur* (National Council of Social Service).
ANON 1956: 'Notes of the Day', *Monthly Musical Record*, lxxxvi: 201–3.
ANON 1964: *A Policy for the Arts* (Government White Paper).
ANON 1965: *Making Musicians* (Gulbenkian Foundation).
ANON 1973: *Curricular Differences for Boys and Girls* (DES Education Survey no. 21).
ANON 1978: *Training Musicians* (Gulbenkian Foundation).
ANON 1984: *The Glory of the Garden* (Arts Council).
ANON 1985: *A Great British Success Story* (Arts Council).
ANON 1990: *Directors' Report and Accounts* (Performing Right Society).
ANON 1991a: *Interim Report* (National Curriculum Music Working Group).
ANON 1991b: *The National Curriculum for Music* (DES).
ANON 1992: *In Tune with Heaven: the Report of the Archbishops' Commission on Church Music* (London).
APEL, W. 1944: *The Harvard Dictionary of Music* (London).
ARNHEIM, R. 1933: *Film* (London).

BACHARACH, A. L. (ed.) 1946: *British Music of Our Time* (Harmondsworth).
BAILEY, P. 1986: *Music Hall: the Business of Pleasure* (Milton Keynes).
BAILY, J. 1990: 'Qawwāli in Bradford: Traditional Music in a Muslim Community', in P. Oliver 1990a: 153–65.
BAILY, L. 1973: *Gilbert and Sullivan and Their World* (London).
BANERJI, S. and BAUMANN, G. 1990: 'Bhangra 1984–8: Fusion and Professionalization in a Genre of South Asian Dance Music', in P. Oliver 1990a: 137–52.
BANFIELD, S. 1981a: 'The Artist and Society', in Temperley 1981: 11–28.
BANFIELD, S. 1981b: 'Aesthetics and Criticism', in Temperley 1981: 455–73.
BANFIELD, S. 1985: *Sensibility and English Song: Critical Studies of the Early Twentieth Century* (2 vols) (Cambridge).
BANFIELD, S. 1986: 'British Opera in Retrospect', *Musical Times*, cxxvii: 205–7.
BARFORD, P. 1958: 'Wordless Functional Analysis', *Monthly Musical Record*, lxxxviii: 44–50.

LIST OF SOURCES

BARFORD, P. 1972: 'Preface to the Study of Music Theory', *Music Review*, xxxiii: 22–33.
BARNARD, S. 1989: *On the Radio: Music Radio in Britain* (Milton Keynes).
BARNES, J. 1976: *The Beginnings of the Cinema in England* (London).
BARNES, J. 1983: *The Rise of the Cinema in Great Britain* (London).
[BARRETT, G.] 1989: 'Editorial', *Organists' Review*, lxxv: 79.
BAUMOL, W. J. and BOWEN, W. G. 1966: *Performing Arts – the Economic Dilemma* (New York).
BAWTREE, M. 1991: *The New Singing Theatre: a Charter for the Music Theatre Movement* (Bristol).
BAX, A. 1943: *Farewell, My Youth* (London).
BEADLE, J. J. 1993: *Will Pop Eat Itself? Pop Music in the Soundbite Era* (London).
BECCE, G. 1919: *Kinobibliothek* (Berlin).
BENJAMIN, W. 1936, R/1970: 'The Work of Art in the Age of Mechanical Reproduction', in H. Arendt (ed.), *Illuminations*, tr. H. Zohn (London): 219–53.
BENNETT, J. R. 1955 : *Voices of the Past, vol I* (Lingfield).
BENOLIEL, B. and ROBERTS, B. 1981: note to recording of Brian: *The Tigers* (Symphonic Movements), UM 3529–31.
BENT, I. 1987: 'Analysis', in Sadie 1980, i: 340–88, rev. and expanded as *Analysis*, with a glossary by W. Drabkin.
BERGER, F. 1913: *Reminiscences, Impressions and Anecdotes* (London).
BESCH, A. 1974: 'The Catiline Conspiracy', *Musical Times*, cxv: 210–11.
BIDDISS, M. D. 1977: *The Age of the Masses: Ideas and Society in Europe since 1870* (Harmondsworth).
BIGSBY, C. W. E. (ed.) 1975: *Superculture: American Popular Culture and Europe* (London).
BIRD, E. 1976: 'Jazz Bands of North East England: the Evolution of a Working Class Cultural Activity', *Oral History*, iv/2: 79–88.
BIRTWISTLE, H. 1971: Preface to score of *Down by the Greenwood Side* (London).
BLACKING, J. 1976: *How Musical Is Man?* (London).
BLACKING, J. 1987: *'A Commonsense View of All Music': Reflections on Percy Grainger's Contribution to Ethnomusicology and Music Education* (Cambridge).
BLACKING, J., FALLOWS, D. and WHITTALL, A. 1980: 'Musicology in Great Britain since 1945', *Acta Musicologica* lii: 38–68.
BLISS, A. 1965: '[Tribute to Michael Tippett]', in Kemp 1965: 34.
BLISS, A. 1970, R/1989: *As I Remember* (London).
BLOM, E. 1942: *Music in England* (Harmondsworth).
BLOM, E. (ed.) 1954: *Grove's Dictionary of Music and Musicians* (5th edn, 10 vols, supplement 1961) (London).
BLYTH, A. 1969: review of Searle: *Hamlet*, *Opera*, xx: 545–8.
BODEN, A. 1992: *Three Choirs: A History of the Festival* (Stroud).
BONAVIA, F. 1928: 'The Music of the Halls', *Musical Times*, lxix: 118–19.
BOON, B. 1978: *Sing the Happy Song: a History of Salvation Army Vocal Music* (London).
BOOSEY, W. 1931: *Fifty Years of Music* (London).

LIST OF SOURCES

BOUGHTON, R. 1911: *Music Drama of the Future* (London).
BOURDIEU, P. 1980: 'The Aristocracy of Culture', *Media, Culture and Society*, ii/3: 225–54.
BOWEN, M. 1981: *Michael Tippett* (London).
BOWEN, M. 1985: 'A Tempest of Our Time', in John 1985: 93–8.
BOYD, M. 1974: 'The Beach of Falesá', *Musical Times*, cxv: 207–9.
BOYD, M. 1980: *Grace Williams* (Cardiff).
BOYES, G. 1993: *The Imagined Village: Culture, Ideology and the English Folk Revival* (Manchester and New York).
BRADBURY, E. 1963: 'Modern British Composers: from *c.* 1925', in A. Jacobs 1963: 339–55.
BRADBURY, M. and McFARLANE, J. (eds) 1976: *Modernism: a Guide to European Literature 1890–1930* (Harmondsworth).
BRADBY, B. 1993: 'Sampling Sexuality: Gender, Technology and the Body in Dance Music', *Popular Music*, xii: 155–76.
BRADLEY, D. 1992: *Understanding Rock 'n' Roll: Popular Music in Britain 1955–1964* (Buckingham).
BRADSHAW, S. 1963: 'Thea Musgrave', *Musical Times*, civ: 866–8.
BRAND, V. and BRAND, G. (eds) 1979: *Brass Bands in the 20th Century* (Letchworth).
BRAY, T. 1975: 'Bantock's "Seal-Woman"', *Musical Times*, cxvi: 431–3.
BRETT, P. 1977: 'Britten and Grimes', *Musical Times*, cxviii: 995–1000.
BRETT, P. (ed.) 1983: *Benjamin Britten: Peter Grimes* (Cambridge).
BRIDSON, D. G. 1971: *Prospero and Ariel* (London).
BRIERLEY, P. (ed.) 1988: *United Kingdom Christian Handbook 1989–90* (London).
BRIGGS, A. 1961–79: *The History of Broadcasting in the United Kingdom* (4 vols, London and Oxford).
BRISCOE, D. and CURTIS-BRAMWELL, R. 1983: *The BBC Radiophonic Workshop: the First 25 Years* (London).
BROUGHTON, V. 1985: 'Another Day's Journey: Gospel Music in Britain', in *Black Gospel: an Illustrated History of the Gospel Sound* (Poole): 133–57.
BROWN, C. 1989: 'Religion', in R. Pope (ed.), *Atlas of British Social and Economic History, since c. 1700* (London): 211–23.
BRUNNING, B. 1986: *Blues: the British Connection* (Poole).
BUCK, P. C. 1905–6: 'Prolegomena to Musical Criticism', *Proceedings of the Musical Association*, xxxii: 155–77.
BURGESS, A. 1986: *The Pianoplayers* (London).
BURGESS, G. 1901: 'Musical London', in G. R. Sims (ed.), *Living London* (London): 216–34.
BURN, A. 1983: 'Geoffrey Poole – an Introductory Note on his Music', *Tempo*, 145: 12–18.
BURN, A. 1988: 'The Hussey Legacy', sleeve note, Cantus recording CAN 301–2.
BURTON, N. 1981a: 'Oratorios and Cantatas', in Temperley 1981: 214–41.
BURTON, N. 1981b: 'Opera: 1865–1914', in Temperley 1981: 330–57.
BUSH, G. 1981: 'Chamber Music', in Temperley 1981: 381–99.

LIST OF SOURCES

CAIRNS, D. 1973: *Responses* (London).
CAMERON, K. 1947: *Sound and the Documentary Film* (London).
CAMPBELL, M. 1975: *Dolmetsch: the Man and His Work* (London and Seattle).
CANNON, P. 1964: 'Morvoren', *Musical Times*, cv: 508–10.
CARDEW, C. 1961: 'The Ledge', *Musical Times*, cii: 707.
CARDEW, C. 1974: *Stockhausen Serves Imperialism* (London).
CARDUS, N. 1957: *Talking of Music* (London).
CARDUS, N. 1970: *Full Score* (London).
CARDUS, N. 1977: *What is Music?*, ed. M. Hughes (London).
CARLTON, M. 1987: *Music in Education* (London).
CARPENTER, H. 1992: *Benjamin Britten: a Biography* (London).
CARR, I. 1973: *Music Outside: Contemporary Jazz in Britain* (London).
CARR, I., FAIRWEATHER, D. and PRIESTLEY, B. 1987: *Jazz: the Essential Companion* (London).
CARR-SAUNDERS, A. M. and WILSON, P. A. 1933: *The Professions* (Oxford).
CHAMBERS, I. 1985: *Urban Rhythms: Pop Music and Popular Culture* (London).
CHATBURN, T. 1990: 'Trinidad All Stars: the Steel Pan Movement in Britain', in P. Oliver 1990a: 118–36.
CHISHOLM, A. 1984: *Bernard van Dieren: an Introduction* (London).
CHISHOLM, E. 1961: 'John Joubert's "Silas Marner"', *Musical Times*, cii: 550–56.
CLARKE, D. 1990: *Language, Form and Structure in the Music of Michael Tippett* (New York).
CLARKE, D. 1994: 'Seeking no shelter . . .' *Musical Times*, cxxxv: 244–5.
CLARKE, S. 1980: *Jah Music: the Evolution of the Popular Jamaican Song* (London).
CLEGG, A. 1986: 'Invitation to a Dance', note to recording CSVL 179.
CLEMENTS, A. 1985: 'Music for an Epic', in John 1985: 65–72.
COBBETT, W. W. (ed.) 1929–30: *Cobbett's Cyclopaedic Survey of Chamber Music* (vol. i 1929, vol. ii 1930, supplement 1963, ed. C. Mason) (London).
COHEN, S. 1991: *Rock Culture in Liverpool: Popular Music in the Making* (Oxford).
COHN, N. 1969: *Awopbopaloobop Alopbambaoom: Pop from the Beginning* (London).
COKER, W. 1972: *Music and Meaning* (New York and London).
COLE, H. 1974: 'The Story of Vasco', *Musical Times*, cxv: 205–6.
COLE, H. 1978: *The Changing Face of Music* (London).
COLE, H. 1989: *Malcolm Arnold: an Introduction to his Music* (London).
COLIN, S. 1977: *And the Bands Played On* (London).
COLLES, H. (ed.) 1927–8: *Grove's Dictionary of Music and Musicians* (3rd edn, 5 vols; 4th edn, 5 vols and supplement, 1940) (London).
COLLES, H. 1945: *Essays and Lectures* (London).
COLLINGWOOD, R. G. 1938: *The Principles of Art* (London, Oxford and New York).
COLLINS, J. 1932: *The Maid of the Mountains* (London).
COLLS, R. and DODD, P. 1986: *Englishness: Politics and Culture 1880–1920* (London, New York and Sydney).
COOK, N. 1987: *A Guide to Musical Analysis* (London).
COOK, N. 1990: *Music, Imagination, and Culture* (Oxford).
COOKE, D. 1959a: *The Language of Music* (London).

LIST OF SOURCES

COOKE, D. 1959b: 'In defence of Functional Analysis', *Musical Times*, c: 456–60.
COOKE, D. 1988: *Vindications: Essays on Romantic Music* (London).
COOKE, M. 1993: sleeve note, *English Anthems*, EMI Classics recording CDC 7 54418 2: 3–5.
COON, C. 1988: *The New Wave Punk Rock Explosion* (London).
COOPER, M. (ed.) 1974: *The New Oxford History of Music: The Modern Age (1890–1960)* (London).
COOVER, J. 1985 : *Music Publishing, Copyright and Piracy in Victorian England* (London).
COPLEY, I. A. 1978: *The Music of Charles Wood: a Critical Study* (London).
COPLEY, I. A. 1979: *The Music of Peter Warlock: a Critical Survey* (London).
COPPER, B. 1971: *A Song for Every Season* (London).
COTTERRELL, R. (ed.) 1976: *Jazz Now* (London).
COVELL, R. 1984: note to recording of Goossens: *Judith*, EMI SLS 3002/2.
COWAN, J. L. 1950: 'The Problem of Modern Opera', in Hill 1950: 61–70.
COWARD, N. 1937: *Present Indicative* (London).
COWLEY, J. 1990: 'London Is the Place: Caribbean Music in the Context of Empire 1900–60', in P. Oliver 1990a: 58–76.
COWLEY, M. (ed.) 1991: *The Mentor Opera Handbook* (London).
CRAGGS, S. 1977: *William Walton: a Thematic Catalogue of his Musical Works* (London).
CRITCHLEY, M. and HENSON, R. A. 1977: *Music and the Brain: Studies in the Neurology of Music* (London).
CROSS, B. (ed.) 1948: *The Film 'Hamlet': a Record of Its Production* (London).
CROSSE, G. 1970: 'Note', sleeve to *Changes*, Argo recording ZRG 656.
CROZIER, E. (ed.) 1945: *Benjamin Britten: Peter Grimes* (London).
CROZIER, E. 1964: 'But Why a Comic Opera?', *Opera*, xv: 658–61.
CRUMP, J. 1986: 'The Identity of English Music: the Reception of Elgar, 1898–1935', in Collis and Dodd 1986: 164–90.
CULSHAW, J. 1949: 'The Objective Fallacy', *Monthly Musical Record*, lxxix: 37–42.
CUTLER, C. 1985: *File Under Popular: Theoretical and Critical Writings on Music* (London).

DAIKEN, M. 1980 : 'Notes on Goehr's Triptych', in Northcott 1980: 40–48.
DART, R. THURSTON 1954: *The Interpretation of Music* (London).
DART, R. THURSTON 1958: 'The Achievement of Arnold Dolmetsch', *Listener*, 6 March : 400–402.
DAUBNEY, B. B. 1979: Benjamin Burrows: the Life and Music of the Leicester Composer (M. Phil thesis, University of Leicester).
DAVIES, J. L. 1985: 'A Visionary Night', in John 1985: 53–62.
DAVIES, P. MAXWELL 1965: 'A Letter', *Composer*, 15: 22.
DAY, T. 1989: *A Discography of Tudor Church Music* (London).
DEAN, W. 1949: 'Music – and Letters? An Impertinent Inquiry', *Music and Letters*, xxx: 376–80.
DEAN, W. 1952: 'Further Thoughts on Operatic Criticism', *Opera*, iii: 655–9.

LIST OF SOURCES

DEAN, W. 1980: 'Criticism', in Sadie 1980, v: 36–50.
DEANE, B. 1978: *Alun Hoddinott* (Cardiff).
DEATHRIDGE, J. 1973: 'England: Music and Society', in Sternfeld 1973: 193.
The Delius Society Journal 1963–: (Maidstone).
DELLAR, F. 1981: *The NME Guide to Rock Cinema* (Feltham).
DEMUTH, N. 1947: *An Anthology of Musical Criticism* (London).
DEMUTH, N. 1952: *Musical Trends in the 20th Century* (London).
DENT, E. J. 1930: 'The Scientific Study of Music in England', *Acta Musicologica*, ii: 83–92.
DENT, E. J. 1931: 'Music and Music Research', *Acta Musicologica*, iii: 5–8.
DENT, E. J. 1935: 'Handel on the Stage', *Music and Letters*, xvi: 173–87.
DENT, E. J. 1940, R/1949: *Opera* (Harmondsworth and New York).
DENT, E. J. 1952: 'Edmund Horace Fellowes', *The Score*, 6: 52–4.
DIBBLE, J. 1992: *C. Hubert H. Parry: His Life and Music* (Oxford).
DICKINSON, A. E. F. 1940: 'The Progress of John Ireland', *Music Review*, i: 343–53.
DICKINSON, A. E. F. 1951: 'The Isolation of Elgar', *Music Survey*, iii: 233–40.
DICKINSON, A. E. F. 1963: *Vaughan Williams* (London).
DICKINSON, P. 1983: 'Lord Berners, 1883–1950: a British Avant-Gardist at the Time of World War I', *Musical Times*, cxxiv: 669–72.
DICKINSON, P. 1988: *The Music of Lennox Berkeley* (London).
DICKINSON, P. 1989: sleeve note, Conifer recording CDCF 167.
DIEREN, B. VAN 1935: *Down Among the Dead Men and Other Essays* (London).
DISHER, M. WILLSON 1938: *Winkles and Champagne* (London).
DOLMETSCH, A. 1916: *The Interpretation of the Music of the XVIIth and XVIIIth Centuries* (London).
DONINGTON, R. 1932: *The Work and Ideas of Arnold Dolmetsch* (Haslemere).
DONINGTON, R. 1963: *Wagner's 'Ring' and its Symbols: the Music and the Myth* (London).
DREYER, M. 1983: review of Josephs: *Rebecca*, *Musical Times*, cxxiv: 763.
DRIVER, P. 1985: 'A Ritual of Renewal', in John 1985: 19–24.
DUCKLES, V. 1981: 'Musicology', in Temperley 1981: 483–502.
DUNCAN, R. 1981: *Working with Britten* (Bideford).
DUNN, G. 1980: *The Fellowship of Song: Popular Singing Traditions in East Suffolk* (London).
DUNSBY, J. and WHITTALL, A. 1988: *Music Analysis in Theory and Practice* (London).
DURANT, A. 1984: *Conditions of Music* (London).
DURANT, A. 1992: 'A New Day for Music: Digital Technologies in Contemporary Music Making', in P. Hayward (ed.), *Culture, Technology and Creativity* (London): 175–96.
DWYER, T. 1967: *Teaching Musical Appreciation* (London).
DYSON, G. 1924: *The New Music* (London).
DYSON, G. 1932: *The Progress of Music* (London).

LIST OF SOURCES

EAST, L. 1975: 'The Problem of Communication – Two Solutions: Thea Musgrave and Gordon Crosse', in Foreman 1975: 19–31.
EAST, L. 1985: 'Stereotypes and Rebirth', in John 1985: 115–26.
EHRLICH, C. 1976, R/1990: *The Piano: a History* (London).
EHRLICH, C. 1985: *The Music Profession in Britain since the Eighteenth Century: a Social History* (Oxford).
EHRLICH, C. 1989: *Harmonious Alliance: a History of the Performing Right Society* (Oxford and New York).
EHRLICH, C. and WALKER, B. 1980: 'Enterprise and Entertainment: the Economic and Social Background, in B. Walker (ed.), *Frank Matcham, Theatre Architect* (Belfast): 21–35.
EISENBERG, E. 1987: *The Recording Angel: Music, Records and Culture from Aristotle to Zappa* (New York).
EISENSTEIN, S. 1943: *The Film Sense* (London).
EISENSTEIN, S. 1951: *Film Form* (London).
ELIOT, T. S. 1948, R/1962: *Notes towards the Definition of Culture* (London).
ELIZALDE, F. 1929: 'Jazz – What of the Future?', *The Gramophone* (February): 392–3.
EMERSON, R. W. 1856: *English Traits* (1903 in *The World's Classics* vol. xxx) (London, Edinburgh, Glasgow, New York and Toronto).
EMMERSON, G. 1971: *Rantin' Pipe and Tremblin' String: a History of Scottish Dance Music* (London).
EVANS, E.(i) 1933–5: *Handbook to the Chamber and Orchestral Music of Johannes Brahms* (2 vols) (London).
EVANS, E. (ii) 1923a: The Perfect Fool', *Musical Times*, lxiv: 389–93.
EVANS, E. (ii) 1923b: review of Holst: *The Perfect Fool, Musical Times*, lxiv: 423.
EVANS, E. (ii) 1929: 'Music and the Cinema', *Music and Letters*, x: 65–9.
EVANS, J., REED, P. and WILSON, P. 1987: *A Britten Source Book* (Aldeburgh).
EVANS, P. 1979 : *The Music of Benjamin Britten* (London).

FEATHER, L. 1986, R/1988: *The Jazz Years: Earwitness to an Era* (London).
FELLOWES, E. H. 1946: *Memoirs of an Amateur Musician* (London).
FERNEYHOUGH, B. 1989: 'Speaking with Tongues. Composing for the Voice: a Correspondence–Conversation [with Paul Driver]', in P. Driver and R. Christiansen (eds), Music and Text. *Contemporary Music Review*, v: 155–83.
'FESTE' [GRACE, H.]: 'Ad libitum', *Musical Times*, lxii (1921): 98–101; lxv (1924): 797–801; lxxiii (1932): 407–11.
FINNEGAN, R. 1989: *The Hidden Musicians: Music-Making in an English Town* (Cambridge).
FLETCHER, P. 1987: *Education and Music* (Oxford).
FOREMAN, [R.] L. [E.]. 1972: 'The British Musical Renaissance: a Guide to Research' (FLA thesis, Cambridge University).
FOREMAN, L. (ed.) 1975: *British Music Now: a Guide to the Work of Younger Composers* (1975).

LIST OF SOURCES

FOREMAN, L. 1983: sleeve note, *Choral Music by Sir Arnold Bax*, Hyperion recording A66092.
FOREMAN, L. 1987: *From Parry to Britten: British Music in Letters, 1900–1945* (London).
FOREMAN, L. 1988: 'Benjamin Britten and "The Rescue"', *Tempo*, 166: 28–33.
FORNÄS, J. 1995: 'The Future of Rock: Discourses that Struggle to Define a Genre', *Popular Music*, xiv: 111–25.
FOX STRANGWAYS, A. H. 1938–9: 'The Criticism of Music', *Proceedings of the Musical Association*, lxv: 1–18.
FRANKLIN, P. 1985: *The Idea of Music: Schoenberg and Others* (London).
FRIEDHEIM, P. 1983: 'Wagner and the Aesthetics of the Scream', 19th Century Music, vii: 63–70.
FRITH, S. 1978: *The Sociology of Rock* (London).
FRITH, S. 1983: *Sound Effects: Youth, Leisure and the Politics of Rock 'n' Roll* (London).
FRITH, S. 1987: 'The Making of the British Record Industry 1920–1964', in J. Curran, A. Smith and P. Wingate (eds), *Impacts and Influences* (London): 278–90.
FRITH, S. 1988a: *Music for Pleasure: Essays in the Sociology of Pop* (Cambridge).
FRITH, S. 1988b: 'Copyright and the Music Business', *Popular Music*, vii: 57–75.
FRITH, S. (ed.) 1990: *Facing the Music: Essays on Pop, Rock and Culture* (London).
FRITH, S. and GOODWIN, A. (eds) 1990: *On Record: Rock, Pop and the Written Word* (New York and London).
FRITH, S., GOODWIN, A. and GROSSBERG, L. (eds) 1993: *Sound and Vision: the Music Video Reader* (London).
FRITH, S. and HORNE, H. 1987: *Art into Pop* (London).
FRITH, S. and McROBBIE, A. 1978: 'Rock and Sexuality', *Screen Education*, 29: 3–19.

GAMMOND, P. and HORRICKS, R. 1980: *Music on Record, vol. I: Brass Bands* (Cambridge).
GÄNZL, K. 1986: *The British Musical Theatre* (2 vols) (London).
GÄNZL, K. and LAMB, A. 1988: *Gänzl's Book of the Musical Theatre* (London).
GARLAND, H. 1957: *Henry Francis Lyte and the Story of 'Abide With Me'* (Manchester).
GEORGE, W. T. 2/1914: *Playing to Pictures* (London).
GIDDENS, A. 1991: *The Consequences of Modernity* (Cambridge).
GILBERT, A. 1980: *The Making of Post-Christian Britain* (London).
GILLETT, C. 1970, R/1983: *The Sound of the City: the Rise of Rock and Roll* (London).
GILLIES, M. 1989: *Bartók in Britain: a Guided Tour* (Oxford).
GLOCK, W. 1952: 'Comment', *The Score*, 6: 3.
GLOCK, W. 1991: *Notes in Advance: an Autobiography in Music* (Oxford).
GODBOLT, J. 1984: *A History of Jazz in Britain 1919–50* (London, Melbourne and New York).
GODBOLT, J. 1989: *A History of Jazz in Britain 1950–1970* (London).
GODDARD, C. 1979: *Jazz Away from Home* (New York and London).
GODMAN, S. 1959: 'Francis Wiliam Galpin: Music Maker', *Galpin Society Journal*, xii: 8–16.

LIST OF SOURCES

GOEHR, A. 1973: 'Poetics of My Music', *University of Leeds Review*, cxvi: 170–85.

GOODWIN, A. 1990: 'Sample and Hold: Pop Music in the Digital Age of Reproduction', in Frith and Goodwin 1990: 258–73.

GOODWIN, A. 1992: Dancing in the Distraction Factory: Music, Television and Popular Culture (London).

GOOSSENS, E. 1951: *Overture and Beginners: a Musical Antobiography* (London).

GRACE, H. and McNAUGHT, W. 1934: 'Edward Elgar. June 2, 1857–February 23, 1934', *Musical Times*, lxxv: 305–13.

GRAVES, R. and HODGE, A. 1940, R/1985: *The Long Week-End: a Social History of Great Britain 1918–1939* (London).

GRAY, C. 1924: *A Survey of Contemporary Music* (London).

GRAY, C. 1934: *Peter Warlock: a Memoir of Philip Heseltine* (London).

GRAY, C. 1947: *Contingencies, and Other Essays* (London).

GRAY, C. 1948: *Musical Chairs, or Between Two Stools: Memoirs* (London).

GREEN, L. 1988: *Music on Deaf Ears: Musical Meaning, Ideology, Education* (Manchester).

GREENE, H. PLUNKET 1935: *Charles Villiers Stanford* (London).

GREENE, R. 1992: 'A Musico-Rhetorical Outline of Holst's "Egdon Heath"', *Music and Letters*, lxxiii: 244–67.

GREENHALGH, H. 1926: 'Please Bring Your Music!', *Music Masterpieces*, 28 (4 November): 128.

GRIDLEY, M., MAXHAM, R. and HOFF, R. 1989: 'Three Approaches to Defining Jazz', *Musical Quarterly*, lxxiii: 513–31.

GRIEVES, J. 1989: 'Acquiring a Leisure Identity: Juvenile Jazz Bands and the Moral Universe of "Healthy" Leisure Time', *Leisure Studies*, viii: 1–6.

GRIFFITHS, P. 1982: *Peter Maxwell Davies* (London).

GRIFFITHS, P. 1985: *New Sounds, New Personalities: British Composers of the 1980s in Conversation with Paul Griffiths* (London).

GRIGGS, C. 1985: *Private Education in Britain* (London).

GRONOW, P. 1983: 'The Record Industry: the Growth of a Mass Medium', *Popular Music*, iii: 53–75.

GROSSBERG, L. 1990: 'Is there Rock after Punk?', in Frith and Goodwin 1990: 111–26.

GURNEY, E. 1880: *The Power of Sound* (London).

HADOW, W. H. 1893–5: *Studies in Modern Music* (London).

HADOW, W. H. 1928: *Collected Essays* (London).

HALE, P. 1991: 'Editorial', *Organists' Review*, lxxvii: 3.

HALL, M. 1984: *Harrison Birtwistle* (London).

HALL, S. and JEFFERSON, T. (eds) 1976: *Resistance through Rituals: Youth Subcultures in Post-War Britain* (London).

HAMILTON, I. 1977: 'The Royal Hunt of the Sun', *Musical Times*, cxviii: 23–5.

HARGREAVES, D. J. 1986: *The Developmental Psychology of Music* (Cambridge).

HARKER, D. 1980: *One for the Money: Politics and Popular Song* (London).

LIST OF SOURCES

HARKER, D. 1985: *Fakesong: the Manufacture of British 'Folksong', 1700 to the Present Day* (Milton Keynes).

HARPER, J. 1990: sleeve note, *The English Anthem, vol. iv: The Twentieth Century to 1960 – from Bairstow to Britten*, Abbey recording alpha CDCA 914.

HARRIES, M. and HARRIES, S. 1989: *A Pilgrim Soul: the Life and Works of Elisabeth Lutyens* (London).

HARRIS, E. 1987: *Henry Purcell's 'Dido and Aeneas'* (Oxford).

HARVEY, J. 1975: 'Composition Teaching at a University', *Composer*, 53/54: 27–8/31–2.

HARVEY, J. 1979: 'Brian Ferneyhough', *Musical Times*, cxx: 723–8.

HARVEY, J. 1980: 'The Composer's View: Atonality', *Musical Times*, cxxi: 699–700.

HARVEY, J. 1986: 'The Mirror of Ambiguity', in S. Emmerson (ed.), *The Language of Electroacoustic Music* (London): 175–90.

HASKELL, H. 1988: *The Early Music Revival: a History* (London).

HATCH, D. and MILLWARD, S. 1987: *From Blues to Rock: an Analytical History of Pop Music* (Manchester).

HEBDIGE, D. 1979: *Subculture: the Meaning of Style* (London).

HEBDIGE, D. 1981: 'Towards a Cartography of Taste 1935–1962', *Block*, iv: 39–56.

HEBDIGE, D. 1987: *Cut 'n' Mix: Culture, Identity and Caribbean Music* (London).

HENSON, B. and MORGAN, C. 1989: *First Hits: the Book of Sheet Music Hits 1946–1959* (London).

HERBERT, T. (ed.) 1991: *Bands: the Brass Band Movement in the 19th and 20th Centuries* (Buckingham).

HEWISON, R. 1981: *In Anger: Culture in the Cold War 1945–60* (London).

HEWISON, R. 1986: *Too Much: Art and Society in the Sixties 1960–75* (London).

HIBBERD, L. 1959: 'Musicology Reconsidered', *Acta Musicologica*, xxxii: 25–33.

HILL, R. (ed.) 1950: *Music 1950* (Harmondsworth).

HIND, J. and MOSCO, S. 1985: *Rebel Radio: the Full Story of British Pirate Radio* (London).

HINDMARSH, P. 1983: *Frank Bridge: a Thematic Catalogue* (London).

HINES, R. S. (ed.) 1970: *The Orchestral Composer's Point of View* (Norman, Oklahoma).

HOBSBAWM, E. and RANGER, T. 1983: *The Invention of Tradition* (Cambridge).

HODDINOTT, A. 1970: 'Peter Racine Fricker', *Music and Musicians*, xviii/12: 30.

HODEIR, A. tr. NOAKES, D. 1956: *Jazz: its Evolution and Essence* (London).

HOGGART, R. 1957, R/1958: *The Uses of Literacy* (London).

HOLD, T. 1972: 'The Music of William Alwyn' *Composer*, 43/44: 22–4/15–20.

HOLST, I. 1938, R/1969: *Gustav Holst* (London).

HOLST, I. 1951: *The Music of Gustav Holst* (London).

HOLT, R. 1989: *Sport and the British: a Modern History* (Oxford).

HOWARTH, E. and HOWARTH, P. 1988: *What a Performance! the Brass Band Plays* (London).

HOWAT, R. 1983: *Debussy in Proportion: a Musical Analysis* (Cambridge).

HOWES, F. 1941: 'The Dead Past', *Music and Letters*, xxii: 252–60.

LIST OF SOURCES

HOWES, F. 1948: *Man, Mind and Music* (London).
HOWES, F. 1957: 'What to Look for in the Programme Note', *The Times*, 29 November: 5.
HOWES, F. 1958: *Music and Its Meanings* (London).
HOWES, F. 1965, R/1973: *The Music of William Walton* (London).
HOWES, F. 1966: *The English Musical Renaissance* (London).
HOWKINS, A. 1989: 'Greensleeves and the Idea of National Music', in Samuel 1989, iii: 89–98.
HUGHES, D. J. 1964, R/1973: 'Pop Music', in D. Thompson (ed.), *Discrimination and Popular Culture* (Harmondsworth): 133–55.
HULL, R. 1932: *Handbook on Arnold Bax's Symphonies* (London).
HUNTLEY, J. 1947: *British Film Music* (London).
HURD, M. 1962, R/1993: *Immortal Hour: the Life and Period of Rutland Boughton*, rev, as *Rutland Boughton and the Glastonbury Festivals* (London).
HURD, M. 1978: *The Ordeal of Ivor Gurney* (Oxford).
HUSTWITT, M. 1983: '"Caught in a Whirlpool of Aching Sound": the Production of Dance Music in Britain in the 1920s', *Popular Music*, iii: 7–31.
HUSTWITT, M. 1985: *Sure Feels Like Heaven to Me: Considerations on Promotional Videos* (IASPM Working Paper no. 6).
HUTCHINGS, A. 1974: 'Music in Britain, 1916–1960', in Cooper 1974: 503–68.
HUTCHISON, R. 1982: *The Politics of the Arts Council* (London).
HUTCHISON, R. and FEIST, A. 1991: *Amateur Arts in the UK* (London).
HYLTON, J. 1934: 'Jazz! the Music of the People', in *The Jack Hylton Song Book*, *Woman's World* supplement, 27 October.

IRVING, E. 1943: 'Music in Films', *Music and Letters*, xxiv (London): 223–35.
IRVING, E. 1959: *Cue for Music* (London).
IRVING, J. 1988: 'Schönberg in the News: the London Performances of 1912–1914', *Music Review*, xlviii: 52–70.

JACKSON, B. 1943: 'Elgar's "Spanish Lady"', *Music and Letters*, xxiv: 1–15, repr. in Redwood 1982: 209–29.
JACOBS, A. 1962: 'At the Musical', *Opera*, xiii: 496.
JACOBS, A. (ed.) 1963: *Choral Music* (Harmondsworth).
JACOBS, A. 1964: 'Notes Before an Opera', *Musical Times*, cv: 818–19.
JACOBS, R. L. 1956: 'A *Gestalt* Psychologist on Music: a Discussion of the Article on *Gestalt* Psychology in *Grove* V', *Music Review*, xvii: 185–8.
JASPER, A. (comp.) 1983, R/1984: *The Top Twenty Book: the Official British Record Charts 1955–1983* (Poole).
JEVONS, W. S. 1883: *Methods of Social Reform and Other Papers* (London).
JOHN, N. (ed.) 1983: *Peter Grimes/Gloriana* (London).
JOHN, N. (ed.) 1985: *The Operas of Michael Tippett* (London).
JOHNSON, E. (ed.) 1971: *Robert Simpson: Essays* (London).
JOHNSON, P. 1964: 'The Menace of Beatleism', *New Statesman*, 28 February: 17.
JOHNSON, H. and PINES, J. 1982: *Reggae: Deep Roots Music* (London).

LIST OF SOURCES

JONES, M. 1990: 'Edgar Bainton: Musical and Spiritual Traveller', *British Music*, xii: 19–40.

JONES, N. 1965: 'Well, What Is Pop Art', *Melody Maker*, 3 July.

JONES, S. 1986: *Workers at Play: a Social and Economic History of Leisure, 1918–1939* (London).

JONES, S. 1988: *Black Culture, White Youth: the Reggae Tradition from JA to UK* (Basingstoke).

JOUBERT, J. 1969 : 'Under Western Eyes', *Musical Times*, cx: 470–73.

KAY, N. 1969: 'Thea Musgrave', *Music and Musicians*, xviii/4: 34.

KELLER, H. 1956: 'KV503: the Unity of Contrasting Themes and Movements', *Music Review*, xvii: 48–58, 120–29.

KELLER, H. 1956–7: 'A slip of Mozart's: Its Analytical Significance', *Tempo*, 42: 12–15.

KELLER, H. 1957a: 'Functional Analysis: Its Pure Application', *Music Review*, xviii: 202–6.

KELLER, H. 1957b: 'Knowing Things Backwards', *Tempo*, 46: 14–20.

KELLER, H. 1957c: 'The Musical Analysis of Music', *The Listener*, 29 August: 326.

KELLER, H. 1957d: 'Wordless Analysis', *Musical Events*, 12: 26–7.

KELLER, H. 1958a: 'The Homecoming of Musical Analysis', *Musical Times*, xcix: 657–8.

KELLER, H. 1958b: 'Wordless Functional Analysis: the First Year', *Music Review*, xix: 192–209.

KELLER, H. 1960: 'Wordless Functional Analysis: the Second Year and Beyond', *Music Review*, xxi: 73–6, 237–9.

KELLER, H. 1969: 'Roberto Gerhard's Two Ears', *The Listener*, 24 July: 121.

KELLER, H. 1987: *Criticism* (London).

KEMP, I. (ed.) 1965: *Michael Tippett: a Symposium on His Sixtieth Birthday* (London).

KEMP, I. 1984: *Tippett: the Composer and His Music* (London).

KENNEDY, M. 1964: *The Works of Ralph Vaughan Williams* (London).

KENNEDY, M. 1968, R/1982: *Portrait of Elgar* (London).

KENNEDY, M. 1972: note to recording of Vaughan Williams: *The Pilgrim's Progress*, SLS 1959.

KENNEDY, M. 1975: note to recording of *Sir John in Love*, SLS 980.

KENNEDY, M. 1977: 'Vaughan Williams Choral Music', note to recording SLS 5082: 4–19.

KENNEDY, M. 1989: *Portrait of Walton* (Oxford).

KENNEDY, M. 1991: 'Hugh Wood', Chester Music brochure (London).

KENYON, N. 1981: *The BBC Symphony Orchestra: the First Fifty Years: 1930–1980* (London).

KERMAN, J. 1985: *Musicology* (London).

KHAN, N. 1976: *The Arts Britain Ignores: the Arts of Ethnic Minorities in Britain* (London).

KING, K. AND BLAUG, M. 1976: 'Does the Arts Council Know What It is Doing?', in M. Blaug (ed.), *The Economics of the Arts* (London): 101–25.

KITSON, C. H. 1914: *The Evolution of Harmony* (Oxford).

LIST OF SOURCES

KNIGHT, G. H. and REED, W. L. (eds) 1965: *The Treasury of English Church Music: vol. v 1900–1965* (London).

KNUSSEN, O. 1993: 'Notes by the Composer', Virgin Classics recording VC 7 59308 2: 10–14.

KRUMMEL, D. W. 1981: 'Music Publishing', in Temperley 1981: 46–59.

LAING, D. 1969: *The Sound of Our Time* (London).

LAING, D. 1985: *One Chord Wonders: Power and Meaning in Punk Rock* (Milton Keynes).

LAING, D. 1991: 'Reviewing the Reviewers', *RPM*, 15: 22–4.

LAING, D., DALLAS, K., DENSELOW, R. and SHELTON, R. 1975: *The Electric Muse: the Story of Folk into Rock* (London).

LAMBERT, C. 1934, R/1966: *Music Ho! a Study of Music in Decline* (London).

LAMBOURN, D. 1987: 'Henry Wood and Schoenberg', *Musical Times*, cxxviii: 422–7.

LANGLOIS, T. 1992: 'Can You Feel It? DJs and House Music Culture in the UK', *Popular Music*, xi: 229–38.

LARKIN, P. 1970: *All What Jazz: a Record Diary 1961–68* (London).

LARSON, R. D. 1985: *Musique Fantastique: a Survey of Film Music in the Fantastic Cinema* (Metuchen, N. J.).

LAURENCE, D. H. (ed.) 1981: *The Bodley Head Bernard Shaw: Shaw's Music* (3 vols) (London).

LAW, J. K. 1985: '"We Have Ventured to Tidy Up Here": the Adapters' Dialogue in *Billy Budd*', *Twentieth Century Literature*, xxxi: 297–314.

LEACH, G. 1980, 2/1989: *British Composer Profiles: a Biographical Dictionary and Chronology of Past British Composers 1800–1979* (Maidenhead).

LEAVIS, F. R. 1930: *Mass Civilisation and Minority Culture* (Cambridge).

LEAVIS, F. R. and THOMPSON, D. 1933: *Culture and Environment: the Training of Critical Awareness* (London).

LE GRICE, M. 1977: *Abstract Film and Beyond* (London).

LEIGH, S. 1984: *Let's All Go Down the Cavern: the Story of Liverpool's Merseybeat* (London).

LeMAHIEU, D A. 1988: *A Culture for Democracy: Mass Communication and the Cultivated Mind in Britain between the Wars* (Oxford).

LEPPARD, R. 1965: review of G. Bush: *If the Cap Fits*, *Music and Letters*, xlvi: 282.

LEVENTHAL, F. M. 1990: 'The Best for the Most', *Twentieth Century British History*, i: 289–317.

LEVY, L. 1948: *Music for the Movies* (London).

LLOYD, L. S. 1947: 'Concerning "Theoreticians" and Others', *Music Review*, viii: 204.

LOEB, D. 1970: 'Mathematical Aspects of Music', *Music Forum*, ii: 110–29.

LONDON, K. 1936: *Film Music*, tr. E. Baisinger (London).

LONG, K. 1972 : *The Music of the English Church* (London).

LONGMIRE, J. 1969: *John Ireland: Portrait of a Friend* (London).

LIST OF SOURCES

McCARTHY, A. 1971: *The Dance Band Era* (London).

MacCOLL, E. 1990: *Journeyman* (London).

MacDONALD, C. 1991: 'Tom Anderson – an Appreciation', *English Dance and Song*, liii/4: 8–9.

MacDONALD, M. 1974–83: *The Symphonies of Havergal Brian* (3 vols, 1974, 1978 and 1983) (London).

MacDONALD, M. 1975: *John Foulds: his Life in Music* (Rickmansworth).

MACDONNELL, J. B. 1860: 'Classical Music and British Musical Taste', *Macmillan's Magazine*, i: 383–9.

McEWAN, I. 1989: Preface to *A Move Abroad*, adapted in *Weekend Guardian*, 2–3 September: 2–5.

MACKERNESS, E. D. 1964: *A Social History of English Music* (London).

MACKERNESS, E. D. 1974: *Somewhere Further North: a History of Music in Sheffield* (Sheffield).

MacKINNON, N. 1993: *The British Folk Scene: Musical Performance and Social Identity* (Buckingham).

McMULLIN, M. 1947: 'The Symbolic Analysis of Music', *Music Review*, viii: 25–35.

McNAUGHT, W. 1935: 'Vaughan Williams's Symphony no. 4', *Musical Times*, lxxvi: 452.

MACPHERSON, S. 1910, R/1940: *Music and Its Appreciation: or The Foundation of True Listening* (London).

MACQUEEN-POPE, W. 1949: *Gaiety: Theatre of Enchantment* (London).

MACQUEEN-POPE, W. 1959: *The Footlights Flickered* (London).

MAIRANTS, I. 1980: *'My Fifty Fretting Years': a Personal History of the Twentieth Century Guitar Explosion* (Newcastle upon Tyne).

MANDER, R. and MITCHENSON, J. 1957: *Theatrical Companion to Coward* (London).

MANNHEIM, K. 1956: 'The Democratisation of Culture', in *Essays on the Sociology of Culture* (London): 171–246.

MANNING, J. 1986, 2/1994: *New Vocal Repertoire: an Introduction* (Oxford).

MANVELL, R. and HUNTLEY, J. 1957, R/1975: *The Technique of Film Music* (London and New York).

MARCUS, G. 1989: *Lipstick Traces: a Secret History of the Twentieth Century* (London).

MARCUS, G. 1993: *In the Fascist Bathroom: Writings on Punk 1977–1992* (London).

MARKS, A. 1990: 'Young, Gifted and Black: Afro-American and Afro-Caribbean Music in Britain 1963–88', in P. Oliver 1990a: 102–17.

MARTIN, B. 1981: *A Sociology of Contemporary Cultural Change* (Oxford).

MARTIN, G. 1979: *All You Need Is Ears* (London).

MARTIN, G. (ed.) 1983: *Making Music: the Guide to Writing, Performing and Recording* (London).

MARWICK, A. 1982, R/1990: *British Society since 1945* (Harmondsworth).

MARWICK, A. 1991: *Culture in Britain since 1945* (Oxford).

MATHIESON, M. 1948: 'Recording the Music', in Cross 1948: 63–4.

MATHIESON, M. and MITCHELL, L. 1947: 'Music: Introducing Muir Mathieson', in Towers and Mitchell 1947: 54–62.

MATTHEWS, D. 1980: *Michael Tippett: an Introductory Study* (London).

LIST OF SOURCES

MAYCOCK, R. 1991: sleeve note, *Mary Wiegold's Songbook: the Composers Ensemble*, CD NMC D003: 3.

MELLERS, W. 1943: 'Rubbra and the Dominant Seventh', *Music Review*, iv: 145–56, repr. in Mellers 1948: 153–70.

MELLERS, W. 1946, R/1950: *Music and Society: England and the European Tradition* (London).

MELLERS, W. 1948: *Studies in Contemporary Music* (London).

MELLERS, W. 1964: 'John Joubert and the Blessed City', *Musical Times*, cv: 814–17.

MELLERS, W. 1967: *Caliban Reborn: Renewal in Twentieth-Century Music* (London).

MELLERS, W. 1973: *Twilight of the Gods: the Beatles in Retrospect* (London).

MELLERS, W. and HILDYARD, R. 1989: 'The Cultural and Social Setting', in B. Ford (ed.), *The Cambridge Guide to the Arts in Britain, vol. viii: The Edwardian Age and the Inter-War Years* (Cambridge): 3–44.

MELLY, G. 1970, R/1989: *Revolt into Style* (London).

MIDDLETON, R. 1972: *Pop Music and the Blues* (London).

MIDDLETON, R. 1981: 'Popular Music of the Lower Classes', in Temperley 1981: 63–91.

MIDDLETON, R. 1990: *Studying Popular Music* (Milton Keynes).

MILLER, R. and BOAR, R., ed. J. Lowe 1982: *The Incredible Music Machine* (London).

MILNES, R. 1972: 'Towards Music Theatre', *Opera*, xxiii: 1067–72.

MILNES, R. 1983: 'William Alwyn and "Miss Julie"', note to recording of *Miss Julie* SRCD 2218.

MINIHAN J. 1977: *The Nationalization of Culture: the Development of State Subsidies to the Arts in Britain* (London).

MITCHELL, D. 1963: *The Language of Modern Music* (London).

MITCHELL, D. 1988: 'Britten's and Auden's "American" Opera', note to Virgin Classics recording of *Paul Bunyan*, VCD 7 90710-2: 31–46.

MITCHELL, D. and KELLER, H. (eds) 1952: *Benjamin Britten: a Commentary on His Works from a Group of Specialists* (London).

MITCHELL, D. and REED, P. (eds) 1991: *Letters from a Life: Selected Letters and Diaries of Benjamin Britten* (2 vols) (London).

MOORE, A. 1993: *Rock: the Primary Text* (Buckingham).

MOORE, J. N. 1987: *Elgar and His Publishers* (2 vols) (Oxford).

MORRIS, R. O. 1935: *The Structure of Music: an Outline for Students* (London).

MORRIS, W. 1962: *Selected Writings and Designs*, ed. A. Briggs (Harmondsworth).

MORTON, B. and COLLINS, P. (eds) 1992: *Contemporary Composers* (London).

MUNRO, A. 1984: *The Folk Music Revival in Scotland* (London).

MURRAY, C. S. 1989: *Crosstown Traffic: Jimi Hendrix and Post-War Pop* (London).

Music Analysis 1982– : (Oxford).

Music and Letters 1920– : (Oxford).

Music Review 1940– : (Cambridge).

Music Survey 1949–52: (London).

Musical Times 1844– : (London).

MYERS, A. 1991: 'Instruments and Instrumentation in Brass Bands', in Herbert 1991: 169–95.

MYERS, R. 1939: *Music in the Modern World* (London).

LIST OF SOURCES

NEGUS, K. 1993: *Producing Pop: Culture and Conflict in the Popular Music Industry* (Sevenoaks).
NEWMAN, E. 1925a: *A Musical Critic's Holiday* (London).
NEWMAN, E. 1925b: 'A Postscript to "A Musical Critic's Holiday"', *Musical Times*, lxvi: 881–4, 977–81, 1076–9.
NEWMAN, E. 1925c: review of Holst: *At the Boar's Head, Musical Times*, lxvi: 413–14.
NEWMAN, E. 1956: *From the World of Music*, ed. F. Aprahamian (London).
NEWMAN, E. 1958: *More Essays from the World of Music*, ed. F. Aprahamian (London).
NORRIS, C. (ed.) 1989: *Music and the Politics of Culture* (London).
NORTHCOTT, B. 1973: 'Jonathan Harvey', *Music and Musicians*, xxi/7: 34–40.
NORTHCOTT, B. 1974: 'Robin Holloway', *Musical Times*, cxv: 644–6.
NORTHCOTT, B. (ed.) 1980: *The Music of Alexander Goehr* (London).
NORTHCOTT, B. 1990: 'The Way We Hear Now', *Independent*, 14 July: 31.
NORTHCOTT, B. 1991: 'Don't Shoot the Critic', *Independent*, 26 January: 29.
NUTTALL, J. 1968: *Bomb Culture* (London).
NYMAN, M. 1969: 'Two New Works by Harrison Birtwistle', *Tempo*, 88: 47–50.

O'CONNOR, N. 1991: *Bringing It All Back Home: the Influence of Irish Music* (London).
OGDEN, C. K., RICHARDS, I. A. and WOOD, J. 1922: *The Foundations of Aesthetics* (London).
O'GRADY, T. 1983: *The Beatles: a Musical Evolution* (Boston).
OLIVER, M. 1975: 'Miscellany: Justin Connolly – Jonathan Harvey – Roger Smalley – Anthony Payne – Tristram Cary – Anthony Milner – Christopher Headington – Robin Holloway – David Ellis', in Foreman 1975: 162–77.
OLIVER, P. (ed.) 1990a: *Black Music in Britain: Essays on the Afro-Asian Contribution to Popular Music* (Milton Keynes).
OLIVER, P. 1990b: *Blues Fell This Morning: Meaning in the Blues* (Cambridge).
ORWELL, G. 1937, R/1962: *The Road to Wigan Pier* (London).
OSBORNE, N. 1984: 'Panufnik at 70', *Tempo*, 150: 2–10.
OSMOND-SMITH, D. 1971: 'Music as Communication: Semiology or Morphology?', *International Review of the Aesthetics and Sociology of Music*, ii: 108–11.
OSMOND-SMITH, D. 1991: *Berio* (Oxford).
OTTAWAY, H. 1971: 'Rubbra's Symphonies', *Musical Times*, cxii: 430, 549.
OTTAWAY, H. 1980: 'Rubbra, (Charles) Edmund', in Sadie 1980 xvi: 292–4.

PAGET, M. M. 1915–16: 'Some Curiosities of Musical Criticism', *Proceedings of the Musical Association*, xlii: 69.
PALMER, C. 1972: 'Walton's Film Music', *Musical Times*, ciii: 249–52.
PALMER, C. 1978: *Herbert Howells: a Study* (Borough Green).
PALMER, C. (ed.) 1984: *The Britten Companion* (London).
PALMER, C. 1990: 'Sir William Walton (1902–1983): *The Quest* – (complete)', note to recording, CHAN 8871: 4–6.

LIST OF SOURCES

PALMER, C. and FOREMAN, L. 1975: 'Richard Rodney Bennett', in Foreman 1975: 108–19.
PAYN, G. and MORLEY, S. 1982: *The Coward Diaries* (London).
PAYNE, A. 1964: 'Alan Bush', *Musical Times*, cv: 263-5.
PAYNE A. 1984: *Frank Bridge – Radical and Conservative* (London).
PAYNTER, J. 1982: *Music in the Secondary School Curriculum* (Cambridge).
PEACOCK, A. 1970: *A Report on Orchestral Resources in Great Britain* (Arts Council).
PEACOCK, A. and WEIR, R. 1975: *The Composer in the Market Place* (London).
PEARSALL, R. 1976: *Popular Music of the 1920s* (Newton Abbot).
PERRY, G. 1981: *Forever Ealing: a Celebration of the Great British Film Studio* (London).
PICK, J. 1981: *The Privileged Arts* (Eastbourne).
PICK, J. 1991: *Vile Jelly: the Birth, Life and Lingering Death of the Arts Council of Great Britain* (Doncaster).
PICKERING, M. 1986: 'White Skin, Black Masks: "Nigger" Minstrelsy in Victorian Britain', in J. S. Bratton (ed.), *Music Hall: Performance and Style* (Milton Keynes): 70–91.
PICKERING, M. 1990: 'Recent Folk Music Scholarship in England: a Critique', *Folk Music Journal*, vi: 37–64.
PIRIE, P. J. 1979: *The English Musical Renaissance* (London).
PLEASANTS, H. 1969: *Serious Music – and All That Jazz* (London).
POPPLEWELL, R. 1984: 'Music in Shetland', in B. Crawford (ed.), *Essays in Shetland History* (Lerwick): 243–53.
Popular Music 1981– : (Cambridge).
Popular Music 1988: vii/3, special issue on music, video and film (Cambridge).
Popular Music 1990 ix/2, special issue on radio (Cambridge).
PORTER, A. 1964: review of Cannon: *Morvoren, Musical Times,* cv: 671.
PORTER, A. 1978: *Music of Three Seasons: 1974–1977* (London).
PORTER, R. 1992: *Myths of the English* (Cambridge).
POTTER, K. 1972: 'The Life and Works of Roberto Gerhard' (MA thesis, University of Birmingham).
PRIESTLEY, J. B. 1934: *English Journey* (London).
PRITCHARD, F. 1988: *Dance Band Days Around Manchester* (Manchester).
PROTHEROE, G. 1975: 'Alexander Goehr', in Foreman 1975: 41–52.
PRUSLIN, S. 1980: note to recording of Birtwistle: *Punch and Judy*, HEAD 24125.
PUDOVKIN, N. I. 1958: *Film Technique and Film Acting* (London).
PUFFETT, D. 1986: 'The Fugue from Tippett's Second String Quartet', *Music Analysis*, v: 233–64.
PULLING, C. 1952: *They Were Singing* (London).

RACE, S. 1956a: untitled article, *Melody Maker*, 5 May: 5.
RACE, S. 1956b: 'Rock-and-Roll on Record', *Melody Maker*, 20 October: 5.
RAINBOW, B. 1980: 'Education in Music: Great Britain, Schools', in Sadie 1980, vi: 22–4.
RAINBOW, B. 1981: 'Music in Education', in Temperley 1981: 29–45.

LIST OF SOURCES

RAINBOW, B. 1989: *Music in Educational Thought and Practice* (Aberystwyth).
RAPÉE, E. 1924: *Motion Picture Moods of Pianists and Organists* (New York).
RAYNOR, H. 1952: 'Towards a Rationale of Criticism', *Music Review*, xiii: 195–205.
REDHEAD, S. 1990: *The End-of-the-Century Party: Youth and Pop towards 2000* (Manchester).
REDHEAD, S. and STREET, J. 1989: 'Have I the Right? Legitimacy, Authenticity and Community in Folk's Politics', *Popular Music*, viii: 177–84.
REDWOOD, C. (ed.) 1982: *An Elgar Companion* (Ashbourne).
REED, P. and EVANS, J. 1987: 'Music for Radio', in Evans, Reed and Wilson 1987: 154–65.
REYNOLDS, S. 1990: *Blissed Out: the Raptures of Rock* (Washington D.C. and London).
RIIS, T. 1989: *Just Before Jazz* (Washington D. C. and London).
RILEY, T. 1988: *Tell Me Why: a Beatles Commentary* (London).
RIMMER, D. 1985: *Like Punk Never Happened: Culture Club and the New Pop* (London).
ROBERTS, D. 1978: review of works by Peter Maxwell Davies, *Contact*, 19: 26–9.
ROCHE, E. 1979: 'Early Music and the BBC', *Musical Times*, lxx: 821–3, 912–14.
ROCHE, E. 1988: '"Great Learning, Fine Scholarship, Impeccable Taste": a Fiftieth Anniversary Tribute to Sir Richard Terry (1865–1938)', *Early Music*, xvi: 231–6 .
ROREM, N. 1974: 'Jesus Christ Superstar', *Harper's Magazine*, 1453 (June 1971), repr. in *Pure Contraption* (New York): 84–5.
ROSCOW, G. (ed.) 1991: *Bliss on Music: Selected Writings of Arthur Bliss, 1920–1975* (Oxford).
ROSENTHAL, H. 1960: review of Tate: *The Lodger, Musical Times*, ci: 570.
ROSSELSON, L. 1979: 'Pop Music: Mobiliser or Opiate?', in C. Gardner (ed.), *Media, Politics and Culture* (London): 40–50.
ROTH, E. 1969: *The Business of Music* (London).
ROUTH, F. 1968: *Contemporary Music: an Introduction* (London).
ROUTH, F. 1972: *Contemporary British Music: the Twenty-Five Years from 1945 to 1970* (London).
ROUTH, F. 1984: 'Rawsthorne's Instrumental Style', *Musical Times*, cxxv: 143–5.
ROUTLEY, E. 1964: *Twentieth Century Church Music* (London).
RUFER, J. , tr. H. Searle, 1954 : *Composition with Twelve Notes* (London).
RUNCIMAN, J. F. 1901: *Old Scores and New Readings* (London).
RUSSEL, M. T. 1993: *James Joyce's 'Chamber Music': the Lost Song Settings* (Bloomington and Indianapolis).
RUSSELL, D. 1987: *Popular Music in England, 1840–1914: a Social History* (Manchester).
RUSSELL, D. 1991: '"What's Wrong with Brass Bands?" Cultural Change and the Band Movement, 1918–c.1964', in Herbert 1991: 57–101.
RUSSELL, I. 1970: 'Carol-Singing in the Sheffield Area', *Lore and Language*, 3: 12–15.
RUSSELL, I. 1973: 'A Survey of a Christmas Singing Tradition in South Yorkshire 1970', *Lore and Language*, 8: 13–25.
RUSSELL, I. 1990: 'The Hidden Musicians', review of Finnegan 1989, *Folk Music Journal*, vi: 87–90.

LIST OF SOURCES

RUST, B. 1961, R/1969: *Jazz Records 1897–1942* (Hatch End).
RUST, B. 1972: *The Dance Bands* (London).
RUST, B. 1977: *London Musical Shows on Record 1897–1976* (Harrow).
RUST, B. 1979: *British Music Hall on Record* (Harrow).
RUST, B. and FORBES, S. 1987, R/1989: *British Dance Bands on Record 1911–1945* (Harrow).
RYE, H. 1990: 'Fearsome Means of Discord: Early Encounters with Black Jazz', in P. Oliver 1990a: 45–57.

SADIE, S. (ed.) 1980: *The New Grove Dictionary of Music and Musicians* (6th edn, 20 vols) (London).
SAMPSON, H. 1980: *Blacks in Blackface* (Metuchen N.J. and London).
SAMSON, J. 1977: *Music in Transition: a Study of Tonal Expansion and Atonality, 1900–20* (London).
SAMUEL, R. (ed.) 1989: *Patriotism: the Making and Unmaking of British National Identity. Vol. I: History and Politics; Vol. II: Minorities and Outsiders; Vol. III: National Fictions* (London and New York).
SAREMBA, M. 1994: *Elgar, Britten & Co: eine Geschichte der britischen Musik in zwölf Portraits* (Zürich and St Gallen).
SAXTON, R. 1991: interview, BBC Radio 3, 11 July.
SCANNELL, P. 1981: 'Music for the Multitude? The Dilemmas of the BBC's Music Policy 1923–1946', *Media, Culture and Society*, iii: 243–60.
SCANNELL P. and CARDIFF, D. 1991: *A Social History of British Broadcasting, vol. I 1922–1939: Serving the Nation* (Oxford).
SCAPING, P. (ed.; comp. C. Green and H. John) 1991: *B[ritish] P[honographic] I[ndustry] Yearbook 1990: a Statistical Description of the British Record Industry* (London).
SCHAEFER, J. 1990: *New Sounds: the Virgin Guide to New Music* (London).
SCHAFER, R. MURRAY 1963: *British Composers in Interview* (London).
SCHOLES, P. 1935: *Music: the Child and the Masterpiece* (London).
SCHOLES, P. 1938: *The Oxford Companion to Music* (London).
SCHOLES, P. A. 1947: *The Mirror of Music, 1844–1944: a Century of Musical Life in Britain as Reflected in the Pages of the 'Musical Times'* (2 vols) (London).
SCHULLER, G. 1968: *Early Jazz* (New York).
SCOTLAND, J. 1930: *The Talkies* (London).
SCOTT, C. 1917: *The Philosophy of Modernism (In Its Connection with Music)* (London).
SCOTT, D. 1989: *The Singing Bourgeois: Songs of the Victorian Drawing Room and Parlour* (Milton Keynes).
SCOTT, H. 1946: *The Early Doors* (London).
SCOTT-SUTHERLAND, C. 1973: *Arnold Bax* (London).
SEARLE, H. 1962: 'Are Twelve-Note Symphonies Possible?', *The Listener*, 29 November: 941.
SENNETT, R. 1991: 'Fragments Against the Ruin' (review of Giddens 1991), *The Times Literary Supplement*, 8 February: 6.

LIST OF SOURCES

SHAPIRO N. and HENTOFF, N. (eds) 1955, R/1966: *Hear Me Talkin' to Ya* (London).
SHARP, C. 1912: *Folk Singing in Schools* (London).
SHARP, G. 1950: 'Some Problems of Musical Criticism', *Music Review*, xi: 130–8.
SHAW, C. 1993: review of Carpenter 1992, *Tempo*, 184: 31–2.
SHAW, R. 1978: *Elitism versus Populism in the Arts* (Eastbourne).
SHAW, R. and SHAW, G. 1988: 'The Cultural and Social Setting', in B. Ford (ed.), *The Cambridge Guide to the Arts in Britain, vol. IX: Since the Second World War* (Cambridge): 3–44.
SHEAD, R. 1973: *Constant Lambert* (London).
SHEPHERD, J., VIRDEN, P., VULLIAMY, G. and WISHART, T. 1977: *Whose Music? a Sociology of Musical Languages* (London).
SHORT, M. 1990: *Gustav Holst: the Man and His Music* (Oxford).
SIEVEKING, L. 1934: *The Stuff of Radio* (London).
SINFIELD, A. 1989: *Literature, Politics and Culture in Postwar Britain* (Oxford).
SMALL, C. 1977: *Music, Society, Education* (London).
SMITH, A. 1991: *An Improbable Centenary: the Life and Times of the Slaithwaite Philharmonic Orchestra 1891–1990* (Huddersfield).
SMITH, R. 1961: 'The Sorry Scheme of Things', *Music Review*, xxii: 212–19.
SORABJI, K. S. 1932: *Around Music* (London).
SORABJI, K. S. 1947: *Mi contra fa: the Immoralisings of a Machiavellian Musician* (London).
SOUSTER, T. 1970: 'Triple Music II', *The Listener*, 13 August: 222.
SPOTTISWOODE, R. 1935: *A Grammar of the Film* (London).
STANFORD, C. V. 1911: *Musical Composition: a Short Treatise for Students* (London).
STASIAK, C. 1991: 'An Analytical Study of the Music of A. Panufnik' (PhD thesis, Queen's University, Belfast).
STERNFELD, F. W. (ed.) 1973: *A History of Western Music vol. V: Music in the Modern Age* (London).
STEVENS, D. 1989: 'Performance Practice Issues on the BBC Third Programme', *Performance Practice Review*, ii: 73–81.
STEVENSON, R. (ed.) 1980: *Alan Bush: an 80th Birthday Symposium* (Kidderminster).
STEWARD, S. and GARRATT, S. 1984: *Signed, Sealed and Delivered: True Life Stories of Women in Pop Music* (Boston and London).
STIMPSON, M. 1991: 'The Cutting Edge', *Music Teacher*, 70 (October): 29–33.
STONE, C. 1933: *Christopher Stone Speaking* (London).
STRADLING, R. and HUGHES, M. 1993: *The English Musical Renaissance 1860–1940: Construction and Deconstruction* (London and New York).
STRAW, W. 1988: 'Music Video in Its Contexts: Popular Music and Post-Modernism in the 1980s', *Popular Music*, vii: 247–66.
SWANN, D. 1994: 'John Foulds (1880–1939)' (unpublished paper, Southampton University).
SWANWICK, K. 1968: *Popular Music and the Teacher* (London).
SWANWICK, K. 1988: *Music, Mind and Education* (London).
SYMONS, D. 1980: 'Tonal Organization in the Symphonies of Egon Wellesz' (PhD thesis, University of Western Australia).

LIST OF SOURCES

TAMM, E. 1989: *Brian Eno: His Music and the Vertical Color of Sound* (Boston).
TAYLOR, A. 1983: *Labour and Love: an Oral History of the Brass Band Movement* (London).
TAYLOR, H. (ed.) 1979: *Selected Essays: Edward J. Dent* (Cambridge).
TAYLOR, P. 1985: *Popular Music since 1955: a Critical Guide to the Literature* (London).
TAYLOR, R. C. 1978: *Art, an Enemy of the People* (Hassocks).
TEMPERLEY, N. 1979: *The Music of the English Parish Church* (2 vols) (Cambridge).
TEMPERLEY, N. (ed.) 1981: *Music in Britain: The Romantic Age 1800–1914* (London).
Tempo, 1939– : (London).
Tempo, 1979: special Holloway issue 129 (London).
Tempo, 1981: special Gerhard issue 139 (London).
THOMPSON, D. (ed.) 1964, R/1973: *Discrimination and Popular Culture* (Harmondsworth).
THOMPSON, L. 1986: 'Spike Hughes vol. II', note to recording FG–409.
THOMSON, D. 1965: *The Pelican History of England vol. IX: England in the Twentieth Century* (Harmondsworth).
THOMSON, J. M. (ed.) 1978: *The Future of Early Music in Britain* (London).
THOMSON, R. 1989: 'Dance Bands and Dance Halls in Greenock', *Popular Music*, viii: 143–55.
TIPPETT, M. 1974: *Moving into Aquarius* (London).
TIPPETT, M. 1980: *Music of the Angels: Essays and Sketchbooks* (London).
TIPPETT, M. 1991: *Those Twentieth Century Blues: an Autobiography* (London, Sydney, Auckland and Johannesburg).
TOMLINSON, F. 1978: *Warlock and van Dieren* (London).
TOOP, R. 1985: 'Brian Ferneyhough in Interview', *Contact*, 29: 4–19.
TOOP, R. 1987: 'Ferneyhough's Dungeons of Invention', *Musical Times*, cxxviii: 624–8.
TOOP, R. 1988: 'Four Facets of "The New Complexity"', *Contact*, 32: 4–50.
TOOP, R. 1990: 'Brian Ferneyhough's *Lemma–Icon–Epigram*', *Perspectives of New Music*, xxviii/2 : 52–102.
TOVEY, D. F. 1935–9: *Essays in Musical Analysis* (6 vols, chamber music supplement 1944) (London).
TOVEY, D. F. 1944: *Musical Articles from the Encyclopaedia Britannica*, ed. H. J. Foss (London).
TOVEY, D. F. 1948: *A Companion to Beethoven's Pianoforte Sonatas* (London).
TOWERS, H. A. and MITCHELL, L. 1947: *The March of the Movies* (London).
TRAUBNER, R. 1984: *Operetta: a Theatrical History* (London).
TREND, M. 1985: *The Music Makers: Heirs and Rebels of the English Musical Renaissance* (London).
TRUSCOTT, H. 1975: 'Two Traditionalists: Kenneth Leighton and John McCabe', in Foreman 1975: 145–54.

VAN DER MERWE, P. 1989: *Origins of the Popular Style: the Antecedents of Twentieth-Century Popular Music* (Oxford).

LIST OF SOURCES

Various 1960: 'Music Critics and Criticism Today', symposium, *Musical Times*, ci: 220.
VAUGHAN WILLIAMS, R. 1953: *Some Thoughts on Beethoven's Choral Symphony, with Writings on Other Musical Subjects* (London).
VAUGHAN WILLIAMS, R. 1963: *National Music and Other Essays* (London).
VAUGHAN WILLIAMS, U. 1964: *R.V.W.: A Biography of Ralph Vaughan Williams* (London).
VAUGHAN WILLIAMS, U. and HOLST, I. (eds) 1959: *Heirs and Rebels: Letters Written to Each Other and Occasional Writings on Music by Ralph Vaughan Williams and Gustav Holst* (London).
VERMOREL, F. and J. 1978: *Sex Pistols: the Inside Story* (London).
VULLIAMY, G. and LEE, E. 1976: *Pop Music in School* (Cambridge).

WALKER, A. 1959: 'Unconscious Motivation in the Composing Process', *Music Review*, xx: 277–81.
WALKER, A. 1962: *A Study in Musical Analysis* (London).
WALKER, A. 1962–3: 'Back to the Couch', *Music and Musicians*, xi/10: 20, 53.
WALKER, A. 1966: *An Anatomy of Musical Criticism* (London).
WALKER, A. 1967: 'A Glossary of the Elements of Graphic Analysis', *Music Forum*, i: 260–68.
WALKER, E. 1946: *Free Thought and the Musician and Other Essays* (London).
WALSER, R. 1993: *Running with the Devil: Power, Gender and Madness in Heavy Metal Music* (Hanover, N.H.).
WALSH, S. 1966: 'A Memory of Violins', *Opera*, xvii : 851–3.
WALSH, S. 1974a: 'Musgrave's "The Voice of Ariadne"', *Musical Times*, cxv: 465–7.
WALSH, S. 1974b: 'The Music of Andrzej Panufnik', *Tempo*, 111: 5–14.
WALTER, A. 1992: 'Angelic Choirs', *Musical Times*, cxxxiii: 278–81.
WALTON, S. 1988: *William Walton: Behind the Façade* (Oxford).
WATERS, C. 1989–90: 'The Americanization of the Masses: Cultural Criticism, the National Heritage and Working Class Culture in the 1930s', *Social History Curators Group Journal*: 22–6 .
WEEDON, B. 1991: 'Mr Guitar', BBC Radio 2 broadcast (13 August).
WESCOTT, S. D. 1985: *A Comprehensive Bibliography of Music for Film and Television* (Detroit).
WESTRUP, J. A. 1943: *British Music* (London).
WESTRUP, J. A. 1946a: 'Frank Bridge', in Bacharach 1946: 75–82.
WESTRUP, J. A. 1946b: 'E. J. Moeran', in Bacharach 1946: 175–84.
WESTRUP, J. A. 1980: 'Partsong', in Sadie 1980, xiv: 257–8.
WHARTON, R. and CLARKE, A. 1979: *The Tommy Talker Bands of the West Riding* (Bradford).
WHATLEY, G. L. 1981: 'Music Theory', in Temperley 1981: 474–82.
WHITCOMB, I. 1972, R/1986: *After the Ball: Pop Music from Rag to Rock* (Harmondsworth).
WHITE, M. J. 1985: 'Haunted by an Old Tradition', *Guardian*, 29 November.

LIST OF SOURCES

WHITELEY, S. 1992: *The Space Between the Notes: Rock and the Counterculture* (London).

WHITTALL, A. 1975: 'Nicholas Maw', in Foreman 1975: 97–107.

WHITTALL, A. 1982: *The Music of Britten and Tippett: Studies in Themes and Techniques* (Cambridge).

WICKE, P. 1990: *Rock Music: Culture, Aesthetics and Sociology*, tr. R. Fogg (Cambridge).

WIENER, M. J. 1981: *English Culture and the Decline of the Industrial Spirit, 1850–1980* (Cambridge).

WILCOX, J. R. 1984: 'Daniel Jones: Some Compositional Traits', *Welsh Music*, vii/6: 14–20.

WILLIAMS, R. 1958: *Culture and Society 1780–1950* (London).

WILLIAMS, R. 1965: *The Long Revolution* (London).

WILLIAMS, R. 1973: *The Country and the City* (London).

WILLIAMS, S. and GODDARD, S. 1950: 'Music in the Theatre: Opera', in Hill 1950: 187–99.

WILLIS, P. 1978: *Profane Culture* (London).

WILSON, S. 1975: *Ivor* (London).

WISHART, T. 1990: 'The Vox Cycle', sleeve note, Virgin Classics recording VC 7 91108-2.

WOODS, F. 1979: *Folk Revival: the Discovery of a National Music* (London).

WRIGHT, D. 1994: 'Clicks, Clocks & Claques: Birtwistle at 60', *Musical Times*, cxxxv: 426–31.

YORK, N. (ed.) 1991: *The Rock File: Making It in the Music Business* (Oxford).

YOUNG, P. M. 1955, R/1973: *Elgar O.M.: a Study of a Musician.*

YOUNG, P. M. 1967: *A History of British Music* (London).

YOUNG, P. M. 1975: 'Alan Bush at 75', *Music and Musicians*, xxiv/12 (December): 18–19.

INDEX

à Kempis, Thomas 410
A–Z 110
Abba 450
ABC 93
'Abide with me' 162
Abingdon 526
Abraham, Gerald 509
absurdity 24
Academy of Ancient Music 528
Academy of Choreographic Art 394
Accident 137
Ace of Clubs 115
acid house parties 85–6
acid rock 90
acoustics 312, 503, 513
Adams, A. Emmett 69
Adams, John 337
Adams, Stephen 45, 61
Addinsell, Richard 27, 131, 132–3, 134
Addison, John
 ballet music 397
 film music 135, 137
Addison, Joseph 365, 427
Adorno, T.W. 34, 331, 342, 509, 516
adult oriented rock (AOR) 103
advertising 34, 49, 123
 see also television
Aeschylus 392, 497
aesthetics 58, 63, 65, 337, 417, 447, 461, 480–1, 486–8, 503–6, 509–10, 514, 516–17
 and taste 30–1, 36–8, 39, 48, 57, 70
 of film 129
 of rock music 79, 80, 84, 91–2, 95, 104–6
Africa 106, 425, 446
 South Africa 372–3; Cape Town 357
African musicians 58
African-American music *see* America (USA) and American influence
African-Caribbean music 36, 97–9, 150
 see also calypso; dub; reggae; ska; West Indian musicians
'Agincourt song' 414
Alaap 157–8
Albania 318
Albion Band 102
Aldeburgh 324
 see also festivals, Aldeburgh Festival
aleatoric music 153, 280, 290, 316–17, 319, 428, 438, 460
'Alexander's ragtime band' 2
Alexandra Palace 357
Alford, Kenneth 69, 151
All Creatures Great and Small 142
All Girls Band 68
Allen, Hugh 30, 510, 511
Allingham, William 469
Alloway, Lawrence 36
Allt, W. Greenhouse 510
Alwyn, William 375
 film music 131, 134
 operas 369, 374
 orchestral music 237–8; Fourth Symphony 282, 290
amateur musicians 5, 40, 69, 71, 74, 85, 91, 99, 101, 145–76, 239, 346, 348, 359, 363–5, 372, 403, 404, 406, 482
 gentleman amateur 503, 517, 523
 incompetence 28
 organists 163
Ambrose, Bert 57, 58, 59, 65, 68, 73–4, 132
Ambrosian Singers 527

America (USA) and American influence 3, 16, 31–4, 36, 48, 50, 52, 57–78, 79–110, 129, 136, 148, 156–7, 159, 162, 232, 274, 284–5, 303, 315, 317, 331, 337, 340, 359, 374, 377, 380, 399, 402, 409, 447, 465, 480, 499, 516
 African-American music 30–1, 34–5, 81–7, 91, 95, 100, 106, 107–8, 158
 early music revival in America 520–1, 524, 528
 Chicago 85, 88, 95
 Detroit 87
 Hollywood 132, 464
 Los Angeles 359
 New York 3, 87, 95, 108, 341, 443, 464
 Princeton 310–11
 San Diego Extended Vocal Techniques Ensemble 447
 Tin Pan Alley 80, 96
 West Coast music 90
 white folk styles 101
 see also Anglo-American relations; jazz; minimalism
American Indian creation myths 392, 498
American Ragtime Octette 57
AMM 318
amplification 65, 81, 119, 120, 122, 124, 129, 402, 428, 444–51
analysis 504–5, 507–8, 510–14, 516–18
 see also Music Analysis
'Anarchy in the UK' 92
Anderson, Alastair 102
Andersen, Hans Christian 376
Anderson, Tom 158
'And her mother came too' 110
Andrewes, Lancelot 463
Andrews, Hilda 523
Andriessen, Louis 337
Anglican music *see* church music
Anglo-American relations 1
 popular music 80
Anglo-Catholic church 521
Animals 88
Anna Karenina 134
anthems 167, 441, 452–63, 522
Aplvor, Denis
 ballet music 397
 operas 370
Apocrypha, settings of 412
Apollinaire, Guillaume 499
Appleford, Patrick 165–6
appropriation 105
Arc de Triomphe 112
archaism *see* early music
architects 41
Aristophanes 370
Arlette 110
Armes, Philip 511
Armstrong, Louis 58, 63–4, 71–2, 77
Armstrong, Thomas 510
Army Air Force Band 74
Arnell, Richard 358
Arnheim, Rudolph 129
Arnold, Denis 511, 515
Arnold, Malcolm 27
 ballet music 397
 film music 135
 operas 369
 orchestral music 237
Arnold, Matthew 29
arrangers 28, 71, 78
 and arrangements 73, 464, 468–9, 474–7, 481, 487

Ars Nova 21
art music (classical music), status, conditions and influence of 5, 6, 28, 89, 90, 100, 103–4, 117, 402, 447, 487, 491
 canon 28–9
art rock 90
art schools 35, 104
art song *see* song, solo
Arthurian romance 384–5
 see also Boughton, Rutland
Arthurs, George 108
Arts and Crafts movement 519
Arts Council 4, 24, 28, 36, 48, 50, 52, 372, 437–8, 443, 529
Ashton, Frederick 394–5
Asian musics 5, 36, 99, 174
 see also bhangra; indipop
Aspects of Love 122
Associated Board examinations 32, 169, 171
Aswad 98
atonality 22, 25–6, 341, 513
 see also serialism and 12-note music
Atwell, Winifred 77–8
Auden, W.H. 131, 359, 399, 431, 439, 472, 480, 484, 489
'Auf Wiederseh'n sweetheart' 78
Austin, Ernest 69
Austin, Frederic 111
Australia 96, 312, 334, 372–3, 410
Austria 50
 Vienna 115–16, 344, 372, 408
Austro-German tradition 2, 40, 286, 372, 485
 see also Second Viennese School
avant garde, the 12–13, 20, 21, 100, 100–4, 169, 292, 303, 306, 342, 487, 488
 cinema 142
'Ave Maria' 70
Axt, William 128
Ayer, Nat D. 109

Babbitt, Milton 301, 310–11
'Baby blues' 110
Bach, Johann Sebastian 33, 70, 180, 395, 407, 420, 431, 441, 526
 revived in performance 522–3, 524; *see also* English Bach Festival
Bach Cantata Club 522–3, 524
Bach Choir 523
Bacharach, Burt 155
back entry singers 162
'Back to life' 95
Bailey, Derek 100
Bain, Aly 102
Bainbridge, Simon
 instrumental music 340–1; *People of the Dawn* 497–8
Baines, William 469
Bainton, Edgar 455
Bairstow, Edward 455, 511
 Organ Sonata 277
Baker, Josephine 107
Ball, Eric 152
Ball, Kenny 77, 99
ballad concerts 69
ballads 29, 108, 111, 122, 348
 contemporary 153
 folk 391
 narrative and choral 403–4, 407, 417, 444
 parlour or drawing-room 59, 61, 69–70, 162
 pop 86, 402
 postwar 31
 rock 91

554

INDEX

royalty 472
sacred 69
sentimental 80
stage 402
see also opera, ballad
Ballads and Blues Club 159
ballet 108, 113, 130, 134, 366, 367, 393–8, 527
 in opera 349, 356, 367
Ballet Rambert 396–7
Ballets russes 393
'Balloons' 60
ballroom dancing 60
Band Aid 93
Band Wagon 132
bands 145, 148, 150, 156–8, 170
 accordion 70–1
 banjo 71
 big 100
 bugle 145
 brass 35, 40, 145–6, 148, 149, 151–4, 155, 168, 174, 175–6, 485
 comic 150
 concertina 145–6
 dance 35, 47, 57–78, 103, 111, 112, 116, 145, 148, 156, 157–8, 175, 323
 drum and fife 145
 jazz 57–78
 kazoo 150
 mandolin 71
 marching 150
 military 79, 145
 percussion 51, 168
 pipe 145, 149; bamboo pipe movement 51, 168
 service 73–4
 showbands 47
 steel 68, 150
 wind 145, 150, 168
 see also country music, groups; folk music, groups; jazz; pop music, groups; recorder, groups; rock music, groups; swing
Banfield, Stephen 511
Banks, Don 135, 312, 439
Bantock, Granville 179, 203, 510, 511
 choral music 154, 430; *Omar Khayyam* 408, 427, 429; operas 349; orchestral music 198, *The Seal-Woman* 349
Barber, Chris 76–7
barbershop singing 150, 439
Bard, Wilkie 112
Barnes, William 470
Barr, Ida 108–9, 119
Barrett, Richard 24, 334
Barrie, J.M. 394
Barris, Harry 61
Barriteau, Carl 67
Barritt, Kennth 510
Barry, John 137–41
Bart, Lionel 120–1
Bartlett, Ethel 274
Bartók, Béla 17, 21, 180, 191, 242, 257, 260, 264, 274, 284, 290, 443, 460, 470
Basie, Count 75
Bassey, Shirley 80
Bates, Django 100
Bath 348
Bath, Hubert 111, 129, 134
Battle of Britain 137
Battleship Potemkin 128
Baudelaire, Charles 486, 489
Bax, Arnold 194, 195, 210, 213, 215, 217, 246, 469
 ballet music 394
 chamber music 248–9; Fantasy-Sonata for harp and viola 248; Nonet 248; Piano Quartet 248; string quartets 249; Viola Sonata 248–9; violin sonatas 248
 choral music 411, 430–2; *Enchanted Summer* 411; 'Mater ora filium' 430; *To the Name Above Every Name* 411; *Walsinghame* 411; 'What is it like to be young and fair?' 437; 'This worldes joie' 430–2, 456
 film music 134
 orchestral music 198–203, 270; *The Garden of Fand* 199; *November Woods* 199; Fifth Symphony 202–3; First Symphony

199–201, 202, 207–8; Fourth Symphony 202; Second Symphony 200, 207–8; Seventh Symphony 202; Sixth Symphony 202; Third Symphony 200–2; Symphonic Variations 199; *Tintagel* 199
 piano music 266, 270–1; First Sonata 270; Fourth Sonata 271; Second Sonata 270–1; Third Sonata 271
 songs 469
Bax, Clifford 437
Bay City Rollers 90–1
Baylis, Lilian 394
BBC (British Broadcasting Corporation), 1, 4, 13, 16, 18, 24, 29–30, 32–5, 39, 48, 52–3, 62, 64, 83, 85, 158, 165, 167, 355, 357, 358, 367, 373, 375, 381, 398–401, 516, 523–4, 525
 Forces' Programme 73–4
 Radio 1 83
 Radio 2 83, 103
 Third Programme 525
BBC Dance Orchestra 58
BBC Jazz Club 64
BBC Radiophonic Workshop 144, 400–1
BBC Singers 403, 430, 522
BBC Wireless Chorus 522
Beat 99
beat poetry 35
Beatles 1, 35, 78, 80, 85, 86–90, 105, 136, 450
 see also Lennon, John; McCartney, Paul
Beats International 95–6
Beaumont, Geoffrey 165
Bechet, Sidney 58, 65
Bechstein Hall *see* Wigmore Hall
Beckett, Samuel 392, 445, 489
Bedford, David 428
 educational music 171–3
 instrumental music 317
Bee Gees 91
Beecham, Thomas 13, 42, 343–4, 524
Beecham Opera Company 343–4, 345, 349
Beethoven, Ludwig van 35, 37, 126, 132, 183, 185, 222–3, 259, 281, 283, 285, 288–9, 309, 407, 422, 423, 452, 478, 529
Beggar's Opera, The 111
Belfast 41
Bell, Clive 30–1
Bell, Graeme 74
'Bells of St Mary's, The' 69
Ben Hur 128, 137
Benjamin, Arthur
 film music 131
 operas 357–8
Benjamin, George 23, 340
 Antara 340; *Ringed by the Flat Horizon* 340; 'Upon silence' 490
Benjamin, Walter 37, 105
Bennett, Arnold 357
Bennett, Richard Rodney 27, 280, 491
 choral music: 'Out of your sleep' 465; *Five Carols* 465; *Sea Change* 439; *Spells* 408
 film music 137, 401, 315
 instrumental music 297, 299–300, 314–15
 jazz scores 315
 operas 374–5
 radio music 401
 songs 484–5, 489
Bennett, Rodney 410
Benslow Trust 147
Benson, A.C. 443
Benson, Ivy 68
Berberian, Cathy 491
Berg, Alban 2, 17, 21, 233, 242, 259–60, 298–9, 321, 359, 360, 377, 380–1, 383, 388, 485
Bergerac 144
Bergmann, Walter 524
Berio, Luciano 315, 392, 491
Berkeley, Lennox 299, 315, 482
 chamber music 253–4; Horn Trio 253–4; Oboe Quartet 253–4; Quintet for piano and wind 254; Second Quartet 253; String Trio 253; Viola Sonata 253; Violin Sonatina 253
 choral and church music 230; *Jonah* 410; 'The Lord is my shepherd' 455; Mass 421; *Missa brevis* 421; *Stabat mater* 421; 'The windhover' 438

operas 367, 368–9; *Castaway* 369; *A Dinner Engagement* 368; *Nelson* 230, 368; *Ruth* 368–9
orchestral music 230–2; Divertimento in B♭ 231; First Symphony 230–1; Flute Concerto 231; Fourth Symphony 231; Piano Concerto 231, 272; Second Symphony 231–2; Serenade for Strings 230; Sinfonietta 231; Third Symphony 231
 piano music 272–3; Concert Studies 272; Five Short Pieces 272; Six Preludes 272; Sonata 272–3
 songs 466, 477, 478–81
Berkeley, Michael 420, 483
Berkoff, Steven 386
Berlin, Irving 1, 2, 57, 108, 119, 464
Berlioz, Hector 155, 189, 198, 401
Bernard, James 135
Berne Convention 45
Berners, Lord 179, 214, 484
 ballets 356, 393–5; *Cupid and Psyche* 395; *Les sirènes* 395; *The Triumph of Neptune* 394, 395; *A Wedding Bouquet* 395
 film music 132, 134
 opera: *Le carrosse du Saint-Sacrement* 356
 orchestral music 206
 piano music 272
Bernstein, Leonard 408
Berry, Chuck 37, 87
Betjeman, John 484, 489
bhangra 3, 99, 157–8
Bible, settings of 368, 392, 405–6, 412, 417, 421, 426, 427–8, 445, 452, 459, 498
Bidgood, Harry 70–1
Big Ben 116
Big Parade, The 128
Bilk, Acker 77, 99
Billion Dollar Baby 137
Billy Liar 137
Bing Boys 109
Binge, Ronald 70
biography 505, 512
Birmingham 41, 77
 see also festivals, Birmingham Festival
Birmingham, University of 490, 509, 511
 Barber Institute 490, 526
Birmingham Conservatoire 510
Birmingham and Midland Institute School of Music 510
Birmingham Post 514–15
Birmingham Royal Ballet 396
Birth of a Nation 128
Birtwistle, Harrison 3, 21, 23, 25, 37, 315, 319, 337, 340, 341, 382–3, 430, 491, 491, 497, 511
 Antiphonies 327; band music 151; *Cantata* 497; *Carmen Arcadiae Mechanicae Perpetuum* 327; Chorales 325; *Down by the Greenwood Side* 385, 391; *Earth Dances* 327; *Endless Parade* 327; *The Fields of Sorrow* 497; *Gawain* 384, 385; *Grimethorpe Aria* 153, 325; *An Imaginary Landscape* 325–6; instrumental music 324–7; *The Mask of Orpheus* 384–5; *Melencolia I* 326, 327; *Meridian* 485; *Monodrama* 390, 391; *Monody for Corpus Christi* 497; music theatre 390–1; *Nenia: The Death of Orpheus* 497–8; *Nomos* 325, 327; operas 381, 384–5; *Prologue* 497; *Punch and Judy* 370, 384, 385; *Refrains and Choruses* 325; 'Ring a dumb carillon' 497; *Secret Theatre* 327; *Silbury Air* 327–8; *Songs by Myself* 497; *Tragoedia* 325–6; *The Triumph of Time* 326–7; *Verses* 325, 327; 'White and Light' 499
Bitter Sweet 113–15, 124
Blacher, Boris 281
Black, Ben 70
Blackall, A.K. 510
Black and White Rag 77–8
Blackboard Jungle, The 85, 136
'Black bottom (of the Swanee River)' 61
Blackburn, Thomas 442
Blackburn, Tony 83
Black Churches 164
blackface *see* minstrelsy

555

INDEX

Blackmail 129
black music and musicians 58, 61, 63, 65, 67–8, 74–5, 87, 97–9, 103, 150, 420
  see also African-Caribbean music; American (USA) and American influence; African-American music; jazz
Black Sabbath 88
Blackwell, Chris 105
Blake, Cyril 67–8
Blake, David 439
  instrumental music 297, 298–9
  operas 376
Blake, Howard 421
Blake, William 223, 394, 421, 439, 443, 445, 471, 472, 478, 488, 489
Blakey, Art 100
Blatchford, Robert 31
Bless the Bride 116
Bliss, Arthur 17, 30, 32, 48, 162, 179, 223, 233, 356, 405, 429, 439–42, 486–7; ballet music 206–7, 395, 396; *Adam Zero* 396; *Checkmate* 396, 397; *Miracle in the Gorbals* 396
  band music: *Kenilworth* 151
  chamber music 250–1; Clarinet Quintet 250; *Conversations* 250; early quartets 250; First Quartet 250–1; Oboe Quintet 250; Second Quartet 250–1; Viola Sonata 250
  choral music: 'Aubade' 437; *The Beatitudes* 421; 'Birthday song for a royal child' 439; 'Mar Porugues' 439; *Morning Heroes* 409; *Pastoral: Lie Strewn the White Flocks* 409; *Shield of Faith* 442; *The World Is Charged with the Grandeur of God* 441–2
  film music 134; *Men of Two Worlds* 134; *Things to Come* 130, 131
  operas 367; *Tobias and the Angel* 358
  orchestral music 206–7, 208; *Colour Symphony* 206; *Meditations on a Theme by John Blow* 207; *Music for Strings* 206; Piano Concerto 206, 219; Violin Concerto 206
  piano music 271
  solo vocal music 445; *Four Songs* 487; *A Knot of Riddles* 487; 'Madam Noy' 487; 'Rhapsody' 487, 488; 'Rout' 250, 487; *Serenade* 487; *Seven American Poems* 487; *Two Nursery Rhymes* 487; *The Women of Yueh* 487
Blitz 120
Blom, Eric 513, 515
Blowzabella 102
'Blue pipes of Pan' 117
blues 81, 85, 87, 95–6, 97, 101, 102, 116, 231, 288, 402, 412–13, 491
  acoustic 159
  see also rhythm 'n' blues
Blunden, Edmund 417, 437
Blyth, Alan 514
Board of Education 168
Boccaccio, Giovanni 368
'Bohemian rhapsody' 93
Bomb the Bass 95
Bond, Graham 88
boogie woogie 73, 78
Boosey, William 45–6, 69
Booth, Webster 70
Boptical Illusion 75–6
Born Free 137
Botsford, George 77–8
Botticelli, Sandro 417
Boughton, Rutland 344, 371, 524
  choral music 419
  operas 345–8, 349, 377, 385; *Alkestis* 348; Arthurian cycle 345–8, *Bethlehem* 346–7; *The Ever Young* 348; *The Immortal Hour* 345–7, 348; *The Queen of Cornwall* 348
Boulanger, Nadia 230, 478
Boulez, Pierre 18, 20, 22, 37, 312, 319, 320, 331, 334, 342, 382, 392
Boult, Adrian 16, 19
Bourgeois, Derek
  band music 151, 153
Bournemouth 246
Bovell, Dennis 205
Bowie, David 91

Bowlly, Al 62, 65, 66
Bowman, James 489, 528
Boyd, Joe 105
Boy Friend, The 119–20, 137
Boys of the Lough 102
Bradbury, Ernest 414, 515
Bradford 164
Bragg, Billy 101
Braham, Philip 117
Brahms, Johannes 12, 156, 179, 252, 265–6, 273, 332, 423, 452, 454, 467, 529
Bratton, J. W. 70
Bream, Julian 477, 525
Brecht, Bertolt 386
Breil, Joseph 128
Breitkopf & Härtel 521
Brett, Philip 359, 526
Breughel, Pieter 326
Brian, Havergal 16, 19, 198, 438
  operas 356
  orchestral music 202–5; 281; Eight Symphony 205; Fourth Symphony 204; Fifth Symphony 204; *Gothic Symphony* (no. 1) 204, 422; Second Symphony 204–5; *Sinfonia tragica* (no. 6) 204
Bric-à-brac 109
Bridge, Frank 13, 17, 19, 189, 192, 232–3, 245, 247, 261–2, 267, 484, 516
  chamber music 239–44, 268; *Divertimenti* 244; Fourth Quartet 243–4; *Noveletten* 240; Phantasie for piano trio 239–40; Phantasy for piano quartet 239–40; Piano Quintet 240; Piano Trio 242–3, 261; Rhapsody Trio 242–3, 261, 270; Second Quratet 240–1; string quartets 239; String Sextet 240; Third Quartet 17, 240–2, 244, 261; *Three Idylls* 240; Violin Sonata 243
  choral music: *A Prayer* 410
  opera: *The Christmas Rose* 355
  orchestral music 194–7; *Enter Spring* 194, 195–7; *Isabella* 194; *Oration* 194, 195–7, 242, 262; *Phantasm* 17, 197; *The Sea* 195; Suite for strings 194; Symphony for strings 194
  piano music 266, 268–70; *Dramatic Fantasia* 268; *A Fairy Tale Suite* 268; *Gargoyle* 270; 'Rosemary' 268; Sonata 268–70; *Three Sketches* 268
  songs 470
Bridge, Frederick 3, 511
Bridge, Joseph 511
Bridge on the River Kwai, The 135
Bridges, Robert 408, 417, 436, 442, 443
Bridson, D. Geoffrey 399, 400
Briggs, Anne 28, 101
Bright, Gerald *see* Grealdo
Brighter London 57
Bristol *see* Western Ballet Theatre
British Broadcasting Corporation *see* BBC
British Film Year 142
British National Opera Company 51, 343–4
Britishness 2–3
  see also Englishness
Britten, Benjamin 2, 15, 17, 18, 20–2, 28, 191, 230, 278–9, 285, 292, 324, 369, 378, 405, 408, 420, 428, 429, 433, 437, 451, 478, 490, 497, 512, 527
  ballet: *The Prince of the Pagodas* 366, 397–8
  chamber music 261–5; *Alla quartetto serioso* 262; Cello Sonata 264; Cello Suites 263–4; (early) String Quartet in D 262; First Quartet 262; *Lachrymae* 264; *Metamorphoses* 263; *Nocturnal* 263; (Phantasy) Oboe Quartet (op. 2) 197, 261–2; Phantasy Quintet 261; Quartettino 261; Second Quartet 262–4; *Sinfonietta* 232, 234, 261–2; string quartets 234, 262–4; Suite for harp 263; Suite for violin and piano 262; *Temporal Variations* 262; Third Quartet 263
  choral and church music 166, 419–20, 421, 431, 436, 443, 455–6, 460; *The Ballad of Little Musgrave and Lady Barnard* 404; *Ballad of Heroes* 419; *A Boy Was Born* 431, 436, 465; *Cantata academica* 420; *Cantata misericordium* 404; *A Ceremony of Carols* 444, 465; *Children's Crusade* 404, 444; *The Company of Heaven* 399; *Festival Te Deum* 421; *Five Flower Songs* 435–6; *Friday Afternoons* 444; *The Golden Vanity* 404; 'Hymn of St Columba' 456; *Hymn to St Cecilia* 431; *Jubilate Deo* 456; *Missa brevis* 460–2; 'The oxen' 465; *Psalm 150* 444; *Rejoice in the Lamb* 460–1; *Saint Nicolas* 404, 419, 421; *Spring Symphony* 419–20, 422–3; *Te Deum in C* 455–6; *War Requiem* 366, 409, 417, 419–20, 421, 422, 423–6, 489, 497; *Welcome Ode* 444; *The World of the Spirit* 399
  film music 131
  operas and church parables 235, 343, 344, 358–67, 373, 374, 377, 384, 400, 431; *Albert Herring* 362, 365, 374; *Billy Budd* 362–5, 367, 368; *The Burning Fiery Furnace* 366; *Curlew River* 366; *Death in Venice* 263, 265, 366–7, 397; *Gloriana* 363, 366, 368, 374; *Let's Make an Opera* (*The Little Sweep*) 362, 365; *A Midsummer Night's Dream* 362, 365–6; *Noye's Fludde* 363–4, 406, 427; *Owen Wingrave* 358, 366; *Paul Bunyan* 359, 365; *Peter Grimes* 2, 4, 234, 236, 263, 358–61, 362, 363, 366, 367, 370, 399, 497; *The Prodigal Son* 366; *The Rape of Lucretia* 360–2, 363, 367; *The Turn of the Screw* 363, 375
  orchestral music 232–7; Cello Symphony 234, 236–7, 279; *Diversions* 233–4; *Men of Goodwill* 400; *Mont Juic* 230; Prelude and Fugue for strings 234; Piano Concerto 234–5; *Scottish Ballad* 234; Sinfonia da requiem 235; Sonata for orchestra 236; Variations on a Theme of Frank Bridge 233–4, 399; Violin Concerto 197,235; *Young Person's Guide to the Orchestra* 234, 431
  organ music 277
  piano music 273–5; *Holiday Diary* 274; Introduction and Rondo Burlesca 274–5; *Mazurka elegiaca* 275; *Night-Piece* 274
  radio music 399–400
  solo vocal music 431, 480; *Canticle IV: Journey of the Magi* 489; *Canticle V* 477; folksong arrangements 474–5; *Our Hunting Fathers* 233, 472; *Phaedra* 485; songs and song cycles 466, 472–8
  broadcasting 32, 49, 123, 129, 239, 398, 522
  see also BBC; Classic FM; radio
Brodsky, Adolf 510
Broken Blossoms 137
Brontë, Charlotte 486
Brontë, Emily 399, 444
Brooke, Rupert 466, 469
Brooks, Shelton 108
Broones, Martin 117
Brown, Christopher 421
Brown, George Mackay 492–4
Brown, Joe 136
Brown, Howard Mayer 511
Browne, William Denis 469
Bruch, Max 180
Bruckner, Anton 281
Bryars, Gavin 318
  Homage to Vivier 318; *The Vespertine Park* 318; *The War in Heaven* 429
Buchanan, Jack 132
Buck, Percy 504, 511
Buckle, Richard 35
Buckley, Reginald 345, 347
buildings 40–1
Bull, John 323
Buller, John 389
Bullock, Ernest 457, 510
Bunyan, John 355, 400
Burgon, Geoffrey
  Mass 421; *Missa Brevis* 421; *Nunc Dimittis* 405; *Requiem* 405, 408, 421; *Revelations* 421; television music 144, 405
Burke, Joe 61
Burnaby, Davy 117
Burne-Jones, Edward 519
Burnett, Earl 65

556

INDEX

Burnett, Richard 529
Burns, Robert 472, 478
Burns, Tito 75
Burrows, Benjamin 469
Bush, Alan 23
  chamber music 258; *Dialectic* for string quartet 216, 258; Quartet in A minor 258; Three Concert Studies 258
  operas 371
  orchestral music 216–17; *The Byron Symphony* 418; 'Nottingham' Symphony (no. 2) 216; Piano Concerto 216–17, 418; Symphony in C (no. 1) 216; Violin Concerto 217
  vocal music 418–19, 438, 478
Bush, Geoffrey 238
  If the Cap Fits 370; Ozymndias' 438; songs 481–2
Bush, Kate 104
Busoni, Ferruccio 469
Butler, Martin 337, 340
Butlin's holiday camps 70
Butterworth, George 468, 469–70
Buxton 41
By Appointment 112
'By the fireside' 67
Bye, Antony 515, 517
Byfield, Jack 70
Byrd, William 430, 521, 522, 524

cabaret 117, 487
Caesar, Irving 67
Café de Paris 58, 67
Cage, John 21
Caird, George 510
Cairns, David 514
cakewalk 107, 413
California Ramblers 62
'call of life, The' 114
Calloway, Cab 64
Calvert, Leon 75
calypso 60, 97
Camargo Society 394
Cambridge University 62, 77, 340, 404–5, 469, 482, 503, 504, 509, 511, 521, 523, 527
  King's College 463, 521, 522
  St John's College 460
Cambridge University Musical Society 524
Campbell, James 67
Campion, Thomas 466
Canada 388
  Banff Music Centre 389
Canetti, Elias 381
Canning, Hugh 514
Cannon, Philip
  operas 370
  vocal music 421, 477
canon, art-music 28–9, 39
cantatas 403–30, 441–2, 444, 460, 465, 471–2, 478, 485, 488, 500
Canterbury Cathedral 371
Capell, Richard 514, 515
capitalism 24, 82, 84, 106
Captive Heart, The 134
'Cara mia' 78
Cardew, Cornelius 21–2, 23, 318, 374
Cardus, Neville 507–8, 514
Careless Rapture 110
Carey, Patrick 441
Carl Rosa Opera Company 358
Carless, Dorothy 67, 73
Carlisle, Elsie 68
carol singing 162
carols 434, 437, 442, 463–5
Carols for Choirs 464
Carnegie United Kingdom Trust 147, 258, 522
Carroll, Lewis 489
Carry On films 135–6
Carter, Benny 63, 67
Carter, Elliott 314, 327, 334, 341
Carter, Sydney 166
Carter, Tim 515
Carthy, Martin 101
Carus, Louis 510
Caruso, Enrico 28
Cary, Tristram 134–5, 312

Casken, John 24, 25
  'A gathering' 463; *Golem* 330, 385–7; *Ia Orana, Gauguin* 486; instrumental music 330
Castling, Harry 117
Catch Us If You Can 136
Cats 121–3
Cavalcade 117
Cavalli, Pietro 527
Celan, Paul 499
Celtic themes and inspiration 69, 199, 345, 346, 349, 385, 466, 481, 489
Chagrin, Francis 134
Challis, John 520
chamber music 33, 41, 161, 280–1, 238–65
Champagne Charlie 132
Champion, Harry 112
chapel music 145, 163–7
Chappell, Herbert 406
Chappell, William 349
Chariots of Fire 142
Charlot's 1925 Revue 110
'Chase me, Charlie!' 115
Chaucer, Geoffrey 348, 368, 414
Cheek-By-Jowl 122
Chekhov, Anton 368
'Cherokee' 75
Chester 408
  Mystery Play 363, 489
Chester, Betty 117
Chetham's School of Music 51
Chew, Geoffrey 37
Chichester 408, 455
Chieftains 102
Child, Harold 443
child prodigies 42
children, music for 158, 167, 403, 406, 444, 464
  children's concerts 32
  opera 362, 363–5, 373–4
  see also schools, music in; youth
children's songs and rhymes 155, 477
Childs, Gilbert 117
Chisholm, Erik 155
Chisholm, George 60, 72, 73
  and his Jive Five 73
choir directors 527–8
choirs and vocal ensembles 40, 175–6, 403–5, 406, 430
  a cappella folk groups 101
  amateur repertoire 154–5
  cathedral 447, 527
  chamber 403
  choral societies 145–9, 156, 171, 174, 403
  church 163–5, 171, 174, 406
    early music 521–3, 527–8
    male voice choirs and ensembles 148, 154, 444, 527
    school 168, 170–1, 406, 444
Chopin, Fryderyk 426
choral drama 345, 348, 371
choral music 402–65
choral songs 442–4
choral symphonies 422–3
chromaticism 180–1, 189, 217, 433, 457
  total 282, 439, 460; *see also* serialism and 12-note music
church music 40, 145, 147–8, 163–7, 174, 452–65
  Anglican 164–7, 404–5, 452–65
  chant, Anglican 180, 275
  evangelical 167
  Nonconformist 167, 457
  opera 363–5, 366, 372
  psalms, Genevan 167
  see also hymns; organ music
cinemas *see* film and film music
Circa 1500 528
Cirencester 324, 406
CLAP 392
Clapton, Eric 80, 88
Clare, John 427, 482, 484
Clark, Petula 86
Clarke, Rebecca
  chamber music 247–8
  songs 469–70
Clash 91

class structure and audiences 29–34, 37–8, 59, 77, 85, 104, 108, 148–9, 170, 174
  authentic working-class culture 74
Classic FM 4
Clements, Andrew 514, 515
Cleobury, Stephen 463
Clerkes of Oxenford 528
Cliff, Laddie 117
Clinton, Gordon 510
Club Eleven 75
Clutsam, George 515
Coal Face 131
Coastal Command 133
Coates, Albert
  operas 357
Coates, Eric 27, 69–70, 396
  Calling all Workers 70; *Dam Busters* march 165; 'The green hills o' Somerset' 69–70; 'Knightsbridge' March 70; *The Selfish Giant* 70; *The Three Bears* 70
Cobbett, W.W. 194, 238–40, 244–6, 248, 255, 261
Cockcroft, Robert 515
Cocker, Joe 97
Coe, Tony 99
Coffin, Hayden 111
Cohen, Harriet 270, 524
Cold War 36
Colditz Story, The 134
Cole, Gracie
Coleman, Edwin 358
Coleman, Ornette 100
Coleridge-Taylor, Samuel 45, 404
Colet Court 121
college 89, 90
colleges of music *see* music colleges
Colles, Henry C. 513, 514
Collier, Graham 100
Collingwood, Lawrance
  operas 357
Collins, Charles 109
Collins, Phil 103
Collins, Shirley 101
'Colonel Bogey' 151
colonial links 372–3
Colosseum 90
Coltrane, John 100
Colum, Padraic 466
Colyer, Ken 76
comedians 112, 132
comic opera *see* opera; operetta
comic songs and singers 108, 110, 112, 115, 119
  see also music hall; variety; vaudeville
commercial music 1, 4, 28, 402, 447
  see also music industry
commissions 281, 290, 337, 358, 360, 375, 377, 393–4, 400, 406, 437–8, 444, 450, 460, 463, 489, 502
commodification of culture 27–38, 84, 104–6
Communards 93
Communism 347, 371
  Party membership 74
community music and singing 32, 161–3
compact discs 529
competitions 157, 175, 404
  test-pieces 151, 152–4
  see also festivals; Leeds, Piano Competition
composers, conditions for 44–6
Composers Ensemble 499–500
composers in residence 404
composers in music 95, 105, 312–13
concept albums 89–90
concert programming 29
conductors 42, 51, 357, 524, 527
congregational music 145, 163–7, 365, 406, 443, 464
Congregationalism 167
Connelly, Reginald 67
Connolly, Justin
  Antiphonies 315
Conrad, Joseph 373, 375
conscientious objection 2
conservatism 9, 12, 16–17, 22, 180, 279, 289–91, 342, 371
  see also Thatcherism
conservatoires *see* music colleges
Consort of Musicke 528

557

INDEX

consumerism 4–5, 32, 82, 84, 104, 106
  see also commodification of culture
Contact 318
contemporary music 529
  folk music 159
Conversation Piece 114–15
Conway, Russ 78
Cook, Nicholas 517
Cook, Will Marion 68, 107
Cook, the Thief, His Wife and Her Lover, The 142–3
Cooke, Arnold 230
  operas 371–2
Cooke, Deryck 506, 513, 516
Coolidge, Elizabeth Sprague 240, 247
Cooper, Martin 514, 515
Co-optimists 117
co-option 80
Copland, Aaron 296, 499
Cooper family 101
copyright 45–6
Copyright Act 46
Corder, Frederick 197–8, 202
Corder, Henrietta 198
Cornwall 162, 344–5, 369, 370, 377
Corries 101
Cosmo Club 68
Cossack Club 67
Costello, Elvis 103
Cotton, Billy 59, 67, 103
Country Dance Tunes 350, 352
country music 85, 87, 103
  groups 157
  songs 162
Convent Garden see Royal Ballet; Royal Opera House
Coventry Carol 465
Coventry Cathedral 419, 459
Coverdale, Miles 459
Coward, Henry 146
Coward, Noël 110, 112–15, 116, 117, 119, 120, 122, 124
Cowie, Edward
  instrumental music 329
Cox, Frederick 510
Crabbe, George 359,435
Craig, Gordon 524
Crane River Jazz Band 74
Cream 80, 88
creative music movement 168
'Crescendo' 113
Crest of the Wave 110
Crichton, Ronald 514
critical theory 4
criticism 503–10, 513–16
composer-critics 508–9
  see also jazz, criticism; journals; newspapers; rock music, criticism
Crombie, Tony 75
crooners 30, 65, 116
Crosse, Gordon 21
Changes 408, 423; instrumental music 315; Memories of Morning: Night 485–6; operas 375–6; Verses in memoriam David Munrow 490; A Wake Again 490
Crossman, Joe 72
crossovers 27, 33, 103–4, 317, 337, 403, 450
Crozier, Eric 362, 368, 421
Cry Freedom 144
CSE curriculum 36
cue sheets 126, 128
cultural issues 79, 104–6, 342, 465–6
counterculture 83, 90, 520
cultural revolution 84
  high, low and middlebrow culture 27–38, 39, 65
  popular culture 487
Culture, Smiley 98
Culture Club 93
cummings, e. e. 439, 484, 489
Cundell, Edric 510
Cunneen, Paddy 122
Cure 92
Curse of Frankenstein, The 135
Curse of the Werewolf 135
Cynewulf 421
Czibulka, Alphons 127

dada 91
Daily Express 162–3
Daily Mail 58, 507
Daily, Telegraph 514
Dalby, Martin
  instrumental music 316
Dale, Benjamin 198
  chamber music 247
Dali, Salvador 484
Dallapiccola, Luigi 207, 296, 392
Damned 91
dance, contemporary 398
dance halls 59
'Dance, little lady' 113
dance music 31, 33, 57–78, 84–5, 91, 95–7, 100, 102, 103, 116, 118, 447, 450
  see also bands, dance; folk music, dance; ritual dance
dances
  popular 59–60, 113–14, 323
  traditional 102
dance-songs 93
Dancing Years, The 110–13
Dangerous Moonlight 132–3
Daniels, Joe 71
Dankworth, John 27, 75, 77, 99–100
  film music 137
Dante, Alighieri 340
Dark Side of the Moon, The 90
Darke, Harold 523
Darling 137
Dart, R. Thurston 511, 519, 525–6
Dartington Summer School 51
Darwin, Charles 24
Dave Clark Five 86, 136
David, Worton 108
Davie, Cedric Thorpe 481
Davies, Cyril 88
Davies, Meredith 510
Davies, Peter Maxwell 15, 21–3, 280, 310, 317, 327, 337, 341, 382–3, 406, 408, 423, 439, 491, 492, 529
Alma Redemptoris mater 323; Anakreontika 492; Antechrist 321; Ave maris stella 319–20, 324; 'The blind fiddler' 492; Blind Man's Buff 492; carols and motets 465; Eight Songs for a Mad King 390–1; 'Fiddlers at the wedding' 492; 'Epitaph' 492; film music 137; First Symphony 22, 323; First Taverner Fantasia 323; Five Pieces for Piano 319; From Stone to Thorn 492–5; Hymn to St Magnus 320, 324, 492; Hymnos 323; Image, Reflection, Shadow 324; instrumental music 319–24; Leopardi Fragments 492; The Lighthouse 384; The Martyrdom of St Magnus 383–4; The Medium 491, 493–7; Miss Donnithorne's Maggot 391; music theatre 390–1; 'My Lady Lothian's lilt' 492; O magnum mysterium 306; operas 343, 381, 383–4; Prolation 319, 320, 321; Psalm 124 324; Revelation and Fall 323, 390–1, 491, 492; Ricercar and Doubles 323; St Michael Sonata 320; St Thomas Wake 323; Second Taverner Fantasia 321–4; Seven In Nomine 321, 323; Strathclyde Concertos 324; string Quartet 323; symphonies 321; Taverner 321, 383; Tenebrae Super Gesualdo 492; Trumpet Concerto 324; Trumpet Sonata 319; Two Pavans 323; Winterfold 492; Worldes Blis 321–4
Davies, (Henry) Walford 32
Davies, W.H. 466
Davis, Carl 27, 137
Davis, Colin 37
Davis, Miles 58
Dawson, Peter 69
Day Lewis, Cecil 438, 439, 443
de la Mare, Walter 410, 466, 469, 471, 472, 480
de Lloyd, David 376
de Valois, Ninette 394, 396
Dean, Winton 517
Deane, Basil 511
Dearmer, Percy 165, 167
Debussy, Claude 12, 13, 17, 179, 180, 182, 188, 189, 191, 192, 195, 199, 246, 265, 318, 345, 346, 413

Decca Debts 62
Deep Purple 88
degrees and diplomas 41, 43, 52
  music graduates 50
Dehn, Paul 368–9
Delius, Frederick 3, 12, 14, 128, 137, 180, 195, 199, 215, 252, 329, 344, 346, 417, 470
  choral music; Appalachia 411; Requiem 411; Song of the High Hills 411
Deller, Alfred 525, 527
Deller Consort 527
demographics 52
Dench, Chris 24, 334
Dene, Terry 86
Denny Sandy 101
Dent, Edward J. 469, 504–5, 506, 511, 523, 524–5, 526
Denyer, Frank 489
Depeche Mode 93
Depression, the 47, 132
Derby 157
Derek B 95
Derrida, Jacques 334
descants 165
Desert Victory 134
DeSylva, Brown and Henderson 61
Deutsch, Otto 509
Devils, The 137
Diack, Michael 155
Diaghilev, Serge 208, 393
Diamonds Are Forever 137–41
Diary for Timothy, A
diatonicism
Dickens, Charles
Dickinson, Emily
Dickinson, Meriel
Dickinson, Peter
  concertos 317; Four Poems of Alan Porter 489; Larkin's Jazz 489; 'Late afternoon in November' 438; Martin of Tours 442; Mass of the Apocalypse 425–6; A Memory of David Munrow 490; Outcry 426–7; Stevie's Tunes 484; Surrealist Landscape 484; The Unicorns 485
Dickson, Dorothy
Dieren, Bernard van
  Chinese Symphony 422; string quartets 249–50; The Tailor 356
digital technology 144
Dillon, James 24, 334–5
d'Indy, Vincent 525
Dinner and Dance 72–3
Dire Straits 103
disc jockeys 33, 83, 95
discos and disco music 49, 85, 91, 93, 95, 97, 157, 402, 447
'Do they know it's Christmas' 93
Dr No 137
Dr Terror's House of Horrors 135
Dolmetsch family 524
  Arnold 519–21, 523, 526
  Carl 524
domestic music 40, 145, 160–1, 174
Don Porto and His Novelty Accordions 70–1
Donegan, Lonnie 85
Donington, Robert 520
Donizetti, Gaetano 343, 370
Donne, John 472, 489
Donnellan, Declan 122
Donovan 90
'Don't cry for me, Argentina' 122
'Don't dilly dally on the way' 109
'Don't have any more, Mrs Moore' 117
Dorchester Hotel 67, 72
Douglas, Craig 136
Dowland, John 263
Dowson, Ernest 466, 467
Draughtsman's Contract, The 142
Drew, David 515
Dring, Madeleine 484
Driver, Paul 514
Drowning By Numbers 142
Dryden, John 438
du Maurier, Daphne 369
du Pré, Jacqueline 51
dub 97
'Dub be good to me' 95–7
dub poets 98

558

INDEX

Dufay, Guillaume 526
Dunbar, Rudolph 67
Dunbar, William 414
Duncan, Ronald 360–2
Dunhill, Thomas 112
Dunsby, Jonathan 515
Dunstable, John 522
Duran Duran 93
Durham University 509, 511
Dykes, John Bacchus 189
Dylan, Bob 90
Dyson, George 179–80, 188, 510
  choral and church music 413–16; 420, 459;
    Agincourt 414; *The Canterbury Pilgrims*
    408, 414–15; *In Honour of the City* 414;
    Jubilate Deo 459; *Nebuchadnezzar* 414–
    15; *Quo vadis?* 408, 416; 'Song for a
    festival' 443

Ealing Film Studios 132, 135
early music 1, 166–7, 278, 323, 404, 489–90,
    500, 519–29
  antiquarianism 519, 522, 523
  archaism 135, 227, 277, 374, 422, 431,
    433–4, 452, 454, 466–7
  authenticity 51, 529
  choral revival 521–3
  Elizabethan revival 524; *see also* Elizabethan
    poetry, settings of
  English fantasias 194, 226; *see also* Cobbett,
    W.W.
  glees 31, 433
  renaissance motets 226, 439, 454
  Tudor music 181–2, 226, 285, 288, 383, 465,
    521–3, 528
  see also folk music; madrigals and madriga-
    lian techniques; mediaeval techniques;
    motets; neoclassicism
Early Music 515, 529
Early Music Centre 529
Early Music Consort of London 528
Early Opera Project 527
Easdale, Brian 134
easy listening 38, 68, 103
eclecticism 33
economic factors 28, 36, 39–53, 58–9, 64, 74,
    76–7, 79, 80, 83–4, 85, 92–3, 104, 106, 142,
    147, 157–8, 160, 174, 406, 472
  charities 162
  industrialization 28–9
Edinburgh 74
  University 506, 511
Edison films 126
Edmunds, Christopher 510
education 4, 32–3, 36–7, 45, 161, 175, 313, 403,
    406
  correspondence courses 175
  early music 529
  higher 36
  master classes 51
  music for self-tuition 43, 159–60
  music teachers 36, 41, 42–4, 47–8, 51, 160,
    168; peripatetic 51
  teaching methods 32
  see also Associated Board examinations; music
    colleges; Rural Music Schools; schools,
    music in; universities
Education Act (1870) 403
Education Act (1944) 84
Edwards, Frederick G. 515
Edwardian age 33, 40, 117
Eisenstein, Sergei 129
Eisler, Hanns 298
eisteddfods 175, 376
Electric Light Orchestra 90
Electric Phoenix 447, 450
electro-acoustic music 6, 23, 153, 312–13, 340,
    374, 385, 400–1, 444–51
electronic instruments 157, 161, 337
electronics in rock music 83, 88, 89–90, 91, 105
  in folk 101, 102
  in musical theatre 124; *see also* amplification
  sampling 105
electro-pop 93
Elephant Boy 131
' 'Leven thirty Saturday night' 65
Elgar, Edward 2, 3, 12–13, 27–8, 39, 128, 137,
    181–2, 189, 192, 198, 203, 296, 208, 213,
    233, 265, 273, 281, 333, 414–15, 429, 437,
    454, 457, 511, 512
  band music: *Severn Suite* 151
  chamber music: Piano Quintet 265; String
    Quartet 240
  choral music 155, 156, 407; *The Apostles* 407;
    Coronation Ode 443; *The Dream of
    Gerontius* 407, 420; *The Kingdom* 407;
    The Music Makers 407
  opera: *The Spanish Lady* 344
  orchestral music: Cello Concerto 298; *Pomp
    and Circumstance* March no. 1 443
Elguera, Amalia 374
Elias, Brian 341
  The Judas Tree 398; 'Peroration' 491
Eliot, George 373
Eliot, T.S. 31, 288, 442, 445, 462, 489
élite tradition 1
élitism 23, 29–36, 39, 41, 174
Elizabeth II 363, 437
Elizabethan poetry, settings of 466–7, 481–2
Elizalde, Fred 61, 62, 63, 65, 72, 77
Ellington, Duke 61, 63–7
Ellington, Ray 68
Ellis, Benedict 464
Ellis, Mary 112
Ellis, Osian 477
Ellis, Vivian 110, 115–16
Ellis Roberts, Richard 399
Embassy Club 57
Emerson, Ralph Waldo 438, 452, 459
Emerson Lake and Palmer 90
Emmerson, Simon 312
Emperors of Swing 67, 73
Empire Theatre Orchestra 125
Empson, William 482
English Bach Festival 527
English Baroque Soloists 528
English Concert 528
English Folk Dance and Song Society (EFDSS)
  158, 159, 477
English language 1, 3, 96, 402
  see also opera, in English
English Madrigal School 522
English Music Theatre Company 388
English musical renaissance 179
English National Opera (ENO) 376, 388, 389
English Opera Group 358, 360, 368, 374, 388,
    527
English School of Lutenist Song-Writers 522
English Singers 430, 522, 524
English Song Award 484
Englishness 3, 179–80, 242
  see also Britishness
Enna, August 128
Eno, Brian 27, 103–4
ENSA (Entertainments National Service Associa-
    tion) 68, 73
Ernst, Max 484
eroticism 86, 88, 412, 472
Escape Me Never 131
establishment, the, 24, 48, 279, 447, 519
ecclesiastical 522
  see also institutions
L'Estro Armonico 528–9
ethnic minority musics (in the UK) 157–8
ethnic musics (worldwide) 330, 334, 402
ethnomusicology and ethnomusicologists 28,
    36
Eton College 77
Euripides 348, 389
Europe and Europeans 100, 285, 319, 329, 331,
    342, 358
  central 111, 386, 509
  eastern 158, 279, 489, 503; choirs 442–3
  refugees from Europe 294–5, 372, 400, 524
  see also operetta; Second Viennese School
Eurythmics 93
Evans, Edwin (i) 507
Evans, Edwin (ii) 16, 47, 244, 349, 507
Evans, Peter 512
Everley Brothers 87
'Everybody's doing it!' 108, 119
Everything Is Rhythm 132
Evita 121–2
exam systems 43, 175
  see also Associated Board examinations
experimental music 21–2, 318

expressionism 17–19, 21, 25, 323–4, 381, 386,
    423, 478, 485, 487, 491
Expresso Bongo 136

Fairport Convention 101–2
Falkner, Keith 510
Fall 92
Falmouth Opera Singers 155
Family 90
Fanshawe, David 425
Far from the Madding Crowd 137
Farman, Ambroise 69
Farncombe, Charles 526
Farnon, Robert 144
Farrant, Richard 522
Farrar, Ernest 268, 469
Farrell, T.R. 162
Fascinating Aida 122
Fauré, Gabriel 156, 195, 230, 246, 265, 405
Fawkes, Wally 74
Fayrfax, Robert 522
Fearon, Alan 137
Feather, Leonard 67, 73, 75–6
Featherstonhaugh, Buddy 64
Fellowes, Edmund 522, 523, 525
Felsenstein, Walter 390
feminism 4
Fenton, George 144
Ferguson, Howard 469
  chamber music 252–3; First Violin Sonata
    252, 273; Octet 252–3
  piano music 273
  vocal music: *Amore languor* 411; *Discovery*
    481; *Dream of the Rood* 411
Ferneyhough, Brian 23–5, 330–2, 334, 337,
    402–3, 422, 446
  Carceri d'invenzioni 25, 331; *Cassandra's Dream
    Song* 331; *Firecycle Beta* 331; *Four Minia-
    tures* 331; *Missa brevis* 421, 446; Second
    String Quartet 331–2; *Sonatas* 331;
    Sonatina 331; *La terre est un homme* 331;
    Time and Motion Study I 331; *Time and
    Motion Study II* 446; *Transit* 331, 446;
    Unity Capsule 331
Ferrier, Kathleen 485
Ferry, Bryan 117
Festival of Britain 48, 68, 355, 362, 372, 443,
    523
festivals 175, 406–8, 460, 529
  Aldeburgh Festival 235, 263, 368, 373, 374
  Batignano Festival 389
  Birmingham Festival 407
  Cheltenham Festival 375
  competitive festivals 32
  Festival of Nine Lessons and Carols 463
  Hoffnung festivals 405
  Leeds Festival 407, 408–9, 410, 412
  Leith Hill Festival 441
  Norwich Festival 407
  Petersfield Festival 414
  St Magnus Festival 337
  Three Choirs Festival 405, 407–8, 410, 414–
    15, 442, 485
  Wexford Festival Opera 375
Fields, Gracie 70, 116–17, 132
Fight for Right 443
Filipotto and Ariotto Tango Band 59
film and film music 23, 46–7, 59, 79, 85, 93,
    111, 116, 125–43, 148–9, 303, 337, 349,
    363, 367, 374–5, 399, 404, 414, 524, 528
  background music 49; and source music
    134, 137, 143
  biopics 137
  cinemas 47, 59
  documentary films 131–2
  feature films 131, 134–5, 137–42, 524
  horror films 135
  intertitles 129
  silent films 40, 46–7, 125–9, 130, 137, 142
  sound films (talkies) 47, 129–31
  theory 129, 130, 131
  film musicals 132, 136, 137
Financial Times 514, 516
Fings Aint Wot They Used to Be 120
Finnissy, Michael 23, 24, 337
  instrumental music 334, 336
  music theatre 392
  vocal music 443

559

INDEX

Finzi, Gerald 412, 413, 429, 469, 483
  chamber music 252
  choral and church music 417, 436–7, 441, 459; *For St Cecilia* 417; 'God is gone up' 459; *In terra pax* 417; *Intimations of Immortality* 407, 408, 415, 416–17; 'Lo, the full, final sacrifice' 442, 459; *Magnificat* 456; *Requiem da camera* 469; *Seven Poems of Robert Bridges* 436–7; 'White-flowering days' 437
  orchestral music 229–30
  solo vocal music 229, 437, 466–7, 471–4; *Dies natalis* 408, 472, 478 485; Hardy songs 471–3, 477; *Let Us Garlands Bring* 467
Finzi, Joy 456
Firbank, Ronald 119
Fires of London 280, 492, 493
Firman, Bert 61, 63
Fischer-Dieskau, Dietrich 474
Fitkin, Graham 25, 104
FitzGerald, Edward 408, 429
Fitzgerald, Ella 79
Flanders, Michael 406
Flanders and Swann 119
Fleet Street Choir 522
Fleetwood Mac 103
Fleming, Marjory 484
Fletcher, Percy 151
Fletcher, Phineas 441
floorsingers 159
'Flower of Scotland' 101
flower power 2, 379
Fo, Dario 392
Foggin, Myers 510
'Fold your wings' 111
folk music 34, 35, 82, 89, 97, 101–2, 103, 105, 157–9, 175, 334, 402, 403, 425
  clubs 101, 159
  contemporary 90, 101
  dance 158, 168, 174, 412
  fiddling 102, 158
  folk-blues 85
  folk-rock 90, 101–2, 105, 157
  folksong 2, 4, 31, 153, 154–5, 166–7, 171, 180–1, 189, 215, 247, 251, 318, 349–53, 355, 420, 434, 442–3, 474–7, 480–1, 487, 508
  groups 101, 157–8, 487
  pipers 102
  see also 'Greensleeves'; Hebridean songs; national songs; traditional music
folk revival
  first 442, 465, 468, 469
  second 101–2, 477
folklore and folkloric styles 86–7, 113, 117, 284, 302, 376–9, 384, 464, 489, 492
  see also mummer' plays; mediaeval morality plays
Folk-Songs for Choirs 442
Follies 122
Follow a Star 116
Fonteyn, Margot 395
football and rugby matches, music at 3, 145, 162–3
Forbes, Robert 510
Forbes, Sebastian 463
Forman, Denis 50
formalism 517
Formby, George 71, 132
Forster, E.M. 362
Forsythe, Reginald 67
Fortner, Wolfgang 207, 296
Fortune, Nigel 515
49th Parallel 133, 443
Foss, Hubert 522
Foulds, John 13, 411
400 Club 67
Fox, Roy
Fox Strangways, A.H. 515
France 11, 44, 50, 53, 358, 382, 471, 519, 525
  literature 472, 480, 484
  Paris 107, 108, 122, 356, 397, 400
  see also IRCAM; SACEM
Franco-Russian style 2, 393–4, 414, 507
Frankel, Benjamin
  film music 135
  symphonies 295–6
Frankie Goes to Hollywood 93

Fraser-Simson, Harold 111
Freddy and the Dreamers 86
French music, influence of 115, 230, 255, 265, 272, 300, 341, 368–9, 395, 404, 467, 478, 486
Fretwork 490, 528
Fricker, Peter Racine 237–8, 284–5
  chamber music 284; symphonies 284–5; 'The tomb of St Eulalia' 489; *The Vision of Judgement* 421
Frog Chorus 80
Fry, Christopher 437, 444
Fuller Maitland, J.A. 514
Functional Analysis (FA) 511–12
funk 85, 97, 101, 402
Furber, Douglas 69
Fury, Billy 86, 136
Future's in the Air, The 131
Futurism 131, 487

Gabriel, Peter 103
Gabrieli, Giovanni 441
Gaelic music 101, 330
  small harp 175
  dance tunes 71
Galpin, Francis William 522
Gance, Abel 137
Gandhi 142, 144
Garbarek, Jan 100
Garden of Weed 67
Gardiner, Henry Balfour 410–11, 455
Gardiner, John Eliot 527
Gardner, John
  Mass in D 425–6; 'O clap your hands' 456
Garland for the Queen, A 437
'Gasman cometh, The' 119
Gaumont-British Studios 129
Gay, John 111
Gay, Noel 116
Gay Deceivers 117
gays 4, 481
gay liberation 2
  see also homosexuality
GCSE curriculum 36–7, 169
Gebrauchsmusik 255, 372
gender issues 4, 42, 91, 104, 149, 157, 163, 174, 491
  see also women and music
General Strike 347
Genesis 90
Gentle Fire 317
George Webb's Dixielanders 74, 77, 157
Georgian poets 465–6, 482
Geraldo (Gerald Bright) 59, 68, 70, 73, 75
Gerard, Teddie 117
Gerhard, Roberto 280, 314, 321, 324–5
  ballet: *Don Quixote* 397
  instrumental music 294, 300–2, 303; *Concert for Eight* 301–2; Concerto for Orchestra 302; First Symphony 300; Fourth Symphony 302; *Gemini* 302; *Leo* 302; *Libra* 302; Second Quartet 301; Second Symphony 300–1; Third Symphony 301, 312
  opera: *The Duenna* 372, 397
  radio music 400
  vocal music: *The Akond of Swat* 488–9
German music, influence of 12, 265, 341, 357, 389–90, 404, 482
German bands 57
  New German School 198
  see also Austro-German tradition
Germany 11, 13, 53, 168, 331, 343, 344–5, 358–9, 371–2, 382–3, 521, 522, 525
  Bayreuth 378
  Berlin 15, 108, 115–16, 371–2, 381
  Cologne 393, 400
  Darmstadt 280
  Hamburg 381
  Leipzig 344, 371, 408
  Munich 357
  Weimar 371
Gerry and the Pacemakers 86
Gershwin, George 75, 116, 480
Gibbons, Orlando 167, 522, 524
Gibbs Cecil Armstrong
  The Blue Peter 112; *The Highwayman* 407; *Odysseus* 416–17; *A Saviour-Born* 464; songs

466, 471; 'While the shepherds were watching' 464
Gibbs, Mike 100
Gideon, Melville 110, 117
Gilbert, Anthony 319, 492
Gilbert, Olive 112
Gilbert and Sullivan 155, 176
Gilliat, Sidney 369
Gillespie, Dizzy 75
Ginsborg, Jane 491
Girl Who Came to Supper, The 115
Gissing, George 45
Glamorous Night 110–11
Glasgow 103, 377
  see also Royal Scottish Academy of Music and Drama
Glasgow Grand Opera Society 155
Glasgow Orpheus Choir 154
Glass, Philip 103–4
Glastonbury Festival 344, 346–8, 524
Glock, William 15, 18, 19, 34, 39, 515
Gloucester *see* festivals, Three Choirs
Gluck, Christoph 155, 525, 527
Glyndebourne Festival Opera 51, 360, 375, 388, 526–7
'Gnu, The' 119
Goble, Robert 521
Goehr, Alexander 313, 319, 321, 340, 382–3, 511
  instrumental music 306–10
  operas and music theatre 309, 383, 390–1, 485
  vocal music 309, 429, 485
Goehr, Walter 19, 134, 400, 524
Gogol, Nikolai 381
Gold, Harry 74
Goldschmidt, Berthold 372
Gonella, Nat 66–7, 71–3
Goodall, Howard 122
Goodman, Benny 72
Goodman, Lord 36
Goodwin, Ron 137
Goodwin and Tabb 128
Goossens, Eugene 128, 179
  chamber music 246–7
  choral music; *The Apocalypse* 410, 428; *Silence* 428
  operas 357
Gordon, Gavin 112, 369
gospel music 97, 164, 337, 413, 494
Gothic Voices 528
Gough, Hugh 521
Gough Matthews, Michael 510
Gounod, Charles 70, 455
Gow, David 438
Gowers, Patrick 144
Gowrie, Lord 50
GPO Film Unit 131, 399
Grace, Harvey 515
Grainer, Ron 120, 144
Grainger, Percy 13, 334, 468, 524
  folksong arrangements 442, 474–6, 487–8
Gramophone, The 64
gramophones 40, 46, 148, 160
Granados, Enrique 372
Grange, Philip 278
  instrumental music 341
  music theatre 393
Grantham, Bill 65
Graves, Robert 335, 466, 482–3
Gray, Cecil 179–80, 206, 246, 249, 272, 508
  operas 356–7
Grayson, Barrie 15
Great Expectations 134
Greed 137
Greek literature 378, 384–5, 425, 480, 492, 497
  see also Aeschylus; Aristophanes; Euripides; Homer
Green, John 62
Greenaway, Peter 23, 142
Greene, Graham 373
Greenfield, Edward 514
Greenhalgh, Herbert 69
'Greensleeves' 135, 442
Greenwood, John 131
Greer, David 511
Gregorian chant (plainsong) 21, 384, 412, 428, 494

INDEX

Gregorian chant (*cont'd*)
  Dies irae 413
Gregson, Edward 151–3
greyhound racing 129
Grieg, Edvard 180
Grierson, John 131
Griffith, D.W. 128, 137
Griffiths, Paul 514
Griller Quartet 238
Grove, George 513
Groves, Charles 37
Grove's Dictionary of Music and Musicians 513–14, 518
Guardian see *Manchester Guardian*
Guest, George 527
Guildhall School of Music and Drama 375, 510, 529
Guiney, Louise Imogen 465
guitarists and their techniques 88, 91, 103, 175, 477
Gulbenkian Foundation reports 52
Gundry, Inglis
  operas 371–2
Gunning, Christopher 135, 144
Gurney, Ivor 466, 469
Guy, Barry 100
Guys and Dolls 116

Hass, Karl 524
Hacker, Alan 497
Hadley, Patrick 411, 465, 469, 477, 488, 511
Hadow, W.H. 30, 503
Hahn, Reynaldo 115
Hale, Binnie 115
Haley, Bill 85
  and the Comets 136
Half a Sixpence 120
Hall, Adelaide 67
Hall, Henry 33, 58, 59, 67, 70, 132
Hall, Marie 44
Hall, Richard 382
Hallé Orchestra 42
Hamilton, Iain 237, 319, 377
  choral music 421
  instrumental music 303, 304, 306
  operas 374–5
Hamlet 134
Hammer Film Studios 135
Hammond, John 74
handbell ringing 145, 149
Handel, George Friederic 45, 155–6, 164, 406, 411
  opera revival 524–5, 526–7
Handel Opera Society 526
Hanover Band 528–9
'Handsworth Revolution' 98–9
Hard Day's Night, A 136
Hardy, Thomas 348, 465, 466, 471–2
Harewood, Earl of 515
Harlan, Peter 521
Harlem Knights 67
Harlem Symphony, A 63
harmonic principles 180
Harper, Edward 408
Harrell, Lynn 510
Harriott, Joe 99
Harris, Albert 66
Harris, Rolf 77
Harris, William 407, 455
Harrison, Jonty 312
Harrison, Julius 407, 421
Hartmann, Karl 207
Harty, Hamilton 30, 409
Harvey, Jonathan 10–11, 22, 23, 24, 25–6, 306, 310–13, 319, 427, 445, 461–3
  Benedictus 310; *Blaki* 313; 'Carol' 465; *Chaconne on Iam dulcis amica* 310; 'The dove descending' 462–3; 'I love the Lord' 462; *Inner Light* trilogy 311–12, 445–6; *Ludus amoris* 408; *Madonna of Winter and Spring, The* 313; *Mortuos plango, vivos voco* 313; *Persephone Dream* 311–12; *Resurrection* 408; *On Vision* 311
Haslemere 521
  Festival 524, 529
Hassall, Christopher 368
Hatch, Tony 144

Hatfield, John 439
Hatfield Broad Oak 522
Hausmusik 529
Havergal, Henry 510
Hawkins, Coleman 64–5, 67, 73
Haydn, Franz Joseph 65, 156, 203, 204, 258, 283
Hayes, Tubby 99
Hazlehurst, Ronnie 144
Head, Michael 464, 466
Heath, Edward 439
Heath, Ted 77
heavy metal 88, 104, 405
Hebridean songs 69, 346, 349
Hedges, Anthony 438
Heera 157–8
Heisenberg, Werner Karl 24
Help! 136
Helpmann, Robert 395, 396
Hely-Hutchinson, Victor 511
Heminway, Maggie 485
Henderson, Gavin 510
Henderson, Ray 67
Henderson, Robert 514
Hendrix, Jimi 88, 90
Heneker, David 120
Henley, W.H. 469
Henry V 130, 134, 135
Henze, Hans Werner 20
Heralds of Swing 72
Herbert, A.P. 112, 116
Herbert, George 442, 460, 470
Hereford see festivals, Three Choirs
heritage industry 52
Herman's Hermits 86
Herrick, Robert 467, 480, 482
Hertfordshire 147
Heseltine, Philip see Warlock, Peter
Hess, Nigel 144
Heyworth, Peter 515
Hicks, Seymour 108
Hildebert of Lavardin 463
Hill, Granville 514
Hilliard Ensemble 527
Hindemith, Paul 17, 208, 213, 217, 219, 230, 253, 255, 284, 289–91, 372, 383, 460
hip-hop 97
Hipkins, A.J. 520
Hired Man, The 122
Hirst, Linda 491
historiography 4, 503, 509, 513
History of Music in Sound 525
Hitchcock, Alfred 129
Hobbs, Chris 318
Hoddinott, Alun 292
  instrumental music 290–1; *Job* 421; operas 376; *Six Welsh Folk-Songs* 481
Hogarth, William 396
Hoggart, Richard 34
Hogwood, Christopher 528
Holbrooke, Joseph 179, 198, 371
  operas 345, 385
Hold, Trevor 482
Hölderlin, Johann 472
Holiday, Billie 117
Hollies 87
Hollins, Alfred 276
Holloway, Robin 21–2, 24, 337
  'Ah fading joy' 438; *Clarissa* 388; *Five Little Songs About Death* 483; *From High Windows* 489; *Georgian Songs* 482; *He-She-Together* 439; instrumental music 331–4; *Lights Out* 482; songs 482, 483; *Wherever We May Be* 482
Holloway, Stanley 117
Holly, Buddy 87
Hollywood see America and American influence
Holst, Gustav 2, 13–14, 179–81, 194, 195, 206, 207, 228, 234, 239, 329, 408, 412, 428, 429, 456, 461–2, 468
  band music: *Moorside Suite* 151
  chamber music 246
  choral and church music; *Choral Fantasia* 408; *Choral Hymns from the Rig Veda* 442; *Choral Symphony* 408, 412; *Dirge for Two Veterans* 409; 'The evening-watch' 459; folksong arrangements 442; *The Hymn of Jesus* 412–13; *Hymns from the Rig Veda* 189; 'I vow to thee, my country' 443; *Ode to Death* 409; *Seven Partsongs* 442; *Six Choruses* 442
  operas 349–52, 356, *At the Boar's Head* 349–52; *The Perfect Fool* 349–51; *Savitri* 189, 349, 353, 360; *The Wandering Scholar* 350
  orchestral music 188–92; *Beni Mora* 189; *Cotswolds Symphony* 188; *Egdon Heath* 191–2, 329; *Fugal Concerto* 191; *Fugal Overture* 191; *Hammersmith* 188; *Japanese Suite* 189; *The Planets* 49, 183, 186, 188–91, 192, 206, 429, 443, 446; *Scherzo* 188; *Somerset Rhapsody* 189
  songs 470, 471
Holt, Simon
  instrumental music 340–1
'Holy City, The' 61
Homer 369, 392, 400
homosexuality 359, 366, 379, 472
Honegger, Arthur 128, 131
honkytonk 85
Honorary Consul, The 142
Honri, Percy 71
Hooker, John Lee 85
Hopkins, Antony
  ballet music 397
  operas 370–1
Hopkins, Bill 491
Hopkins, Gerard Manley 438, 441–2, 488–9
Horn, Trevor 105
Horovitz, Joseph
  band music 151
  choral music 405, 406
  operas 370–1
Horsbrugh, Ian 510
Hosier, John 510
Hosken, Pearce 522
Hot News 64
house music 85, 95
Housman, A.E. 466, 469, 470–1, 480–1, 482
Howarth, Elgar 151, 153
Howells, Herbert 15, 429, 511, 524
  band music: *Pageantry* 151
  chamber music 246–7, 251
  choral music 417–18; *Hymnus paradisi* 408, 416–19; *A Kent Yeoman's Wooing Song* 417; *Missa sabinensis* 407, 417; *Sine nomine* 417; *Sir Patrick Spens* 417; *Stabat mater* 417
  church music 166, 457–9, 461, 464–5
  Keyboard music 276–7; clavichord: *Howells' Clavichord* 277; *Lambert's Clavichord* 277
  organ: 'De profundis' 277; 'Master Tallis's testament' 277; Psalm-Preludes 276–7; Rhapsodies 277; Second Sonata 277; Six Pieces 277; Sonata 276
  songs 466, 471
Howes, Frank 514–16
Hoyland, Vic 341
  music theatre 392
Hubbard, Frank 521
Huddersfield 146, 161
Huddersfield Choral Society 147
Hudson, W.H. 478
Hughes, Arwel 376
Hughes, Don Anselm 522
Hughes, Donald 35
Hughes, Herbert 514
Hughes, Patrick 'Spike' 33, 62–3, 65, 67, 77
Hughes, Ted 376, 489
Hugill, Andrew 318
Hugo, Victor 472
Hulbert, Jack 132
Hullo, Ragtime! 57, 108
Hullo, Tango! 108
Human League, The 93
humanism 19, 23, 417
Humphris, Ian 464
Hungary 294
  Budapest 359
Hunt, Edgar 524
Hunter, Alberta 67
Hupfeld, Herman 59
Hurd, Michael 406
Hussey, Walter 455, 460
Hutchings, Arthur 509, 511
Hutchings, Ashley 101

INDEX

Hutchinson, Leslie 67
Hyde, Joseph 445
Hyde Park concert 38
Hylton, Jack 58, 63, 65, 66, 67, 70, 73, 132
hymns 3, 162, 165–7, 180, 189, 275, 365, 428, 443–4, 464, 484, 494

'I feel free' 80
'I said goodbye' 110
'I should be so lucky' 93–5, 96
'I took my harp to a party' 116
'I vow to thee, my country' 443
Ibberson, Mary 147
identification signals 143–4
ideology 28–9, 31–5, 80, 84, 90, 104, 106, 130, 142, 318, 526
'If you were the only girl in the world' 109
'If your kisses can't hold the man you love' 116
'I'll follow my secret heart' 114
'I'll see you again' 114
'I'm on a see-saw' 116
'Imagine' 80
imperialism 12, 23
impresarios 108
   see also record producers
impressionism 486
improvisation 88, 112, 168–9, 317–18
IMS see International Musicological Society
In a Persian Market 47
In Dahomey 107
incidental music 123, 126, 128, 137, 399
   see also radio, music for
Incorporated Society of Musicians (ISM) 147
Incredible String Band 101
Independent 514
independent cinema 142
Indian classical music 161
indie music 92
indipop 92
insularity 15, 207
institutions 6, 40–53, 279
instrumental effects
   cascading strings 70
instrumental ensembles 51, 52, 280–1, 423, 487–90
   early music 489–90, 528
   new music 490–500
   see also opera, chamber; orchestration and arrangement
instruments, musical 42, 48, 161, 175
   bagpipes 102
   concertina 71, 102
   guitar 159–60, 161, 166, 402, 477, 490, 493
   harp 477, 480
   harpsichord 489–90, 493, 520–1, 523
   in bands 58, 156–60
   manufacture, sale and maintenance 160–1; in early music 520–1
   melodeon 71
   non-standard 489
   pianola 46
   piano 40, 48, 403; and keyboards, amateur status of 160–1
   tuition in schools 169–70
   ukelele 71; banjolele 71
   viols 489–90
   see also bands; early music; gramophones; jukeboxes; orchestras; technology
intellectual contexts 2–5, 9–26, 40
Intermodulations 317
International Musicological Society (IMS) 506
International Society for Contemporary Music (ISCM) 207, 251, 506
'Internationale' 418
internationalism 4, 15, 17, 20, 22, 422, 516
Intimate Opera Company 358, 370–1
IRCAM (Institut de Recherche et de Coordination Acoustique/Musique) 10, 312–13, 340
Ireland, John 215, 216, 232, 246, 269–70, 455
   band music: *A Comedy Overture* 151 (*see also below* orchestral music: *A London Overture*); *A Downland Suite* 151
   chamber music 239, 244–5; Cello Sonata 245; early string quartets 244; Fantasy-Sonata for clarinet and piano 245; First Violin Sonata 244, 267; Phantasie-Trio (no. 1) 244; Second Violin Sonata 244–5; Sextet 244; Third Piano Trio 245; Trio in E minor (no. 2) 244

choral and church music: 'Greater love hath no man' 452–5; 'The hills' 437; 'Man in his labour rejoiceth' 443; *These Things Shall Be* 407, 418
film music 134
orchestral music 192–4; *Concertino pastorale* 193–4; *The Forgotten Rite* 193; *Legend* 193; *A London Overture* 194 (*see also above* band music: *A Comedy Overture*); *Mai-Dun* 193; Piano Concerto 193–4, 219; *Satyricon* 194
piano music 266–8, 270, 'Amberly Wild Brooks' 267; *Decorations* 266–7; 'For remembrance' 267; 'In a May morning' 267; 'The island spell' 266; *London Pieces* 267; 'Moon-glade' 266–7; Prelude 267; 'Ragamuffin' 267; Rhapsody 267; *Sarnia* 267–8; Sonata 267; Two Pieces 267
songs 466, 471–3, 267; *Five Poems by Thomas Hardy* 471; *Five XVIth Century Poems* 467; 'Her song' 472; 'Spring sorrow' 466; 'The trellis' 472–3
Irish influence 199, 215, 250, 318
   see also Celtic themes and inspiration; Northern Ireland
Irish traditional music 102, 103, 156, 158
   Anglo-Irish traditions 87
Iron Maiden 88
Irving, Ernest 129, 131, 132, 134
ISCM *see* International Society for Contemporary Music
Italian influence 298–9, 368, 478
Italy 343, 358, 388–9
   Milan 359
It's a Wonderful World 77
'It's just a memory' 110
'It's the talk of the town' 66
It's Trad, Dad! 136
'It's unanimous now' 62
Ives, Charles 288, 309, 313–314, 323–4, 334

Jackson, Edgar 61, 63, 64, 65, 75
Jackson, Ellis 67
Jackson, Francis 460
Jackson, Jack 67
Jackson, Stephen 464
Jacobean Ensemble 526
Jacobs, W.W. 345
Jaeger, August 443
Jaffa, Max 103
Jagger, Mick 38, 81–3, 88
Jamaica 97
James, Harry 73
James, Henry 363, 366, 367, 374
James, Margaret 168
James, Sid 135
James Bond films 136–41
Janáček, Leoš 2, 405, 411
Janis, Elsie 109
jazz 3, 4, 6, 30, 31, 33, 34–5, 57–78, 97, 99–101, 103, 105, 110, 150, 157, 175, 402, 412–13, 415, 420, 464, 487, 491, 499, 526
   Archer Street 74
   authenticity 74, 77
   bebop 74–6; bop 100
   criticism 33
   definitions of 61–5
   Dixieland 74, 76
   double bass, use of 62
   free 100
   hot versus sweet opposition 71
   improvision 61–2, 66–7, 90, 100
   influence of 116, 135, 137, 214, 231, 271–2, 274, 337, 395, 439, 484
   modern 99–101, 103, 379
   New Orleans 61–2, 74, 77
   revivalist 74, 75, 76–7 99, 157, 176
   saxophonists 100
   symphonic 33, 58
   trad 99
   see also blues; ragtime; swing
Jazz Singer, The 129
Jazz Warriors 100
jazz-rock 35, 90
Jenkins, Cyril 151, 154
'Jerusalem' 443
Jesus Christ Superstar 121–2

Jethro Tull 90
Jewel in the Crown 144
Jewish music and musicians 65, 156
Jill Darling 116
jingles 3, 143–4, 402
jive 60
John, Elton 91
John Alldis Choir 403
'John Bull's girl' 108
'John, come kiss me now' 351–3
John Rae Collective 100–1
Johnson, Ken 'Snakehips' 67, 73
Johnson, Linton Kwesi 98
Johnston, Johnny 144
Jolly, Prof. 125
Jolly Roger 111–12
Jolson, Al 129
Jones, Daniel 281
Jones, Gwyneth 122
Jones, Philip 510
Jones, Tom 80
Jonson, Ben 344, 357, 439, 482
Jordan's Syncopated Orchestra 58
Joseph and the Amazing Technicolor Dreamcoat 120–1
Josephs, Wilfred 290
   ballet music 398; operas 369; Requiem 421; television music 144
Joubert, John
   'All wisdom cometh from the Lord' 456; choral symphonies 422; *Herefordshire Canticles* 408; 'O Lorde, the maker of al thing' 456; 'O praise God in his holiness' 456; operas 373; *Rorate coeli* 430; *Te Deum* 421; 'Torches' 464; works with early music instrumentation 490
journalism 63, 514–16
journals 35, 64, 437–9, 503, 512, 515–15, 529
   see also criticism
Joy Division 92
Joyce, Archibald 45
Joyce, James 439, 445, 450–1, 467, 469, 489
Joystrings 166
Juana Inés de la Cruz, Sor 439
Judas Priest 88
jukeboxes 34, 79, 162
jump 85
'Jumpin' Jack Flash' 81–3
Jung, Carl 2, 377–9, 384

Kagel, Mauricio 389, 393
karaoke 162
Keats, John 411
Keel, Frederick 466
'Keel Row' 314
'Keep the home fires burning' 110
Keighley, Thomas 151
Keller, Hans 19, 510–12, 515, 516
Kellog, Shirley 109
Kelly, Jo Ann 97
Kelly, Frederick 469
Kemp, Ian 378, 512
Kennedy, Jimmy 59, 70
Kennedy, Michael 37, 355, 512
Kennedy, Nigel 28
Kent 74
Kent Opera 388, 526, 527
Kenton, Stan 68
Kenyon, Nicholas 515
Kerman, Joseph 517
Kern, Jerome 108, 115
Ketèlbey, Albert 47, 68–9, 70
   'Amaryllis' 127; *In a Monastery Garden* 68–9; *In the Mystic Land of Egypt* 68; *In a Persian Market* 47; *The Sacred Hour* 69; *Sanctuary of the Heart* 68
Keyes, Sidney 478
Keynesian economics 48
Kevs, Ivor 511
Killing Fields, The 142
Kimbell, David 511
King, Mary 491
King Crimson 90
Kingdom for a Cow, A 119
King's College, Cambridge *see* Cambridge University
King's College, London *see* London University

562

INDEX

King's Singers 403, 447, 527
Kinks 88
Kipling, Rudyard 445
Kirchen Band 60
Kirkby, Emma 527
Kirkpatrick, Jess 65
Kirkup, James 437
kissing duets 108
Kit and the Widow 122
Klages, Ray 67
KLF (Kopyright Liberation Front) 95
Kneller Hall 44
Knighton, Tess 515
Knussen, Oliver 21, 24
    instrumental music 340; operas 388; Second Symphony 485; vocal music 492, 497, 499
Kodály, Zoltán 294, 443
Kolisch Quartet 240–1
Korner, Alexis 88
Kreisler, Fritz 28

Labé, Louise 478
Lady Betty 122
Lady Caroline Lamb 137
Lady Luck 117
Ladykillers, The 135
Laine, Cleo 28, 99–100
Lalandi, Liam 527
Lambert, Constant 17–18, 29, 33, 65, 179, 189, 206, 210, 213, 414
    ballet music 214, 393–5, 524; *Horoscope* 395; *Pomona* 395; *Romeo and Juliet* 393–4, 397; *Tiresias* 395;
    criticism 508
    film music 134
    orchestral music 214–15; *Aubade héroïque* 214; Piano Concerto 214
    piano music 271–2; Sonata 214, 272; *Trois pièces nègres pour les touches blanches* 272
    vocal music: *The Rio Grande* 395, 412–13; *Summer's Last Will and Testament* 413, 414; *Two Songs* 488
Lambert, John 315
Lamond, Frederick 44
Lancashire 146, 329, 372
'Land of hope and glory' 28, 443
'Land of Might Have Been, The' 111
landscape 327–30, 334, 340
Landowska, Wanda 521
Lange, Lee 78
Langer, Susanne 516
Langford, Gordon 153
Langford, Samuel 514
language *see* English language
Larkin, Philip 34–5, 482, 489
Latham, Alison 515
Latin, settings of 421–2, 459
Latin American influence 340, 413, 450
    dances 59–60, 71
Lauder, Harry 129
Lawes, Henry 167
Lawrence, Gertrude 115, 117
Laye, Evelyn 113
'Layla' 80
le Fleming, Christopher 466, 469
Le Grice, Malcolm 142
Leader, Harry 73
Lear, Edward 488–9
Leavis, F.R. 32, 34
Led Zeppelin 88
Ledger, Philip 510, 527
Leeds 74, 369
    Piano Competition 274, 407
    see also festivals, Leeds Festival
LeFanu, Nicola
    instrumental music 329
    music theatre 460, 483–4
    vocal music 460, 483–4
Legge, Robin 514
Legge, Walter 49
Lehar, Franz 111, 115, 155
Leigh, Fred W. 109
Leigh, Walter 111–12, 131, 230
Leighton, Kenneth 511
    instrumental music 289–90
    vocal music 460; *Animal Heaven* 489; *Crucifixus pro nobis* 441; *Earth, Sweet*

Earth 478; 'Give me the wings of faith' 456; masses 421; *Three Carols* 465
leisure provision and industry 29, 59, 93
Lemare, Edwin, H. 70
Lennon, John 80, 86–7, 120, J236, 155
    see also Beatles
Lennon, Robert 153
Lennox, Annie 28, 93
Leopardi, Giacomo 229, 492
Leppard, Raymond 370, 527
lesbians 4
    see also homosexuality
Leslie, Henry 403
Lester, Richard 136
'Let the great big world keep turning' 109
Levy, Louis 129, 131
Lewis, Alun 478
Lewis, Anthony 509, 510, 511, 523, 525, 526
Lewis, Archie 68
Lewis, Jerry Lee 85
Lewis, (Percy) Wyndham 487
Lewis, Philip 62
Lewis, Vic 68, 74
lexicography 513
liberalism 19, 22
library music 142
Lichfield 408
Lido Lady 119
Ligeti, György 340–1
light listening *see* easy listening
light music 27, 33, 47, 68–70, 78, 151, 153, 153, 165–6, 171, 414
light opera 70, 162
    see also operatic societies; operetta
light orchestras 70
Lillie, Beatrice 110
'Limehouse blues' 117
Lindsay, Vachel 406
Lion in Winter, The 137
Liszt, Franz 14, 193, 194, 198, 199, 266, 270, 272, 296, 413
literacy, musical 175
Little Richard 87
liturgical factors 164–5
Liverpool 101, 103
    merseybeat and Merseyside traditions 86–7
    University 509
Livingston, Jerry 66
Lloyd, A.L. 158–9
Lloyd, George 281
    operas 348–9
Lloyd, Jonathan 341, 491
Lloyd, Marie 108–9
Lloyd Webber, Andrew 1, 27, 111
    musicals 120–3
    Requiem 405
Lloyd Webber, W.S. 510
Locke, Matthew 525
Loesser, Frank 116
Logue, Christopher 483, 497
Lombardo, Guy 72
London, music in 1, 13, 16, 41–2, 44, 47–51, 57–8, 64, 67, 74, 75–6, 90, 103, 107–24, 129, 137, 159, 343–89, 504, 507, 519, 523, 528–9
    Almeida 122
    Barbican 122
    Bloomsbury 520
    clubs 58, 72, 90
    South Bank 24, 48, 276, 390, 529
    swinging London 88
    Westminster Abbey 404
    Westminster Cathedral 431, 460
    see also Lyric Theatre, Hammersmith; music colleges; music hall; Promenade Concerts; Royal Albert Hall; West End
London Baroque 528
London Calling 113
London Classical Players 529
London Coliseum 41, 526
London College of Music 510
London County Council 375
London Festival Opera Company 525
London Filmmakers' Cooperative 512
London Hippodrome 57
London Palladium 63–4
London Sinfonietta 280, 327, 330, 337, 341
London Symphony Orchestra (LSO) 42, 128
London University 516

Loose Tubes 100, 337
Loppert, Max 514
Lorca, Federico Garcia 397, 400,489
'Lord of the dance' 166
Loss, Joe 59, 73, 77, 103
lottery, national 53
Lough, Ernest 28
'Love changes everything' 122
'Love is the sweetest thing' 66
'Love will find a way' 111
Love Story 134
Lovelace, Richard 469
Lucie-Smith, Edward 484
Lumsdaine, David 312
'Dum medium silentium' 460; *Hagoromo* 312
Lumsden, David 460, 510
Lute Society 524
Lutosławski, Witold 316
Lutyens, Edwin 488
Lutyens, Elisabeth 19, 491
    film music 135
    instrumental music 303–6
    operas and music theatre 380–1; *Infidelio* 381, 389; *Isis and Osiris* 381; *The Numbered* 381; *The Pit* 381; *Time Off? Not a Ghost of a Chance!* 381
    vocal music 304, 478, 488; *Akapotik Rose* 488; 'The egocentric' 488; Motet 'Excerpta tractatus-logico philosophici' 488; 'O saisons, ô châteaux' 488; *Quincunx* 304–5; 'Requiescat' 488; *Stevie Smith Songs* 484; *And Suddenly It's Evening* 488; *The Valley of Hatsu-se* 488; 'Verses of love' 439
Lynn, Vera 68, 71, 74, 78
Lyric Theatre, Hammersmith 111–12
Lyttelton, Humphrey 77, 99

M/A/R/R/S 95
Macari Brothers 70
McCabe, John 292–510
    band music 151; instrumental music 289–90; *Notturni ed alba* 485–6; *Rain Songs* 489; 'Les soirs bleus' 489; *Stabat mater* 421; *Visions* 439
McCartney, Paul 80, 84, 86–7, 120, 136, 155
    Liverpool Oratorio 405
    see also Beatles
McClaren, Malcolm 91
McColl, Ewan 101, 158–9, 162, 477
MacDiarmid, Hugh 478, 489
MacDonald, Calum 515
McEwan, Ian 420
McEwen, John 510
McGegan, Nicholas 527
Machenzie, Alexander 510
    operas 344
Mackintosh, Cameron 122
McLaughlin, John 90
MacLeish, Archibald 490
Macleod, Fiona (William Sharp) 346, 466
MacMillan, James 342
    instrumental music 337, 338; 'Scots song' 499
McNaught, William (i) 515
McNaught, William (ii) 515
MacNeice, Louis 400, 437
Maconchy, Elizabeth
    chamber music 261, 284, 370
    operas 370
    vocal music 442, 465, 477
McPeake family 102
Macpherson, Stewart 30
McQuater, Tommy 60, 72, 73
McTell, Ralph 101
Madden, Edward 77
Maderna, Bruno 392
Madness 93
madrigals and madrigalian techniques 285, 403, 412, 430–411, 454, 466, 522
    The Triumphs of Oriana 437
Maeterlinck, Maurice 346, 357
Maggie May 120
Magine, Frank 60
Magritte, René 484
Mahabharata 349
Mahler, Gustav 12, 21, 283, 294, 323, 333, 344, 422, 485
Mahler 137

563

INDEX

Maid of the Mountains, The 111
Malcolm, George 525, 527
Mallarmé, Stéphane 489
Malta GC 134
'Mama' 38
Man in the White Suit, The 135
Man Who Knew Too Much, The 131
Manchester 42, 51
 see also Royal Manchester College of Music; Royal Northern College of Music
Manchester Guardian 514
Manchester School 382, 384, 390–1, 392
Manduell, John 510
Mann, A.H. 521, 523
Mann, Thomas 366
Mann, William 35, 514
Manning, Jane 491–2, 497, 499
Mantovani, Annunzio 70, 103
Maoism 318
Marchant, Stanley 510, 511
marches 108
Marie Rambert Dancers 394
Markova, Alicia 394, 396
Marlborough School 170
Marley, Bob 97, 99
Marlowe, Christopher 375
Marsden, Evan 69
Marsh, Roger
 instrumental music 330
 music theatre 392, 405
 vocal music 405, 447, 450–1, 491, 499
Martin, George 78, 105
'Martini' theme 144
Martland, Steve 23, 27, 104
 instrumental music 337, 339
Marx, Karl 24, 509, 516
 Marxism 4
'Mary from the dairy' 117
Mary Wiegold's Songbook 499–500
Maschwitz, Eric 117–18
Masefield, John 466, 470
Mason, Ben 137
Mason, Benedict 318
Mason, Colin 514, 515
mass culture 27–38, 168
 singing 162–3
Massenet, Jules 455
masses 421–2, 425–7, 441
Massine, Leonide 113
Master of the King's Musick 134
 see also Bax, Arnold
Matcham, Frank 41
materialism 31
 see also consumerism; economic factors
Mathias, William
 choral and church music 421, 427, 460; 'A refusal to mourn the death, by fire, of a child in London' 438; Lux aeterna 408; 'Make a joyful noise' 460; Missa brevis 421; Te Deum 421; This Worldes Joie 427; World's Fire 422
 instrumental music 290–1
 operas 376–7
Mathieson, Muir 131, 132–3, 134
Matrix 497
Matthay, Tobias 44
Matthews, Colin 21, 24
 instrumental music 330
 vocal music 486
Matthews, David 341, 485
Matthews, Jessie 113, 117, 132
Matumbi 98
Maunder, J.H. 164
Maupassant, Guy de 362, 376
Maw, Nicholas 21
 instrumental music 292–3; Life Studies 292–3; Odyssey 26, 293; Personae 293; Sinfonia 292, 293; Sonata for two horns and strings 292; String Quartet 292
 chamber music 292
 operas 374–5
 vocal music: Nocturne 292; Scenes and Arias 375, 485–6; Six Chinese Lyrics 293
Mayall, John 88
Maybrick, Michael see Adams, Stephen
Mayerl, Billy 27, 60, 111, 132
Mayfair Hotel 58, 72
Me and My Girl 116

Mechanical Copyright Protection Society (MCPS) 49–50
media, influence of the 29, 83, 105, 136, 165, 528, 403, 529
 see also broadcasting; radio; television
mediaeval morality plays 384, 406
mediaeval music in revival 524, 526, 527–8
mediaeval poetry 411, 442, 465, 484, 486, 488–9, 497
mediaeval techniques 310, 320, 323, 437, 465, 490
Meek, Joe 105
Meisel, Edmund 128
Mekons 103
Melachrino, George 70
Mellers, Wilfrid 18, 227, 516–17
melodrama 113, 126, 402
Melody Maker 61, 62, 63, 64, 74, 157
Melos Ensemble 280–1
'Memory' 122–3
Men of Two Worlds 134
Mendelssohn, Felix 45, 156, 365, 411–12, 415–16
Mendoza, Joe 369
(Yehudi) Menuhin School 51
Mérimée, Prosper 356
'Merry Xmas everybody' 80
Meskill, Jack 67
Messager, André 119
Messiaen, Olivier 21, 207, 265, 307–10, 319, 340, 355, 368, 460–3
metaphysical poets, settings of 459
Metcalf, John 388, 389
Meyerbeer, Giacomo 343
Meyerstein, E.H.W. 487
Michael, George 97
Michelangelo Buonarroti 299, 439, 472, 477
Mickey-Mousing 135, 137
middle English settings 392
Midlands 42, 99
midsummer operas 344, 367
'Mild green Fairy Liquid' theme 144
Miley, Bubber 61
Millay, Edna St Vincent 487
Miller, Glen 72–4
Miller, Jimmy 73
Miller, Max 116–17, 132
Mills, Florence 107
Mills, Irving 60
Milner, Anthony 408, 422
Milnes, Rodney 515
Milton, John 485
Milton Keynes 159, 169, 174
mime 385, 492
Mine Own Executioner 135
minimalism 2, 23, 25, 103–4, 317, 337, 451
 holy minimalism 428
 subminimalism 24
Ministry of Information 132, 134
Ministry of Labour 64
Minogue, Kylie 93–4
minstrelsy 423, 487
 blackface 57, 71, 106
Misérables, Les 122
'Misery Farm' 62
Miss Saigon 122
'Mississippi mud' 61
Mr Cinders 115–16
Misty 98
Mitchell, Donald 18, 19, 512, 515, 517
mod culture and music 85, 88, 95
modality 62–3, 87, 93–4, 100, 101, 120, 167, 181, 279, 285, 308, 310, 329, 353–4, 427, 428, 431, 454, 457, 461–3, 471
 octatonic scales 418, 439, 457–8, 463
modernism 9–26, 34, 38, 61, 75, 180, 283–4, 291, 341–2, 280, 382, 385, 391, 429, 452, 481–4, 487, 507, 508, 524
Moeran, E.J. 436, 468, 469, 484
 chamber music 252
 choral music: Nocturne 410; Songs of Springtime 433–5
 orchestral music 215–16; Cello Concerto 216; Lonely Waters 215; In the Mountain Country 215; Rhapsody (no. 3) for piano and orchestra 216; Serenade 216; Sinfonietta 216; Symphony in G

minor 215–16, 252; Violin Concerto 216; Whythorne's Shadow 215
 songs 466, 467, 470
Molière (Jean-Baptiste Poquelin) 358, 370, 376
Monckton, Lionel 108, 109
Monkman, Phyllis 117
Monks, Victoria 108
Monnot, Marguerite 117
Monsieur Beaucaire 119
Montague, Stephen 450
Monteverdi, Claudio 429, 437, 497
 revival 524, 525, 527
Monteverdi Choir 527
Montgomery, Bruce 135
Monty Python's Flying Circus 405
mood-music 128, 142
'Moonlight and roses' 70
Moonlighting 142
Moore, George 519
MOR (middle-of-the-road) 103
moral and ethical considerations 30, 84, 278, 283, 411, 420
More, Hannah 438
Moret, Neil 70
Morgan: a Suitable Case for Treatment 137
Morison, Duncan 69
Morley, Christopher 515
Morris, R.O. 226
Morris, William 519
Morrison, van 28
Morrow, Michael 528
Morse, Theodore 77
Morton, Jelly Roll 72
Mossolov, Alexander 131–2
Most, Mickie 105
motets 430, 441
Motorhead 88
Move 88
Mozart, Wolfgang Amadeus 377, 378, 527, 528
mouldy fig 76
Muldowney, Dominic 337
'Mull of Kintyre' 84
mummers' plays 391
Munch, Edvard 491
Munrow, David 28, 51, 490, 528
Murder on the Orient Express 137
Murdoch, Iris 377
Murray, Gilbert 348
Musgrave, Thea 280, 377
 band music 151; Beauty and the Beast 398; instrumental music 313–15, 316; Mary, Queen of Scots 374, 377; operas 360, 374; vocal music 439, 490
Music Analysis 515, 516
Music Analysis Conference 516
Music and Letters 512, 515
music clubs and societies 52
music colleges 41, 43–4, 52, 123, 503, 510, 521, 529
 centres of excellence 52
Music Curriculum Association 37
Music Group of London 280–1
music hall 4, 31, 35, 39, 41, 43, 45, 47, 59, 69, 70, 71, 88, 107–24, 126, 132, 135
 Alhambra 125
 Collins, Islington Green 117
 Empire 125
 Metropolitan, Edgware Road 117
Music Hath Charms 132
music industry 4, 28, 37, 40, 47, 53, 86, 88, 91, 104, 120, 159
Music Lovers, The 137
Music Party 529
Music Review 512, 515
Music Survey 18, 512, 515
music theatre 381, 383, 389–93, 399, 451, 490, 492, 493–7
music videos 93, 142
Musica Britannica 523, 525–6
Musica Reservata 527–8
musical appreciation 32 39, 48, 53, 168
Musical Copyright Act 45
musical theatre and musicals 4, 107–24, 149–50, 153, 155, 165, 346, 389, 402
musical comedy 4, 45, 107–9, 112–16, 118–21
 see also film musicals
Musical Times 437–9, 465, 515, 517

564

INDEX

Musicians' Union 42–3, 64, 73
musicology and musicologists 35, 447, 482, 503, 505, 506, 516–18
   early music 466, 519–29
   editions 521–3
   new musicology 517
   thematic catalogues 518
musique concrète see electro-acoustic music
Muslims 161
Musorgsky, Modest 388, 478
Muzak 79
'My bonny boy' 251
'My generation' 88
'My sweet Virginia' 67
Myers, Stanley 142
mythic opera 377, 379, 384–7
myths in music 31, 443, 446

Napoleon 128, 137
Nash, John 487
Nash, Paul 487
Nash Ensemble 280
Nashe, Thomas 413
national anthem 47
National Curriculum 36–7, 53, 169
National Early Music Association (NEMA) 529
National Federation of Music Societies (NFMS) 147
National Learn-the-Organ Year 163
national songs 27–8, 101, 153, 171, 443–4
   see also folk music, folksong
National Theatre, Royal 4, 337
National Youth Orchestra 51
nationalism 4, 12–17, 279, 420
   national self-definition 3, 412
   patriotism 59, 414
nativity plays 346–7, 355
Naylor, Edward 455
Neel, Boyd 524
Neiburg 66
Neighbours 144
Nelson, Stanley 65
neoclassicism 17–18, 216, 222, 230, 273, 274, 292, 300, 309, 321, 331, 370, 431, 474, 481, 484
neo-baroque devices 217, 219, 222, 279, 357–8, 378, 394, 407, 451, 471–2, 477, 490
Neruda, Pablo 489
Nesbit, Max 71
'Neville was a devil' 109
new age 103–4
New Babylon 128
new complexity 24, 331, 334, 340, 341
New Grove Dictionary of Music and Musicians, The 53
New Lindsey Theatre Club 119
New London Chamber Choir 404
New London Consort 528
New Mayfair Dance Orchestra 65
New Order 92
New Philharmonia *see* Philharmonia Orchestra
New Queen's Hall Orchestra 529
New Simplicity 23
New Symphony Orchestra 42
Newcastle-upon-Tyne 58
Newley, Anthony 120
Newman, Ernest 13, 350, 359–60, 504–6, 507, 513, 514, 515
Newman, Sidney 511
News at Ten 144
Newsom Report 170
newspapers 503, 514–16
   see also criticism; journals
Niblo, Fred 137
Nice 90
Nicholas and Alexandra 137
Nicholas Nickleby 134
Nichols, Red 61
Nichols, Robert 410
Nicholson, George 491
Nicolai, Otto 351
Nicolson, Harold 34
Niecks, Friedrich 511
Nielsen, Carl 18, 20, 283
Nieman, Alfred 439
Nietzsche, Friedrich 29, 411
Night Mail 131
Nightingale, Mary 69

Nights at the Comedy 119
Nipjm 111
Noble, Ray 65–7, 75
'Noël nouvelet' 464
noise music 131
nonconformism 520
Noorman, Jantina 528
Norrington, Roger 527, 529
Northampton 455
Northcott, Bayan 405, 514
Northern Ireland 3, 102, 156, 160
   Belfast 102
Northern Music Theatre 392–3
northern soul 85
Northumbrian small pipes 102, 175
Norwegian traditional music 158
Norwich *see* festivals; Norwich Festival
nostalgia
   golden age 523
   see also heritage industry
Novello (publisher) 45, 437–9
Novello, Ivor 69, 110–13, 115, 116, 120, 122
Novello Book of Carols, The 464
novelty genres 80
'Now be thankful' 101–2
nuclear protest 2
nursery rhymes 155
Nyman, Michael 23, 27, 142–3, 337, 391
Nymph Errant 119

'O sole mio' 38
Oakenfold, Paul 105
Oakland, Ben 60
Obey, André 362
O'Brien, Richard 120
Observer 515
Ocean, Billy 97
October 128
Odessa 157
Offenbach, Jacques 112
Ogdon, John 273, 382–3
'Oh! you beautiful doll' 109
'Oh, you nasty man' 67
O'Hear, Anthony 37
O'Hogan, Betsy 69
Oklahoma! 116, 119
Old Chelsea 118–19
'Old Father Thames' 69
old time 103
Old Vic Theatre *see* Vic-Wells Ballet
Oldfield, Mike 103, 142, 317
Oldham, Arthur 397
Oldham Press 64
Oliver! 120–1
Oliver, King 74
Oliver, Stephen
   operas 388–9
      television music 144
      vocal music 460
Oliver Twist 134
Olivier, Laurence 134
Olleson, Edward 515
On With the Dance 113–114
opera 1, 28–9, 41, 48, 50–1, 107, 111, 112, 120, 121, 343–89, 399, 401, 407, 420, 485
   ballad 350–1, 376
   chamber 349, 350, 360, 363, 368, 369, 370, 372, 374, 384, 389, 393
   early opera revival 490, 524–5, 526–7
   in English 343–4, 358, 372, 376, 525
   in Greek 389
   in Welsh 376
   librettos 347–8
   puppet 358, 385
   rock 89, 120–2
   verismo 359, 377
Opera 515
Opera Factory 388
opera houses 41
operatic societies 145, 149–50, 155–6, 524–5, 526–7
operetta 107, 108, 109, 110–16, 122, 124, 359
Operette 114
oratorio 42, 45, 155–6, 399, 405, 406–30, 523
Orchestra of the Age of Enlightenment 527, 528
orchestras 41–2, 46, 48, 49, 51, 52, 280–1
   amateur 145–9, 171

and early music 523, 527, 528–9
   cinema 46–7, 125–9
   see also light orchestras
orchestration and arrangement 28, 130, 181, 187, 189, 195, 198, 207, 227, 265, 280–1, 345, 524, 525
   see also instrumental ensembles
Ord, Boris 522, 527
Ord Hume, James 151, 152
Orff, Carl 168, 414
organ music 275–7
organists 40, 404–5
organs, theatre and cinema 103, 126, 129
Oriana Madrigal Society 430, 522
oriental influences 90, 366, 397, 489
   Chinese literature 472, 480
   gamelan 289, 397, 490
   Indian music 89, 428
   Japan 366; literature 488; noh drama 392, 397
   Peking Opera 318
Original Dixieland Jazz Band 57, 59
Orr, C.W. 465, 469, 480
Orr, Robin 511
   opera: *Full Circle* 377
Orton, Richard 317
Orwell, George 34
Osborne, John 35
Osborne, Nigel 23, 511
   I Am Goya 490; instrumental music 330; operas 388
O'Shea, Tessie 115
O'Sullivan, Seumas 466, 470, 471
'Other people's babies' 116
Others 2, 106
Our Nell 111
Out of Africa 137
Over She Goes 111
Overlanders, The 134
Overton, Aida 107
Ovid 263
Owen, Morfydd 469
Owen, Wilfred 409, 423–5, 489
Oxford 372, 388
Oxford University 404–5, 503, 509, 511, 521, 525
Oxford University Opera Club 525
Oxford University Press 411, 529
Oyster Band 102

Pacific 1860 115
pacifism 359, 366, 383–4
Page, Christopher 526
'Painting the clouds with sunshine' 61–2
Palestrina, Giovanni Pierluigi da 37, 407
palm court 103
Palmer, Geoffrey Molyneux 469
pantomime 111, 374, 391, 394
Panufnik, Andrzej
   symphonies 284
Paolozzi, Eduardo 488
Paradise nightclub 72
Paranoiac 135
Parish, Mitchell 60
'Parisian Pierrot' 113, 119
Park Lane Group 281
Parker, Charlie 75
Parker, Clifton 134
Parker, Elizabeth 144
Parker, Evan 100
Parker, Jim 144
Parnell, Jack 74
parody 107, 280, 310, 317, 323, 386, 392, 423–5, 439, 493
Parratt, Walter 511
Parrott, Andrew 527
Parry, Hubert 3, 15, 31, 179, 181–2, 183, 192, 197, 229, 436, 506, 510, 511
   choral music 408, 443
Partch, Harry 489
partsongs 155, 403, 429, 431–41, 444
Pasadena Roof Top Orchestra 78
Passage to India, A 142
Passing Show of 1912, The 108
Pasternack, Boris 388
pastiche 111, 114–15, 119, 130, 137, 357, 371, 383–4, 394, 396, 406
pastoralism 217, 252, 262, 279, 324, 329, 395, 411, 412, 414, 417, 441, 481

565

INDEX

pastoralism (cont'd)
  see also landscape; Vaughan Williams, Ralph, *Pastoral Symphony*
patronage 4
Patterson, Paul 316–17, 427
  Brain Storm 450; *The Canterbury Psalms* 408; *Cataclysm* 153; *The Circular Ruins* 317; Concerto for Orchestra 317; *Cracovian Counterpoints* 317; *Fusions* 312, 316–17; *Magnificat and Nunc dimittis* 460; *Mass of the Sea* 408, 425; *Requiem* 421; Sinfonia for Strings 317; *Sonors* 316; *Stabat mater* 421
Pavarotti, Luciano 38
Payne, Anthony 491
  instrumental music 329
  vocal music 442, 460, 463
Payne, Jack 58, 59, 67, 70
Paynter, John 169
Peacock Report 52
'Peanut vendor, The'
Pears, Peter 365, 368, 399, 420, 474, 478, 497
Pearson, Johnny 142, 144
Peel, John 83
Pelissier's Follies 117
Penderecki, Krzysztof 317, 389
penillion 175
'Penny Lane' 89
pensioners 162
Pentangle 101
Perchance to Dream 110–11
Percival, Allen 510
performance practice, historical 519–29
performers 6, 50–2
  early music 521–9
  orchestral 42–4, 46–8
  see also bands; choirs; conductors; instrumental ensembles; organists; pianists; pop music, groups; professional music and musicians; rock music, groups; string quartets; violinists
performing rights 44–6, 49–50, 83
Performing Right Society (PRS) 47, 49–50
Perkins, Carl 87
Perle, George 307
permissiveness 22
Pet Shop Boys 93
Petrassi, Goffredo 207
Pfitzner, Hans 383
Phantom of the Opera 27
Philharmonia Orchestra 49
Philharmonic Society 42
Philips, Peter 522
Phillips, Sid 72–3
Philomusica Orchestra 526
Phono-Bio-Tableau Films 129
Piaf, Edith 117
pianists 43, 46, 64, 78, 407, 524
  fortepianists 529
piano music 45, 69, 111, 265–75
  novelty piano 413
Picasso, Pablo 487
Piccadilly Dance Orchestra 78
'Piccadilly trot, The' 108
'Pick and slap' 62
Pierné, Gabriel 70
Pierrot Players 390, 492
Pine, Courtney 100, 103
Pink Floyd 90
Pinski Zoo 100–1
Piper, John 395
Piper, Myfanwy 367, 376
Piranesi, Giovanni Battista 331
plainsong *see* Gregorian chant
Plainsong and Mediaeval Music Society 522, 524
Plath, Sylvia 429, 485, 489, 498
'Play to me, gypsy' 59
Players' Theatre Club 119
Playford, John 349
Pleeth, William 51
pluralism 21–3, 26, 175, 292, 318, 331
  see also permissiveness
poetry 403–4, 465–6, 489
Pogues, the 103
pointillism 303
Polish influence 316–17, 330, 427
politics 22–3, 29–38, 40, 74, 76–7, 80, 106, 122, 158–9, 168, 169, 216–17, 232, 318, 330,
337, 344, 347, 371–2, 376, 420, 466, 489, 517
  see also ideology
Polo, Danny 65
  and his Swing Stars 73
Poly Styrene 104
Poole, Geoffrey 341, 429, 439
'Poor little Pierrette' 119
'Poor little rich girl' 113–14
'Poor Uncle Harry' 115
pop art 36
pop music 35, 49, 53, 79–106, 119, 122, 402, 428, 443, 450, 500
  and glitter 90–1
  cantatas 404, 405–6
  chart-orientated 80
  in church 165–6
  groups 35, 36, 157
  new pop 93
  in school 51, 53, 169, 171
  see also music industry; music videos; rock/pop antinomy
pop musicals (film) 136
Pop Will Eat Itself 95
Pope, Alexander 442
popular classics 27–8, 121
popular music 1, 4, 5, 6, 19, 22, 27–38, 39, 45, 47, 50–2, 57–176, 317, 337, 379, 386, 402, 420, 464, 480–1
  show business styles and practices 79, 80, 91
  'well-made' popular song 31
populism 38, 39, 83, 482
Porgy and Bess 116
Porter, Andrew 514–16
Porter, Cole 113, 119
Portman, Rachel 144
postmodernism 10, 36, 38, 103, 104, 106, 280, 303, 317, 337, 340, 341–2, 385, 481, 517
Poston, Elizabeth 466, 469
Poulenc, Francis 230, 265, 272, 368, 369
Poulton, Diana 520
Power, Lionel 522
Powers, Anthony 341
Pre-Raphaelite Brotherhood 519
Presley, Elvis 1, 85, 86, 88
Preston, Simon 404, 527
Pretenders, the 93
Price, Curtis 510, 511
Price, Tim Rose 425
Prick Up Your Ears 142
Priestley, J. B. 33, 367
Printemps, Yvonne 115
Prior, Maddy 101
Private Lives 114
Pro Cantione Antiqua 527
Procul Harum 90
professional music and musicians 5, 28, 40–4, 46–8, 50–2, 74, 101, 150, 155, 156–7, 359, 363–5, 404, 406, 518
  chamber ensembles 238–9
  institutions 175
  organists 276
  studio musicians 49
  see also performers
programme notes 506–7
progressive pop 35
  see also rock music, progressive rock
Prokofiev, Sergey 213, 264, 372, 394, 405
Promenade Concerts 4, 35, 48, 428, 429
Prospero's Books 142
Pruslin, Stephen 384
psychedelic blues-rock 90
pubs, music in 79, 99, 119, 120, 145, 161–2
  drinking songs 444
publishing 44–6, 64, 83, 107, 159, 406, 521
  sheet music sales and culture 40, 47, 83, 160; song-sheets 58
Puccini, Giacomo 2, 111, 359, 369, 397, 423, 500
Pudovkin, N. I. 129
Puffett, Derrick 515
'Pump up the volume' 95
Punjabi folk music 157–8
punk rock 91–2, 103, 104
punks 99
Puppets 110
Purcell, Henry 155, 171, 234, 265, 323, 526
  opera revival 524–5, 527
Purcell Operatic Society 524

Purcell Quartet 529
Pushkin, Alexander 472
psychology 505

Quadrophenia 137
Quasimodo 488
Quatermass Experiment, The 135
Queen 90, 93
Queen's Hall 41
Queen's Hall Orchestra 42
Quilter, Roger 469
  choral music 410
  theatre music 112
  songs 467–8, 481–2

Rabelais, François 357
Rabin, Oscar 59, 73
Race, Steve 31, 75, 79
racism 30–1, 376
radio 32–4, 40, 47–9, 58, 64, 69, 73–4, 83, 85, 103, 120, 132, 148, 160, 523–4, 528
  music for 355, 372–3, 375, 381, 398–401
  pirate radio stations 83
  pop radio 79, 95–6
  see also broadcasting; disc jockeys
Radio Rhythm Club 64
Radio Rhythm Club Sextet 64
Radio Times 33
RAF Dance Orchestra *see* Squadronaires
'Raggedy doll' 110
ragtime 57, 61, 108–10, 117, 159, 413
Raine, Kathleen 482
Rainier, Priaulx
  chamber music 284
Rajah of Rajpore 155
Ralton, Bert 57–8
RAM *see* Royal Academy of Music
Rambert, Marie 394
  see also Ballet Rambert
Rameau, Jean-Philippe 525, 527
Ramsey, Basil 515
Rands, Bernard 315, 392
  Mésalliance 315; *. . . in the receding mist* 315; *Wildtrack pieces* 315
Rankl, Karl 358
rap 85, 95, 97, 379, 402, 447
Rastafarian themes 97
Rattle, Simon 37
Ravel, Maurice 179–80, 206, 246–7, 265–6, 375, 388
raves 106
Rawsthorne, Alan 229, 252, 289
  ballet: *Madame Chrysanthème* 397
  chamber music 217, 255–7; Clarinet Quartet 256; Concerto for ten instruments 255; early string quartet (lost) 256; Oboe Quartet 257; Quintet for piano and strings 257; Quintet for piano and wind 256–7; Second Quartet 256; Suite for flute, viola and harp 255; Third Quartet 257; Viola Sonata 255–6; Violin Sonata 256–7
  choral music 411, 437
  film music 134
  orchestral music 217–20; Cello Concerto 220; Concerto for String Orchestra 219; Concerto for two pianos 220; Cortèges 219; First Piano Concerto 219, 273; First Symphony 219–20; First Violin Concerto 219; Oboe Concerto 219; overtures 219; Second Piano Concerto 219, 273; Second Symphony 217, 220; Symphonic Studies 217–19, 255; Third Symphony 217, 219, 220–1, 282, 289–90
  piano music 273
Raybould, Clarence 366
RCM *see* Royal College of Music
Reach for the Sky 135
Rebello, Jason 100
record companies 32, 58–9, 64, 83, 86, 91–2, 93, 112, 524, 529
  Columbia 57, 64, 524
  Decca 59, 62, 70, 74–5, 524
  EMI 59
  Esquire 75
  Levy's 64
  HMV (Gramophone Company) 57, 65, 168, 524, 525

566

INDEX

record companies (cont'd)
  Parlophone 64, 75
  Vocalion 74–5
  Zonophone 61
record producers 95, 105, 123–4
recorder 489–90, 521, 522, 524
  groups and consorts 51, 164, 168, 171, 428
records and recordings 1, 47–9, 58, 62, 64, 67, 70, 83–4, 85, 92, 105, 120, 123, 129, 131, 159, 157, 239, 275–6, 398, 472, 499–500, 521, 523–4, 528
  tape 40, 49, 83, 312, 398, 400
Red Byrd 490
Red Peppers 115
Red Shoes, The 134
Redcliffe concerts for British Music 281
Redgate, Roger 334
Redlich, Hans 509
Redpath, Jean 101
Reed, Henry 437
Rees, Gordon 72–3
Rees, Leonard 514
reggae 97–9, 103, 105
regional factors 50, 154
Reimann, Aribert 389
Reich, Steve 317, 341
Reith, John 32, 48, 53
Reizenstein, Franz 372, 421
relativism, cultural 36, 39, 50
religion 136
  music in 5, 148; non-Christian faiths 164; *see also* church music; Salvation Army
religious observance 156, 163–7
religious songs 477
Renaissance Singers 527
Rendell, Don 99
Réti, Rudolph 509, 511
Revolver 89
revue 108–11, 113, 115, 117, 119
rhetoric 402–3, 409, 422, 424–6, 446, 472, 474, 491, 499
  elocution training 403
Rhys, Jean 486
Rhythm 64
Rhythm Clubs 64
Rhythm Maniacs 62
rhythm 'n' blues 81, 85–8, 90, 97
Rhythmic Eight 61
Rice, Tim 121
Richard, Cliff 86, 136
Richards, Keith 83
Richardson, Samuel 388
riff tune 72–3
Rihm, Wolfgang 22
Riley, Howard 100
Riley, Terry 317
Rilke, Rainer Maria 489
Rimbaud, Arthur 472, 488, 489
Rimmer, William 151
Rise and Fall of Ziggy Stardust and the Spiders from Mars, The 91
Ritterman, Janet 510
ritual dance 159
ritualism 23–4, 384, 391
Roadside Picnic 100–1
Robert and Elizabeth 120
Roberton, Hugh 154
Roberts, Richard 510
Robertson, Harry 135
Robertson, Rae 274
Robeson, Paul 67
Robey, George 111–112
Robinson, Paul 137
Rock Around the Clock 85, 136
'Rock around the clock' 84, 85
Rock Around the World 136
rock music 31, 35, 50, 77, 78, 79–106, 111, 121, 122, 136, 175, 379, 398, 402, 405
  authenticity 80, 91, 105
  and charity fund-raising 79, 93
  criticism 35
  death of rock 106
  dole-queue rock 92
  groups 157, 174, 487
  heavy rock 88, 90
  lovers' rock 97
  progressive rock 90–1, 100, 101, 103
  soft rock 103

stadium rock 28, 90
see also jazz-rock
rock 'n' roll 30–1, 34, 77, 79, 84–7, 91, 96–7, 104, 105
rock/pop antinomy 80, 90–1
rockabilly 85, 87
rock-steady 97
Rocky Horror Show, The 120
Rodgers and Hammerstein 28, 116, 155
Rogers, Eric 135–6
Rolling Stones 81–3, 85, 88
Rollini, Adrian 61
Rollins, Sonny 100
romanticism 12, 14, 16, 18–19, 21, 24, 34, 80, 104, 112, 124, 281, 342, 369, 374, 420, 433, 466, 470, 523
  neo-romanticism 24, 250, 332–4, 482
Ronald, Landon 510
'Room in Bloomsbury, A' 119
'Room with a view, A' 113
Rootham, Cyril
  Second Symphony 422; *The Two Sisters* 355
roots music 159
Roper, Stanley 510
Rorem, Ned 121–2
Ros, Edmundo 60, 68
Rosa, Carl *see* Carl Rosa Opera Company
Rose, Denis 75
Rose, Vincent 67
Rosenthal, Harold 370, 515
'Roses of Picardy' 69
Rosseter, Philip 466
Rossetti, Dante Gabriel 470
Rossini, Gioacchino 28, 155, 156
Rossini's Accordians 71
Rostal, Max 51
Rostropovich, Mstislav 236
Roussel, Albert 230
Roxburgh, Edwin 317
Roy, Harry 68, 71, 72, 132
Royal Academy of Music (RAM) 44, 197–8, 370, 510, 529
Royal Air Force (RAF) 73
Royal Albert Hall 41, 162, 411
Royal Ballet 396, 398
Royal College of Music (RCM) 44, 197, 206, 232, 248, 261, 352, 455, 510, 519, 524, 529
Royal Festival Hall *see* London, music in, South Bank
Royal Manchester College of Music 382, 510
Royal Musical Association 503
Royal Northern College of Music 510
Royal Opera House (Covent Garden) 48, 52, 111, 112, 128, 348–89, 393, 526–7
  Garden Venture 393
Royal Scottish Academy of Music and Drama 510
royalties 45–6
Rubber Soul 89
Rubbra, Edmund 217, 238, 281
  chamber music 254–5; Cello Sonato 255; First Piano Trio 255; Oboe Sonata 255; Second Violin Sonata 255; string quartets 254–5
  choral music: *Missa a 3* 422; *Missa brevis* 241; Ninth Symphony (*Sinfonia Sacra*) 422; *Veni, Creator Spiritus* 441–2
  orchestral music 226–9, 254; Fifth Symphony 226, 228; Fourth Symphony 228; Piano Concerto 228–9; Second Symphony 227–8; Seventh Symphony 229; Sixth Symphony 229; Third Symphony 226, 227–8; Viola Concerto 228–9
  songs 477, 488
Rubens, Paul 108, 109, 110
'Rufty tufty' 350, 352
Run Rig 101
Runciman, John 504
Rural Music Schools 32, 147
Ruskin, John 370, 478
Russell, Ken 137
Russell, Kennedy 112
Russia 371
  St Petersburg 357
Russian literature 392, 393
Russian music, influence of 191, 264, 357, 393–4
  see also Franco-Russian style
Rutland, Harold 515

Rutter, John 442, 460
  carols 464; *The Falcon* 423; *Lichfield Canticle* 408; 'Praise ye the Lord' 460; Requiem 405
Ruttmann, Walther 132

Sablon, Jean 117
SACEM (Société des Auteurs, Compositeurs, et Editeurs de Musique) 44, 46
sacred music 175
  concerts 163–4
  see also church music
Sackville-West, Edward 400
Sadie, Stanley 514, 515, 517
Sadler's Wells 394
  Ballet 395–7
  Opera 51, 357–9, 367, 370–1, 373, 375
  see also English National Opera; Vic-Wells Ballet
'Sailing' 91
Sainsbury's Choir of the Year 404
St John of the Cross 421, 489
St Michael's Singers 523
St Teresa of Avila 480
Saki 369
Salad Days 120
Salding, John 515
Salford 162
Salvation Army 151
Salzedo, Leonard
  ballet music 397
Sammons, Albert 44
Samuel, Harold 524
Samuel, Rhian 481
Sanderson, Wilfrid 69
Sarton, May 481
Satie, Erik 131, 179, 206, 272, 317, 318
satire in music 110, 124, 349, 356, 375
'Satisfaction' 88
Saturday Night and Sunday Morning 137
Saturday Night Fever 91
Saturday Night Jump 72–3
Savoy Havana Band 58
Savoy Hotel 59, 62, 72
Savoy opera *see* Gilbert and Sullivan
Savoy Orpheans 58
Savoy Tango Album, The 59
Sawer, David
  music theatre 393
  radio music 393, 401
Saxton, Robert 24, 25, 38, 491–2
  instrumental music 340
Scala, Primo 59
  and His Accordion Band 71
Scarlatti, Domenico 394
scat 72
scenas, dramatic 485–6
Schehadé, George 376
Schenker, Heinrich 311, 447, 516
Schnabel, Artur 15
Schoenberg, Arnold 13, 17–19, 21, 180, 189, 214, 230, 242, 253, 257, 258, 262, 284, 292, 293–300, 319, 329, 372, 380–2, 390, 393, 423, 478, 483, 485, 487, 491, 492, 509, 511
Scholes, Percy 32, 48, 53, 168, 515
Schönberg, Claude-Michel 122
Schubert, Franz 252, 273, 452, 483, 488
Schumann, Robert 22, 332–3
schools, music in 3, 32–3, 36–7, 51, 79, 145, 150, 167–73, 174, 405, 444
  boys' schools 170
  private schools 170
  see also education
Schütz, Heinrich 415, 441
scientific research 517–18
Scotland 3, 44, 71, 101, 103, 160, 337, 388
  folk music 101–2, 154, 481
  literature 463, 472, 478
  opera 377
  Orkney 324, 337, 383
  pipe bands 149
  traditional and dance music 156, 158
  see also Edinburgh; Glasgow; Hebridean songs; Scottish Opera Scots dialect
Scots dialect 477–8
Scots-Irish traditional music 102
Scott, Charles Kennedy 430, 522

567

INDEX

Scott, Cyril 27, 179
  choral music 411
  piano sonatas 266
Scott, Francis George 478
Scott, Ronnie 75, 77, 99
Scott, Walter 348
Scott of the Antartic 133–4
Scottish Early Misic Consort 490
Scottish Opera 375, 388
Scottish Theatre Ballet 397–8
Scratch Orchestra 318
Scruton, Roger 37
Seamen, Phil 99
'Searching for lambs' 247
Searle, Humphrey 19, 296–7
  operas 381–2; partsongs 439; Second Symphony 296–7
seaside resorts 42
  shows 58, 115, 117
Second Viennese School 240–1, 374, 380, 516
Secret Ceremony 137
secularization 147–8
Seeing Stars 117
Seiber, Matyas 400, 509
  instrumental music 294
  vocal music 443, 488–9
Sendak, Maurice 388
'Serenade in the night' 59
Sgt. Pepper's Lonely Hearts Club Band 35, 89
serialism and 12-note music 4, 19, 20, 23, 135, 214, 216, 217, 220, 256, 278–80, 282, 284, 291, 293–312, 313, 316, 317, 319, 321, 363, 372, 375, 376, 380–2, 397, 428, 438–9, 460–2, 481, 483, 484, 486, 493
  see also Second Viennese School
Servant, The 137
Severini, Gino 487
Sex Pistols 91–2
Sexton, John 78
Shadows 86
Shaffer, Peter 375
Shakespeare, William 349, 351–3, 362, 365–6, 379, 389, 393, 414, 443, 467
Shand, Jimmy 102, 156
Shapiro, Helen 136
Sharon, Ralph 75–6
Sharp, Cecil 31, 32, 168, 349–50, 352, 403, 468
Sharp, Geoffrey 515
Sharp, William *see* Macleod, Fiona
Shaw, Geoffrey 443
Shaw, George Bernard 347–8, 430, 504, 519
Shaw, Hank 75
Shaw, Martin 167
Shaw, Roy 36
Shawe-Taylor, Desmond 359, 514
'She loves you' 87
She Shall Have Music 132
Shearing, George 64
sheet music *see* publishing
Sheffield Musical Union 146
Sheldon, A. J. 515
Shelley, Percy Bysshe 372, 438, 294
Shelton, Anne 68
Shepherd's Bush Pavilion Theatre 129
Shepp, Archie 100
Sheppard, Andy 100
Sheppard, John 522
Sheridan, Richard Brinsley 344, 372
Shetland Islands 158
'Shipmates o' mine' 69
Shipp, Jesse A. 107
Shostakovich, Dmitry 128, 216, 227, 264, 360, 414, 441
Show Boat 115
Sibelius, Jan 17–20, 22, 195, 198, 202, 210, 212, 214–16, 228, 283, 284, 451
Side Saddle 78
'Sidewalks of Cuba' 60
sight-singing 403
signature tunes 70, 79, 143–4
Signorelli, Luca 417
Simon, Moises 59
Simon, Paul 155
Simple Minds 92
Simpson, Robert 18, 22, 282–3, 289
  band music 156
  string quartets 20, 283
  symphonies 20, 282–3

Sinatra, Frank 79
singalong genres 80
sing-songs 162
Singcircle 404, 447, 450
singers 472–4
  ballad 103
  baritones 490
  blues 85
  boy trebles 404–5
  countertenors 489–90
  early music 527–8
  folk-rock 101
  jazz 68
  new music 447; sopranos 490–500
  pop 447
  see also crooners
singer-songwriters 101, 104
Siouxsee and the Banshees 104
Sitwell family 356
  Edith 373, 487, 489
  Sacheverell 394, 412, 488
Six, Les 382
Sixteen, The 528
sixties, the 4, 19, 379
  see also flower power
ska 97, 99
Skellern, Peter 80
Skelton, John 414–15, 460
Skempton, Howard 23, 318
Skidmore, Alan 100
skiffle 85, 86, 157, 158
Skryabin, Alexander 13, 242, 265
Skyrockets 72–3
Skull, The 135
Sky 103
Slade 80, 90–1
Slater, Montagu 370
Slits 104
Smalley, Denis 312
Smalley, Roger
  'The crystal cabinet' 439–41; instrumental music 317; *Missa brevis* 421, 439
Smart, Christopher 421, 460
Smith, Dave 318
Smith, Nicola Walker 491
Smith, Stevie 429, 483, 484, 489
Smith, Tommy 100
Smith Brindle, Reginald 18, 438
Smiths 92
Smyth, Ethel 4, 371
  operas 344–5; *The Boatswain's Mate* 344–5; *Entente cordiale* 345; *Fête galanta* 345; *The Wreckers* 4, 344, 370
  The Prison 422
snobbery 130
social clubs, music in 161–2
social dance 157
social and democratic factors 27–38, 83, 86, 278, 337, 402–3, 420, 529
socialism 22, 29, 418
Society of British Composers 13
Society of Recorder Players 524
Society of Women Musicians 486
sociology 104–6, 517
Söderström, Elisabeth 485
Soft Lights and Sweet Music 132
Soft Machine 35, 90
Sohal, Naresh 438
Solitude 66
Solomon 44
'Someday I'll find you' 114
Somers, Debroy 58
Somerville, Jimmy 93
'Something in the atmosphere' 109
Sondheim, Stephen 122
song 430, 445, 497
  chamber song 500
  solo (art) 404, 444, 465–85, 490, 499–500
song-and-supper 119
Song of Ceylon 131
Songmakers' Almanac 482
Sorabji, Kaikhosru 17, 132, 508
soul 85, 91, 97, 402
  electric-soul 91
Soul II Soul 95
sound effects 126, 129, 131
sound system 97
Souster, Tim 144, 312, 317–18

Soutar, William 472, 478, 499
Southall 174
Souther Maid, A 111
Southern Syncopators 58
Soviet Union *see* Russia
Spain and Spanish influence 302, 372, 397, 400
Spandau Ballet 93
Specials 99
Spencer Davis Group 88
Spenser, Edmund 455
Spinners 101
Spitalfields Festival 529
Spohr, Louis 156
sponsorship 52–3
Spottiswoode, R. 129
'Spread a little happiness' 115
Spread It Abroad 117–18
Springfield, Dusty 104
Spring-Rice, Cecil 443
Squadronaires 73, 77
Squire, J. C. 466
Squire, William Barclay 523
Stadlen, Peter 514
Stainer, John 164, 441
Standford, Patrick 421, 422, 431–3
Stanford, Charles Villiers 2, 128, 171, 179, 181, 191, 192, 197, 202, 232, 239, 247, 265, 268, 437, 452, 455, 468, 511
  choral and church music 404, 444, 452
  operas 344
Status Quo 80
Steel Pulse 98–9
Steele, Tommy 80, 86, 136
Steeleye Span 101
Stein, Erwin 509
Stein, Gertrude 395
Steiner, Rudolf 445
Stephens, James 466
Stept, Sam 62
Stevens, Denis 525, 526
Stevens, John 100
Stevens, Wallace 482, 489
Stevenson, Robert Louis 376, 470
Stevenson, Ronald 444
Stewart, Jean 245
Steward, Rod 91
stinging 137
Stobart, Kathy 68
Stock, Aitken and Waterman 93–5
Stockhausen, Karlheinz 20, 23, 311–12, 317, 319, 320, 331, 382, 491
Stoker, Richard 438–9
Stone, Christopher 33
Stone, Lew 60, 65, 66–7, 71–3
Stop the World – I Want to Get Off 120
Storch, Eberhard 78
'Story of Peter Pan, The' 113
Strachey, Jack 117–18
Stranglers 91
Strauss, Johann 112, 375
Strauss, Richard 12–14, 179, 189, 333, 345, 357, 372, 375, 377, 396
Stravinsky, Igor 2, 12, 13, 17–18, 20–1, 179, 180, 188, 189, 191, 192, 206, 208, 226, 230, 232, 272, 274, 279, 284, 285, 286, 288, 292, 306–7, 309, 314, 330, 372, 378–9, 388, 389, 398, 405, 412, 423, 428, 429, 430, 438, 451, 460, 488, 490, 491
'Strawberry fields forever' 89–90
Streamline 116
street music 145, 161–3
Street Singer, The 111
Strindberg, August 369, 374
string quartets 51, 52, 281
Stroheim, Erich von 137
Stroud 347
Stuart, Charles 515
Stuart, Leslie 45, 108
Stubbs, John Heath 485
subjectivity 3
subsidies 28, 44, 49–50, 52–3, 343, 529
Suffolk 162, 362, 366, 376
Sullivan, Arthur 112, 152, 429
  see also festivals, Aldeburgh Festival
Sullivan, J. W. N. 30
  see also Gilbert and Sullivan
summer schools 51, 346
Summer Holiday 136

INDEX

Summers, Dorothy 70
Sunday Times, The 35, 505, 514
Sunset Boulevard 122
supper dances 58
Surman, John 100
surrealism 391, 428, 481, 482, 484
Sussex 101, 158
Swann, Donald *see* Flanders and Swann
Swanwick, Keith 169
Swarbrock, Dave 101
Swayne, Giles 341, 429–30, 446
Sweden 50
    dances 168
    Stockholm 359
Sweet 90–1
swing 33, 72–4, 103, 111
Swing Along 117
Swing for Roundabout 67
Swing Music 64
Swinging Blue Jeans 86
Swingler, Randall 418
Sylvester, Victor 60
Symes, Marty 66
Symons, Arthur 466
Synge, J. M. 352
synthesized scores 144

T. Rex 90–1
Tabs 110
Tagore, Rabindranath 470
Tails Up! 113
Tallis, Thomas 167, 446
Tallis Scholars 404, 528
Tamblyn, Bill 464
Tan, Melvyn 529
Tantivy Towers 112
tape recording *see* records and recordings
'Ta-ra-ra-boom-de-ay' 107
Tarkovsky, Andrei 330
taste *see* aesthetics, and taste
Tate, Phyllis
    opera: *The Lodger* 370
Tauber, Richard 118–19
Tausky, Vilem 395
Tavener, John 3, 25, 431
    instrumental music 330
    vocal music 427–8; *The Apocalypse* 3, 428; *Akathist of Thanksgiving* 428; *Akhmatova Requiem* 428, 430; *Cain and Abel* 427; *Canciones españolas* 489; *Celtic Requiem* 427–8; *Ikon of St Seraphim* 428; *In alium* 427–8; *Little Requiem for Father Malachy Lynch* 428; *Requiem for Father Malachy* 428; *Resurrection* 428; *Risen!* 428; *Three Surrealist Songs* 484; *Ultimos ritos* 428; *We Shall See Him as He Is* 408, 428; *The Whale* 427–8
Taverner, John 383, 522
Taverner Choir 527
Taylor, Cecil 100
Taylor, Cyril 167
Taylor, Eric 511
Tchaikovsky, Peter Ilich 132, 137, 198, 484
'Teach me to dance like Grandma' 113
techno-dance 95
technology 1, 21, 39–40, 47–9, 82, 88–9, 92, 95, 105, 126, 129, 130, 144, 148, 160, 162, 175, 312–13, 444–5, 472, 523–4, 529
    see also amplification; broadcasting; computers in music; electro-acoustic music; electronics in rock music; film and film music; gramophones; radio; records and recordings; sound system; television; video
teddy-boys 30, 86
Teddy Bears' Picnic, The 70
television 49, 93, 111, 120, 123, 134, 137, 148, 149, 165, 528
    commercials 38, 49, 79, 80, 142, 143–4
    music 3, 49, 79, 93, 142–4
    opera 357, 358, 366, 367, 370, 376
Temperance Seven 78
Tempo 515
Ten Years After 90
Terry, Richard Runciman 431, 521–2, 523
Tertis, Lionel 248
Teschemacher, Edward 69
Teyte, Maggie 112
Thatcher, Reginald 510

Thatcherism 22, 50, 92–3
theatre and theatres 41, 47, 130
    eighteenth-century stagecraft 527
    see also music hall; West End
theatre clubs 119
theatre music 27, 100, 123, 126
    see also incidental music
Them 88
Theodore and Co. 110
theory, music 509–10, 513–14, 516–18
    see also critical theory
'There's an angel watching over me' 110
'These foolish things' 117–18
Thiman, Eric 167, 475
Thin Lizzy 88
Things to Come 130, 131
This Year of Grace 113
Thomas, A. F. Leighton 515
Thomas, Dylan 438, 489
Thomas, Edward 482
Thomas, Gavin 515, 517
Thomas, Mary 491–2, 497
Thompson, Francis 407, 421
Thompson, Herbert 515
Thompson, Kevin 510
Thompson, Leslie 67
Thompson, Richard 101
Thomson, John 515
Thorne, Gordon 510
Those Magnificent Men in Their Flying Machines 137
Three Musketeers, The 128
Tickell, Katherine 102
'Till the boys come home' 110
Tilley, Vesta 129
Tilmouth, Michael 511
timbre 11, 217, 303, 487, 493
Times, The 35, 452, 514, 516
Timms, Colin 511
Tina 109
Tinker, Tailor Soldier, Spy 405
'Tiny flat in Soho Square, A' 119
Tippett, Keith 100
Tippett, Michael 2, 15–18, 21, 22, 27, 30, 34, 37, 207, 237, 252, 278–80, 285–9, 292, 302, 309, 314, 321, 330, 368–9, 386–9, 408, 512, 517, 529
    chamber music 258–60, 378; First Quartet 258–9; Fourth Quartet 288–9, 379; Second Quartet 222, 259–60, 285; Third Quartet 259–60, 285
    choral and church music 420, 429–30; *A Child of Our Time* 259, 410 420, 422; *Crown of the Year* 444; 'Dance, clarion air' 437; *Four Songs from the British Isles* 443; *Magnificat and Nunc dimittis* 460–2; *The Mask of Time* 16, 420, 428, 429–30; 'Music' 444; *The Vision of St Augustine* 420, 429; 'The windhover' 438
    criticism 509
    operas 343, 367, 376, 377–80, 420; *The Ice Break* 379; *King Priam* 223, 279, 285, 378–9; *The Knot Garden* 288, 379; *The Midsummer Marriage* 222–3, 289, 368–9, 377–8, 484; *New Year* 358, 379–80
    orchestral music 220–6; Concerto for Double String Orchestra 220–2, 223, 285, 288, 289; Concerto for Orchestra 285–7; Fantasia Concertante on a Theme of Corelli 223; First Symphony 222–3; Fourth Symphony 288; Piano Concerto 223, 229; Second Symphony 224–5, 281, 285, 289; Symphony (in B♭) 220; Third Symphony 288, 302, 420; Triple Concerto 288–9
    organ music 277
    piano music 266, 273–5; First Sonata 274; Fourth Sonata 288; Second Sonata 285, 286; Third Sonata 288
    solo vocal music: *Boyhood's End* 478; *Byzantium* 485; *The Heart's Assurance* 273, 478–9
toasting 97
Tolstoy, Leo 375
Tom Jones 137
Tommy 89, 120, 137
Tommy Steele Story, The 136
tonality and neo-tonality 22, 303–4, 313, 317, 319, 333, 341, 429, 452. 513
tonal backlash 22, 25–6

tonic sol-fa 175
Tonight at 8.30 115
Toop, Richard 23–4, 25
Toovey, Andrew
    Adam 334; *Ubu* 370
Torrance, Leo 69
Tough at the Top 116
Tovey, Donald Francis 208, 505, 506–7, 511–12, 513
The Bride of Dionysus 355
Townshend, Pete 79, 91, 137
    see also Who
Townswomen's Guilds, National Union of 149
Toye, Geoffrey 396
Tracey, Stan 100
Tracy, Arthur 71
trade unions 45, 46
    see also Musicians' Union
traditional music 31, 32, 73, 101–2, 105, 156–9, 162, 351
Traherne, Thomas 472
Trakl, Georg 390–1, 485, 489, 497
Tranpani, Tulio 78
travellers 160
Treacher, Graham 392
Treorchy Zulus 150
Trials of Life, The 144
Trimble, Joan 358
Trinidad All Steel Percussion Orchestra 68
Trinity College of Music 44, 510
Trocadero Cinema, Elephant and Castle 63
Trotsky, Leon 2
Trowell, Brian 511
Tubular Bells 103
Tucker, Sophie 116
Tudor Church Music 522, 523
Tudor Singers 522
Turnage, Mark-Anthony 3, 337
    Entranced 337; *Greek* 3, 358–6; *Her Anxiety* 498; *Lament for a Hanging Man* 498–9; *Leaving* 429; *Night Dances* 337; *Three Screaming Popes* 337
Turner, Bruce 99
Turner, John 78
Twentieth Century Church Light Music Group 165
Twickenham 74
'Two little boys' 77
Two Tone bands 99
Tye, Christopher 522
Tyler, James 528

UB40 99
UFO 90
Ultravox 90
Under Milk Wood 100
Under the Clock 108
Under Your Hat 116
underscoring 142
unemployment 129
Unicorn Theatre Group 526
unison songs *see* choral songs
universities 35, 40, 43, 50, 51, 52, 53, 404–5, 503, 509, 511, 514
    polytechnics 51, 53
urban folksong 4, 82–3
USA *see* America

Vacek, Karel 59
Valmouth 119
Varèse, Edgard 21, 301, 324
variety 58, 63, 64, 71, 86, 103, 108–9, 115, 116, 129
vaudeville 129, 386
Vaughan, Henry 459
Vaughan Williams, Ralph 2, 12–17, 19–20, 120, 165, 167, 191, 192, 194, 198, 199, 201, 207, 210, 214, 215, 220, 230, 233, 239, 246, 247, 252, 261, 278, 279, 281, 329, 412, 414, 428, 512, 523, 524
    ballet music: *Job* 183, 394–5, 397, 411
    chamber music 245–6
    choral and church music 411, 429, 442, 446, 459–60; *Benedicite* 441; *Dona nobis pacem* 409–10, 417, 420, 446, *Five Mystical Songs* 470; *Five Tudor Portraits* 407, 411, 414–15; *Flos campi* 412, 446, 470; *Hodie* 408, 411, 465; 'The Hundredth Psalm'

569

INDEX

choral and church music (*cont'd*)
441; Mass in G minor 431; 'The new commonwealth' 443; 'O taste and see' 459; *Sancta civitas* 411; *A Sea Symphony* (Symphony no. 1) 181, 407, 408–9, 411, 429; *Serenade to Music* 414; *The Shepherds of the Delectable Mountains* 355; 'Silence and music' 437; *Three Choral Hymns* 459; *Three Shakespeare Songs* 436; *Toward the Unknown Region* 409; 'Whitsunday hymn' 459
film music 133–4, 443
operas 349, 350–5, 356; *Hugh the Drover* 350–1; *The Pilgrim's Progress* 355, 400, 411, 417; *The Poisoned Kiss* 355; *Riders to the Sea* 352–5; *Sir John in Love* 351–3
Orchestral music 179–88; Eighth Symphony 187; *English Folk Songs* suite for military band 251; Fantasia on a Theme by Thomas Tallis 181–2; Fifth Symphony 185, 187, 353, 355; Fourth Symphony 17, 183–5, 187, 188, 200, 202, 235, 246, 273, 353; *The Lark Ascending* 182; *A London Symphony* (no. 2) 182, 187, 200; Ninth Symphony 187, 200; *Norfolk Rhapsodies* 181; *Pastoral Symphony* (no. 3) 182–3, 185, 187, 199, 207–8, 430; *Sinfonia antartica* (no. 7) 133–4, 187, 353; Sixth Symphony 20, 185–6, 187, 200, 353
piano music 270
radio music 400
songs 470–1, 488
Vautor, Thomas 417, 466
Venuti, Joe 64
Verdi, Giuseppe 204, 343, 349–50, 351, 360, 365, 369, 373, 375, 377, 405, 423
Verlaine, Paul 472, 486
vernacular art 484
Verne, Mathilde 44
Versatile Four 58
'Very thought of you, The'
Victorian age and values 14, 30, 32, 39, 40–1, 344, 403–4, 463–4, 465, 520
Vic-Wells Ballet 394–5
video 49, 84, 159
Vieuxtemps, Henri 519
Viñao, Alejandro 450
Vinter, Gilbert 151, 153
Viola da Gamba Society 524
violinists 43, 44, 46
Vivaldi, Antonio 224, 451
vocal music 402–500
vocal styles and techniques 34, 72, 110, 112, 119, 122, 123–4, 390, 425, 477, 489–500, 527–8
extended vocal techniques 388, 391, 392, 438, 444–51, 460, 491, 493
parlando 381
in rock music 80, 81, 86, 91, 93, 106
Sprechstimme and *Sprechgesang* 116, 374, 438, 497
see also crooners; rhetoric; singers

Wadland, Peter 124
Wadsworth, Edward 487
Wagner, Richard 12, 180, 181, 189, 198, 333–4, 343, 345, 347, 348, 349, 356, 358, 363, 373, 377, 385, 396, 407, 454, 455
Wagner, Wieland 378
Wales and Welsh music 3, 162, 290–1, 421
opera 376–7
University Council of Music in Wales 146
see also choirs and vocal ensembles, male voice; eisteddfods; *penillion*; Welsh National Opera
Wales, Roy 510
Walker, Alan 512
Walker, George 107
Wall, The 90
Waller, Fats 64
Wallis, C. Jay 62
Walsh, Jimmie 117
Walter, Bruno 344, 485
Walton, William 17, 194, 215, 221, 230, 234, 237, 252, 356, 437, 438
ballet music 394, 395–6

chamber music 251–2; Piano Quartet 251; String Quartet (1923) 251; String Quartet in A minor 251; Violin Sonata 251–2
choral and church music 413–16, 420; *Belshazzar's Feast* 405, 407, 410, 414–16, 447; *In Honour of the City of London* 414; *Missa brevis* 421; 'Set me as a seal upon thine heart' 455; *Te Deum* 421
film music: *Battle of Britain* 137; *Escape Me Never* 131; *Hamlet* 134; *Henry V* 130, 134, 135
operas 360, 367–8
orchestral music 206, 207–14; Cello concerto 213; First Symphony 210–13, 220; *Portsmouth Point* 191, 207–8; *Scapino* 368; Second Symphony 213–14, 282; *Sinfonia concertante* 208; Variations on a Theme by Hindemith 213; Viola concerto 208–10, 213, 250, 251; Violin Concerto 212–13
piano music 271
radio music: *Christopher Columbus* 400
solo vocal music: *Anon in Love* 477, 478; *Façade* 206, 207, 368, 394, 395, 445, 487; *Song for the Lord Mayor's Table* 478
war *see* World War, First; World War, Second
Ward, David 401
Wardour Street English 348
Warlock, Peter (Philip Heseltine) 13, 466, 469, 523, 524
choral music 434, 465
songs 434, 444, 466, 470; *The Curlew* 242, 470, 486; 'Consider' 486; 'The Lover's maze' 467
Warner Brothers 129
Warren, Raymond 421
Warsaw Concerto see Addinsell, Richard
Water Gipsies, The 116
Waterhouse, John F. 515
Waters, Muddy 85
Watersons 101
'Watkins ale' 413
Waugh, Evelyn 33–4
walking songs 69
'We all stand together' 80
'We shall overcome' 28
Weatherly, Frederick 69–70
Webb, George *see* George Webb's Dixielanders
Webern, Anton 20–1, 26, 303, 304, 331
'Wedding jazz, The' 110
Wee Papa Girl Rappers 95
Weedon, Bert 159–60
Weelkes, Thomas 430
Weill, Kurt 119, 337, 386, 423
Weir, Judith 24, 377
'Ascending into heaven' 463; *The Bagpiper's String Trio* 340; *Blond Eckbert* 388; 'Don't let that horse' 492; *Isti mirant stella* 340; *King Harald Sails to Byzantium* 340; 'Illuminare, Jerusalem' 463; *King Harald's Saga* 430, 388; *Lovers, Learners and Libations* 490; *Missa del Cid* 425; *A Night at the Chinese Opera* 388; *The Ride over Lake Constance* 340; 'The romance of Count Arnaldos' 499; *A Serbian Cabaret* 340; *Scotch Minstrelsy* 481; *The Vanishing Bridegroom* 388
Welch, Denton 481
welfare state 48, 84
'We'll gather lilacs' 111
Wellesz, Egon 509
Incognita 372; instrumental music 294–5, 296; 'The leaden echo and the golden echo' 488–9
Wells, H. G. 131
Welsh, Alex 99
Welsh National Opera 376–7, 388
Wembley FA Cup final, music at 162–3
Wen, Eric 515
Wesley, S. S. 441
West End 1, 119, 346, 394, 443
Daly's Theatre 108
Gaiety Theatre 108, 110, 117
Lyceum Theatre 348
New Theatre 112
Palace Theatre 122
Savoy Theatre 112; *see also* Gilbert and Sullivan

Shaftesbury Theatre 107
see also English National Opera; Royal Opera House; Sadler's Wells
West Indian musicians 58, 68, 78, 98
West Side Story 119
Westbrook, Mike 27, 100
Western Approaches 134
Western Ballet Theatre 398
Westminster 347
Westminster Cathedral 521–2, 527
Westrup, J. A. 194, 215, 243, 509, 511, 515, 523, 525, 526
Wham 93
Wheeler, Kenny 100
Wheen, Natalie 4
'When I'm sixty-four' 78
'When the saints go marching in' 74
'When Yuba plays the rumba on his tuba' 59
Whenham, John 515
'Where are the songs we sung?' 114
Where the Rainbow Ends 112
Whitaker, David 135
White, John 318, 438
White, T. H. 400
Whiteman, Paul 57–8
Whitfield, David 78
Whiting, John 375
Whitlock, Percy
Organ Sonata 277; Organ Symphony 277
Whitman, Walt 409, 419, 438, 499
Whittaker, W. G. 510
Whittall, Arnold 511, 516
Whittier, John Greenleaf 443
Who 79, 88, 89, 120, 137
'Who will buy?' 120–1
Who's Hooper? 110
'Widows are wonderful' 109
Wiegold, Mary 491, 499–500
Wiener, Martin 9, 11
Wigmore Hall 41
Wilbye, John 430
Wilde, Marty 86
Wilkinson, George Jerrard 469
Willcocks, David 442, 464, 510, 527
Williams, Bert 107
Williams, Grace 376, 421
Williams, John 103
Williams, Joseph 43
Williams, Peter 511
Williams, Raymond 35
Williamson, Malcolm 290
ballet music 398; church music 165; *The English Eccentrics* 389; *Mass of Christ the King* 421; operas and music theatre 373–4; Third Symphony 422; *The Violins of Saint-Jacques* 373–4, 376
Williamson, Sonny Boy 85
Williamson, Steve 100
Wilson, Garland 67
Wilson, Sandy 119
Wilson, Steuart 510
Winchester 408
wind players 44
Windsor, Barbara 135
Windsor Castle 125
'Wings of sleep, The' 111–13
Winnick, Maurice 72
Winwood, Steve 97
Wishart, Peter 490
Wishart, Trevor 104, 312, 429–30
Anticredos 447; *Red Bird* 447; *Vox* 446–50
'With one look' 122
Wittgenstein, Ludwig 488
Wolf, Hugo 471
Wolfe, Humbert 470
women and music 4, 6, 42, 45, 46, 68, 104, 149, 163, 166, 174, 443, 528
adolescent girls 150
composers 69, 481
girls' schools 170
'Ladies' choirs 149, 155
Women's Institutes 149, 443
Wood, Charles 13, 344, 511, 516
choral music 409
operas 344
Wood, Haydn 69
Wood, Henry 13, 42

570

INDEX

Wood, Hugh 491
   instrumental music 297–9
   vocal music: *Four Logue Songs* 483; *Robert Graves Songs* 482–3; *Scenes from Comus* 485–6; 'To a child dancing in the wind' 439
Wood, Peggy 113
Wood, Ursula 437
Woodhouse, Violet Gordon 521, 524
Woodstock Music Festival 38
Woolf, Virginia 482
Woolrich, John 499
Woolworth's 34
Worcester *see* festivals, Three Choirs
word-setting 350, 383, 425, 428, 429, 436, 462, 472, 478–9, 482–3
Wordsworth, William 417
Workers' Education Association 371
working men's clubs 162
Working Week 103
world music 103, 105, 159, 420, 425
World War, First 1–2, 9, 13, 24, 31, 46, 57, 59, 109–10, 164, 180, 197, 203, 206, 207, 244, 268, 356, 407, 409, 410, 411, 443, 469, 471, 523

World War, Second 1, 3, 9, 15, 33, 38, 64, 73–4, 118, 132–4, 147, 207, 343, 358, 371, 402, 408, 516
'World weary' 113
Wray, J. 510
Wright, Lawrence 64
Wulstan, David 528
Wurlitzer organs 129
Wylie, Elinor 487
Wynter, Mark 136
Wyss, Sophie 474

Yanks 137
Yardbirds 88
Ye Olde English Swynge Band 73
Yeats, W. B. 375, 438, 439, 466, 470, 477, 485, 486, 489, 490, 498
Yellen, Jack 67
Yellow submarine 136
'Yellow submarine' 80
Yes 90
Yes! Uncle 109
York
   Minster 452
   University 392–3
   Early Music Festival 529

Yorkshire 142, 162
   Airedale Opera 155
Yorkshire Jazz Band 74
Yorkshire Post 515
'You'll never walk alone' 28, 443
Young, Douglas 439
Young, Jimmy 83
Young, Lester 75
Young, Paul 97
Young Communists 74
Young England 111
Young Ones, The 136
Young Tradition 101
youth 42, 75, 85
   county bands 151
   movements 145, 150
   orchestras 51, 220, 239
   teenagers and teenyboppers 79, 84, 90

Ziegler, Anne 70
Zinovieff, Peter 384, 497